THE PSYCHOBIOLOGY
OF MIND

BOOKS BY WILLIAM UTTAL

Real Time Computers: *Techniques and Applications in the Psychological Sciences*

Generative Computer Assisted Instruction (with Miriam Rogers, Ramelle Hieronymus, and Timothy Pasich)

Sensory Coding: *Selected Readings* (Editor)

The Psychobiology of Sensory Coding

Cellular Neurophysiology and Integration: *An Interpretive Introduction*

An Autocorrelation Theory of Form Detection

The Psychobiology of Mind

THE
PSYCHOBIOLOGY
OF
MIND

WILLIAM R. UTTAL
The University of Michigan

 LAWRENCE ERLBAUM ASSOCIATES, PUBLISHERS
1978   Hillsdale, New Jersey

DISTRIBUTED BY THE HALSTED PRESS DIVISION OF
JOHN WILEY & SONS
New York   Toronto   London   Sydney

Lawrence Erlbaum Associates, Inc., Publishers
62 Maria Drive
Hillsdale, New Jersey 07642

Distributed solely by Halsted Press Division

Library of Congress Cataloging in Publication Data

Uttal, William R.
    The psychobiology of mind.

    Bibliography: p.
    Includes indexes.
    1. Neuropsychology.   2. Mind and body.
3. Psychobiology.   I. Title. [DNLM: 1. Brain—
Physiology.   2. Psychophysiology. WL103 U93p]
QP360.U87   599'.01'88   78-1443
ISBN 0-470-26316-4

Printed in the United States of America

As ever, for Michan

Contents

Preface

At the Beginning–July 29, 1974

I commence work on this book with the greatest trepidation and humility. In the last few months, I have studied a large amount of material relevant to the theme on which I propose to write. From this survey has come a re-appreciation of the extreme difficulty one unavoidably encounters in dealing with any reductionistic analysis of mental functions (The Mind-Body Problem) and of the enormity of the contributions of the many distinguished experimentalists and theoreticians throughout a history of interest in the problem that literally must be measured in millenia. There is no question that, from the earliest writings of the Greek scientist-philosophers through the great sages of the Middle Ages to the modern psychobiologists, there has been a monumental concern with what is probably history's most profound question: What is the relation between the body and the mind?

In light of the consequence of this subject matter and its extensive history and abundant literature, how could any contemporary scientist possibly undertake the task of presenting a discussion of this material? The answer to this query is founded on the twin advantage enjoyed by contemporary workers: recency and history itself. The last few decades have seen extraordinary conceptual developments and a vast accumulation of new and relevant empirical knowledge. What had been solely the topic of philosophical speculation has now become the matter of laboratory investigation; what had been issues of debate are now open, at least in part, to the direct observations of instruments of measurement and analysis that workers only a few years ago could not have imagined. The plain and simple fact is that there has been a leap in our neuroscientific and psychological knowledge in the last three decades that must be measured in orders of magnitude. This new knowledge has brought a depth of understanding about the mind-brain problem to the psychobiological scientific community at large that allows even workers of modest talent to attempt tasks that the best and brightest of previous eras had sensibly avoided. We must never forget, however, that the very existence of an active, modern program of inquiry into the many aspects of the mind-body problem is itself based upon the fact that there is a lengthy history of continued concern with the problem. The least experienced or most marginally talented student of the problem today stands on the "intellectual shoulders" of the great men of the past and possesses the enormous advantages of the accumulated knowledge, insight, and wisdom that were denied to his predecessors, no matter how profound their genius.

As knowledge about the brain and mental processes has accumulated, the mind-body problem has changed. Today's mind-body problem is not the same as that of the Greeks, of medieval times, or of even the early twentieth century. Like so many other examples in scientific history, some of the classic and most important questions are not as often answered as they are discarded or reformulated in context with contemporary empirical developments. So it is in this book that the question of mind-body interaction or equivalence (depending upon one's perspective) will be restated and dealt with in a somewhat different manner than has been previously employed. Some of the classic problems will be ignored, rather than solved, for the very simple reason that they are no longer meaningful in light of our contemporary data and understanding; in their stead, new issues have arisen that will take the place of some of these obsolete problems.

However, it should also be clearly understood that other momentous and fundamental issues remain both valid and unanswered. Solutions to some of the most important problems remain as elusive today as they were in Aristotle's time. For all of our sophisticated instrumentation, we still have no idea of how the brain's function is transmuted to the personal self-awareness that must certainly be considered to be each individual's greatest treasure. We have made progress with some problems of the neural correlates of rather simple mental functions, and a perspective is emerging, but as yet there is no psychobiology of mind that comes close to completion. However ambitious the title of this book, the fact must be acknowledged at the outset.

Thus, the function of this book will be to review the history, restate the issues, acknowledge the difficulties, and survey the present empirical knowledge in pursuit of its main goal—the elucidation of the conceptual foundations of the mind-body problem. At this point—as I set out on this task—I assume that whatever view of the nature of the relation of the body and the mind that emerges will most certainly have been anticipated by some sage somewhere in the history of classic philosophy or modern psychobiology. This volume can at best hope to only partially integrate the diverse bodies of knowledge that have accumulated; it is quite unlikely that any totally new or universally comprehensive theory will emerge. Yet, even within the context of this limited goal, it is interesting to note that in this problem area there have been very few attempts to carry out this type of integrative review at any time in the several decades just past. The books devoted to the problem of brain and mind have been basically unintegrated reports by groups of specialists that concentrate on highly specific subtopics [see, for example, Scher (1962), Eccles (1966), or Corning and Balaban (1968)] or simple textbooks that tabulate without synthesizing. Only a few contemporary psychobiologists, most notably John C. Eccles (1973a) and Karl Pribram (1971), have even attempted to create a general synthesis of the fundamental psychobiological issues in the study of the mind-body problem.

This book will be different from most of these predecessors in numerous regards. It will be composed of the writing of a single person—less than expert in each of the fields discussed, and thus less qualified to deal with each than any of a number of others who might have undertaken specific portions of this task.

The sheer volume of material makes the task especially difficult for a single author. As I start to write, frankly, I am not sure how long this book is going to be. When I first thought of writing this volume, I conceived of it as a brief summary of the contemporary state of the mind-body problem as viewed from the perspective of the late twentieth century. The more I thought about it, however, the more I realized that that approach would result in a superficial and inadequate analysis and that each topic must be sufficiently supported by empirical data to prevent simply another vacuous pseudophilosophical outburst of personal convictions. But where to stop? The book itself, as it evolves, must answer this question as the material leads naturally from one topic to another. When I am exhausted, or the most pertinent material is, then the book will be finished.

Although my goal is to use a broad brush to cover a wide canvas, one has only to look at the abundance of literature in psychobiology and the other neuro- and behavioral sciences to realize that there is no possibility that every topic that should be covered will indeed be discussed. The material, quite simply, is growing faster than it can be summarized, and, even if the current growth suddenly stopped, the already available material would be overwhelming. How does one deal with such a problem? There is only one way: The *general principle* and the *illustrative example* must substitute for the *exhaustive list.*

Thus, the abstraction of general principles is not only a practical necessity, but also the major goal of this undertaking. I honestly do not think that an exhaustive encyclopedia would either be much fun to write or very useful to anyone If there is any single contribution that would most satisfy me, it would be the knowledge that when someday in the future this book is finished, something of a meaningful pattern has been brought to the seemingly random array of empirical studies with which we have been inundated.

In selecting and abstracting from among the vast literature of psychobiology, of course, I am certain to offend many of the dedicated workers who have given so much of their lives to work in this field. It is inevitable that I am not going to be able to cite all of the relevant or important experiments or theories. The only conceivably successful strategy to achieve the goal I have set for myself is to draw an example here, or an idea there, as I try to extract and construct a meaningful message, and then to hope that, in the end, the synthesis makes sense as a whole rather than merely as a concatenation of the parts. This is the way science must work. However much energy has been expended on battles of priority of discovery or invention and whatever gains have been made in the solution of practical problems, the major payoff of the considerable investment in science is the global understanding of nature by the whole human community. All of us whose work has gone uncited and unrecognized at one time or another, as well as those who must, of necessity, be overlooked in the pages of this volume, can draw some comfort from the fact that knowledge sometimes has strange ways of being communicated throughout the scientific community. Some sound ideas and properly run experiments have had less impact than a few studies that are obviously absurd but which magically become seminal by virtue of the very blatancy of their incorrectness.

It is within this context of an emphasis on general conceptual principles and overall order that I plan to do two things that may upset certain of my psychobiological colleagues. First, I plan to insert, at each of the appropriate points in the discussion, historical summaries in a deliberate effort to place contemporary topics within their long-term context. Without a sense of history, this science, as any other human undertaking, would be worthless and would stand isolated from the overall symphony of human endeavor. Second, I plan to place related discussions of methodology and technical background at the points in the book at which they will be most pertinent to the topic under discussion, rather than to lump them entirely at its beginning. This experiment in organization, I can anticipate at the outset, is going to break the rhythm of the book in some instances. Nevertheless, I believe that the freshness of such relevantly placed mini-reviews may help to make the substantive material more understandable. I believe this approach to be particularly necessary in psychobiology, in which the technological foundations are so intimately intertwined with the data obtained and the theories generated.

The title of this book places it, very intentionally, in the mainstream of my work over the last twenty years. This volume attempts to provide a conceptual structure for a psychobiology of mind just as my earlier book, *The Psychobiology of Sensory Coding* (1973), did for the more restricted topic of sensory communication. Some of the general principles that became evident to me as I worked on that earlier manuscript begged for generalization to other areas of psychobiology. If the delight that I have gained simply from working on these two volumes can be transferred to a few readers, then all of my efforts will have been adequately rewarded. If some new insight, generally useful to the community of my fellow psychobiologists, should emerge, I shall indeed rejoice.

And so, with this plan and these preconceptions, I lay this preface aside. I will pick it up again some time from now when I am looking over the final pages of the manuscript.

At the End–October 1, 1976

I have just finished the final version of this manuscript and now lay it aside to complete the preface that I began over two years ago. Looking at the stack of paper that has resulted, I am filled with surprise. Surprise that the project went as fast as it did and surprise that it is really done. Looking over a few of the pages it seems incredible to me that some of the early ideas had actually taken on the particular final form that they did. I am also somewhat surprised, in retrospect, at the overall organization of ideas in this final draft. Writing this book was a dynamic process, and the final organization was based on a trichotomy of issues that I did not expect at the outset. The three main themes of psychobiology, as I now see them, are localization of function in brain (a problem at the macro-anatomical level), representation or coding (a problem at the microanatomic level), and dynamic change (a problem that transcends not only the anatomic levels but also the functional levels of molecular, chemical, physiological, and behavioral analysis).

Most particular research studies fit fairly well within this trichotomy. This classification scheme, I now am convinced, provides a conceptual metastructure that allows systematic categorization of new experiments in a way that has made it much easier for me to understand the implications and contributions of empirical developments as they are encountered. I hope it will do the same for the readers of this volume.

I must certainly acknowledge that the main reason the work went so well was the help I had from a number of people and organizations. Of especially great importance to me in the last two years has been the NIMH Research Scientist Award that I have held since 1971. Also my co-workers Lucinda Quackenbush and Thelma Tucker have given so much of the energy to this project that I find it hard to simply say that I acknowledge their efforts. I am truly and deeply appreciative of their loyalty and competence.

A number of my colleagues at the University of Michigan have read chapters and made significant contributions to their improvement. As ever, I bear the full responsibility for any stupidity in interpretation or technical error, but when I imagine what this book might have been without the help of such colleagues as Robert K. Lindsay, Maija Kibens, Sarah Winans, Jim Greeno, J. Bradley Powers, Daniel Green, and Lester Rutledge, I am especially grateful for the share of their busy time they spent reading and commenting on rough drafts.

I also have been most fortunate to have had a superior working relationship with a remarkable publisher. Erudite, profoundly literate, supportive, and ever a better friend, Larry Erlbaum retains the tradition of close personal relationships and high scholarly standards and goals that are increasingly rare in the highly commercialized publishing industry these days. It has been an honest pleasure to have had the kind of interactions with him that have characterized the writing of this, my third Lawrence Erlbaum Associates book. Psychology, as a science, also owes a special debt to Larry for his faith in work that is not directed at the most elementary levels and that is, therefore, not destined to make enormous profits.

Larry also put me in touch with two outstanding scholars who read the entire manuscript and made many helpful suggestions. One, H. Phillip Zeigler, of City University of New York and the American Museum of National History, had helped me with a critique of an earlier book, and his willingness to do so again was a pleasant surpirse. Phil's insight into desirable reorganization was of special value. Wally Welker of the University of Wisconsin became a new friend whose insight and wisdom into the multifaceted field covered by this book has added much to the quality of the final version. His sharp critique of early drafts, in particular, removed both technical absurdities and literary clumsiness.

I owe a continuing debt to my original mentor in psychobiology, Donald R. Meyer. Don's brilliance, wisdom, and high standards have served as models for a generation of his students, among whom I am proud to be included.

There was also a group of distinguished scholars with whom I have little personal contact but whose writing stimulated me and inspired some of the general views and concepts about which I have written. Among this group are almost all of the few systematizers in the neurosciences, philosophy or psychology who have sought, as I have, to find some order in the chaos that appears to characterize the empirical literature. Should such distinguished scholars as Janos Szentágothai, John C. Eccles, Karl Pribram, Herbert Feigl, J. R. Kantor, Richard F. Thompson, E. Roy John, or A. R. Luria ever encounter this book, they will see some of their influence clearly demonstrated even when my response to certain points they highlighted may have been more reaction than acceptance. Many others of less reknown, needless to say, have also stimulated the development of my ideas in sometimes subtle and indirect ways.

I also must note that in some of the chapters of this book (particularly Chapters 6 and 7) I have liberally adapted sections of my own previous writing. Reworking the material and updating it proved to be a far less onerous task than attempting to rewrite material on which I had already achieved a sense of closure.

The subject index and final proofreading of the page proofs of this work were done by Katherine Noto, whose dedicated competence it is also a pleasure to acknowledge.

I also owe a special debt of gratitude to my new colleagues at the Institute for Social Research at the University of Michigan for the opportunity to join this remarkable and cordial community of scholars. Their encouragement to pursue this project during this last year was especially important. I am especially grateful to Angus Campbell, Robert Kahn, Steven Withey, and Thomas Juster for their continued maintenance of a personal and intellectual environment that makes the Institute for Social Research the most pleasant, stimulating, and productive place to work I have ever seen.

It has, however, been my greatest source of inspiration to have shared my life so far with a remarkable and talented woman, my wife May. Her never-ending enthusiasm for life, my constant surprise and delight as she demonstrates some new artistic talent or expresses some new depth of wisdom, and her companionship and love have made everything that I have done possible. To Michan, as usual, this book is lovingly dedicated.

WILLIAM R. UTTAL

Acknowledgments

In the development of this book I have depended on art work, tables, and quotations from many sources. In each case, use in the book has been with the permission of the publisher and, whenever possible, also with the explicit written permission of the original author or artist. I am particularly grateful to the many distinguished scholars who have generously contributed their personal time to locate some old photograph or negative or have parted with what, in many instances, was a particularly precious reprint of an obviously well-received publication. The author's and publisher's permission for the use of each figure or table has been indicated in the appropriate caption.

In the following list, I express my appreciation to the authors and publishers who have permitted me to utilize quotations of 50 words or more. The pages in this book on which the quotations appear are indicated in italic in parentheses.

Academic Press

Leiman, A. L., & Christian, C. N. Electrophysiological analyses of learning and memory. In J. A. Deutsch (Ed.), *The physiological basis of memory.* New York, 1973. *(564-565)*

Posner, M. I. Psychobiology of attention. In M. S. Gazzaniga & C. Blakemore (Eds.), *Handbook of psychobiology.* New York, 1975. *(329)*

Ranck, J. B., Jr. Studies on single neurons in dorsal hippocampal formation and septum in unrestrained rats. Part I. Behavioral correlates and firing repertoires. *Experimental Neurology,* 1973, *41,* 461-531. *(486)*

American Association for the Advancement of Science

John, E. R. Switchboard versus statistical theories of learning and memory. *Science,* 1972, *177,* 850-864. *(542-543)*

Kety, S. S. A biologist examines the mind and behavior. *Science,* 1960, *132,* 1867-1969. *(11-13, 206)*

American Physiological Society

Disterhoft, J. F., & Olds, J. Differential development of conditioned unit changes in thalamus and cortex of rat. *Journal of Neurophysiology,* 1972, *35,* 665-579. *(593)*

Kandel, E. R., & Spencer, W. A. Cellular neurophysiological approaches in the study of learning. *Physiological Reviews*, 1968, *48*, 65-134.   *(565)*

American Psychological Association

Kantor, J. R. The evolution of mind. *Psychological Review*, 1935, *42*, 455-465.   *(205)*

Pribram, K. H., & McGuinness, D. Arousal, activation, and effort in the control of attention. *Psychological Review*, 1975, *82*, 116-149.   *(329, 329-330)*

Stellar, E. The physiology of motivation. *Psychological Review*, 1954, *61*, 5-22.   *(228)*

Thompson, R., & Myers, R. E. Brainstem mechanisms underlying visually guided responses in the rhesus monkey. *Journal of Comparative & Physiological Psychology*, 1971, *74*, 479-512.   *(309, 311)*

Annual Reviews, Inc.

Kupfermann, I. Neurophysiology of learning. *Annual Review of Psychology*, 1975, *26*, 367-391.   *(564)*

Appelton-Century-Crofts

Hilgard, E. R. *Theories of learning.* New York, 1948.   *(77)*

California Institute of Technology

McCulloch, W. S. Why the mind is in the head. In L. A. Jeffress (Ed.), *Cerebral mechanisms in behavior (The Hixon Symposium).* New York: Wiley, 1951.   *(19)*

Consultants Bureau/Basic Books, Inc.

Luria, A. R. *Higher cortical functions in man.* Authorized translation by Basil Haigh. 1966, Consultants Bureau Enterprises, Inc., and Basic Books, Inc., Publishers, New York.
                                                     (287)

Luria, A. R. *The working brain: An introduction to neuropsychology.* 1973, Penguin Books Ltd., Basil Haigh translation, Penguin Books Ltd. 1973, Basic Books Inc., Publishers, New York.   *(354)*

Encyclopedia Britannica Education Corporation

Koch, S. Behaviourism. In *Encyclopaedia Britannica* (Vol. 3). 1968, by Encyclopaedia Britannica, Inc.   *(514)*

Harper & Row, Publishers

Luria, A. R. *Human brain and psychological processes.* New York, 1966.   *(259, 287)*

Institute of Electrical & Electronics Engineers, Inc.

Lettvin, J. Y., Maturana, H. R., McCulloch, W. S., & Pitts, W. H. What the frog's eye tells the frog's brain. *Instititute of Radio Engineers (Proceedings)*, 1959, *47*, 1940-1951.
                                                  (443, 444-445)

International Universities Press

Cobb, S. (In S. Cobb, H. M. Fox, P. H. Gates, S. Gifford, P. H. Knapp, A. O. Ludwig, W. F. Murphy, C. Mushatt, E. V. Semrad, J. L. Weinberger, & F. Deutsch) Is the term "mysterious leap" warranted? In F. Deutsch (Ed.), *On the mysterious leap from the mind to the body.* New York, 1959.   *(206)*

Macmillan Company

Wundt, W. Vorlesungen uber die Menschen und Thierseele. In W. S. Sahakian (Ed.), *History of psychology: A source book in systematic psychology.* Itasca, Ill.: Peacock, 1968.
                                                     (205)

Macmillan (Journals) Ltd.

Hodgkin, A. L., & Huxley, A. F. Action potentials recorded from inside a nerve fibre. *Nature*, 1939, *144*, 710.   *(376)*

Massachusetts Institute of Technology Press

Rosenblueth, A. *Mind and brain: A philosophy of science.* Cambridge, Mass., 1970
(206)

McGraw-Hill Book Company

Minsky, M. Steps toward artificial intelligence. In E. A. Feigenbaum & J. Feldman (Eds.), *Computers and thought.* New York, 1963. *(43-44)*

Mouton and Company

Eccles, J. C. Preface. In E. P. Polten, *Critique of the psycho-physical identity theory.* The Hague, 1973. *(81)*

Polten, E. P. *Critique of the psycho-physical identity theory.* The Hague, 1973. *(50, 51)*

Neurosciences Research Program

Lennenberg, E. H. Language and brain: Developmental aspects. *Neurosciences Research Program Bulletin,* 1974, *12,* 513-656. *(317, 322-323)*

New York University Press

Feigl, H. Mind-body *not* a pseudoproblem. In S. Hook (Ed.), *Dimensions of mind: A symposium.* New York, 1960. *(60, 60-61)*

Plenum Publishing Corporation

Szentágothai, J. Memory functions and the structural organization of the brain. In G. Ádam (Ed.), *Biology of memory,* New York, 1971. *(195)*

Pontificia Academia Scientiarum

Eccles, J. C. (Ed.). *Brain and conscious experience.* New York: Springer-Verlag, 1966. *(6, 7)*

Princeton University Press

Penfield, W., & Roberts, L. *Speech and brain-mechanisms.* Princeton, N.J., 1959 *(549)*

Psychonomic Society

Teyler, T J., Baum W. M., & Patterson, M. M. (Eds.). Behavioral and biological issues in the learning paradigm. *Physiological Psychology,* 1975, *3,* 65-72. *(513)*

Random House

Reprinted by permission from *The Random House Dictionary of the English Language,* The Unabridged Edition, ©1966, 1973 by Random House, Inc. *(200-202)*

Rockefeller University Press

Miller, N. E. Certain facts of learning relevant to the search for its physical basis. In G. C. Quarton, T. Melnechuk, & F. O. Schmitt (Eds.), *The neurosciences: A study program.* New York, 1967. *(517-518)*

Zanchetti, A. Subcortical and cortical mechanisms in arousal and emotional behavior. In G. C. Quarton, T. Melnechuk, & F. O. Schmitt (Eds.), *The neurosciences: A study program.* New York, 1967. *(342)*

Routledge & Kegan Paul, Ltd.

Smythies, J. R. (Ed.). *Brain and mind: Modern concepts of the nature of mind.* London, 1965. *(205)*

Society of Experimental Biology

Lashley, K. S. In search of the engram. In D. G. Stein & J. J. Rosen (Eds.), *Learning and Memory.* New York: Macmillan, 1974. [Reprinted from *Society of Experimental Biology Symposium No. 4: Physiological Mechanisms in Animal Behaviour.* Cambridge University Press, 1950, pp. 454-482] *(538-539)*

Springer-Verlag, New York, Inc.

Eccles, J. C. *The physiology of synapses.* Berlin, 1964.   *(619)*

Charles C. Thomas, Publisher

Swammerdam, J. Experiment to demonstrate contraction of frog muscle. In J. F. Fulton & L. G. Wilson (Eds.), *Selected readings in the history of physiology.* Springfield, Ill., 1966.
                                                                                             (367)

Wistar Institute Press

Ling, G., & Gerard, R. W. The normal membrane potential of frog sartorius fibers. *Journal of Cellular and Comparative Physiology,* 1949, *34,* 383-385.   *(377)*

Yale University Press

Cassirer, E. *The philosophy of symbolic forms* (Vol. 1). *Language* (R. Manheim, trans.). New Haven, 1953.
                                                                                             (358)

Part I

BASIC CONCEPTS

1
A Survey and Introduction

A. THE PROBLEM

For millenia, since the emergence of consciousness and symbolic thought, our species has been concerned with a set of problems of such magnitude that all other issues of philosophy, science, and practical technology pale to insignificance in comparison. This set of problems concerns the nature of the relationship between our physical bodies and the insubstantial—but no less real—mental life of which each of us is personally aware. The search for an explanation of this relationship has come to be known as the *Mind-Body Problem,* an issue of such consequence that one philosopher (Schopenhauer, 1788-1860) referred to it as *The World Knot*—a play on words both of magnitude and of complexity.

At the dawn of human consciousness, man must have asked about the difference between the vitality of a living friend and the lifeless corpse into which he might so suddenly be transformed. The implications of the difference between the dead and the living, in contrast to the personal self-awareness of each individual, were profound, yet also compellingly straightforward; each man is forced to ask—Will "this" happen to me, too? Each man and each society is concerned with the problem. History is dominated by examples of the impact of this concern: The architecture, the literature, the wars, and other geopolitical interactions all show the effect of the popular, religious, philosophical, and scientific concern with the fundamental perplexity of the mind-body relationship. The folkways of man's daily life and his relation to his fellows, his psychology, and his attitudes toward kinsmen and strangers, all may be traced back to the basic urge to untie the "world knot."

What is the solution to the mind-body problem in general, in detail? The answers to these questions have varied over the numerous epochs of human history, but generally it can be agreed that man has attempted to determine the

3

relationship between his body and his mind by generating theories or explanations that provide satisfactory answers in the context of the intellectual and technological environment of each epoch. The answeres were, at various times in history, based upon premises that either treated the mind as a separate and distinct entity (the soul) that survived the body or, in total contrast, treated the mind as nothing more than the function of a material information processor. If there is any consistency among the classic explanatory models, it is that the mind has been taken as a real thing, as an entity that itself must be explained and related. In light of these classic models, the modern concept of mind as a process, rather than a thing, is a highly revolutionary development. Curiously, the concept of the body—another aspect of the problem—has been somewhat more variable in spite of the fact that it is more tangible. From time to time, various organs have been proposed to be the seat, locus, or receptacle of the mental processes.

Throughout all of this speculation and theory, however, the problem has been: How is it that the body of man transmutes the physiological processes into the mental states the existence of which each individual is totally confident because of his own personal self-awareness? This question, or some variant of it, is asked by all men, whether they be philosophers or farmers, at one time or another. Although the technical sophistication of the philosopher may obscure the great personal issue—Will "my" consciousness survive the inevitable decay of "my" body—his concern does not differ in quality from the most primitive worries about personal survival. Apparently, something about man's evolutionary heritage and his ability to process symbols impels each of us to seek to survive both as a species (sex is pleasurable) and as an individual (life, in general, is sweet and filled with experiences, pleasant or not). Whatever selective forces operate to guarantee the survival of our species and individuality have also led to the multifaceted expression of the will to survive, the most universal expression of which has been the urge to find some form of personal immortality.

And yet, all around us is evidence of death and the transitory nature of our personal physical existence. It is hard to avoid the fear of a similar termination of mind or spirit in light of this evidence. Our species has evolved self-awareness and has been provided with the ability to analyze the nature of its own consciousness only to find that the results of that analysis promise only terminal unconciousness. What a cosmic joke that is!

This "joke" is an exaggerated example of the kinds of considerations, primitive and elemental, in man's mental life, that have led to the human preoccupation with the many aspects of the mind-body problem and to the development of all of the many solutions that have permeated human history. For example, the many theologies, in spite of the social utility of their ethical codes, primarily represent the responses of the collective urgency of many individuals to find a solution to the mind-body problem and to answer the question of personal continuity after death.

Early in human history, the proposed answers to the mind-body question came mainly from prophets and philosophers, but beginning in the Middle Ages with the emergence of a more modern quantitative and experimental scientific tradition, formalized finally in the writings of Francis Bacon (1561-1626) and René Descartes (1596-1650), a trend away from purely philosophical or theological solutions occurred. A completely different theoretical and empirical approach, placing mind within the domain of biology, has gradually been substituted for metaphysical and theological speculations.

Psychobiology, the culmination of this trend, is a new interdisciplinary science that has evolved from experimental psychology on the one hand, and neurophysiology on the other. The basic axiom of modern psychobiology is that it is possible to compare and relate the observations obtained in the psychological laboratory with those forthcoming from the neurobiological sciences. So far, psychobiology is a correlative science in the first approximation, but the adequate biology of mind (the true or valid psychobiology) that will ultimately evolve must be more than that now at hand. It must seek to reduce the psychological observations to their underlying, unique, necessary, and sufficient neural determinants to whatever extent possible.

The proposition of a psychoneural or mind-body equivalence is the basic credo of the present volume. The idea that it is possible to compare and relate mind and body has within it an implicit commitment to one particular solution to the mind-body problem. The reader should not underestimate this point; this credo directly and absolutely implies that there is a basis of comparison that goes far beyond simple concomitancy—one, in fact, that implies an *equivalence* and not just a *correlative* correspondence between the two domains. Simply put, this approach contends that the mind and the body are related in such a basic manner that without the body, the mind does not exist. This explicit statement of the basic premise of modern psychobiology involves a philosophical position that is highly likely to have a massive impact on human society. This idea of equivalence is, therefore, not simply another theoretical utterance of interest solely to a few specialists, but a concept that could affect our attitudes toward social systems, education, national politics, and international conflict.

It should also be acknowledged that the idea of psychoneural equivalence is a relatively unpopular credo and one for which there is still no general acceptance even among scientists. Furthermore, many people express this point of view in some aspects of their lives while ignoring or rejecting it in others. The psychobiologist, like any individual human being, is likely, in fact particularly likely, to dichotomize his professional and personal lives because of the dual pressures of his work and the society to which he is subject.

In spite of the gentle and compromising tendency on the part of each of us to agree that each person should decide the issue for himself, the premise of mind-body equivalence implicit in modern psychobiology conflicts in a fundamental way with the predominant theologies of our society, and that conflict is becoming increasingly explicit today. The contradiction between the premise of this small science and the personal philosophies of most people living today may be a profoundly important world issue of the next few centuries even in comparison to the more practical problems of population and food supply. Such a fundamental disagreement is almost guaranteed to offend some thoughtful people as the implications become more generally known. Although mind-body equivalence is a relatively recent development, and it takes an astonishingly long time for even the most relevant (to problems of daily life) ideas to percolate from the studies of scientists and philosophers to the communally accepted body of wisdom, this conflict is certain to ensue. And when it does, the idea of mind-body equivalence is so personally and institutionally threatening that the intellectual upheaval may be enormous. Like evolution, which shook nineteenth century thinking to its foundations and which has not even yet been universally accepted, the problem of psychoneural equivalence, far more recent and probably far more influential because it deals with each man's future rather than the species' past, may dominate human intellectual activity in the centuries to come.

For the present, however, we play some curiously inconsistent games of intellectual duplicity. An interesting example of an attempt to draw an arbitrary line between the equivalence premise of psychobiology and a conflicting idea strongly held by another part of human society, can be read in a dialogue quoted in the preface of the report (Eccles, 1966) of an extraordinary scientific meeting held at an even more extraordinary location. John C. Eccles organized a conference on brain and conscious experience that was held at the Vatican City under the auspices of a little-known but highly prestigious organization: the Vatican Academy of Science. Eccles reports in his prefatory remarks to the volume that, during the planning of the meeting, he was informed that: "the Academy by its constitution has for aim to promote the study and progress of the physical, mathematical and natural sciences and their history. Thus the discussion of philosophical questions is excluded" [Eccles, 1966, p. vii].

But as may be obvious to the reader, many psychobiologists feel that this greatest of all philosophical issues is precisely the content of the natural science we know as psychobiology—the actual topic of that meeting. Eccles found that it was hardly possible to follow the prohibition of the Chancellor of the Vatican Academy and summed the problem up very well in his reply:

I fear that some of your concern derives from the different linguistic usages that we have. For example, to me all sciences have a philosophical basis and it is generally agreed that there is a philosophy of science which is in fact basic to all scientific investigations and discussions. Certainly when one comes to a Study Week devoted to brain and mind it is not possible to exclude relations with philosophy, though I agree that there are certain philosophical questions which the Academy would be well advised to avoid. I do not think that any of the proposed subjects fall into this category [Eccles, 1966, pp. vii-viii].

In spite of this exchange and without Eccles knowledge, the following statement was distributed by the church hosts to all of the participants of the meeting, further expressing the view of the Academy on this matter.

> As to the meaning of the term "consciousness," the Study Week intends that it strictly designates the psychophysiological concept of perceptual capacity, of awareness of perception, and the ability to act and react accordingly.
>
> Consequently, the subject which the invited scientists are requested to discuss, has to be duly delimited by this semantic acceptation, which is of a strictly scientific character.
>
> It is obvious, that every extrapolation of the meaning of the term "consciousness" leading the subject into an extrascientific field, would be contrary to the spirit of the Study Week [as quoted in an article by H. Schaefer in Eccles, 1966, p. 522].

Obviously, as this dialogue exemplifies, modern approaches to the solution of the mind-body problem are sensitive matters and trespass on some very deeply held beliefs. The premises of psychobiology, unspoken though they may be, are patently "philosophical"; it would reduce both the Vatican meeting and the science of psychobiolgy to absurdities to have ignored the reasons for which some strange little experiments, indeed, are carried out. It would not really be worthwhile, nor could it possibly have any long-range effect, to attempt to build arbitrary boundaries between the subject matter of this science and the great related problems of human existence. We must face the fact that the two statements of the issue are one and the same; both priest and psychobiologist speak to the same matters even though they have quite different concepts of what are their respective "best" solutions.

In the last few paragraphs, I have set the stage for what follows by trying to spell out, in a rather informal manner, the nature of the mind-body problem, the intended topic of this book. The remainder of this chapter will be aimed at achieving the two further introductory goals. Section (B) defines what I believe to be some of the main issues that collectively constitute the great mind-body problem. Section (C) describes the detailed plan of the remainder of the book.

B.   SUBISSUES IN THE MIND-BODY PROBLEM

The mind-body problem, as has been suggested, can hardly be considered a single issue or a simple question; rather it is a mixture of many different subproblems of varying degrees of intricacy. Some of the subissues encountered in the study of the mind-body problem are matters of global epistemology; others are matters of minute technical detail. It seems quite clear that all scientists working in the sister fields of psychology and neuroscience are more or less directly attacking some specific aspect of the mind-body problem. This assertion has been most emphatically made for neuroscientists by a distinguished neurophysiologist, G. A. Horridge, when he said, simply and clearly, that "The aim of neurobiology is the explanation of behavior" (Horridge, 1969, p. 1). Similarly, all psychologists, no matter how alien their personal approach may be to neurophysiological reductionism, contribute to an increasingly precise definition of what exactly we mean by mind. In recent years those who seek to specifically resolve the mind-body problem have come to be encompassed within the general rubric of psychobiology.

A simple statement that the aim of psychobiology is to determine the relationship between the mind and the body may, however, leave the philosopher or scientist who is really interested in doing something concrete floundering. The very diffuseness of the problem when stated in this general way makes it impossible to answer it in any practical manner; the problem must be subdivided into workable units that the philosopher or scientist can deal with in a realistic fashion. In carrying out such a division, not only is the content of the problem made concrete and workable, but also the intellectual nature of the problem itself is more critically defined.

The discussion to be presented in this section will attempt to identify the main conceptual and technical issues that collectively define the contemporary status of the mind-body problems but will not descend to the details of individual experiments. Some problems to be discussed are issues for philosophers; some are problems for neurophysiologists; others reside in the domain of psychobiologists or more classically oriented psychology. Collectively, these subproblems are the mind-body problem. There is a basic order to the presentation of the subissues in the following list. I will first discuss the more general and philosophical subissues and then turn to the more empirical and technical.

1. What are "Good" Psychobiological Questions?

Not too surprisingly, in an area as complex as that of the mind-body problem, one of the initial difficulties is being certain that one has actually posed questions that are both important and resolvable. It is interesting to note that even the idea that the mind-body problem exists has been challenged by some operationalistic and positivistic philosophers, most notably Ludwig Wittgenstein (1889-1951), in this century. In his later years, Wittgenstein recanted on even the positivistic position that the mind-body question could be understood only in terms of empirical observations and simply assumed that it was a "bad question" that is probably not resolvable.

A major portion of the resistance to the mind-body problem as a researchable question is the fact that some still doubt that consciousness, self-awareness, or whatever it is that is meant by the term "mind," is amenable to observation and measurement. Another factor leading some to the conclusion that the mind-body problem is not a researchable question was the behavioristic orientation of much of mid-twentieth century psychology. In rejecting the mind as an observable, as the behaviorists did under the influence of their operationalist and positivistic predecessors, the importance of the question of its relation to the body was also thrown out.

The historic justification of the mind-body problem as an issue, it still must be admitted, depended in large part on the subjective importance of one's own personal self-awareness prior to the rush of new laboratory developments in this century. But since then, substantial evidence for the validity of the question lies in the magnitude of the scientific and popular effort devoted to the pursuit of the problem, regardless of what epistemologists might feel about the formalities of the question. It may not be possible to prove the logical validity of the mind-body problem, but it is difficult to avoid the conviction that the problem, as stated, is real and important to a very large number of people.

Another reason that attempts may have been made to define the problem out of existence by some philosophers has been hinted at by Feigl (1958), who suggests that: "Many of the philosophical positions at least since the 18th century were primarily motivated, I strongly suspect, by the wish to avoid the mind-body problem [p. 372]."

Considering some of the implications (for example, the transitoriness of personal consciousness and the invalidity of many religious beliefs) of many of the modern scientific solutions to man's attitude toward his own continuity and his conception of the role of his species in the universe, it is easy to understand how some thoughtful people may be quite eager to avoid the issue entirely. In this context, it is interesting to note that in most contemporary textbooks of physiological psychology, there is almost a deliberate avoidance of the social, personal, and religious implications of the empirical data. A clear and unequivocal statement of what the study of the mind-body problem might mean to human thought simply is not a typical part of even those books that are incontestably dealing with just that issue.

2. Is Reductionism Possible?

One major theme of science is the continued effort to explain one level of inquiry by showing how its mechanisms and processes arise out of mechanisms of some lower or more microscopic level. This theme is called *reductionism.* In metallurgy, for example, explanations of the behavior of metals are sought in terms of their atomic structures, and explanations of atomic structures are sought in the basic physical forces holding the components of the atoms together.

Reductionism is also the foundation upon which the entire science of psychobiology is built. Psychobiologists seek to explain behavioral observations in terms of the neural substrates that are presumed to account for them. Some philosophical and scientific schools (e.g., the Gestalt tradition) like the positivistic philosophies, have questioned the idea that any process can be reduced to the attributes of mechanisms at a more microscopic level. They note in many instances that novel properties of the higher level emerge as a result of the particular pattern of *organization* of the parts and processes of the lower level and not because of the *characteristics* of the individual parts themselves. Thus, they suggest that prediction from lower levels to higher levels purely on the basis of aggregation is not possible. In physics the problem has been sharply focused in discussion of statistical theories of gases [e.g., the classic work by J. H. Jeans (1940) on the theory of gases]. The physicist asks: Given the total information about the nature of molecules and the rules for their interaction, could we describe the pressure in a container of gas? In other words, given all of the necessary information about the components, can the global properties of the aggregate be predicted?

The debate over the answerability of this question is a theoretical one: All agree that the huge number of atoms makes prediction based upon calculation of the individual atom's dynamics completely impractical. No one asserts that all of the necessary information about the positions, velocities, and interactions between all particles in a container of gas could be made available. So the controversy rages over matters of interpretation and theories of the nature of reality. Is the behavior of the aggregate theoretically, although not practically, predictable from the sum of the characteristics of the parts, or is there some new and emergent property that arises unpredictably when components are accumulated in great numbers?

One of the major difficulties in resolving this issue is that the complete specification of the characteristics of the parts includes a description of the *relations* between the parts. But, these relations are often not observable until the parts have been accumulated into the whole and the forces of interaction have the opportunity to manifest themselves. Obviously, this is an epistemological issue of considerable complexity—indeed, it was and is a continuing dilemma for physicists. Throughout his life the great physicist-mathematician Albert Einstein (1879-1955) believed that "God would not play dice with the universe," an eloquent expression of the idea that deterministic rules, and thus reductive analysis, must govern even those systems that must be dealt with statistically because their parts are so numerous. On the other hand, various distinguished physicists, including such a luminary as Niels Bohr (1885-1962), felt that the statistical methods used by physicists actually reflected an innate randomness and indeterminacy of the universe.

Perhaps the only way to handle this epistemological controversy for psychobiology, in particular, is to simply accept the premise that reductionism is a valid concept. The idea of reductionism is so deeply embedded in the research in this field that rejection of this premise would be exceedingly counterproductive at this stage of the science. We must, therefore, accept two basic psychobiological axioms: The first states that psychological properties arise out of physiological processes, and the second acknowledges that it is possible to seek explanations of psychological functions by observing these physiological processes. Reductionism, therefore, is the *sine qua non* of modern psychobiology, and the ultimate goal of psychobiology is to answer the question: What are the necessary and sufficient structures and associated processes to account for specific mental/behavioral taxonomic units?

3.   What Is The Proper Level of Inquiry?

Once the goal of reductionism of mental states to their physiological substrates
is accepted as the main task of contemporary psychobiology, it is appropriate to
next consider what is the appropriate level of reductionism. The issue in this case
arises from the fact that there are many aspects or levels of the physical nervous
system on which the attack may be concentrated. The metabolic and circulatory
functions, for example, are certainly important to the physiologist, but are they
of significance to the psychobiologist, other than in a supporting or indirect
manner? The answer to this question if fairly easy: No, they are probably not!
The aspects of the brain that correlate most closely with our mental life are
probably quite distinct from these essentially service functions. Although a
failure in circulation, or more emphatically, of brain circulation in particular,
could easily result in unconsciousness, the effect would have to be considered
to be quite indirect.

However, suppose that the question of an appropriate level of inquiry was
posed in a different manner. Suppose that one was asked to decide between the
action of single neurons or of chunks of the brain as being uniquely associated
with some mental state. In this case, and in spite of the fact that many modern
psychobiologists have strong personal commitments to one neural level or the
other as being the "key" level, there is a great deal of difficulty in providing an
answer to this query with which all would agree.

Perhaps this point can be more clearly illustrated by consideration of an
amusing allegory that was written by a distinguished contemporary neuroscientist, Seymour Kety of the National Institute of Mental Health. Kety (1960) considers the difficulty of determining the most appropriate level of inquiry by
comparing the mind-body problem to the analysis of a new discovery—books—
suddenly presented to some scientists who exist in a hypothetical bookless
society. He writes:

> Let us imagine a community with inhabitants who are of high intelligence and quite
> civilized except that they have never seen a book and have developed other means
> for the transmission of knowledge. One day a million books appear in their midst,
> an event which arouses so much curiosity and consternation that they decide to es-
> tablish a scientific institute to study them. They set up this institute by disciplines
> and establish a policy that each scientist may examine these objects only with the
> tools and techniques and concepts of his discipline.
>
> The first laboratory to be organized is the Laboratory of Anatomy. There the
> workers study these strange objects for a while, and their conclusion reads like this:
> "The specimen is a roughly rectangular block of material, covered ventrally and dor-
> sally with two coarse, fibrous, encapsulated laminae approximately three millimeters
> thick. Between these lie several hundred white lamellae a fraction of a millimeter
> thick, all fastened at one end and mobile at the other. On closer inspection, these are
> found to contain a large number of black surface markings arranged in linear group-
> ings in a highly complex manner.
>
> By that time the chemists have appeared on the scene. The first chemist to get
> hold of a specimen burns it, and satisfies himself that it obeys the law of conserva-
> tion of matter and is therefore in his province; he may even compute the energy

release per gram on complete oxidation. Next comes the analytical chemist, who discovers first its elementary composition but later breaks it down less completely into pure compounds; he also reports traces of elementary carbon, "which are probably impurities." Before I forget to mention it, one day a chemist accidentally drops a colored solution on one of the pages and by serendipity discovers paper chromatography, which lies around for 25 years before someone figures out what to do with it.

Then there are the biochemists, who slice the book and mince it and, best of all, homogenize it (because on the slices and mince they can still see those black contaminants, while the homogenate can be centrifuged to remove them, permitting them to work with a Pure System). But all of these chemists have an uncomfortable feeling that though what they are doing is important, the real answers will come from the fellow down the hall who has just arrived and is still polishing his bright and expensive equipment—the molecular biologist.

With the self-confidence which comes from the adulation of the less fundamental sciences, he is anxious to begin work on the book he has selected because someone has told him that it is biased and distorted. Having hung a sign over his door which reads, "No twisted book without a twisted molecule," he proceeds to search for the molecule. By repeated extraction, centrifugation and ultracentrifugation, electrophoresis, hydrolysis, and repolymerization, he finally isolates a pure substance, free of the carbon particles, and—what is even better—a macromolecule, and a twisted one at that. Figure 1-1 represents his version of the fundamental nature of the book, which many will recognize as a current hypothesis of the structure of cellulose.

Simultaneously, the physiologists have been attacking the subject. Unlike the biochemists, they have read the report from the anatomists and proceed to study and speculate upon why and how the pages are attached on one side. They study the movement of the pages as the book is riffled and derive complex equations to describe it. Then a biophysicist discovers that in an appropriate electrostatic field the graphite deposits produce discontinuities in potential. Fine microelectrodes are developed to pick these up, and amplifiers and oscilloscopes to display them. The biophysicist discover by sticking these electrodes into the book in various places that those which do not break off will pick up signals, some of which are reproducible. They develop thousands of tracings of these signals, and call in the cyberneticist to help uncode them. The signals are recorded on miles of magnetic tape and fed into huge computers. Excitement mounts when, in a particular region extending over a few millimeters in a certain book, one of them discovers on a particular day that, for a few minutes before he damaged the source of the signals, a tremendously complex pattern appeared which was reproducible but incomprehensible. This pattern is fed into the data reducers and the computers, which can generate and test thousands of hypotheses per minute. Finally, the electric typewriter begins to print; a meaning has been found in that complex pattern—it reads "THE."

By this time the behavioral scientists have been admitted to the institute and begin to study the problem. They are a strange lot. Some of them have read the reports of the anatomists, the chemists, and the physiologists, but many of them don't seem to care. Most will admit, if pressed, that the book is material in nature, that it obeys material laws, that it and its contents are nothing more than a highly specialized arrangement of chemical substances. But they don't slice the book, and they don't purify its chemical components—in fact, they seem to feel that it is improper to do so. Instead, they ask questions peculiar to their disciplines and look in the book for the answers. The first one likes to count, so he counts the number of letters in the words and comes up with a frequency distribution of the words by their length (Fig. 1-2). He finds a preponderance of four-letter words, forms a hypothesis that the book

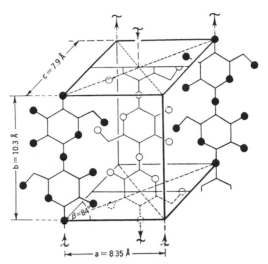

FIG. 1.1   A model of the molecular structure of cellulose. (From Kety, ©1960, after K. H. Meyer; caption from Kety, ©1960, with the permission of Wiley/Interscience, Inc.)

is a modern novel, and ventures a prediction that it will be a best seller and also banned by the Postmaster General. Then he looks for particular words and counts them and confirms the hypothesis. His colleagues join him, asking other general questions and finding their answers in the content of the book. They learn a great deal about classes of books, how they differ from one another, and what their effects are on the community. Although the behavioral scientist has learned much about the nature of books—infinitely more, in certain areas, than the physical scientist—his techniques falter in the area of the individual book, its characteristics, and his ability to make entirely reliable predictions about it. If it is important to learn something about the individual book, then there is need for a technique which can read it completely. Such a technique has not yet appeared, but some progress has been made in its development.

Finally, the book is brought in desperation to the psychoanalyst in the hope that he will be able to read it. That he does not do precisely, but instead asks the author to select portions and read them while he listens. Of course, the author is biased and reads what he wants to read, or, if there is "good transference," those passages which he thinks the analyst would like to hear. And the analyst himself doesn't always hear with equal acuity but, depending on his school or on his preconceived notions, is deaf to greater or lesser portions of the data [Kety, 1960, pp. 1867-1869].

Kety's allegory, of course, is a humorous and insightful reflection of the state of psychobiology and the neurosciences today. We, too, see neuroscientists of all sorts ranging from molecular biochemists to behaviorally oriented workers trying to determine the nature of the relationship between the mind and the body. It seems, however, that just as in Kety's allegory, we must also assume that many of the neurosciences today are concerned with phenomena that do not directly pertain to the mind-body problem. The electrochemistry of the neuron is exceedingly important to neurophysiologists, and it most certainly

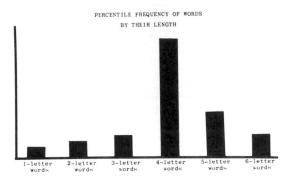

FIG. 1.2   Percentile frequency of words arranged according to their length in a particular book. (Figure and caption from Kety, ©1960, with the permission of The American Association for the Advancement of Science.)

is an intrinsically important problem. Whatever the brain does, it does because of neuronal biochemistry. But, in fact, the essence of the mind-body problem lies at a different level, the level at which information patterns are processed. We can probably safely assume that barring some practical constraints, the mind could exist even if neurons were built on some other structural basis than the sodium-potassium-chloride ion chemistry on which it is known to be based. We may conclude that it is the organizational pattern of the parts rather than the nature of the parts that is probably the correct level of inquiry with regard to the specific subject matter of the mind-body problem.

It should be noted, however, that even if the researcher's attention is restricted to this level of neuroanatomical organization, the problem of defining the most appropriate level still remains acute. Perhaps nowhere is this point made better than in Welker's (1976) elegant conceptualization of the many levels at which organizational neuroanatomy can be studied, reproduced in Fig. 1-3. There are, in short, levels within levels that preclude a precise answer to this important problem at the present time.

4.   Is Mind Measurable?

It is also surprising to note how many scientists, particularly those in fields other than psychology, still would not agree that psychological states, as observed in explicit behavior, are actually measurable in the same sense as physical parameters. Part of the problem arises because of the difficulty in defining mental states and the dimensions of consciousness. However, much progress has been made by assuming that these dimensions can be measured and that mind, even though it may require a different mathematical treatment than the measurement of length, for example, is susceptible to measurement and quantification through the intermediary of behavior.

Psychophysics, the body of techniques and data relevant to the relations

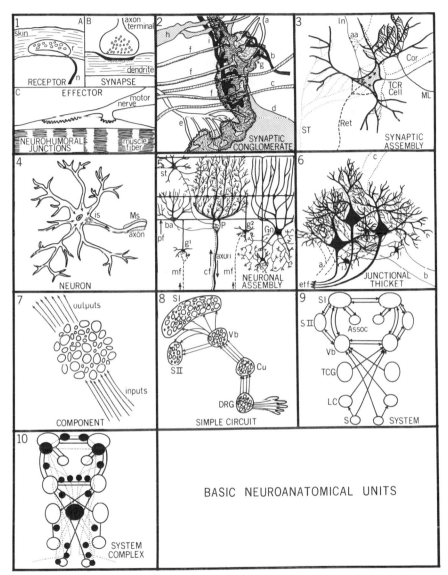

FIG. 1.3   The problem of defining the appropriate level of neural organization at which to search for the essential correlates of mind is exceedingly complex. In this schematic drawing, Welker has insightfully noted the multiple levels that can be examined. A full description of the significance of each of these levels of neural organization can be found in Welker (1976). (From Welker, ©1976, with the permission of Lawrence Erlbaum Associates.)

between the dimensions of physical stimuli and the dimensions of sensory experience, has made enormous progress toward an understanding of the relatively simple information processing carried out by sensory systems. Enjoying the advantages of a clearly defined referent, the physical stimulus, sensory psychophysics has progressed perhaps further than any other research program toward an understanding of this aspect of the mind of man. Both the relative simplicity of the neural structures involved and the predominantly unidirectional flow of information as well as the conceptual anchor provided by the physics of stimuli have helped to place sensory psychophysics among the most mature of the psychobiological sciences. Interestingly, many of the concepts from this field (e.g., spatial interaction) are now becoming increasingly important in some of the more complicated areas of cognitive psychology.

The general problem of how one links the world of numbers and quantitative measurements to a world of mental processes that are essentially nonnumerical (how long is a thought and how much does it weigh are essentially meaningless questions) is a massive intellectual effort by itself. I claim no expertise in the basic premises and paradigms of mathematical psychology, so the interested reader may want to look at the very important two-volume work by Krantz, Luce, Suppes, and Tversky (1971) for a thorough and scholarly approach to the problems of measurement in psychology. The point to be made here is only that most, if not all, psychological processes are assumed in this volume to be susceptible to mathematical description, quantification, and analysis.

5.   Are Psychological Processes Localizable in Specific Regions of the Brain?

One of the great experimental themes of psychobiological research concerns the matter of the localization in the brain of specifically defined psychological functions. Specific sites mediating learning, vision, sex drives and many other functions from the psychological taxonomy have been sought over the past century using such techniques as ablation of cortical masses and evocation of neuroelectric responses with various kinds of environmental stimuli, or conversely evocation of behavioral responses with stimuli applied to the brain. This search expresses, in a highly concrete manner, the premise intrinsic to this approach, that these functions might have relatively narrowly defined loci in the nervous system. There are, however, in spite of this large effort, such a substantial number of conceptual as well as anatomical complications involved in the search for these specific loci that a special effort is required to ensure that the issue is well-defined.

So often in scientific work we tend to see what we want to see. The implicit acceptance of the premise of localization as an operating paradigm [see Kuhn (1970) for a discussion of what is meant by a scientific paradigm] often limits the nature of one's conclusions. In spite of the fact that the search for localization is a main theme of modern psychobiological research, there is considerable experimental evidence suggesting that no narrow localization exists for most psychological processes. Lashley's studies of memory, so aptly summed up in the classic paper "In Search of the Engram" (Lashley, 1950), led him to the conclusion that there was no specific storage place for memories, but rather the relevant brain mechanisms are widely and diffusely distributed throughout the brain. Modern work has generally tended to support this conclusion for memory. The question must be asked separately for other psychological functions.

The premise of localization has had an extensive history, emerging first in classic Greece, and then growing through the highly specific theories of the phrenologists and the faculty psychologists to modern localization theory. But today, the general idea of localization as well as the particular assignments of functions to particular areas of the brain are being challenged in a number of laboratories. Localization now appears to make most sense when spoken of in terms of complex interconnecting communication links rather than in terms of narrowly circumscribed integrative functions.

There are several sources of this challenge to classical localization theory. Some researchers have suggested that certain of the localization effects obtained in experiments in which parts of the brain were ablated may have been confounded by feedback, feedforward, and inhibitory effects characteristic of highly interconnected systems. Others have pointed out that while the brain and its parts are reasonably well-defined structures, the psychological constructs that are being localized are not, and this imbalance in precision of definition invariably leads to some confusion. Finally, there is considerable concern being expressed today about the level at which localization might be sought. Should one look for functions in single cells or in larger chunks of brain? This is questioned in spite of the fact that localization has classically been a "chunk" problem. In the following discussion, we consider each of these subissues in turn.

a.   What Is the Role of Interactions in the Interpretation of Localization Experiments?

To replace the strict localization doctrine and the idea of quasi-independent centers, new perspectives have emerged concerning the interrelationship of the parts of the brain. One new perspective referred to as a system or cybernetic approach has been stimulated by the notions of such mathematicians as Norbert Wiener (1894-1964) as well as by such biological observations as the opposition of antagonistic muscles made by Charles S. Sherrington (1857-1952) and the lateral inhibitory interactions in the invertebrate eye made by H. Keefer Hartline (Hartline, Wagner, & Ratliff, 1956). This approach stresses the importance of interaction, feedback, and feedforward among the various circuits of a highly interconnected brain. System effects such as these make the problem of localizing functions exceedingly complex, for if two or more parts of the brain are reciprocally interconnected, it is entirely possible that the removal of one of them could produce a change in the response pattern of all of the involved parts. Cascaded inhibition (disinhibition) may simulate excitation, and thus the activation of a distant inhibitor may actually result in an increased local response mediated by a nearby inhibited inhibitor. In such a system, one functional role for a given center might thereby be suggested, when, in fact, an entirely different functional role is played by that center. Needless to say, many of our most cherished convictions about brain organization may have to be reconsidered in the light of these new ideas.

b.   What Is It That Is Being Localized?

Another difficulty with attempts to localize functional roles is that our classification of psychological functions leaves much to be desired. A wide variety of behavioral functions have been classified, for one or another historical or empirical reason, into highly artificial categories. However, it is not certain a priori that each of the conventionally existing categories of behavior, invented as an organizing concept or theoretical construct, must necessarily have a discrete biological correspondence in brain. Although it seems clear that sensory experience, for example, must have some kind of specific and localized neural concomitant, is it possible to extend this same kind of neural hypothesis to all other psychological constructs? Is motivation, a concept that really pertains to the likelihood of emission of any one of many possible behaviors momentarily available to the organism, likely to have an equivalent neural correlate in the brain?

The general question thus arises: What forms of behavior are proper targets of research that seeks their particular anatomic loci, and what forms of behavior represent more general parameters of mind that may not be localizable into a particular brain region? Chapter 5 presents an anatomy of mental processes that clarifies into which of these two categories a particular behavioral descriptor might best fit.

c.   Should Localization Be Sought at the Microscopic or Macroscopic Level?

The final perplexity of the issue of localization is ultimately related to the level of inquiry. Assuming that a given mental process is actually localizable by some empirical procedure there remains the problem of deciding at what level of brain structure the search for the structural equivalent should be carried out. Should gross ablation techniques be employed to determine which lobe of the brain is associated with a particular function, or should the search be carried out at microscopic levels among individual neurons and their connections? If the latter approach seems more appropriate, localization at the cellular level becomes a matter of understanding the interconnection patterns of neural nets with greater or lesser degrees of regularity.

This, then, also brings us back to an even older and more general form of the question of the physical locus of the mind. Why, indeed, must we assert that the brain is the site of mental processes? Perhaps the best answer to this very general question can be found in the details of the most specific level, that of the interconnected neural nets just discussed. The answer has been best put by Warren McCulloch (1894-1969) in 1951:

Why is the mind in the head? Because there, and only there, are hosts of possible connections to be formed as time and circumstance demand. Each new connection serves to set the stage for others yet to come and better fitted to adapt us to the world, for through the cortex pass the greatest inverse feedbacks whose function is the purposive life of the human intellect [p. 56].

Obviously, the problem of localization, both as a concept and as the historical sequence of an extensive series of experiments is immensely complex. In Chapter 5 this issue is considered in great detail but from a slightly different point of view than is usual. Rather than stressing the correspondence between one neural mechanism and one psychological process, this chapter concentrates on the broad issue of localization elaborating on some of the conceptual problems briefly alluded to earlier in this section.

6.   Analogy or Homology?

A major conceptual difficulty currently facing psychobiology concerns the problem of how one should deal with *processes* that seem to be very similar to each other but which are generated by *mechanisms* which are not amenable to direct observation. The question raised is: Does a similarity in the course of a process imply an equivalence of underlying structure? In other words, if we should, for example, observe similarities in some spatiotemporal aspects of the behavior of two organisms, must this necessarily lead us to the conclusion that identical, or even similar, mechanisms are underlying these observed behaviors?

To make this point more concrete, consider the following situation. Two systems, one simple and one complex, are observed to exhibit inhibitory interactions between sequential stimuli. Does this mean that a simple temporal interaction that can be observed when one dissects the simpler one is necessarily the mechanism of the similar process in the more complex system?

When the question is posed in this way, most physical scientists, as well as psychobiologists, would quickly agree that it is theoretically impossible to make the logical leap from the observed mechanisms to the unobserved one. They would concur with mathematicians who note that given only the "solution" to a problem (i.e., the behavior may be thought of as the solution or output of the problem posed by the mechanism's structure), there is no way to retrace the derivation of that solution to determine the nature of the original problem. In other words, numerical solutions, either simple arithmetic or complex differential equations are not reversible; the answers do not project back uniquely to a single problem even though the problem may have a unique solution.

Psychological processes are, in this same sense, solutions or functions of the physiological mechanisms that produce them. And like the situation in mathematics when solutions are not unique, very similar processes can be produced by very dissimilar mechanisms. The psychobiologist is no more able to refer back to a unique mechanism to account for some observed process than the mathematician.

In the rush of scientific observation and publication, however, the fact that one cannot go directly from behavior to mechanism is often ignored. Many investigators have observed behavior of one kind or another and have even demonstrated that it is the function of a single highly specific mechanism. However, when the same *mechanism* is imputed to another process that is similar to the first only to the extent that there is a correspondence in the time course or spatial pattern of the response there is the considerable potential for error. In large part this difficulty has been engendered because of what appears to be a confusion of what is meant by the terms *analogy* and *homology,* the essentials of a more general conceptual issue that is now considered in detail.

The terms analogy and homology are borrowed from structural biology and evolution. Lorenz (1974) eloquently defines the two terms. By analogy, he notes, biologists refer to the relationship between structures that perform the same function but have different embryological origins. Figure 1-4 shows two analogous structures that have evolved to solve the problem of visual input. In each case, however, the embryological and evolutionary origins are quite different although all of the analogous structures accomplish the same functions. Homologies, on the other hand, are structures of similar embryological or evolutionary origins that differentiate to play distinct functional roles. Figure 1-5, for example, shows how the anterior appendage of the generalized vertebrate skeleton has evolved into wings, paddles, or legs, respectively, different functions from structures of identical embryological origin.

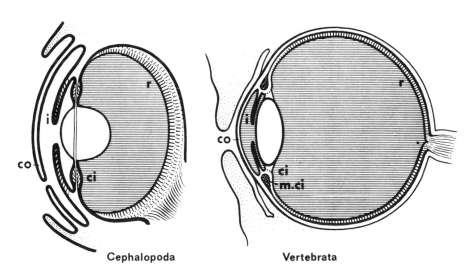

Cephalopoda   Vertebrata

FIG. 1.4 Analogy displayed in the visual organs of two quite different species. Each of these eyes has structures that perform the same functions, and the overall arrangement is strikingly similar. However, the embryological and evolutionary origins of the eyes in the cephalopod octopus and the vertebrate primate are totally different. These analogous structures reflect an evolutionary convergence to solve a similar problem rather than a common origin. (From Lorenz, ©1974, with the permission of The Nobel Foundation.)

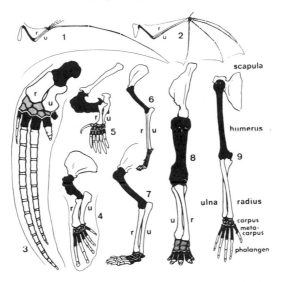

FIG. 1.5   A collection of homologs. Each of these vertebrate forelimb structures, though performing quite different functions, has evolved from a common embryological origin. (From Lorenz, ©1974, with the permission of The Nobel Foundation)

A continuing task for scientists is to avoid the confusion between analogies and homologies. Contrary to Lorenz' assertion for biology, however, I do not believe that the problem for psychobiology lies in the danger of "mistaking a homology for an analogy." Psychobiology's greater danger lies in just the opposite direction—mistaking an analogy for a homology—that is, misinterpreting similarities between two functions as being indicative of identical underlying mechanisms.

To make this point more concrete, let us consider a particular example. Psychologists often observe evidence of perceptual interactions between several visual stimuli presented in close proximity to each other. One of the classic cases of spatial interaction is the simultaneous contrast phenomenon. The effect is such that stimuli surrounded by one kind of contrasting field appear different than when they are surrounded by another kind. For example, as shown in Fig. 7-17, a grey will appear darker when surrounded by a light area than when it is surrounded by a dark area. In other cases, the size or the color of an object may vary as a function of its surround.

Neurophysiologists, on the other hand, often observe processes of reciprocal interaction between neurons. One neuron may inhibit the action of a neighbor in a way that is quite similar to the psychological process of simultaneous contrast. There is, in these cases, a very strong tendency on the part of some psychobiologists to assume that the two processes—simultaneous contrast and neuronal interaction—are thus homologs of each other and that the simultaneous contrast phenomenon can be "explained" or "reduced to an equivalent form of neural interaction. However, if one looks very carefully at the two phenomena, it turns out that the analogy itself is only a superficial first approximation and that there are many pieces of evidence that suggest gross differences between the two phenomena (see Chapter 7 for a complete discussion of this issue). As one example of discrepancy, the simultaneous contrast phenomenon is continuous and uniform over the entire contrasted area, although all forms of lateral interaction involve highly regular distance functions. The neural interaction declines as the space between the interacting parts increases, whereas the simultaneous contrast phenomenon seems to be independent of distance.

The point to be made by this example is that these two processes, though analogous to at least some degree, are probably mediated by completely different neural mechanisms located in quite different parts of the nervous system. Thus, the similarities between the two processes should not be interpreted to mean that there are equivalent similarities between their underlying physiological mechanisms.

As another example emphasizing the difference between homology and analogy, we may consider some important differences recently observed between the mammalian and avian nervous system. Nauta and Karten (1970) have pointed out that the region of the bird's brain that receives the primary visual and auditory projections—the external striatum—has a very different embryological origin than the cerebral cortical area that is the primary projection area for this sense modality in the mammalian brain. However, it may be assumed that analogous visual functions are being processed by these two different structures in spite of the fact that they have different embryological origins. Furthermore, although it has not been definitively established as fact, the known differences in the cellular arrangement of the avian striatum and the mammalian occipital cortex suggest that these analogous functions may indeed be the results of entirely different neuronal integrative processes.

Both of these examples indicate that even processes that seem to be identical at first glance should not be assumed to be necessarily the result of the function of equivalent structures. Therefore, some very simplistic psychobiological models based entirely on such process analogies may have to be reconsidered. Unfortunately, while it is relatively easy to distinguish between analog and homolog when one is dealing with anatomical material, it is not as easy to make the same distinction in the domain of the mind-body problem. For this reason, it is exceedingly important to keep this issue in mind so that the epistemological error of analogy-homology confusions may be made as infrequently as possible.

This same issue may be raised with regard to another often used technique in psychobiology. Because of the simplicity of their nervous systems, it is frequently desirable to use invertebrate specimens as models of more complex behavior in vertebrate specimens. Suppose that two behaviors that appear to be functionally very similar are observed in an invertebrate and a vertebrate. Does this necessarily mean that if one were able to discover the neural mechanism underlying the invertebrate behavior, that one has also explained the vertebrate process as well? Obviously at this point, the answer to this question has to be "no." There is every reason to be suspicious of this kind of generalization, because psychobiological analogies of this sort, as we have seen, do not necessarily reflect homologous mechanisms, even within the vertebrate classes.

7. Emergence of Higher-order Properties from Microproperties: The Fundamental Issue of Representation

Another subissue of considerable concern within the more general mind-body problem deals with the emergence of global patterns from concatenation and organization of the component parts of any system. In the present context, the specific system being dealt with, of course, is the brain, and the component parts are the individual neurons of which it is composed. The global patterns are of two kinds: One includes the psychological processes and conscious self-awareness, and the other includes the compound neurological electropotentials such as the electroencephalograph. It is generally accepted that the organization of the components into a patterned system gives rise to higher-order global properties that are not evident when one studies the components alone. This is not, in any way, meant to imply that there is an emergence of totally novel or *unpredictable* characteristics but rather that the organizational patterns that are implicit in the components can only become explicit when the components are put together. The assertion of philosophers of determinism is that given the complete set of specifications of the components, the features of the aggregate will be predictable. However, it should be remembered that the nature of the interactions between the units as well as the nature of the units themselves must be included in the "complete" set of specifications. Thus, the rules of interaction are a necessary part of any deterministic theory or explanation.

The practical issue in the case of the mind-body problem is that the analysis of a neural network into its components often leads to a loss of the very information that is the actual target of the inquiry. The arrangement of the parts of the network is discernible and measurable only as long as the network exists. Similarly, in the psychophysical laboratory whole new sets of relations and important facts are often encountered when one goes, for example, from the study of problems associated with the perception of a single dot to the study of how we see a pattern of dots. In another work (Uttal, 1975a), I have shown that the overall arrangement of a pattern of dots is a strong determinant of the pattern's detectability in masking backgrounds, even when the stimulus energy (i.e., the number of dots) remains constant. This is only a modern expression of the Gestalt tradition so popular a few decades ago.

A major theme of contemporary neurophysiological research is now directed toward the study of groups of neurons, their interactions, and the idea of ensemble action as distinguished from either individual neuronal or compound responses. As important as this theme is certainly going to be, it must also be understood that it is extremely difficult to do research on neural ensembles with our current technology, tuned as it is to study individual neurons. The practical limits of the number of neurons that can simultaneously be impaled with microelectrodes, the huge mass of data that can be so quickly accumulated, and the difficulty in most vertebrate preparations of linking the electrophysiological records with specific cellular structures, all make this a problem area in which progress will be slow. Yet, in spite of this technical difficulty, the problem of studying the patterned action of networks of neurons is among the most important issues of modern science and certainly among the foremost tasks of modern psychobiology.

The problem of the correspondence of psychological processes to the activity of neural networks is closely linked with philosophical debates among the proponents of determinism and indeterminism. Philosophers and physicists have argued for years whether or not the premise of predicting global behavior from a full knowledge of the characteristics of the parts is valid in principle, if not in practice. Indeterminists suggest that it is not just a matter of practical difficulty, but that it is theoretically impossible to go from the sum of the parts to the whole. Determinists, on the other hand, suggest that the difficulty is only a practical one, and if we are unable to predict global behavior from the parts, it is only because the number of interacting variables exceeds our computational capabilities. Whatever the resolution of this controversy, it is true that contemporary science is very much deterministic in principle although often indeterministic in practice.

The most general term that can cover all of these scientific and philosophical perplexities and the problem of the emergence of molar behavior from what is essentially a discrete nervous system is *representation.* The fundamental problem of representation is to determine how discrete neural processes can serve as the transactional equivalents of molar psychological processes. The problem of representation, in fact, constitutes one of the major research issues of modern psychobiology. An enormous amount of both empirical research and speculative theorizing has been aimed at the elucidation of the relationship between the two domains, some of which are reviewed in Chapters 6 and 7.

8.   Isomorphism, Nonisomorphism, and Coding Theory

In the preceding discussion, in which the focus was on the problems of the emergence of a pattern from the aggregation of its parts, brief mention was made of the school of Gestalt psychology—a theoretical position that was popular in the 1920s and 1930s. The emphasis in the Gestalt tradition was that the overall organization of a stimulus pattern was critical for cognition. This view contrasts with the atomistic orientation of modern behaviorism, which is much more likely to invoke local features than global arrangements. The Gestalt mode of *description* of mental activities has much to offer to those interested in global pattern effects and the action of aggregates and may be a more meaningful approach to psychobiological processes than the atomistic approach proposed by many alternative psychological theories. However, when the Gestalt psychologists proposed neurophysiological theories of perception, they turned to simplistic models that had considerably less to offer than did their descriptive statements. Their main psychobiological premise was isomorphism, the idea that spatial neuroelectric patterns in the brain were geometrically identical to corresponding mental states. The only concession (and for isomorphism any concession may in fact be irretrievably damaging) that the strict isomorphists would make on this issue was that the neural representation might be topological, i.e., that the geometrical relationships between the parts might not be congruent to the perception although the general arrangement must still be maintained.

Topological isomorphisms of this kind allow a "rubber sheet"-like distortion. But even such a modest form of distortion opens the door to consideration of more profound symbolic and indirect representations. For if the arrangement of the parts of real stimulus shapes can be topologically distorted when represented in the brain and perceptual order maintained, what logical difficulty is there in assuming that the order of the parts cannot also be varied without perceptual effects? Indeed, like all forms of coding and representation, there is no a priori "best" form of representation for mental states. One language is as good as another as long as one knows the rules of semantics and syntactics. The representation of any pattern, even geometrical forms, is possible with a totally disordered array if one has a set of translation rules to reconstruct the original pattern. The television set is a perfectly good example of this sort of disordered representation. A two-dimensional replica of some scene is produced on the surface of a phosphorescent screen from a one-dimensional time-varying signal transmitted from some distant station where the original scene was present. Yet the transmitted signal represents the original scene in a highly disordered manner. Adjacent points on the two-dimensional surface are not necessarily adjacent to each other during the one-dimensional time scan of the raster lines. It is only when the one-dimensional signal is displayed that the original spatial relationships are restored. Although human observers can utilize the two-dimensional spatial display better than the one-dimensional time function, there is no other criterion of priority or goodness that makes the scene in one encoded form superior to the scene in the other. The same information is available in both forms.

The translation of the original two-dimensional scene into a one-dimensional time function is said to be a processing of *encoding*. A code may be defined as the set of symbols used to represent some pattern *and* the rules involved in their use and translation.

As a matter of fact, it turns out that our nervous system also encodes stimulus patterns in much the same way as a television transmitting station, translating from one stimulus dimension to another with which it may not be isomorphic. For example, acoustic signals, in which pneumatic pressure varies along temporal dimensions, are translated to spatial patterns at the level of the cochlea and at other levels of the ascending pathways. Indeed it seems as if this sort of interdimensional encoding and reencoding is the norm as information is passed through the various pathways of the nervous system. At each stage of encoding, the new representation is very likely to be nonisomorphic with that of the preceding stage.

How does the brain sort out this nonisomorphic and chaotic representation of the various messages coursing through it? Obviously, it is able to accomplish this feat because the "rules" for decoding information are built into the nervous system. Equally obvious, then, is the fact that the doorway that was opened a crack to nonisomorphism by the Gestaltists' acceptance of the principle of topological representation is now thrown wide open by modern coding theory. There is no longer a need for any sort of a dimensional isomorphism, because it is entirely possible to represent any dimension by any other.

Acceptance of the perspective of coding theory also rather neatly resolves many other classic problems of psychobiological equivalence. The major premise of coding theory—any dimension is capable of representing any other dimension—is directly antithetical to isomorphically oriented theories. Thus there is no difficulty in explaining why we do not see the world upside down as a result of the inverted retinal image or why the world does not move when the eye moves. These questions and other quaint historical oddities became immediately answerable within the context of a theory involving a system of codes or cues able to *symbolically represent,* rather than *geometrically replicate,* external stimulus patterns. Therefore, coding theory, and the perspective that is associated with it is an important escape hatch from many pseudoquestions that inadvertantly arose from the descriptive theories that preassumed dimensional isomorphism. Once freed from that trap, attention can be directed toward problems specified by the biology of the organism rather than derived from the superfluous structure of theoretical models.

9. What Is the Nature of Consciousness?

Students of the mind-body problem constantly return to the problem of consciousness as the prototypical issue. Yet consciousness is perhaps the most elusive of the many targets of psychobiological research. The reasons for this elusiveness are very simple to discern. Consciousness is a process that is monumentally private—only *I* can experience *my* own intrapersonal self-awareness. Any speculations or measurements concerning the consciousness of others can only be derived from an analogistic extrapolation based on the premise that there is no reason to assume that *I,* as an individual conscious entity, am unique. *My* fellow man, who is similar to *me* in so many other ways, must also possess this important common characteristic. However, it is exceedingly difficult, if not impossible, to prove that this is indeed the case. The problem is made no less (or more) difficult if we consider the matter of consciousness in computers or lower animals as opposed to other men. In all of these cases, we are limited to observations of behavioral responses of one sort or another. There is no satisfactory procedure to distinguish between a cleverly designed automation and a being that exhibits the same sort of self-awareness of which *I* am personally conscious.

It is relevant to consider the problem of consciousness in animals in general and household pets in particular. It had long been fashionable among students of the mind-body problem to avoid this question entirely while accepting, more or less explicitly, that consciousness was necessarily to be found in their fellow men. But what an arrogant species-centrism that attitude reflects! Anybody who has enjoyed the company of a household pet could hardly tolerate the rejection of its self-awareness. Given that he is without speech and without manipulative hands, the dog, for example, responds in perfect adaptation to his situation and with what appears to be a full range of emotions. It is very difficult to conceive that these animals do not experience the same sort of conscious awareness we ascribe to our fellow *homo sapiens.*

Nevertheless, this is a highly untestable hypothesis, and it is obvious that the problem of consciousness is a terrible tangle. It is also obvious, however, that the question of consciousness is at the heart of the mind-body problem. Without self-awareness, there would be no mind-body problem, no psychobiology, and very little else of our culture and history. All other aspects of this great "world knot" would become almost entirely matters of circuit diagrams and tracings of how certain outputs originate from certain inputs—if anyone spent any time on such intellectual matters at all. Therefore, the study of consciousness—as difficult a problem as it is—is of considerable concern, and there are many ways in which modern psychobiologists have approached the problem. But clearly, any attempt to define consciousness will have to be done within the constraints of the operations used in the surgery and the behavioral laboratory if we are to avoid a total collapse into prescientific modes of thought.

The issue of the nature of consciousness has an important corollary associated with it. This related question is: What is the proper subject matter of psychology? For many centuries consciousness and related processes of self-awareness were specifically the issue of concern. The rise of positivism and operationalism, philosophies that stated that variables could only be defined in terms of the measurements or operations that were used to measure them, led to the emergence of a psychology that rejected introspection as an experimental tool. The mind, elusive consciousness, was simply declared to be outside of the realm of scientific psychology, and behavioral responses, motor and verbal, were declared to be the only appropriate subject matters of this science. In recent years, however, this strong operationalistic trend has been reversed, and it is becoming increasingly appreciated that in addition to the overt behavior of the organism, there are many other implicit states that must affect its existence. Herbert Feigl (1958), for one, now asserts that the proper subject matter of psychology is the set of "raw feels," the inner self-awareness that each person directly experiences from sensory stimuli. Behavior is but a meter, an external indicator, of these internal conscious experiences.

To clarify this point and to illustrate that psychology is no different than any other science, an analogy may be drawn between psychology and astronomy. Both sciences have the same difficult problem in that their pertinent subject matter, conscious experience in the one case and stars and galaxies in the other, cannot be examined first-hand. Rather, the scientist has to turn to various in-direct indicators to find out what is happening in his universe of inquiry. The astronomer collects tiny samples of light that have been travelling through the cosmos for thousands and millions of years to find out about distant stars; the psychologist observes verbal and motor responses, which are also very indirect, to find out about the mind. But in both cases it should be made very explicit that the instrument of measurement is not the subject of the science. We are interested in astronomy because we want to know about stars, and we are in-terested in psychology because we want to know about our minds; tired light and behavior are merely vehicles carrying us to the understanding of these in-trinsically exciting topics.

10.   Can the Mind Affect the Brain and Other Parts of the Body?

Manipulation of brain structure affects its functioning in ways that are expressed in mental processes. The opposite question can also be asked: Does the mind affect the brain? There is a strong possibility, however, that this is a pseudoques-tion that is of the same genre as the questions, "does the mind affect the mind" or "does the brain affect the brain?" Nevertheless, popular convention through-out history has been that it is possible to produce changes in the physiology of the body by altering one's psychological state, and many modern scientific developments bear evidence in this regard [for example, the recent demonstra-tions by such distinguished psychobiologists as Neil Miller (e.g., Miller & Dwor-kin, 1974) have shown that it is possible to train subjects to control autonomic as well as somatic nervous functions].

However, there is a certain circularity about the question of mental control of the body when it is viewed from the position of a theorist who feels that the mind is nothing but a function of the brain. If the mind is simply a reflection of the state of the brain, then mental control of the brain or other physical parts of the body is, in actuality, simply another means of the brain affecting the body through the more or less usual channels. That a person can be taught to control these functions only reminds us of the fact that the brain is plastic and can be driven from one state to another by fluctuations of the environment. Thus, there appears to be an enormous semantic difficulty in defining exactly what is meant by this question, in spite of the enormous popular interest in such fads as transcendental meditation, yoga, and consciousness-varying devices of one sort or another, and the nearly universal acceptance of the idea that the mind directly affects the body.

11.   What Is the Nature of Learning: What Is Its Relation to Growth and Development?

A major concern in our approach toward a definition of consciousness, particu-larly in the last century, has revolved around the fact that both the nervous sys-tem and behavior are plastic. That is, both structure and function change as a function of prior experience. Learning research dominates much of experimental psychology today, and some of the most distinguished psychobiologists are involved in a search for the "engram"—the neural state change that corresponds to behavioral flexibility. It is now believed that learning is a process that is not highly localized in the brain. Lashley's pioneering work resulted in the currently universally accepted conviction that distributed action, rather than a high degree of localization, was the rule. Most workers now search for neuronal plasticity at the cellular, synaptic, or biochemical level in many different regions of the brain.

Although considerable attention has been directed toward synaptic properties, and synapses in some situations seem to change their properties as a result of use, no one has yet demonstrated a unique association between synaptic properties and learning in a convincing way. Other investigators have suggested that macromolecular changes are the correlates for learning, though here, too, no one has yet offered a convincing explanation of how such macromolecular means of storing information might be rapidly read out when a memory is recalled.

It should be noted that there is no a priori inconsistency between these two possible explanations of learning—synaptic change and macromolecular involvement. Synaptic growth, if that is the basis of learning, would certainly not be inconsistent with the involvement of macromolecules. However, the role of transfer ribonucleic acid (RNA_t), for example, in a synaptic or network theory of learning would be very different than that proposed by those who suggest that the molecular structure itself is the storage medium. Rather, these growth-directing molecules would be involved in altering the conduction probabilities at the synapse.

It seems more probable that some aspect of the neural network changes than that experimental information is encoded in molecular structure, but the nature of that change is yet to be established. Given that this change is likely to be highly distributed, (i.e., the storage of a memory is due to changes that occur throughout the brain), there are some enormous technical obstacles that must be overcome before we will be able to understand the information storage retrieval processes of memory.

In spite of the popularity of many imaginative contemporary models of memory, it seems certain that for short-term memory, at least, it is unlikely that any synaptic growth or macromolecular involvement could occur as quickly as is required. Rather, some aspect of the neural circuit that has the ability to change fairly rapidly must be involved. Other forms of memory, however, that involve very long-term storage may involve synaptic or macromolecular mechanisms. The recent thrust in memory research has been to acknowledge a hierarchy of multiple forms of memory (iconic, short-, medium-, and long-term), and there may be an equal number of different mechanisms involved and thus a different "explanation" for each. The problem of memory would then be complicated by the additional requirement that the means of communication between the different levels of memory would also have to be elucidated. We would certainly like to discover how information is passed from the mechanisms that underlie short-term memory to those that underlie long-term storage.

Another important issue concerns phenomena of very long-term storage and gradual behavioral plasticity. How does one distinguish between behavioral or structural changes that are the result of experience and those that are the result of the fairly normal growth of the individual? This, of course, is a form of the classic nature-nurture controversy that has played such a central role in psychology throughout its history. The contemporary examination of this question emphasizes many of the interactions that exist between growth and learning—one not being possible without the other in almost all practical situations. The relationship between the two modes of change remains an important issue in psychobiology.

12.   The Technical Issues

Finally, we come to a large number of subissues that are not quite as esoteric and philosophical as the ones already discussed. These are the basic technical problems that stand between the investigator and the solution of the broader issues. For example, any solutions to the conceptual problems surrounding the issues of mind and brain depend upon clear and definitive statements of what we mean by brain. Defining the brain is the subject of neuroanatomy. The parts of the brain must be described and their interconnecting tracts identified so that we not only know what its parts are, but also how these parts are tied together into a working system. Any theory, which proposes a model of interaction between parts of the brain, that is not in accord with neuroanatomy is obviously going to be inadequate from the start.

Another important set of technical issues concerns the various external agents that may act on the brain to produce changes in its function and thus in overt behavior. The action of drugs, surgery, electrical or thermal shock, and trauma on mental states and behavior are among the most important clues that we have available to us today in our quest for understanding of the mind-brain problem. Often data in these areas are obtained in situations that are highly undesirable to scientists trained to esteem precisely controlled laboratory environments. For sound reasons, experimentation involving drugs and surgery on humans solely for the purpose of extending knowledge is considered to be unethical by most psychobiologists and other neuroscientists. Surgical intervention into the human body is acceptable only when there is a valid therapeutic reason for the surgery. For example, surgical treatment of the epilepsies has been a source of considerable knowledge regarding the localization of brain function in man. The work of Wilder Penfield (for example, Penfield & Rasmussen, 1950) and his colleagues is most notable in this regard. Similarly, human drug experimentation is, in general, prohibited in our society except where there is a high probability of therapeutic payoff or desperate need on the part of the patient.

Changes in the structure of the brain produced by injury also provide a fortuitous set of data, but obviously these "natural" experiments do not provide neat ablations or otherwise well-controlled situations. Thus most clinical data are "dirty" as a result of being recorded under unacceptable conditions in uncontrolled situations. Nevertheless, one does with what one has, and "dirty" or not, in many cases the only information we have on some aspects of brain structure and chemical effects comes from anecdotal and fortuitous cases of this kind.

Another technical area of considerable contemporary interest concerns the growth and development of the brain both as a result of normal maturation and as a function of experimental alterations in the concentration of various chemicals or other environmental factors. Recent experiments have shown that many specific chemical substances must be present at an exact concentration at a specific time in the course of the brain's development, or abnormal growth patterns will result. Growth, development, and regeneration patterns in the brain are now, in some instances, being compared to corresponding stages in behavioral development. This group of topics represents a major and interesting set of subissues in the mind-brain problem.

The action of hormones, natural products of the endocrine glands of the body, on both growth and behavior is also a major current interest in many psychobiological laboratories. Hormones affect behavior in some highly precise ways, regulating sex and eating among many other behaviors, but are still dependent upon interactions with the stimulating environment to produce their effects.

One of the most active methodological approaches in psychobiology is that of electrophysiology—the study of the electrical signals that can be picked up with appropriate electronic recording instruments. Electrical signals from various parts of the nervous system are important indicators of the action of the nervous tissue that produces those signals. Although there is still a considerable doubt about the exact significance and role of many of the signals detected with micro- and macroelectrodes, there is currently no more abundant source of information about the action of the nervous system and its component cells than that obtained electronically.

Finally, there is the enormous body of technical knowledge accumulating in the experimental psychology laboratories, where the many aspects of the behavior of humans and lower animals are studied. In a way this knowledge sets the stage for much of the work that is done in the neurophysiology laboratory. It is becoming increasingly clear that the more interesting physiological problems are those that are associated with the search for explanations of some form of behavior.

These and a host of other technical problems are the active daily pursuits of a large number of psychobiologists today. In the previous sections of this chapter, I have tried briefly to introduce the mind-body problem by discussing it in a fairly general way. However, if this book is to achieve its goal, this general introduction must be made more concrete by specifically detailing the current state of knowledge in this field. The next section outlines the plan of the book.

C.   PLAN OF THE BOOK

Obviously, the mind-body problem is not a single issue but a constellation of technical and philosophical questions, all of which can contribute to the all-important search for an understanding of how our body structures are associated with our mental processes. The main purpose of this book is to review and survey the contemporary state of data and theories relating to this association. The goal is to bring some order and systematic understanding out of the apparent chaos of the babel of the laboratory and the glut of the highly esoteric and detailed studies that fill the scholarly journals. This book is intended to be an interpretive and synthetic presentation, in the sense that it will strive more to explicate general principle than to be an exhaustive encyclopedia of experimental results. In doing so, I shall probably be restating the modern status of the mind-body problem rather than solving it. The "world knot," as persistent as it has been throughout history, is itself constantly in a state of evolution.The mind-body problem today is not what it was a century ago and not what it will probably be a century from now.

To achieve the goal of integration and synthesis of this continuously changing field, the material surveyed will have to be organized in quite a different manner than has been previously employed. This book will not be organized as, for example, is Thompson's (1967) distinguished text in terms of the classic areas of psychology or of neural anatomy. Rather than chapters centered on, for example, the hippocampus and emotion or on the reticular activating system and arousal, this book is organized in general accord with the problems and issues that were described in the preceding parts of this chapter. Therefore, one of my chapters deals with the concept of localization in its entirety. The ramifications of this topic in many parts of the brain and for many psychological states are discussed in a general way that seeks to emphasize the general principles.

Overall, the book seeks to achieve a synthesis rather than an analysis of the mind-body problem. The book, therefore, is organized according to the following plan. Chapter 2 commences the discussion by turning to the past—the history of philosophy and theory of the mind-body problem. It is included with some trepidation and with the expectation that some readers, expert in technical psychobiology, will find this material inappropriate and uninteresting. But it is presented with the absolute conviction that this material is of prime importance; to ignore its existence will cause us to suffer the fate of all who have done so in the past—to accept intellectual repetition. Chapter 2, therefore, spells out the various points of view regarding the mind-body problem as they have developed over the centuries and attempts to point out the specific controversies as well as to candidly examine the limits of each view.

The anatomy of the central nervous system is then considered in Chapter 3. This is an obvious and necessary body of technical knowledge required for a complete understanding of the material discussed in subsequent chapters. Although there may be some debate about the detailed locus of specific psychological functions, all agree today that the organ of mind is the central nervous system. The anatomy of the central nervous system is presented in a sequence ranging from a conceptual model showing the overall functional arrangement, through an increasingly detailed description of the various major centers, to a microscopic analysis of the neuronal network arrangement of certain well-ordered centers. This latter material is a rapidly emerging body of knowledge that was not discussable even a few years ago; however, we are now beginning to understand quite a bit about the organization of a few structures like the retina, the cerebellum, and even the cerebral cortex.

Chapter 4 pursues another sort of anatomy, but one that is far more difficult to present in a way that will satisfy all readers. This chapter deals with the structure of psychological concepts. In this discussion, an attempt is made to define an "anatomy" of the mind by developing a classification of what psychologists are currently studying.

Chapters 2, 3, and 4 are, therefore, preparatory to the material discussed in the remaining chapters in that they deal with the conventional fields of philosophy, anatomy, and psychology. The main theme of the rest of the book, however, is patently psychobiological, i.e., direct comparisons will be made between the data that are obtained in psychological experiments and from biological observations. The remaining chapters each emphasize a particular aspect of the mind-body problem as viewed by current psychobiologists.

Chapter 5 deals with what is perhaps the classic area of "physiological psychology"—the problem of localization of function in the nervous system. This chapter is approached from a macroscopic point of view that uses, as its prototypical research tool, ablation (surgical amputation) or block inactivation of nervous tissue. A wide variety of specific behavioral tests are then applied to determine the effects of these blocks or ablations. Chapter 5 also presents that poorly controlled but vitally important body of knowledge that comes from the surgery when human subjects are treated for injury, malignancy, or those ill-defined organizational disorders that result in the epilepsies. The general conclusion drawn in this chapter is that precise, circumscribed, and unique localization is not likely to be the actual biological condition. Rather, we shall see that almost every portion of the brain is involved in almost every behavioral act in one way or another, and it is the interaction between the parts that defines the emitted behavior.

Chapters 6 and 7 deal with the problems of representation and coding. In an earlier work (Uttal, 1973), I dealt with some of the problems of neural encoding in a relatively restricted area of psychology—the sensory processes. The discussion of neural encoding for the senses is greatly simplified by the structural and organizational simplicity of receptor organs, but the general principles that emerged in that work have become models for the comparable coding processes that must be occurring when any of the more complex mental processes are active. This chapter brings this material up to date as well as spells out in detail what is meant by coding and representation theory in contemporary thinking.

Another goal of Chapter 6 is to consider some cellular neurophysiological issues that are of increasing concern to modern psychobiologists. In the bright light of modern developments, some of the classic laws of neurophysiology are taking on a somewhat different meaning than they possessed when originally presented. To place them in proper context without recapitulation of an elementary neurophysiology text, a brief list of neurophysiological principles is also presented in this chapter.

Following the presentation of this background material in Chapter 6, Chapter 7 is devoted to a review of examples of the most important findings in the field of representation. Because the field is so large, the visual system has once again been selected as a model for all representation theory, and only visual data is considered as it was in Chapter 5. The premise that the principles so elucidated for vision are applicable to all of the other perceptual fields seems to be generally acceptable today. Chapter 7 also includes a discussion of some highly exciting new work regarding the representation of cognitive, emotional, and motivational processes.

Chapters 8 and 9 deal with one major field of psychobiology—that of learning and memory. I have chosen not to include this material in the previous chapters, in which many psychobiological relations between localized structure and function or between representation changes and behavioral adaptations are drawn, for a number of reasons. First, there is, as I have noted, an increasingly strong conviction among many psychobiologists that learning and memory are not highly localized functions; the physiological processes that are involved in memory seem to be distributed throughout wide regions of the brain. Second, the field of learning is of such great breadth and contemporary interest that a separate discussion of this material seems warranted, simply to avoid skimping on this important topic. Third, much of the theorizing about possible neural or chemical mechanisms underlying learning is not aimed at the "chunk" level that underlies the main theme of Chapter 5. Rather, many physiological theories of learning deal with the cellular and even subcellular (synaptic and molecular) levels and thus the problem is also closely related to the problems of representation discussed in Chapters 6 and 7.

Finally, Chapter 10 summarizes what has been said over the many pages of the earlier chapters by presenting a list of emerging principles as a brief statement of a modern theory of mind and brain. The list of principles is intended to make the important generalities and developments discussed during the course of the book more explicit.

Clearly, this book is not complete. There are many subfields that cannot be covered in adequate detail. The field of psychochemistry, to which only passing allusions are made, is simply too massive to be incorporated into these pages without disastrous effects. A wide variety of prescientific "pop" psychologies seem to have something to say about the mind-body problem, but their message is still obscure and mainly unanalyzed by rigorous empirical procedures and critical theoretical insights. The problems of consciousness as studied by research anesthesiologists might also have been a rich source of wisdom.

In a sense, however, these topics are somewhat outside of the theme of this book. Many pages from now I assert that the critical aspect of any resolution of the mind-body problem is the relationship of the mental process to the state of networks of neurons and nuclei. These other media, although demonstratively capable of producing effects, do so in ways that are quite unknown at the present time and that are probably indirect. So they, like many other relevant bodies of wisdom or hope, are not included in this book.

As this introductory chapter clearly indicates, this book is based upon premises and axioms that are relatively specifically defined. It is my contention that such an explicit statement of the premises upon which a book is based is always desirable, and, in the case of psychobiology, vital. This particular topic is of relevance to all men. From the study of the philosopher, to the laboratory of the experimental scientist, to the daily concerns of each of our fellow men, the mind-body problem exerts a compelling social and intellectual force. It always has and probably always will. The ultimate purpose of this book is to determine just where we are in our progress toward a general solution to this problem at this stage of the twentieth century.

2
History of the Mind-Body Problem

A. INTRODUCTION

The subject of theories of the mind is an exceedingly technical and complicated field of philosophical and scientific history. There are many terms that are exceedingly abstruse with a great variety and subtlety of meaning and referents. There are many views, concepts, methods of approach, historical trends, and perceived ranges of subject matter. The mind-body problem, as we saw in Chapter 1, is really a number of overlapping subproblems with explanations that are not mutually exclusive on the one hand, or all inclusive on the other. Some are comprehensive, some limited, some extreme, some mild, some obviously absurd, and some seductively plausible.

A problem in this chapter, therefore, will be to keep from losing the current perspective as brief resumes of the many alternative views are presented. This is a special problem with this material, because the criteria for distinguishing among the alternative theories of the mind are often only those of internal consistency and completeness, parsimony, or more usually, just plain vested interests based on value judgment rather than empirical testing. Therefore, the reader should keep in mind from the beginning the main points that will be elaborated at the end of this chapter, namely, that modern psychobiology is monistic, reductionistic, and mechanistic. Psychobiology assumes only one level of reality and considers body and mind to be related in the same way as are a machine's structure and its function.

Unfortunately, this brief preliminary statement of a psychobiological credo is telegraphic and probably cryptic at this point. It is for this reason that we must take this excursion into philosophy and history. The words used in this credo must be defined in order for the reader to understand the implications of the sentences of which they are a part. Hopefully, at the end of this chapter, the significance of the main philosophical assumptions underlying the modern science of psychobiology will be clear enough that the real meaning of the experiments that will be discussed in later chapters will be intelligible.

As one explores the massive amount of recent literature expressing the many views of philosophers and scientists concerning the mind-body problem, a major fact quickly emerges. The problem of the relationship of mind and body is extremely complex from a philosophical and logical point of view as well as from an empirical-technical one. Yet there appears to be a relatively complete disregard on the part of most contemporary philosophers for the enormous amount of empirical physiological information that has accumulated in recent years. It also seems as if there is an equal lack of concern on the part of many physiologists and psychologists for the philosophical antecedents and implications of their work. For example, physiologists all too often seem to accept, without critical consideration, the fact that the electrical responses to physical stimuli obtained in their laboratories correspond directly with the psychological responses that may be generated by the same physical stimuli. Philosophers, on the other hand, mainly seem to be operating as if the last 30 years of progress in neuroscience and psychobiology laboratories had never occurred. They appear to either be disinterested in the literature or unaware of it.

How did such cross-discipline apathy develop? The answer probably lies in the sociological structure of modern science. Specialization and compartmentalization have increasingly become the rule in recent decades; there are vanishingly few universalists around these days. The magnitude of the contemporary scientific data base has made it necessary for almost all of a psychobiologist's intellectual energies to be committed to absorbing and contributing to the body of knowledge in but a single, narrow, scientific topic.

How can this situation be improved? One way to assist the psychobiologist is to present a brief review of the philosophical and historical issues. By directing attention in this chapter to the main issues and selecting a few especially important examples, a meaningful introduction can be made to the sort of thinking that has characterized the various theories seeking to relate mind and body during the historical past. This chapter will therefore be aimed at an exposition of the historical continuity of the mind-body problem.

In developing such a history, one might hope to demonstrate a certain historical or intellectual evolutionary sequence. However, as we shall see, this is not to be the case. There are a number of controversial, antagonistic, and opposed positions, but all of them have antecedents dating back to the classic Greek philosophies. It appears that no one contemporary philosophy can be considered to be any more modern than any other. Nevertheless, at one time or another, a particular position may have been dominant. From about 700 to 1600 A.D., the "Age of Faith" in Will Durant's (Durant, 1950) terms, a tradition was dominant that was mainly based on theological concepts. A general acceptance of both Christian and Moslem theological and Aristotelian philosophical doctrines dominated much of Western thought during that period. The emergence of empirical science under the intellectual influence and leadership of Francis Bacon (1561-1626) and René Descartes (1596-1650), in particular, strongly influenced the next 300 years. Cartesian dualism may probably be considered the dominant metaphysical theme of that period during which the intellectual tide shifted from theological to technical philosophical and nontheological interpretations of mind.

In recent times, two significant opposing philosophical strains—a mechanistic-reductionistic monism asserting unity of mind and body, and the linguistic-positivistic perspective that rejects the meaningfulness of the question itself—have grown within the symphony of answers that have been proposed to the mind-body problem. Nevertheless, each of these alternative points of view has been present throughout each historical period. Contemporary mechanistic monisms had their antedecents in Democritus' atomism, and there appears to be a reemergence of Cartesian interactionism today as the linguistic-positivistic philosophies have declined in influence.

In spite of its importance, the mind-body problem, it should be remembered, is only one of the great philosophical issues. There are a number of closely related problems that are intertwined with it in the literature of the past millenia. Thus, issues of metaphysics and epistemology have given rise to particular orientations and perspectives that, while impinging directly on the particulars of the mind-body problem, are conceptually distinct from it. Therefore, to keep the many threads of the discussion straight and to avoid confusing the several issues, I preface the discussion of the mind-body philosophies with a brief consideration of some of these other issues.

This chapter subsequently reviews the main solutions to the mind-body problem that have been offered and presents a brief statement of what the implicit philosophical orientation of contemporary psychobiology is in order to alert the reader to biases in later interpretations of the data.

B.   THE GREAT PHILOSOPHICAL ISSUES

It is easily appreciated that problems of epistemology (the theory of the methods of acquiring knowledge) and metaphysics (the theory of the nature of reality) are intricately intertwined with the mind-body issue. Indeed, the history of these sciences is so entangled with the mind-body issue that it is often difficult to be sure which issue is actually being discussed. A simple way to keep the three issues separate is to acknowledge that the task of epistemology is a strategic one—how to go about acquiring knowledge about reality. The task of metaphysics is a substantive one—What is the nature of that reality? The mind-body problem, however, is a more circumscribed issue dealing specifically with the relationship between mental experience and the bodily mechanisms that might underlie it.

The interrelationships between the three problems—how do we acquire knowledge of reality? what is the nature of reality? what is the relationship between mind and body?—are so intricate that each must be considered as being an integral part of the other two. Understanding nature, whatever form its "reality" may take, is the goal or target of the methods that are explored by epistemology, and mind is the vehicle that executes these methods, motivates the search, and is the repository of the understanding. Clearly, to understand epistemological methods is not to understand nature, nor is to solve the mind-body riddle equivalent to finally explicating the advantages or disadvantages of one or another epistemological method. But the continued approach to the solution of any one of these problems feeds forth on the ultimate understanding of the others.

To clarify these issues and to explicate what the opposing stands have been in the classic debates in the areas of epistemology and metaphysics, let us consider these two particular philosophical fields in somewhat greater detail.

1. The Metaphysical Controversy: Idealism Versus Realism

The great metaphysical issue is the question of the nature of reality. Since the time of Plato (427?-347 B.C.) and Aristotle (384-322 B.C.), the main antagonists in this great debate have been realism and idealism. Those philosophers who counted themselves realists (or sometimes physicalists or materialists) championed the idea that the only basic reality is the physical universe. They further asserted that physical entities exist independent of whether or not they were observed by any sentient being.

Opposed to this simple, straightforward (or as it is sometimes called, "naive") realism, is a philosophy of idealism, the concept that the physical universe exists only to the extent that it becomes part of the thought processes of some observer. Because reality can be understood only through the senses and because sensed objects are thus mental, the simple (or "naive") idealist asserted, the basic reality must reside in the ideas of men rather than in the fabric of some physical material.

Idealism and realism were not evolutionarily related, that is, one did not grow out of the other nor can one be considered more modern than the other. Plato, for example, taught a modified idealism that rejected the notion of the primacy of the physical universe. To him, the important aspects of the universe were ideas or archetypes that existed independent of both the physical world and the mind of man. Aristotle, his student, on the other hand, was a realist. To him, the objects of nature had properties that had priority regardless of the relationship between the observer and the physical universe or between the physical universe and the "idea" of the physical universe.

In the seventeenth century, a similar, but in some sense simpler, sort of schism still existed. Observers such as John Locke (1632-1704) promulgated a philosophy that could not be construed to be anything other than a strict realism. Locke asserted that there was a real physical environment even though we are constrained by the limits of our sensory apparatus in acquiring full knowledge of it. On the other hand, Bishop George Berkeley (1685-1753) contemporaneously championed a classic form of idealism. Berkeley denied the very existence of the physical world and maintained that reality consisted only of minds and ideas. While Berkeley did not suggest that matter dematerialized when it was not observed, he did believe that the continued existence of matter was due to its being continuously sensed by an omnipresent God.

Idealism obviously can be carried to extremes. For example, the notion that only the mental aspects of the world are meaningful has been extended by some philosophers to the notion that the only reality is personal experience, and all other sensory representations of the outside world are meaningless. David Hume's (1711-1776) theory of phenomenalism is an example, but a more extreme point of view usually referred to as *solipsism* concentrates on the role of personal sensory experiences to the exclusion of everything else. Solipsism, in rejecting knowledge except that directly experienced by one's self, is usually considered to be intellectually destructive and counterproductive, because it cuts man off from even considering the nature of the universe in which he resides or sharing knowledge with his fellows. Epistemological solipsism only makes this restriction a problem in strategy; metaphysical solipsism, more seriously, makes this a matter of the ultimate nature of reality.

These are the classic, and perhaps most extreme, stands in the controversy over whether the ultimate nature of reality could best be described as being locked to the characteristics of a constant material universe or, contrariwise, dependent upon mental processes in sentient observers. Today, philosophers rarely debate this particular issue. Dominating contemporary science is an almost universal acceptance of the fact that the material universe exists, although our perception of it must be inferred from coded neural messages, and will continue to exist despite the role played by our fragile, transient, and mortal species. The naive idealistic argument has been severely damaged by modern atomic- and astrophysics. Events, even at these micro- or macroscopic levels, occur with well-defined and measurable histories. Light is now universally accepted as traveling at a finite velocity because of the work of Albert Einstein (1879-1955). On arrival at some detector, it can be seen that light is loaded with vestigial indications of its past and thus possesses a real history. For example, the red shift observed in light coming from extragalactic sources is highly suggestive that not only are the sources distant but also that the light took a considerable period of time to arrive here. Thus the existence of time, space, and reality without the intervention of human perception is compellingly asserted. Other examples of physical events in both the microcosm and macrocosm could be listed to bolster this argument for realism, but it is not necessary. All readers of this book come from an age that easily accepts material realism. It is the cornerstone of the modern scientific paradigm.

2. The Epistemological Controversy: Empiricism Versus Rationalism

While metaphysicians debated the ultimate nature of reality, epistemologists were embroiled in a controversy concerning the best strategy to be used in searching for answers to metaphysical questions. The issue of strategy has crystallized over the years in two opposing camps: that of the empiricists on the one hand, and that of the rationalists on the other. Briefly, the respective positions can be summarized as follows. Empiricists supported the contention that the only means of gathering knowledge that would help us understand the reality of the universe is the strategy of direct experience with nature. Empiricism, thus, heavily depends upon the senses and the process of human perception as the main avenue through which understanding can be achieved. In modern science, a hearty commitment to empiricism is embodied in the heavy emphasis on experimental science.

Rationalists, on the other hand, supported the contention that knowledge could mainly be attained through the use of logical processes. In fact, the emphasis on reasoning was so strong that the most ardent of the rationalists assumed that sensory experience could, in many instances, actually obstruct the true understanding of a problem. It was suggested that illusions, the false representation of real-world stimuli by the sense channels, and other limits on the perceptual processes, might distort, rather than elucidate, the nature of reality. Rather, the rationalists asserted that the deductive powers of mathematics and logic represented the ideal manner of acquiring knowledge. In the days when most human intellectual energy was directed at acquiring knowledge about the supernatural, rationalism stood at its zenith. Arguments concerning proofs of God's existence, for example, could hardly be solved empirically, because there was no conceivable "meter" that could be used to experimentally measure His influence.

Such great historical figures as Plato, St. Augustine (354-430), and Descartes championed the rationalistic approach. Equally important philosophers such as Aristotle, Thomas Hobbes (1588-1679), John Stuart Mill (1806-1873), David Hume, and John Locke were the proponents of the empiricistic approaches.

In recent years, the classical empiricism that stressed the experiential strategy as the main means of accumulating knowledge has evolved some very extreme positions. The logical positivists of the Vienna circle of the 1920s, for example, stressed an epistemology that was classically empirical in its emphasis on sensory experience as the only source of knowledge. However, it added the idea, antithetical to the solipsistic view, that the experience must be public and sharable. This led the logical positivists, the most influential of whom included the eccentric Ludwig Wittgenstein (1889-1951), into studies of language and communication. Much of their philosophy concerned the meaning of language and its role in defining reality, as well as mind, for individual members of a community (see, for example, Maslow, 1961).

In large part, logical positivism was a purely European empiricism until the emigration of many of its adherents to the United States in the years prior to World War II. In America, the special history and resources of the country had led to the earlier emergence of pragmatism, a related but distinct extension of empiricism, under the leadership of Charles S. Peirce (1839-1914). Peirce's general philosophical position was that ideas and knowledge are only meaningful in the context in which they can be used to locate and describe material (and, implicitly, useful) objects.

Another American philosophy quite similar to logical positivism in its hyper-empirical stance was the philosophy of operationalism proposed by Percy W. Bridgman (1882-1961). Operationalism extended empiricism to its ultimate by saying that reality does not depend so much on the aspects of the material object as it does on the operations that are used to make measurements of that object. Bridgman's background as a physicist obviously was a strong influence in the development of this perspective.

For psychologists, the particular evolutionary development of the empirical perspective that has, until very recently, dominated so much of modern experimental psychology was the school of behaviorism. Its founder, John B. Watson (1878-1958), attempted to extend empirical principles to psychology and to totally discard the concept of mental processes in order to make the subject matter of psychology comparable in its objectivity to physics or chemistry. Psychology, under this influence, became nonmentalistic and, some say, slavishly imitated what was an inappropriate model in its mimicry of modern physics. Mind was held by Watsonian behaviorists to be an invalid concept, and only behavior, as explicitly defined by precisely specific laboratory operations, could be considered within the appropriate content matter of "scientific" psychology.

In recent years, there has been a trend away from this naive form of behaviorism, which dominated laboratories prior to the 1960s, and a rebirth of interest in problems such as imagery, thinking (problems that can be attacked only with introspective methods despised by the behaviorists), and the physiological basis of perception. Such books as those of John Anderson and Gordon Bower (1973), Walter Kintsch (1974), and Alan Richardson (1969), reflect this emerging new interest in such mental processes as imagery and cognition. The interested reader is directed to an especially sensitive review of the rise and influence of behaviorism in psychology by S. Koch (1968).

This is only a very brief review of two great philosophical issues, the nature of reality (the field of metaphysics) and the most appropriate strategy to learn about that reality (the field of epistemology), both of which are intimately intertwined with the mind-body problem. In the next section, attention is directed particularly to the mind-body problem and the various answers that have been proposed to it by theologians, philosophers, and neuroscientists through the centuries.

C.   PROPOSED SOLUTIONS TO THE MIND-BODY PROBLEM

As we have noted previously, the importance of the mind-body problem is elo-quently evidenced by its great antiquity. Another reflection of the importance of this central human perplexity is the great variety of answers that have been proposed by one or another philosopher, scientist, or theologian over the millenia. To bring order to these various theories of the relationship between the mental and the physical aspects of human existence, it is well to note that there are three broad classes of philosophies within which each of the many theories may be included. This trichotomy is based mainly on the attitude that each theoreti-cian takes with regard to the relationship of the mind and the body. On the one hand are the *dualisms* and *pluralisms*—those philosphies whose metaphysical stance is that the mind and the body are separate and distinct in some funda-mental ways, with dualisms including two domains and pluralisms including three or more. The traditional theologies, with their emphasis on the immortality of the soul, are typical of the dualistic or pluralistic views of nature.

On the other hand, the main opposition to dualisms and pluralisms is usually framed in terms of explanations that are in one way or another based on the pre-mise that mind and body are really one and the same. Such single-domain theories are referred to as *monisms*. Historically, it can be seen that there has been a trend away from dualistic or pluralistic explanations to more monistic explanations; however, as we shall see, this is not universally true.

Although there appears to be no historical priority of dualisms in favor of monisms, or contemporary logical advantage of monisms over dualisms, there is a suggestion by Marvin Minsky (1963) that certain logical arguments exist for assuming that a dualism is the most likely philosophy to emerge when a machine or a man first begins to analyze the nature of his own reality. In an exceedingly interesting statement, Minsky asserts:

If a creature can answer a question about a hypothetical experiment, without ac-tually performing that experiment, then the answer must have been obtained from some submachine inside the creature. The output of that submachine (representing a correct answer) as well as the input (representing the question) must be coded descrip-tions of the corresponding external events or event classes. Seen through this pair of encoding and decoding channels, the internal submachine acts like the environment, and so it has the character of a "model." The inductive inference problem may then be regarded as the problem of constructing such a model.

   To the extent that the creature's actions affect the environment, this internal model of the world will need to include some representation of the creature itself. If one asks the creature "why did you decide to do such and such" (or if it asks this of itself), any answer must come from the internal model. Thus the evidence of in-trospection itself is liable to be based ultimately on the processes used in constructing one's image of one's self. Speculation on the form of such a model leads to the amusing prediction that intelligent machines may be reluctant to believe that they are *just* machines. The argument is this: our own self-models have a substantially "dual"

character; there is a part concerned with the physical or mechanical environment—
with the behavior of inanimate objects—and there is a part concerned with social and
psychological matters. It is precisely because we have not yet developed a satisfactory mechanical theory of mental activity that we have to keep these areas apart. We
could not give up this division even if we wished to—until we find a unified model to
replace it. Now, when we ask such a creature what sort of being it is, it cannot simply
answer "directly"; it must inspect its model(s). And it must answer by saying that it
seems to be a dual thing—which appears to have two parts—a "mind" and a "body."
Thus, even the robot, unless equipped with a satisfactory theory of artificial intelligence, would have to maintain a dualistic opinion on this matter. [Minsky, 1963, p.
449]

In sum, Minsky is thus supporting the notion that there is an essential primitive-
ness of a dualistic self model that can only be replaced when one knows enough
to propose a plausible monistic explanation. This quotation is the only instance
to come to my knowledge in which dualisms and monisms have been placed in
either a logical or historical order on grounds other than irrelevant value judgments.

The monism-dualism controversy may also be expressed in other philosophical terms concerned with the ways in which phenomena in one domain of inquiry are related to those in another. The dualistic or pluralistic philosophies are
explicit in their axiomatic stance that the mental and the body functions represent two or more quite different aspects of reality, and, though they may interact, philosophers of these schools would assert that the one is not translatable
to the terms, linguistic or otherwise, of the other. Materialistic (as opposed to
idealistic—a minority view) monists on the other hand strongly assert the axiom
of mechanism—namely, that mental terms can be "explained" in or "reduced"
to the terms of the underlying physical components and principles. Materialism,
or as it is often known—physicalism or mechanism—is thus usually associated
with the general premise of reductionism in philosophy. Reductionism asserts
that any level of reality or discourse may be explained in terms of lower levels
and those lower levels in terms of even lower levels until all phenomena are explained in terms of the basic physical-mechanical principles of electrical charge,
mass, and acceleration. Thus, the reductionists believe that, in principle, mental
processes can be reduced to neurophysiological terms, which themselves can be
reduced to chemical terms, which can in turn be reduced to the terms of atomic
physics. Modern psychobiology is patently reductionistic and mechanistic in
this way.

Such a position, however, is not without its own intellectual perplexities. We
must not forget the message of Kety's allegory quoted in Chapter 1. For any
problem that is as multileveled as the mind-body problem, there will always remain the question of what is the optimum level of inquiry as well as the problem
of transition between levels.

Table 2-1 lists the major positions discernible within the monism-dualism-
pluralism trichotomy. Included also are a number of other points of view that

TABLE 2-1

Past and present theories of the relationship between mind and body.

Dualisms	Pluralisms	Monisms	Rejectors of the issue
Plato's dualism	Occasionalism	Democritus' atomism	Solipsism
		Aristotle's formism	
Classic theologies	Eccles and Popper's trialism	Berkeley's monistic idealism	Phenomenalism
Vitalism	Ornstein's multiaspect theory	Epiphenomenalism or automation theory	Bridgman's operationalism
Panpsychism		Spinoza's double aspect theory	Positivism
Descartes' interactionism		Neutral monism	Logical positivism
Psychoneural parallelism		Emergent evolution and the emergence hypothesis	Behaviorism
Kohler's isomorphism		The identity hypothesis	
Polten's interactionism		Neuroreductionistic theory	
		Mach's network hypothesis	
		Cybernetic theory	
		Coding theory	
		Ryle's dispositional monism	
		Modern psychobiology	

reject the question of whether the mind and body are separate entities or simply different aspects of a unified reality. Classical logical positivism, for example, treats the mind-body problem by denying the validity of the question itself. Instead, such philosophies propose that we are only able to consider the data that we have used in the context of the language used to describe them and/or the operations involved in measuring them.

In concluding this introduction to a general classification of the mind-body philosophies, it is appropriate to note that at least one modern philosopher of the problem suggests that the three positions (monism, dualism, and pluralism) may not be as distinguishable as I have indicated. Globus (1973), while essentially arguing against a simple form of monism or psychoneural identity theory, has proposed that both dualistic and monistic views are really subject to the same sort of criticisms and in fact are complementary to each other. He says that: "A complete account of reality entails more than mind, more than matter, and something different from both mind and matter [p. 1133]."

It is not clear whether Globus is thus a monist or a dualist or whether he adheres to a theory that is classifiable in either of the categories. He, himself, asserts that the main point is one of complementarity, in Niels Bohr's sense; namely, materialism and idealism are both adequate models of a single universal reality as long as they are not used simultaneously, just as the wave and particle models of matter cannot be used simultaneously. He thus raises the questions of whether the type of categorization proposed for this chapter is itself appropriate. Globus concludes by suggesting that he has proposed a means by which the scientist is able to "maintain the spirit of dualism while in no way compromising his materialist account," a point of view, as we shall see, that seems internally inconsistent, and from my point of view, not justified by allusion to the complementarity principle.

Now let us briefly consider the various philosophical positions proposed as answers to the mind-body problem.

1.   The Dualisms

a.   *The Classical Theologies*

From the dawn of human consciousness, man has sought to explain the phenomena of his daily existence by attributing to natural objects supernatural intelligence and conscious intervention. At the most primitive levels, individuals attributed concerned intelligence to inanimate objects rather than considering them as unconscious and uninterested. The earliest protoreligions must have been simple animisms or panpsychisms that extrapolated from the human's intrapersonal awareness of his own consciousness to the idea that all natural objects possessed a similar consciousness. Thus rocks, trees, water, and weather, all of which affected human affairs, were attributed conscious and often male-volent intelligence. The relationship of the individual human to the individual "spirits" of the natural environment became exceedingly important in man's daily life. When natural objects altered the course of the human existence, bringing pain or social disruptions, means of propitiating the indwelling spirits had to be invented by problem-solving men. The primitive dialogues with and sacrifices to animistic spirits easily evolved into the sophisticated prayers and rituals just as the animisms themselves evolved into complex polytheisms of a more general kind. No longer were the spirits merely individual intelligences associated with specific natural objects, but they became much more powerful and personalized, though disembodied, gods and goddesses. As religious philosophies became more complex, the forest spirits, formerly only as powerful as the individual human, were transformed into sentient beings whose powers vastly transcended those of individual men.

Yet, the early religions were still framed in the context of the multiple forest spirits; they were always polytheisms reigned over by multiple gods who themselves were not individually omnipotent. Each new god struggled in some Olympian arena, as man did in his battlegrounds, for supremacy, goods, or glory. Fallen (often "fallen" to the heavens where they were immortalized in stellar constellations) and thus not omnipotent, gods filled the myths of all lands. Gods, like men, were born of parents, lived, and ultimately died.

In the second millenium B.C., Amenhotep IV (Pharaoh of Egypt from 1379-1362), perhaps for the first time in human history, proposed the notion of a single omnipotent sun god. Although this theme of monotheism did not take permanent root in his society (Amenhotep may have been murdered by the conservative priests of the state polytheism), his ideas may have been influential in stimulating the desert peoples of the Middle East to the development of the extremely sophisticated monotheisms (Judaism, Christianity, and Mohammedanism) that predominate in Western civilization today. These essentially monotheistic religions represent the contemporary end-product of the theologic evolutionary process just described. However, monotheism, as we shall see, is not tantamount to monism. Most monotheisms are, quite to the contrary, intrinsically dualistic.

If the main function of religion was to provide a metaphysical theory of all of life, it also served another important function by providing a framework for the individual's conception of his own personal immortality and thus of the nature of his own consciousness. The theological ideas of personal immortality that emerged were curiously antique, for just as the primitive animisms did for the individual objects of nature, the newer theologies ascribed to each person an individual soul that was separate enough from the body to be perpetuated even when the body had decayed. While the details of the afterlives, the heavens, hells, and the reincarnations differed from one religion to another, one of the central tenets of almost all religions is some sort of conscious personal immortality. That idea, the concept that the mind, or soul, can survive the body, is the essence of theological dualism.

b. Nontheological Dualisms

In addition to the important role of the mind-body problem in theological history, it has also played a central role in the history of nontheologically oriented philosophical discussions concerning the nature of metaphysical reality. Although these discussions have been carried on among a much smaller group of philosophers than the vast number of people concerned with religious matters, and the esoteric writings have had nowhere near the enormous audience of the holy books of the various religions, the dialogue among technical philosophers has also been influential in human thought.

The mind-body problem was explicitly discussed as a separate conceptual issue by the classic Greeks. Both Anaxagoras (500?-428 B.C.) and Plato were philosophical dualists who championed the notion of the separate existence of the mental and physical domains. In a similar vein and from a perspective that some might even feel is at least partly monistic, Aristotle fathered the closely related theory of vitalism—the philosophy that animate organisms differ from inanimate objects by virtue of the possession of some unique life fluid, process, or principle that is not reducible to the terms of physics and chemistry. While vitalism is not strictly a theory of mental and physical separateness, it is a type of dualism suggesting that there are nonphysical aspects to life that can not be explained in terms of the physical details. Aristotle's more specific philosphy of the relation of the mind and body, on the other hand, is considerably more explicitly monistic, as we shall see.

Descartes' interactionism. The modern history of philosophical solutions to the mind-body problem probably began in the seventeenth century with the writing of René Descartes. Descartes was an extraordinary man who contributed to both philosophical theory and to more practical matters of mathematics and physics. His invention of analytic geometry—the union of algebra and geometry— was instrumental in the enormous growth of technology and science in the subsequent centuries. In the context of the present book, his role as a philosopher and more specifically as a metaphysician is of primary interest. In 1641, Descartes' metaphysics was presented in a work, the title of which most clearly defines his dualistic perspective: *Meditations on First Philosophy, in which the Existence of God and the Distinction between Mind and Body Are Demonstrated.* In this book and other works, Descartes spelled out a dualistic answer to the mind-body problem that has come to be called *interactionism.* Descartes' main contribution was to place the mind in the realm of the natural rather than the supernatural, thus making an exceedingly important step forward from the theological interpretations of the scholastic philosophers and St. Augustine's (354-730), works that had dominated the previous millenium.

The main premise of mind-body interactionism, that mind and body are distinct and separate entities, is prototypical of the dualistic point of view, but Descartes added to this axiom the specific idea of interaction between the two to explain the many observed instances of mind-body correspondence. It was his thesis that mind and matter do interact with each other and that either is capable of "causing" effects in the other. Just as the body could affect mental processes, the mind was also capable of affecting physical processes.

The central difficulty of the philosophy of interactionism, however, lies in achieving a precise definition of causation and this, itself, is a major philosophical perplexity. Descartes' interactionism, however, was straightforward enough, even to the point of his suggesting a site at which the mental and bodily processes might actually carry out this interaction. The site he proposed was the pineal gland, even then well-known through anatomical studies and certainly centrally enough located in the human brain to appear to be of special significance. It was not until centuries later that the pineal gland was appreciated for what it really is, a vestigial photoreceptor that has mainly secretory (endocrine) functions in living mammals.

Although strongly influenced by his contemporary religious environment (he once stopped publication of one of his books because of possible difficulties with the church), Descartes and his concept of a dualistic interactionism have been considered by some to be the starting point of most modern (nontheological) dualisms. Many of the later theories were specific reactions to Descartes' ideas, and thus his importance as a seminal contributor to the philosophy of the mind-body problem is unquestioned.

Leibniz and Hartley's parallelism.   The main thesis of the classic parallelistic philosophy, usually originally attributed to Gottfried Wilhelm Leibniz (1646-1716) and more fully developed by David Hartley (1705-1757), is that the dualistic cleavage between mind and matter is so great that the two domains are totally incapable of causal interaction in the manner proposed by Descartes. Thus Leibniz and the succeeding parallelists asserted that mental processes and bodily functions usually correspond only because both are identically affected by the same stimuli. In reality, they said, the correspondence between the two is only fortuitous; it is definitely not causal in whatever sense one would like to use the word. Neither the mental aspects nor the physical aspects cause or produce the other, but, as Leibniz analogized, they are in agreement just as two clocks would be in agreement when started at the same time. The agreement between mind and body is due not to interaction, but to a parallel response to a common history. Parallelism, therefore, describes a philosophy of a mind-body problem that is characterized by a noninteracting dualism.

Kohler's psychoneural isomorphism.   Another theoretical position which is sometimes included within the rubric of dualisms (although it is not necessary to do so if one considers it to be a purely physiological rather than a philosophical argument) is Wolfgang Kohler's (1887-1967) *psychoneural isomorphism.* Basically, Kohler was attempting to describe how neural mechanisms represented percepts. In doing so, he suggested a highly specific model in which the dimensions of the neural response were actually isomorphic (of the same shape) in at least a topological (i.e., rubber sheet distortions are acceptable) manner with the dimensions of the percept. He felt that the two domains—the brain states and the mental percepts—were so tightly linked by this similarity in shape that observations in one domain—behavior—could provide unequivocal information about phenomena in the other—brain fields. Thus Kohler believed that behavioral observations were sufficiently dimensionally isomorphic with neural events that behavioral observations could tell us something about brain fields. Obviously this point of view is in sharp contrast to coding theory (see the discussion later in this chapter and in Uttal, 1973) which allows for nonisomorphic but encoded representations of percepts.

It is not entirely clear from Kohler's writing whether he and his colleagues of the Gestalt school felt that the two aspects—similarly shaped brain electric fields and global, holistic perceptions—were actually expressions of one form of reality, making them monists, or whether quite to the contrary they, as most later writers (Boring, 1942: Kaufman, 1974) thought, were actually metaphysical dualists. Generally, however, Gestalt psychoneural isomorphism is included among the parallelisms—one with a highly specific neurophysiology based on cortical electric fields.

This specificity of the Gestalt physiological field theory, unfortunately, was also its downfall. It has been clearly demonstrated (Sperry, Miner, & Myers, 1955; and Lashley, Chow, & Semmes, 1951) that the insertion of gold or tantalum pins and sheets into the cortex, which would be expected to short out any cortical electrical fields, had virtually no effect on performance in laboratory animals. Therefore, isomorphic electrical fields could not possibly be the correlates of the perceptions in the way suggested by the Gestalt theorists.

Polten's contemporary interactionism.   Polten is a modern idealistic dualist who has embodied his arguments for a modern interactionism within the framework of a particular critique of Feigl's identity theory.[1] Polten (1973) states very emphatically:

> I remove all known objectives to a dualistic interactionism, and go so far as to upset the old problem by maintaining that matter cannot act on matter apart from nonmaterial entities. More than that, the general picture which I put forward is that mind precedes matter in every relevant way, i.e., psychologically, logically, epistemologically, ontologically, chronologically, and normatively.
>
> I contend that old rationalist methods must be rejuvenated, and new techniques developed, in order to take account of the complete general nature of the universe. For contemporary empirical science can only lead us to the doors of the world of mind; it does not have the keys to unlock them [p. 274].

---

[1] Identity theory is discussed in a later section of this chapter.

Polten presents as his alternative to the identity hypothesis a metaphysical dualism, a form of interactionism, that involves two forms of reality: the entities of the inner mental world and the external physical world, respectively. Then, at another level, he also proposes two distinct levels of perceptual experience. The first is an "inner sense" that reflects our awareness of inner mental states, and the second is an "outer sense" that reflects our awareness of the material universe in which we are physically embedded. Introspection, according to Polten, is the function of the "innermost core of the mind—entitled the pure ego" (p. 19), and this pure ego itself is a part of the mental world.

Polten's proposed form of interactionism between the mental and physical realities appears to be more or less the classic one. The crux of the interaction question is: Can the mind affect the brain? (It is agreed by all philosophers and neuroscientists—monists and dualists alike—involved in this great debate that the body must certainly be able to affect the mind.) But as with so many of the philosophical conjectures on this question, the argument becomes circular; it then is difficult to tie down the exact meaning of a particular answer. For example, in rejecting the results of some hypothetical superneurophysiological experiment in which corresponding brain states were shown to be present on a one-for-one basis for all psychological processes, Polten (1973) says: "For it might be the case that every private mental event in the inner sense, even spaceless mathematical thought, continuously has brain events as its *effect*, and that a brain event which seems to be the *cause* of a subsequent mental event is really itself the *effect* of a prior mental event [p. 242]." As a general model of his point of view, Polten presents the diagram shown in Fig. 2-1. Unfortunately, his view runs so counter to the flow of modern monistic materialism that it is unlikely to have a serious impact on contemporary thinking concerning the mind-body problem.

Thus we can see that interactionism and parallelism are the two main themes of dualistic philosophies. Although each differs with regard to the degree of causal relation between the mental and physical domains, they both adhere to the main metaphysical premise of dualism, namely, that the mind and the brain are separate levels of reality in terms of their fundamental nature and not just in terms of the operations or language that must be used to examine each. In addition to the consistency with classic theological thinking that such a perspective affords, dualisms also reflect the practical realities of extensive scientific research. Whether or not the mental and the physical realms are truly separate, the experimental procedures used to explore each have been historically quite distinct.

The distinctions between ancient and modern dualisms are essentially summed up in terms of the degree of interaction that is proposed between the two domains of mind and body. Modern medical psychosomaticists are perhaps implicitly dualistic in the sense that they attribute a considerable amount of effective influence of what they call mind on bodily states and functions, but the linkage is tight and direct. Classical dualism, particularly the parallelisms, hypothesize a much looser relationship between mind and body.

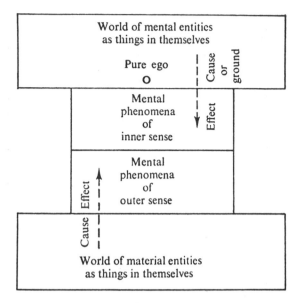

FIG. 2.1   A diagram illustrating Polten's conception of the relationship between the mental and physical domains. (From Polten, ©1973, with the permission of Mouton and Company.)

2.   Some Pluralisms

The position of the dualists that mind and matter were epistemologically separate is also a key premise of a small group of philosophies that, in addition, assumed that there were states of reality other than mind and matter. Pluralisms, as such philosophies are called, are relatively few in number, yet have been recurrently proposed for centuries.

One of the main issues around which the various mind-body controversies revolve is the difficulty of explaining how mental states and body states could correlate, as they obviously do, in so many different situations. Injury to the body brings on painful mental states and common observation attested to the fact that mental states could also affect the body. Was there some sort of a cause and effect relationship between the two domains; was there some sort of common fate due to a parallel sensitivity; or was there some sort of intervention on the part of other states of reality?

All pluralisms seem to be based on the general premise that by multiplication of the number of components in a system, the interactions between the original lesser number of components become more easily explained. This implies that concrete mechanisms can be substituted for abstract processes with some increase in simplicity. However, it often seems that this is not the case, and both the complexity and the number of potential interactions simply increase as new components are added.

a. *Geulincx and Malebranche's Occasionalism*

In the late seventeenth century there was a considerable reaction against the Cartesian dualistic notion of interactionism. At one extreme, was Leibniz' proposition of a noninteracting dualism consisting of parallel but independent domains of mind and matter. At about the same time, however, a more theologically oriented philosophy was also introduced by Geulincx (1624-1669) and Malebranche (1638-1715), which they called *occasionalism*, that was explicitly pluralistic. Their idea, like that of the classic dualistic positions, was that there was a complete separateness of mind and body. They proposed, however, that the parallel operation of these two levels of reality was accounted for in terms of a third level of reality—an actively involved God who was neither mental nor physical in the same way as the mind or body of man. Thus they proposed the idea of a continuous miracle to explain the correspondence of mind and matter. The role of God in this tripartite universe was to coordinate the actions of the physical and mental domains so that they were concurrent. Although the two domains appear to causally interact, in fact, they were totally independent and did not interact at all; their correspondence occurred only on the "occasion" of God's intervention. According to the occasionalists, the mental and the physical domains followed separate laws while God himself followed another set of natural laws that were not interpretable in the terms of either mind or body.

Therefore, occasionalism may be appreciated in terms of its exceedingly close relationship to classical theology. Although the formulation of this particular perspective is in terms of a more technical form of philosophy than the traditional church might be willing to support, occasionalism is clearly a theological theory. The notion of a continuous miracle and the omnipresent and ever-influential intervention by a supernatural force is quite distinct from most of the other philosophies with which we will be concerned.

b. *Popper and Eccles' Tripartite Reality*

Lest it be misunderstood that pluralisms are more or less antique philosophies that grew out of classical philosophy or medieval scholasticism and subsequently faded from the philosophical scene, our attention should now be directed toward what may seem to some to be a philosophical curiosity. Elsewhere in this chapter I have asserted that modern neurophysiology is implicitly monistic. In fact, some would claim that a philosophy of mind-body unity is inexorably implicit in its search for the physiological mechanisms associated with mental processes. Yet, curiously enough, a modern pluralism has been eloquently championed by a man who, perhaps better than any other, might be called the dean of modern neurophysiology. John C. Eccles received the Nobel Prize in 1963 for his distinguished work in neurophysiology and has authored a number of the most important integrative summaries of modern thinking on the synapse (Eccles, 1964), the cerebellum (Eccles, Ito, & Szentágothai, 1967), and general neurophysiology (Eccles, 1953, 1957). In short, his credentials are impeccable and his scientific achievements outstanding in all regards. Yet John C. Eccles' personal philosophy, as summed up in a recent statement (Eccles, 1970) and in a more general book on the brain (Eccles, 1973a), indicates that this very important modern scientist has read out of his experimental results a very different interpretation than have most contemporary neuroscientists.

John Eccles is explicitly a pluralist. He adheres to a view of the universe suggested by the eminent philosopher Karl R. Popper that involves three levels of reality. The first level of reality, or as Eccles calls it "World 1," is the world of physical objects and states including the material portion of the nervous system. "World 2" is the world of mental activities, or as he terms them "states of consciousness," and "World 3" is the world of man's culture and knowledge. The components of this tripartite reality are shown in Fig. 2-2. The essence of the mind-body-culture problem to Eccles revolves around the possible manner in which these three levels of metaphysical reality interact with each other. Just as with dualisms, the degree of interaction becomes the critical issue in his philosophy.

As a neurophysiologist, Eccles goes far beyond most philosophers in pointing out the specific anatomical structures that play significant roles in this pluralist universe. On the other hand, he finds it easy to accept, in exactly the same manner as Polten (see our earlier discussion), the notion of two classes of perception:

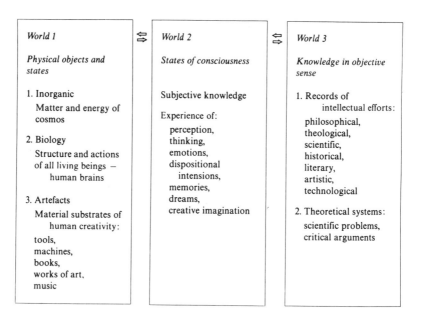

FIG. 2.2   The three worlds of reality according to Eccles and Popper. See text for details. (From Eccles, ©1970, with the permission of Springer-Verlag, Inc.)

an inner sense responsive to World 2 mental processes and World 3 stored memories, and an outer sense responsive to the stimuli impinging from the external World 1. The central interpreter of all of these sensory impressions is accepted, again in agreement with Polten, as a form of "pure ego." As incongruous as it seems in a modern neurophysiological text, Eccles refers specifically to this pure ego as being in many ways equivalent to the theological use of the word "soul."

The pathways of interaction between Eccles' three worlds are summed up in Fig. 2-3. While he very carefully qualifies his discussion as only a conceptual model, Eccles concretely charts the flow of interactions between the various components of the three worlds. To understand this figure, we should first note that World 1 and World 3 have been further subdivided in his schema. First, World 1, composed of the physical universe, can be seen to consist of three different categories. The first part—World 1a—is the external physical universe; the second part—World 1b—is the world of communication media and includes books, films, and all of the other objects whose function is *to store* information rather than *to be* information. The third part—World 1c—is the physiological and anatomical mechanisms of the body and includes the receptors, effectors, and the other portions of the peripheral and cortical nervous system.

An exceedingly interesting point is that World 3, the culture and store of knowledge, is also divided into two distinguishable categories. World 3a is composed of the information that is contained in World 1 storage media, such as books and films, and World 3b consists of the information contained in storage media, such as the memory banks of the human brain, whatever they are. Eccles stresses the essential similarity of these two information stores by putting them in the same category. This is an important logical point which emphasizes the secondary role of the physical nature of the storage medium in contrast to the primary role of the stored information in any discussion of information representation.[2]

Over the years, Eccles has been particularly interested in the idea that there is a "Liaison Brain" that is particularly necessary (and perhaps sufficient) to mediate the interaction between the World 1 brain states and World 2 mental states. Based primarily on Roger Sperry's work on the split brain preparation (see Chapter 5), Eccles now feels that the liaison brain is probably some part of the dominant cerebral hemisphere now thought to be most concerned with verbal and conscious behavior.

The flow of information in Fig. 2-3 now becomes clear. World 2, conscious, mental, and experiential, is in two-way communication with the physical, anatomical, and neurophysiological aspects of the World 1 nervous system, which itself is in two-way communication with the World 3 external culture through the afferent and efferent pathways.

---

[2]The reader may be interested in rereading Kety's allegory in Chapter 1 again at this point in the light of this new emphasis.

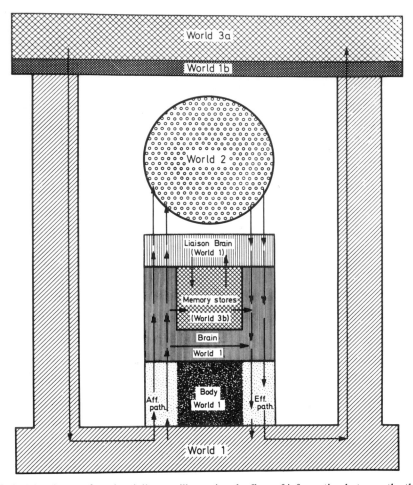

FIG. 2.3   A more functional diagram illustrating the flow of information between the three levels of reality in Eccles' and Popper's schema. Note that, according to these neuroscientific philosophers, both libraries (1b) and the brain itself are part of the physical world (1), but their contents are considered to be information and culture that are a part of world 3, objective knowledge. (From Eccles, ©1970, with the permission of Springer-Verlag, Inc.)

Eccles' attitude toward the relationship of the three domains is perhaps made most clear by his philosophy concerning the persistence of Stage 2 processes after cessation of neurophysiological function. In his most explicitly philosophical work, Eccles (1970) cites "the conscious existence that inevitably ends in death for tyrants as well as for the enslaved and the free. It is this reality that each of us has to face—or refuse to face [p. 189]!" Obviously Eccles believes that the linkage between World 1 and World 2 is very tight and that an afterlife is not likely.

c.   *Ornsteins' Multiple Aspect Theory*

Writing in specific opposition to the mind-body identity theory as well as to Ryle's dispositional monism (discussed later in this chapter), Ornstein (1972) has proposed in its stead a "multiaspect theory" of the relationship between the mind and the brain that he suggests lies halfway between Cartesian dualism and the reductionism of Feigl's identity theory (which is discussed later in this chapter). However, in developing his notion of a universe with multiple aspects that must be studied relatively independently and in which the linguistic terms of one aspect help little to explicate the others, Ornstein seems to be describing what is essentially a pluralistic view of reality rather than an intermediary between monism and dualism.

Specifically, Ornstein suggests that there are four aspects of mind. They are the *experiential* (what we feel), the *neural* (what is going on in the nervous system concomitant to the experience), the *behavioral* (what the organism is doing), and the *verbal* [what a man (uniquely) may say about what he is doing]. The identification of each of these aspects, Ornstein suggests, is necessary for assuming that mind exists in any given situation. A fifth aspect of his pluralism is the *body*—composed of the organic states that lead to the four levels of mind. This body category, according to Ornstein, also includes the receptor responses to stimuli from the external world.

The main thrust of Ornstein's theory is that reductionism from one level to another never works; it only leads to infinitely smaller categories that are inexplicable themselves. In thus rejecting reductionism and turning to this sort of pluralism, Ornstein multiplies many of the difficulties that are generated by the dualistic position. Rather than mind-body interactions alone, a whole new collection of dynamic interactions between all of his five aspects becomes a problem demanding solution. Whether this is a true expression of the ultimate nature of reality or merely a philosopher's invention, it is difficult to say. In any event, most contemporary psychologists would be unwilling to accept his fourfold separation of mental processes.

3.   Some Monisms

The basic premise of the monistic philosophies is that there is only one kind of reality, in spite of the fact that there might be practical difficulties from time to time and from instance to instance in demonstrating the true metaphysical unity. The classic historical antecedent of the monistic philosophy can be found in the teachings of Democritus (460-370 B.C.), a contemporary of Plato. Democritus was primarily a natural philosopher (today we would call him a physicist), who taught that all matter is made up of a relatively small group of units or atoms. Thus he is often given credit for anticipating modern atomic theory, although the conceptual basis of his point of view and modern physics could not differ more. In addition, Democritus suggested that mental substance was also, like material substance, made up of the arrangement of similar kinds of atomic elements. As such, he saw mental processes as emerging directly from the primitive physical properties, and, in this regard, his view is one very much in accord with the basic premise of the most modern monism.

Although much of classic Greek philosophy was concerned with the relationship between a mind and a body that were viewed as two very independent entities, Democritus' inclusion of mental processes within the limits of his atomistic theory of nature, as well as Aristotle's description of mind as the "form of the body," strikes a familiar and modern monistic chord. Clearly, monism, although gaining wider popular appeal as a philosophical position in recent years, is not really such a modern idea. Whereas the word "monism" may have become a part of the philosopher's vocabulary only a few centuries ago, its antecedents may be found quite early in philosophical history.

An important point that should be made before we embark on our brief review of the many monistic philosophies is that they are not mutually exclusive. In many cases they are not so much alternatives to each other as they are complements that enhance each other's description of reality. With that thought in mind, let us now consider some of the classic and modern monistic points of view.

a. *Berkeley's Monistic Idealism*

Although monisms are usually associated with mechanisms, materialisms, or physicalisms (i.e., those philosophies that assert that the ultimate nature of nature must ultimately be reducible to the terms of physical reality), it should also be noted that some monistic philosophers have suggested just the opposite view, namely, some form of monistic idealism. In this case, the single ultimate form of reality would be mental or ideational, rather than physical. The metaphysical philosophy of Bishop George Berkeley, for example, must certainly be placed in this unusual category of nonmaterialistic monisms. In denying the existence of matter independent of the reality that is attributed to it by the act of perception by some sentient being, man or god, Berkeley was in fact giving support to the monistic notion of a single form of reality. Unlike modern materialistic reductionists, however, who believe that mind arises out of ultimate physical reality, Berkeley was championing a view that matter arises out of some ultimate mental or spiritual reality. In so doing, incidentally, he set the stage for the historical emphasis on perception that has characterized much of modern psychology.

b. *Epiphenomenalism*

Most monisms, other than Berkeley's idealism, are patently mechanistic or physicalistic and assert that the mind is solely the resultant of some physical (electrochemical) process in the brain. Epiphenomenalism, on the other hand, asserts that mind emerges from this physical process in a relatively passive and insignificant manner. Mind is but an epiphenomenon of physical action "secreted by the brain as the liver secretes bile." However, the actual emphasis in debates that pit, for example, epiphenomenalism against dualistic parallelism, or for that matter against modern psychosomatic medicine, is on the degree of causal interaction between the mind and the body. Epiphenomenalism's essential premise is that mind cannot interact to any degree with body to cause changes in the body. Any "mental process" is merely the reflection of some unobserved physical state of the body that itself is the true antecedent of some other bodily change.

Another feature of epiphenomenalism is the assertion that our enormous concern with mental processes is the result of the creation of a set of pseudoproblems that have been engendered solely by the egocentrism of human beings. Thus, epiphenomenalism transforms mind into a second-order byproduct of physical processes that categorize man's behavior as more or less automatic. It thus is often referred to as automaton or automation theory.

c. Spinoza's Double Aspect Theory

Some monists, such as Benedictus Spinoza (1632-1677), while attributing a basic unity to the mind and the body, suggest, however, that there is a fundamental epistemological and practical difficulty in measuring both domains with the same instruments. They suggest, therefore, that though the mind and the brain are expressions of one and the same reality, they appear to an observer to be separate, because he observes two different aspects of this single reality due to the different measurements that are required for each set of observations. Double aspect theory, therefore, tends to deny any form of physiological reductionism in practical fact, but accepts it in theory and principle.

d. Neutral Monism

Neutral monism is another monism that ascribes primacy to a single form of reality, but in this case, that fundamental form is neither mental nor physical. The fundamental reality, from the point of view of the neutral monist, is the sensory experience itself. Neutral monism thus assumes that all mental and physical entities are derived in some way from the sense experiences, which themselves are considered to be epistemologically neutral, i.e., the product of neither bodily nor mental processes. By placing the emphasis in the determination of natural reality on the role of the observer, neutral monists come close to the Berkelian notion of an idealistic monism. Both are egocentric in the sense that the observer's actions take priority in the definition of the ultimate nature of reality. The difference is that Berkeley's idealism gives priority to the mental states per se, while neutral monism declines to define the exact nature of the sensory experience. It thus remains neutral on the exact nature of reality. It is, however, fully committed to the notion of a single form of reality.

e.   Emergence and the Hypothesis of Emergent Evolution

Another philosophy that assumes that there is but one form of reality has come to be called the "emergence hypothesis." According to this theory, the concatenation of parts into a compound structure results in the emergence of new properties that could not have been predicted even from full knowledge of the nature of the parts and the microdetails of their interactions. In the light of this emphasis, it is clear that emergence runs completely contrary to the basic premise of reductionism—the philosophy that the higher levels of observation can ultimately be explained in terms of the lower levels. Therefore, emergence theorists like Henri Bergson (1859-1941), who proposed a comprehensive theory of emergent evolution, or Father Pierre Teilhard de Chardin (1881-1955), a paleontologist who was especially concerned with the evolution of mind, whether speaking of the evolutionary emergence of behavior or of new physical properties, claim that the grouping of parts is more important than the parts themselves.

There is, of course, a practical difficulty in defining exactly what is meant by the term "nature of the parts" that may spuriously lead to emergent-type theories when, in fact, they might be logically untenable. The perplexity is, that if one is to know the "part" fully, he must also know about the nature of the interactions it will undergo with other parts when many parts are compounded into a global organizational structure. To be fully aware of these interactions requires concatenation, but to concatenate is to allow "emergent" properties to become manifest. Therefore, there is a paradox inherent in determining all that must be known of the parts, and thus emergence theory in some fundamental sense may be logically frail. Nevertheless, the essence of emergence theory is the stress that it places on the emergence of new and unpredictable properties even when all microdetails are known. Whereas both the emergence hypothesis and reductionism are patently monistic with regard to their metaphysical stance—both are physicalistic—it is clear that the two approaches differ fundamentally with regard to the part-whole relationship.

f.   The Identity Hypothesis

In the twentieth century, another form of materialistic monism, known as the psychoneural identity hypothesis, has gained wide currency among philosophers and neuroscientists. The essence of modern identity theory is that mental and brain processes are one and the same, i.e., metaphysically indistinguishable. The leading exponent of the identity hypothesis, Herbert Feigl (most particularly see Feigl, 1958), and others have made the point that any sensory, perceptual, or mental experience is nothing more, nor less, than a brain state. The main premise of the identity hypothesis is that the brain state is equivalent in all regards to the psychological process and vice versa. Perhaps the simplest way to make this form of radical monistic materialism concrete is to note that it essentially asserts that function and structure are inseparable and that the pattern, state, arrangement, or action of a group of neurons *is* mental process with a vigorous emphasis on the word *is* in its strongest sense of equivalence.

Another more formal way to look at the significance of the identity hypothesis can be framed in linguistic terms. A particular phrase may have both a *connotation* and a *denotation*. In common usage, as well as in technical philosophy, denotation refers to the actual meaning of a phrase, and connotation refers to the suggested meaning of a term that is in addition to its actual meaning. The term "actual meaning" in the case of the mind-body problem would essentially imply the same concept as the word "reality" as used previously in this chapter, i.e., the thing itself. "Suggested meaning," on the other hand, implies a concept that exceeded reality—a model with superfluous components. Thus in these terms, the words brain and mind *connote* different things, but the identity theorist would assert that they actually *denote* one and the same thing. Differences in connotation are due to the practical difficulties of measurement, not to the actual facts of nature. Feigl (1960) makes this same point, much more eloquently:

> Certain neurophysical terms denote (refer to) the very same events that are also denoted (referred to) by certain phenomenal terms. The identification of the objects of this twofold reference is of course logically contingent, although it constitutes a very fundamental feature of our world as we have come to conceive it in the modern scientific outlook. Utilizing Frege's distinction between *Sinn* ("meaning," "sense," "intension") and *Bedeutung* ("referent," "denotatum," "extension"), we may say that neurophysiological terms and the corresponding phenomenal terms, though widely differing in *sense*, and hence in the modes of confirmation of statements containing them, do have identical *referents* [p. 38].

Other modern philosophers have also supported the identity hypothesis; in addition to Feigl, metaphysicists associated with identity theories include S. C. Pepper (1891-1972), J.J.C. Smart, and D.M. Armstrong (e.g., Armstrong, 1962), although the version of some of these philosophies is often called *central state materialism*. In recent years, however, there has been a considerable rebound against this point of view. Perhaps the most vigorous critique has been that of E.P. Polten, whose work we have already discussed. Polten's (1973) stand—"The human mind is not identical with the central nervous system [p. 20]"—by antithesis helps to define exactly what is meant by the antagonistic view of the identity hypothesis. Another vigorous critique has come from Ornstein (1972) who suggests as an alternative, a multiple aspect theory, which has also already been discussed in the section on pluralisms.

Despite these criticisms, the contemporary version of identity theory, particularly as championed by Feigl, has a considerable amount of support among both philosophers and psychobiologists. Feigl (1960) himself has best summed up some of the advantages implicit in this particular solution to the mind-body problem:

> Does the identity theory simplify our conception of the world? I think it does. Instead of conceiving of two realms or two concomitant types of events, we have only one reality which is represented in two different conceptual systems—on the one

hand, that of physics and, on the other hand, where applicable (in my opinion only to an extremely small part of the world) that of phenomenological psychology. I realize fully that the simplification thus achieved is a matter of *philosophical* interpretation. For a synoptic, coherent account of the relevant facts of perception, introspection, and psychosomatics, and of the logic of theory-construction in the physical sciences, I think that the identity view is preferable to any other proposed solution of the mind-body problem [p. 41].

g. *Neuroreductionistic Theories*

The advent of optical microscopy in the seventeenth and eighteenth centuries, ultimately to provide the observational basis for the demonstration of the existence of cellular components (neurons) in the nervous system (see Fig. 2-4 for one of Leeuwenhoek's early drawings), led to a major new approach to the relationship between mind and brain. Based on the generally accepted notion that mental function is associated with the operation of the nervous system and the fact that the brain is itself made up of these elementary neuronal units, this new form of monistic metaphysics suggested that the interactions among networks of neurons were the bases of all mental function. This type of neuroreductionistic network theory is patently monistic and mechanistic and deals, for the first time in history, with what certainly are the true building-blocks of nervous tissue and thus probably of mind. In their emphasis on interaction among these elemental units, neuroreductionistic theories represented a major step toward understanding the mind-body problem.

The first major proponent of a cellular network type of neuroreductionist theory was probably Ernst Mach (1838-1916). The reader is directed to Ratliff (1965) for a brilliant review of Mach's philosophy in general and his theory of how contour intensification, the well-known subjective brightening and darkening of edges called "Mach Bands," could be produced by the inhibitory interaction of neurons in the visual pathway. Mach was exceedingly explicit about the fact that he was dealing with interacting discrete neurons rather than fields of some sort of neural energy that could conceivably have been invoked to produce analogous explanations. Thus he set the stage for a number of other workers of the twentieth century who were to propose explanations of other psychological processes based on the action of neural nets.

Two main lines of development from Mach's work may be discerned. The first has resulted in the enormous growth of empirical studies in the neurophysiological laboratory that are more or less explicitly committed to uncovering single neuron correlates of mental processes. The second is the vigorous development of network models of idealized neurons that might serve as theoretical explanations of some of the same mental processes.

The first line of development was highly stimulated by the extraordinarily fruitful work of H. K. Hartline (see, for example, Hartline, Wagner, & Ratliff, 1956) and his colleagues on the compound eye of the horseshoe crab, *Limulus*

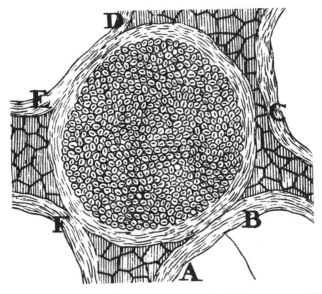

FIG. 2.4   Leeuwenhoek's drawing (circa 1719) of the individual neuronal fibers in a compound nerve. (Courtesy of Pergamon Press.)

polyphemus. The simplicity of this organism's eye and the orderly way in which the photoreceptor neurons were interconnected made it possible to show highly specific correspondences between neural interactions in *Limulus* and certain aspects of human perception such as contour intensification. These correspondences are extremely compelling. The basic network process of lateral inhibitory interaction was observed in this preparation for the first time (even though Mach had speculated some such process must exist) and has been generalized to a wide variety of other possible perceptual processes, although often in a most uncompelling manner (see Chapter 7 for a discussion of some of the misapplications of this principle).

In the past decade, the discovery of specific spatio-temporal feature sensitivities of individual neurons by such workers as David H. Hubel and Thorsten Wiesel (for example, see Hubel & Wiesel, 1962) and Lettvin, Maturana, McCulloch, & Pitts (1959) has led to another burst of laboratory activity and the continued development of the concept that the response patterns of single cells individually underlie perceptual processes. This material is also considered in greater detail in Chapter 7.

The second line of development from Mach's work is the one that is more germane to the topic of this discussion, for it includes the many theoretical studies that have become the embodiment of what certainly must be a specific monistic philosophical solution to the mind-body problem. Collectively, these studies proceed under the implicit assumption that global molar behavior of the whole organism can be deduced from the concatenated action of networks of interacting, but individual, neurons. The specific question these theories seek to answer is most clearly expressed as follows: How can we go from the properties of the individual neuron, increasingly well-known from neurophysiological studies, to the molar properties of behavior? As easy as it is to put the words of this question together, it is not so easy to answer it. There are unfortunately no satisfactory specific answers to this modern and exceedingly intricate expression of the mind-body problem. What these models emphasize, however, is that it is the interaction of the neurons in the networks that is the key to the answer, rather than the properties of the individual cells.

If any one person may be considered to be the father of this modern network theoretical approach, it would have to be Warren S. McCulloch (1898-1969), whose two papers with Walter Pitts, "How we know universals: The perception of auditory and visual forms" (Pitts & McCulloch, 1947) and "A logical calculus of the ideas imminent in nervous activity" (McCulloch & Pitts, 1943) were milestones in the development of the basic concept of neural network theory. In the first of these papers, Pitts and McCulloch combined anatomical, mathematical, and behavioral data in what was probably at that time a unique manner. Many of the ubiquitous assumptions of the lateral spread of effect and of the value of a multilayered, parallel network processing have become standard concepts in neural modeling even if some of the details of their model can no longer be supported. Modern works like that of Dodwell (1970) and Uttal (1975a) on the same topic look surprisingly similar when considered in this regard.

In retrospect, however, the McCulloch and Pitts (1943) paper is biologically flawed because it dealt with a logical calculus that depended exclusively upon all-or-none spike action potential as the means of neuronal interaction. We now know that graded potentials play an important information processing role in the brain. However, many of the theorems explicated in that paper would be useful reading to some of the most recent neural-net modelers. One of the networks proposed by Pitts and McCulloch (1947) to account for the functions of the auditory cortex is presented in Fig. 2-5.

A direct intellectual descendent of McCulloch and Pitts' work is the Perceptron, an invention of Frank Rosenblatt (1928-1971). The Perceptron is also a neural-net model of perception but adds two new features: adaptive behavior, or learning, rather than fixed interconnectivity, and random, rather than regular, interconnection patterns. The general thesis of the adaptive, random-network Perceptron is spelled out in detail in Rosenblatt's (1962) book, and the mathematics of Perceptron-like structures are further developed in Minsky and Papert's (1969) book.

Figure 2-6 depicts a typical three-layer Perceptron in which the first layer is composed of sensors. The second layer is a group of learning units with variable weightings at the interconnections, and the third layer is the response or decision layer.

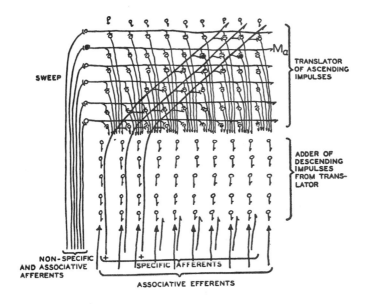

FIG. 2.5 An early neural network theory of mental processes. This particular network models the function of the auditory cortex. (From Pitts & McCulloch, ©1947, with the permission of Pergamon Press.)

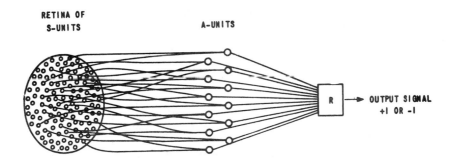

FIG. 2.6 A simple diagram showing the three-layered, but random, organization of a typical perceptron. (From Rosenblatt, ©1962, with the permission of Spartan Books.)

More recently, other workers have applied similar neural network models to the explanation of perceptual and learning processes. Dodwell's (1970) and Deutsch's (1955) works in vision are of special importance. Anderson (1972) has also developed a model of learning and memory based upon interconnections between two groups of neurons with variable synaptic strengths. Grossberg (1973) has generalized from the simple simultaneous linear algebraic equations used to describe the Hartline data (see Ratliff, 1965, chap. 3) and the steady state descriptions handled by the linear algebraic models listed by Ratliff (1965, p. 122) to a system of differential equations that describes the dynamic changes in the *Limulus* eye evoked by transient stimuli. Grossberg's study is an important mathematical plausibility test that explores the possible stable configurations into which neurons with specific inhibitory and excitatory interconnections can be arranged. Figure 2-7 shows one of the simple nets whose stability is discussed in Grossberg's work.

It is not possible to describe fully all the ideas involved in each of these neurophysiological models, just as we could not deal at this point with all of the neurophysiological data. In general, we can see that the combined mathematical

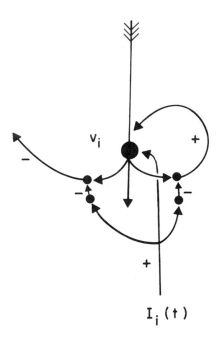

$$v_i$$

$$I_i(t)$$

FIG. 2.7   Schematic drawing of a hypothetical simple neuronal net possessing the special property that it can inhibit an old circulating pattern of activity while at the same time initiating a new pattern. (From Grossberg, ©1973, with the permission of Elsevier/North-Holland, Inc.)

and neurophysiological-anatomical approach, exemplified by all of these models, has received considerable attention in recent years. It is germane to note, however, that collectively they represent a unique philosophical approach to the mind-body problem which asserts that mind is the function of the neural network. This new approach has some highly specific assumptions built into it that differ greatly from the single cell approach. The premises of the latter are characterized by the axiom of the selective filtering function of individual neurons as opposed to parallel processing by networks of neurons. Some of the logical differences between the two approaches encountered when one begins to deal with networks or ensembles of cells have begun to be considered as a distinct topic themselves. The reader may be interested in looking at discussions of such matters in Sommerhoff (1974), Katchalsky, Rowland, and Blumenthal (1974), and Szentágothai and Arbib (1975), all of which discuss the conceptual basis of the neural network approach.

h.   *Cybernetic or Information Processing Models*

Another clearly monistic theme in modern thinking about the mind-body problem consists of the ideas implicit in a group of theories that attempt no particular neurophysiologizing at all, but instead concentrate on the information flow among hypothetical functional centers or units. Two relatively independent but equally important ideas permeate this line of thought. One is concerned specifically with the feedback and control properties of self-governing systems, which has come to be called *cybernetics* and which deals mainly with the arrangement of the channels through which information flows between processing units.

The other idea is closely related, but emphasizes the nature of the processing units. This alternative but closely related view has arisen mainly within the field of experimental psychology. Constrained from analysis of human behavior into its anatomical components by ethical and technical obstacles, a large number of contemporary psychologists have decided to deal with hypothetical models of the processes that are developed on the basis of behavioral observations. Thus, for example, in the view of these psychologists, the study of the processes of memory or learning is much more reasonable than the explication of the specific neural processes that might be involved in the storage of information. It must be clearly remembered, that the figures presented in this section are drawings of hypothetical *processes* and not of structural *components*.

Much of the work on cybernetics, or information processing, models was stimulated by Norbert Wiener (1894-1964), who was the foremost student of time series analysis in this century. Wiener (1948) was a mathematician and an eclectic scientist who had a remarkable ability to see how abstruse mathematics could be applied to problems of human psychology and physiology. It must be noted that his notions of cybernetic feedback control in biology are the intellectual descendants of the earlier work on feedback and reciprocal inhibition that had characterized the thinking of such a distinguished neurophysiologist as

Charles S. Sherrington (1856-1952). However, Wiener's introduction of formal mathematical modeling to such biological processes was a profound contribution.

Modern proponents of the cybernetic or information processing theories of mind include M. Arbib (1972) and W. R. Ashby (1960). In all of their theories, the emphasis of the system is on a network of interacting anatomical centers. Figure 2-8, for example, shows a sample flow diagram modeling the cybernetic organization of the visual nervous system. Note especially in this example that the emphasis is on the nature of the feedforward and feedback interconnections.

Many modern psychological theories, such as that of Broadbent (1958), Atkinson and Shiffrin (1968), or Sperling (1967), are information processing theories that are very similar to those cybernetic ones just mentioned, although the interacting units in this latter case are more often psychological entities such as "short-term memory" rather than anatomical units such as the "cerebellum." Furthermore, the emphasis in these information processing theories is on the interconnected processing units rather than the interconnecting pathways. Figure 8-4 displays a sample of this sort of information processing model, and the reader may wish to look ahead at this diagram.

i. *Sensory Coding Theories*

Sensory coding theories, although restricted to a highly specialized aspect of neural information processing (how neural signals represent the incoming sensory information patterns and their perception), are also an important prototype of a more general monistic approach to the mind-body problem. The key metaphysical premise of sensory coding theory—that the afferent message is totally represented by the pattern of neural action potentials—is clearly a monistic position. It is very specifically assumed that there is no a priori requirement for isomorphic or dimensionally similar representation of an input pattern by the neural code, such as that suggested by Kohler and discussed earlier in this chapter. For example, a temporal stimulus pattern may be represented by a spatial pattern (as high frequency acoustic energy is on the basilar membrane of the cochlea). The idea is that as long as the nervous system has the rules of information translation built into it, one code is as good as another for representation of any message.

The idea that dimensional similarity is not required for neural representation of sensory processes is also implicit in Pepper's (1960) defense of identity theory, as well as in Rosner's (1961) rejection of the need of linear relationships between neural coding dimensions and psychophysical dimensions. In this regard, sensory coding theory may be seen as a general alternative to any hypothesis that requires isomorphism or parallelism between stimulus, neural response, and behavior. All that is required to represent any stimulus pattern is a system of coding symbols and the rules for their use. Although the symbols and dimensions may differ (i.e., the stimulus, the behavior, and the neural representation

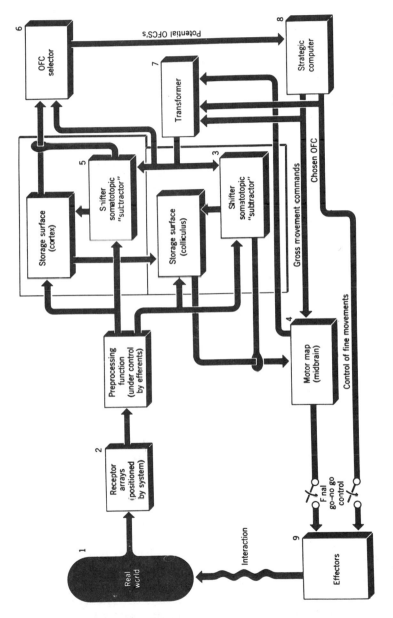

FIG. 2.8 An example of a cybernetic model of a portion of the nervous system. This theoretical approach emphasizes the interconnections between functional blocks such as the "transformer" and "strategic computer." The functional blocks have little direct relevance to the anatomical structures that actually are known to be involved in the two visual systems modeled here. (From Arbib, ©1972, with the permission of Wiley/Interscience, Inc.)

may be nonisomorphic), an equivalence of information is maintained that is adequate for the neural state to be tantamount to the psychological state.

Sensory coding ideas were probably first made explicit in the papers presented in the notable symposium volume (Rosenblith, 1961) on sensory communication. The major ideas have recently been summarized in Perkel and Bullock (1968), Uttal (1972, 1973), and Uttal and Krissoff (1968). I believe that extrapolation of the basic concepts of coding theory, from relatively peripheral processes to the most intricate problems of the central nervous system and cognition, can be accomplished without too great a stretch of logical credibility.

j. Ryle's Dispositional Monism

Gilbert Ryle, an important contemporary student of the mind-body problem, has reacted against both the dualism of Descartes and the modern reductionistic monisms that he believes downgrade the role of the mental processes. Although Ryle is clearly a monist, he has been greatly influenced by the linguistic approaches of the logical positivists. He has suggested (Ryle, 1949) that in order to salvage a significant role for the mind, it should be considered a set of dispositions or tendencies, or in the terms of a closely related terminology, a set of weighting factors that reflect the propensity of an individual to behave in a particular way. But even as Ryle relegates these mental processes to a role in which they have no physical substance of their own, he reaffirms the basic premise of the physicalistic monism that the mental processes arise out of or reflect the action of the material substrate. By attributing the role of behavioral weighting factors to mind, Ryle attempts to remove any separate existence of the mind as "the ghost in the machine." Such a separate existence he believes is only a "philosopher's myth."

Ryle does not, however, believe that the rejection of dualistic thinking allows us to ignore the mental aspects of our existence. An important part of his philosophy is that the group of dispositions that we call mind is public rather than private and as such is amenable to observation. Thus Ryle comes quite close to associating himself with the behavioristic tradition, which is described later, that asserts that only observable behavior is important. Influenced though he is by the operational perspective, it must be kept in mind that Ryle is clearly a material monist, and for him the sole essence of reality is physical.

k. Sperry's Emergent Interactionism

It would not be inappropriate at this point to briefly mention a controversy that has arisen over a recent statement by R. W. Sperry (1969) with regard to the mind-body problem. Sperry, a distinguished American psychobiologist, has made a highly significant contribution to the study of consciousness by analyzing the behavior of animals and humans who have had transections of the great band of axons between the two hemispheres of the brain known as the corpus callosum. His work has shown that it is possible to disassociate human consciousness and animal behavior into what appear to be two independent and separate "minds" as a result of the callosal transection.

In a recent paper, Sperry (1969) suggested that mental processes, which emerged from the concatenated action of myriad neural elements, could in some way affect the action of the very neurons from which they arose. Sperry believes that the concept of mental effects on the brain is not antimonistic in any way because the origin of mind must be dependent on the action of neurons. However, once those neurons have created what we call mental states, he suggests that the mental states are able to feed back and produce actual physical neural changes.

D. Bindra (1970) has responded to this suggestion by noting that he believes Sperry's paper really confuses two issues. The first issue is Sperry's acceptance of the concept of the emergence of a holistic mental state from a manifold of individual neural states. Bindra also finds this point acceptable and in agreement with much of modern scientific thinking. However, Bindra feels that the second issue in Sperry's argument is, in fact, implicitly dualistic. To him, the action of mind on brain is an essentially circular argument that leads to a "brain-mind-brain" sort of thinking. That circularity, according to Bindra, is actually the basis of a "nonhypothesis" that allows "a retreat (towards pre-nineteenth century vitalism) into a comfortable metaphysical dualism," in spite of Sperry's protestations to the contrary.

Sperry's (1970a) reply to Bindra's critique is mainly based upon the notion that his approach would return mind to "objective science." But it may also be argued that it already has been returned by the decline of radical behaviorism and the logical positivistic traditions in the last half century. Furthermore, Sperry's work on the behavioral effects of brain splitting itself (discussed in detail in Chapter 5), as Bindra also pointed out, is one of the best examples of this new scientific concern with mind and consciousness.

It should be understood that Sperry's position is not in any way a minority view. Much of the exceedingly popular work in modern psychosomatic medicine and behavior therapy and biofeedback is based upon the presumption that some sort of causal influence can be exerted on bodily functions by mental processes. Even if one considers this to be an action of brain processes on brain processes, such an action of mind on mind, without the intervention of alterations in the physical environment, would essentially be a dualistic concept.

l. *Modern Psychobiology*

This list of monisms should also briefly mention the particular metaphysical position most often implicit yet all-pervasive in the work of modern psychobiologists. I have already made repeated mention of various instances of this point of view in these first two chapters. However, for closure, it should be noted that the empirical association of behavioral and physiological measures, which is the prevailing paradigm of this emerging science, is itself the expression of a physicalistic reductionism quite similar to and yet, by virtue of its heavy emphasis on experimentation, distinct from the most philosophical arguments previously presented.

Simply stated, modern psychobiology seeks to explicate those correlations between neural *structure* and mental or behavioral *function* in a way that allows the investigator to distinguish between the instances that are merely correlational and concomitant and the instances that represent a true expression of a structure-function identity.[3] In dealing either with neurons, brain nuclei, theoretical nerve nets, or data from ablative psychosurgery, on the one hand, and information obtained by behavioral and introspective observation, on the other hand, psychobiology constantly asserts a monistic philosophy that theoretically and pragmatically embodies the postulate that there is an essential unity of mind and body.

4.   Rejections of the Mind-Body Problem

In the preceding three sections of this chapter, I have considered three general but distinct types of solutions to the mind-body problem—dualism, pluralism, and monism. Regardless of the differences among the various answers, all of the scientists and philosophers who have suggested such solutions to the "world knot" have done so from a position that is based upon the premise that the answers are proposed to a worthy and meaningful question. On this they all agree. However, this issue of the validity of the question itself is very controversial. Many philosophers have argued that the mind-body problem is an issue that is an improperly stated, ill-formed, unanswerable, or "bad" question and, therefore, should be rejected as a topic of inquiry. Many of the philosophers who reject rather than attempt to solve the issue based their studies of mind on theories of language or on epistemological positivism. Some of these linguistic or positivistic approaches have historical antecedents dating back to classic Greek philosophy.

a.   *Solipsism*

Classic solipsism is a form of rejection of the mind-body problem that places extreme emphasis on the one particular aspect of mental activity that is largely ignored by some of the other philosophies of rejection—perception. To the solipsist, the only form of reality that can exist is the introspective self-awareness of one's own experiences. The solipsist would assert that no information could possibly become available that could speak to the nature of reality of either matter or the minds of other individuals. Solipsism, in this sense, is a pessimistic

---

[3]This is a very complicated issue discussed in detail in Chapter 6 in terms of the signs-codes controversy in studies of sensory coding.

philosophy with regard to the hope of understanding the nature of reality if it is concerned with the problem at all. Not only does it isolate the individual from his fellow humans and consider the mind-body problem unsolvable, but also, much worse, it does not propose any alternative route to the understanding of the nature of human existence. Solipsism's lack of fertility makes it a dead-end—correct or not. It is usually rejected by all students of the mind-body problem and instead used as an example of the "reductio ad absurdem" to which certain arguments can lead.

b. *Phenomenalism*

Phenomenalism is similar in some respects to solipsism, but its impact on philosophical thought has been much greater due to the fact that it carries with it a possible means of acquiring knowledge. Thus it is a fruitful rather than a dead-end epistemology. Phenomenalism's similarity to solipsism lies in the fact that it, too, gives priority to sensory experience as the main, and perhaps the only, way to acquire knowledge about the external universe. Phenomenalism thus questions the reality of the material universe, but in a practical manner and only to the extent that it denies the direct measurability and examination of it. It, therefore, is a step away from solipsism and toward those philosophies that stress the primary importance of the operations used to measure nature, rather than of nature itself. The philosophy of phenomenalism may thus be considered as a precursor of the following positivistic and operationalistic philosophies.

c. *Positivism*

The epistemology of the British empiricists (e.g., Locke, Hume, and Mill) was founded on the assertion that experiment and observation were the sole means of gathering knowledge about the nature of reality. From this position evolved another point of view, *positivism*, which professed that the significant metaphysical questions themselves were simply not answerable with the empiricistic methods. Thus the empirical data, it was reasoned by the positivists, became primary, and the metaphysical questions had to be rejected as nonsense. Ernst Mach is usually considered to have been the main proponent of the philosophical doctrine of positivism in the nineteenth century.

Positivism has on occasion been used as a substitute for theology. Auguste Comte (1798-1857) proposed a metaphysics that taught that all questions of the reality of nature as well as theological speculation only hinder man's intellectual evolution. Comte essentially rejected the mind-body problem and associated himself with the position that it was only empirical observation of which we could be sufficiently positive to accept as meaningful.

Positivism, as both an epistemological and a metaphysical statement, can thus be seen to be closely tied to the emergence of empirical science. Although many of the British empiricists were metaphysical dualists, they were also epistemological positivists.

d. Logical Positivism

Positivism and empiricism evolved further in the twentieth century into an extreme form known as *logical positivism*, which was the most explicit of all of the rejectionist theories in regarding the mind-body problem as a meaningless question. The logical positivists mainly centered around the so-called "Vienna Circle," which consisted of such philosophers as Rudolph Carnap (1891-1970), Otto Neurath (1882-1945), Hans Reichenbach (1891-1953), and Moritz Schlick (1882-1936). This group was especially influenced by the early work of one of the most remarkable philosophers of the twentieth century—Ludwig Wittgenstein.

The philosophy of the Vienna Circle proceeded under the central premise that the methods of modern scientific empiricism were the sole route to acquiring knowledge about the universe. Not only did they reject the intended content of the metaphysical issues, but they asserted that the sensory and experiential route to knowledge championed by the earlier empiricists was meaningful only to the degree that it could be shared and made public. The private introspective route to knowledge through personal experience was discarded along with the rationalistic and speculative approach of theoretical induction. This emphasis on the public and interpersonal demonstration of empirical fact led to extensive and critical concern with the medium of interpersonal communication—language—and this indirectly to the modern emphasis on psycholinguistics evident in the attention paid to the writings of such contemporary linguists as Noam Chomsky.

Wittgenstein's personal work, as well as that of many of the members of the Vienna Circle, was largely directed toward understanding the various aspects of language. The meaning of words and the use of language became a very important topic as descriptors of the nature of whatever portion of reality that we, as experimenting human beings, were able to know.

The role of Ludwig Wittgenstein in modern philosophy is so pervasive and important that it is important to briefly discuss his views at this point. The use of the plural word *views* is especially significant in this case because, even though Wittgenstein's earlier thoughts were the source of the basic concepts of the Logical Positivists, his later teaching repudiated many of the premises that he had contributed to this school of modern epistemological thinking.

Wittgenstein's first book, *Tractatus Logico-Philosophicus* (1922), was the result of his early association at Cambridge with Bertrand Russell (1872-1970) and dealt, if one can constrain its contents to a single phrase, with the study of the methods of logic, mathematics, and language, and specifically with the problem of what actually can be achieved with these methods. Other than one other article, Wittgenstein published nothing else in his lifetime (although he was a prolific writer of notes), and his further impact rested almost exclusively on his role as a teacher and discussant in the classes he taught at Cambridge University. The main points of his later thinking were published as a series of notes prepared from dictation to his students and known as *The Blue and Brown Books* or *Preliminary Studies for the "Philosophical Investigations"* (Wittgenstein, 1958 edition). The final work of his career, *Philosophical Investigations* (Wittgenstein, 1953), was published after his death and dealt more generally with a number of philosophical topics including the meaning of such terms as meaning, imagining, and proposition. In this work, a main theme of Wittgenstein's writing was a critique of his own earlier work as expressed in the *Tractatus* and that of his mentor, Bertrand Russell. Russell, indeed, acknowledged that Wittgenstein's arguments were so compelling that he too was forced to accept them and modify his earlier opinions. Specifically, Wittgenstein challenged in the latter work (Wittgenstein, 1953) the dependency of logical positivism on the formal logic and mathematics that he had so vigorously championed in his youthful writing. Thus, he was essentially repudiating the very foundations of the philosophy of the Vienna Circle to which he had contributed so much.

In neither of his two most important works, the *Tractatus* nor the *Investigations*, does it appear that Wittgenstein speaks directly to the mind-body problem, other than to reject it as a mere nonquestion. Rather he is most concerned with the metaproblems that revolve around the definition of the terms of the mental and physical languages. His role in the discussion we have just presented, therefore, is peripheral, but his impact on the most influential of the rejectionist philosophies warrants considerable attention to his thinking.

Although Wittgenstein rejected the validity of the mind-body problem (he suggested it should be "dissolved" rather than "resolved"), it must also be acknowledged that his two major works were extremely influential in reviving interest in the discussion of mind as a scientific subject matter. In fact, the content of his poetic and disorganized *Philosophical Investigations* may be said to actually represent one definition of what it is that we call mind.

e.   *Bridgman's Operationalism*

The revolution that occurred in modern physics around the turn of the twentieth century stirred up a number of philosophical perplexities that had laid dormant for years. The very nature of matter and the basic physical dimensions became difficult to intuitively appreciate in light of the new Einsteinian relativistic principles. Intuition, so useful in a Newtonian world, was a hindrance in the universe of Einstein. This sort of conceptual difficulty led some physicists to question what they were actually measuring when they carried out measurements in the laboratory. At least a few came to the conclusion that it was not possible to define the nature of *what* they were measuring independent of the nature of *how* they were measuring it. Therefore, the *process* of measurement used in executing a given experiment became of greater importance to the definition of nature than the *referent* of the measurement.

Such a philosophy has come to be called *operationalism*. Operationalism was formalized for physics by P. W. Bridgman (1927). It is of consequence for psychology and contemporary perspectives of the mind-body relationship mainly because of parallel evolution of modern psychological behaviorism. The impact of behaviorism on the mind-body problem was critical, for the emphasis there was on the ultimate nature of mind and body. By giving priority to the operations and measurements in the realm of psychology, however, a major difficulty was engendered: The essential subject matter of the science is altered. The study of the events of intrinsically unobservable inner consciousness (mind) changes to the study of extrinsically observable motor and verbal responses (behavior).

f.   Watson's and Skinner's Behaviorism

As I have noted, the operational philosophy in physics, which placed the greater share of the emphasis on the process of measurement rather than the referent of the measurement, had a counterpart in modern psychology—*behaviorism*. This philosophy is an epistemological methodology that played such a dominant role in American psychology in the twentieth century that it actually changed the metaphysical assumptions of a generation of psychologists. As originally proposed by Watson (1913), behaviorism sought to remove mind entirely from the psychological sciences. It was, in part, a vigorous reaction against the introspective structuralism that flourished around the turn of the century under the leadership of E. B. Tichener (1867-1927). Access to all introspective and intrapersonal experiences was simply denied to the tools of science, and only the overt behavior of the organism, as publicly measurable, was considered to be of consequence. Watson's behaviorism has also been called *S-R Psychology* because of its emphasis on the observation of *R*esponses elicited by specific *S*timuli.

The rejection of the introspective and the conscious aspects of man's experience had an enormous practical effect on the subject matter of psychology between 1920 and 1960. The study of sensation and perception, which were essentially private and intrapersonal, was reduced, and such subject matters as learning, much more amenable to interpretation as observable performance changes, became much more popular in psychological laboratories. Similarly, the central role of physiological work was considerably reduced in central importance for the psychologist cum behaviorist. Measuring motor or linguistic responses rather than postulating their possible physiological mechanisms became the main goal of mid-twentieth century behavioral psychology. Sadly, the mind-body problem lay in limbo within the confines of the single science best equipped to deal with it.

In recent years, there has been a return of interest in the physiological mechanisms of behavior and of sensory and perceptual research as the antimentalistic tradition of behaviorism has declined. This renaissance has also been stimulated very directly by the enormous progress that had been made in the neurosciences between 1940 and the present.

Behaviorism stimulated the growth of theoretical models that were in some ways quite different than those popular today. Most behavioristic theories of learning [see, for example, those of Guthrie, 1952; Tolman, 1932; and Hull, 1943 (even though Hull, at least, was quite mathematical)] were strictly limited to descriptive statements of the functional relationships between observed responses and controlled stimuli; they sought assiduously to avoid "speculation," either physiologically or mathematico-deductively, about any possible underlying mechanisms. Ernst R. Hilgard (1948), a distinguished modern behaviorist, makes this point of view very clear:

> In view of the lack of knowledge of what actually does take place inside the organism when learning occurs, it is preferable not to include hypothetical neural processes in the definition of learning. We know that learning takes place. We should therefore be able to define what we are talking about without reference to any speculation whatever. This position does not deny that what we are calling learning may be a function of nervous tissue. It asserts only that it is not necessary to know anything about the neural correlates of learning in order to know that learning occurs [p. 5].

In view of the many modern psychobiological attacks on the problem of the physiological basis of learning, it is apparent that the void of knowledge to which Hilgard refers may be in the process of being at least partially filled (see Chapter 9).

The orientation of a behavioristic mathematical theory is clearly discernible in the writing of Clark L. Hull (1884-1952) whose algebraic models were solely descriptive. In his formalization of learning (Hull, 1943), simple functional correspondences were established between the stimulus dimensions and the response dimensions that could be shown to be related to them. When internal states, or, as he called them, intervening variables, were hypothesized, they were framed solely in terms of other processes that might conceivably represent the tendency of a response to be emitted rather than in terms of any possible physiological mechanism that might have been doing the processing.

For example, consider Fig. 2-9. This summary diagram of Hull's description of latency effects in learning is constructed from some observable and measurable values (N = number of reinforcements; h = number of hours of food deprivation; $_st_r$ = response latency) and from some hypothetical intervening variables ($_sH_r$ = habit strength; D = drive strength; $_sE_r$ = reaction potential). However, none of these intervening variables is even remotely physiological. They are merely other processes, not directly observable, that might contribute to the observed response characteristics when a measured stimulus impinges upon the subject.

Following the decline of this radical form of behaviorism and the increased availability of neurophysiological data, mathematical models of learning and perception that hypothesized specific neural explanations became much more common. The neuroreductionist models of Anderson (1972) and Grossberg (1973) and others, such as those described in Ratliff's (1965) book, are patently physiological in nature because they deal with interactions among realistic, if not real,

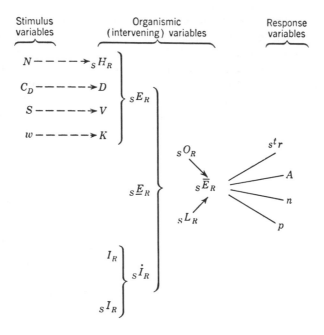

FIG. 2.9   A totally behavioral "Hullian" model of mental processes that is completely isolated from any anatomical considerations. The psychological processes and variables invoked here do not depend on any neurological explanation or theory. Abbreviations are defined in the text. (From Marx & Hillix, ©1973, with the permission of McGraw-Hill Book Company.)

neurons. This sort of neural modeling represents a distinctly different conceptual thrust than does Hull's totally descriptive model.

An even more radical form of behaviorism than the Hullian descriptive model can be discerned in a totally antitheoretical approach championed by B. F. Skinner (e.g., Skinner, 1938), who steadfastly champions a position that has culminated in some controversial recent application to social theory. In a recent book, Skinner (1971) asserts that man should be "shaped" to certain desirable social ends by behavioral modification techniques that are totally devoid of any attempt to understand the origins of the maladaptive behavior. In these two regards (i.e., the denial of the desirability of a formal model and the support of a policy of behavior change without understanding the root causes), Skinner represents an antitheoretical view that is perhaps the most extreme example of twentieth century radical behaviorism.

Other changes in classic behaviorism have occurred in recent years. The passionate reaction of behaviorism against Titchener's introspectionism has been counterbalanced in the last twenty years with a revival of interest in cognitive approaches stressing the inner processing of information by an integrating, thinking, and thoroughly conscious entity. But during most of the twentieth century, it must be acknowledged that it was Watson's behaviorism that dominated experimental psychology. Along with the emphasis on operationalism and empiricism went an almost total lack of concern with the metaphysical question of the relationship between mind and body that is the theme of this book.

Finally, a distinction should be made between two uses of the word *behaviorism*, which reflect quite different meanings. The distinction has been made by Ducasse (1960) between behaviorism as a philosophical resolution of the mind-body problem and behaviorism as merely a methodological approach to the study of mind. In the former case, the philosophical position that behavioral responses represent the only relevant subject matter of the science of psychology is asserted; mental constructs are thus denied tangible reality. This position is a metaphysical behaviorism.

On the other hand, as a methodology, behaviorism reflects the realities of a practical difficulty. It is the case that the only route to understanding mental processes must be through the study of behavior, whether it be in terms of muscular responses or verbalizations of introspective experiences. But, to those who hold this methodological view of behaviorism, the subject matter of psychology is, as it always has been, mental states, and the subject matter of psychobiology is the relationship between brain states and these mental states. This position is an epistemological behaviorism.

D.   A FINAL SUMMARY AND A PSYCHOBIOLOGICAL CREDO

This, then, brings my brief review of the philosophy and history of the mind-body problem to the final section of this chapter. I have surveyed only a few of the many postulated solutions to the mind-body problem, including some that were dualistic, some that were pluralistic, some that were monistic, and some that simply rejected the whole problem by refusing to consider the question as "good." The organization of this chapter was quite arbitrary, and there is always some residual question regarding into which of the four categories one or another of the various philosophical stances might have best been placed. Some philosophers would have preferred, for example, to have placed what I believe to be Gilbert Ryle's dispositional monism among the philosophies of rejection. As another example, some of the seventeenth century writers, who at first seem to champion modern sounding philosophies, are frequently found to be actually referring to theological concepts that suggest that their dualistic metaphysics may not have been as physicalistic as they seemed.

If the intended goal of this second chapter has been achieved, an objective statement about the various competing positions has been presented. However, with material such as this, it is incredibly difficult to be totally objective; viewpoints that I sincerely believed to be absurdities are difficult to discuss in a disinterested manner without so labelling them. It is clear that complete objectivity cannot be achieved in a discussion of the material of this chapter.

What grounds are there then for choosing one or another of the philosophical stands as the foundation on which the rest of the book is built, or, for that matter, as the appropriate credo of the entire psychobiological community? As twentieth century scientists steeped in the empirical-theoretical tradition, most of us would idealistically prefer that after reviewing the data, a rational decision could be made on the simple basis of the observed facts. Despite the rather naive views of many modern scientists, this sort of idealized scenario is probably not to be found very often, even in the case of the simplest experimental situation. Theories and models exist as surrogates for complete knowledge, for the simple reason that there is incomplete evidence for almost everything. The naive model of a totally objective science collapses in almost every instance that one penetrates its fragile surface. What is always found inside is something like a working "paradigm" (Kuhn, 1970) that substitutes for a totally objective analysis.

If one can appreciate the difficulty in naively applying a simplistic model of experimental and theoretical science to some problems of lesser complexity, then imagine how much more difficult it is to apply the same rules of evidence, induction, and deduction to the most complicated issue in human history—the mind-body problem. There is, furthermore, a corresponding practical obstacle to the understanding of the mental aspects of the nervous system. This is the problem already alluded to several times as the intrinsic intrapersonal privacy of experience. Although we are all aware of our own personal experiences and consciousness, the only road that the psychologist has to study conscious experience in others in through the medium of expressed behavior. Thus there will always be a sort of indirectness about the psychophysical data.

In light of the many limitations on our empirical and theoretical attacks on the mind-body problem, it is not surprising that the metaphysician, like the laboratory scientist, has been forced to rely upon other criteria than empirical validation to make his point. These other criteria include internal consistency, intellectual productiveness, completeness, parsimony, and even in many cases, personal values. I frankly believe that there is little in the way of empirical proof that could suddenly persuade a materialist-monist to accept the view of an interactionist-dualist, or vice versa, for the very simple reason that each bases his decision on these "softer" criteria.

This fact leads to what are apparently some very peculiar inconsistencies. Although, it seems reasonably clear, at least to this writer, that modern psychobiology is explicitly based on a unified or monistic premise of mind-body relationship, in our time we can observe such an extraordinary anomaly as the distinguished neurophysiologist, John C. Eccles, embracing a pluralistic philosophy. This is so in spite of the fact that his contributions to neurophysiology are among the most profound and his opportunity to observe the neurophysiological basis of behavior may be among the most complete in human history. In spite of this, one cannot read his very important monographs without feeling a sense of curious internal inconsistency.

How can such apparently internally inconsistent views come about? I believe that they naturally occur when the road to the solution of problems of great importance are obstructed by empirical hindrances, i.e., when a problem is not solvable by direct observations at the same level of discourse as the problem. In such situations, people often turn to value judgments or value-loaded interpretations of consistency or completeness, for guidance and then make their decision on the basis of aesthetics, some sort of personal consonance, or maximum pay-off.

The words of John Eccles clearly illustrate the role that is played by such value judgments. In his preface to Polten's (1973) critique of the identity theory, Eccles (1973b) makes the following statements:

> If Feigl is right, then man is no more than a superior animal, entirely a product of the chance and necessity of evolution. His conscious experiences, even those of the most transcendent creative and artistic character, are nothing but the products of special states of the neural machinery of his brain, itself a product of evolution. If Polten is right, man has in addition a supernatural component, his conscious self that is centered on his pure ego. Thus with his spiritual nature he transcends the evolutionary origin of his body and brain, and in so far could participate in immortality [p. xii].

Even though Eccles' purpose in making this comment was to emphasize the ultimate importance of the mind-body problem and the enormity of the potential effects of either proposed solution, it is clear that this is a value-loaded statement. Attend particularly to the phrase "are nothing but," on the one hand, and "could participate in immortality," on the other. These phrases have such enormous emotional loading that no further information is needed to resolve the mind-body problem for any individual at any point in human history. "I, as an individual," almost all men would say, "do not want to be nothing but a machine and do, with all my being, want to participate in immortality." How could a mess of psychological data countervail that sort of value-loaded argument?!

The point of this discourse is not to resolve the issue or to reject one or another of the positions; this would not satisfy anyone at this point. Rather, it is to emphasize that the decision to opt for one or the other of the antagonistic metaphysical positions is not one that is going to be resolved by empirical data or inductive or deductive logic, but, in almost all cases, it will necessarily be based on softer criteria including ones based on emotion, values, and intuitive and aesthetic judgments of consistency, completeness, or productiveness.

What, then, is the metaphysical position assumed by contemporary psychobiology? I believe that it is important to explicitly answer this question to inform the reader of any potential bias that might be reflected in the handling of the empirical matter of the second half of this book. In brief, I believe that psychobiologists implicitly assume that we live in a world that is:

Mechanistic and physicalistic,
Realistic,
Monistic,
Reductionistic,
Empiricistic,
Methodologically behavioristic,

and is not

Idealistic,
Dualistic or pluralistic;

and thus not

Parallelistic or interactionistic,
Rationalistic,
Emergenistic,
Vitalistic,
Operationalistic or logically positivistic,
Metaphysically behavioristic.

Now, within the context of the discussion in this chapter, let me be more specific about what each of these terms means.

The orientation of most contemporary psychobiologists to the mind-body problem is mechanistic and physicalistic in the sense that it gives priority to matter and asserts that the form or process of mind arises out of the action of that matter. It distinguishes between matter on the one hand and form or process on the other, as linguistic entities, but in a way that asserts that process or form is totally dependent on the arrangement of the matter. It is thus realistic in the sense that no mental processing is required for matter to maintain its reality. There is an essential asymmetry in this view; mind is a function of body, but body is not influenced by mind in any simple way that might satisfy our current pop psychologists.

This position is, thus, monistic in assuming that there is only one form of ultimate reality—that of matter and its arrangements in time or space. Furthermore, it is reductionistic in assuming that terms and objects of psychological discourse, as well as all other biological processes, are reducible in theory, if not in practice, to the terms and components of the physical world. Thus all levels of organization of matter should be understood ultimately by being reduced to lower levels without the introduction of extra physical principles. Such a view is also antiemergenistic in that it assumes that, if it were possible to have total knowledge of the parts, including the nature of their interactions, we would know all there is to be known about the whole. Nothing new emerges from concatenation that is not in principle predictable from the elements.

This approach to the mind-body problem is empirical in the sense that observation and experimentation are considered absolutely necessary. However, some psychobiologists modify this empiricism to a certain degree by asserting that the data accumulated in any particular experiment are of no fundamental importance themselves. It is only in terms of its role as a set of clues to the inductive development of global understanding and broad theoretical insight that laboratory research is of any consequence.

Another characteristic of contemporary psychobiological philosophy is that it is methodologically behavioristic. Behavioral observation is thought, of necessity, to be the only method available for determining the characteristics of mind. However, most psychobiologists are not dogmatic (in Ducasse's terms) or metaphysical behaviorists, because they do not necessarily believe that the content matter of psychology is behavior: Behavior is only the instrument; mental process is the content.

Finally, most psychobiologists, I believe, are interested in the relationship between neural and mental responses, not with the relationship between the stimuli of the external world and the mental response or between the stimulus and the neural response. Figure 2-10a makes this relationship diagrammatically clear and stresses the fact that, lacking the anchor of the stimulus, the psychobiologist has some very difficult conceptual problems that are unique to his approach, above and beyond that of the classical neurophysiologist or psychologist. The rest of this book spells out the nature of those special problems.

It should be noted, however, that this diagram is really only a procedural one stressing the relationships sought by the psychologist, neurophysiologist and psychobiologist respectively. It may be that Fig. 2-10b reflects the actual biological situation more accurately in the terms of the philosophical position we have just described. Stimuli directly produce neurophysiological responses but mental states are produced only to the extent that these neural changes occur. The connection between the neurophysiological changes and the mental states, however, are not symmetrical. In spite of the many popular "mind over matter" cults so prevalent today, as we have seen, there is a considerable question as to the validity of the feedback loop from mind to body. This alternative model may, therefore, more accurately reflect the position of contemporary psychobiology.

This, then, is a brief statement of the philosophical history and current premises of modern psychobiology and thus, of the orientation of this book. Admittedly, this world view represents a set of biases, prejudices, and personally selected premises that are no more provable than those of any competitive philosophy. By making these premises explicit, however, perhaps the rest of this book may gain in consistency and coherence. Make no mistake, psychobiology does take an advocate position, but one that at least appreciates that

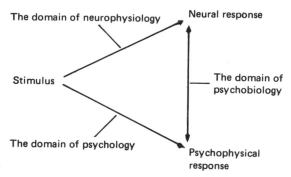

FIG. 2.10A One possible model of the relationships among the stimulus world, the neuro-physiological responses, and the psychophysical responses. Neurophysiologists and psychologists have traditionally considered separate sets of problems from those now scrutinized by psychobiologists. But many of the older data are of relevance and provide suggestive, if not direct, evidence toward the solution of psychobiological problems. (From Uttal, 1973.)

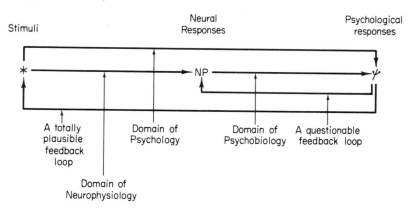

FIG. 2.10B A more realistic model of the relationship among the physical, neural, and mental domains, emphasizing the conceptual difficulty of assuming a direct effect of mind on brain even though modern monism strongly asserts the direct effect of brain on mind.

the duel is not to be won by weight of facts in the near future but rather by the slow evolution of value structures and the ultimate elegance and fruitfulness that have characterized all successful intellectual pursuits throughout human history.

In the remaining portions of the book, I turn from philosophy to the task of seeking to understand exactly what the current scientific status of the mind-body problem is. There occurs one shift in terminology that should be explicitly mentioned. Up to this point, the great task has been referred to as the search for a solution to the mind-*body* problem—the classic phraseology. From this point on, however, I refer to the mind-*brain* problem. In today's scientific arena, the part of the body in which the mind must be sought is the brain. Warren McCulloch's comment, which concluded the previous chapter, that this is necessary because it is only in the brain that we find the myriad possibility of interconnections necessary for consciousness, is a strong logical argument for the primacy of the brain. Modern laboratory science links the two—brain and mind—irretrievably and uniquely. The discussion of the body is therefore a discussion of the brain. I define by anatomical discourse what the brain really is, then define mind, and then by examining the scientific literature in the field see how the two domains are interrelated in terms of empirical fact. In so doing, the goal is not to accumulate and catalog facts, but rather to develop a synthetic perspective and integrative paradigm that hopefully will place the mind-brain problem in a more modern and more sharply defined context than has been previously possible.

3
Neuroanatomy

A. INTRODUCTION

The debate over the anatomical locus of the mind is of great antiquity. Plato, as I have noted, thought it was located in the brain, but Aristotle suggested that the brain only cooled the blood and that the mind was actually localized in the heart. However, if there is any single fact that is noncontroversial in the arena in which the mind-body problem is debated today, it is that the seat of mental functions is at least contained within the limits of the central portions of the nervous system and more than likely the essential parts are to be found in the brain. Thus, to meaningfully continue my consideration of the modern status of what I shall now refer to as the mind-brain problem, it is absolutely essential that a foundation of anatomical knowledge of the central nervous structures be established. The purpose of this chapter, therefore, is to explore neuroanatomy in a structural, rather than a physiological or functional, manner. My discussion will not consider all parts of the nervous system in equal detail; for example, I will deal only briefly with the more peripheral receptor or effector structures and pay only passing attention to the communication links that convey information between the periphery and the central nervous system.

The rationale for this constraint on the breadth of the subject matter in this chapter is that mental processes are certainly more dependent upon the integration of neural information in the more central portions of the nervous system than upon the communication of patterns of information to and from the brain. The reader interested in the anatomy and function of the peripheral sensory systems might wish to look at other books by Geldard (1972), Somjen (1972), or Uttal (1973) for more complete presentations.

An important distinction is made in this chapter between two aspects of neuroanatomy. I deal, on the one hand, with the *macroanatomy* of those structures that are large enough to be examined directly with the naked eye or with very low-power magnification at most. I am also, on the other hand, concerned with the *microanatomy* of the neurons that make up these macroscopic structures. Although knowledge of the macroanatomy of the brain, particularly with regard to the interconnections among some of the macroscopic centers or nuclei, is still growing, the truly fundamental breakthrough of the last few decades has been with regard to the microscopic anatomy and cellular organization among ensembles or aggregates of neurons and their interconnections. We now know something about the pattern of neuronal network interconnections in the retina, the spinal cord, the cerebellum, the hippocampus, the thalamus, and the cerebral cortex, as well as a great deal of the anatomy of the individual neuron. This microanatomical knowledge is now so rich that, as we begin to understand the specific features of interconnections that have evolved, we are becoming tantalizingly close to being able to explain the way in which neural structure underlies behavioral functions at least in some simple systems.

This chapter is organized according to the following plan. After this brief introduction, the techniques that are used to determine anatomic detail at both the macroscopic and microscopic levels are considered. Technique is a major focus in neuroanatomy for it is not quite as direct and easy as a novice might initially guess to determine even the gross features of the anatomy of the central nervous system. The original structural theme, which is reasonably uncomplicated, is obscured by both phylogenetic evolutionary and ontogenetic developmental changes. The most important change is the differential growth of the original subdivisions of the primitive brain, which results in some areas being completely enveloped by others. Furthermore, the dividing lines between various distinct functional and structural centers are often not sharply demarcated in freshly dissected or fixed but unstained tissues. Specific stains or specialized electrophysiological techniques must usually be used to distinguish one part of an apparently amorphous mass from another. Some recently developed techniques, also useful for the study of neuroanatomy, allow visualization of selected regions or pathways by introducing substances into them in the living brain that can be radiographically or chemically labeled during the normal metabolic process. These neural structures can subsequently be identified in slices of brain tissue. Some of these techniques are considered in detail in later parts of this chapter.

At the microscopic level, the difficulties in explicating neuroanatomy are even more formidable. Images of individual cells must be enormously magnified before they can be examined (some important cellular structures are only a fraction of the wavelength of visible light in size). At this level of microstructure (the domain of the optical microscope) and ultrastructure (the domain of the electron microscope), optical and electronic microscopic techniques are exceedingly important and thus are considered in some detail.

The discussion will then turn to the embryological development of the brain. There is perhaps no better way to understand the complex nature of the mature human nervous system than to observe its development during the embryonic development from a simple to a more complex structure. The arrangement of the constituent parts and the relations between them become strikingly clear as the ontogenetic sequence is followed.

I then consider the macrostructure of the mature brain and point out the substructures of which it is composed. The main goal of this section is to provide a working knowledge of macroneuroanatomy so that discussion of structure-function relationships to be presented in later chapters are meaningful and clear. I have especially strived, therefore, to provide a discussion which places the various components in a reasonable structural and conceptual framework.

The next section of this chapter deals with particular examples of the microanatomy of the central nervous structures that are currently understood. Finally, in the last section of this chapter, I have tried to draw together the various pieces of microanatomical information discussed in the previous section and extract from them the general principles of neuronal organization.

Throughout this chapter, I concentrate as much as possible on the anatomy of the human nervous system. As noted earlier, the human brain appears to be the highest embodiment of organic evolution as evidenced by the complexity of behavior and culture it encodes and represents. However, to avoid any unwarranted "species-centrism," it should also be noted at this point that the human brain is not the largest or even the most complex in appearance. Simple criteria of brain size or convolution complexity do not place man at the head of the list. Consider, for example, Fig. 3-1, which compares the brain of a porpoise, a cetacean, with that of a human. The enormous and heavily convoluted cetacean structure clearly exceeds the human brain both in its total weight and in the size of its forebrain. Similarly, reference to a brain-weight-to-body-weight ratio is

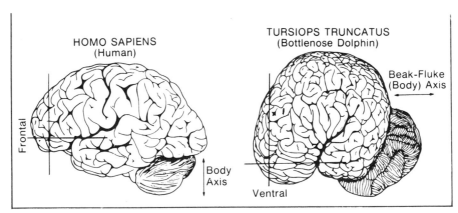

FIG. 3.1   A diagrammatic comparison of the brain of the human and the bottlenose dolphin drawn to approximately the same scale. Note that the dolphin's brain is both larger and more heavily convoluted than the human brain. (From Earley, ©1974, with the permission of The New York Academy of Sciences.)

inadequate to establish man's neuroanatomical primacy. Even the humble tree shrew has a better brain than does man on the basis of this criterion.

A much better criterion, however, is the encephalization quotient suggested by Jerison (1976). The encephalization quotient (E.Q.) is defined by him to be equal to the actual brain size divided by the expected brain size. The expected brain size, in turn, is predicted by an expression of the following form for the function relating brain size to body size:

$$E = .12 \, p^{2/3}$$ (Equation 3-1)

where E is brain size and p is body size. This expression is a best fit to a large

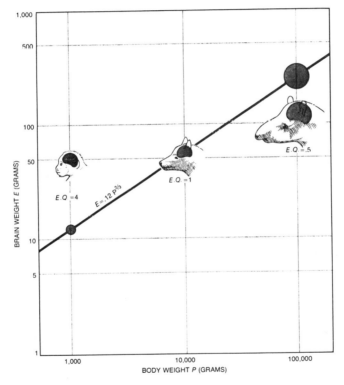

FIG. 3.2 A chart plotting the encephalization quotient for several representative mammals. The encephalization quotient is the ratio of the animal's actual brain size to its expected brain size. The expected brain size is calculated from an arbitrary expression that best fits the family of mammals. It has the form: expected brain size = .12 body weight$^{2/3}$. The fact that the monkey's actual brain size is four times greater than expected gives it an encephalization quotient of 4, whereas the tapir's half-again smaller-than-expected brain size gives it an encephalization quotient of .5. (From Jerison, ©1976, with the permission of *Scientific American.*)

body of measurements made for a wide variety of modern mammals. The criterion works fairly well as shown in Fig. 3-2. A small but smart monkey has a high E.Q. because its brain size is larger than predicted for all mammals, and a dumb but large tapir has a low E.Q. because its brain is smaller than would be predicted by the expression for expected brain size. The E.Q. is thus a corrected and improved measure in comparison to a simple brain-weight-to-body-weight ratio.

The criterion of excellence of the human brain, however, is probably not so much one of gross structure as it is a measure of the intricacies of cellular organization. It is at that level that the crux of the mind-brain problem in contemporary psychobiology is currently to be found. However, to be perfectly blunt, it must be admitted that we still have only the crudest idea of what it is about the detailed connections of the human brain that allow it to create language, thought, or self-awareness, and biological criteria of brain excellence remain elusive. Nevertheless, a major premise of this work is that all of our culture and mental life is somehow explainable in these terms and these terms alone.

Finally, a brief comment should be made at this point to dissipate a common negative attitude of students on their initial encounter with the study of anatomy. Anatomy is usually presented in a rather tedious manner. Rote memorization of the component parts, for some inexplicable reason, has traditionally been the pedagogic method of choice. But modern neuroanatomy is extremely sophisticated, elegant, and, even more important, an intrinsically highly organized body of knowledge. The evolutionary and embryological development of the nervous system may be viewed in terms of dynamic processes and even in terms of mathematical elegance that would excite and enthuse even the least interested student of classical anatomy. The development of structures like the brain can be couched in the terms of topology—the mathematics of those aspects of form that remain invariant, in spite of any rubber-sheet kind of distortions. One of the most exciting problems in modern evolutionary studies of neuroanatomy, for example, is the determination of the homologous structures of various central nervous systems in different animals. The problem is to determine which structures have common evolutionary origins (i.e., are homologs of each other) in spite of the fact that they may be very much dislocated or deformed when compared in the adult animals of different species.

To distinguish between analogs and homologs is not always easy. In the course of evolution, simpler structures may grow, assume new shapes, or, far worse, even fuse with portions of other structures to create new centers that are the evolutionary product of two or more preceding structures. For example, in his outstanding series of volumes on comparative neuroanatomy, Kuhlenbeck (1967) compares the anatomy of the anterior (telencephalic) portion of the brain in a series of vertebrates in two most informative figures. Figure 3-3 shows a cross-section through the brain of a cyclostome, an amphibian, a reptile, a bird, a marsupial, and man. In the primitive vertebrate, the cyclostome, each half

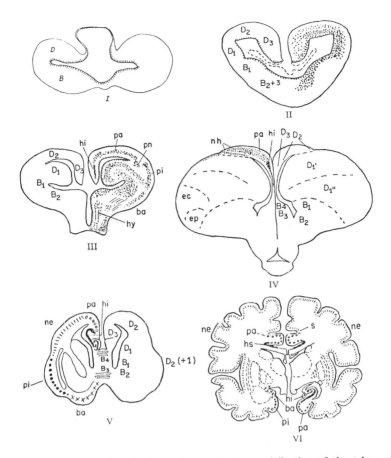

FIG. 3.3   Diagrams showing the increasing anatomic specialization of the telencephalon in six different vertebrates: Cyclostome (I), amphibian (II), reptile (III), bird (IV), and mammals (V, VI). I. Larval *Petromyzon* (Ammocoetes). II. *Triton* (urodele amphibian). III. *Cistudo* (Turtle, reptilian pattern). IV. *Columba* (avian pattern). V. *Didelphys* (marsupial, *Metatheria;* generalized mammalian pattern). VI. *Homo*. Abbreviations indicated are: B = basal neighborhood; ("fundamental telencephalic basal longitudinal zones"); D = pallial, i.e., dorsal neighborhoods ("fundamental telencephalic pallial longitudinal zones"); ba = basal cortex; ec = ectostriatum of Edinger; hi = hippocampal cortex or formation; hy = hypothalamus; ne = neocortex; nh = homologon of neocortex (in birds); pa = parahippocampal cortex; pi = cortex of piriform lobe; and pn = primordium neopallii (in reptiles). (Figure and caption information from Kuhlenbeck, ©1967, with the permission of Academic Press.)

of the telencephalon is divided into only two regions, one basal and one dorsal. As one ascends the phylogenetic tree, however, these two primitive regions grow, become more complex, and subsequently subdivide into numerous daughter structures. Comparably labeled areas in Kuhlenbeck's drawings for different species show the course of this evolutionary diversification.

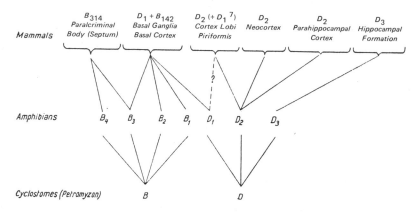

FIG. 3.4   Diagram of the progressive evolution and specialization of the primitive basal (B) and dorsal (D) neighborhoods of the cyclostome's brain into the much more complex regions of the mammalian brain. (From Kuhlenbeck, ©1967, with the permission of Academic Press.)

In Fig. 3-4 Kuhlenbeck makes this sequence of developing and diversifying brain structure as one ascends the phylogenetic tree even more specific and graphic. Starting at the bottom of the figure, he shows how the two primitive basal and dorsal regions are transformed first in amphibia and then ultimately multiplied into the many structures of the advanced mammalian brain. Kuhlenbeck's analysis is but one example of the many ways in which homologous structures may develop from more primitive undifferentiated structures in lower animals. As the brain becomes more complex, these homologous structures take on new functions that were not present in the primitive ancestor.

There has, furthermore, been a general revival in recent years of studies that compare neuroanatomy across species. Comparative neuroanatomy received a strong reinvigorating stimulus from the insightful and germinal paper by Hodos and Campbell (1969). Recent studies by such workers as Cuenod (1974) and Karten (1969) have helped to define homologies between mammalian thalamic structures and the telencephalon of birds using microanatomic, electrophysiological, and behavioral studies. Although the range of problems that have come to be called *comparative neuroanatomy* is somewhat outside of the scope of this book, the reader may find much to excite his interest in this emerging field of neuroanatomic research.

The embryological or ontogenetic approach is another avenue by means of which neuroanatomy may be studied. Embryology emphasizes the dynamic rather than the static features of anatomy stressed in conventional neuroanatomy courses and texts. Any of the approaches—the evolutionary, the comparative, or the embryological—can serve as the central conceptual theme and provide the organizational framework that helps make the understanding of neuroanatomy both pleasant and easy. In this chapter, the embryological theme is stressed.

I now turn to a discussion of the methods and instruments that are used to determine the macroscopic and microscopic structure of the central nervous system.

B.   ANATOMICAL RESEARCH PROCEDURES

Modern anatomical research is blessed with a variety of methods that can help to determine both the gross and microscopic structure of nervous tissue. A useful, but not completely exclusive, dichotomy can be made between techniques suitable for the study of macrostructure and microstructure, respectively.

However, before I begin this discussion, it is worthwhile to explicitly state what the goals are in the application of neuroanatomical techniques. Neuroanatomy may be considered to have three specific target questions that it seeks to answer:

1.   What are the major and macroscopic subdivisions of the nervous system?
2.   What are the connections between the major subdivisions?
3.   What is the arrangement of the cellular components (neurons) and what relation does this microscopic arrangement have to the macroscopic subdivisions?

The techniques that I describe in the following sections all seek to answer one of these three questions. In modern neuroanatomy not all of the techniques that produce descriptive statements of morphology are made possible by special staining or microscopic techniques. Some are based on physiological techniques (e.g., the evoked potential) that demonstrate anatomical facts through the medium of functional, rather than structural, observations.

With this orientation in mind I now separately consider some of the macroscopic and microscopic techniques used for the study of neuroanatomy.

1.   Techniques for the Study of Macrostructure

a.   Gross Dissection

Clearly, the major source of knowledge about the macrostructure of the brain is simple dissection. A considerable amount of information can be obtained once the brain and/or spinal cord are removed from their bony encasements. Methods of laboratory dissection for teaching neuroanatomy or for autopsy have become highly standardized in the last century as training in gross anatomy has progressed to its current almost routine level of development.

The first stage of examination of the gross structure of the central nervous systems of man and animals is carried out with simple tools. A blunt probe or similar dissection instrument is usually recommended so that tissues may be separated along their natural lines of demarcation rather than along artificial lines of surgical incision. On the basis of this simple sort of gross dissection, the brain may be separated into a number of structural subunits. Various swellings, lobes, and macrostructures are immediately apparent.

The next stage of examination of the gross structure would be to ask if any substructure can be seen within the various lobes. In general, the answer to this question is negative. For example, note Fig. 3-5, which shows both a lightly stained slice of the brain of a rat and a map of many of the centers that are

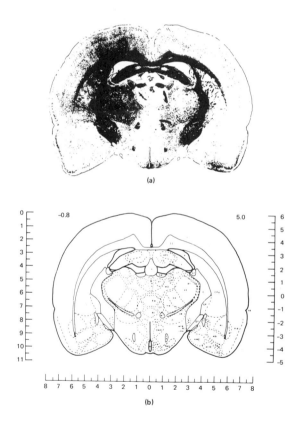

FIG. 3.5   Photograph (a) showing the appearance of a lightly stained section of the brain of a rat and a stereotaxic map (b) with abbreviations of some of the many known centers and nuclei of the same section. Because most of these centers and nuclei cannot be seen in the original photograph, it is clear that they have had to be tediously traced by degeneration, evoked potential, and other anatomic locating procedures. (From Pellegrino & Cushman, ©1967, with the permission of Plenum Publishing.)

known through other procedures to exist in this same region. Obviously, in the freshly sliced or lightly treated brain, there are no grossly discernible lines of demarcation between the various centers and tracts, and little of the enormous complexity of the mammalian brain is apparent to the naked eye. Therefore, other procedures have to be used to demarcate the invisible boundaries between these structurally and functionally distinct units. These other procedures are described in the following subsections.

b.   Evoked Potential Techniques

Electrical stimulating and electronic recording procedures are often used to trace out the anatomy of the subunits of the central nervous system. The procedure typically involves activation of one portion of the nervous system with a stimulus and simultaneous probing for the evoked electrical responses in other locations. The stimulation may be accomplished in a number of ways. Adequate (optimal physical energy) stimuli may be applied to the normal receptor channels (the eye or the ear, for example); electrical stimuli may be used to activate almost any region of the nervous system; or chemicals may be applied to a portion of the brain. A wide variety of other chemicals can also be used to stimulate the brain. Some do so by simply irritating the neurons with nonphysiological conditions; others mimic the normal activating mechanism by which neurons communicate—the chemical neurotransmitters. An electrophysiological recording system may then be used to determine the regions of the brain or spinal cord that are subsequently activated by the stimulus.

One of the major problems with this technique is that a very large number of remote regions can be activated by any stimulus due to what is often a surprisingly abundant interconnectivity. In most mammals it seems as if stimulating any region of the brain activates almost all other regions. For this reason, the most powerful application of this evoked potential technique has been the analysis of sensory systems that are sufficiently simple in organization so that afferent conduction pathways can be directly traced. Much of what we know of the localization of sensory functions in the cortex has come about through the application of this evoked potential approach.

The modern master of the evoked brain potential technique for mapping the sensory regions of the brain is Clinton Woolsey of the University of Wisconsin. For example, Fig. 3-6 shows one of his maps of the localization of auditory stimuli of varying frequencies on the cat cerebral cortex (Woolsey, 1961). Each of the many traces in this figure indicates a typical oscilloscopic response obtained at a particular point on the cortex when a single frequency auditory stimulus is presented. Thus, a different map is produced for each stimulus frequency by moving the electrode to a number of different points and observing the local variation in response as the identical stimulus is repeated over and over again. The stimulus frequency is then changed and the mapping repeated to produce the set of drawings shown in this figure, each of which represents the map of

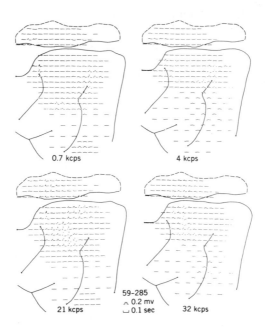

FIG. 3.6   Maps of the electrical activity produced in the primary auditory portion of the brain of a cat with four different frequencies of acoustic stimulation. Note the shift in evoked response pattern with variations in frequency. Each of the many recorded traces on each of the four plates was produced by a separate positioning of the electrode. (From Woolsey, ©1961, with the permission of The M.I.T. Press.)

brain responses for a single frequency. It is important to note that the localization of the response for each frequency is not precise, rather there is only a gradual change in response magnitude as one moves the recording electrode over relatively large portions of the cortex. This fact leads to one of the great limitations of the evoked potential technique. It is not possible to discriminate simple electrotonic spread of response from true overlapping representation through the application of this technique alone.

c.   Degeneration Techniques

If an axon is disconnected from its cell body, the axon will die. This is due to the fact that the metabolically important structures of a cell are located in the cell body; the processes extending from the cell body, the axons and dendrites, therefore cannot survive alone. This fact has been used as a useful adjunct to the stimulation and recording and dissection techniques for tracing central nervous pathways. If a cut is made that severs the axons forming a pathway, there will appear over the next few days a neurological lesion or region of degeneration along the entire pathway, terminating at the synaptic junctions of the cut axons.

Tracking the course of the degeneration is an exact means of mapping the course of the pathway and thus defines the tract's route between its point of origin and its termination at the next synapse. Figure 3-7 shows a prepared slice of the superior colliculus of a hamster showing the granulated appearance of a sharply circumscribed degenerated region produced by removing the contralateral eye. Because the cell bodies of the ganglion cells in the retina are destroyed by enucleation, this operation produces degeneration of the axons of the optic nerve— degeneration that can be traced into the superior colliculus, in this case, as well as into the thalamus.

Axonal degeneration of this sort is known as *anterograde degeneration*. Degeneration of a cell body can also occur when the axon is cut loose. This is a result of *retrograde degeneration* and is usually exhibited as a systematic change in the intracellular structure of the cell body (the perikaryon) following amputation of the axon. Nauta and Gygax (1954) have developed this technique to a high degree of utility. When axons in the peripheral nervous system are severed,

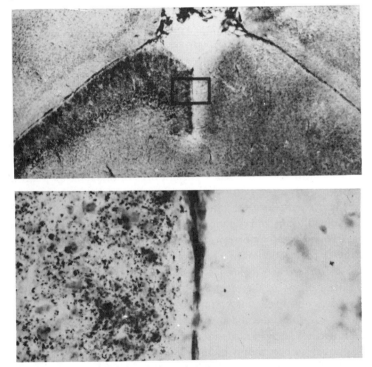

FIG. 3.7   Micrograph of a degenerating tract in the superior colliculus of a hamster. This degeneration was produced by removing the contralateral eye of the animal a week prior to the time it was sacrificed and the histological sample taken. The evidence of degeneration is the accumulation of the dense granular material, a phenomenon shown in more detail in the more highly magnified lower photograph. (A photograph of a sample collected by G. Schneider, reproduced courtesy of L. Heimer, ©1970, and Springer-Verlag, Inc.)

retrograde degeneration is often reversible, and the perikarya giving rise to those axons may return to normal after their regeneration. In the primate central nervous system, however, even though regenerative sprouting occurs, full regrowth seems to be blocked by the dense packing of the constituent neurons and glia. Transsynaptic degeneration has also been reported adding a further means of studying pathways, but one that is complicated by the involvement of several sequential neurons and producing not nearly as crisp results as mononeural degenerations.

d.   Gross Autoradiography

The fact that photographic film is sensitive to electromagnetic radiations other than visible light means that silver halide emulsions can also be used as a powerful means of elucidating brain structure. Radiographic techniques depend, in large part, upon the fact that the brain is a metabolizing organ and, therefore, may take up particular substances at particular locations as it goes through any of a large number of chemical cycles. If, however, the metabolic process is abruptly stopped (by killing the animal), the tissue will retain any radioactively labeled and metabolically active substances at concentrations approximating their abundance at the time of death. Slices made from the dead animal's brain, when subsequently placed in contact with a thin sheet of sensitive emulsion, can leave an "autoradiograph," because the persisting radioactivity will expose the film. In this way, it is possible to track the time course of some metabolic process by sacrificing a number of animals at regular time intervals following the injection of some metabolite. The procedure can thus be used to determine the regions in which the metabolic process may or may not have occurred, or to compare the relative amount of activity, and thus of metabolite uptake at different locations.

An excellent example of the latter application of this technique is the work of Eichenbaum, Butter, and Agranoff (1973). Their particular experimental goal was to determine whether or not protein synthesis in the brain was actually inhibited by the introduction of a known protein inhibitory substance—puromycin dihydrochloride. Their technique involved the introduction of the puromycin into a localized region of the brain through a cannula inserted through the skull. Quantities of radioactively tagged amino acids, the constituent building blocks of proteins, were then injected into the femoral vein of the animal. These injected amino acids had been made radioactive by substituting radioactive Carbon 14 for the usual carbon atoms in their molecular structure. Carbon 14 has a radioactive half-life (the time it takes half of the material to radioactively decay) of many thousand years, and its radioactivity is, therefore, persistent and virtually constant over the full course of the experiment. Because radioactive decay is a nuclear event and, therefore, will be totally unaffected by any subsequent chemical processing, and because the half-life is so long, the "tagged" amino acids would leave a trace on the film corresponding to the places and amounts in which they were incorporated during life into the specimen brains—that is, into whatever regions of the brain were actively producing proteins.

The question asked by Eichenbaum and his colleagues was: Would the regions of the brain that had been perfused with the protein synthesis inhibitor, puromycin, take up any of the amino acids? Following the sacrifice of the monkey used in this experiment, slices of the brain were prepared and laid on photographic films for several weeks—the long exposure required by the low level of radioactivity present in these relatively safe laboratory chemicals. Figure 3-8 shows one of the autoradiographs they obtained when the photographic film was developed. Two prints of the same photograph are shown. The first is the raw autoradiograph; the second has been modified by outlining, with a dotted line, the lighter area in which there appears to have been no uptake of the radioactive amino acids. Because this is the region into which the puromycin had been injected, the compelling conclusion is that this inhibitor did indeed block the normal synthesis of protein in a relatively sharply circumscribed area. In addition, the autoradiograph indicates another feature of brain protein synthesis. The region of darkening shown in the photographs indicates that the synthesis of brain protein occurs mainly in the outer rind of the cerebrum and very little in the underlying regions.

If drugs can alter the metabolism of certain substances at particular locations in the brain, one is also tempted to ask if induced or stimulated activity can also cause such an alteration. This question has been considered by Kennedy, Des Rosiers, Jehle, Reivich, Sharp, and Sokoloff (1975) who showed that the uptake of deoxyglucose (also tagged with Carbon 14) was correlated with the amount of induced neural activity. For example, Fig. 3-9 shows two different

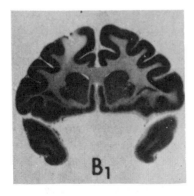 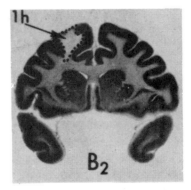

FIG. 3.8   Autoradiographs showing the zone of inhibition of protein synthesis produced by the injection of a protein formation-inhibiting substance. The animal was sacrificed one hour after the injection and the material quickly fixed. B_1 shows the unretouched autoradiograph, and in B_2 the region of protein synthesis inhibition has been outlined. (From Eichenbaum, Butter, & Agranoff, ©1973, with the permission of Elsevier/North-Holland Biomedical Press.)

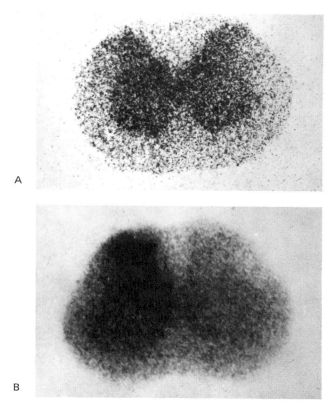

A

B

FIG. 3.9   Autoradiographs showing the effect of repeated stimulation of the sciatic nerve of a rat. *A* shows the results from a normal control, whereas *B* shows the effect (darkening of the dorsal horn) produced by the stimulation. This combined stimulation-autoradiographic procedure has allowed the investigators to track out the pathway of this nerve. (From Kennedy, Rosiers, Jehle, Reivich, Sharpe, & Sokoloff, ©1975, with the permission of The American Association for the Advancement of Science.)

autoradiographs of sections of the spinal cords from two rats. Figure 3-9a is the autoradiograph of a normal rat; Fig. 3-9b is the autoradiograph of a rat that received repeated stimulation of the sciatic nerve. Clearly, a much greater density of exposed silver grains is present in the dorsal horn of the cord of the stimulated rat. Thus, the induced activity presumably increased the metabolism and thus the uptake of the deoxyglucose by a substantial amount, particularly in this region. It is also a direct conclusion that the sciatic nerve projection passes through this part of the spinal cord, a very useful anatomic datum.

e.   Lesions—Permanent and Temporary

The identification of the various parts of the brain is only one of the goals of gross neuroanatomy; another important task, as I previously noted, involves tracing out the neuronal connections between the many identified nuclei. To accomplish this goal, it is often useful to interrupt a possible pathway to determine if there is a physiological or degenerative effect. The interruption may have some effect on the elicitation of a compound action potential, for example, in some location when a stimulus is applied either to a sensory receptor or to some other part of the nervous system, or produce degeneration in a distant locus because fibers course to that region. The most obvious means to interrupt a pathway is simple surgery. A region of the brain may be surgically ablated or removed by suction or a possible pathway transected with a scalpel cut. However, surgery of this sort is almost always irreversible, and it is often desirable to produce a "lesion" that is only temporary. Temporary blockages of neural activity, comparable to a permanent lesion, can be produced chemically by the application of ion exchange beads (Butcher & Fox, 1968) which temporarily depletes ions necessary for normal function, by topical application of potassium chloride (Leao, 1947) or other chemicals, by administration of anesthesias, or even thermally. Fish, for example, can be totally anesthetized by immersion in ice water because neuronal activity varies with temperature; a procedure that is entirely reversible. More precise localization of temporary thermal blockages of function can be produced if one applies a cooling element to a particular portion of the brain rather than cooling the whole animal. A particularly efficient way of doing this is to use a Peltier junction. Peltier junctions are cooled simply by the passage of electricity through two dissimilar metals. (Running current through such a device in the opposite direction will heat the junction.) "Thermodes" of this sort have been developed especially for biological use by Hayward, Ott, Stuart, and Cheshire (1965). One of their thermodes is shown in Fig. 3-10.

2. Techniques for the Study of Microstructures

a. Optical Microscopic Histological Techniques

The optical microscope has played and will continue to play an important role in mapping the microstructure of the central nervous system. However, to use a microscope to observe what are normally transparent tissues, special techniques must be employed to make the cells visible.

The classic microanatomical technique has been to use some dye or stain that is relatively specific to a particular kind of tissue. Whatever the staining technique of choice, there is some characteristic of the neuron that makes a particular region selectively sensitive to the acquisition of some staining substance. The membrane may be selectively permeable, there may be some special metabolic interaction with a given chemical, or axonal transport may move injected materials from one portion of the cell to the other. Any stain that did not selectively operate on some portion of the preparation would simply leave the anatomist with a monochromatically colored, rather than a black and white, preparation, with no real gain in the ability to discriminate between different structural

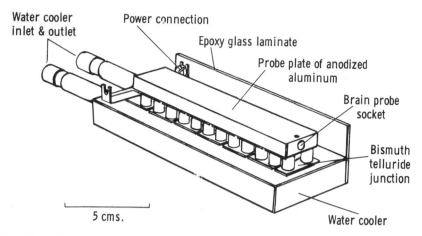

FIG. 3.10 A Peltier cooling unit for use with a brain probe. The probe itself is inserted in the socket indicated and is cooled by conduction from the Peltier unit. (From Hayward, Ott, Stuart, & Cheshire, ©1965, with the permission of Medical Research Engineering.)

elements. Thus, there are stains like toluidine blue, which are believed to bind to the RNA in the Nissl substance that is concentrated in the cell body, and others like the silver-based stains, which act in little-understood ways to selectively stain all parts of some cells including the axons and dendrites, but, mysteriously, to completely unaffect other nearby cells. Many pictures of whole neurons have been processed with a technique known as the Golgi silver impregnation method. In this procedure, crystals of silver chromate fill the cell completely, and thus it is really not so much a "staining" technique as it is a sort of "fossilization" procedure. In other silver staining techniques, such as the Holmes and Bodian procedures, the silver atoms combine with intracellular neurofibrillar elements, thus achieving a true stain of the cell parts rather than a replacement of them.

The silver staining technique, known as the Nauta stain (Nauta & Gygax, 1954), and more recent modifications of it such as the Fink-Heimer technique (Fink & Heimer, 1967), are particularly useful because they act selectively on degenerating axons. With these stains, fibers can be traced from one part of the brain to another by separating the axon from its cell body and observing the course of the subsequent anterograde degeneration microscopically.

Other optical techniques have also been developed that allow unstained nervous tissue to be observed. The phase contrast microscope takes advantage of minute differences in the refractive index of different parts of individual cells, thus allowing the microscopist to observe virtually unaltered tissue. With this type of microscope, it is possible, in some instances, to actually see a living cell going through its normal metabolic activities.

Fluorescence techniques, which allow examination of tissues in a form very close to their natural states, have also been developed. However, the fluorescence technique usually involves some specialized preparation of the tissue including the injection of special fluorescent dyes, which cannot always be done with living cells. Typically, the tissue is frozen and then dried in a vacuum. The prepared tissue is then placed in a special microscope whose light source is rich in ultraviolet rays. Different tissues pick up different amounts and kinds of dyes and thus fluoresce in different colors when they are exposed to the ultraviolet light. It is this secondary emission of light that is seen by the observer, rather than the incident ultraviolet light, filtered and absorbed as it is by the stained slice of tissue (and, in any case, invisible to the eye). The particular color with which the cell fluoresces can thus be a clue to which cells are histochemically alike or perhaps, even more important, functionally similar.

A recent development (Stretton & Kravitz, 1968) in fluorescence microscopy takes advantage of a special dye known as Procion yellow. This dye has a number of important advantages. One of the most significant is the fact that it is relatively harmless to a living neuron. It is, therefore, possible in some preparations to inject this material into a physiologically responsive cell through a micropipette and, for a short time, to observe the anatomy of the living cell while simultaneously recording its electrophysiological signals. Another important advantage is that the neuronal membrane seems to be very impermeable to the Procion yellow dye. Thus, all of the dye remains within the single neuron into which it is injected, but it is also capable of diffusing to most of its branches. Therefore, if the injection is properly done, a cell can be microscopically examined as if it were perfectly isolated from its neighbors.

Procion yellow fluoresces in the yellow portion of the spectrum when irradiated by a bluish light; most cells that do not contain this dye will fluoresce with a much paler natural greenish color. The injected cell including most of its smaller ramifications, therefore, stands out clearly. The dye is also stable during normal fixation procedures and remains intact in serial sections so that it can be examined microscopically postmortem. Figure 3-11 shows a Procion yellow electron micrograph and graphic reconstruction of a neuron in the stomatogastric ganglion of a lobster (Selverston & Mulloney, 1974). Related dyes that fluoresce in other colors (e.g., Procion brown or brilliant red) have also been developed. Another relatively harmless intracellular dye composed of cobalt compounds that are electron opaque has also been reported (Pitman, Tweedle, & Cohen, 1972).

An important breakthrough in fluorescence microscopy is the even more recent development of immunofluorescent techniques (Geffen, Livett, & Rush, 1969). This histochemical technique allows the histologist to place fluorescent materials in particular parts of single neurons by taking advantage of antibody-antigen reactions. The procedure involves the preparation of antibodies by injecting purified antigens (or target substances) into living animals. After a period

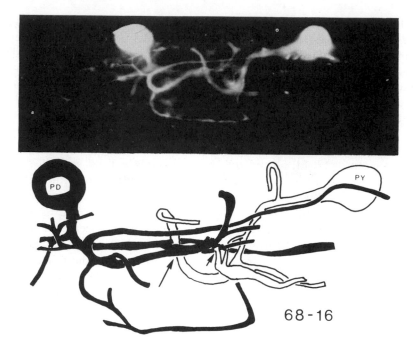

FIG. 3.11 A pair of neurons in the stomatogastric ganglion of a lobster fluorescing after injection with Procion yellow and a graphic reconstruction of these two cells. (From Selverston & Mulloney, ©1974, with the permission of The M.I.T. Press.)

of time specific antibodies for these antigens can be isolated by biochemical processes from the blood serum of these animals. These antibodies treated with fluorescent materials can then be placed in contact with excised neural tissues where they will react with the tissue so that the fluorescent materials are loaded preferentially into the portions of the cells rich in the target antigen, or substances closely linked to it, for which the antibody had been specifically produced. Individual portions of cells will fluoresce under microscopic examination in proportion to the amount of the antigen present. Thus, not only does this method provide a means for tracking neurons, but it also provides a means of performing a quantitative microchemical analysis of the chemicals present in particular neurons. Figure 3-12 (from Goldstein, 1972) shows a typical immunofluoresce response in the neurons of the superior cervical ganglion of the rat.

Another microscopic tracer technique of increasing popularity involves the use of tracer proteins such as horseradish peroxidase. This particular protein has a peculiar and very useful property. It is able to enter a neuron only near the cell body and the axonal or dendritic terminations (Sellinger & Petiet, 1973), but it cannot pass through the axonal membrane. Once inside the cell, however, horseradish peroxidase is conveyed by axonal transport mechanisms along the axons (Kristensson, Olsson, & Sjostrand, 1971; LaVail & LaVail, 1972; Lynch, Gall,

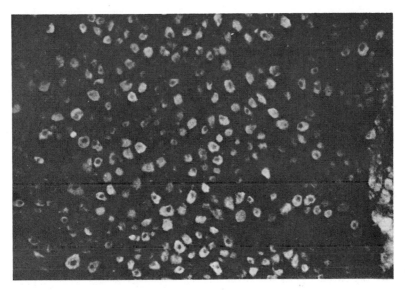

FIG. 3.12   An immunofluorescent micrograph of neurons in the rat's superior cervical ganglion. These cells are responding to the presence of the enzyme dopamine-β-hydroxylase.
(From Goldstein, ©1972, with the permission of Plenum Publishing.)

Mensah, & Cotman, 1974). Thus the protein can be perfused into a localized
brain area where it will enter the cell body and subsequently be transported
through the axons to distant loci. Microscopic examination of tissues stained
with reagents specific to horseradish peroxidase thus can determine whether or
not there are direct connections between the perfused region and the distant
centers. Because horseradish peroxidase is not able to enter the cell through
axons, any fibers that merely pass through a perfused region will not be affected
by the treatment. A cell body must be present for the "tracer" to be picked up
in the perfused region. Figure 3-13 shows a preparation traced with this technique.

By taking advantage of the fact that another region in which the protein can
enter the neuron is the axon terminal, the process of neuronal tracking with
horseradish peroxidase can also be reversed. Kievit and Kuypers (1975), for
example, have traced fiber connections from terminals located in the frontal
and parietal cortex back to cell bodies located in the hypothalamus and basal
ganglia by perfusing the substance into these regions of the cortex. This reverse
action occurs because horseradish peroxidase migrates particularly well in a
retrograde direction (i.e., opposite to that of the normal axonal cytoplasmic
streaming) as well as in an anterograde direction. An excellent review of the
retrograde transport method is found in an article by LaVail (1975).

A full review of several different tracer techniques for studying the internal
structure and routing of individual neurons with optical and electron microscopes is reported in an article by Lasek (1975).

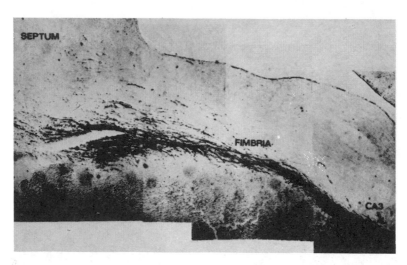

FIG. 3.13   A micrograph of neurons in the brain stem labeled with horseradish peroxidase. This enzyme's inability to permeate axonal membranes provides another method for tracing the course of axons. (From Lynch, Gall, Mensah, & Cotman, ©1974, with the permission of Elsevier/North-Holland Biomedical Press.)

b.   The Electron Microscope

The range of magnifications that we have considered so far fall within the capabilities of the optical microscope. However, in recent decades, neuroanatomists have realized that many of the important structural elements of neurons are even smaller than the 1500-2000 power maximum magnifications obtainable with visible light microscopes. Many of the intracellular components, including the membrane, are too small to be fully resolved at these levels of magnification and, furthermore, many of the components display even more detailed microstructure that is extremely important in understanding their function. The development of ever more powerful microscopes has been, therefore, a major goal of microanatomists for many years.

Because of diffraction effects produced by the interaction of wave fronts from the much magnified individual light waves, however, there is no realizable way of improving the magnifying properties of any optical microscope to distinguish between two adjacent points that are closer than a certain minimum amount. That is to say, even with perfect optical elements, the wavelength of the utilized radiation specifies a minimum separable distance (resolving power) for any magnifying system. An estimate of the maximum possible resolving power of any given magnifier is given by Eq. 3-2, which is seen to be a function of both the wavelength of the radiation and the geometry of the magnifying system:

$$r = \frac{.5\lambda}{NA} \qquad\qquad \text{(Equation 3-2)}$$

where r is the resolving power (the minimal separable distance achievable by the magnifier); λ is the wavelength of the utilized radiation; and NA is the "numerical aperture" of the magnifying system. For optical microscopes, the numerical aperture is defined by:

$$NA = \mu \sin \theta \qquad \text{(Equation 3-3)}$$

where μ is the index of refraction of the medium through which the light passes, and θ is half the angle subtended by the lens.

Under optimum conditions of viewing, using an appropriate fluid immersion system and appropriately slanted light pathways, the numerical aperture of a microscope using visible light can only be as great as 1.5. Therefore, the resolving power of the best quality optical microscope is limited to about a third of the wavelength of the magnifying light. The shortest visible blue light that can be seen under normal conditions is about 380 or 400 nm. Resolving power is thus limited to separations of about 130 or 140 nm.

Through the use of even shorter wavelength electromagnetic radiations such as ultraviolet light and special photographic or electronic detection systems, resolving power can be extended even further. Finally, however, the problems of lens transparency and of lens aberrations begin to take over, and the limits of the optical microscopes cannot be extended by any means.

Unfortunately, this technological limit prohibits optical methods from distinguishing many of the microanatomical structures of biological concern. As one important example, the lamellar layers of the outer segment of a retinal rod are only 50 Å thick[1] (see Porter & Bonneville, 1968, p. 181), and it is at this ultramicroscopic level that most significant transductive phenomena occur. Synaptic gaps also are very small, of the order of 20-200 Å, and here too the important structures are far beyond the limits of resolution of optical microscopes. Alternative means of increased magnification are, therefore, necessary if one is to have fuller information about the details of microstructure.

Equation 3-2 leaves two different routes open in the search for a means to improve the resolving power of a magnifying system; the wavelength of the radiation may be decreased, or the numerical aperture of the system may be increased. For many practical reasons, it has generally not been possible to greatly increase the numerical aperture of any magnifier; the optical or electrical properties of lenses and magnets seem to be recalcitrant to technological improvement in this direction. Therefore, it has been necessary to work on the other variable in the equation—the wavelength of the radiation used in the magnifying process. This strategy is facilitated by the fact that visible light is but one small region of the continuum of electromagnetic energies and wavelengths that spans the energy spectrum from long, low-frequency radio waves to the ultrahigh-frequency equivalents of some of the basic particles of matter as they are accelerated to high velocities. A beam of electrons, just like a light ray, has wave properties associated with it that result in the fact that it can be refracted, reflected, and focused by appropriate "lenses." The "lenses" that can accomplish

[1]An Angstrom unit (Å) is equal to 10^{-10} meters or 1/10 of a nanometer.

this for the electron beam, however, are not made of glass or quartz but must be either electrostatic plates or electromagnetic coils identical to those used in an oscilloscope or a commercial television set. The key result is that 1 nm.; rather than 130 nm., resolution can be achieved with such lenses.

Like optical microscopes, there are two types of electron microscopes—reflection and transmission—and each type requires a special and appropriate technology of specimen preparation. In the transmission electron microscope, extremely thin cross sections of specimen tissues must be prepared to minimize the absorption and thus the associated heating of the electron beam. To achieve such thin cross sections, ultramicrotomes, which are capable of slicing a section to a fraction of a micron in thickness, are routinely used. Blades made from specially fractured pieces of glass are usually required for these instruments. For reflection electron microscopy—a process specialized for the examination of the surface detail of a specimen—special metallizing techniques have been invented. In this process, a thin coating of a metal, especially selected for its ability to reflect electrons, is sputtered onto the surface of the specimen. These reflected electrons are then guided to a fluorescent screen or photographic film. Figure 3-14 is an example of a transmission electron micrograph of a spinal motor neuron from a cat.

An important new development in electron microscopy has been the recent availability of the scanning electron microscope. This device has the advantage of having an enormous depth of field—so great in fact that in many instances solid objects appear to be in focus over their entire surface. Figure 3-15 shows a set of scanning electron micrographs showing a progressive increase in magnification of a neuron from a neuroblastoma, a tumor that consists of a relatively immature and unspecialized type of neuron. The three-dimensional property of the scanning electron micrograph is graphically displayed in these photographs.

The scanning electron microscope operates on the basis of the secondary ejection of electrons from the specimen after its surface is bombarded with the primary electrons produced by the electron gun of the microscope. The key point is that not all loci on the surface of the specimen are bombarded simultaneously; instead, a highly focused beam of electrons sequentially "scans" each point in synchrony with the "painting" of an image on a cathode-ray oscilloscope. It is this sequential scanning procedure, similar to that used on an ordinary television, that is the basis of the name of this form of the electron microscope, as well as of the great depth of focus. Very often, the specimen is coated with some metal, capable of being vaporized and deposited in a coating only a few angstrom units thick, to increase the number of secondary electrons.

A recent modification of the scanning principle uses x-rays as the probe rather than an electron beam (see, for example, Warner & Coleman, 1975). X-rays eject electrons from the material under study on the basis of the atomic number of the constituent atomic elements making up the material. Therefore,

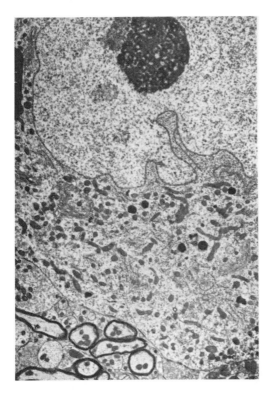

FIG. 3.14   A transmission electromicrograph of a motor neuron from the spinal cord of a rat showing the flat map-like representation obtained with this type of microscope. (Courtesy of C. S. Raine of the Albert Einstein College of Medicine.)

the number of emitted electrons will vary as a function of the chemical composition either of the original preparation or of the coatings that selectively adhere to particular parts of the original material. Although the most recent photographs produced by this novel x-ray scanning electron microscopic principle do not have the dramatic three-dimensional properties of the conventional scanning electron microscope, the technique has the potential of making some anatomic structures visible that were previously beyond the range of other laboratory instruments.

An especially striking way of visualizing the three-dimensional structure of a neuron using a combination of electron microscope and computer techniques has been developed by Cyrus Levinthal and his research group at Columbia University (Levinthal, Macagno, & Tountas, 1974). Their technique requires that a series of sequential cross sections of a neuron be photographed with a transmission electron microscope. The pictures are then digitized (converted to numeric representations) and entered into a digital computer for processing. The computer draws pictures like the one shown in Fig. 3-16. The capability of the

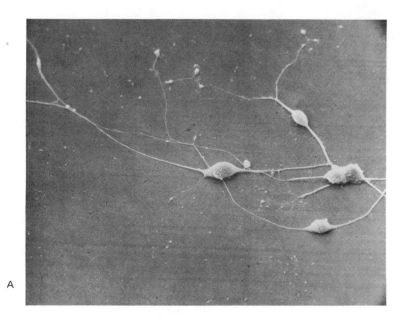

A

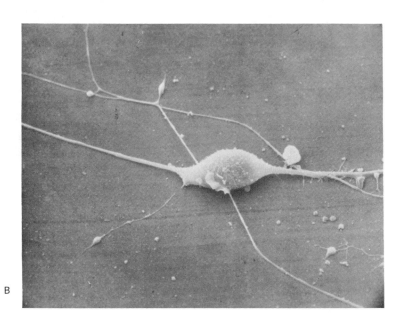

B

FIG. 3.15 Four progressively magnified scanning electronmicrographs of abnormal neurons from a mouse tumor showing the great depth of field and resulting three-dimensional effects

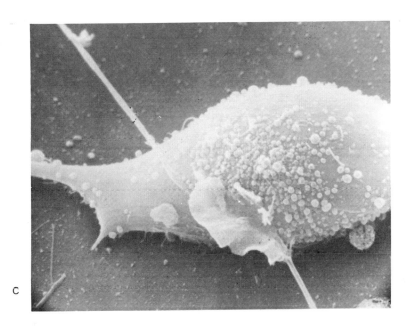

C

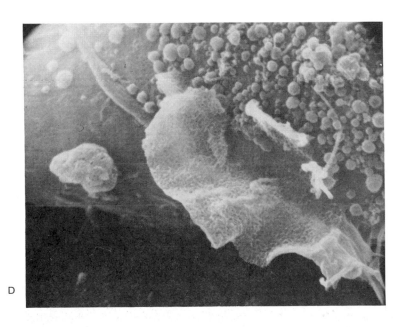

D

obtainable with this type of microscope. $A - \text{X570}; B - \text{X1400}; C - \text{X5500}; D - \text{X13,860}$. (Courtesy of J. Harkins of the University of Colorado.)

FIG. 3.16   Reconstructions of receptor cells from the eye of the water flea using the computer technique described in the text. (From Levinthal, Macagno, & Tountas, ©1974, with the permission of The Federation of American Societies for Experimental Biology.)

computer program is such that the reconstructed image of the neuron can be rotated at will on the face of a display oscilloscope thus giving the anatomist the opportunity to almost "turn the neuron over in his hands." One difficulty with this technique is that a massive number of photographs must be taken and substantial amounts of such data analyzed for the reconstruction of each neuron.

c.   Microelectrode Recording

Another exceedingly important and popular technique for tracing the microscopic or cellular structure of the nervous system involves the use of microelectrodes—minute probes made of metal or salt-solution filled glass pipettes that have dimensions comparable to those of the neurons and their processes themselves.

Microelectrodes may be made small enough to penetrate the interior of the neuron without destroying its membranes or affecting its function. A microelectrode can, therefore, record the potential difference between the inside and the outside of a single cell if a reference electrode is placed in the extracellular environment. To study the smallest neurons, microelectrode tips must be drawn as small as 1/10 of a micron. Eventually even cells punctured with these tiny electrodes become less responsive, indicating damage to the neuron, but a skilled electrophysiologist can often keep a microelectrode-penetrated cell alive for periods of up to several days. Apparently the initial puncture itself does less harm than is done by subsequent tissue movements around the electrode tip. These movements may enlarge the puncture wound to such an extent that the cell's self-healing properties no longer work.

To use these minute recording elements, relatively massive mechanical devices are required to stabilize and manipulate them. Heavy stereotaxic instruments with three-dimensional control are used to bring the tip of the microelectrode into the general region (a particular nucleus or lamina) of interest in the brain, in accord with an atlas of the brain developed for the particular animal under investigation. However, after the microelectrode tip is grossly placed by the stereotaxic instruments, the sampling of individual neurons in all mammalian preparations is largely a fortuitous process. The final placement of the microelectrode is controlled by micromanipulators capable of placement precision as small as 1 micron. But the process is a more or less blind exploration until a responsive cell is indicated on the electronic recording or audio monitoring equipment.

Although the microelectrodes are small, the fact that the stereotaxic manipulators are large has resulted in a severe limitation on the number of microelectrodes that can be inserted simultaneously into a single preparation. This is a serious handicap, particularly now that we understand that some of the most important aspects of neural activity may be in terms of their function as elements in an interacting network.

Microelectrode equipment of this sort is generally used to record the physiological reactions of individual neurons to stimulation of many different kinds. Among many other applications, pathways can be traced, the efficacy of neurochemicals can be evaluated, and dynamic changes in neurophysiological response can be examined as a function of experience. I present a more complete discussion of the technique in Chapter 8 and consider many examples of its use in the second half of this book.

d. Microautoradiographic Techniques

Although the autoradiographic and degeneration techniques were previously presented in the section on methods of macroanatomical research, it should be noted that these processes may also be applied at the level of microanatomy. Using these techniques on a microscopic level, it is possible to track individual neurons as they course between different nuclei or even between particular layers of tissue within a given nucleus (e.g., see the work of Lasek, Joseph, & Whitlock, 1968), to study the ways in which certain chemicals are created or deposited in particular parts of individual neurons, or to measure the rate and amounts of protoplasmic transport through axons.

Modern microautoradiographic techniques depend, as do the gross techniques, upon the application to living tissue of some radioactively tagged material that is a metabolite or that may be incorporated by normal physiological processes into the new substance that is built by the neuron. For this reason, it is very convenient to use radioactively labeled or tagged amino acids—the basic building blocks of proteins. Another fact that makes these methods useful for tracking the connections of individual neurons is that the newly created proteins are very often transported by the normal axonal transport mechanisms from the cell body where they are manufactured to distant portions of the cell where they are usually used.

An excellent example of the way in which this technique can be used to study the microanatomy of the nervous system is seen in the work of Neale, Neale, and Agranoff (1972). Their study was aimed at determining the particular layers of the optic tectum of the goldfish brain to which retinal ganglion cell fibers are connected. The darkening shown in Fig. 3-17 and the histogram of grain counts shown in Fig. 3-18 observed in the various levels of the brain make it clear that the ganglion cell axons project mainly to the external plexiform layer of the contralateral optic tectum of the goldfish.

Autoradiographic techniques can also be used with the electron microscope to achieve an even further level of magnification into the ultramicrostructural range. To do so, however, requires the use of special photographic emulsions with very small grain size, because it is the developed silver grain that is the actual target of the electron microscope beam rather than the original biological material itself. Because individual silver grains develop as a whole, the limit of resolution of this technique will ultimately depend upon the technological capability to achieve small grain size.

A comprehensive review of microscopic autoradiographic techniques in tracing axonal connections can be found in a paper by Cowan, Gottleib, Hendrickson, Price, and Woolsey (1972).

e. Freeze Fracture Techniques

To achieve an even higher degree of anatomical magnification and dissection, a new technique known as *freeze fracturing* is now being used. Freeze fracturing allows the neuroscientist to actually split the plasma membrane of a neuron so that the interior structure can be examined with electron micrographic techniques. The material to be observed is usually frozen in liquid freon at a temperature of about -150 °C. The specimen is then placed in a vacuum at a slightly higher temperature (-115 °C), which causes it to rupture. Figure 3-19, for example, is a drawing made by Raviola and Gilula (1975) of a synaptic ridge and some associated structures at the base of a monkey photoreceptor cell. This drawing shows how the membrane at the bottom of the picture fractures, exposing its

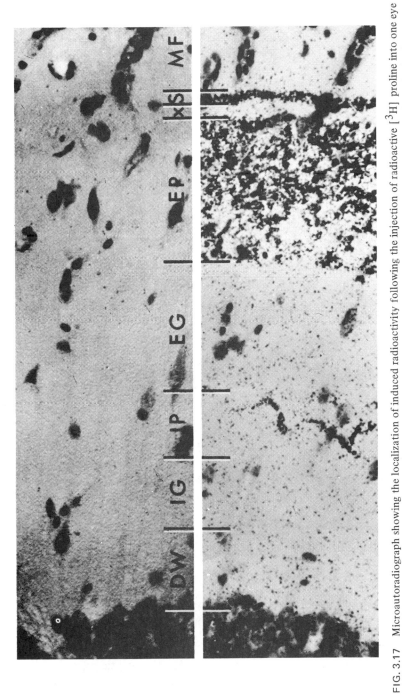

FIG. 3.17 Microautoradiograph showing the localization of induced radioactivity following the injection of radioactive [³H] proline into one eye of a goldfish. There is little induced radioactivity in the ipsilateral tectum (upper photograph), but there is a striking band of activity in the contralateral external plexiform layer (lower photograph). Layers indicated are: *CT* = pial connective tissue; *MF* = marginal fiber; *S* = "outer" synaptic; *X* = undefined; *EP* = external plexiform; *EG* = external portion of central gray; *IP* = internal plexiform; *IG* = internal portion of central gray; *DW* = deep white; and *PV* = periventricular. (From Neale, Neale, & Agranoff, ©1972, with the permission of The American Association for the Advancement of Science.)

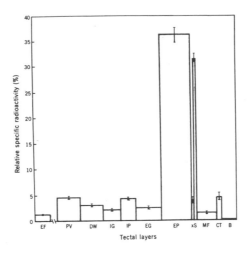

FIG. 3.18 Histogram of the relative amount of radioactivity in the contralateral cortex of the goldfish using the procedure described in the text and the type of autoradiograph shown in Figure 3.17. This technique has thus effectively demonstrated the region of the goldfish tectum to which the optic nerve neurons project. (From Neale, Neale, & Agranoff, ©1972, with the permission of The American Association for the Advancement of Science.)

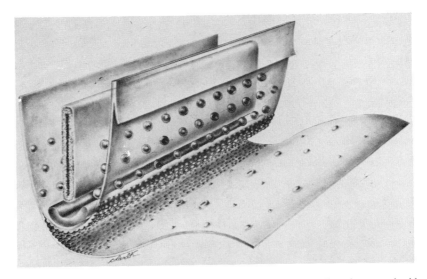

FIG. 3.19 A conceptual drawing developed from freeze fracture studies of a synaptic ridge at the base of a photoreceptor in the eye of a monkey. The thin ribbon-like structure (above) is the presynaptic wedge-shaped projection of the foot of the photoreceptor cell. The grooved membrane that surrounds it is the postsynaptic membrane of a horizontal cell. The membrane of the horizontal cell has been split open as it would be by the freeze fracturing technique to show the *A* face (with the particles attached) and the *B* face (with the pits) of the membrane. (From Raviola & Gilula, ©1975, with the permission of The Rockefeller University Press.)

116

inner structure. The portion of the membrane that is attached to the cytoplasm of the cell is referred to as the *A* face. The portion that adjoins the extracellular space is referred to as the *B* face. Certain intramembrane granules and particles are seen to selectively adhere to either the *A* or *B* face after the fracture has occurred.

The fractured membranes can then be shadowed with some electron opaque material and examined in a scanning electron microscope to produce such extraordinary pictures as that shown in Fig. 3-20. This figure displays the synaptic arrangement at the base of a rod. This electron micrograph, also made by Raviola and Gilula (1975), shows a synaptic ridge clearly demarcated by the characteristic particulate nature of this portion of the fractured membrane.

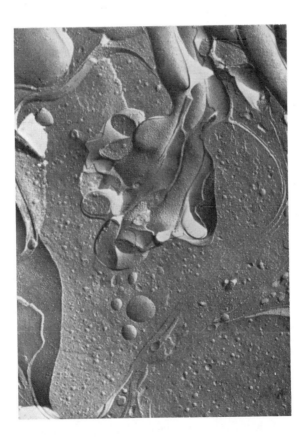

FIG. 3.20   A scanning electron microscope photograph of a freeze fractured tissue of the kind leading to the conceptualization in Figure 3.19. This micrograph shows the exposed inner surfaces of the various membranes involved in a photoreceptor-horizontal cell synaptic complex. (From Raviola & Gilula, ©1975, with the permission of The Rockefeller University Press.)

The full potential of the freeze fracturing technique is yet to be explored, but clearly this powerful tool extends the anatomist's vision down into the ultramicroscopic regions at which some of the most important neural processes must occur.

These then are some of the major techniques used for studies of macro- and microanatomy of nervous tissue. In the brief review that is presented in this chapter, it is not possible, of course, to give the complete details of all of the techniques we have mentioned. The reader who is in need of, or interested in, greater technical detail is directed to two series of books (Thompson & Patterson, 1973, 1974a, 1974b; and Myers, 1971, 1972) totally dedicated to the methodological issues. To more fully understand the goals and results of the structural explorations that use these methods, it is now necessary to consider the embryological development of the nervous system.

C. THE EMBRYOLOGICAL DEVELOPMENT OF THE NERVOUS SYSTEM

The anatomy of the mature nervous system is exceedingly complicated by the enlargement and resultant overlapping of the primitive antecedent structures during development. Therefore, the mature nervous system is sometimes difficult to comprehend in an effective and intuitive manner. However, gross neuroanatomy can be made more easily understandable if we consider the brain's embryological origins and development. I shall not dwell on the magnificence of the process, nor on the amazing similarity among the developing embryos of many vertebrate species. Nevertheless, every reader should note the extraordinary fact that no one seems to be able to read even the dullest textbook of embryology without an overt expression of amazement and fascination. Should the reader be interested in looking over an especially excellent text, he is directed to Hamilton and Mossman (1972), the major guide for the following discussions, which spells out in far greater detail than does this brief summary the full grandeur of this process of prenatal development.

The embryological study of the nervous system is important because it provides several different sources of information about the adult nervous system. Specifically:

1. The adult plan of the nervous system is superficially complicated but can be understood, in principle, if it is considered to be an outgrowth of the basic plan laid down during embryological development.

2. Embryological development (ontogeny) is a partial recapitulation of the evolution of the species (phylogeny). Embryology is, therefore, one of the main contemporary clues to the details of evolutionary development over the millenia.

3. Microembryology (the study of the development of individual neurons) is an important potential source of information concerning the development of

certain kinds of behavior and possibly even the recovery of function following injury or of learning in adult animals.

Embryological development is initiated by the fertilization of an egg cell, or ovum (produced by the female), by a male sperm cell. Each of these germ cells (or gametes) is characterized by the fact that it possesses only half of the number of chromosomes (structures containing the genetic materials or genes which stain especially deeply during cell division) found in all other cells of the body. Both ova and sperm are, therefore, said to be haploid with regard to the full complement of chromosomes. Upon fertilization, the two sets of haploid chromosomes unite to form a single fertilized cell, or zygote. The zygote, now possessing a full set of chromosomes (and then said to be diploid), begins an extraordinary process of cellular multiplication by cleavage and chromosomal duplication. From this primitive beginning come, ultimately, both the brain and mind of man.

The processes of cellular cleavage of the zygote does not at first result in any increase in its physical volume, because no new metabolic materials are absorbed at this early stage. The fertilized ovum divides again and again, but in doing so, each of the daughter cells, or blastomeres, is progressively reduced in size. This process continues until a cluster of cells known as the *morula* (as shown in Fig. 3-21a) is formed.

The blastomeres of the morula continue to divide until approximately one hundred cells are present. At this point, the next important stage in the process

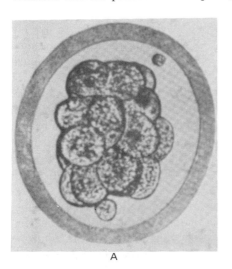

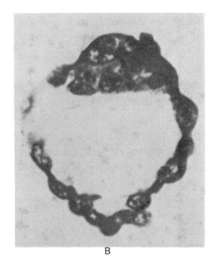

A   B

FIG. 3.21   (A) A macaque monkey morula consisting of the 16 daughter cells of the originally fertilized ovum. No cavity has yet been formed within the morula. (X300). (B) A human blastocyst showing the primitive cavity and the thickened mass of cells from which the nervous system will ultimately evolve. (X600.) (Both figures from Hamilton & Mossman, ©1972, with the permission of The Macmillan Press Ltd.)

of development occurs: The unstructured cluster of cells that was characteristic of the morula begins to take on a simple structure. A cavity within the innermost group of blastomeres forms, and these cells migrate to form a single-layered, hollow sphere called the *blastula*, or *blastocyst*. A human blastula is shown in Fig. 3-21b.

Up to this point, the protoembryo has been mobile and has been moving along the fallopian tube, away from the ovary—the gland that had produced the ovum. However, at the blastocyst stage, the embryo implants itself in the wall of the uterus and commences to grow in volume, from this point on to be nourished by nutrients that it receives through the point of attachment. At the site of this original contact, the wall of the uterus will later be transformed into the placenta.

It should be noted in Fig. 3-21b that the blastula is not a uniform sphere. Rather it has a slightly thickened polar region known as the inner cell mass. Shortly after implantation, the cells of the inner cell mass begin to differentiate into three different types, which subsequently make up three layers known as the *ectoderm, mesoderm,* and *endoderm.* We are particularly interested in the ectoderm because it is from this layer that the nervous system will ultimately emerge. Figure 3-22a shows the trilayered appearance of the inner cell mass at this point in the development of the embryo.

Up to this stage, the embryology of the individual blastula is almost irrelevant to neuroanatomy, simply because there is no hint yet of the development of even a prototypical nervous system—all of the blastomeres are more or less identical. At this point, however, the cells of the embryo begin to exhibit sufficient specialization and differentiation to allow us to attend solely to those aspects of subsequent embryological development that are to result in neural structures. Figure 3-22a also shows the ectodermal region from which the structures of the nervous system will ultimately develop. The first sign of the specific development of the nervous system proper is the formation of a slight depression in the ectoderm as shown in Fig. 3-22b. This depression, known as the *neural groove*, deepens as development of the embryo progresses, then invaginates, and finally separates from the ectodermal issue of its origin (which goes on to produce the epithelium) to form a partially (and, ultimately, completely) closed tube running the length of the embryo.

The failure of the neural groove to close completely to form the neural tube can lead to a large number of anomalies in the organism when it is born. The cerebral cortex, for example, is formed from the most rostral end of the tube—the portion that closes last. Failure of this portion to close can lead to a total absence of the cerebrum—a condition known as *anencephaly*; failure to close elsewhere can lead to postnatal openings along the vertebral column frequently involving malformations of the spinal cord—a condition known as *spina bifida*. (See Leck, 1974, for a fuller discussion of such embryological failures in neural development.)

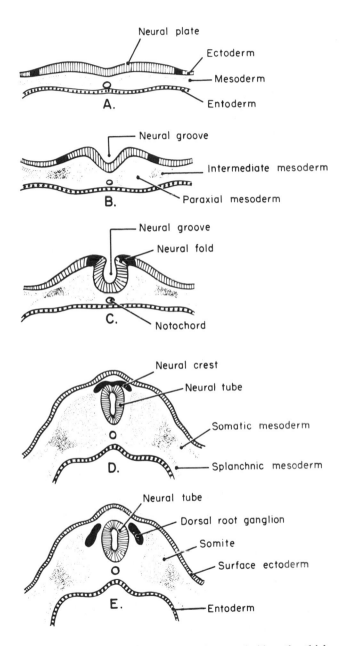

FIG. 3.22 Successive stages of development of the neural ridge, the thickened layer of cells seen at the top of the blastocyst in Figure 3.21(B). It is from the primitive neural plate that the entire nervous system develops by a process of invagination and entubularization into the neural tube. (From Carpenter, ©1976, with the permission of Williams & Wilkins Company.)

The further development of the neural groove into the neural tube, is shown in Fig. 3-22c, 3-22d, and 3-22e, respectively. The primitive neural tube is the progenitor of the central nervous system. As we shall see, a realization of the fact that the tube-like organization persists until adulthood gives conceptual order to the superficially disorganized anatomy of the mature central nervous system.

On either side of the original neural groove, another band of ectoderm is also slated to play an important role in the development of the nervous system. This tissue, shown in Fig. 3-22, likewise descends into the embryonic mesoderm along with the neural tube and forms the structure known as the *neural crest* (see Fig. 3-22d). It is from the neural crest that the peripheral sensory (somatic and visceral) and autonomic (visceral motor) neurons are to be formed.

Let us now change our point of view. For the most part, up to now we have been looking at cross sections of the developing tube. Now let us consider a longitudinal view of the entire tube. The simple, single-cell layered neural tube is shown diagrammatically in Fig. 3-23a. On this drawing three prototypical regions are indicated by different shading and stippling. These three rostral re-

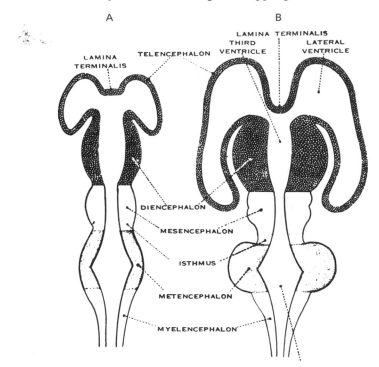

FIG. 3.23   Transverse sections of the developing neural tube showing the early development of the various portions of the central nervous system. *A* and *B* are two successive stages. (From Hamilton & Mossman, ©1972, with the permission of The Macmillan Press Ltd.)

gions include the forebrain (the prosencephalon or proencephalon), the midbrain (the mesencephalon), and the hindbrain (the rhombencephalon). These three rostral regions will ultimately develop into the brain and brain stem, and the more caudal portions of the neural tube will undergo a much less dramatic embryological development to form the conceptually simpler spinal cord.

Figure 3-23b shows the next stage in the extraordinary growth of the three regions of this rostral protobrain. The primitive prosencephalon separates into two distinct regions—the telencephalon (ultimately giving rise to the cerebral hemispheres) and the diencephalon (ultimately giving rise to the thalamus, hypothalamus, and visual apparatus). The fact that the retina, the optic nerves and tracts, and the optic chiasma are produced by an extrusion (first called the *optic vesicle*, then the *optic cup*, and, finally, the *retina*) from the diencephalon is the reason that the retina and other optic structures are considered to be part of the central, rather than the peripheral, nervous system.

The primitive mesencephalon begins a process of differentiation that will give rise to the colliculi and the crus cerebri, and the rhombencephalon also subdivides as embryological development continues into the metencephalon (ultimately giving rise to the cerebellum and pons) and the myelencephalon (ultimately giving rise to the medulla). Table 3-1 outlines this series of sequential specializations.

TABLE 3.1

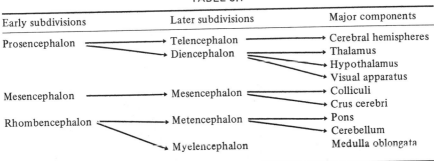

Early subdivisions	Later subdivisions	Major components
Prosencephalon	Telencephalon	Cerebral hemispheres
	Diencephalon	Thalamus
		Hypothalamus
		Visual apparatus
Mesencephalon	Mesencephalon	Colliculi
		Crus cerebri
Rhombencephalon	Metencephalon	Pons
		Cerebellum
	Myelencephalon	Medulla oblongata

The progressive specialization of the three primitive protoregions of the rostral portion of the neural tube into the subdivisions of the mature mammalian brain. Also shown are some of the main regions and nuclei within each of the later subdivisions.

Figure 3-24 shows the further development of this tubular theme as the embryo continues to grow and cells continue to specialize. In particular, note the great swelling that occurs in the telencephalon. This ontogenetic swelling is so great that the mature cerebral hemispheres in man and many other vertebrates will ultimately overlie and hide much of the underlying diencephalic structures. Another great swelling occurs on the dorsal side of the metencephalon that will ultimately become the mature cerebellum.

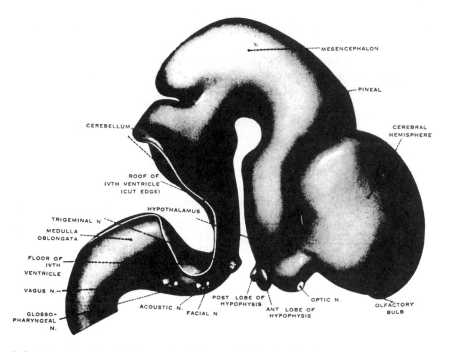

FIG. 3.24   The later development of the neural tube showing the swellings that form the various nuclei and the beginning of the twisting and folding that give rise to the great apparent complexity of the mature central nervous system. In spite of this apparent complexity, the basic tubular theme is maintained in the adult. (From Hamilton & Mossman, ©1972, with the permission of The Macmillan Press Ltd.)

In addition to the embryological development of the major regions I have already discussed, the embryological development of individual neurons is also exceedingly interesting. The primitive unspecialized ectodermal cells of the neural tube and the neural crest must undergo an unbelievable degree of differentiation and specialization as they metamorphose from the simple unspecialized ectodermal cells of the embryo into the many different kinds of neurons and other accessory cells in the mature nervous system. For example, Fig. 3-25 shows the specialization of the single original kind of neural crest cells into several of the many different kinds of peripheral neurons found in the mature organism. It must not be forgotten, however, that the basic "blueprints" or genotype for all of the diversified forms of mature neurons are encoded in the genetic materials (DNA) of the nucleus of all of the cells regardless of their ultimate development. Which particular forms, or phenotypes, will actually be expressed from this basic all-inclusive genotype will depend upon the chemical environment, including that produced by its neighbors, that the developing neurons experience as they divide and specialize.

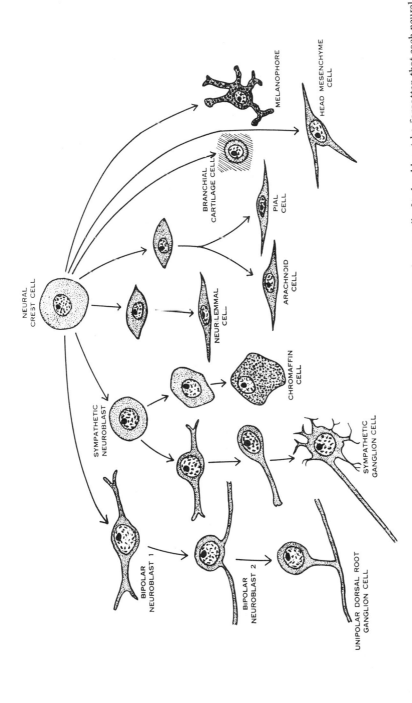

FIG. 3.25 Specialization into the various types of neurons from the prototypical neural crest cells. It should not be forgotten that each neural crest cell is also a daughter cell of the single original fertilized ovum. All of its descendants, like all of the other cells in the body, contain the total genetic map. (From Hamilton & Mossman, ©1972, with the permission of The Macmillan Press Ltd.)

An interesting aspect of the embryological development, as well as of regenerative growth, of nervous tissue concerns the manner in which individual neurons seem to grow to particular target locations. It appears that the growth of neurons, as well as their specialization, is also determined by chemical influences expressed by one neuron on another. It is almost as if the growth of neurons is, in some way, directed to particular "tagged" locations by biochemical mechanisms that we still do not understand completely.

An early suggestion that chemical specificity existed came from the work of Sperry (see, for example, Sperry, 1951). In some of his early studies, Sperry transected both optic nerves in frogs and then observed behavioral responses following crossed nerve regeneration. Though this experiment was originally invoked to show that each eye took over the relatively normal function of its opposite, it is more interesting to note that following regeneration the retinotopic map was preserved. Thus, it appeared that the original connections had regenerated with regard to some sort of chemical specificity that was built into the original genetic blueprint. Figure 3-26 shows the logic behind this experiment.

More recently, Jacobson (1968a, 1968b) has observed regeneration of optic nerve fibers in the South African clawed frog (*Xenopus laevis*) and has also found a highly specific point-to-point reconstruction of the original course of the optic pathway. These results also support the idea that there was some form of chemical specificity that controlled the path taken by either the embryologically developing or the regenerating fibers.

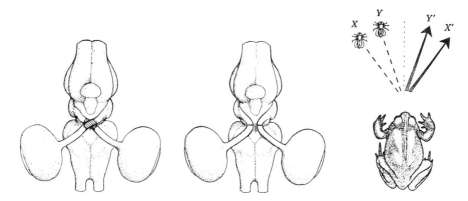

FIG. 3.26   Diagram showing the logic of Sperry's crossed optic nerve regeneration experiment. The experiment showed reversal of the function of the two eyes following regeneration, but more germane to this discussion, the retinotopic map also seemed to be reproduced. This most probably can be attributed to specific chemical effects guiding the development of the nervous system. (From Sperry, ©1951, with the permission of Wiley & Sons, Inc.)

The notion of chemical specificity as a guide to embryological development thus seems to be an important hypothesis of modern neuroembryology. An important point, well worth reiterating, however, is that the details of this chemical specificity, like all of the other details of embryological development, are solely contained in the genes of the original single zygote. Even the interaction between the genes and the chemicals that differentiate and guide structure is, in the final analysis, coded in the genes themselves.

Willmer (1970) has helped to clarify some of these issues involved in the embryological development of neurons by suggesting the following fourfold classification scheme for the influences that affect cytological development:

1. *The Genome*—the full gene pool.

2. *The Hegemon*—the part of the gene pool that is actually operating to define structure at any moment.

3. *The Econome*—the nongenetic intracellular influences that determine which parts of the total gene pool will be expressed. The econome includes such factors as the chemical produced by the ribosomes, the Golgi apparatus, and other cell inclusions.

4. *The Agoranome*—the nongenetic extracellular influences such as hormones, nutrition, contact guidance, and the influence of other neurons and glia.

My favorite analysis of this problem, however, is the much more graphic listing of factors that can affect the development of neural circuits that has been prepared by Welker (1976). It is reproduced here in Fig. 3-27.

Willmer and Welker each emphasize the fact that both intrinsic and such extrinsic factors as nutritional support during prenatal development, early experience of the neonate, and later experiences of the mature organism, can affect the details of neural organization. However, the entire plan, whatever the final outcome, is contained in the relatively simple sequential codes of only four molecular bases—adenine, guanine, cytosine, and uracil. The story of macromolecular sequences and the way in which this material is replicated during cell division is not a necessary part of this book, but the newly emerging understanding of the process itself is one of the true "Copernican revolutions" of science.

This then is a brief discussion of the early embryological origins of the nervous system. The most germane point to keep in mind is the fact that all of the complex structures described in the next section of this chapter develop from elaborations of the primitive and simple tubular structure originally arising in the blastula. Neuroanatomy can be best understood if this single fact is kept in mind. Not only are the various lobes and centers outgrowths of this tubular protoform, but also the enclosed fluid-filled cavities (or ventricles) are the embryological extensions of the original cavity that lay within the primitive neural tube. Now I consider the macrostructure of the mature human nervous system.

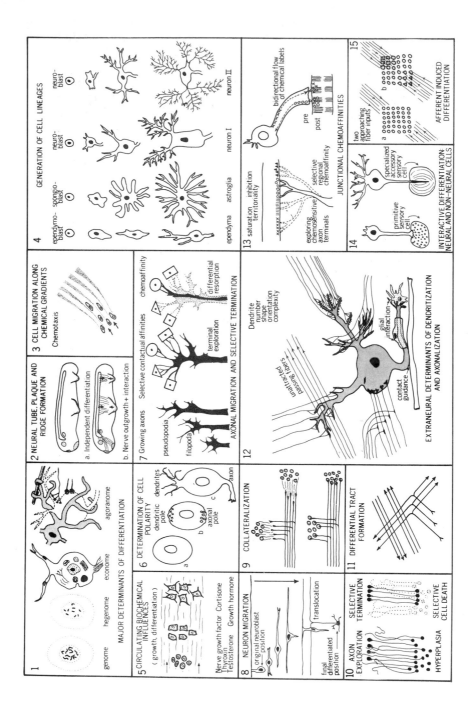

1 MAJOR DETERMINANTS OF DIFFERENTIATION

genome   hegenome   econome   agoranome

5 CIRCULATING BIOCHEMICAL INFLUENCES
(growth, differentiation)

Nerve growth factor   Cortisone
Thyroxin   Growth hormone
Testosterone

8 NEURON MIGRATION

original neuroblast position

translocation

final differentiated position

10 AXON EXPLORATION

SELECTIVE TERMINATION

HYPERPLASIA   SELECTIVE CELL DEATH

6 DETERMINATION OF CELL POLARITY

dendrites
dendritic pole
axon
axonal pole

9 COLLATERALIZATION

11 DIFFERENTIAL TRACT FORMATION

2 NEURAL TUBE, PLAQUE AND RIDGE FORMATION

a. Independent differentiation

b. Nerve outgrowth + interaction

3 CELL MIGRATION ALONG CHEMICAL GRADIENTS

Chemotaxis

7 Growing axons   Selective contactual affinites   chemoaffinity

pseudopodia

filopodia

terminal exploration   differential resorption

AXONAL MIGRATION AND SELECTIVE TERMINATION

12

Dendrite
number
shape
orientation
complexity

glial interaction

unattracted passing fibers

contact guidance

EXTRANEURAL DETERMINANTS OF DENDRITIZATION AND AXONALIZATION

4 GENERATION OF CELL LINEAGES

ependymo-blast   spongio-blast   neuro-blast   neuro-blast   neuro-blast

ependyma   astroglia   neuron I   neuron II

13 saturation   inhibition   territoriality

exploring chemosensitive axon terminals   selective regional chemoaffinity

bidirectional flow of chemical labels

pre

post

JUNCTIONAL CHEMOAFFINITIES

14

primitive sensory cell

specialized accessory sensory cell

INTERACTIVE DIFFERENTIATION: NEURAL AND NON-NEURAL CELLS

15

two approaching fiber inputs

a   b

AFFERENT INDUCED DIFFERENTIATION

128

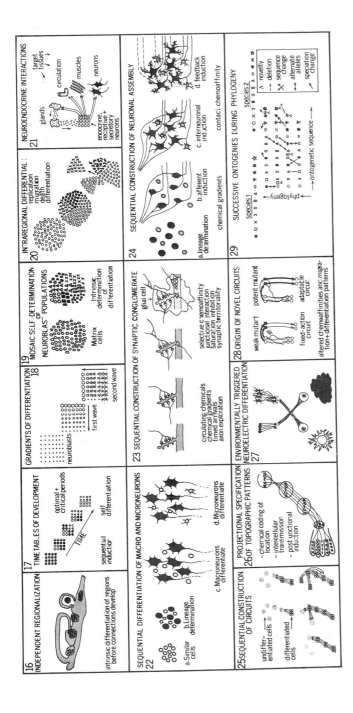

FIG. 3.27   A host of different factors can influence the specific patterns of neural organization during the development of the individual. In principle, these factors determine which of the genotypic elements will be embodied in the final phenotype. Wally Welker of the University of Wisconsin has brilliantly illustrated these many forces in this set of drawings. (From Welker, ©1976, with the permission of Lawrence Erlbaum Associates.)

129

D. THE GROSS ANATOMY OF THE MATURE
CENTRAL NERVOUS SYSTEM

1. A Conceptual Model

Now that I have traced the embryological development of the nervous system, and hopefully have made the importance of the tubular protoform clear, I am in a position to consider the details of the anatomy of the mature human central nervous system. However, to attain maximum clarity of exposition, it is still necessary for a moment more to operate at a diagrammatic rather than a precisely pictographic level. Figure 3-28 is a highly diagrammatic sketch of the mature human nervous system showing its development based upon the tubular theme that was shown in Figs. 3-23 and Fig. 3-24. Because this drawing is so highly schematic and distorts the actual physical locations of some of the major features, the reader may also wish to simultaneously study Fig. 3-31, which gives a more realistic external view of the developing neural tube. Note especially the twists or flexures not shown in the diagrammatic presentation. It should also be noted that this more realistic drawing is that of a 46.5 mm. (about 10 weeks after conception) embryo. Beyond that point of development, the swelling of the cerebral and cerebellar hemispheres begins to obscure the basic tubular arrangement of the nervous system.

Another aspect of the nervous system not shown in either of these drawings is its essential bilateral symmetry. Each of the structures shown (with the exception of the pineal body and the hypophysis or pituitary body) is actually composed of similar (mirror image) left and right sides. Interconnections between the two sides, as well as between the various centers themselves, are also developing increased complexity during the embryological period. Tracking the course of these connections is one of the main tasks of modern neuroanatomy.

To help orient the reader in the following discussion, I use a vocabulary that may be strange to some readers. It is one that is designed to be consistent with human anatomy. To locate a particular structure in relation to others, we must be able to define its location in terms of three different dimensions. The first of these dimensions runs along the long axis of the body. I refer to the direction pointing toward the toes or the base of the spinal cord as the *caudal* (tail) direction. The direction pointing toward the head end shall be referred to as the *rostral* (nose) direction. For something to be "more rostral" than another structure means that it lies more toward the nose or head end than toward the tail or foot end of the organism. The axis of the second dimension is defined in terms of a line running from the belly (front) to the back of the body. The direction pointing to the back is called the *dorsal direction*, and that pointing to the front is called the *ventral direction*. The third, or left-right, dimension is rarely invoked because of the general bilateral symmetry of the nervous system. Rather than refer to the left side or the right side of the body—terms that are ambiguous unless the dorsal or ventral direction of view is defined—I more often use the

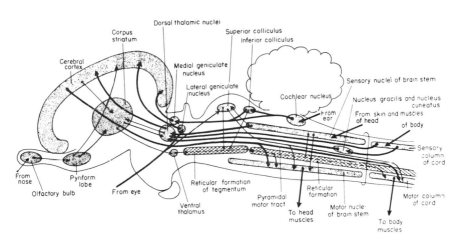

FIG. 3.28 Schematic drawing of the adult mammalian nervous system showing the basic tubular arrangement and indicating many of the major nuclei. This diagram has been distorted to emphasize the basic anatomical organization of the various parts. (From Romer, ©1949, with the permission of W. B. Saunders Company.)

terms *medial* (close to the center line or plane of symmetry) and *lateral*, or dorsal and ventral to emphasize whether some structure is either close to the central core of the nervous system or displaced more to the sides, front, or back of the body. Figure 3-29 sums up this dimensional system.

Another set of terms relating to clusters of neurons, the constituent building blocks of the nervous system, is also important in the discussion to follow. The word *neuron*, of course, refers to a single nerve cell. The words *axon* and *fiber* are synonymous and refer to the main elongated extension of an individual neuron. The extension is specialized for long-distance transmission. Other parts of the neuron include the *perikaryon*, or cell body, and the *dendrites*, or dendritic arborization. The latter structures are mainly input elements into a given neuron. Because they often possess very extensive ramifications, they represent the main medium through which multiple inputs can be integrated to effect the neuron in highly variable ways. Figure 3-30 shows a typical peripheral transmission neuron and a central integrating neuron.

Both fibers and neuronal cell bodies are usually grouped into separate clusters within the nervous system. A band of axons outside of the central nervous system is referred to as a *nerve*, and within the central nervous system it is referred to as a *tract*. Groups of cell bodies outside the central nervous system are referred to as *ganglia*, and inside the central nervous system they are referred to as *nuclei*. The word *center* within the central nervous system is a general term that is used to generically define a particular structure, often a nucleus, but also often

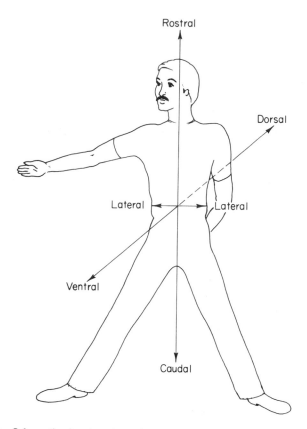

FIG. 3.29   Schematic showing the axis system used to describe the directions, relations, and locations of various brain structures.

a larger portion of tissue that for one reason or another is to be distinguished from its surround. The term *center* is usually used in descriptions of functionally, rather than anatomically, distinguished regions.

Figure 3-31 indicates a number of the major main structures that we have already mentioned as well as a few that are newly introduced. Starting at the most rostral end of the drawing, we see the great swelling of the isocortex or "neopallial" cortex, phylogenetically the most recent portion of the cerebral hemispheres, that will ultimately overhang and cover most of the rest of the underlying structures in man. Immediately beneath this huge "nucleus" is another region of cerebral cortex—the paleopallium, or older portion of cortex—that is mainly made up of the amygdala, the prepyriform cortex, and the septal region among others. This region and some other subcerebral centers had been referred to in the past as the *rhinencephalon*, indicating its original close relation to the olfactory parts of the brain, but are now more often termed collectively as the

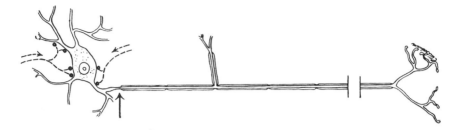

FIG. 3.30A   A typical transmission neuron specialized for the communication of information over long distances by means of a heavily myelinated axon of great length. In this case,
the neuron shown is a motor neuron. (From Bodian, ©1962, with the permission of The
American Association for the Advancement of Science.)

FIG. 3.30B   A typical integrating
neuron specialized for the localized interaction of neural information. There is, in this case, no
main axon, but rather the dendritic tree is greatly elaborated.
This particular neuron is a Golgi
type II neuron from the kitten
brain. (From Scheibel & Scheibel,
©1963, with the permission of
Elsevier/North-Holland Biomedical
Press.)

limbic system. The archipallium (or archicortex) is mainly made up of the hippocampus. The term allocortex refers to the paleopallium and the archipallium
inclusively. The origin of all of these cortical regions is the swelling of the most
rostral portion of the primitive neural tube.

The basal nuclei and the thalamus, immediately caudal from the main cerebral regions, originate from swellings of the interior of the primitive neural tube
at regions nearly on the midline. The basal nuclei are found at the base (i.e.,
at the more caudal end) of the cerebrum and are part of the telencephalon.

The thalamus is mainly thought of as one of the great sensory relay stations
of the brain, passing messages from the lower centers to the cerebral hemisphere.
However, because it also receives information from the cortex this is something
of a misconception. In reality, the motor nuclei of the thalamus play exceedingly
important roles in motor function just as its sensory nuclei play important transmission and integration roles in sensory function. Just caudal to the thalamus
and the hypothalamus lies the portion of the brain stem known as the *midbrain.*

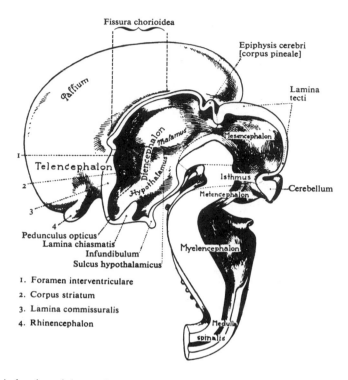

Fissura chorioidea

Epiphysis cerebri
[corpus pineale]

Lamina
tecti

Pallium

Mesencephalon

Thalamus

Diencephalon

Telencephalon

Isthmus

Cerebellum

Hypothalamus

Metencephalon

1

2

3

4

Pedunculus opticus
Lamina chiasmatis
Infundibulum
Sulcus hypothalamicus

Myelencephalon

1. Foramen interventriculare

2. Corpus striatum

3. Lamina commissuralis

4. Rhinencephalon

Medulla
spinalis

FIG. 3.31 A drawing of the nearly mature nervous system showing the various regions and the relationship among the major nuclei. Note particularly the maintenance of the tubular schema. (From Spalteholz & Spanner, ©1967, with the permission of Bahn, Scheltema, & Holkema.)

The midbrain is primarily made up of a series of relay and integrative stations for both ascending sensory and descending motor information. On the dorsal side of the human midbrain lie the two pairs of inferior and superior colliculi, which together make up a general region known as the *tectum* or *roof*. The colliculi are especially important relay stations for sensory information. Ventral to these structures, or on the ventral side of the human midbrain, lies the crus, or floor, a region through which many sensory and motor tracts pass up and down the central nervous system.

In the hindbrain, the pons contains a number of important nuclei and also has many important tracts passing through it without synaptic relays. The cerebellum of the hindbrain is primarily a center for motor control but does receive some sensory information, notably from the proprioceptive and vestibular receptors. The medulla oblongata is richly endowed with a wide variety of ganglia and tracts and is also one of the important relay stations for the somatosensory pathways. The spinal cord is mainly a collection of giant tracts, but many nuclei and synaptic connections are also present there.

Now that a general conceptual organization of the central nervous system has been presented and the tube-like arrangement emphasized, we can move on to consider a more realistic description of the appearance of the many constituent centers. Figure 3-32, for example, is a picture of the complete central nervous system of an adult human as it would appear if the dissection had been carried out through a ventral approach. The true spatial relations and relative sizes of the cerebral hemispheres, the brain stem, and the spinal cord are more clearly evident in this picture than in the diagram of Fig. 3-28. Figure 3-33 is a side view of the brain alone. This figure clearly emphasizes the fact that almost all of the

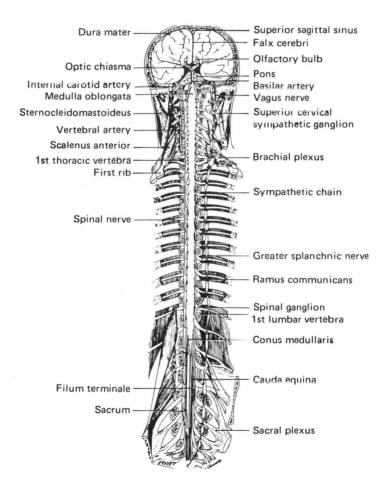

FIG. 3.32   Drawing of the central nervous system as it would appear in a gross dissection approached from the front. (From Goss, ©1973, after Hirschfeld & Leveille, with the permission of Lea & Febiger, Publishers.)

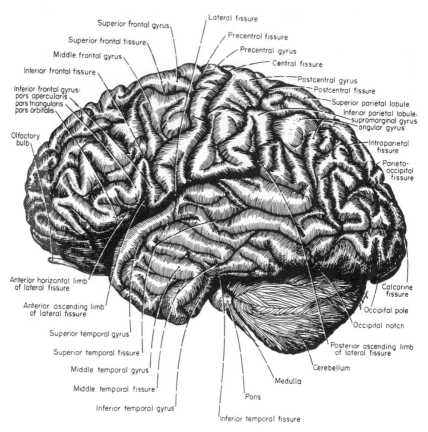

FIG. 3.33 The left side of the brain showing the various external features and the most common names of the sulci and fissures. (From Crosby, Humphrey, & Lauer, ©1962, with the permission of Macmillan Publishing Co.)

underlying structures have been hidden by the mushrooming of the cerebral structures of the telencephalon. When one looks at the brain from this perspective, virtually all that is to be seen is the exterior of the neocortex, a bit of the cerebellum peeking out from underneath, and the brain stem and spinal cord protruding in the caudal direction.

I now turn to a more detailed anatomical discussion of each of the main regions mentioned in this introductory section.

2. The Cerebral Hemisphere

The massive cerebral cortical mantle is the main sight when the excised brain is examined in a gross dissection. An external view of the cerebral cortex shows it to be an irregularly convoluted structure crevassed with many fissures (or sulci), which divide large numbers of convolutions (or gyri) from each other. Some of the fissures are very pronounced and divide the cerebral hemispheres into major lobes, and others are more shallow depressions and merely subdivide the major lobes into smaller individual convolutions.

The convoluted and divided structure of the cerebral cortex serves an obvious function. It is a means of increasing the surface area, or perhaps more properly, the volume of the outer cortical rind of the cerebrum, and thus provides the opportunity for a greater complexity of interactions and, thus, presumably, higher intelligence. The increase in convolutional complexity is clearly evident as one compares the cerebrum of various vertebrates. The brain of a fish is deficient in neocortex and smooth. A dog has a small number of sulci and a few convolutions, but man has many (see Fig. 3-33). We have already noted that the brain of most cetaceans is even more convoluted and of considerably greater volume than that of man. Useful casting techniques for making models of the gross morphology of the brain have been developed by such workers as Welker (1967).

A major question concerning the nature and origins of the surface convolutions of the cortex can be raised. Are the convolutions functional, reflecting actual boundaries between regions that serve differing purposes, or, quite to the contrary, are they merely random processes arising because of simple mechanical forces resulting from the swelling of the cerebral mass? The fact that different lobes may seem to have sharply different functional properties is not, in fact, a convincing answer to this question. Even with random folding, such apparent functional arrangements would be produced as the actual cortical distances between different regions are obscured.

This point can be made clear by considering Fig. 3-34. Here we see that the lobes of this hypothetical cerebral cortex seem to be sharply selective representations for different body parts. It is clear, however, that the selectivity is largely based upon the nature of the folding of the cerebral surface. Lobes appear to be physiologically separate, and there appears to be an abrupt line of discontinuity only because two portions of the surface, which are very distant from each other as measured along the surface of the cortex, fortuitously adjoin due to the invagination of the gyrus. Sharply different functions between lobes thus appear to be the case even though continuous and overlapping representation may be a much better description of the organization of the cerebral cortex.

A fruitful collaboration of neurologists and mechanical engineers (Richman, Stewart, Hutchinson, & Caviness, 1975) has provided some insight into this problem. These workers note that there are actually three different types of sulci. The large primary and secondary sulci are relatively constant from one human brain to another, but the tertiary sulci seem to be almost random in their configuration. Richman and his colleagues have developed a mathematical model of the development of the tertiary sulci (which they do not necessarily feel also describes the larger fissures) that suggests that the minor fissures are simply fortuitous mechanical enfoldings produced by the buckling of the cortex as it grows.

FIG. 3.34   A schematic drawing showing how the sulci may appear to have sharply demarcated functional localization but how this apparent sharp localization may be an artifact arising from the enfolding of the cerebral mantle. The true state of affairs may be better characterized as a gradual shift in localized representation as one moves along the surface of the cortex. (From Welker, ©1973, with the permission of S. Karger AG, Basel.)

The buckling of the cortex is quite closely related, they observe, to the relative thickness of the layers of the cortex. To support this view, they cite the wide variability of the enfolding found in brains with abnormal thickness. "Lissencephalic" infants show a very small number of sulci and also exhibit an abnormally thickened inner cortical layer, whereas "microgyric" infants display an abnormally large number of small gyri and a markedly thinner than normal inner cortical layer. The buckling, therefore, that produces the sulci seems to be due to a simple mechanical response to the growth of the extensive surface area, at least for the minor sulci. Not too much significance should, therefore, be ascribed to the otherwise unremarkable lines of demarcation observed on the surface of the brain. The fact that tertiary sulci seem to be the result of purely mechanical pressures does raise the possibility, at least, that the primary and secondary ones also are similarly produced. The constancy in their form from one animal to another may simply reflect the common genetically determined gross brain structure.

This rejection of a physiological significance of sulci is not a universally agreed upon position. Many comparative psychobiologists feel that there is a regular physiological pattern that corresponds to the anatomic arrangement of the convolutions of the mammalian brain. Examples of this view can be seen in reports by Welker and Seidenstein (1959), Welker and Campos (1963), Radinsky (1969), and Welker (1973). Welker and Campos (1963), for example, have studied the brain of the *Procyonidae*, the family of mammals that includes the raccoon, coati-mundi, and lesser panda among others. They recorded evoked potentials from the surface of the cerebral cortex produced by somatosensory stimuli applied to various portions of the animal's body. They observed what they believed to be a close correspondence between the particular cerebral regions to which various body parts projected and the sulci and gyri that were anatomically defined on the surface of the cerebrum. They concluded, unlike Richman and his colleagues, that the sulci were, therefore, not fortuitous, but were physiologically significant.

The counter argument to Welker and Campos' view is that the gyri separate regions that are actually very far apart topologically, and this segregation of function among the gyri may be more apparent than it is real. Welker and Campos note as counter-counter argument, however, that the conformation of the sulci varies from animal to animal in a way that seems to correspond not only to the projections of the sensory evoked potential, but also to the relative behavioral difference (degree of use of paws or snouts) among the various animals. Figure 3-35 shows the arrangement of the sulci, the electrophysiologically defined projection regions, and the receptive areas on the surface of the bodies of three of the Procyonidae.

At the present time it is probably not possible to give a definitive answer to this question of the physiological significance of the sulci of the mammalian brain. If sulci were physiologically significant, we would be able to assign greater confidence to a powerful tool of paleopsychobiological research. The technique is based on the empirical fact that in many mammals other than the primates (an unfortunate exclusion), the pia and dura maters are sufficiently thin so that the pattern of the cortical fissures and sulci is actually impressed into the inside of the skull as it matures. By filling a fossil skull with a quick hardening plastic (which can be removed from the skull through the foremen magnum), a mold, or endocast, approximating the structure of the unfossilized and long-ago deteriorated brain can be obtained. The anatomical and technical aspects and implications of this part of the strategy are fairly straightforward. However, paleopsychobiologists must make highly specific assumptions that a particular sulcus is associated specifically with somatosensory processes, for example, to extend the concept to an analysis of fossil behavior as a distinct from fossil anatomy. These assumptions, as we have seen, are, at least in some circles, controversial. For the reader interested in pursuing this problem further, by far the best source is Jerison's (1973) analysis of the evolution of the brain.

The cerebrum is usually divided by anatomists into a number of major lobes—the frontal, temporal, parietal, and occipital. Figure 3-33 also indicates many of the names of the secondary convolutions that divide the major lobes.

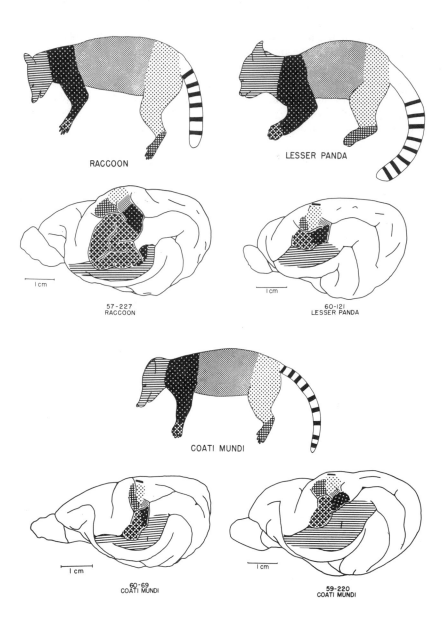

RACCOON

LESSER PANDA

57-227
RACCOON

60-121
LESSER PANDA

COATI MUNDI

60-69
COATI MUNDI

59-220
COATI MUNDI

FIG. 3.35 Schematic diagrams showing the apparent functional significance of the sulci in three members of the Procyonidae. The regions of the body have been keyed to the particular regions of the somatosensory cortex in which they produce electrical activity. The coati mundi brain regions have been shown for two animals to indicate the degree of interspecimen variability that is obtained even when the same species is studied. (From Welker & Campos, ©1963, with the permission of The Wistar Press.)

Although we shall not consider the microscopic structure of the cerebrum at this point (this is dealt with later in this chapter), one important mapping system of the cerebral surface is based upon the cellular architecture (a subject known as cytoarchitectonics, i.e., the science of the arrangement of cell types in nuclei) of the cerebral cortex. This system of cortical regions, developed by Brodmann (1909) and shown in Fig. 3-36, has had some remarkable successes in recent years as it has been repeatedly shown that the cytoarchitectonically defined "Brodmann regions" are often highly correlated with equally distinct electrophysiological properties.

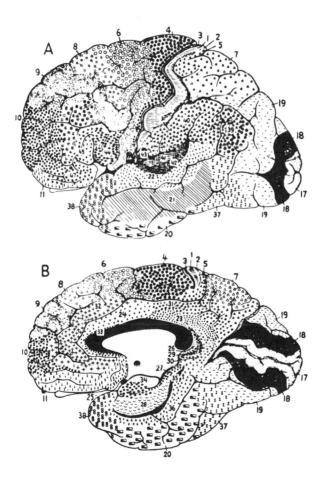

FIG. 3.36 Brodmann's maps of the cerebral hemispheres. In these maps, Brodmann has defined certain (numbered) regions of the brain on the basis of cytoarchitectonic criteria. (From Brodmann, 1908.)

The two halves of the cerebral cortex are linked together by great bands, or commissures, of axons that are whitish in color. These connecting bands include the corpus callosum and the anterior commissure. As we shall see later in this book, these connecting bands play an important role in coordinating the mental functions mediated by the two cerebral hemispheres. Surgical transection of the corpus callosum and the anterior commissure can actually lead to the emergence of two seemingly independent states of consciousness in the same human.

When the brain and spinal cord are dissected and observed without any special preparation, there is little indication of this rich array of pathways that convey neural information, either between the periphery and the higher portions of the brain or among its constituent parts, except for a slight color difference. Most interconnecting tracts of the central nervous system are composed of axons with a myelin sheath and thus display a whitish cast. Nuclear regions, which are made up mostly of neuronal cell bodies and unmyelinated axons and dendrites, are, in contrast, pinkish gray.

The greatest nucleus of all, of course, is the grayish outer mantle of the cerebral cortex, but beneath the cerebral cortex lies a large number of other important nuclei that play critical roles in brain function. Figure 3-37 is a cross section through the brain showing the approximate location of the most significant of these nuclei. The most important include the caudate nucleus, the putamen, the globus pallidus, the substantia innominata, the claustrum, and the amygdala. Although the nomenclature of these cerebral nuclei is extremely variable from one anatomy text to another, collectively these lower cerebral nuclei are often referred to as the *basal nuclei,* or historically and inappropriately but more often, as the *basal ganglia.* Certain subgroups of these basal nuclei are also referred to by special names, such as the *corpus striatum*, or incorporated along with other noncerebral structures into aggregates with common functions, such as the limbic system.

Many tracts of myelinated fibers course between these basal ganglia and the cerebral cortex conveying neural signals in either an afferent (progressing from the peripheral to the central nervous system) or efferent (progressing from the central to the peripheral nervous system) direction. Identification of the complete range of all of the nuclei, their subdivisions, and the interconnecting pathways is beyond the intended purpose of this chapter, but the reader is referred to any of the excellent modern texts on neuroanatomy (e.g., Crosby, Humphrey, & Lauer, 1962; Truex & Carpenter, 1969; or Carpenter, 1976) for a complete discussion of the many conducting pathways of the brain.

3. The Limbic System

To modern psychobiology, among the most important of the various interconnected clusters of cerebral and brain stem nuclei is the group known as the *limbic system.* The limbic system is an organized and interacting group of struc-

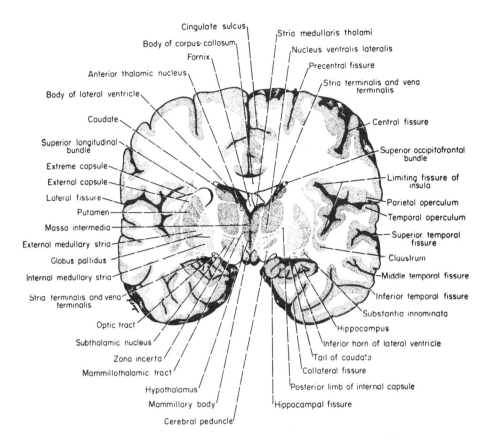

FIG. 3.37 A cross-sectional diagram of the human brain to show the relationship between the cerebral cortex and many of the important subcortical nuclei. (From Crosby, Humphrey, & Lauer, ©1962, with the permission of Macmillan Publishing Co.)

tures that was originally thought to be solely associated with the olfactory system but is now believed to play a much more general role in emotion and learning (Papez, 1937) in the higher vertebrates.

Although exactly which neural nuclei are to be considered constituents of the limbic system is a judgment that tends to vary from one author to another (for example, the hypothalamus is included by some and excluded by some), Walle Nauta, in an informal communication, has presented what is probably the most authoritative taxonomy of the components of the limbic system. Nauta first distinguishes between three major subdivisions of the limbic system. Some limbic structures, he states, are subcortical brain stem mechanisms; others are classified as belonging to either the paleo- or allocortex; and others are more properly considered to be portions of the juxtallocortex, a region of transition between the phylogenetically older allocortex and the evolutionarily more recent

TABLE 3.2

Allocortical components	Juxtallocortical components	Subcortical components
1. Olfactory bulbs	1. Presubiculum	1. Amygdaloid complex
2. Hippocampus	2. Cingulate gyrus	2. Septal region
a. Ammon's horn	3. Fronto-temporal cortex	3. Some thalamic nuclei
b. Dentate gyrus		4. Some hypothalamic nuclei
3. Pyriform lobe		5. Caudate nucleus
a. Prepyriform cortex		6. Midbrain reticular formation
b. Periamygdaloid cortex		7. Habenular complex
c. Entorhinal area		8. Mammillary bodies
		9. Preoptic nucleus

Components of the limbic system classified according to the portion of the brain with which these components are usually associated. (This table is adapted from some informal notes by W. J. H. Nauta and J. V. Brady dated June 1955.)

neocortex. Table 3-2 lists the components of the three subdivisions of the limbic system according to Nauta's taxonomy.

The organization of the limbic system is now known in much better detail than it was in 1937. Figure 3-38 is a block diagram of the main interconnections. Figure 3-39 is a more pictorial view showing essentially the same information but with a more realistic spatial arrangement.

The centers of the limbic system are interconnected by a number of major tracts including the fornix and the temporoammonic and subicular tracts. According to Powell and Hines (1974), the various nuclei of the limbic system may be thought of as an interface between the cerebral cortex and the lower centers of the brain stem, particularly the thalamus and the hypothalamus (if not included as a part of the limbic system proper). The limbic system also seems to play important regulatory roles in the general function of other brain areas. Excision of various portions may have exceedingly complex inhibitory or excitatory effects on brain physiology and behavior including learning, emotion, and motivation. For an excellent modern discussion of the structure and function of the limbic system, the reader is referred to an especially insightful monograph by Isaacson (1974).

4. The Corpus Striatum

An important subgroup of basal nuclei is collectively referred to as the *corpus striatum*. The corpus striatum is usually considered to consist of the globus pallidus and the putamen (which together are known as the *lenticular nucleus* because of their combined lens-like shap) and the caudate nucleus. Unlike the limbic system, which has complex behavioral effects on motivation, learning, and emotion, the corpus striatum seems to be more closely allied with those portions of the cerebral cortex and lower centers, like the cerebellum, that are involved in motor function. The general relationship of the corpus striatum and other basal nuclei is shown in Fig. 3-40.

5. The Thalamus

Anatomically and physiologically the thalamus can best be understood as the major relay station for sensory fibers entering the telencephalon from the brain stem and for motor fibers leaving the telencephalon for the brain stem. Although not all sensory fibers and tracts that emmanate from the thalamus are direct connections from afferent inputs to the telencephalon (some project to other brain stem loci or send signals to the cortex that have been integrated from a variety of inputs), relaying sensory messages is the main function of this very important center. There are, however, also a number of thalamic nuclei that have motor functions. A particularly good drawing showing the placement of

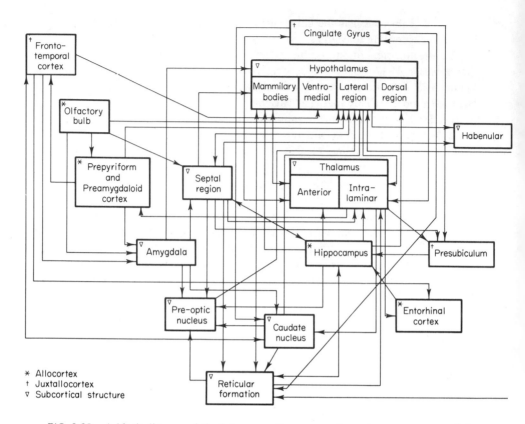

FIG. 3.38 A block diagram of the interconnections among the various components of the
limbic system. Each region has been coded as belonging to the allocortex, the juxtallocortex,
or the subcortical regions respectively. (This drawing is adapted from some informal notes
by W. J. H. Nauta and J. V. Brady dated June 1955.)

the thalamus with respect to the cortex and some of the basal ganglia can be
seen in Fig. 3-41.

The thalamus is made up of a large number of subsidiary nuclei. Over 40 distinct nuclei subserving one function or another have been specifically identified.
This complex of nuclei would make an indecipherable mess out of any attempt
to draw a coherent diagram of thalamic anatomy. Therefore, only the main nuclei are usually shown in drawings of the thalamus.

Another convenient way of handling this diversity of thalamic nuclei is to
categorize clusters of them into single groups purely on the basis of their geo-
graphic location within the thalamus. For example, there is a cluster of nuclei
known as the *midline nuclear group* that consists of four distinguishable nuclei.
This categorization is based entirely on the neuroanatomic locus and does not
refer to the functional relationships that might exist between these nuclei. Table

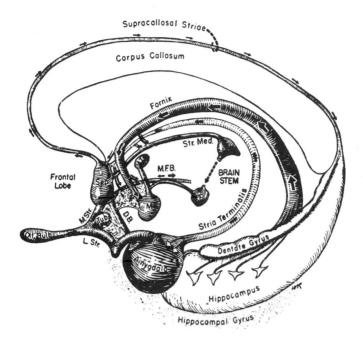

FIG. 3.39   A more realistic depiction of the spatial relationships of some of the components of the limbic system. (From MacLean, ©1949, after Krieg, with the permission of Elsevier/ North-Holland, Inc.)

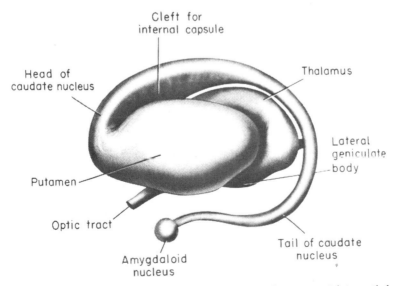

FIG. 3-40   A drawing of the spatial relationships among the corpus striatum, thalamus, and Amygdaloid nucleus. (From Carpenter, ©1976, with the permission of Williams & Wilkins Company).

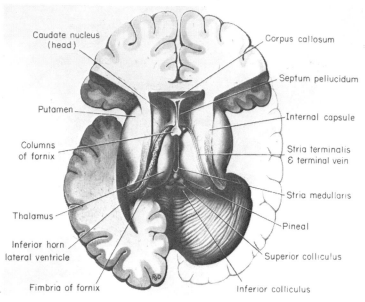

FIG. 3-41 A drawing of the spatial relationships of some of the main structures at the base of the cerebrum. (From Carpenter, ©1976, with the permission of Williams & Wilkins Company.)

3-3 (from Carpenter, 1976) lists these geographically determined categories and the major nuclei within each group. The location of a few nuclei and their functions are made more diagrammatically explicit in Fig. 3-42.

6. The Hypothalamus

The hypothalamus lies on the ventral side of the brain stem and is made up of a group of nuclei clustered around the infundibulum (the stalk of the hypophysis or the pituitary body). Although the hypothalamic region is very small and its several nuclei do not all appear to be discrete anatomical structures, these nuclei may make important contributions to the control and regulation of a large number of exceedingly important body functions, such as thermoregulation, water balance, eating and drinking, and sexual behavior, etc. Hypothalamic nuclei, as part of the limbic system, are also thought to play an important role in directing and controlling motivation and emotional responses. The names of the major hypothalamic nuclei are shown in Fig. 3-43. Table 3-4 lists, in a more

TABLE 3.3

A. Anterior nuclear group 　　1. Anteroventral nucleus (AV) *R* 　　2. Anterodorsal nucleus (AD) *R* 　　3. Anteromedial nucleus (AM) B. Medial nuclear group 　　1. Dorsomedial nucleus (DM) 　　　　a. parvocellular part *A* 　　　　b. magnocellular part *SC* C. Midline nuclear group 　　1. Paratenial nucleus 　　2. Paraventricular nucleus 　　3. Reuniens nucleus 　　4. Rhomboidal nucleus D. Intralaminar nuclear group 　　1. Centromedian nucleus (CM) *SC* 　　2. Parafascicular nucleus (PF) *SC* 　　3. Paracentral nucleus *SC* 　　4. Central lateral nucleus *SC* 　　5. Central medial nucleus *SC* E. Lateral nuclear group 　　1. Lateral dorsal nucleus (LD) *A* 　　2. Lateral posterior nucleus (LP) *A* 　　3. Pulvinar (P) *A* 　　　　a. medial part 　　　　b. lateral part 　　　　c. inferior part	F. Ventral nuclear group 　　1. Ventral anterior nucleus (VA) 　　　　a. parvocellular part (VApc) *R, SC* 　　　　b. magnocellular part (VAmc) *R, SC* 　　2. Ventral lateral nucleus (VL) 　　　　a. oral part (VLo) *R* 　　　　b. caudal part (VLc) *R* 　　　　c. medial part (VLm) *R* 　　3. Ventral posterior nucleus (VP) *R* 　　　　a. ventral posterolateral (VPL) *R* 　　　　　aa. oral part (VPLo) *R* 　　　　　bb. caudal part (VPLc) *R* 　　　　b. ventral posteromedial (VPM) *R* 　　　　　i. parvocellular part (VPMpc) *R* 　　　　c. ventral posterior inferior (VPI) *R* G. Metathalamus 　　1. Medial geniculate body (MGB) *R* 　　　　a. parvocellular part (MGpc) *R* 　　　　b. magnocellular part (MGmc) 　　2. Lateral geniculate body (LGB) *R* 　　　　a. dorsal part *R* 　　　　b. ventral part H. Unclassified thalamic nuclei 　　1. Submedial nucleus 　　2. Suprageniculate nucleus 　　3. Limitans nucleus I. Thalamic reticular nucleus (RN) *SC*

The thalamic nuclei classified according to their respective location in the thalamus. The most commonly used abbreviations are indicated in parentheses. A further classification criterion has been used to indicate whether the nuclei are mainly relay (R) or association (A) in function or have major subcortical (SC) connections. (From Carpenter, ©1976, with the permission of Williams & Wilkins Company.)

organized fashion, the various hypothalamic nuclei. It is important to note, however, that the search for understanding of the roles of the various nuclei forms an active body of research and that, as we shall see in Chapter 5, much current theorizing about hypothalamic function may be obsolescent.

7. Other Centers of the Brain Stem

The arrangement of many of the nuclei of the brain stem can be seen in Fig. 3-44. The region referred to as the *brain stem* terminates rostrally at the level of the basal nuclei. In this figure, the paired lateral geniculate nuclei of the diencephalic thalamus can be seen to lie just rostrally to the two superior and the

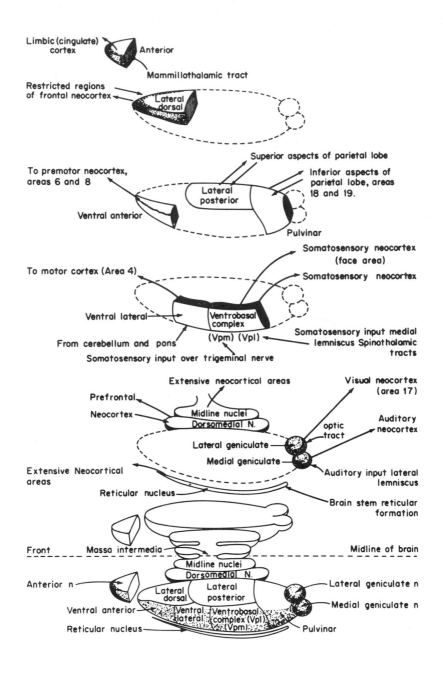

FIG. 3-42 Diagrammatic representation of the spatial relationships of the various nuclei of the thalamus. (From Isaacson, Douglas, Lubar, & Schmaltz, 1971.)

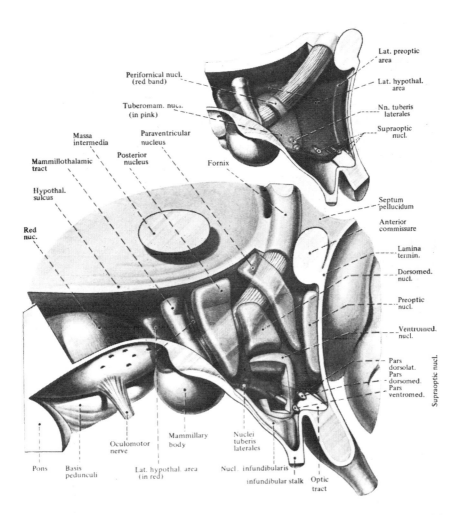

FIG. 3-43 Diagrammatic representation of the spatial relationships of the various nuclei of the hypothalamus. (From Haymaker, Anderson, & Nauta, ©1969, with the permission of C. C. Thomas, Publisher.)

two inferior colliculi that make up the tectum or roof of the mesencephalon. Ventral to the colliculi, but not visible in this picture, is the crus or floor of the mesencephalon.

The superior colliculi are multilayered mesencephalic structures composed of five discrete layers. The superior colliculi are primarily involved in visual function, and the inferior colliculi are enlarged but unlayered structures composed of rather smallish cells. These latter nuclei are mainly involved in auditory information transmission. Other nuclei of the mesencephalon are grouped within the

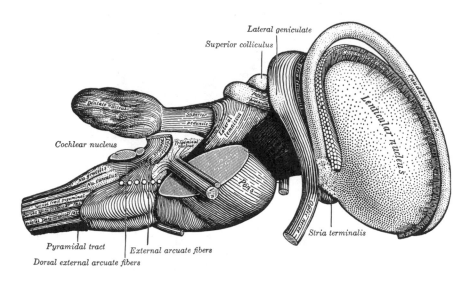

Labels on figure: Lateral geniculate · Superior colliculus · Lateral geniculate · Dentate nucleus · Superior peduncle · Lateral lemniscus · Trigeminal nucleus · Cochlear nucleus · Lenticular nucleus · Caudate nucleus · Pons · Stria terminalis · Pyramidal tract · External arcuate fibers · Dorsal external arcuate fibers

FIG. 3-44 A diagrammatic view of the side of the brain stem to show the spatial relationships among the various components. (From, Goss, ©1973, with the permission of Lea & Febiger, Publishers.)

TABLE 3.4

A. Anterior group
   1. Preoptic periventricular area
   2. Median preoptic nucleus
   3. Medial preoptic nucleus
   4. Lateral preoptic nucleus
   5. Suprachiasmic nucleus
   6. Anterior hypothalamic nucleus
   7. Paraventricular nucleus
   8. Supraoptic nucleus
   9. Diffuse supraoptic nucleus

B. Middle group
   1. Lateral hypothalamic area
   2. Tuberomammillary nucleus
   3. Lateral tuberal nucleus
   4. Arcuate nucleus
   5. Ventromedial hypothalamic nucleus
   6. Dorsomedial hypothalamic nucleus
   7. Dorsal hypothalamic area

C. Posterior group
   1. Posterior hypothalamic area
   2. Perifornical nucleus
   3. Posterior periventricular nucleus
   4. Premammillary nucleus
   5. Supramammillary nucleus
   6. Medial mammillary nucleus
   7. Lateral mammillary nucleus
   8. Nucleus Intercalatus

The major hypothalamic nuclei classified according to location. (Translated from Haymaker, Anderson, & Nauta, ©1969. Courtesy of Charles C. Thomas, Publisher.)

region known as the *tegmentum* and include those neurons whose axons make up the trochlear nerve, the oculomotor nerve, and portions of the trigeminal nerve. The central gray and the red nuclei and the substantia nigra are also found in this region. There is also a continuation of the reticular formation from the lower portions of the brain stem to be found here as well as at most other levels of the brain stem. Most of the other structures in this mesencephalic portion of the brain stem are tracts passing through the mesencephalon connecting higher and lower centers. Some of these tracts contain fibers that synapse on mesencephalic nuclei and other fibers that pass through without making any synaptic contacts.

Also shown in Fig. 3-44, is the brain stem enlargement known as the *pons*, which makes up almost the entirety of the ventral portion of the metencephalon. Dissection of the pons demonstrates that it is composed of two distinctly different portions. The more ventral part is mainly composed of fiber tracts, and the more dorsal part is composed of a number of important nuclei including nuclei of other portions of the trigeminal nerve, the facial nerve, the abducens nerve, and part of the eighth (auditory) nerve. It also contains a nuclear structure known as the *superior olive.* Also found in the pons are a number of minor nuclei called the *pontine nuclei.*

The medulla oblongata is the most caudal end of the brain stem—the adult derivitive of the myelencephalon. It, too, is composed of a number of important nuclei and tracts. The main nuclei, as well as the spatial relationship of the medulla to the rest of the brain stem structures, are shown in Fig. 3-45.

8. The Cerebellum

Second only to the great telencephalic cerebral hemispheres, the most conspicuous portion of the brain is the cerebellum, a metencephalic center that is especially involved in motor control functions. In addition to its somatic motor functions, the cerebellum also appears to be involved in important ways in autonomic functions. For example, stimulation of the cerebellum seems to produce wide-ranging inhibitory actions on breathing. It is also possible to surgically induce rage reactions by cerebellar surgery similar to those produced by limbic lesions.

Recent evidence (Bernston, Potolicchio, & Miller, 1973; and Ball, Micco & Berntson, 1974) suggests that the cerebellum also may be involved in fairly complex behavior beyond that usually ascribed to it in the past. These studies showed that eating, grooming, and other oral responses, which were clearly not simple motor automatisms, were elicited by electrical stimulation of various regions of the cerebelli of both rats and cats. The simple concept that the cerebellum is merely a controller of more or less automatic motor responses, therefore, would seem to be in need of radical revision.

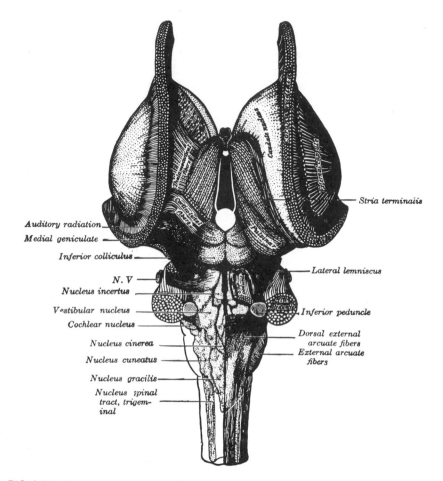

FIG. 3-45 A diagrammatic view of the top of the brain stem to show the spatial relationships among the various components. (From Goss, ©1973, after Weed, with the permission
of Lea & Febiger, Publishers.)

The cerebellar cortex also possesses, as does the cerebral cortex, a topographic type of mapping of the body that can be elicited by applying tactile
stimuli which produce evoked potentials that can be recorded with macroelectrodes placed on the cerebellar surface. Auditory, vestibular, and visual responses
can also be detected by appropriate recording procedures in certain portions of
the cerebellum.

Emerging between the most caudal portion of the colliculi and the most rostral portion of the medulla, the cerebellum is seen to be a richly and finely convoluted structure with both an outer nuclear mass and an underlying region of
whitish tracts consisting of myelinated connecting fibers. These fibers from three

pairs of tracts—the superior, middle, and inferior cerebral peduncles. The superior peduncles are primarily composed of fibers leaving the cerebellum, and the middle and inferior peduncles convey information to it. The richness of the very fine convolutions that are typical of the human cerebellum can be clearly seen in Fig. 3-46. A better view of the outward appearance of the cerebellum can be seen in the two plates of Fig. 3-47, which show the external aspects of the structures as they might be viewed from both the dorsal and ventral directions.

The cerebellum has a number of deep-lying nuclei somewhat analogous to the basal ganglia of the telencephalon. Four pairs of major cerebellar nuclei are usually listed: the dentate nucleus, the emboliform nucleus, the globosus nucleus, and the fastigial nucleus. More on the microscopic structure of the cerebellum appears later in this chapter.

9. The Spinal Cord

Finally, in our descent through the central nervous system, we come to the spinal cord, the elongated caudal portion of the original neural tube. The spinal cord is in part made up of great tracts of richly myelinated fibers conveying sensory and motor information to and from the periphery of the body, but it also contains a large number of nuclear structures in its central core. Figure 3-48 is a

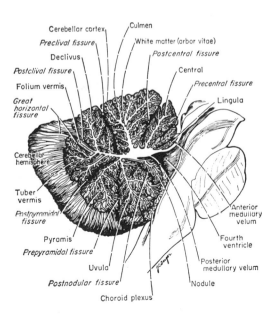

FIG. 3-46 A cross section through the cerebellum to demonstrate the very intricate structure of this important brain component. (From Crosby, Humphrey and Lauer, ©1962, with the permission of Macmillan Publishing Company.)

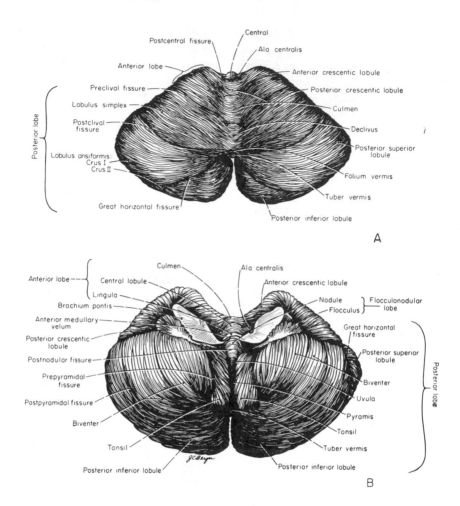

FIG. 3-47   Exterior views of the dorsal (A) and ventral (B) sides of the cerebellum indicating the various lobes and fissures. (From Crosby, Humphrey, & Lauer, ©1962, with the permission of Macmillan Publishing Company.)

cross section of the spinal cord at about the level of the second cervical vertebra. The cord is seen to be composed of two distinctly different regions. The central portion consists of a more or less butterfly-shaped, gray structure that is mainly composed of a variety of rostro-caudally elongated nuclei, which in turn consist largely of unmyelinated cell bodies and dendrites. The outer whitish portion of the spinal cord surrounding this central butterfly is made up of a system of tracts consisting of many myelinated axons. Many of the nuclei of the central grey matter and many of the tracts of the outer white matter are shown in Fig. 3-48. However, since not all of these nuclei and tracts extend the full length of the cord, not all are visible in the figure.

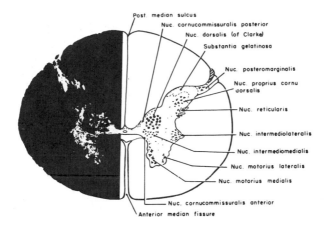

Post. median sulcus
Nuc. cornucommissuralis posterior
Nuc. dorsalis (of Clarke)
Substantia gelatinosa
Nuc. posteromarginalis
Nuc. proprius cornu dorsalis
Nuc. reticularis
Nuc. intermediolateralis
Nuc. intermediomedialis
Nuc. motorius lateralis
Nuc. motorius medialis
Nuc. cornucommissuralis anterior
Anterior median fissure

FIG. 3-48   A cross section of the thoracic portion of the human spinal cord indicating some of the spinal nuclei found at this level. (Courtesy of M. B. Carpenter of Pennsylvania State University.)

The nuclei of the central, gray, butterfly-shaped region are unusual when compared to those of the rest of the nervous system; they are typically elongated structures extending along many vertebrae rather than the prototypically ovoid nuclear shape in the brain. In fact, a few of these elongated nuclei actually extend the full length of the spinal cord. An example is the substantia gelatinosa, a structure thought to be intimately involved in the conduction and modulation of pain experiences (Melzack & Wall, 1965). Others, like the phrenic nucleus, extend only within the span of a few cervical vertebrae. A full description of the extent of each of the spinal nuclei is shown in Fig. 3-49. This figure also indicates the general locus of each nucleus by indicating in which of the three major horns of the butterfly-shaped center core they are to be found.

10.   The Ascending and Descending Reticular Systems

The reticular formation consists of a group of nuclei in the central core of the brain stem. Anatomically the reticular formation has been described as an almost structureless "reticulum" of cells that lack the linear ordering of the usual afferent pathways. But some of the cells may be very long, diffusely branching at all levels of the brain stem. In addition to the specific sensory nerve tracts that pass to the sensory cortical areas, there are collateral sensory inputs to the ascending formation that have been physiologically, if not structurally, defined from all sense organs. The output of the ascending reticular formation is a general and nonspecific spatio-temporal pattern of signals that is conveyed to almost all parts of the forebrain. These nonspecific outputs seem to produce a state of activation or excitement in these cortical regions, which many researchers, most notably Moruzzi and Magoun (1949), believe may correspond in some way to

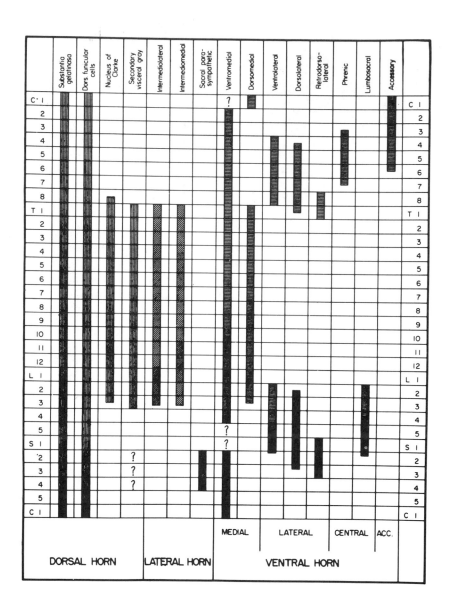

FIG. 3-49 Schematic diagram of the extent of the spinal nuclei within the various levels of the spinal cord. Abbreviations indicated are: *C* = cervical; *T* = thoracic; *L* = lumbar; *S* = sacral; and *C* = coccygeal. The relative lateral location of each nucleus within the spinal cord is also indicated. (From Crosby, Humphrey, & Lauer, ©1962, with the permission of Macmillan Publishing Company.)

the psychological states of attention, awareness, and consciousness. The reticular activating system, which is responsible for these arousal effects, is defined as the afferent portions of the reticular formation and the pathways and structures through which it influences activity in the telencephalon. A similarly diffuse descending reticular system, involved in motor function at the spinal cord level, is also known.

11.   A Comment

In this discussion of the gross anatomy of the central nervous system, I have concentrated on the development of an intuitive understanding of the three-dimensional structure of this complex organ and on establishing a familiarity with the relative location and size of the various centers or nuclei that are contained within it. However, the total mass of all of the nuclei is much less than the mass of the interconnecting tracts that course from one nucleus to another. It now would be desirable to discuss the pathways connecting the nuclei. However, this is impossible because the number of interconnections that exist is enormous and a list would serve no purpose. It is sufficient to note that as anatomical research progresses, it seems that all conceivable interconnections have been found. Almost everything seems to be connected to almost everything else, at least within the brain and brain stem, and at least indirectly. The only way out of this dilemma is to be selective; therefore, only a *few* interconnecting systems are discussed, mainly within the confines of the later chapters of this book to which they are relevant. Although this is not a completely ideal solution, it is the only practical one.

E.   THE GROSS ANATOMY OF THE PERIPHERAL NERVOUS SYSTEM

The peripheral nervous system, the network of nerves and ganglia that exists outside of the central nervous system and that extends to all portions of the body consists of two parts. One part is composed of the somatic nerves that both send motor (efferent or outward-going) signals to the striated voluntary muscles and receive sensory (afferent or inward-going) signals from the sensory receptors. A general idea of the extent of the somatic peripheral nervous system is obtained by viewing Fig. 3-50.

The other part of the peripheral nervous system is also both efferent and afferent and both sends motor signals to and receives sensory messages from the smooth muscles and internal organs of the body. This second part is known as the *autonomic* system. Its motor component, in turn, is composed of two parts: the sympathetic and the parasympathetic portions.

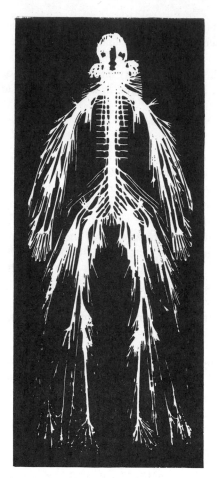

FIG. 3-50   Photograph of a dissection of the entire nervous system now in The Johns Hopkins University Medical School.

Communication between the central nervous system and peripheral tissues, muscles, and sense organs is accomplished through two sets of nerves—the spinal and cranial nerves. The spinal nerves enter or leave the central nervous system at the level of the spinal cord. Figure 3-51 shows the many spinal nerves and identifies the various regions of the cord from which they emanate, as well as the motor groups activated by each. The other set, that communicate with the central nervous system, the cranial nerves, enter at the level of the brain. Figure 3-52 shows the origin of each of the cranial nerves, and Table 3-5 more completely lists the names and functions of each.

The spinal nerves enter and leave the spinal cord through the efficient duplex system shown in Fig. 3-53. The fibers are segregated on the basis of their function according to a rule known as the Bell-Magendie Law. According to this

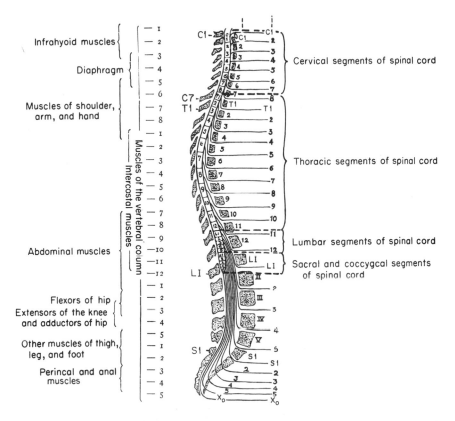

FIG. 3-51   Drawing shows the ventral spinal motor roots and indicates the various muscles driven by each root and its level of origin. Letters labeling each root represent the general level from which it emanates: C = cervical; T = thoracic; L = lumbar; S = sacral; and X = coccygeal. Numbers indicate the particular root. A similar system of dorsal roots constitutes the pathway for incoming sensory messages. (From Ranson, ©1959, with the permission of W. B. Saunders Company.)

functional-anatomical law, the afferent and efferent fibers are segregated so that sensory fibers enter through the dorsal roots and motor fibers emanate from the ventral roots.

The peripheral autonomic system consists of some nerves that are exclusively autonomic in function, but all purely autonomic nerves merge with somatic nerves to enter and leave the spinal cord and brain through the dorsal and ventral roots. The two portions of the autonomic system, the sympathetic and the parasympathetic, generally are antagonistic to each other in their function. For example, the parasympathetic system produces neural signals that contract the iris of the eye; the sympathetic system's effect is to dilate the iris. Nowadays, however, it is somewhat more usual to emphasize the anatomic, rather than the functional, distinction between the two. As shown in Fig. 3-54, sympathetic nerves

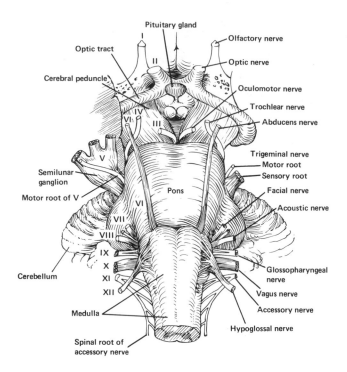

FIG. 3-52   A ventral view of the brain showing the point at which the cranial nerves enter the brain. (From Chusid, ©1976, with the permission of Lange Medical Publications.)

originate in the thoracic and lumbar regions of the spinal cord, and parasympathetic nerves have their origins in the cranial and sacral regions of the spinal cord. This figure also shows one of the dual chains of sympathetic ganglia that run parallel to the spinal cord.

F.   ORGANIZATION OF SELECTED CENTRAL NEURAL NETWORKS

We now turn the gross anatomy of the central and peripheral nervous system to a consideration of the microscopic neural structure, or *cytoarchitectonics*, of a few regions which, happily, for one reason or another, are now fairly well-known. To fully appreciate the significance of this discussion, however, the reader must be sufficiently familiar with cellular neurophysiology to be able to understand the nature of individual neurons and their interactions with each other. For a brief introductory discussion, the reader is referred to Chapter 6.

Unfortunately, a full discussion of cellular neurophysiology cannot be included in this chapter without making it cumbersomely large. Fortunately, there are a

TABLE 3.5

Number	Name	Functions
I	Olfactory	Smell
II	Optic	Vision
III	Oculomotor	Eye movement
IV	Trochlear	Eye movement
V	Trigeminal	Masticatory movements
		Sensitivity of face and tongue
VI	Abducens	Eye movement
VII	Facial	Facial movement
VIII	Auditory vestibular	Hearing
		Balance
IX	Glossopharyngeal	Tongue and pharynx
X	Vagus	Heart, blood vessels, viscera
XI	Spinal accessory	Neck muscles and viscera
XII	Hypoglossal	Tongue muscles

The cranial nerves and their functions. (Adapted from Thompson, ©1967, with the permission of Harper & Row Publishers.)

number of texts that concentrate specialized attention on this body of knowledge, and the reader is referred to any of them for a more complete discussion. Some of the better ones include: Aidley (1971), Ochs (1965), Hodgkin (1967), Schmidt (1975), Stevens (1966), and last, but hopefully not least, Uttal (1975b). A brief summary is also presented in chapter six.

In the following sections of this chapter, I concentrate on the microanatomy of neurons and the ways in which they can be organized into functional networks by describing a few of the structural arrangements that have been observed in the central nervous system. The discussion concentrates on the three-dimensional arrangement of neurons into arrays or networks in the various structures of the nervous system. This emphasis has been selected for a number of reasons. Among the most important is one that has already been mentioned: the fact that the information processing function of the nervous system is more dependent upon the structural and logical arrangement of the components than upon the biochemical nature of the components. It is a basic premise of this book that any kind of computational unit arranged in the same pattern could probably produce the same network functions, although in some cases with different time scales.

We shall be only minimally concerned at this point with the neurochemistry of neurons or with their individual shape or form. Shape or form will be important to us only within a secondary context of how the geometry of the cell might help to define the kinds of interconnections that are possible.

The concept of the neuronal network is central in the following discussion and, as we shall see later, to the entirety of the psychobiology of mind. A network may be functionally defined, for the purposes of this discussion, as a systematically interconnected, three-dimensional structure made up of connecting lines and nodes of communication and interaction. But in a broader sense, achieving an adequate definition of the term "neural network" is the main purpose of this entire section. Finally, after considering various examples, I have described a more or less prototypical arrangement of neurons that is itself a conceptually complete definition of a network.[2]

1.   The Retina

A particular aspect of the nervous system that will not be dealt with in very great detail in this book (it has already been a main object of discussion in my earlier work, Uttal, 1973) is the anatomy of the peripheral sensory pathways. However, a most useful and interesting simplified diagrammatic comparison of four of the major systems has been prepared by Szentágothai. This diagram, shown in Fig. 3-55, is an excellent brief summary of this important body of material.

I consider in some detail, however, the neural network of the retina, a structure that, as I have already noted, is considered a part of the central nervous system by reason of its embryological origin. One of the most up-to-date analyses of the primate retina has been carried out by Dowling and Boycott (1966). Their summary drawing (shown in Fig. 3-56) has become something of a classic and is reproduced here as an example of the detailed knowledge of neural organization that can be obtained in the relatively simple structures of sensory re-

---

[2]I would like to point out that there is one name that will repeatedly appear in the following discussion. This is the name of Janos Szentágothai, a Hungarian neuroanatomist, who has made a most remarkable series of contributions in this field. Professor Szentágothai combines excellence in microscopic neuroanatomy with an artistic bent. In addition, he apparently has an almost unsurpassed ability to visualize the three-dimensional organization of the intricate interconnections among neurons that are most often observed in only two dimensions under the optical or conventional transmission electron microscope. His contributions in elucidating the complex networks of many of the centers of the central nervous system have been outstanding. In the following discussion, a collection of his drawings are featured, each of which is probably unique not only in its pictorial clarity but also in its conceptual fruitfulness. As we progress through the following discussion, I am happy to acknowledge that the written and artistic contributions of this master cytological neuroanatomist were my main guides in learning about these wonderful nets. Not only has his published material been of great help, but Professor Szentágothai's cordial cooperation in sending me preprints and photographs is gratefully acknowledged. The importance of the transition from the shadows of micrographs to his drawings is best evidenced in the figures presented in this section.

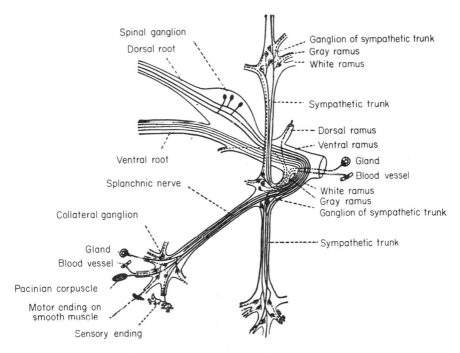

Spinal ganglion
Dorsal root
Ganglion of sympathetic trunk
Gray ramus
White ramus

Sympathetic trunk

Dorsal ramus
Ventral ramus
Gland
Blood vessel

Ventral root

Splanchnic nerve

White ramus
Gray ramus
Ganglion of sympathetic trunk

Collateral ganglion

Sympathetic trunk

Gland
Blood vessel

Pacinian corpuscle

Motor ending on
smooth muscle

Sensory ending

FIG. 3-53 Arrangement of the autonomic nervous system showing one of the chain of ganglia running parallel to the spinal cord. The autonomic system contains both sensory and motor fibers. (From Ranson, ©1959, with the permission of W. B. Saunders Company.)

ceptors. Dowling and Boycott used conventional transmission electron microscopes to determine the organization of this network. For some more recent retinal anatomy, the reader is referred to Boycott and Kolb (1973), Dubin (1970), and Sjöstrand (1976).

Sjöstrand's work in particular provides a much more realistic view of the very great complexity of the retina than is apparent in the highly diagrammatic drawing prepared by Dowling and Boycott. Sjöstrand uses serial sections of electron micrographs to produce a three-dimensional view of the complicated interconnections that are possible. Figure 3-57, for example, is a sketch of the intertwinings to be found at the foot of the photo receptors in a rabbit retina.

The primate retina is, as has been known for many years, composed of three layers of neurons—receptors, bipolars, and ganglion cells—with lateral cross connections provided by amacrine and horizontal cells. Physiologically the most peripheral cells in the neural chain are the photoreceptors themselves. But the retina is inverted with the receptors at the back of the eye; light must pass through all of the retinal elements to reach the receptors. Two kinds of photoreceptors are known to be present in the primate retina: *rods* and *cones*. The two types of receptor cells are distinguished not only on the basis of their

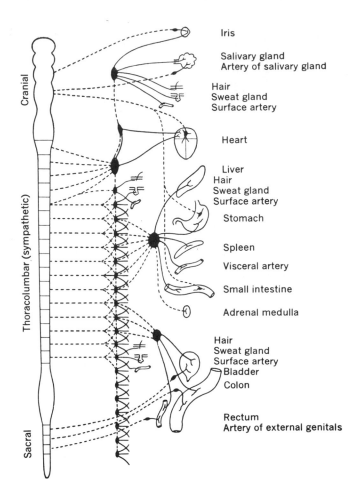

FIG. 3-54 Arrangement of the efferent or motor portions of the autonomic nervous system. This drawing shows the anatomic division of the sympathetic (thoracolumbar) and parasympathetic (sacral and cranial) components and the internal organs supplied by each division. (From Mountcastle, 1968, after Cannon from Bard.)

shape, but also on the basis of their constituent photochemicals and the way in which the discs of their outer segments (seen in Fig. 3-58) are revitalized. Rods shed the discs as the discs migrate to the tip of the rod; cone discs are permanent. (For details, see Uttal, 1973, chap. 3.) Beneath the receptor level is a layer of multiple and reciprocal synaptic interconnections known as the *outer plexiform layer.* Horizontal cells located at the level of the outer plexiform layer interconnect various receptors to each other laterally across this layer. Various types of bipolar cells make the inner nuclear layer and convey incoming signals from the receptors toward another region of rich synaptic interconnection, the

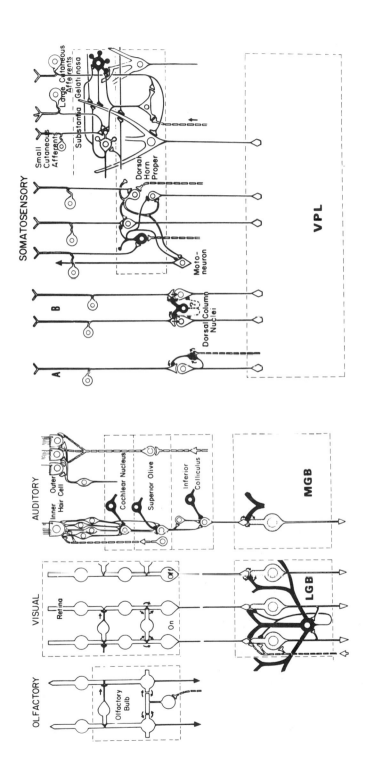

FIG. 3.55 A highly simplified schematic drawing of the arrangement of neurons in the various receptor structures. (From Szentágothai & Arbib, ©1975, with the permission of The Neurosciences Research Program.)

167

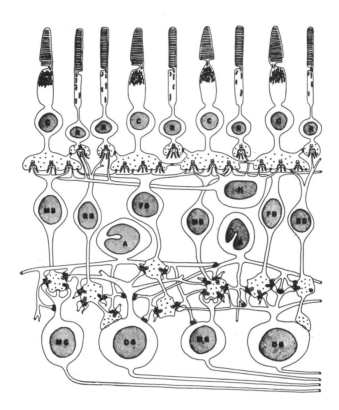

FIG. 3-56   A more realistic representation of the neural connections in the primate retina. Abbreviations indicated are: *R* = rod; *C* = cone; *MB* = midget bipolar neuron; *RB* = rod bipolar neuron; *FF* = flat bipolar neuron; *A* = amacrine cell; *H* = horizontal cell; *MG* = midget ganglion cell; and *DG* = diffuse ganglion cell. (From Dowling & Boycott, ©1966, with the permission of The Royal Society.)

inner plexiform layers. At this latter layer, there is found an additional class of horizontally interconnecting neurons known as *amacrine* cells. Amacrine cells convey signals laterally among the bipolars as well as among the ganglion cells that make up the innermost layer of the retina. The axons of the ganglion cells make up the optic nerve and tracts and convey visual afferent information to the brain.

Although we are not specifically interested in the retina or any of the other sensory receptors in this volume (the reader who is so oriented may wish to study the very important volume by Rodieck, 1973, which comprehensively describes the structure and function of the vertebrate retina), this structure does illustrate a number of general principles that will recur in many of the presentations to follow. Because of the relative organizational simplicity of the retina, these general features are somewhat more evident there than they are in some of

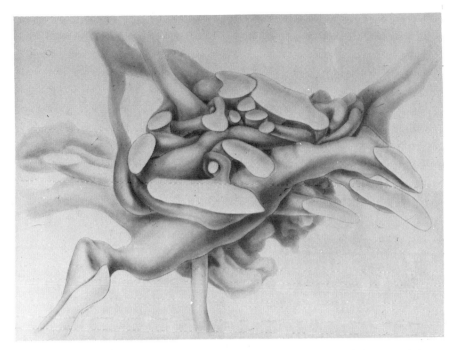

FIG. 3-57   An even more realistic three-dimensional reconstruction of the synaptic inter-connections in the outer plexiform layer of the rabbit retina (From Sjöstrand, ©1974, with the permission of Academic Press.)

the more central structures, and it is useful to make some of these features ex-plicit at this point.

For example, it should be noted that there is a clear layering of the neurons in the retina. Vertical lamination is a recurrent theme throughout neural cyto-architectonics. It should also be noted that there are repeated instances at each of the two plexiform layers of another fundamental form of neural interaction—the lateral interconnective. Clearly, point-to-point transmission of signals imping-ing upon the retina, by private wires, to the more central portions of the nervous system is highly unlikely. Rather, there is an elaborate horizontal and divergent system of interconnections that makes the response at any point deep in the pathway a function not only of the receptors immediately in line with it, but also of a widespread distribution of the surrounding receptors. Both neural con-vergence and divergence are, therefore, simultaneously involved in defining the flow of information in this three-dimensional lattice-like arrangement.

All of these properties emphasize the importance of neural integration—the process by which signals from multiple sources are mixed and modified. The pat-tern of signals that emerges from a neural net is not topologically identical to the one that entered. Within circumscribed limits set by the span of the inter-active effects produced by the lateral connectives, all points are influenced to a

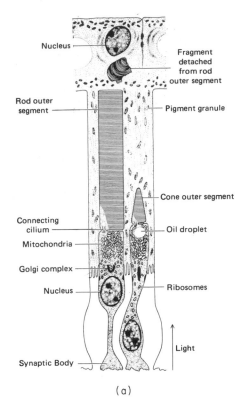

(a)

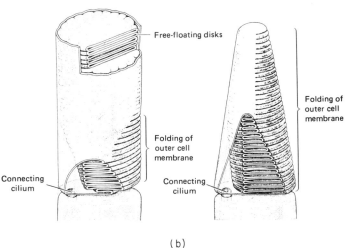

(b)

FIG. 3-58   Drawings of the rod and cone of the frog retina; (A) and (B) are at successively greater stages of magnification [(A) is from Young, ©1970, with the permission of *Scientific American;* (B) is reproduced by courtesy of Richard W. Young of the University of California at Los Angeles.]

certain degree by all others. It is this mixture of incoming information at each point to produce a new pattern of neural response that, in turn, underlies the great flexibility and variability of all aspects of human mental life.

I now proceed to consider some of the known organizational patterns of other portions of the central nervous system. The general order of the discussion is in terms of an ascent from the spinal to the cerebral level. However, as we ascend in the nervous system, we also see a general trend toward an increasing complexity of neuronal arrangement.

2.   The Spinal Cord

We have already seen in Fig. 3-48 how a gross dissection of the spinal cord displays a duplex cross section characterized by a central, butterfly-shaped gray nuclear mass surrounded by a more peripheral region mainly composed of myelineated fiber tracts. When the dissection is magnified (to the cellular level), the gray nuclear matter is found to be typically arranged in laminae, or layers, and columns that run longitudinally along the length of the spinal cord.

The general functional arrangement of the neurons of the spinal cord's gray matter is shown in Fig. 3-59, a reproduction from one of Szentágothai's most important papers (Szentágothai & Réthelyi, 1973). This conceptual diagram is based upon his research and also that of Scheibel and Scheibel (1966; 1968; and 1969). The view in this figure is from the ventral side of the spinal cord. The macrostructure of the gray nuclear core can be seen in this figure to be made up of constituent lamina labeled by the code numbers I, II, III, IV, and IX,[3] as well as a central cylindrically shaped region. Two other smaller columns of cell bodies can also be seen in this diagrammatic presentation, one lying just outside the larger cylinder and one centered within the cylinder. The entire mass of the gray matter is surrounded, of course, by the myelinated axons of the white matter contained within the peripheral featureless region shown in this drawing.

Just what are these lamina and columns? Clearly, they do not represent sharply demarcated regions within the spinal cord or any of the other centers that I discuss. Rather they are defined on the basis of more subtle anatomical criteria. The variously shaped volumes represent the hypothesized regions within which particular neurons exert their influence and within which the dendritic and axonal arborizations of the neuron may be distributed. Thus, a neuron whose dendritic tree is flattened in one dimension, yet quite extensive in another, will define a flattened slab-like region, within which it can interact with its neighbors. Neurons that ascend through some center with a more or less uniform (in

---

[3]This nomenclature skips the numbers V-VIII for a historical reason. Szentágothai believes that the original schema of lamina proposed by Rexed (1954) misconstrued the cyclindrical central structure to be a series of lamina that included some that were labeled V, VI, VII, and VIII. Newer studies suggest that these particular lamina do not exist, in fact, and Szentágothai has replaced them with the cylinder. Nevertheless, Rexed's schema of lamina numbering had been so ingrained in the literature that it is still conventionally used for the other existing lamina.

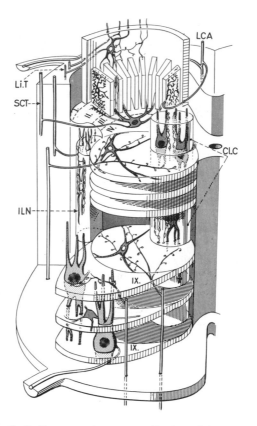

FIG. 3-59   Szentágothai's diagrammatic conceptualization of the spinal cord. Note the five main lamina I, II, III, IV, and IX and the geometrical volumes defined by the organization of the individual neurons. Abbreviations indicated are: *Li.T.* = Lissauer's tract; *LCA* = large cutaneous afferents; *SCT* = spino-cervical tract; *Cl.C.* = Clarke's column; and *ILN* = Sympathetic intermediolateral nucleus. (From Szentágothai & Réthelyi, ©1973, with the permission of S. Karger AG, Basel.)

all directions) spread of their dendrites will define columns, and structures that are organized so that only particular kinds of cells are to be found at certain depths will exhibit layered structural characteristics.

The three-dimensional regions that Szentágothai defines in his diagram and uses to emphasize the action space of a given neuron or cluster of neurons, therefore, exist only in the abstract. They represent his best judgment of the spatial organization into which these particular tissues are arranged. They must be considered as organized in a representational sense rather than in terms of truly circumscribed three-dimensional structures that might someday be teased apart by a clever dissector. What these drawings represent, therefore, is a statement of the three-dimensional pattern of interconnection among various kinds of neurons. Although they do not provide any information about the detailed interconnections between neurons contained within them and the cells of adjacent volumes, this type of information is of major importance in the development of our understanding of the cellular organization of central nervous centers and nuclei.

As I have said, Szentágothai defined the spinal three-dimensional lamina and cylinders shown in Fig. 3-59 on the basis of the orientation of their constituent cell bodies and their dendritic arborizations. For example, he notes that Lamina I is made up of a layer of medium-sized neurons whose cell bodies are arranged tangentially to the walls of this layer and which are, for the most part, oriented along the axis of the spinal cord. Lamina II is made up of smaller neurons that are the typical residents of the spinal nucleus known as the *substantia gelatinosa.* The neurons are arranged so that the abundant arborization of their processes runs mediolaterally across the lamina. These neurons, therefore, form a secondary organizational pattern of small radial "plates" that fill the Lamina II space and also extend across the boundary into Lamina III. Lamina III itself is made up almost entirely of the dendritic branches of these Lamina II neurons and is not distinctly occupied by any other special cell type. Lamina III, therefore, is extensively criss-crossed by many fibers that pass from Lamina II to Lamina IV. Spinal Lamina IV is made up mainly of neurons that receive dendritic connections from Lamina II, and from those passing through Lamina III, and send out major axons to form the spinocervical tract of the white matter. Their cell bodies and fibers mainly lie in a mediolateral plane, and their dendrites mainly interconnect among the neurons at the same rostrocaudal level of the spinal cord.

According to Szentágothai, the large central cylindrical core of the spinal gray matter shown in Fig. 3-59 is made up of a cellular arrangement that mimics a rostrocaudally oriented stack of poker chips. Each "chip" in the stack contains a number of different kinds of neurons, but only one—the Renshaw cell—is indicated in this drawing, and its horizontal orientation defines each of the "poker chips." Lamina IX, in large part making up the region called the *ventral horn,* consists of longitudinally oriented, large motor neurons that transverse a number of the "chips" in the large cylindrical cord. Each of these motor neurons, therefore, receives many synaptic inputs from the various "chips" and sends an axon out through the ventral nerve root to motor units of the periphery.

The two smaller columns shown in Fig. 3-59 represent the sympathetic intermediolateral nucleus and a nucleus known as *Clark's column.* In each of these columnar nuclei, unlike the large central column, the cell bodies are arranged with their main axes longitudinal to the spinal cord, i.e., running along its length.

In sum, the cellular structure of the spinal cord can be seen in Szentagothai's drawing to be arranged in a pattern that begins to make sense only when observed in a three-dimensional manner. Although the details of the individual synaptic contacts are not emphasized in this drawing, it is clear that the information flow allows for both longitudinal and horizontal flow of information, exactly analogous to the kind of organization found in the retina, although made considerably more complicated by a larger variety of neuron types. Like the retina, the flow of neural information at any one point in the spinal cord is always subject to modification and integration by the information pattern of other points.

In conclusion, the spinal cord exhibits considerable regularity of structure and thus an overall simplicity of organization. Its structure is sophisticated enough to be able to mediate some forms of behavior exclusively within the cord's own neural networks and without reference to the more involved neural systems of the higher levels of the nervous system. In particular, reflexive actions, simple stereotyped responses to what are typically considered noxious—or tissue-damaging—stimuli, are probably handled entirely by spinal network mechanisms. I also show in Chapter 8 that spinal learning now seems to have been irrefutably demonstrated. However, these types of sensory-motor information processing, although very useful, are only a part of the role of the spinal cord. Perhaps more important is its role as a route for fiber tracts conveying signals between the periphery and the central nervous system.

Before continuing this discussion of the cytoarchitectonics of higher centers in the central nervous system, it is important to reiterate that these geometrical building blocks, used by Szentágothai in his reconstruction of spinal cord tissues, do not in fact exist. The boundaries of each block are only conceptual in the sense that a rather irregularly shaped neuron may only vaguely define their extent. No such demarcations would be observed microscopically, no matter how excellent a microscope or staining technique was used. Rather, the point made by Szentagothai is that, in spite of the apparent chaos of structure observed at the cellular level, there is in fact a high degree of orderliness when the neurons are viewed in assembly at this and at other levels of the nervous system.

3.   The Lateral Geniculate Body of the Thalamus

As an example of the cytoarchitectonics of a thalamic relay, I consider Szentágothai's conceptualization of the lateral geniculate nucleus, an important synaptic junction in one of the several visual pathways. The lateral geniculate nucleus is the first synaptic relay point in the pathway from the retina to the visual neocortex. It is here that the long axons of the retinal ganglion cells synapse with the neurons that project to the visual cortex.

The lateral geniculate body is also observed to be a laminated structure in all animals in which it is present. In some species, like the domestic cat, the lamination consists of only three distinguishable layers as shown in Fig. 3-60a. Between the layers labelled A and A_1 and between A_1 and B, there are two less well-defined zones best defined as "interlayers." In primates, however, the lateral geniculate body is more complex and is composed of six distinct layers, each of which, according to DeValois, Abramov, and Jacobs (1966), carries a different encoded form of visual stimulus information. An example of the layering in the primate lateral geniculate nucleus is shown in Fig. 3-60b.

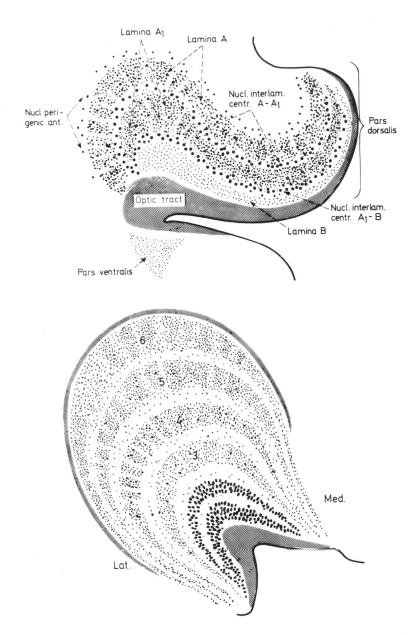

FIG. 3-60 (A) A schematic drawing of the layers of the lateral geniculate body of a cat. Note particularly the different size cells in the different lamina and the fact that there are really only three main lamina. (B) A schematic drawing of lateral geniculate body of the monkey. Note particularly that in this primate there are six distinct layers. (Both figures from Szentágothai, ©1973a, with the permission of Springer-Verlag, Inc.)

The optic tracts lie just ventral and caudal to the lateral geniculate nucleus, and the afferent fibers from this primary visual pathway ascend into the lateral geniculate body. They then pass through the various lamina in sequence synapsing with other neurons that proceed on to the cerebral cortex. Figure 3-61 is Szentágothai's conceptualization of the way in which the neurons are organzied in the cat's three-layered lateral geniculate. Axons of the ganglion cells emerge from the optic nerve and rise in almost perfect vertical lines through the various layers. At various levels in this ascent, a certain proportion of the incident axons terminates in an arborization that defines a cylindrical shape. These conceptual

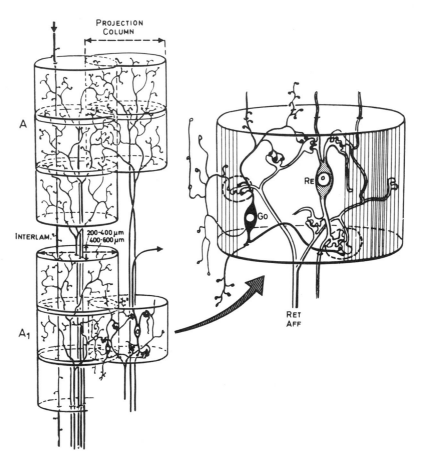

FIG. 3-61   A schematic drawing of the regular organization of the neurons in the lateral geniculate body. Abbreviations indicated are: Ret Aff = retinal afferents; Re = relay cells; and Go = Golgi type II cells. Note that in spite of the apparent disarray there is a great deal of order in this structure if one properly considers the volumes defined by the dendritic arborizations of the various neurons in general rather than the idiosyncracies of each cell. (From Szentágothai, ©1973a, with the permission of Springer-Verlag, Inc.)

cylinders define functional and structural regions in which elaborate synaptic interactions occur.

The general arrangement of the cylinders (Fig. 3-61) is like a group of parallel columns, each column consisting of a stack of these cylinders. The cylindrical regions are variable in height, and synaptic contacts are made at all levels within each column. Consequently there is considerable overlap of synaptic inputs to the cylinder both vertically and horizontally.

Within each cylinder, each ascending ganglion cell axon makes synaptic contact with two types of cells. One of these is the next transmission neuron—the relay cell—in the chain to the cortex. The other is a characteristically shaped neuron, which Szentágothai refers to as a Golgi-type cell, that is specialized for lateral (horizontal) transmission among the cylinders. These Golgi-type cells, therefore, provide a potential means for lateral interaction and neuronal integration between cylinders at all of the layers of the lateral geniculate nucleus.

One other very important type of neuron is found in these synaptic cylinders. Descending from the cortex are long axons with multiple synaptic contacts within all lamina of the lateral geniculate nucleus. These neurons provide a means for centrifugal (efferent) signals to be integrated with the centripetal (afferent) signals from the retina. The details of the neuronal interconnections in the lateral geniculate body are shown in Fig. 3-62.

In sum, the organization of this portion of the thalamus also displays the same kind of lamination and lateral cross connectives observed in the retina and the spinal cord. In addition, the microanatomy of this thalamic nucleus illustrates a form of columnar organization that will also be found at higher centers of the central nervous system.

4.   The Cerebellar Cortex

The cerebellum is a remarkable structure that is mainly responsible for the coordination of motor responses, but as we noted, is also involved in some other more complex behaviors. The beauty of the cerebellum, in the context of our present anatomical discussion, is that its internal neural architecture is exceedingly specific and orderly yet complex in terms of the behavioral sequences it controls.

Many of the important facts of cerebellar organization have been known since the time of the pioneering microneuroanatomist Ramon y Cajal (1911). But there is a continual accrual of new information about this important structure, much of which has been summarized in two notable monographs (Eccles, Ito, & Szentágothai, 1967; and Szentágothai & Arbib, 1975), as well as in a remarkably clear and cogent article (Llinás, 1975).

Figure 3-63 is a drawing prepared from numerous microphotographic investigations of the structure of the cerebellar cortex. In the cerebellum, the cortex can be seen to be composed of three layers: an outermost "molecular" layer,

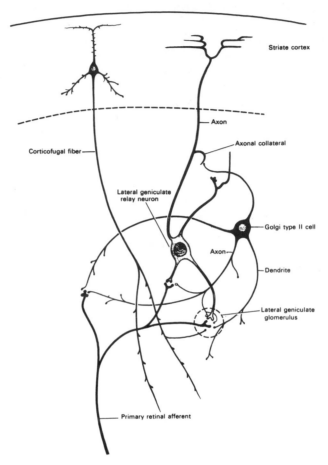

FIG. 3-62   A more detailed drawing of the arrangement of the cells in a single volumetric cylinder (see Figure 3-61) in the lateral geniculate body. (From Carpenter, ©1976, after Szentágothai, 1970, with the permission of Williams & Wilkins Company.)

a middle "Purkinje cell" layer, and an inner "granular" layer. The arrangement of the neurons shown in this figure is quite uniform over the entire expanse of the cerebellar cortex, the external morphology of which, the reader may recall from Fig. 3-47, is highly convoluted and fissured. Another feature that makes description of the cytoarchitectonics of the cerebellar cortex relatively easy (compared to the much more complex cerebral cortex, for example) is that the number of different kinds of neurons that are found there is very small. In fact, only five types of cells are usually listed as making up most of the mass of the cerebellum. In addition, there is not thought to be any microanatomic or cyto-architectonic specialization of regions of the cortex analogous to the differentiation underlying the Brodmann areas of the cerebral cortex.

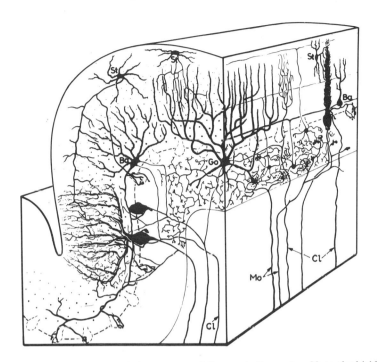

FIG. 3-63   The arrangement of the neurons of the cerebellar cortex. Note the highly regular array. Abbreviations indicated are: Cl = climbing fibers; Mo = mossy fibers; St = stellate cells; Ba = basket cells; and Go = Golgi cells. The cerebellar glomeruli are outlined with dotted lines, and the large conspicuous Purkinje neurons are typified by the cell near the fold on the left. (From Eccles, Ito, & Szentágothai, ©1967, with the permission of Springer-Verlag, Inc.)

The five types of cells, in order of their depth below the cerebellar cortical surface according to Szentágothai are:

a. *The stellate neuron.*   Stellate neurons are found in the outermost layers of the cerebellar cortex. As seen in Fig. 3-63, they have a relatively oval cell body (or perikaryon) and a uniformly distributed dendritic arborization.

b. *The Purkinje neuron.*   Purkinje neurons are large cells whose axons constitute the main efferent routes for signals emerging from the cerebellar cortex. The dendritic brush of these cells is very extensive but is curiously flattened with an extensive arborization in one plane and a very flat cross section in the other. This curious structural arrangement of the purkinje cell is shown in Fig. 3-64.

c. *The Golgi neurons.*   Golgi neurons are also very large cerebellar neurons somewhat similar in shape to purkinje neurons. However, the arborization of their dendritic trees is similar in all directions and is not compressed in any one plane. Furthermore, the Golgi neuron does not have a single, or greatly elongated, main axon. Rather, its axon is multiply branched and also forms an irregular arborized structure mainly in the layers closest to the cortical surface. The

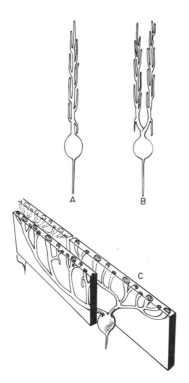

FIG. 3.64 Three diagrams illustrating the peculiar flattening of the dendritic arborization of the cerebellar Purkinje cell. A and B show two typical microscopic views, C is a three-dimensional cross section. (From Eccles, Ito, & Szentágothai, ©1967, with the permission of Springer-Verlag, Inc.)

dendritic brush, however, is made up of a collection of more or less straight dendrites that extend, as do the dendrites of the purkinje cells, toward the surface of the cerebellum. Figure 3-65 shows the typical shape of a Golgi-type cerebellar neuron.

d. *The basket neuron.* The basket neuron is a relatively small cell, much like the stellate cell, but with a typically much more asymetrical dendritic arborization. The oval cell body gives rise to many dendrites, which project toward the outer regions of the cortex, and a single axon which projects laterally to the cell bodies of purkinje neurons of the same layer of the cerebellar cortex. Thus, like the stellate and the Golgi neurons, it is primarily capable of serving as an interneuron for lateral signal integration within the cerebellar cortex.

e. *The granule neuron.* Granule neurons are grouped together in the so-called granule layer. These cells receive afferent signals from other portions of the nervous system, as well as from other cerebellar neurons by means of claw-shaped dendritic branches. The granule cell sends a single major axon up to the molecular layer of the cerebellar cortex where it branches to form one fiber in an extraordinarily regular parallel arrangement of transverse-running fibers. These parallel fibers from the numerous granule cells form a highly regular structure reminiscent of a crossbar switch in a telephone central station.

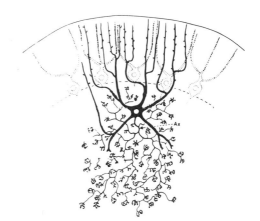

FIG. 3.65   A more detailed view of a typical cerebellar cortex Golgi cell. Note particularly the extensive arborization of the axon (Ax). (From Eccles, Ito, & Szentágothai, ©1967, with the permission of Springer-Verlag, Inc.)

In addition to these five types of neurons within the cerebellar cortex, there are three classes of fibers entering and leaving the cerebellar cortex that have also been described. One is the efferent axon of the purkinje neuron that I have already mentioned. It conveys the result of cerebellar cortical information processing to deep nuclei of the cerebellum and thence to other portions of the nervous system. The other two axon types are afferent fibers that bring information into the cerebellar cortex. The first kind of afferent fiber is defined as the class of "mossy fibers." Mossy fibers are axons that originate from nuclei in the spinal cord, medulla, and pons. They represent the main inputs to the granule cells. The other set of inputs—those known as the climbing fibers—are the axons of neurons that have their cell bodies in the inferior olive of the brain stem. These fibers relay neural signals mainly from the spino-olivary tract of the spinal cord and synapse at many different layers within the cerebellum. Their synaptic terminals can be identified on the basket cells, the purkinje cells, and the Golgi cells.

In summary, we can see that though there are an enormous number of individual neurons present in the cerebellum, they are of only a few kinds. The relatively small number of different cell types and the extreme regularity of cerebellar cytoarchitectonics suggest that the overall function of this center is relatively consistent throughout. Input signals enter the cerebellum along the climbing and mossy fibers and selectively activate the various interneurons contained within this great nucleus. Through the integrative action of both excitatory and inhibitory synaptic functions, the regular structure of the cerebellum leads to the emission of coordinated patterns of signals along the axons of the purkinje cells.

This flow of information has been pictorially summed up in an extraordinarily insightful drawing by Szentágothai, which is shown in Fig. 3-66. To make the progressive flow of information more apparent, he has inverted the purkinje cells

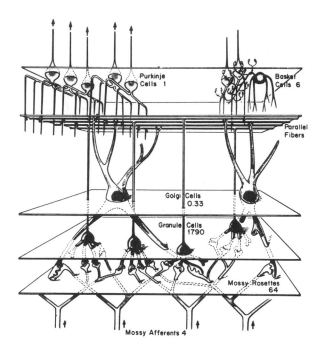

FIG. 3-66   An ingenious diagrammatic sketch of the organization of the cerebellar cortex. In this drawing, the cerebellar cortex has been unfolded so that the cells that enter it do so from the bottom of the figure whereas those that leave do so from the top of the figure. In actual fact, both the afferent and efferent fibers enter from the bottom. (From Szentágothai & Arbib, ©1975, with the permission of The Neurosciences Research Program.)

and basket cells and, rather than having their outputs flow out in the same direction from which the mossy and climbing fibers (which are not shown in this figure) entered the cortex, the purkinje cell efferents emerge from the top of the picture. This figure emphasizes the precise loci at which the most important synaptic contacts occur and the uniform flow of information among the several layers and points of potential lateral interconnection. With the exception of the highly unusual layer of exceedingly regular parallel fibers, the structure of cerebellar cortex appears strikingly similar to the cellular arrangement of some of the other centers already discussed. Lamination (layering), horizontal interconnectives, and both excitatory and inhibitory connections are obviously necessary for the functioning of the cerebellum. Although the cerebellar architecture is not identical to the other centers, it should be increasingly clear that a more or less general three-dimensional neuronal matrix is common to all of the structures considered so far.

5.   The Cerebral Cortex

We now come to the highest level and most complicated neural aggregate of all: the cerebral neocortex. Here the interconnections are both far more intricate and numerous than at any other level of the nervous system as would be expected from its far more complex functions. Furthermore, there are many more distinct types of cells in the cerebral cortex than in the lower centers. Unlike the cerebellar cortex, where only five cell types were involved, over 50 cell types have already been identified in the cerebral cortex, and the problems in comprehending its functional organization are considerably more complex. However, I have already reviewed some general principles that may help to clarify the basic structure of even this cerebral mass.

The neuronal arrangement in the cerebral cortex has been the object of study for many years. Szentágothai, who as usual will be our modern guide through this network, notes (Szentágothai, 1972; 1973b) that many of the basic principles of cerebral cortex organization were fully understood by the neuroanatomical workers who preceded him. These include Ramon y Cajal (1911), Lorente de No (1938), and Sholl (1956), all of whom made important contributions to cerebral cytoarchitectonics.

To understand the cerebral cortex, it is first necessary to appreciate that it, like the cerebellar cortex and the thalamus, among many others, is also a laminated structure. Figure 3-67, for example, shows the arrangement of the lamina at Brodmann's region 17. Unlike the cerebellar cortex, the afferent fibers that convey information into the cerebral cortex do not enter and synapse at the most superficial layers. Rather, many of the axonal fibers that come from the thalamus, from the other hemisphere via the corpus callosum, or from any of the other commissures that feed the cortex, pass without synapsing through the bottom two layers (layers V and VI) of the cortex. It is only in the central lamina, layer IV, that most of these fibers terminate by synapsing with cortical neurons. Only some small proportion of the afferent fibers pass through all of the cortical lamina and synapse within the outermost Lamina I.

A key simplifying concept to keep clearly in mind when one is considering the cytoarchitectonics of the cortex is that the efferent, or output, fibers from the cerebral cortex consist almost exclusively of the long axons of a single kind of neuron—the pyramidal cells—so-called because their cell bodies are generally pyramidal in shape. The dendritic tree of each of these pyramidal cells is also shaped quite characteristically. Near their base, the dendrites are directed horizontally across the lamina of their origin; the dendrites emerging from the apex of the neuron body are generally aligned perpendicularly to the surface of the cortex. This arrangement is shown in Fig. 3-68.

Two classes of motor fibers may be distinguished on the basis of their ultimate destination. One class contributes to the so-called *pyramidal motor system*, the axons of which descend without synapsing to the spinal cord. It is only in

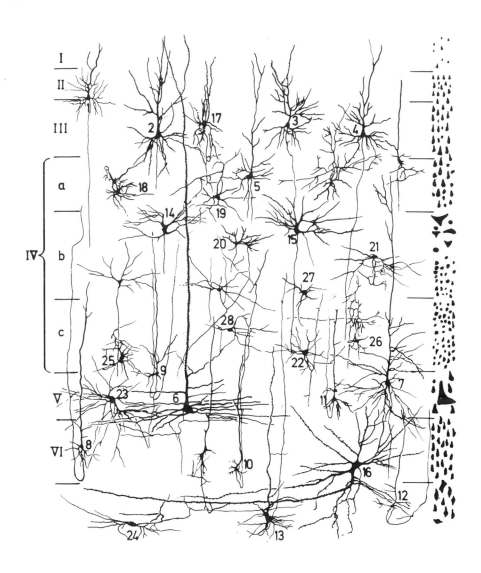

FIG. 3-67 A diagram of the neuron types found in six layers of the human visual cortex. On the right-hand side, only the cell bodies have been drawn to illustrate the different distribution of cell sizes found in the different layers: typical pyramids (1-7), short pyramid — mainly with ascending axons (8-13), large Cateogry I stellates of Cajal (14, 15), giant fusiform lamina VI (16), Category II stellates (17-24), and midget stellates (25-28). (From Szentágothai, ©1973b, after Shkolnik-Yarros, with the permission of Springer-Verlag, Inc.)

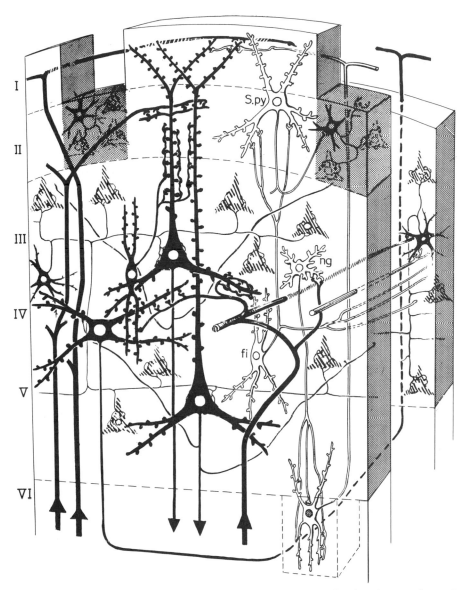

FIG. 3-68 A diagrammatic sketch of the human visual cortex showing the general organization of the main classes of neurons. The structure is highly regular with each cell typically restricted to a well-defined region. The large cells in Layers III and V are pyramidal cells whose axons make up the main afferents from this region of the cortex. The lightly colored cell in Layer IV, sending a lateral connective to adjoining regions of the cortex, is a Type I stellate cell. The afferent axons on the left, which make synaptic connections in Layers I and II, are typically from the corpus callosum. Abbreviations indicated are: fi = fusiform interneuron; S. Py = small pyramid; and ni = neurogliform interneuron. (From Szentágothai, ©1973b, with the permission of Springer-Verlag, Inc.)

185

the spinal cord that these fibers synapse with the final motor neurons to convey signals directly to motor fibers of the muscles. Incidentally, the pyramidal motor system is not so named because its fibers are the axons of *pyramidal cells*, but rather because these fibers pass through a *pyramidally shaped* region in the brain stem.

The other class of fibers emanating from the cerebral cortex also ultimately activates muscle units, but the pathway of members of this class is much more circuitous. Axons of this second type may synapse at any one of a number of places in the brain stem or even in the basal nuclei of the cerebrum. This second class of efferent fibers from the pyramidal cells make up one portion of the brain substructure known as the *extrapyramidal motor system*. Other fibers that make up the extrapyramidal tracts may have their origins in cell bodies of the cerebellum among many other possible sources. In addition to these two motor systems, there are, of course, other efferent pathways emanating from the cerebral cortex. Tracts run from the cortex to the cerebellum, to the thalamus, to the basal ganglia, across the corpus callosum and to many other portions of the ipsilateral cortex itself that are not actually a part of either the pyramidal or extrapyramidal motor system.

The cerebral cortical laminae identified in Fig. 3-67 appear more clearly demarcated if one considers only the cell bodies, which appear on the right side of this figure. Although there is considerable controversy about the specific naming of the layers in the human cerebral cortex, it is only information like that illustrated in this atlas of cell body shapes that is able to give a coherent overall picture of the cortical laminar structure.

As indicated previously, over 50 different kinds of neurons are distinguishable within the various laminae of the cerebral cortex. Szentágothai (1973b) has suggested an arbitrary categorization scheme that brings some order to this distressing multiplicity of cell types. He distinguishes between two general types within which are to be found a number of component subtypes. The first general type, collectively known as *Type I cells*, includes the large pyramidal cells, some other pyramidal-like cells, fusiform cells, and more regularly shaped stellate cells. All four of these cell subtypes are shown in Fig. 3-68.

The second general type of neurons includes those that Szentágothai refers to as *Golgi Type II cells*. These include basket-type cells, stellate cells with widely distributed axonal arborizations, cells with horsetail-like axonal arborizations, midget cells, and others that differ only slightly from these prototypical subtypes. Two members of this second type are also shown in Fig. 3-68.

In addition to these two types of neurons, there are also a number of different kinds of axons coursing into and out of the cerebral cortex whose cell bodies are located elsewhere. The various sensory fibers relayed from the thalamus are among the most numerous; they synapse mostly in the fourth layer of the cortex. But there are also many other fibers that come from other parts of the cerebrum and brain stem, most notably those from the opposite side of the brain.

These latter fibers typically synapse, not in the fourth layer as do the sensory fibers, but rather in the uppermost first and second layers of the cortex. Other fibers from the nonspecific brain stem nuclei (e.g., the ascending reticular activating system) are also found to terminate in widely distributed regions throughout the cortex. Furthermore, axonal connections between adjacent regions of the cerebral cortex are found running just beneath the bottom-most sixth layer.

Now let us consider Fig. 3-68 in greater detail. First, the reader should again note that there are three different kinds of afferent axonal connections that convey information into a specific slab of cortex. Some fibers, as we have noted, come via the corpus callosum and other commissural connectives. These fibers tend to synapse in the outermost layer, Lamina I, very often within the apical arborization of very large pyramidal cells. In addition, there are afferents entering various loci of the cortex that come from other cortical locations. These are very often the axons of Szentágothai's Type I stellate cells, whose cell bodies are located in layer IV. Their axons tend to synapse in layer II. The third class of cortical afferents are the fibers from the sensory relay nuclei of the thalamus. For example, visual information enters the cerebral cortex from axons that originated in cells of the lateral geniculate body. These axons most often synapse in layer IV of the visual cortex.[4]

There are a number of possible points at which sensory signals may synapse, but the details are not yet fully understood. These fibers may synapse with the large pyramidal cells, whose axons are the main efferent fibers; they may synapse with the Type I stellate cells whose axons communicate with other parts of the cortex; or they may synapse with that special type of cell, referred to above, that possesses the horse-tail-shaped dendritic trees and via these axons connect to the pyramidal cells. Alternatively, the route may be through some very uninteresting-looking "neurogliaform" cells that connect to some layer VI cells, which themselves then connect to layer I cells. Unfortunately, the exact details of the synaptic connections are not yet known.

Another important feature that has not yet been emphasized, which obviously must play a critical role in intracortical circuitry, is that an inhibitory subsystem must be present to dampen the activity produced by the manifold excitatory inputs. If some kind of inhibitory synaptic system were not present, then a single input to a highly interconnected excitatory net of this kind, or even a spurious spontaneous response, would be able to trigger universal neural activity and place the organism in a "status epilepticus." Obviously, no organism could evolve and survive without inhibitory connections.

[4]It is interesting to note that neurons of layer IV of the somato-sensory cortex exhibit very simple sorts of trigger feature sensitivity, but that the neurons of layers I, II, and III, as well as V and VI, exhibit more complicated trigger sensitivities. This hierarchy reflects additional levels of processing in these layers beyond that carried on in the IVth layer and emphasizes that layer IV is probably the entry point for most cortical afferents (Gerhard Werner, 1974).

In the cortical network, some workers have suggested that inhibition is a special function of the basket-type cells. In Fig. 3-68, this hypothesis is supported because, as Szentágothai notes, the basket-type neurons tend to have multiple axons that carry signals to a wide variety of pyramidal cells. This is the sort of widely distributed geometrical organization that would be required for a generalized inhibitory stabilizing system.

Interconnections among the various parts of the cerebral cortex are also abundant. Various kinds of cells are indicated in this figure that communicate directly, via their own laterally arranged axons, through a single horizontal layer. Others send connectives vertically coursing upward or downward through narrow columns of the cortex.

Another important feature of this conceptual model of the cortical neurons is the family of three-dimensional action spaces of neurons and coordinated groups of neurons, similar to those already described for the lower centers. However, unlike the situation in these lower centers, there is an increased complexity in the cerebral cortex due mainly to the fact that there are more layers and more different types of neurons.

Nevertheless, some general organizational principles can be proposed that greatly simplify the superficial complexity of cellular arrangement in the cerebral cortex. Once again, it is Szentágothai who provides us with the simple and helpful conceptual model. Figure 3-69 is a more up-to-date and less complete schematic of cerebral cortical cytoarchitectonics (Szentágothai, in press). The most notable feature of this figure is its emphasis on the specification of the three-dimensional spaces that define the regions of influence of particular cell types and clusters.

The reader should first note in this new diagram that a number of horizontal planes have been added for clarity. These planes, however, are simply aids to three-dimensional visualization, and they do not, as Szentágothai emphasizes, represent the boundaries between the different cortical laminae. Only sensory afferents are shown in this figure, in contrast to Fig. 3-68, which depicts the other afferent fibers as well. The sensory afferents terminate on four different types of cells. The critical point, in the context of the present discussion, is that the information that terminates on one of these cell types is more or less restricted to a sharply defined vertical column in the cortex. Although this information may ascend or descend the volumn, there is little horizontal spread of neural signals between these columns.

Physiological evidence for columns of this sort was observed first by Mountcastle (1957) in somatosensory cortex and then later by Hubel and Wiesel (1962) in visual cortex. In both cases, these workers observed that electrode penetrations along these perpendicular (to the surface of the cortex) columns recorded neuronal responses activated by restricted classes of peripheral stimuli. These electrophysiologically defined columns, it has now been suggested, may be the functional expression of the structural organization of the cortical neurons now

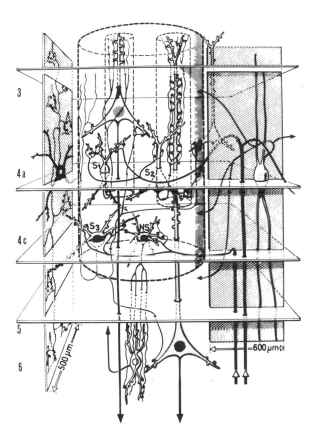

FIG. 3-69   A simplified block diagram of the organization of the cerebral cortex as defined by the volumes of interaction of the individual neurons. The Roman numerals on the left indicate the cortical lamina. S_1 and S_3 are two kinds of spiny stellate neurons; S_2 is a "star pyramid." NS is another kind of stellate cell characterized as being nonspiny and neurogliform. Note the entry of the afferents into the system at level 4. The other major cell types are defined in the text. (From Szentágothai, in press.)

demonstrated anatomically by Szentágothai. I shall discuss the current status of the theory of cortical columns in detail in Chapter 7.

In addition to this vertical columnar form of organization, there are also two other vertical organization patterns of the neurons found throughout a typical portion of the cerebral cortex. These vertical planes are shown in Fig. 3-69 where it can be seen that these two planes are oriented perpendicularly to each other, and their planar shape is defined by the orientation and projection of the axons and dendrites of the neurons contained within them.

The first of the two planes, shown on the left side of Fig. 3-69, is defined by the arborization of basket neurons. The dendrites and axons of basket neurons of this class are flattened, and although they run both up and down and across the plane, they do not pass out of the indicated plane. On the right side of Fig. 3-69, a perpendicular plane is defined by a peculiar H-shaped stellate neuron. Although the orientation of the plane is different, the arborization of this neuron is also limited to the indicated plane.

Szentágothai believes that the first of these two planes, the one on the left, specifically represents the region of inhibitory influence exerted by the basket neurons, which, he thinks, selectively inhibit pyramidal neurons. The H-shaped stellate neuron, on the other hand, is more probably an excitatory unit and may act to integrate the responses of a number of pyramidal neurons, as well as other cell types, that intersect with the plane defining its action space.

In conclusion, it should be reemphasized that these conceptual planes, cubes, and columns are not visible anatomical entities; they are merely regions of most probable influence, and they certainly are not as sharply demarcated as indicated in these idealized drawings. They do, however, attest to the fact that the brain is a highly organized structure and is not arranged in a random fashion. Szentágothai (in press) concludes that the neural tissue might be considered, in a certain sense, to even be quasicrystalline. Because of its nearly regular structure, he believes, it is far more likely to operate by emphasizing patterns of interaction across a distributed network of neurons than by virtue of any special properties of individual neurons. I have made this same point, which is quite contrary to much popular contemporary theorizing, on the basis of psychophysical data (Uttal, 1975a).

6. General Principles of Cytoarchitectonic Organization of the Central Nervous System

It is easy to become discouraged and assume that neural organization is so complex that we will never be able to understand how it might work. However, as we look over the various structures that have been considered so far in this chapter, it seems as if there does exist some general anatomic scheme that is common to all of these levels of neural information processing. The neurons of the spinal cord and the cortex, for example, are clearly not randomly scattered throughout the tissue of the various nuclei and centers. Order, rather than randomness, is the rule. Specific types of cells are found in specific places with specific kinds of synaptic connections. In the following section, I list a number of general principles of neural organization that do minimum violence to the known differences between the various centers, yet still emphasize the many ways in which they are cytoarchitectonically similar.

a. Three-Dimensional Lattice Arrangement (see Fig. 3-70a)

Perhaps the most omnipresent feature to appear in all of the structures we have discussed—from the retina to the cortex—is a basic three-dimensional, parallel lattice arrangement of the constituent neurons. All of the nuclei display a relatively regular organizational pattern that is not distributed as a plane or as a serial chain of units but almost universally in a way that stresses the three-dimensional volume arrangement. This simple parallel latticed organization suggests that the brain is quite unlike the digital computer, a device to which it is often compared.

The modern digital computer (properly referred to after its inventor as the von Neumann machine) is organized in a very different manner than these chunks of brain tissue. Almost all computer functions are carried out serially in the computer's logical structure. One input typically leads to one output, and intermediate steps are sequenced in serial fashion from one instruction to the next. Although some simple parallel information flow occurs as "bits" organized into computer "words," and although there have been some recent attempts to form parallel central processors, almost all modern computers are essentially serially organized. It is mainly for this reason that the mathematics of modern computer science have been so inapplicable to the modeling of brain functions. In fact, it should be acknowledged that, in general, we have no very good mathematical expressions for modeling neural network functions, nor do we have a long tradition of dealing with parallel processing of the sort that goes on in three-dimensional lattices, be they neural or electronic, numerical or nonnumerical.

b.   Layers and Columns (see Fig. 3-70b)

A direct corollary of the principle of the lattice-like arrangement is that the important neuronal nets are very likely to display some sort of layering. The layers may be either horizontal (perpendicular to the main flow of neural signals) or vertical (parallel to the flow of neural signals). Horizontal lamination is common in many nuclei and may be observed with relatively low power magnification. Vertical segregation is generally more subtle and may be columnar rather than planar.

c.   Multiple Inputs and Outputs (see Fig. 3-70c)

All of the three-dimensional neural nets previously considered have multiple inputs that are widely distributed over the afferent or input side of the receptor or nuclear space. Similarly, multiple outputs are usually distributed to multiple destinations from the efferent or output side of any nuclear mass.

d.   Multiple Lateral Connections (see Fig. 3-70d)

All of the neuronal nets that we have discussed are also heavily laterally interconnected. There are ubiquitous neuronal links that convey information patterns from a cell at one place in a horizontal layer or level to another place in the same layer or level. These lateral connectives are often reciprocal and may be either inhibitory or excitatory or both.

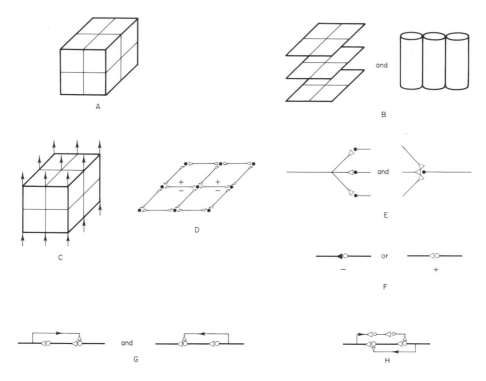

FIG. 3-70   The basic modes of arrangement and interconnection in neural tissue: (A) the basic cubical arrangement; (B) lamina and columns; (C) the predominantly unidirectional flow of information; (D) reciprocal excitation and inhibition; (E) divergence and convergence; (F) excitation and inhibition; (G) feedforward and feedbackward; and (H) temporal dispersion due to multiple pathways of different lengths and reverberation.

e.   Spatial Divergence and Convergence (see Fig. 3-70e)

It is also apparent that the effects of any signal that enters a three-dimensional neuronal lattice at any given input point will affect a large number of output points. This is the classic principle of organization known as *spatial divergence.* It is also the case that the output at any point will represent the effects of the inputs at many different points, reflecting the principle of spatial convergence. Therefore, there is, by definition, no possibility of any private wiring system for any receptor or motor unit. Information flow is always the integrated and modified resultant of a variety of inputs and can be expected to produce many outputs. This concept is considered in greater detail in Chapter 7.

f.   Inhibition as Well as Excitation (see Fig. 3-70f)

There is also an a priori requirement that some substantial portion, perhaps a majority, of the synapses that occur at the terminals of the myriad synaptic contacts of the three-dimensional lattice must be inhibitory. Otherwise the system would be in a constant state of universal excitement after the very first input signal, and no coherent adaptive response to complex stimuli would be possible.

g. Feedforward and Feedbackward (see Fig. 3-70g)

Another organizational property universally found in these neuronal nerve nets is some sort of feedbackward and feedforward communication links. Feedforward, in this particular case, refers to the communication of information through a connecting link that skips over some intermediate synapses, layers, or nuclei. Feedbackward refers to the organizational pattern in which information is passed back from some locus close to the output to some locus close to the input. In this manner the output can act to alter the input. Obviously, a hierarchy of feedback and feedforward systems must exist in the total nervous system.

h. Reverberation and Temporal Dispersion (see Fig. 3-70h)

The fact that there is feedbackward and feedforward as well as spatial divergence means that a pattern of output signals will generally be of longer duration than the initiating pattern of input signals, because multiple path lengths lead to a distribution of arrival times of single input signals at distant destinations. There is, furthermore, the possibility that signals may reexcite themselves through feedback mechanisms to perpetuate the response until some sort of inhibition or fatigue cancels the echoing loop. Thus, a number of organizational properties tend to temporally as well as spatially disperse the signals.

i. Directionality

Another implicit property of neural lattices that must be made explicit is the notion of a natural directionality or orthodromicity. I have repeatedly referred to both input sides and output sides of the lattice, and this defines a natural directionality of the main flow of information. In general, this directionality cannot be reversed. Directionality is imposed mainly because chemical synapses conduct in only one direction—from the presynaptic neurosecretory region to the postsynaptic neurochemical receptor region. However, added impetus to monodirectionality is also introduced by the refractory period of axons. Refractory periods—the period of inexcitability after action potentials—prevent a neuronal fiber from retrofiring backward in an "antidromic" direction under all but the most extraordinary conditions.

j. Quasicrystalline Arrangement

Finally, because of the structural order that becomes apparent in the light of the many studies of Szentagothai and other microneuroanatomists, it is clear that it may not be very appropriate to accept his suggestion that these neuronal lattices act as quasicrystals. Just as the regularity of spacing and geometric order of the microscopic structure of a true crystal leads to some macroscopic behavior, it may be that structural regularities in the neural lattice underlie some observed molar behavior on the part of organisms. Recent attention (Pribram, Nuwer, & Baron, 1974; John, 1972; and Uttal, 1975a) to "holographic" or autocorrelation-type theories, in which lattices of distributed but unspecialized neurons collectively perform functions often attributed to highly specialized individual neurons, has been extremely influential in suggesting an alternative manner in which these neural nets may perform their evolved functions. This problem is dealt with more extensively in Chapter 7, which is more concerned with the problems of neural representation.

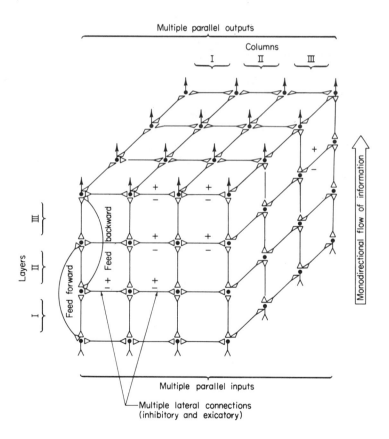

FIG. 3-71   A conceptual model of the arrangement of neurons in the nervous system embodying most of the basic modes of interconnection and organization described in Figure 3-70. Although the nervous system never looks as neat and orderly as shown, there is a great deal of intrinsic order.

Figure 3-71 is a summary drawing of a hypothetical, protypical slab of neuronal tissue that includes all of these fundamental characteristics. In a general sense, this prototypical neuronal cube represents the fundamental operating form of almost any portion of the central nervous system. It is within prototypical networks like this, representing a possible basic anatomical-functional unit building block of the central nervous system, that we would now localize all of the neuronal functions that are equivalents to psychological functions. A major task of modern psychobiology will be to develop a quantitative analysis of how "computation" is carried out in such networks.

If this heavily interconnected matrix of neurons seems to be approaching an unfortunately high degree of generality, one might also consider another important fact about the nervous system. Some authorities believe that any neuron is connected to any other neuron by a very small number of intervening steps. This neurophysiological embodiment of the "small world" effect has been best summed up by Szentágothai (1971) himself:

Considering the "lightning" speed with which messages can be stored away and even more with which they may be retrieved, one has also to speculate on how quickly information from any given site of the CNS might reach any number of other sites. This would mean in anatomical terms: how many synapses, on the average, would be needed in order to reach from a given neurone any other possible neurone of the CNS? Although we have no direct information at hand in answering this question, the number is remarkably low if one tries to think it over from what we know about CNS connectivity in general. It would be a fair guess to assume that the number ought to be somewhere around ten—as an order of magnitude. Restricting this speculation to the cerebrum, the number might even be reduced by a factor of two. This means that within ten synapses any point of the CNS would be connected—potentially—with any other. Consequently, the nervous system could be regarded, with minor restrictions, as something like a continuous medium [p. 24].

There is probably no better way to end this chapter, which has concentrated so heavily on the discrete neurons and nuclei of the nervous system, than by this quotation with its insightful suggestion that the discrete elements cooperate in some manner to produce what appears to be continuous behavior at the molar level. Much of the rest of this book will be directed at an elucidation of just how that transition occurs.

4

An Anatomy of the Mind

1. INTRODUCTION

1. Apology

As stated in Chapter 2, the ultimate goal of psychobiology is to determine the critical relationships between the structure of the brain and the processes of mind. In Chapter 3 I developed an anatomy of the brain. It is the purpose of this chapter to develop a corresponding anatomy of the mind. Just as Chapter 3 spelled out the structural units of the nervous system, the goal of this chapter is to spell out the units of process that make up the various components of our mental life.

This discussion specifically seeks to determine what mind is considered to be in contemporary thought, what the mental processes are, what behavioral indicators are available as clues to the intrapersonal mental states, and what instruments and procedures can be used to measure behavior and thus mind. The larger or holistic constructs that have been used to describe mental processes such as perception, motivation, learning, and thinking, are identified. These are the major categories and also the units of the conceptual framework that provide order to the contemporary scientific science of mind—experimental psychology.

This chapter does not attempt to do some things. It does not come to grips with some of the more complex aspects of mental life such as intelligence, personality, or that most elusive of all mental components, consciousness. In large part these grander issues must be considered to be composed of combinations of more fundamental mental processes. This chapter also does not consider, except in passing example, any more detailed analysis of mental functions to even simpler forms of behavior, a process emphasized by those psychologists who call themselves "experimental analysts of behavior." These more finely divided behavioral "atoms" are only invoked as necessary to make specific points in the chapters that follow. Nor will I be concerned with the ontogenetic development of mental processes. Developmental psychology is a field of such enormity and complexity and is in such a state of flux that it would only be abused by the brief attention it could receive in this chapter.

In spite of these intended limitations, I must candidly admit that this is the chapter that pleases me the least and, if I am not mistaken, will please most psychobiologists the least of any in this book. The task that I can, at best, only briefly and vaguely carry out is gargantuan! Nevertheless, most psychobiologists have been totally remiss in even preliminary attempts at an adequate classification of psychological processes for which they seek neurophysiological correlations, and I believe the rest of the book would suffer without this chapter. However, it should also be admitted that it is possible that the task attempted here is, in fact, impossible. At least some psychologists feel that the data are simply not yet available to produce a universally acceptable anatomy of the mind.

Another difficulty is that the problem of levels of explanation alluded to in Chapter 1 has an analog in any attempt to develop an anatomy of mind that is particularly troublesome. The psychobiologist is constantly faced with the formidable question: What is the most appropriate mental unit for which to seek some neurophysiological correlate? Not only is this a complex problem, but it is probably not even a consistent one. The "most appropriate" mental units must certainly vary with the level of task complexity. The "best" level varies from a simple mental act to a more complex one as the experimental design progresses from a reflex, to a consummatory act like drinking, to learning, to problem solving, to such complex mental conglomerates as personality. This difficulty produces a characteristic imbalance in most psychobiological experiments. Great attention is usually given to the precise placement of the microelectrode or the surgical ablation; little to the precise conceptual identification of the behavior to be measured. Many psychobiological experiments are seriously flawed in this regard, and the specification of the mental states (or even the behaviors) being studied is sometimes exceedingly fuzzy. Only a few psychobiologists like Welker (1971), Hinde (1970), and Fentress (1973) have ever paid serious attention to this problem.

2. Apologia

What, then, does justify even the limited goals of this chapter? The answer to this question can best be made concrete by referring to an anecdotal experience. One of the most startling experiences of my teaching career occurred a few years ago during a meeting with an entering class of experimental psychology graduate students. Curious to know how they perceived the subject matter that was to be the target of the careers on which they were embarking, I asked them three questions. First, what is psychology? Second, what is experimental psychology? Finally, what is mind? To say the very least, the answers were exceedingly disappointing. Here was the absolute cream of the graduate student body in experimental psychology, and yet none of them was able to even suggest what it was that they were studying, or what they were going to be doing, other than to cite a few examples of current research.

In retrospect, it was, of course, an unfair set of questions; these are surprisingly complicated issues, and quick answers to such questions almost always result in definitions that are essentially circular. (Mind is what psychologists study! Psychology is the science of mind or behavior! Intelligence is what I.Q. tests measure!) It is probably the case that good answers to these questions cannot be given in a few words.

As noted earlier, a satisfactorily precise definition of mind is a major undertaking, and one fraught with linguistic, philosophical, and technical hazards. However, whatever the difficulties, it is still necessary to strive for a more precise definition of mind if the goal of this book is to be achieved. We shall also see how the approach to a definition simultaneously leads to an understanding of the meaning of the terms *psychology* and *experimental psychology*. Without a definition and anatomy of mind, the search for an understanding of the relationship between mind and body becomes vacuous. The best answer to the question of justification of this chapter is that whatever can be done must be done to avoid this trap of nebulosity. The intended purpose of this chapter, therefore, is to establish at least a first approximation to a satisfactory definition of mind, and in addition, to develop the beginnings of an analytic approach to the study of mental processes. However superfluous this task may seem to some behavioristically oriented psychologists or neurophysiologically oriented psychobiologists, such a definitional and categorizational framework is a necessary precursor to the discussion in succeeding chapters.

As I look back to the previous chapter on neuroanatomy and begin this one, I appreciate how wonderfully easy it was to create an anatomy of the brain. Although the structure of the brain is complicated, there is a simple and general underlying anatomical theme—the expansion into the mature brain during the embryological development from the primitive neural tube. Furthermore, the anatomy of the brain is "real," concrete, straightforward, and physically interpretable, even if it is structurally complex due to the many intertwined parts. The neuroanatomy was conceptualized in a simple and direct manner by reference to physical sturctures that had specific and intuitively reasonable dimensions of shape, size, and location. The various parts of the brain could thus be measured, separated, and dealt with in terms of physical dimensions for which we humans have a powerful repertoire of measuring instruments, in addition to an existing conceptual anchor. Substructures of the brain do not coexist in the same space; there are precise and coherent boundaries between these substructures that can be observed either with a microscope or with a recording electrode.

The mind, on the other hand, is much more difficult to conceptually comprehend. Whatever mind is, it is not localizable in space, and its component parts are not describable in terms of the measures of size, mass, and shape to which we are intuitively anchored. Thus, we do not have a physically distinct, concrete reference system against which to test our hypotheses of "mental anatomy" as we do have when we test our hypotheses of neuroanatomy against the observed structure of the brain.

Perhaps even more frustrating in the quest for a definition and classification of mental processes is that the mind is composed of a set of processes that are redundant, overlapping, interacting, and, just possibly, they may not be actually demarcatable from each other. Rather, we shall see that any aspect of mind measured by the techniques of modern experimental psychology is so closely linked to almost any other that there is always some question of just precisely which aspect it is that is being measured. Indeed, as one surveys the abundant literature of modern experimental psychology, it is completely obvious that the same experimental paradigm, the same task, and the same data can be used as a means of studying several different and supposedly independent processes.

However unanchored these mental processes may be to convenient physical measures or to clearly defined, concrete structures, such practical difficulties should not be interpreted to mean that the measuring instruments available to psychologists are, in any fundamental sense, less adequate or less precise than those available to anatomists. The difficulty lies not in the problem of how one goes about measuring mental processes, but in that of defining what is to be measured. In this chapter, I also describe some of the methods used by psychologists in their search for measures of mind.

There is a curious perplexity implicit in this discussion that should be faced from the beginning. In spite of the fact that the brain is easy to describe and analyze because of its structural concreteness, and although the mind is, in fact, very difficult to understand because of its lack of concreteness, almost everyone concerned acts as if the opposite were true. Most people are quite willing to admit that they are not experts on brain anatomy; yet, almost everyone is an expert on the mind and on human behavior in general. However, the reader should make no mistake; the exposition of a mental anatomy is much more difficult than the development of a neuroanatomy.

One of the reasons that it is difficult to communicate *inter*personally about the mind is that most of the important observable aspects of mind are patently *intra*personal and thus not easily communicated, except through indirect means. The indirect communication medium in all known cases is behavior, seen, heard, felt, smelled, or tasted, despite the ubiquitous persistence of popular nonscientific parapsychology. It is a limitation of modern scientific experimental psychology that we have no means of describing "raw feels" (as Feigl calls them) to each other, except through the indirect route of behavioral observation.

It is very important to keep clear the distinction between *intra*personal mental processes and *inter*personal behavioral transactions. As we have seen, the lack of clarity of this distinction led to a metaphysical solution by the logical positivists and behaviorists that was terribly unsatisfying. The behaviorist might propose language (Wittgenstein, 1922; 1953), art (Langer, 1953; 1967), or some other form of behavior as the metaphysical reality, but in each of these cases, it was a lack of such a clear distinction between interpersonal behavioral responses and the intrapersonal mental processes that misled them to identify behavior with mind.

B.   TOWARD A DEFINITION OF MIND

How does one begin to search for a definition of a word such as *mind*? Words are entities whose denotative meaning is a matter of consensus, and a first approximation to what most people mean by mind, reflecting social and linguistic evolution, can thus be reasonably sought in a good modern dictionary. Next, I consider what some of the most important thinkers of modern times have had to say about their interpretation of the word, and then I move on to explore the substance of the subject of modern experimental psychology in order to abstract the essence of what the word *mind* means in practice as well as in theory.

1.   Dictionaries

The first thing to do in our search for a definition of mind is simply to consult a dictionary. Although a conventional dictionary is not a technical document, the definitions that it contains do encompass generally accepted views of the use of any word. For example, the following definition of the word *mind* is found in the 1966 edition of the *Random House Unabridged Dictionary:*

mind (mind), *n.*

1. (in a human or other conscious being) the element, part, substance, or process that reasons, thinks, feels, wills, perceives, judges, etc.: *the processes of mind.*

2. *Psychol.* the totality of conscious and unconscious mental processes and activities of the organism.

3. intellect or understanding, as distinguished from the faculties of feeling and willing; intelligence.

4. a particular instance of the intellect or intelligence, as in a person.

5. a person considered with reference to intellectual power: *the greatest minds of the time.*

6. intellectual power or ability.

7. reason, sanity, or sound mental condition: *to lose one's mind.*

8. a way of thinking and feeling; disposition; temper: *To my mind, it was a foolish mistake.*

9. opinion or sentiments: *to change one's mind.*

10. inclination or desire: *to be of a mind to listen.*

11. purpose, intention, or will: *Let me know your mind in this matter before Tuesday.*

12. psychic or spiritual being, as opposed to matter.

13. a conscious or intelligent agency or being: *an awareness of a mind ordering the universe.*

14. remembrance or recollection: *Former days were called to mind.*

15. attention; thoughts: *He can't keep his mind on his studies. Maybe this will take your mind off your troubles.*

16. *Rom. Cath. Ch.* a commemoration of a person's death, esp. by a Requiem Mass. Cf. month's mind, year's mind.

17. (*cap.*) Also called Divine Mind. *Christian Science.* the concept of the noncorporeal as the single source of life, substance, and intelligence. Cf. mortal mind.

18. bear or keep in mind, to remember: *Bear in mind that the newspaper account may be in error.*

19. cross one's mind, to occur suddenly to one: *A disturbing thought crossed her mind.*

20. give someone a piece of one's mind, *Informal.* a. to express an uncomplimentary opinion bluntly. b. to reprimand; scold: *I'll give him a piece of my mind for telling such a lie!*

21. have a good mind to, to intend to; feel tempted or inclined to: *I have a good mind to leave you here all alone.*

22. have half a mind to, to be almost decided to; be disposed toward.

23. know one's own mind, to be firm in one's intentions, opinions, or plans; have assurance: *She may be only a child, but she knows her own mind.*

24. make up one's mind, to decide; resolve: *He couldn't make up his mind which course to follow.*

25. meeting of minds, complete agreement; accord: *A meeting of minds between the union and the employer seemed impossible.*

26. on one's mind, constantly in one's thoughts; of concern to one: *The approaching trial was on his mind.*

27. presence of mind, ability to think and to remain in control of oneself during a crisis or under stress: *She had enough presence of mind to remember the license plate of the speeding car.*

28. put in mind, to cause to remember; remind: *The reunion put us in mind of our college days.*

29. to one's mind, in accord with one's judgment or opinion: *To my mind, she'll always be an unpleasant person to deal with.*

—*v.t.*

30. to pay attention to, heed, or obey (a person, advice, instructions, etc.).

31. to apply oneself or attend to: *to mind one's own business.*

32. to look after; take care of; tend: *to mind the baby; Who's minding the store?*

33. to be careful, cautious, or wary concerning: *Mind what you say.*

34. to feel concern at; care about.

35. to feel disturbed or inconvenienced by; object to (usually used in negative or interrogative constructions): *Would you mind handing me that book?*

36. to regard as concerning oneself or as mattering: *Never mind his bluntness.*

37. *Dial.* to perceive or notice.

38. *Dial.* a. to remember. b. to remind.

—*v.i.*

39. to obey.

40. to take notice, observe, or understand (used chiefly in the imperative): *Mind now, I want you home by twelve.*

41. to be careful or wary.

42. to care, feel concern, or object (often used in negative or interrogative constructions): *Mind if I go? Don't mind if I do.*

43. to regard a thing as concerning oneself or as mattering: *You mustn't mind about their gossiping.*

44. never mind, don't bother; it is of no concern: *Never mind—the broken glass will be easy to replace.*

[ME *mynd(e)*, OE *gemynd* commemoration; c. Goth *gamunds*; akin to L *mens* mind]

—Syn.

1. reason. MIND, INTELLECT, INTELLIGENCE refer to mental equipment or qualities. MIND is that part of man which thinks, feels, and wills, as contrasted with body: *His mind was capable of grasping the significance of the problem.* INTELLECT is reasoning power as distinguished from feeling; it is often used in a general sense to characterize high mental ability: *to appeal to the intellect, rather than the emotions.* INTELLIGENCE is ability to learn and to understand; it is also mental alertness or quickness of understanding: *A dog has more intelligence than many other animals.*

6. MIND, BRAIN, BRAINS may refer to mental capacity. MIND is the philosophical and general term for the center of mental activity, and is therefore used of intellectual powers: *a brilliant mind.* BRAIN is properly the physiological term for the organic structure which makes mental activity possible (*The brain is the center of the nervous system.*), but it is often applied, like mind, to intellectual capacity: *a fertile brain.* BRAINS is the anatomical word *(the brains of an animal used for food)*, but in popular usage, it is applied to intelligence (particularly of a shrewd, practical nature): *To run a business takes brains.*

10. bent, leaning, proclivity, penchant; wish, liking.

11. intent.

14. memory.

30. mark.   [from *Random House Unabridged Dictionary,* 1966, p. 911, with the permission of the publishers].

It is clear, as one reads this example of tedious dictionary prose, that a common thread connects all of the different definitions. In each and every case, whether the word is used as a noun (3), or as a verb (30), or even when it refers to a material body (5) rather than to a mental state, the common emphasis running through all of the various uses of the word is on some aspect of the process rather than on the material structure. Thus, the word may be used in a highly specific sense as a synonym for memory (19), or attention (26), or any of the number of other processes mentioned. But, in all cases, it refers to actions, or at least to structures that are distinguished by the dynamics of their performance rather than their locus, mass, or shape.

A second observation about these many definitions of mind is that the referent is not a singular or unitary entity but rather is very often a composite that gathers within a single rubric a large number of more elementary mental functions. The question of the relationship of these elementary functions is discussed shortly.

This definition from an unabridged dictionary is thus an eclectic one and may, with some interest, be contrasted to the highly abridged technical definition that is found in a good medical dictionary, for example, *Stedman's Medical Dictionary* (Stedman, 22nd ed., 1972). Here the definition of mind is much more abbreviated. The medical dictionary says only: "[A.S. gemynd] the Psyche; the organ or seat of consciousness, remembering, reasoning, and willing [p. 787]." Although this definition also implies that mind is an aggregate of a number of processes, its emphasis is quite different. It strongly suggests that mind is a concrete entity—one that is comparable to any other tissue or "organ" of the body, and one that can be localized sufficiently well to be identified as the "seat" of the mental processes, which are then exemplified. The definition is, therefore, expressed in the structural terminology of the anatomist or biomedical practitioner and not in the process terms of the psychologist. It contrasts sharply, in this regard, with the definitions from the unabridged dictionary.

2. More Technical Definitions

This, then, is a beginning but, as previously noted, it is hardly possible to give an adequate definition of mind in a few words. Dictionaries, in their telegraphic style, tend to suggest and obscure rather than to reveal and sharpen. One next step in the search for a complete and adequate definition is to consider the writings of thoughtful men who have wrestled with this problem throughout history. Is it possible that, in their definition, they have circumscribed a set of topics that may lead us to a satisfactory anatomy of mind? Obviously, a number of authors have dedicated more or less complete monographs in their attemps to define mind (see, for example, Polten, 1973; Kantor, 1971; Scher, 1962; Hook, 1960), and it is the content of the entire works that must be considered to be their definition. But are there also capsule definitions that can help us toward our goal?

Some authors (e.g., Russell & Russell, 1962) have said that a definition of mind is not an attainable goal at the present time. All that can be done now, they argue, is to provide the groundwork prerequisite to achieving a definition by spelling out all of the different aspects of the meaning of mind. The Russells assert that no brief definition is going to satisfy those who demand complete closure.

It should also be noted that a number of workers have sought to discuss the use of the term *mind* without coming directly to grips with its actual meaning. Thus, by avoiding the issue, these authors implicitly make the assumption that the popular, consensual, or common-law notion of what the word mind means, reflective as it is of history and linguistic evolution, may be as good as can be done.

Accepting such a weak form of definition, however, is not without its perils. The content matter of psychology is defined in large part by what is specifically meant by mind at any point in history. Thus the nature of the psychological theories and even the empirical data base are very sensitive to the currently accepted definition of mind. On these grounds, we should not be satisfied with such consensual definitions, no matter how difficult it may be to obtain a more precise one.

There are, fortunately, a number of writers who have accepted the challenge posed by the need for a more rigorous definition of mind and who have contributed to its contemporary technical concept. In the following paragraphs, several definitions of mind are quoted. My goal is to present these definitions juxtaposed in a way that allows us to determine if there is any common thread of agreement upon which to base a rigorous definition.

First, let us consider St. Thomas Aquinas' (1968) definition of mind, an example of a classical dualistic view:

> The principle of intellectual activity, which we term the human soul, is a bodiless and completely substantial principle.
>
> This principle, also termed the mind of intellect, can act without the body having an intrinsic part in the activity. Nothing can act independently unless it be independent [p. 23].

This still popular view is not the sort of definition with which psychobiologists feel very comfortable. Hopefully, our discussion in Chapter 2 clarified this point. Yet, even St. Thomas, in the depths of his dualism, begins to suggest a theme that has persisted—that of action.

Remember also at this point the discussion of Chapter 2, where it was noted that there are other definitions of mind that, though much more modern, are as equally unfruitful as St. Thomas'; for example, the positions of the logical positivists and the behaviorists who equate mind with behavior, and Ryle's (1949) suggestion that the mind is but the artificial creation of a "category mistake." Ryle, in rejecting both idealism and materialism, rejected any denotive meaning for the word mind, other than as a catchall for the "dispositional intent" of the organism—an almost useless teleological concept.

Both of these approaches, that exemplified by Ryle's linguistic "mistake" and theological dualism, are, of course, extreme positions. Both offer little in our search for a definition of mind that can guide scientific research. One approach—positivism—denies, for either pragmatic or metaphysical reasons, the very existence of mind; the other approach—dualism—gives mind an independent existence, which isolates it from the realm of modern science. Interestingly Beloff (1962), a distinguished modern dualist, has pointed out that parapsychological observations are the only really cogent arguments for the dualistic point of view; and if that suspicious source of difficult-to-replicate data should fizzle out, as many expect it will, then he, at least, feels that all will be lost for the dualistic position.

Ryle's approach, on the other hand, denies the most immediate datum of all, that of self-awareness. For if mind does not exist, what is the explanation for the unique, individual experience of self-awareness?

The middle view—that mind exists but only in intimate and inseparable relation to the body—is the one to which most psychobiologists now ascribe. It is a view that stresses the fact that mind and brain are but two aspects of the same metaphysical reality; and that both are real, measurable, and researchable. One is mechanism, and the other is the action of the mechanism.

Let us now survey how the meaning of the word *mind* has been expressed by a number of more or less modern philosophers, psychologists, and neuroscientists in a way that is more consistent with this middle view. First, I turn to the father of modern experimental psychology, Wilhelm Wundt (1968):

> What now is the *nature of mind?*. . .Our mind is nothing else than the sum of our inner experiences, than our ideation, feeling, and willing collected together to a unity in consciousness, and rising in a series of developmental stages to culminate in self-conscious thought and a will that is morally free. At no point in our explanation of the interconnection of these inner experiences have we found occasion to apply this attribute of mentality to anything else than the concrete complex of idea, feeling, and will. The fiction of a transcendental substance, of which actual mental content is only the outward manifestation, a fleeting shadow-picture thrown by the still unknown reality of the mind,—such a theory misses the essential difference between the inner and the outer experience, and threatens to turn to mere empty show all that lends solid value and real significance to our mental life [p. 128].

Note that Wundt also emphasizes the notion of a complex of subprocesses.

And now a few nutshell definitions of mind as expressed by a number of current psychologists and philosophers. First, an eminent philosopher, Smythies (1965):

> If we start off with an unambiguous ostensive definition of sense-data—as I have attempted to do—we can use this then to define 'mind' to account for one important meaning of this complex word in the sense of *conscious* mind. We can say that X's mind is X's collection of sense-data, images, thoughts, emotions and his Ego. 'Mind', of course is used in *other* senses to include his capacities, intelligence and certain features of his personality—psychological aspects of 'mind'; whereas my definition covers its much-neglected existential (even *anatomical*) aspects [p. 102].

Next, from one of the most thoughtful critics of modern psychology, Kantor (1935):

> Mind is individual. There is no such thing as mind in general. The psychologist who thinks of mind in any other way is hopelessly lost in the morass of mysticism. Moreover, mind is essentially a phenomenon pertaining to particular organisms or persons. Furthermore, mind is not a substance or quality, but action—the ways in which an individual adapts himself to the things and conditions of his milieu. Now psychological action is always interaction. This means that if I take one of two things offered me, I do so because of an effect that thing has upon me. Both I and the thing are mutually acting upon each other. It appeals to me and I am attracted to it. This interactional process has evolved during the course of my psychological life. Psychologists refer to this evolution as the individual's reactional biography. To trace out the evolution of all the myriads of such interactions summed up by the term *my mind*, means to study as many as possible of the billions of specific conditions which are the unique and indispensable features of that evolution [p. 456].

Kantor's definition, it should be noted, also stresses the notion of mind as individualistic and as process.

From an elementary textbook by a distinguished physiological psychologist, Hebb (1958):

> Mind is an activity of the brain and our knowledge of it is chiefly theoretical, *inferred from behavior* rather than being obtained directly from self-observation [pp. 2-3].

From an equally distinguished neuroscientist, Rosenblueth (1970):

> Under the expression mental states or events I am including all our conscious experiences, sensations, feeling, emotions, thoughts and reasonings, doubts, beliefs, desires, volitions, and also our memories of these experiences. The fact that we have memories has several consequences: it gives us a consciousness of a temporal succession of events; it allows us to compare present with past experiences; and it permits us to integrate a personality, a mental "I" with a history and some continuity not interfered with by sleep and other periods of unconsciousness.
>
> I wish to emphasize that I am not postulating the existence of "minds" as individual independent entities with specific properties and laws, but only that of mental events. In addition, I am referring exclusively to mental processes of which someone is aware, and I am excluding the possibility that there may exist similar unconscious processes [p. 66].

Or from John Eccles (1970), whose modern trialism was extensively discussed in Chapter 2:

> I feel that there is still confusion in the use of such words as mind, mental, mentality, which in some extremely primitive form are even postulated as being a property of inorganic matter! Hence I have refrained from using them, and employ instead either "conscious experience" or "consciousness" [p. 64].

Or from a congress of psychoanalysts (Cobb, 1959):

> Mind is the integration in action, the relationship of one part of the brain to another. The physical integers or units are the nerve impulse. Mind is a function of the brain just as contraction is a function of muscle or as circulation is a function of the blood-vascular system [p. 11].

and (Murphy, 1959):

> The term "mind" is a holistic concept embracing conscious and unconscious mental phenomena as well as identity and character [p. 22].

And finally, from an important modern neuroscientist, Kety (1960):

> There remains one biological phenomenon, more central to psychiatry than to other fields, for which there is no valid physiochemical model and (or so it seems to me) little likelihood of developing one; this is the phenomenon of consciousness—the complex of present sensations and the memory of past experience which we call the mind [p. 1867].

In the following section I have tried to abstract the common features of all of these definitions.

3. Common Features of Definitions of the Word *Mind*

Although the preceding definitions of mind come from authors with a wide variety of backgrounds and philosophical orientations, there is a common thread of agreement throughout all of them. In the following section, I examine that common thread, tabulate the fundamental characteristics, and list the thematic aspects of a more complete and general definition of mind.

1. Mind is an individual and not a community process. With the exception of a few obscure uses of the word (in ways that usually turn out to be more closely related to the technical, sociological, or anthropological use of the word *culture*), mind is always used as a descriptor of processes that are going on within the limits of a single individual, never in a community. A "meeting of the minds" is a literary metaphor, not a scientific device.

2. If mind is truly individualistic in the manner described in (1), it is by definition intrapersonal. Direct interpersonal communication of primary mental states or actions, therefore, is not possible.

3. Although mind is intrapersonal and individualistic, and thus inaccessible to direct observation by others, it is by no means unreal, supernatural, or unmeasurable. There are many ways of communicating information about mental states interpersonally, including language, art, and simple observation of behavior, as well as formal techniques for observing, describing, and measuring behavior in the psychological laboratory. However, all interpersonally observable behavior of this sort must be considered to be media of communication of intrapersonal mental processes and neither the subject matter of psychology, or the equivalent, in any sense other than as a symbolic indicator, of the intrapersonal aspects of the mind. In other words, the fact that mind must be observed through the medium of behavior does not mean that mind is a metaphysically invalid concept. The reality of astronomical bodies or nuclear particles is not usually rejected because they must be observed and measured through the medium of transmitted light or recoil reactions, nor should the reality of mind be rejected because it must be observed through the medium of behavior. The fact that mind can only be measured by using behavior as an indicator is a practical, and not a metaphysical or conceptual, constraint.

4. Mind is process or function and is not material. Mind is not an organ, rather it is a function of material organs. It is no more reasonable to separate the functions of mind from the mechanics of the brain than it is to separate the process or action of rotation from the mechanics of a wheel or motor. Mind is not an "ectoplasmic bile" secreted by the brain but more akin to the act of secretion. Mind is, in this sense, the result of the spatio-temporal pattern of organization of material components and not any part of the material components themselves. This notion of mind as action, process, or form has a long history. It was the essence of Aristotle's concept of mind and was implicit in the psychology of William James (1890).

5. Intrapersonal mind is indistinguishable in most regards from a host of other philosophical, theological, and scientific near-synonyms like "consciousness," "awareness," "soul," or the "true ego." Substituting these words for mind serves no useful linguistic function and, in most cases, even further confuses the issue by introducing irrelevant and superfluous meanings. Such a substitution does not alleviate the difficulties encountered in defining the complex and multivariate referent of the term. However, the word "consciousness" is particularly important, for it has acquired many additional connotations beyond that of the word *mind*. Consciousness now often specifically refers to awareness, but even more specifically, we shall see in later sections of this chapter how it can be more clearly understood if its meaning is restricted to its near-synonym "attention."

6. Finally, we have to consider the problem of whether or not mind is an aggregate of relatively independent subprocesses or whether it is a holistic entity of which the subprocesses are only selective reflections resulting from our research procedures. This is a particularly sensitive and difficult matter because most experimental psychologists today would assert that they study only one of the "subprocesses" at a time. Most psychological researchers today identify themselves as either students of perception or learning or performance rather than of the whole mind. If, however, at some level of reality, the mind is actually holistic, then each of the experimental paradigms, although supposedly designed to study one isolated subprocess, is, in fact, suffering from a bad case of "the blind men and the elephant" syndrome. Certainly, upon close scrutiny, it becomes extremely difficult to completely segregate any psychological measurement procedure so that we can be sure that it is examining only a single one of the many possible subprocesses of mind. Indeed, any experiment, no matter how carefully designed, does always seem to involve almost all of the input, cognitive, memorial, and output process that can be conceived of, at least to a degree. Thus mind, from an operational point of view, does seem to be inherently holistic and not divisible into parts. Psychology, obviously, has not yet come to grips with this problem.

Although we cannot resolve this issue completely now, it is clear that modern psychologists constantly strive to *analyze* mind, and ubiquitous in the modern empirical psychological approach is a continued effort to find paradigms that will probe only one or another aspect of mind. Yet it is common to find that students of memory, perception, and performance are all often carrying out exactly the same type of experiment. There is the disturbing possibility, therefore, that current attempts to analyze mind are basically fallacious and have little bearing on this central and important issue.

I have now surveyed the views of many previous workers and attempted to extract from them some essential areas of common agreement. The definition of mind thus distilled is a very general and preliminary one, however, and while setting some limits, is not precise enough to act as an experimental guide.

Another, more operational, approach toward a definition of mind is to simply assert that mind is nothing other than a complete description of the subject matter of modern scientific psychology. In the following section, I consider this alternative approach as a means of achieving a more precise definition of mind.

Before I consider this approach to a definition of mind, however, it should be noted that it too can only result in an imperfect answer to a very difficult question. Such an approach suggests that whatever mind is, it is to be a function of the time at which it is measured. The minds of the tenth, twentieth, and thirtieth centuries would be very different from each other if this approach were taken too seriously. It might be better to qualify the following discussion by indicating that the entries to be made in the anatomy are only the currently measurable, quantifiable, and assayable aspects of mind. These are the aspects of which contemporary psychology has an operational grasp. This is not, however, to say that this "mental" anatomy is all there is to mind, or that the portions now in sight are all there ever will be, but rather that these are the parts now amenable to psychobiological comparisons. And that, dear reader, is the name of the game we are playing in this book.

C. THE SUBJECT MATTER OF PSYCHOLOGY AS A DEFINITION OF MIND

1. Introduction

I now undertake briefly to review what practitioners of the modern science of experimental psychology believe to be the subject of their investigations. By defining the subject matter of psychology as fundamentally the study of mental processes measured by specific behavioral tests, we can bring an operational concreteness to a definition of mind. Although this approach is useful, it too is admittedly flawed, first by the fact that scientific psychology at any given point in its development need not necessarily be (nor, for that matter, is it likely to be) all-inclusive of every aspect of mind. Thus, it would be impossible for even an army of psychologists to be studying all aspects of mental processes at any one time.

Second, this approach is flawed by the epistemological fact that the convenient analyses of mental processes may not serve biological reality as well as they serve experimental psychologists. The point is that psychologists place a restrictive emphasis on the particular laboratory manipulations that they perform by means of criteria of accessibility, instrumentation, and/or complexity. In addition to limiting the scope of empirical research, these constraints also dictate the construction of concepts and theories of mind in a manner that may distort our view of the actual underlying metaphysical reality (see Chapter 2). A term like *perception*, for example, conveniently emphasizes the information-acquisition aspects of the organism for the experimenter; but the question remains—Are the actual processes denoted by terms like learning, perception, and performance really separable, or is this separation forced upon the experimenter in the laboratory simply an artifact? Can a perception experiment be done without involving memory or learning or without the intervention of some sort of thinking or problem-solving process?

These questions are not simply esoteric philosophism, rather they are fundamental to our acceptance and evaluation of new knowledge. Indeed, very basic and practical considerations are vitally involved in these questions. For example, if mind is, in fact, unitary and is best considered holistically rather than as an aggregate of parts, what then becomes of the enormous body of work done on localization in various portions of the brain of the subprocesses, most of which must be considered to be spuriously analyzed from this point of view? If memory is, in fact, distributed throughout the brain, as most psychobiologists would assert (see Chapters 8 and 9), is it meaningful to look for a particular anatomic locus that is uniquely or even mainly associated with mnemonic processes? In this context it is clear that a host of empirical laboratory and conceptual questions arise that are loaded with the utmost significance for psychobiology. Although we cannot yet resolve the controversy between mind as an aggregate of independent though interactive processes on the one hand, and mind as a holistic unity on the other, neither can we ignore it.

2. Schools, Methods, and Approaches

a. Introduction

There are a number of ways to ask what experimental psychology is about. In order to determine what aspects of mind have come under empirical scrutiny, one might, for example, look at the various divisions of a large department of psychology, or at the practical fields of modern applied or therapeutic psychology, or even at the theoretical schools of thought that have dominated one or another stage of psychological history. Obviously, all of these possible sources of insight would be misleading in one way or another in our attempt to define mind, because each approach reflects but a small portion of the total problem. However, by considering these approaches, we may learn something about the nature of mind.

Let us begin by considering what at best can be only a very indirect clue—the administrative structure of modern psychology departments. They are usually divided into subsections or areas that might, at first glance, seem to demarcate content areas: Physiological, experimental, mathematical, clinical, developmental, social, and personality are usually found in most large departments. In some of the larger or more specialized departments, sections on behavioral genetics, engineering, comparative, and community psychology, are also found. A few departments even have areas that specialize in psychological history or psychopharmacology.

Do these subject areas comprise the full content of modern psychology? The answer to this question is unequivocally no! Surprisingly, a little reflection leads to the conviction that all of these administrative areas define methodological approaches rather than the content matter of psychology itself. Perception may be studied from the point of view of the experimentalist in a laboratory, from the point of view of perceptual development in infants, from the point of view of its physiological correlates, or even from the point of view that is concerned with abnormal perception in clinical cases. Similarly, learning is a phenomenon that is of common interest to faculty and students associated with many of the areas or subsections.

Looking over these organizational structures, I conclude that psychology, as it is administered in modern universities, is often more concerned with methodologies than it is with the content. Although there is something to be learned from this organization, it is, therefore, obviously not a definitive clue to the nature of the mind that we are searching for. It is instead a useful description of the methodologies of contemporary psychological science.

Another somewhat more deceptive but equally inadequate list of psychological subject matters may be found within those areas that have come to be called *applied psychology*. For example, intelligence and personality are terms that some say denote the subject matter of psychology. Unfortunately, these semipopular concepts are not very useful because they are composites of many much more fundamental aspects of mental process. Intelligence, for example, although a practical and useful notion and, to many laymen, one of the "basic" components of mind, more properly should be considered a conceptual oversimplification. It is quite obvious to the psychologist that intelligence is an uncritical composite of many of the perceptual, cognitive, and response aspects of mind that can be much more sharply defined.

Another direction that we might take in this search for the subject matter of psychology, and thus for a definition of mind, is to consider the theoretical schools of thought that have characterized the history of psychology. A comprehensive review of such intellectual superstructures as associationalism, structuralism, functionalism, behaviorism, and Gestalt psychology may be found in Marx and Hillix (1973), and one could now add to this list the information-processing-physiological approach, which is so dominant in modern psychology. But once again, these schools of thought are better considered as approaches and points of view rather than as actual content matter.

Where, then, can we go in our quest for a definition of mind through an examination of the content matter of psychology? I would propose that the best place would be to the psychological laboratory itself and to the reports therefrom for clues to the mental processes that the experimental psychologists think they are studying. In doing so, however, we must be continuously careful to distinguish between these mental processes (the true object of the investigations), the dependent variables that are measured, and the tools that are used for the measurement. Response dimensions and behavior are important, but they are not, to reiterate this critically important point, the subject matter of psychology.

Before listing the basic psychological processes that may be considered to collectively constitute mind, it is necessary to ask if there is any obvious scheme of categorization into which the various processes could be organized. One scheme for classifying mental processes is a tripartite division consisting of input processes, central or cognitive processes, and output processes. This trichotomy is recently derived from modern information and communication theories but, as we saw in Chapter 2, has antecedents in antiquity. In attempting to apply this scheme to mental processes, it became clear, however, that the concept of "input" includes only a single subject matter (sensory processes), and the concept of "output" refers only to motor performance and (perhaps) to some less germane aspects of speech. It also became clear, upon a little reflection, that neither of these two categories really is at the heart of what is meant by mind in contemporary psychology.

The study of sensory processes, for example, may be thought of as including two subdivisions. The first is a neurophysiological analysis of the signaling methods used by afferent mechanisms. The second is a phenomenological analysis of a set of relatively simple and discrete psychophysical phenomena that may, indeed, be more appropriately incorporated into the rubric of the central cognitive processes collectively referred to as *perception*. Furthermore, descriptions of the mental processes that lead to motor or linguistic performance also turn out to include many cognitive aspects that are better subsumed under other central headings (for example, decision making). The effects of muscular mass, efferent neural coding, and neuromotor interactions are, like sensory coding, not at the core of the subject matter either. Therefore, both afferent signaling and efferent performance processes are not considered in the following list.

When we weigh these restrictions, what is meant by mind becomes much more closely identifiable with those topics that collectively make up the subject matter of *cognitive* psychology, and it is to these topics that I turn in hope of achieving an adequate definition of mind. This circumscription of the inquiry, itself, is also a step forward in our quest. I now can be somewhat more precise as I note that mind is to be defined in terms of the set of processes studied by experimental *cognitive* psychologists. Similarly, just what cognitive psychology denotes also takes on a more precise significance as we likewise constrain its broad scope to the central-nervous-system-mediated set of processes that only incidentally involve the purely communicative aspects of the efferent sensory and afferent motor nervous systems.

b.   Mind as Experimental Cognitive Psychology's Object of Study

The next step in further sharpening this emerging definition of mind is to list and briefly describe the relevant cognitive processes. A review of a wide variety of materials, including modern journals, texts, and, most helpfully, the outline of an introductory survey for entering experimental psychology graduate students at The University of Michigan led to the cluster of processes listed in this section.

Again, it is necessary to remind the reader that it is appreciated that the concepts in this list are overlapping in some ways, redundant, and mutually nonexclusive. Thus perception is not a process that exists independently of memory and learning or attention. This list is merely one among many ways of categorizing these mental processes that have, through historical precedent, behavioral overtness, or introspective insight, already become evident to psychologists. In the future, certain of these categories may be expected to coalesce into single more inclusive concepts. Moreover, new functions not yet explicitly identified or recognized may emerge. The list presented here is but a contemporary, not an ultimate, classification of the anatomy of mind. The reader should not forget that the philosophy underlying this analytic anatomy of mind may ultimately be shown to be completely erroneous. In providing this classification system, I may, in fact, be committing the same error I warned against a few pages earlier—namely, ignoring the fact that the true nature of mind is holistic and indivisible. If that should prove to be the case, the reader may best look upon this suggestive list as a set of descriptors of that holistic unity, rather than as a list of quasi-independent processes.

Perception.   Perception may be described as the relatively immediate mental processing of relatively well-defined input stimulus patterns. The study of perception deals with phenomena of varying levels of complexity ranging from the detection of simple impulsive (brief transient) stimuli, such as flashes, clicks, or taps, to the processing of complex real-world stimuli, such as the moving talking pictures with simultaneous somesthetic stimulation that make up the multimodel confusion of our daily lives.

Perceptual processing cannot be distinguished from sensory processing in any manner other than the complexity of the stimulus. Classic "sensory" psychologists traditionally dealt with the simplest responses to the simplest monodimensional stimuli, while perceptual psychologists traditionally dealt with more complex stimuli that required more elaborate forms of stimulus information processing. The classical dichotomy between the two concepts has become almost meaningless in contemporary psychology. Such topics as form recognition, space perception, pitch and hue discrimination, illusions and constancy phenomenon, and perceptual adaptation, all fall within the rubric of perceptual studies. Currently the main difference between sensory and perceptual psychology is that sensory psychologists generally tend to have some physiological explanation or interpretation of the phenomena they study, and perceptual psychologists generally do not. Clearly, however, this is a highly unstable base upon which to build definitions, and most psychobiologists agree there is little operational reason to distinguish between the two fields now.

Learning.   Learning has been defined as a change in behavior resulting from experience. The study of learning, so defined, emphasizes changes in mental states or behavior over time as a result of the organism's experiential history, rather than the immediate responses that serve as indicators of its momentary state. I elaborate considerably on this definition of learning in Chapter 8.

Behavior variability or learning has been the object of an enormous amount of research attention during the last forty years. The dynamics of learning are studied by observing changes in motor performance, in the retention of verbal materials, or in a host of other tasks. Closely related to the study of learning, but perhaps not identical, is the study of memory. One distinction between the two is that learning may be considered as the dynamic process of acquiring behavioral change, and memory is the quasiphysical mechanism and method by which information is stored or the stored information itself.

Students of memory are more likely to be studying the storage properties of short-term or long-term memory mechanisms by using simple assay tasks that supposedly require a minimum of information processing; students of learning usually emphasize the processes of acquisition, decay, and interference, as well as the specific effect of stimulus variables that must be manipulated to change behavior over time. Clearly, however, the separation between the two topics, the acquisition of information on the one hand, and the storage of information on the other, is at best a tenuous dichotomy. In fact, distinctions made between the learning process and the memory are usually based on nothing other than slight differences in the interests and experimental paradigms of the respective researchers. This is particularly so in light of many of the developments in the information processing approach to learning and memory that have characterized psychology since World War II. From that point of view, the actual mechanism of memory can be examined only in terms of some of the transformations that occur during the storage and acquisition of learned information.

Thinking.   A third cluster of mental processes of interest to experimental psychologists includes such extraordinarily complex actions as thinking, problem solving, decision making, concept and category formation, and creativity. Human thinking and the related processes represent, from some points of view, the latest in the evolution of mental process, just as the human brain represents the most advanced step in the evolution of neural structure. But, what are thought processes and how do they differ from perception, for example? Obviously, thinking must contain perception as a subprocess and vice versa, but whereas the emphasis is on the immediacy of the processing of the input stimulus in perception, with respect to thinking and problem solving, the emphasis is on the construction of new behavior on the basis of the integration and rearrangement of previous multiple inputs and preexisting percepts. Thus defined, thinking approaches the previous definition of learning; the residual distinction is the purely empirical operational fact that laboratory studies of thinking emphasize relatively diffusely defined and previously stored information, and learning studies in the laboratory emphasize the changing responses to relatively more sharply defined stimulus inputs as a result of experience.

It should be clear at this point that the empirical difference between perception, learning, and thinking is one based mainly on differences in the time history of the stimulus. Perception deals with the immediate stimulus; learning deals with the sequence of relatively sharply defined stimuli in the past; and thinking deals with quite diffuse stimuli or memories of stimuli that may have occurred over a prolonged past of unknown duration.

I might also note that throughout history some of our most distinguished psychologists have championed the hypothesis that even the most conventional forms of perception itself are akin to problem solving. For example, the classic rationalist view finds modern expression in Neisser (1967) and Kolers' (1970) support of the so-called "constructionist" position that asserts that every stimulus provides only the clues or cues for a percept and that each must be "problem solved" before the percept develops. Misleading cues cause such false solutions as visual illusions or perceptual constancies. Such nonveridical responses should be attributed, they say, to the misinterpretation of symbolic cues rather than to any distortion in the peripheral neural representation of the stimulus.

Emotions.   Another major target of psychological investigation is a cluster of concepts that includes the so-called affective states or emotions. These mental processes are also particularly elusive of definition because they involve actions and feelings that are essentially "value judgments" by the organism of the biological utility of various internal physiological states and external stimuli. Thus the inferred (by the experimenter) processes of pleasure, anger, rage, love, hunger, and pain, are all subsumed into this concept cluster on the basis of the overt approach or escape behaviors associated with them.

On the other hand, although all affective states must necessarily be inferred in others on the basis of approach or avoidance or even gestural, postural, and expressive behaviors, it is clear that the pleasure or pain induced by any particular stimulus situation is highly intrapersonal in the sense proscribed for all mental states. Indeed, there is a classic example of the difficulty in basing our definition of such internal mental states on observations of the emitted responses. In the surgical laboratory, students must be constantly warned that an animal that may have been immobilized by the injection of curare or curare-like drugs is still sensitive to painful experiences, even though they cannot exhibit escape behavior. Curare and similar drugs act on the neuromotor junctions in a highly selective manner; however, these chemicals do not affect the sensory pathways. Thus an animal can be in extreme pain as a result of surgery even though totally unresponsive. The extrapolation to human behavior is direct: Overt expressions of misery are not the necessary concomitants of deeply distressed mental states. Actors may mimic distress without feeling it, and a person may not exhibit distress while feeling it.

Drives and motives.   Closely related in concept to emotional responses, and indeed perhaps synonymous from some points of view, are the psychological and physiological determinants that impel organisms toward particular forms of consummatory behavior. The drives or motivational forces lead to some of the basic instinctual-type behaviors, such as eating, drinking, sleeping, and sexual behavior, necessary for the perpetuation of the species or the individual. Psychobiologists are particularly interested in whether or not these almost universal forms of organic behavior are innate or acquired during the course of development of particular species. Some extraordinarily strong drive states or motives such as the drive for status, money, or recognition that are regularly observed in man, obviously transcend the more basic, physiologically driven motivational states, for they are not as directly related to the immediate physiological needs of the organism. Quite to the contrary, it is obvious that many drives are learned. Yet some linkage must be established between these acquired reinforcing objects and the more fundamental physiological needs. Alternatively, the objects of acquired drives may somehow assume some impelling or rewarding force in their own right. In either case, the effectiveness of the original or secondary drives clearly arise as a result of experience; it would be terribly difficult to champion any argument that suggested the idea that the value of a little piece of green paper was innate.

Another perspective from which to consider this problem of drives and motives is that acquired drives are the result of a sort of problem solving. The acquisition of money, for example, can be interpreted as a necessary intermediate or even symbolic step in the consummation of some more basic motivational need. Thus, just as stressed earlier for perceptual problems, the separation of these motivational mental states from some aspects of learning or problem solving is exceedingly difficult.

Attention and consciousness.   Somewhere within the complex of processes that we call *mind*, the single aspect that has been most difficult to handle and most provocative of philosophical dialogue has been the problem of attention and consciousness or self-awareness. How is it that an individual can be aware of himself? For that matter, what does it mean to be "aware of one's self," or further, what is it that is aware of what? All of these questions immediately lead to conceptual dilemmas as well as to dualistic theologies because of a possible logical paradox inherent in the process of self-observation. When Descartes said *"cogito ergo sum,"* he was formalizing what had been for millenia the basic source of all religious, philosophical, and scientific concern with the problem of mind. The intrapersonal self-awareness that each of us has of his own exitence is the most primitive, most compelling, and most powerful force in human society. Everything else in human culture flows from this "superfact."

The significance of the controversy about consciousness revolves around two alternative explanations of self-awareness: One position assumes that self-awareness is the best evidence for the separate (dualistic) existence of mind; the other position asserts that self-awareness is but another (emergent) process of brain action. This controversy is not going to be resolved in this book nor will it be solved by either philosophical or empirical laboratory methods in the near future. Quite simply, this is the essence of Schopenhauer's "world knot." However, it is clear that we are beginning to be able to study some aspects of self-awareness, and thus we are making progress toward describing if not fully understanding it. The work on vigilance, for example, exemplifies a direct experimental attack on this problem. The reader is particularly directed to the important work of Broadbent (1958; 1971) for an elegant and complete consideration of the line of research.

Can the enormously overloaded term "consciousness" also be operationally defined? Often the term is used to refer to a general arousal level, but alternatively it is closely related, in practice, to what I have called *attention*. The state of arousal of an animal, as evidenced by its attentive behavior, is clearly an experiment of the same genre as a vigilance experiment with human observers in a simulated radar observation experiment. Studies of sleep and wakefulness are, likewise, intimately interrelated with the notions of arousal and attention.

A major controversy in modern psychology, therefore, is: Can any mental process be unconscious? In the sense in which we have defined attention, there is no question that unconscious mental processes exist. We can do things inattentively, like driving while talking. Similarly, many autonomic functions go on totally "below" the level of consciousness or attention. The notion of a preconscious or subconscious is, therefore, clearly within the scope of modern empirical psychobiology.

The difficulties that have been associated with attempts to define attention, arousal, or awareness over the years make it clear that the semantic, philosophical, and technical difficulties involved in defining consciousness are immense.

These, then, are the major clusters of mental processes that can be identified as the objects of attention in the laboratory investigations of experimental psychologists. These categories of research topics thus serve as pointers toward a definition of mind.

c. Welker's Taxonomy of Covert Mental Processes

Welker (1971) has also developed a taxonomy of mental processes that is comparable in intent to the effort at classifications made in the previous sections and, perhaps, superior in execution. Because so many of his terms have already been discussed, I limit my consideration of his taxonomy to a presentation of Table 4-1.

Perhaps the most important general point to make is that Welker too considers mind to be defined as a system of states and processes that are the direct derivatives of the operation of specific neural networks or circuits. Although his taxonomy differs in detail, it is conceptually consistent with that presented in the previous section.

TABLE 4-1

The repertoire of intrapersonal mental states. (From Welker, ©1976, with the permission of Lawrence Erlbaum Associates.)[a]

Conceptual category	Specific concepts
Inactive states	Sleeping, unaware, unconscious, inattentive
Arousal processes	Activation, arousal, alerting
Awake states	Aware, conscious, alert, vigilant
Attentive states	Alerting, attending, expectancy, scanning, focusing, detection, vigilance, sensitivity, orientation
Specific-reactivity processes	Mobilization, threshold, set, preference, aversion, differentiation, image, expectancy, fixed action pattern, scanning, focusing, attitude, perception detection, hallucination, goal orientation, sensitivity, excitation, orientation, hallucination, goal orientation, sensitivity, excitation, orientation, discrimination, tendency, illusion, displacement, identification
Cognitive states and processes	Perception, thinking, planning, purpose, judgment, guessing, trying, will, wish, hypothesis, evaluation, imitation, cognitive content, expectancy, set, decision, insight, optimizing, competence, self actualizing, recognition, reasoning, understanding, concept formation, abstraction, symbol formation, cognitive map, cognitive model, ideation, aim, creativity, innovation, volition, plasticity, confidence, certainty, effectance, choice, purpose, assumption, conception, goal orientation, seeking
Integrative processes	Generalization, consolidation, judgment, introspection, deduction, homeostasis, programming, mediation, repression, inhibition, facilitation, insight, fixation, plasticity, closure, abstraction, assimilation, feedback, planning, ideation, learning, transaction, creativity, conditioning, symbol formation, association, integration, summation, irradiation, re-afference, displacement, incubation, regulation

Experiential processes	Perception, detection, insight, confidence, introspection, perception, discrimination, surprise, confusion, competence, knowing, symbolizing, feeling, empathy, knowing,
Motivational processes	Energy, attitude, compulsion, interest, homeostasis, optimizing, thirst, love, aspiration, hope, perseverance, craving, disposition, appetite, preference, aversion, fear, hate, joy, will, wish, drive, need, habit strength, volition, urge, curiosity, hunger, anger, anxiety, value
Affective states	Tension, boredom, sensitivity, joy, emotion, anxiety, conflict, surprise, satiation, anxiety, love, preference, aversion, impact, desire, passion, amusement, sentiment, longing
Learning processes	Discrimination, familiarization, symbolization, consolidation, incubation, learning, insight, fixation, abstraction, imprinting, conditioning, generalization, deduction
Reinforcement processes	Impact, meaning, significance, reward, reinstatement, reinforcement, inhibition, suppression, repression, trace, engram, facilitation, closure, feedback
Other change-type processes and states	Adaptation, adaptation level, satiation, suppression, feedback, forgetting, creativity, innovation, plasticity, inhibition, recovery, displacement, habituation, dishabituation, accommodation, disinhibition
Fixation states and processes	Persistence, fixation, instinct, habit, generalization, fixed action pattern, stereotypy, consistency
Memory processes	Memory (immediate, delayed), recall, habit, recognition, amnesia, forgetting, retention, trace, engram, storage, retrieval
Ability states	Discrimination, learning set, perception, achievement, adaptability, habit, acuity, capability, capacity
Maturational processes and states	Critical period, growth, differentiation, readiness, histogenesis, neurogenesis, regionalization, induction, morphogenesis, pattern formation, organization

[a]Behaviorally and phenomenologically derived concepts, constructs and intervening variables referring to hypothesized, internal, central and covert phenomena, functions, states, contents, and processes.

d.   Some Thoughts and Caveats

There are a multitude of other mental processes that might also be mentioned. One has only to look at the monumental encyclopedias of *Philosophy* (Edwards, 1967) or *Psychology* (Eysenck, Arnold, & Meili, 1972; and Goldenson, 1970) to begin to appreciate the range of contemporary human concern with mental processes. However, many of these other processes that might be included in the categorization already discussed are only popular or ill-defined rather than empirical and scientific issues. For example, the issues of intent and will are ubiquitous in discussions of the nature of mind, but each may be subsumed either within the problem-solving cluster or in terms of motives and attention. There is little in the laboratory that speaks directly to the nature of these kinds of mental activity. Thus, in the preceding categorization, I have constrained the discussion and, therefore, limited the scope of our definition of mind to those aspects currently under active laboratory research scrutiny. Within this limited context, mental processes have been at least partially defined for which we can legitimately expect to find physiological and anatomical correlates.

Within the context of the classification of mental processes, there are a number of important points that still must be made quite explicit. First, reconsider why it is necessary to carry out this exercise. The main reason is simple enough: It is the only way to begin to understand what the rest of this book is all about. It makes no sense to search for the anatomical locus of a particular mental process or to examine the effect of some chemical on some mental process unless there is some agreement as to what the process is.

There is also another caveat, to which I have previously alluded, that should be reiterated at this point. Perhaps this most important warning of all concerns the issue of the metaphysical reality of all that has been presented so far in this chapter. Readers should not be misled by the organization of this chapter to assume that it is being suggested that mental processes represent something separate and distinct from other biological processes simply because they have been abstracted from the total mind-brain complex. Rather, this chapter is but a necessary prerequisite and pedagogic tool to add order and coherence to the specifically correlative chapters that follow. Although this chapter is intended to emphasize mental processes, remember that the key idea throughout the entire discussion has been that mind is the process and action of a material substrate—the central nervous system. Thus, while accepting the metaphysical reality of mental process (we, as individuals, are aware), we neither accept the Platonic and Cartesian idea that mind is separable from brain (dualism), nor agree with Ryle's rejection of the concept of mind as only a "category mistake."

A closely related matter concerns the problem of isomorphism and symbolism with regard to stimulus representation. A stimulus pattern may be represented in either of two ways. First, the representation may be in terms of some isomorphic representation that maintains the geometric relationships among the parts of the stimulus. A map, for example, is an isomorphic representation of some geographical area, as a pictograph is of some physical object. Second, a stimulus pattern may also be represented by a symbolic process. A verbal description of an object, for example, does not maintain the geometry but rather substitutes for geometry certain descriptors or equivalences that serve the coding function without maintaining the one-for-one topological relationships. Similarly, coded languages like written English or the binary number system are symbolic rather than isomorphic means of representing information patterns.

The specific impact of this kind of symbolic representation theory in the context of the present discussion is that we must always remember that all research on mental processes can be considered from the viewpoint of either isomorphic or symbolic representation. It is very difficult to tell from comparisons of the input and the output of a system whether the message was represented isomorphically or symbolically within the inner structure of the system. Thus it is a matter of preference with regard to how a particular process will be modeled until one takes the system apart and looks at its inner workings.

Some psychobiologists would prefer to conceptualize their observations as being strictly isomorphic, and it is possible to do so. Phenomena such as visual illusions can be interpreted in terms of hypothetical distortions produced in a spatially or temporally isomorphic encoded replica of the stimulus within various levels of the ascending visual pathway. Distortions can be attributed to lateral inhibitory interactions, for example, or by the loss of redundant portions of the stimulus pattern. This approach, which emphasizes geometrical interaction among the parts of a stimulus in the more peripheral portions of the nervous system, leads to the assertion that most illusions and many thought processes retain isomorphism to their original dimensionality from the point of entry into the receptors to the highest levels of neural processing.

However, an alternative approach, based not on isomorphism but on symbolic representation, would assert that stimuli only convey cues. Thus according to this view, the symbolic representation of a figure, such as a square, for example, could lead to the same sort of perceptual processing as that of the isomorphic model. Certainly we are able to imagine a   □   when we hear or read the word "square." This difference between symbolic representation and isomorphism, therefore, is important for understanding what is meant by mind. It is clear that both isomorphic and symbolic representations are but two alternative means of expressing functional properties and do not themselves reference anatomical structures.

Finally, there is an enormous interest in contemporary psychology with the mental processes that are expressed in language. Language is best described as an output process rather than a central cognitive or mental event itself. Yet, it is truly, if anything can be so called, the "mind-scope" through which mental processes can be best observed. More than any of the other measures of mental activity, the structure of language reveals some of the underlying cognitive processes. Nevertheless, language is not mental activity; it is a form of behavior and, therfore, is not included within the categories presented in the preceding list. Language may be a clue to the way in which people think, solve problems, perceive images, and learn, but it is not mind; it is but another form of behavior, despite the vigorous assertions of the logical positivists who stated that because language was the medium of mental response par excellence, it was identifiable in a metaphysical as well as a practical sense with what is meant by mind.

D.   MEASURES OF MIND

In Chapter 3, I described the instruments used in the study of neuroanatomy and neurophysiology. Having shown that micro- and macroelectrodes, microscopes, radioactive tracers, and the like are the measuring instruments for evaluating neural responses and structures, it is now appropriate to discuss the measuring instruments for the evaluation of psychological responses. However, to do so, I must first consider what sort of response variables are available to the psychological investigator. Only then can I meaningfully describe the instruments that are available for the measurement of those responses.

There are, of course, three separate levels of this discussion that must not be confused. First, there are the intrapersonal mental states themselves that are, from my point of view, the true subject matter of psychology. The next level includes the interpersonally observable actions which in the aggregate we call *behavior.* They signal something about the nature of the underlying mental processes. Third, there are the instruments and research procedures that are used to measure the behavioral responses. A major weakness of modern psychology is that the measures and the responses are often confused with the mental states, and thus the goals of this science are often blurred.

I endeavor in this section to make explicit the properties of the latter two levels—the responses and the instruments for measuring those responses. This should clarify the distinction between the measure and the means of measurement and more clearly distinguish both response measures and the measuring instruments from the underlying mental states.

There is, however, even in this technical area of measurement and response, a major philosophical issue intertwined with the practicalities of the keys, buttons, and protocols. This issue concerns the adequacy of the reflections of the inner mental states by various behavioral responses. Is the relationship really as direct as was just suggested?

The problem of a possible mistaken association between measures of behavior or electrophysiology and mental processes is put into sharpest relief in the context of the quite uncritical and overenthusiastic association of mental and behavioral dimensions observed in the current fad of biofeedback training. There is a thoroughly fallacious association implicit in this enormously popular movement between some behavioral and neural response categories and mental processes. This misassociation is clearly evidenced when the electrical signals from the brain, the muscles, or skin are erroneously associated with mental processes. It is quite clear, for example, that though highly correlated, a physiological variable like the galvanic skin response (GSR) is not identifiable with mind.[1] It is merely a frequent concomitant or indicator of emotional states. Although all would agree that this skin response is not to be identified with mental processes (how few of us would place mental processes in the epidermis), it is somewhat more seductive and conceptually difficult to keep the distinction straight when we are dealing with the relationship between such electrophysiological responses as brain potentials like the electroencephalograph (EEG), on the one hand, and mental processes, on the other. Both classes of response, the mental and the electrical, come from the brain, and there is a strong tendency therefore to assume that the EEG is more closely related to mental processes than is the GSR. In fact, there is no more direct evidence to link the former than the latter to mind. The origins of the EEG are obscure, but the basis of its purported link to mind is correlative in exactly the same way as the GSR. It would require rigorous experimental tests of the necessity and sufficiency of any such electrophysiological signal to determine whether or not it could be identified (as distinguished from being correlated) with some underlying mental state. Certainly, there are mental and physiological processes that occur simultaneously as a result of their common sensitivity to some stimulus, but it is far more difficult than so far realized by the biofeedback folk to establish the direct representative association.

Likewise, the entire pseudoscience of polygraphy, or "lie detection," is based upon a massive misinterpretation of how such electrophysiological variables are related to mental states. There are many other variables that can influence a polygraphic response than the truth or falsity of an assertion by the subject. "Lie detection" is at best, only a measure of autonomic activity, and there is little basis for the idea that certain autonomic states are linked with verity.

Similarly, training either one's muscles or brain potentials by means of the so-called biofeedback procedures, though it may be attention diverting (as are many other games), is not the same as altering one's mental state. This pseudoscientific approach neglects the fact that EEGs can be altered without changing mental state and vice versa. In spite of the fact that mental states often change during the course of a biofeedback training session, there is little reason to assume that such changes in mental state are not mediated by indirect means such as distraction or relaxation. This critique does not mean that biofeedback training is worthless; control over physiological variables can serve some useful therapeutic functions. The point is, however, that the quasitheoretical explanations for the direct effectiveness of biofeedback procedures on the alteration of men-

---

[1]The GSR is a change in skin resistance as a function of some external stimulus conditions.

tal states that are implicitly based on an identification of EEG and mental states are logically nonsensical from a psychobiological point of view.

Similarly, the cult that has grown up around transcendental meditation seems to hardly be justified from a scientific point of view. There is no support for the supposition that transcendental meditation produces some unique state of consciousness. Indeed, recent research (Pagano, Rose, Stivers, & Warrenburg, 1976) have shown that there is little to be distinguished between the EEG phases that are produced by a "transcendentally" meditative state and a good afternoon nap of the same duration. Further, in a study with similar goals and results, Michaels, Huber, and McCann (1976) have shown that there is no difference in the plasma levels of epinephine, norepinephrine, and lactate for groups of subjects who have meditated and those who simply rested. Thus meditation is indistinguishable from a brief rest both electrophysiologically and biochemically. Unfortunately, people want so much to believe in all of these mysterious techniques that even such thoroughly solid empirical debunking will probably not contribute much to a more rational attitude.

This digression aside, I now turn to the more concrete aspects of the response dimensions and the psychological instruments used to measure them.

1.   Dimensions of Behavior

As has been repeatedly pointed out, there is little to argue against the idea that, for a number of practical reasons the study of mind is necessarily confined to the observation of those interpersonally communicable responses we collectively call *behavior*. Therefore, if we are to understand psychology and the measurement of behavior, it is necessary to know what classes of responses are available to the experimenter for study and investigation. In this section, I consider the repertoire of physiological and behavioral responses that have been used by psychologists in their quest for clues to the underlying mental states.

a.   Electrophysiological Responses

Electrophysiological signals from the nervous system, particularly the compound action potentials (electrovoltages that are the summation of many individual neural responses such as the electroencephalograph and the electroretinogram), are one class of responses available for psychological research. There is considerable confusion as to whether or not these behavioral variables should be considered signs or codes (Uttal, 1967, 1973; and see also Chapter 6), i.e., merely concomitants of mental processes or true identity relations. Nevertheless, a wealth of data has been accumulated concerning the concomitant variation of compound brain particularly with fluctuations in the psychological state (see, for example, Cobb & Morocutti, 1967; Regan, 1972; Donchin & Lindsley, 1969). In far fewer but much more extraordinary cases, single neuron recordings have also been correlated with psychological states in human subjects to understand sensory coding (Marg, Adams, & Rutkin, 1968; Hensel & Boman, 1960).

Nonneural electrophysiological responses have also been widely used by psychologists, including the electromyogram (responses from muscles and muscle cells) (Basmajian, 1974) and the galvanic skin response (resistance changes in the skin or in other tissues) (Prokasy & Raskin, 1974).

b. Chemical Responses

Just as organisms generate electrical responses, they also secrete a wide variety of chemicals. Assays of the circulating hormones in the blood stream, or the amount and chemical quality of saliva secreted in the mouth, for example, are also assumed by many workers to reflect variations in inner psychological states. In recent years, a considerable amount of attention has been directed toward the neuro- or psychochemistry of the brain—particularly the secretion of synaptic transmitter substances. I have much more to say on this topic in Chapter 9.

c. Simple Motor Responses

Motor responses consisting of relatively discrete movements are one of the most important categories of response utilized in psychological laboratories. Button-pushing has become almost a ubiquitous tool in a wide variety of behavioral research. Discrete responses of this kind are particularly useful because they represent sharp and precise points of decision in otherwise continuous mental processes. A button-push might, for example, indicate the end of a period of decision making or of processing some visual stimulus. Thus, reaction-time measurements have been used for years to determine the time required for various mental processes to occur. They have, for example, been important sources of information in the search for a solution to whether mental processes can go on simultaneously (in parallel), or whether they must be processed one after the other (in serial) (see Sternberg, 1969). They can also serve as a clue to the relative complexity of various psychological processes.

d. Complex Motor Responses

Very often in field settings, observation of more complex motor behavior than button-pushing becomes the necessary form of data acquisition. The appetitive behavior of man and animals—their eating, fighting, copulating, striving for power or tokens, are all best observed as integrated patterns of response rather than as simple motor twitches. Generally, such field studies are required for two reasons. First, they are required when the expenses and difficulties of acquiring and maintaining a subject population are too great to justify the microscopically controlled laboratory conditions. Second, they are required if it is likely that bringing the subject population into the laboratory would disrupt the overall behavior pattern to such an extent that the responses the investigator intends to observe would be seriously modified. On the other hand, a major limiting characteristic of field observation is that the multivariate stimulus conditions, almost always present in the field, are usually very poorly controlled.

Perhaps the best categorization scheme of the full range of both simple and complex motor responses available has been developed by Welker (1971) specifically in the context of intraspecies comparisons and the evolution of behavior. His scheme is reproduced in Table 4-2.

e. Language

As I have noted, a fruitful avenue for the study of mind is through the medium of language. Language, either in its oral form (speech) or in a written form, is a wonderfully rich source of information—indeed, often too rich and complex to be fully understood. We are just now beginning to develop a truly empirical science of psycholinguistics. Especially significant is the work of Chomsky (1957, 1965). The use of language as a response medium in the laboratory, as opposed to its use by poets or novelists, is often best pursued by careful design of highly circumscribed situations such as exemplified by the model "environments" of simple games like "GO," checkers, or chess.

On the other hand, a free, unstructured flow of language operating in an unconstrained environment, perhaps better than any other response mode, provides a systematic set of introspective clues into the underlying structure of human thought processes. Although introspection was in enormously bad repute as a valid psychological response mode during the heyday of behaviorism, there has been a resurgence of interest in this wide-open window to mental action in recent years.

2. Methods of Measurement

Just as electrophysiologists have developed a large number of sophisticated electronic instruments and mathematical procedures to process the responses of neurons, psychologists have developed equally sophisticated systems of instruments and procedures for evaluating the cognitive process described previously and reflected in the response dimensions mentioned in the preceding section. In this section, I briefly consider the range of methods and procedures available to psychologists for the measurement of mind.

a. Psychophysical Procedures

It is common knowledge that when a physical stimulus (such as light) varies in one or another of its dimensions (such as luminosity), the variation is experienced as a corresponding change in the dimensions of a sensation (such as brightness). The historic premise of psychophysics has been that it is possible to determine the exact form of the relationship between the dimensions of the physical stimulus and the dimensions of the sensory experience. After all of the

mathematical and methodological complexities are sifted out, the real achievement of psychophysics that remains is the set of functions or, as they are
known, *the psychophysical laws*, that describe how sensory information is processed by humans.

It should be noted that there are many dimensions of sensory experience.
Just as a stimulus may vary in intensity, spatial and temporal extent, or pattern
and form of physical energy, the sensory experience may vary in perceived
magnitude, duration or extent, and quality. The task of psychophysics, to relate
the stimulus dimensions to the sensory dimensions, is complicated by the fact
that there is not always a simple relationship between a single stimulus dimension and a unique psychophysical dimension. For example, although the loudness of a sound is determined mainly by the intensity of the acoustic stimulus,
it is also affected by the frequency of that stimulus. (See my discussion of this
important topic in my earlier book, Uttal, 1973.)

A major goal of psychophysics has been to determine the exact form of the
law or functions that relate stimulus intensities and sensory magnitudes. Most
of the earlier psychophysicists (Weber, 1834; and Fechner, 1860) and most
psychophysicists up until the middle of the twientieth century felt that the
relationship between stimulus intensity (S) and sensory magnitude (ψ) was,
both in general and specifically, best described by a logarithmic function (i.e.,
$\psi = \log S$) for many different sensory modalities under many different conditions. In recent years, alternative functional relationships have been proposed, the most famous of which is S. S. Stevens' (Stevens, 1970, 1971) power
function (i.e., $\psi = S^n$). Which law is correct is entirely a matter of experimental measurement—neither can be "proven" by theoretical deductions alone.
A further problem is that both functions sometimes fit the same set of data
fairly well over a narrow range of the stimulus dimension, especially when the
exponent n of the power function is small. Unfortunately, however, it seems to
be the case that neither the power nor the logarithmic function is universally
applicable to all relationships between stimulus intensity and perceived magnitude over the full range of the stimulus dimension.

In recent years, the failure of both the logarithmic laws and power laws has
led to alternative formulations of "the" psychophysical law. Some new formu-
larizations that have been suggested include a hyperbolic tangent law of the form
(Lipetz, 1971):

$$\psi = \frac{1}{2} + \frac{1}{2} \tanh Sw \qquad \text{(Equation 4-1)}$$

where Sw, in this case, is the stimulus intensity in logarithmic units; and Alpern,
Rushton, and Torii's (1970) expression:

$$\psi = \frac{\psi_{max} S}{(S + S_{1/2})} \qquad \text{(Equation 4-2)}$$

where ψ_{max} is the maximum subjective response and $S_{1/2}$ is the stimulus
strength at which the psychological response is one half of the maximum.

TABLE 4-2

The repertoire of interpersonally observable behaviors. (From Welker, ©1976, with the permission of Lawrence Erlbaum Associates.)[a]

1. *Simple reflexes* include muscle twitches and quivers, myotactic (stretch) reflexes, reciprocal "inhibition" of antagonists, lengthening reactions (inverse myotactic reflexes), positive supporting (magnet) extension reactions, negative supporting reactions, ipsilateral extensor reflexes, crossed extension reflexes, bilateral intersegmental (crawling) reflex "figures," startle reflexes, scratch reflexes, mouth wiping (by tongue, head, hand, or foot) reflexes, head and body shaking reflexes, skin-flick reflexes, urination and defecation reflexes, panting, breathing (inspiration, expiration), gasping, choking, coughing and sneezing, and vomiting reflexes, rooting, mouthing, and biting reflexes, licking, swallowing reflexes, clasping and grasping (hand or foot) reflexes, pinna, tympanic, and eyeblink and squinting reflexes, lip and other facial reflexes, lordosis, pelvic thrust reflexes, nystagmus and saccadic and drift eye movements, and narial dilatation reflexes. The simple responses listed above primarily involve striated muscle, but the effects of nonstriated muscle responses may also be observed as the following list illustrates: milk let-down reflexes, bladder and anal reflexes (retentive and releasing), piloerection, gastric and intestinal reflexes, pupillary dilation, lens accommodation, uterine and vaginal reflexes, penile erection and ejaculation reflexes.

2. *Postures and postural changes* include immobile sitting and standing, leaning, lying (supine or prone), sprawling, crouching, curling up, squatting, balancing, hanging, floating, urination and defecation postures, rearing, hopping, placing, stretching, yawning, tonic head-neck-body reflexes, righting (free fall and supine) reflexes (optic, labyrinthine), labyrinthine acceleratory reflexes, and labyrinthine positional reflexes, "freezing" immobilization (e.g., of neonatal kittens when carried by head or scruff of neck). The adjustive recovery from a particular assumed posture (such as stretching) must also be considered as a postural change.

3. *Locomotor sequences* change body locus either in space or usually more specifically with respect to certain types of environmental stimuli, and in such cases may also involve orientation sequences (see below). Locomotor patterns include: walking (quadrupedal, bipedal, bimanual), running (trotting, pacing, cantering, galloping), lunging, charging, creeping, crawling, stalking, dragging, struggling, wriggling, climbing (up or down), rolling, somersaulting, sliding, circling, backing up, skipping, flying, gliding, hopping, sideling, swinging, brachiating, dropping, leaping, jumping, rearing, bucking, diving, surfacing, swimming, and floating.

4. *Simple receptor orientation sequences* include head turning, nodding, lifting, and fixation, eye opening, eye fixation (visual "grasp"), ear turning, sniffing (polypnea), tasting, licking, biting, touching, poking, grasping, holding, batting, dropping, releasing, rubbing, tapping, pushing, pulling, slapping, scratching, twisting, throwing (by proboscis, mouth, hands, feet, or tail).

5. *Simple "fixed action" patterns.*
   (a) *Ingestion (eating and drinking) related components* include mouthing, biting, lip and tooth grasping, grazing, browsing, nibbling, tasting, chewing, cudding, lapping, sipping, drinking, licking, sucking, swallowing, "chop" licking, and lip smacking.

(b) *Elimination related components* include site selection, scratching, digging, squatting, leg lifting, immobilized straining postures, urinating and defecating, parturition, postural recovery, urine and fecal covering, and "scenting" or gland secretion "marking."

(c) *Sexual related components* include (1) *Courtship sequences* such as partner, orientation, and selection, approach, "teasing," chasing and retreating, dancing vocalization, body and facial displays or gestures, strutting, specific postering and "presenting," orogenital and oroanal (nose, lip, and mouth) contacts, biting, sniffing, blowing, sucking, kissing, licking, caressing, nuzzling, and embracing; and (2) *Copulatory and orgastic sequences* include partial and complete mounting (male), immobilization and lordosis (female), clasping and grasping of mate, pelvic thrusting, masturbation, orgasm and ejaculation, dismounting, separation, and after-reactions (rolling, running, cavorting, vocalizing).

(d) *Maternal related components* include licking, nosing, nuzzling, handling, holding, carrying, retrieving and piling, nipple presenting and nursing, huddling and covering, cradling, corraling of offspring.

(e) *Escape, defense and attack related components* include immobilization (freezing), cringing or submission postures and gestures (e.g., rolling over on back), cowering or running away; crouching, stalking, threat gestures and displays, hissing, tail erecting, twitching or slapping, abortive charging, full charge and chasing, bunting, biting, tearing, holding and pinioning, grasping and shaking, hitting, clawing, kicking, sneak attacking, leaping upon and wrestling, growling, barking, grunting, squealing, and screaming.

(f) *Other instinct sequences* include grooming, washing, preening, licking, picking and scratching specific body zones, shaking, awakening, going to sleep, sleeping, "dreaming," nest material retrieval and nest construction, burrowing, digging, excavating, retrieving, holding, carrying, packing, shredding, arranging, weaving, piling, and territorial marking (with urine, feces, or glandular secretions) chest beating, various vocalization patterns (cooing, babbling), spitting, blowing, bucking, bathing, basking, cooling, painting, building, wrecking and testing, purring, and claw protraction and retraction.

(g) *Miscellaneous gestures, displays and social components* include grimaces, tail twitching, ear retraction, eye squinting, lip retraction and tooth baring, protective gestures and postures, smiling, kissing, nuzzling, hugging, huddling, tickling, grabbing, grappling, taking, stealing, staring, gaze avoiding, scratching, specific muscle tensions or relaxations, imitation, encouragement, beckoning, begging, avoidance, separation, mouth sounds, vocalizations (whining, purring, hissing, squealing, etc.), pacing, exhilaration, excitement, restlessness and agitation, rocking, clasping, and self biting and autisms.

6. *Complex organized response sequence aggregates* include exploration, searching or hunting (for food, shelter, escape, a mate, novelty, etc.), building, territorial demarcation, identification and maintenance, games (hide and seek), housekeeping, and various social "structuring" and interactive behaviors.

---

[a]Most of these behavioral sequences are seen only in adult animals or at least in those old enough to have developed complete or matured patterns.

All of these laws do a fair job of fitting the psychophysical functions for a few situations and a poorer job in generalizing to a large number of situations. In general, each of them fails to fit too wide a variety of data to be truly qualified as "the" psychophysical law. What they do have in common is the notion of compression, or in the particular case of Stevens' Power Law, the possibility of modeling either compressed, linear, or expanded function, depending upon the nature of the exponent.[2]

Considerable evidence has been accumulated both in favor of and opposed to the notion of a general power law description of psychophysical functions. A strongly supportive analysis can be found in Stevens (1970, 1971) or in Marks (1974). A more critical analysis can be found in my earlier book (Uttal, 1973). In that volume the criticisms are based upon the fact that a power law can be used to fit almost any monotonic function (it is too general) upon poor fit with data (Luce & Mo, 1965; Zinnes, 1969), particularly with regard to unpooled results from individual subjects, and upon the existence of multibranched functions in many situations (Barlow, 1965) for which power law theorists have proposed simple functions.

The most robust conclusion to which one is irresistibly drawn by a close scrutiny of the data is that, in fact, none of these proposed "laws" of perceived magnitude satisfactorily fulfills the universal role for which it is proposed. This probably means that the actual functions relating stimulus and magnitude dimensions are actually far more complicated than any of the relatively simple forms proposed by the various theoreticians. Indeed, there is a real possibility that there is no universal psychophysical law for perceived magnitude but rather a host of different functions for different situations. Nevertheless, these theoretical proposals and the background research that led to them have played a very important role throughout the history of experimental psychology. Not only did this type of research stimulate a massive theoretical effort, but also it provided an impetus for the development of a family of highly standardized psychophysical techniques. Two main categories of these procedures may be identified. One has been referred to as the set of classic psychophysical procedures, (Corso, 1967; and Stevens, 1951), and the other, a post-World War II development, is based upon a Theory of Signal Detection (Tanner & Swets, 1954; and Green & Swets, 1966).

It is important to remember that the purpose of psychophysics is not to measure stimuli or to determine *their* characteristics. That is the domain of physics. Rather, psychophysics is a psychological science designed to measure the information processing characteristics of the *observer* and to determine how he processes and transforms the incoming information, and thereby to understand further the nature of human mental activity.

---

[2]Exponents less than 1 describe compressed functions; exponents equal to 1 describe linear functions; exponents greater than 1 describe expanded functions.

Classical psychophysical procedures.   Over the years, a wide variety of specialized research methods have been developed to achieve psychophysical goals. Some of these methods have helped to establish the line between the stimuli that are discriminable and those that are indiscriminable. For example, psychophysics was, and still is, very much concerned with determining absolute sensory thresholds—the particular value of the stimulus that indicates the border between the sensed and the unsensed. Other research sought to measure differential thresholds—values indicating the minimum size of a difference between two stimuli that could be "just noticed" as a difference. Additional methods were designed to measure the ability of a subject to evaluate stimuli or sensory dimensions that lacked metricized units. Psychophysical methods involving ranking and ordering, for example, can also be used to measure comfort, goodness of form, or other such nonnumerical dimensions.

Generally, the classical research methods of psychophysics asked the subject to state "yes" or "no" to, or to respond in some other simple way to, a prototypical question of the form: Did you see (or hear, or feel, or taste) that stimulus? Or, he might be asked to indicate whether two stimuli were the same or different, or to make some adjustment of a test stimulus with respect to a certain standard. Careful control of the spatial or temporal order of presentation of stimuli thereby enabled the experimenter to determine the mathematical functions relating dimensions of the stimulus and dimensions of the sensation. Different values of the stimulus could be either presented randomly (Method of Constant Stimuli) or presented in ascending or descending order until a threshold was reached (Method of Limits, or Staircase Method). The subject might be asked to halve or double a standard stimulus (Method of Fractionation) or to modulate one stimulus until it was equal to another (Method of Adjustment). Each of these methods has particular advantages allowing it to overcome one or another artifact that might serve to distort the actual shape of the sensory function. The reader is referred to Corso (1967) and Gescheider (1976) for more complete discussions of these procedures.

Modern psychophysics has added considerable support to the idea that human psychological properties are quantifiable and measurable equally as well as the stimuli that elicit these responses. S. S. Stevens, the "father" of modern psychophysics, believed so strongly that the human can do a very creditable job of directly estimating certain sensory experiences that subjects in many of his experiments were simply given a standard stimulus and then asked to state the relative magnitude of a similar stimulus by assigning a number to it. His Method of Direct Magnitude Estimates was a fundamental change from the earlier psychophysical methods which attempted to reduce the complexity of the subject's task by asking for only the simplest possible judgments of equality or threshold estimates to determine the psychophysical functions.

The important point about all of the procedures mentioned in this section is that they were all designed to reduce the subjects' repertoire of possible responses to the simplest decision. Simplification of the subject's response repertoire reduces the uncertainty and multivariate nature of real-life situations to highly abstracted laboratory situations which are amenable to all of the rigid control and manipulation that is deemed to be desirable in the experimental laboratory. However, a penalty is paid for the exertion of this control. The simplification of the real world reduces the range of variables that were studied. The heavy commitment to the dimensions of intensity and perceived magnitude, among the many that could be studied, in the classical psychophysical laboratories was one result of this fetish for control. Another penalty was the almost total exclusion, until the second half of the twentieth century, of the study of complex cognitive phenomena from the experimental laboratory.

The Theory of Signal Detection.[3]   Because no simple psychophysical law adequately describes all attributes of the functions relating psychophysical to stimulus dimensions, the notion that data accumulated in psychophysical experiments reflect multiple influences became apparent. Another influence on the development of modern psychophysical methodology was the emerging awareness that there was some question of the actual existence of thresholds. It was apparent from the beginning of psychophysical research that thresholds were not sharp lines of demarcation between the sensed and the unsensed. Rather, thresholds always turned out to be statistical regions within which the probability of detection varied. As a result, thresholds have always been defined in probabilistic terms (e.g., percentage of presentations that were detected). This led directly to statistical theories of the interface between the sensed and the unsensed. Furthermore, in some cases, it appeared that thresholds might be as low as the minimum possible amount of physical energy of the stimulus; for example, one quantum in one retinal rod could be perceived. Results of this kind led to the development of a new form of psychophysical methodology, which has come to be called "The Theory of Signal Detection."

The Theory of Signal Detection arose fortuitously as a combination of a number of different factors. Most important was the fact that the problem of target detection in psychophysics was obviously analogous to the problem of target detection with radar or signal detection in other electronic systems. Therefore, it was a natural development that some of the mathematical notions developed by engineers to describe the sensitivity of communication systems (see particularly Peterson, Birdsall, & Fox, 1954) were eventually applied to psychological detection problems. A number of important differences in the basic philosophy of the two approaches, however, make it important for the reader to understand the unique approach of modern psychological signal detection theory in the form first presented by Tanner and Swets (1954) and more fully developed by Green and Swets (1966).

---

[3]Much of the material in this section is abstracted from a discussion in Uttal (1973).

To understand the nature of these conceptual differences, we must note that signal detection theory, as it was originally developed, was a procedure for the analysis of the efficiency of transmitters, communication links, and receivers with *known* noise characteristics. Thus signal and noise amplitudes were directly observable and could be used to define quantitatively the detection characteristics of radar and radio sets. The theory of signal detection as it has been applied by psychologists, however, is an attempt to do something quite different with the same mathematical machinery. Psychologists using signal detection theories are, in general, attempting to infer what the invisible signal-to-noise characteristics and detection characteristics of an invisible communication system are on the basis of measures of its external behavior. Their use of the theory of signal detection, therefore, is based upon a number of assumptions that are not part of the original theory. It is, in a sense, a form of mathematical backtracking from a solution to a problem!

The idea of "noise" takes on a quite different meaning in the psychological context than it does in the electrical engineer's world. To the psychologist, "noise" includes such factors as variability in the decision criteria that are being used from trial to trial, spontaneous noise in the neural communication links, and "noise" in the subjective estimates of the likelihood and payoffs involved in any given decision. Clearly, this is quite a bit more complex than the communication noise in a radiotelegraph. Nevertheless, the processes can be considered to be analogous.

It should be noted that the only data that are needed for most psychophysical signal detection experiments are the proportion of the total responses to which a subject said "yes" when there was, in fact, a signal present (the hit rate), and the proportion of times in which he said "yes" when there was, in fact, no signal present (the false alarm rate). From these two simple sets of data, useful and significant characteristic measures of the subject's performance can be derived. Furthermore, if certain assumptions are made, the characteristics of the signal-to-noise ratio with which the subject seems to be operating can also be estimated.

An important advantage of the signal detection model is that it allows the psychologist to distinguish between *sensitivity* measures and *decision* measures. To understand fully how these factors may be derived, we shall have to consider in detail the meaning of some of the basic concepts used in the system. First, let us consider the form in which data are generated and analyzed in a signal detection experiment.

An important general notion, which has been introduced by the signal detection theorists, is that there are probability values that characterize the number of times a target will be correctly detected, as well as equivalent functions for the number of times false alarms will be reported. These probabilities are reflections of the invisible noise distributions in the system. As stated above, there are two possible responses, which can be given with varying probabilities in a simple yes-no type of psychophysical experiment (Yes, I saw it—No, I did not see it) and also two possible stimulus conditions that must be considered (There was a signal present—There was no signal present).

Four probabilities are thus defined:

1. The probability of reporting a signal when one was present
    $P(S/s)$ A Hit
2. The probability of reporting a signal when none was present
    $P(S/n)$ A False Alarm
3. The probability of not reporting a signal when one was present
    $P(N/s)$ A Miss
4. The probability of not reporting a signal when none was present
    $P(N/n)$ A Correct Rejection

This information could be represented in a two-dimensional table, but there is a much more graphic and explicit means of more fully representing the relationships of the response probability functions as various parameters of the situation change. This is the now well-known ROC (Receiver Operating Characteristic) curve, a sample family of which is shown in Fig. 4-1. The ROC curve simply plots the hit rate against the false alarm rate. Thus, points at the lower left-hand corner of the graph represent the performance of a subject who is essentially responding so conservatively that he is, in fact, saying no to almost everything.

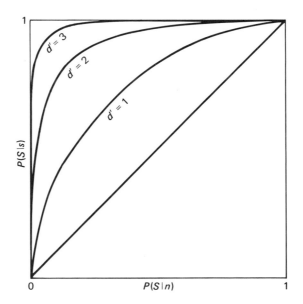

FIG. 4-1   Receiver operating characteristic (ROC) curves plotted for three different levels of d', assuming equal variances of the two distributions of Figure 4-1. Unequal variances would tend to make the ROC curve asymmetrical. (From Green & Swets, ©1966, with the permission of Wiley & Sons, Inc.)

Thus, although he is rarely making the error of the false alarm, he is also rarely correctly reporting the presence of any true signals. As the subject's criteria change, perhaps as a result of the instructions given to him, he may become more and more liberal. Points would then be plotted that tend more toward the other end of the graph where his hit rate is very high, but where his false alarm rate may also approach 100%. Thus, where the subject is performing on a given ROC curve at any given time is a measure of his decision criterion rather than his sensitivity.

The formal measure that is used to describe this criterion level or response threshold in the theory of signal detection is β (beta), which is a measure of the level of the tendency to report a signal at which the subject expects he can maximize the value of his decision. It is, in other words, a variable threshold beyond which the subject will say that a signal was present. The measure β, then, is determined by the subject's conception of the odds and of the values he associates with the possible outcomes, and it is presumably selected by the subject to maximize his return. β may be varied experimentally by varying the instructions and the payoffs given to the subject.

The other major descriptor required is a measure of the sensitivity of the system. Remember that in the old electrical engineering world, the conditions of signal and noise were directly observable. The experimenter could then plot a pair of curves such as those shown in Fig. 4-2. The first curve represents the distribution of the noise alone; the second curve represents the distribution when signal and noise are both present. For example, the first curve might represent a histogram of the intervals between random noise pulses in a pulse-modulated system. When a signal is added to this noise, the interval distribution would shift as spikes occurred more frequently due to the presence of the signal pulses. The band-pass of the system might or might not change, and thus the standard deviation of the curve representing signal plus noise may or may not also change.

For the purposes of most of our discussion, it will be a useful simplification to assume both that the standard deviation remains constant and that the two curves are both normal. In this situation, an objective measure of the discriminability of the signal can be given in terms of the relative degree of overlap of the two curves. Formally, a useful discriminability measure for this situation in which all of the parameters are known could be expressed as:

$$d = \frac{M_1 - M_2}{\sigma} \qquad \text{(Equation 4-3)}$$

The ability of a given instrument to distinguish signal from noise could be calculated with this equation, in which M_1 is the mean of the pure noise distribution, M_2 is the mean of the signal-plus-noise distribution, and σ is the common standard deviation.

It should be noted that d is a measure of the overlap of the two curves. When there is only a small difference between the two means there will be a substan-

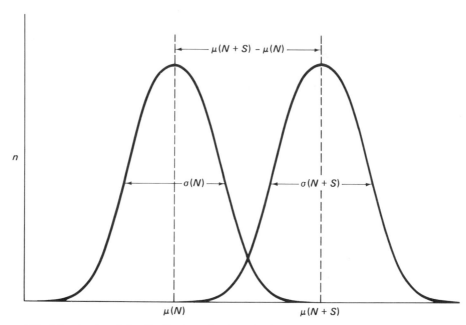

FIG. 4-2   A plot of the distribution of a hypothetical variable for noise distributions with and without a signal. This is the basic model from which most signal detection descriptions of experimental data are derived. μ (N) is the mean of the distribution containing noise along; μ (N + S) is the mean of the distribution that contains both signal and noise; σ (N) is the standard deviation of the distribution containing noise alone; σ (N + S) is the standard deviation of the distribution that contains both signal and noise. Note the region of overlap of the two curves in which it is uncertain from which distribution a particular event was obtained. The horizontal axis represents the range of possible scores; the vertical axis represents the number of times (n) a score occurred. (From Uttal, 1973.)

tial amount of overlap of the two curves, and it will be difficult to determine if a particular instance belonged to the noise or the noise-plus-signal distribution. Sensitivity is, therefore, said to be low. When the difference is great, then there is a lessened probability that instances drawn from each distribution will lie in the common overlapping region, and sensitivity will be high. Similarly, the narrower the distribution (the smaller its standard deviation), the less likelihood of overlap for a given M_1 and M_2. The important thing to remember is that d is an estimate, which can be made purely and uniquely on the basis of message characteristics if they are known.

In the psychological situation, however, we usually do not know all of the characteristics of the noise; it is invisible and is only indirectly reflected in our observations of the responses made by the subject. However, it is assumed that there is an equivalent sort of probabilistic distribution and an equivalent sort of noise and, furthermore, that a measure of sensitivity of discrimination that will operate in exactly the same way can be defined. This analogous measure of discriminability d' (pronounced "dee prime"), which includes the effects of all of the "invisible internal noise" as well as any external stimulus noise, can be defined as:

$$d' = \frac{M_1 - M_2}{\sigma}$$ (Equation 4-4)

where M_1 and M_2 are the means of the two psychological distributions, one containing the signal and one not, and σ is their common standard deviation.

The crucial point to remember is that in the application of the theory of signal detection in a psychological experiment, the two hypothetical distributions, which we are discussing, are really implicit in the behavior of the subject and usually cannot be made truly explicit. Thus, M_1, M_2, and σ are values that, for all practical purposes, really can never be precisely defined or measured. What we can do is extricate from our data an estimate of d', which tells us something about discriminability and informs us of the shape of the ROC curve. The ROC curves thus suggest but do not define the exact form of these hypothetical distributions.

Nevertheless, the analysis can be pushed somewhat further if we are willing to make certain simplifying assumptions. Specifically, we may assume that the two distributions have some standard shape. We may make assumptions about their normality and the equality of variance, for example. When we have done so, we are assuming a shape for these distributions and, therefore, may apply normal probability tables or other statistical tools to make further estimates of the nature of the invisible noise. It is most important to remember, however, that these simplifying assumptions are only that and are not rigorous solutions to the problem.

Differences in effective d' will show up as shifts in the position of the entire ROC curve as shown in Fig. 4-1. Increased discriminability reflected by a larger d' puts more and more of the area of the ROC graph underneath the curve.

What "discriminability" or d' actually means in a given experiment depends upon the experimental design. In a detection experiment, it might be a measure of the ease with which a given stimulus can be correctly detected with any one of a number of different psychophysical techniques. But it can also have a slightly different connotation in experiments on recognition, intelligibility, and even memory. Although the particular shape of the ROC curve and the area included under it empirically specify a particular d', that d' cannot be used to characterize the mean and standard deviation of the invisible noise distribution without making the simplifying assumptions mentioned previously. Rather, d' is used as an empirical dependent variable in experiments in which the effects of varying some stimulus parameter on a subject's performances are desired to be measured. It can, further, be used to compare the sensitivity of a set of subjects when the experimental conditions are held constant.

Because it is possible to compute from known stimulus characteristics the best that any internally noise-free observer (operating as an omnipotent statistician) could do, signal detection theorists have also developed the notion of an *ideal observer*. This theoretical ideal observer can be used as a standard to estimate the additional effects introduced by the invisible noise within the subject. The ideal observer would typically have a d'_{ideal} equal to the square root of twice the signal-to-noise ratio in the external stimulus.

An index of efficiency η' can be formulated for any situation in which we know the specific characteristics of the stimulus and thus d'_{ideal} and in which an experiment can provide an estimate of the subject's sensitivity d'_{subj}. This index of efficiency is usually defined as:

$$\eta' = \left(\frac{d'_{subj}}{d'_{ideal}} \right)^2$$

(Equation 4-5)

As noted earlier, one of the very important notions that both stimulated and was reinforced by the theory of signal detection is the idea that the threshold, once almost the *sine qua non* of psychological theories of sensory performance, may, perhaps, no longer be a valid psychological construct. Reviewing the details of the preceding discussion and, in particular, the probabilistic notions of discrimination between signal and noise, the idea that there is a critical lower limit on the sensitivity of an observer may seem somewhat hard to justify. As an alternative, the signal detection theorists have suggested that we may want to consider the possibility that what "threshold" determinations measure is not so much a lower limit of sensitivity as it is something about the decision criteria that is being momentarily used by a subject. Thus, where the classical psychophysicist would place the blame for the lower bound of sensitivity on the characteristics of d', the signal detection theorist would consider "thresholds" to be a characteristic of β, in other words, response rather than sensory thresholds.

Green and Swets (1966) discuss this point and note that there are several reasons to consider that the notion of the absolute sensory threshold is either an artifact of either some of the older experimental paradigms or of shifting decision criteria. First, they note that the threshold is a theoretical construct, which is highly variable in several different ways. There is the matter of variability in values obtained even when precision of measurement is rigorous. For example, even in neurophysiological experiments, the "threshold" for spike elicitation seems to vary from moment to moment. Second, there is also a matter of criterion or psychological variability in many different detection experiments, which add substantial amounts of variance. Third, differences in psychophysical technique give substantial differences in threshold estimates. Fourth, there is a set of situational factors that influence detectability: the contrast between the target and the background, the time since the last stimulus, and the general status of the subject. Finally, in many situations, Green and Swets note, the detection of signals is one that is not so much a matter of the absolute energy in the stimulus and the background and the history of both.

A further complication, as I have already noted, is that under certain conditions, the "threshold" may turn out to be so very low indeed as to make the notion of a lower limit almost meaningless. Hensel and Boman (1960), for example, have shown that a single spike action potential elicited in the peripheral somatosensory nerve of a human subject can be psychophysically detected. Hecht, Schlaer, and Pirenne (1942) have shown that under appropriate conditions, as few as 5 to 8 quanta of light can give rise to a visual experience in a measurable proportion of the presentations, and only 1 quantum need be absorbed by a given receptor for this threshold experience.

Considered from an empirical point of view, we must also note that values of the estimates of thresholds are always falling as new psychophysical procedures are applied. The theory of neural coding may be relevant here. We so often find that the differential effects of some stimulus pattern previously thought to be "below threshold" can be detected in some new situation in which a judgment is demanded along some other sensory dimension. Although this is not a compelling argument for the absence of thresholds, it does suggest that, at least historically, we have been almost always wrong in our estimates of the lower limits of sensitivity to one or another stimulus dimension, except in those instances in which the threshold is assumed to be as low as it theoretically can be. Unfortunately, it is not possible to resolve the issue completely at the present time. It is a complicated controversy that depends also upon exactly what kind of a theory of the threshold one is discussing.

Signal detection theory helps to alleviate many of the problems of psychophysics by focusing attention on the joint effects of sensitivity and decision criteria rather than on the sensitivity alone. More complete descriptions of the procedures and implications of a modern psychophysical version of the theory of signal detection can be found in Coombs, Dawes, and Tversky (1970), and Corso (1967), or for what is perhaps the most rigorous discussion, Green and Swets (1966).

b. Learning Paradigms

There is a substantial difference between the paradigms of research used in the study of learning on the one hand and in the study of sensation and perception on the other. In general, the sensory psychologists seek to determine the properties of the sensory systems independent of the effects of the preceding sequence of stimuli. The student of learning on the other hand is interested exactly in the effect that the sensory psychologist sought to exclude—the long-term influence of the sequence of stimuli that the organism had undergone.

Thus, except for special situations such as those involved in sensory preconditioning or adaptation, most psychophysical experiments strive to maintain constant conditions so that the repeated representations of a stimulus will produce a stable sequence of responses. The assumption in the typical psychophysical experiment is that the organism's environment, both internal and external, is sufficiently stabilized so that variability in measurement is just that, random variability alone, and will not reflect any trend or experientially defined instability.

Studies of learning, on the other hand, are designed mainly to emphasize the changes in the performance as a result of experience. Therefore, such studies systematically present controlled sequences of stimuli. Thus the typical learning experiment usually has two levels of stimulus manipulation. One level provides a sequence of stimuli that is presented to the subject with the specific intent of altering some aspect of his internal mental state. The other consists of a probe or test stimulus that is used only to assay the effects of the experienced stimuli and to determine the course of that experience. A major problem arises from the fact that some test probes, which are intended to be innocuous, may have substantial effects on the experiential status of the subject. There is a sort of psychological principle akin to that Heisenberg uncertainty principle operating in the behavioral lab, too.

For example, Jones and Holding (1975) have shown that even a single test trial can lead to the initiation of the decay of persistent perceptual after-effect known as the *McCullough (1965) phenomenon.* No decrement in performance is observed simply as a result of the passage of time. If that first test trial is not given for delays that may be as long as six months, the initial response remains virtually constant. Clearly, the probe test stimulus in this case is exerting a profound influence itself on the process under examination and in no sense may be considered innocuous.

The major focus in studies of learning is usually the preparatory phase in which the learning experiences are presented in a controlled manner. Classic learning methods have included such procedures as serial presentation of stimuli, classical conditioning, and instrumental conditioning among many others. I elaborate on these methods in Chapter 8 wherein a more complete definition of learning, partially dependent on the operational characteristics of the relevant research paradigms, is developed.

c. *Choice and Discrimination Procedures*

Another major class of psychological research methodologies that has attracted considerable attention requires that the subject make a decision between alternatives. The reaction time to make a choice is one simple and powerful measure of underlying psychological information processing. To obtain this measure the subject is asked, for example, to depress one of several keys depending upon some characteristic of the stimulus pattern. By appropriately designing the stimulus combinations, a number of workers believe that they have been able to use choice reaction times, as they are called, to interpret the underlying cognitive processes involved in decision making (Donders, 1868) or acquisition of information from memory (Sternberg, 1966). The reader should also see Ratcliff and Murdock (1976) for a good recent review.

Another example of the choice or decision paradigm is the classical "Y maze" used in animal experiments. Determination of an ability of an animal to distinguish the presence or absence of a pheromone (a chemical effective for sensory communication) is one application of this paradigm. The affective (attractive or aversive) properties of a given stimulus can also be determined by placing an animal in a decision-making task of this type.

Discrimination tests can be combined with learning paradigms to evaluate the course of the acquisition of some discrimination skill. Learning of form discriminations (for example, Sutherland, 1964) or black-white discriminations (for example, Meyer, Dalby, Glendenning, Lauber, & Meyer, 1973) have often been used in this manner. Delayed response tests (for example, Jacobsen, 1935; and Fuster, 1973), in which a choice must be made after a prolonged period in which the animal cannot view the stimuli, also are commonly used in the study of frontal lobe function, for example.

The simple examples of choice behavior so far mentioned are almost inconsequential compared to the kind of choices that humans must make in their daily lives. Variables of risk and, perhaps even more important, of inferred risk, as well as the interaction of multiple valences, make human decision making one of the most complex areas of human cognitive psychology. Nevertheless, considerable progress has been made in studying risky decision making. The work of Clyde Coombs and his colleagues is particularly notable in this field (Coombs & Meyer, 1969; Coombs & Huang, 1970).

Other decision-making paradigms have also come into vogue in recent years. One of the most interesting is the notion of using small groups of subjects interacting within the rules of highly structured games, like the Prisoner's Dilemma (Rapoport & Chammah, 1965; and Guyer, Fox & Hamburger, 1973), to explore decision-making criteria and cognitive processes. Games of this sort are particularly interesting because they can be designed to require a particular kind of cooperation among the players. If that cooperation in decision making is not forthcoming, all of the participants lose; if it is forthcoming, all will win. The game-like, decision-making experiment, therefore, becomes a model in microcosm for the study of the social and political macrocosm. Unfortunately, the results of these experiments suggest that the ways in which people usually make decisions are disappointingly inconsistent with those cooperative and collaborative interactions that are necessary for their collective success. A complete taxonomy of 2 X 2 games, of which the Prisoner's Dilemma is only one example, can be found in Rappoport and Guyer (1966).

d. *Field and Protocol Observations*

The psychophysical, learning, and decision-making paradigms all involve highly precise control of the experimental situation. As we have noted in our introductory discussion of these response dimensions, there are many situations in which the abstraction of the real world into a manipulatable model situation would not work. Many complex situations are not reducible to the requirements of the laboratory without the loss of their essential characteristics and meaning. Thus psychological researchers have also developed techniques for the study of situations more closely approaching the natural environment.

One example is the classic field study, which literally may be carried out in the natural habitat of the organism under study. Consider, for example, the problem of studying the behavior of a band of primates. To remove these animals from their natural environment and place them in a laboratory situation would not only be inconvenient and expensive, but would also, without a doubt, disrupt the normal social and physical interactions to a sufficient extent that would distort the important psychological processes. How much easier and better it would be, as an alternative strategy, to take the experimenter to the jungle than to take the jungle to the experimenter! Field observations, therefore, represent a powerful means of observing complex behavior patterns. Some contemporary workers like George Schaller (1963, 1967, and 1972) and Jane Van Lawick-Goodall (1968, 1971) have made some remarkable progress in standardizing field observational procedures and have drawn some important conclusions by literally living with gorillas, lions, chimpanzees, and wild dogs in their natural environments. Their insights could not possibly have come from highly abstracted laboratory observations.

A related form of naturalistic observation is that of the protocol—a detailed statement of the thought processes of a subject as verbalized by him during the course of the problem solving. Protocols may be very formal or very informal. The subject may have a complete monologue electronically recorded and transcribed for subsequent content analysis by computational linguistics procedures using extremely sophisticated digital computer programs. On the other hand, an introspective protocol may be very informal. The classic nondirective approach of psychoanalytical therapy is a form of protocol analysis of the thought processes of a patient who is simply speaking out loud to convert the covert mental processes into overt behavioral (linguistic) statements.

A particularly interesting example of the laboratory application of protocol collection and analysis procedures is illustrated by the work of Kerwin and Reitman (1973). These cognitive psychologists are interested in the thought processes involved in problem solving. They chose to use the Japanese board game of "Go" as a model of a more general cognitive situation. This popular (in the Orient) game is particularly suitable for research, because the rules of the game and the win situation are relatively simple and well-defined even though there are a large number of playing stones and, thus, possible interactions between stones.

Figure 4-3 shows the layout of a "Go" board. The following excerpt from Kerwin and Reitman (1973) is a transcript of a tape recording of the thought processing of a player with a rather high level of proficiency. The game is played simply by placing stones on the board (a placement is indicated in the transcript by the coordinates of a deposited stone) until the opponent's stones are completely surrounded. The thought processes recorded in this protocol involve only one move—the 25th. The dialogue (which includes some technical "Go" terms for various standard positions and moves) picks up after the 24th placement of the game and terminates with the next placement, the 25th stone.

Placement 24:
Okay, let me consider. That seems to be the most palatable thing for black, but it's definitely too low in the circumstance. A high invasion at J-4 is the only one possible because of the feature of this move at F-5, forcing a response over here around E-7, and then this one at J-5 and now black is in very bad shape. The question is the best way to go about it. Clearly, white can do this (white F-5 and black E-7). It is clear

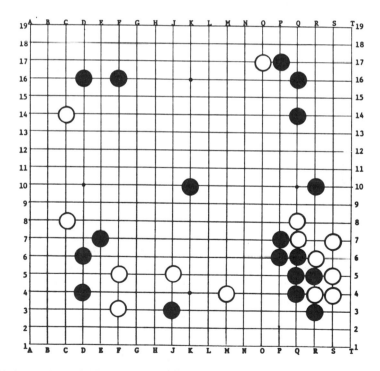

FIG. 4-3 A Go board situation as considered by the introspective subject in the text. (From Kerwin & Reitman, 1973.)

black must play E-7 because he cannot afford to be blocked in; and then here (white J-5). Now black is in some real difficulty with this J-3 stone. But perhaps there might be a better way of going about it. That is, perhaps this way. (White J-5 first.) Then maybe black would only be able to play here at G-4 and now white could push up a couple of times; white F-4, black G-5, white F-5, etc., to block off the black D-4, D-6 group. But I think maybe—let's see what effect this will have on the left side? That is, over here around C-11. He plays over here and I play there [plays not speci-fied]. That's a very big loss. His kake at E-7 is not so great because I'm considering some uchikomi [of C-3 corner?]. I'm thinking that this development he has various plays in here on the west side, but since I was anticipating treating these stones at C-8 and C-14 lightly from the beginning, this is not such a great cost. For him to go here at E-7 and then here at D-9 if I give this C-8 stone up is not so fruitful a develop-ment for black. And there are difficulties here at J-5,—not reinforcing this one at F-3 may make trouble for me. So I think I'll just play [probably E-5]—let me think again [probably considering again white F-5, black J-5]. He can play that tobi at J-5, but that [probably white F-5, black J-5, white E-7] absolutely requires an an-swer. And it will be very unfavorable for him underneath. That is, there is some conceivability—I'm thinking that I'll move here at F-5 and he should move here at E-7 and then this move at J-5 is just completely favorable for white. But what if he doesn't do that and goes here; white F-5, black J-5, white E-7. Well now, this move at E-7 is very favorable for white, closing in the corner and absolutely requiring some re-sponse in this area (black C-3). And I would think that from that point I would con-tinue to develop this M-4 stone, looking at two black positions [J-3 and J-5 group, and Q-4 group] that I think are attackable, and figure that black is—well, there are different ideas. I figure this is extremely favorable for white (boxing in black D-4 and D-6) and also this is favorable for white (referring to H. Dia. 25/27) because this J-3 stone is kind of getting swallowed up, is mochikomi. Black will have a difficult time to develop it—trying to live in this south side area is definitely taboo because the strength it would give white would make this Q-4 area very weak. I think I'll play this way as best. Let's see, your 24 was uchikomi at J-3 [Kerwin & Reitman, 1973, pp. 14-16].

It is obvious that a much deeper insight into the thought processes of this "Go" player has been obtained by asking him to introspect in this overt manner than could have been obtained by simply observing his behavior—the moving of the stones. Language in this protocol paradigm plays a role of the utmost impor-tance in helping us to understand the many intermediate mental steps that lay between the two overt motor responses of placements 24 and 25. Perhaps even more important, however, is the fact that by using a well-structured model situa-tion like the game of "Go" and verbal protocol reports, Kerwin and Reitman have been able to delve into the general ability of humans to deal with problems at a level of complexity that is more characteristic of human life than is the overly simplistic situation of many laboratory experiments.

e.   Questions and Surveys

Finally, in this list of methods that can be used to gain information about mental processes, we should not overlook the most common method of all—the conversational interaction between two people. We are constantly, in our daily life, as well as in the laboratory, communicating information about our mental states to our fellow human beings. We ask and answer questions all the time about our thoughts and attitudes. However, even the dialogue has been formalized into the highly technical and sophisticated survey research procedures that play an exceedingly important role in psychological and social science research today.

Fact and opinion surveys can be used to study a wide variety of mental processes varying from future buying plans to attitudes toward people of other races to the causative social factors that may lead to mental pathologies. In the psychological laboratory we also often ask for subjective interpretations of what people see, or what they remember, even in situations in which discrete responses have been carefully elicited. Deep understanding sometimes is obtained in this fashion that eludes all of the strategies that depend upon simple behavioral measures.

An interesting example of this is the work of Schuman (1972). During the latter days of the Vietnam War, a consensus seemed to be growing in the United States disapproving of the war. Eighty percent or more of the population indicated when surveyed that they thought the war was a mistake. Schuman, however, showed that there was a deeper level of analysis that made the interpretation of the simple disapproval much more meaningful. When people were interviewed in depth it turned out that there were actually two totally opposite reasons for the disapproval of the war. University students and faculties were negative because they were morally outraged at what the United States was doing in Vietnam and because *both* Vietnamese and Americans were being killed there. On the other hand, the negative attitudes in most nonuniversity communities was based upon the fact that the United States Army was not doing well there and too many of *our* troops were being killed there!

E. SUMMARY

This then brings us to the end of what at best can be an incomplete and, for many readers, an unsatisfying attempt to describe an anatomy of mind or to produce a satisfactory definition of mental process. Clearly, the scientific community has not proceeded far enough in the development of philosophy, science, or that interdisciplinary area in which I have been working to provide a definition that is so compelling that it would be accepted by most readers. It is also true that the highly emotionally loaded nature of the problem would make even a precise definition, acceptable by scientific criteria, unacceptable to some whose belief structures are in conflict with such a definition. When I attempt to define mind, I am dealing with the most precious, most important, and most personal part of humanity. I noted at the outset of this book, the cosmic nature of the joke of an evolution that could produce consciousness and yet, at the same time, the awareness that awareness itself is to be limited to a brief few years. Not all are willing to accept the implications of that "joke," and thus there are powerful forces that serve to perpetuate definitions of mind that go beyond the monistic or process emphasis it has been given in this chapter.

To sum up this chapter, consider the following nutshell definition of the mind. Briefly, I have sought to transmit the message that mind is the main process or action of the nervous system. Inherent in this approach is the concept that the process cannot exist without the structure. Self-awareness, consciousness, or attention—whatever one wishes to call that intrapersonal self-knowledge to which each individual is solely privy—is presumed to be a natural, material-based process that emerges at some appropriate level of organic evolution and neural complexity.

In no way are these mental processes independent of the structure of the nervous system, nor is any nonphysical law or function that is not implied in the rules of interaction of basic physical or chemical processes required for self-awareness to occur. To reiterate a useful metaphor—mind is to the nervous system as rotation is to the wheel.

It is important, furthermore, to distinguish between mind, on the one hand, and the behavior that is observed as an indicant of mental process, on the other. It is also equally important to keep separate the experimental paradigm or methodology used to measure behavior from the behavior itself. The specification of these three quite distinct domains—mind, behavior, and measurement procedures—is necessary to avoid the conceptual confusion introduced by the ultrapositivistic behaviorism that dominated psychology for so much of this century and which denied psychology the very essence that made it a coherent and special branch of science.

What I hope I have accomplished with this chapter is to have provided at least a useful and pragmatic definition of the term *mind*. Some usable definition of this sort is a necessary prerequisite for the discussion in many of the subsequent chapters. Whether we are discussing the localization of the mechanisms underlying some mental process or the effect of some drug on some other aspect of mind, it is essential to have some sort of a conceptual agreement as to the nature of mind and its constituent processes.

This completes the introductory portion of this book. I have stated fairly explicitly what is meant by the mind-body problem by contemporary workers and have provided a historical review of the solutions that have been proposed in the past. I have also provided an anatomy of the brain and at least a partial anatomy of the mind. The next step is to consider a variety of topics, each of which deals with a particular aspect of the mind-body problem. Thus, each of the following chapters discusses a set of research findings that deals specifically with some particular strategy of research in which comparisons, correlations, and associations are made between aspects of mentation and nervous system anatomy or physiology. These topics collectively make up the science of psychobiology.

Part II

MIND-BRAIN ASSOCIATIONS
AND CORRELATIONS

5

Localization of Mental Functions:
A Network Point of View

A. INTRODUCTION

1. The Issue

In what part of the brain does a particular mental process occur? What a simple and direct question this seems to be—at first reading. This query embodies the most obvious line of psychobiological experimental inquiry and is almost dictated by the requirements of therapeutic manipulation: How could one possibly cure a "brain" ailment unless one could identify the place in which the difficulty lay? The theory of brain organization that asserts that particular psychological functions are mediated by particular brain loci is, therefore, the logical next development of the fundamental premise that the brain is the seat of mental life and that its parts and their organization define our mental activities. This theoretical point of view is founded on the corollary assumptions that the brain can be analyzed into demarcatable anatomical structures (as described in Chapter 3) and the mind into separable functions (as described in Chapter 4).

However, at second reading, both from the perspective of the philosopher and in the harsh light of experimental research, the very meaning of the question itself begins to blur, and when examined in more detail, it appears to be neither simple nor direct. We are forced by recent developments to at least raise the possibility that the question of localization of mental process may be a "bad question" in at least some of its aspects.

There has been a continuing controversy between those who championed sharp localization of particular mental functions in specific neural structures (I refer to this position as radical localization theory) and those who thought that the brain probably acts as a homogeneous unit with some sort of mass or equipotential action (I refer to this position as radical homogeneity theory). But, it has not always been the case that the validity of the question itself was considered prior to a discussion of the technical and empirical details that underlay the specific associations that have been made between the parts of the brain and the processes of mind. Prior to the last few years, physiological psychology textbooks almost always implicitly assumed, seemingly axiomatically, that relatively sharp localization of function was the true state of affairs and that the problem is simply one of making the correct associations. Most modern researchers likewise, until very recently, have only asked questions of the class: What change in behavior will occur if I ablate this particular portion of the brain? In doing so, however, a large number of conceptual, logical, technical, and biological issues are ignored. The proposition now emerges that the strong forms in which questions of localization are usually framed into the laboratory, as well as many of the answers that had hitherto exclusively associated a particular portion of the brain with a specific psychological process, are probably conceptually flawed.

Indeed, the actual biological facts concerning the localization of the function in the brain may be quite different than the conventional view of radical localization theorists. We see in this chapter that a point of view is developing among the leaders of contemporary psychobiology that stresses that a large number of neural structures is almost always involved in even the simplest mental response, and further, that most structures seem to be involved with more than one response. At the very least, the problem is now appreciated to be very much more complex than had been previously thought. At the very most, the whole concept of localization may be a frail theoretical structure that has arisen only because of its deceptive simplicity, or because it was very difficult to deal with some of the alternatively more diffuse models in the experimental laboratory, even though these models may be more valid descriptions of biological reality. Fortunately, theories that deviate from data do not persist; those built on foundations of oversimplification or a misleading pragmatism typically do not stand the tests of time. Under the pressure of new findings, it does appear that radical localization theory is indeed being reinterpreted by contemporary psychobiologists.

On the other hand, it is clear that any competing theory based on radical homogeneity, mass action, or equipotentiality is also going to prove to be unacceptable in light of the fact that different sorts of behavioral changes do occur with different probabilities when different parts of the brain are injured. The brain is not, therefore, even to a first approximation, operating on the basis of any sort of total mass action or universal homogeneity. The evidence for this is clear in the range of deficits produced in a wide variety of psychological processes by brain lesions. For example, Fig. 5-1 shows a recent summary (Schaltenbrand, 1969) of the types of deficits that are *most likely* to appear when lesions are produced in particular parts of the mantle of the cerebral cortex. This figure should be compared directly to Fig. 5-2, which is a modification of the classic Brodmann area map of cytoarchitectonic areas shown in Fig. 3-36. In both of

FIG. 5-1 A map (plotted on a Mercator projection) of the surface of the cerebrum showing a hypothetical localization of particular psychological functions. These functions include such cryptic and general terms as Bewegung (movement) and Haltung (posture) as well as more specific terms such as Reich-hirn (smell brain). Obviously this chart is not very much more developed than the phrenological theories of a hundred years earlier. It does suggest however, the sort of thinking about the localization of brain functions that were still current in some circles even as recently as the late 1960s. (From Schaltenbrand, ©1969, with the permission of Georg Thieme-Verlag.)

these figures, the diagram of the brain has been distorted, according to the rules of the Mercator Projection, to allow us to observe both the top and the side of the cortex simultaneously. The general impact of this map of psychological deficits produced by widely varying sizes and placements of cortical lesions, as well as all of the others throughout history that have attempted to make this same point, is to emphasize the fact that the cerebrum, at least, is by no means homogeneous. There *are* some differences in function that may be attributed to the various regions.

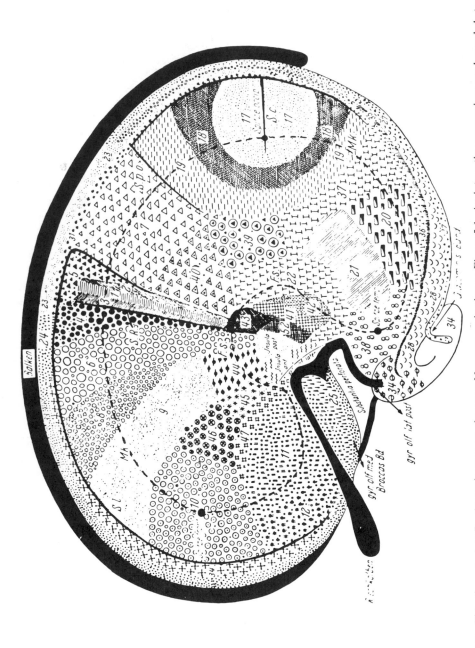

FIG. 5-2 This diagram plots Brodmann's areas on the same Mercator projection as Figure 5-1. An interesting comparison can be made between the suggested localization of function in that figure and the architectonically defined regions in this one. (From Denning, ©1966, with the permission of Georg Thieme-Verlag.)

Because of such obvious weaknesses in both radical localization and radical homogeneity theories, psychobiological theory is now impelled toward a third intermediate point of view—one in which the various parts of the brain do have some special properties, but one in which these properties are exhibited in highly complex manners as multiple nuclei interact to encode psychological processes. In this chapter, I develop the position that it is most likely that this third view, with its emphasis on the interactions that must occur between the components of a system of interconnected brain parts, will prevail. Rather than specific localization of individual functions in sharply defined loci, on the one hand, or massive homogeneity, on the other, the contemporary view presented here emphasizes multiple interacting components, nonunique localization of function, and multiple roles for many brain regions. Although some neural structures are shown to play a central or key role in certain mental functions, no portion can be solely and uniquely involved with any particular psychological function.

At a simple level, this emerging systems view may be analogized in terms of the structure of the link *chain* shown in Fig. 5-3. Cutting any link will lead to a failure of the chain, but the continuity of the chain is not associated with the integrity of any one link to any greater extent than any other—all links are equally critical. If a number of chains are connected in parallel, as in Fig. 5-4, then the analogy may be extended to show how the failure of a single link, and thus of one chain, may not even be totally fatal to the performance of the system, even though it may change the way in which, for example, some suspended object might be balanced in this metaphor of mind.

We should not stretch this metaphor too far, however, for the brain is neither a chain nor an interlocked group of chains. It is a much more complicated net of interacting components in which the components do more than mutually support each other. It is at least three-dimensional and, because the state of the interconnections probably varies from time to time, it should best be considered to be four-dimensional. The point being made, however, is that in a complicated system of interacting components, all of which contribute to the performance of some global function, the function may respond to damage of any of the components in very complicated ways; indeed, in ways that are not within the power of our analytic methods to predict, even when the number of components is smaller and the kinds of interactions much simpler than those known to be found in the brain.

FIG. 5-3   A hypothetical model of an interactive structure modeling one possible theory of the brain. See the text for details. Obviously this model of brain organization is inadequate. It is highly unusual for all brain function to cease when an individual neural "link" is broken.

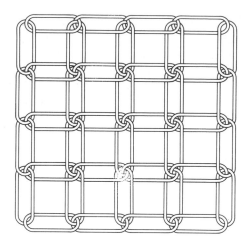

FIG. 5-4   A somewhat more realistic conceptual model of the brain. When a given neural "link" is broken, the system typically does not fail completely but usually rearranges itself to accomplish many of the same functions of which the original network was capable.

Indeed, it seems as if the frontier of the formal analysis of neurological networks is currently at the level of only two and possibly three neurons. Dagan, Vernon, and Hoyle (1975) and Perkel and Mulloney (1974) have debated the optimum description of behavior in simple nets composed of only two or three synthetic neurons—a technique pioneered by Harmon (1961). If contemporary biomathematicians have difficulty resolving the behavior of such a small number of idealized interconnected neurons, it is somewhat discouraging to contemplate the task of analysis posed by the entire nervous system, populated as it is with so many vaguely defined neural substructures.

In the previous pages of this introduction, I have explicitly been seeking to avoid the use of the word *center,* but I am no longer able to do so. The term is ubiquitous in contemporary psychobiology and slips into the discussion that follows all too often. It, therefore, deserves some special attention at this point. The term *center* is a very vaguely defined word. It is not, in fact, exclusively an anatomical term, but more often it must be considered a psychobiological term. A center is usually defined operationally as an anatomical region that, when perturbed, affects certain behaviors in some observable way. Therefore, a center may be a single portion of a nucleus, a nucleus, or a group of nuclei, or perhaps even a major proportion of the brain. If the reader remembers that this word is most often an operationally defined psychobiological term and only rarely based on anatomy alone, its confusing usage can be appreciated, if not clarified.

There is, however, a more fundamental conceptual problem associated with the use of the word *center.* Its use implies that there is some central, key, or most important neural structure on which other influences may play, but which is the ultimate controller or repository of some psychological function. In spite of the fact that it will be very difficult to eradicate this word from either psychobiology or from this book, it must be appreciated that this perspective of a central locus is fundamentally in error from the point of view that I develop in this chapter. There is virtually no remaining psychological function (other than in the sensory or motor communication systems) that research now strictly localizes in any single "center." The use of the word, therefore, is conceptually misleading. Rather than a model that hypothesizes a main focus or center, psychobiologists now should be turning to concepts that embody systems of interacting loci ("centers" only in some weaker sense of the word) within which the mechanisms for a given psychological process are distributed.

If this new point of view stressing networks of nuclei prevails, then the deficiency in our methodology for studying such distributed systems mentioned in the previous paragraph is an even more serious problem in the study of the mind-brain problem than previously appreciated. Nevertheless, the main purpose of this chapter is to champion such a network point of view as a modern substitute for the concepts of radical localization and centers.

There are a number of interrelated conceptual and biological obstacles that make the task of resolving the problems of brain localization of psychological function into such a network theory quite refractory. In the next section, I consider some of these obstacles that prevent psychobiologists from obtaining a final resolution of the localization question.

2. Conceptual and Biological Complexities in the Localization Issue[1]

As I have noted, the issue of whether there is sharp localization of function or diffuse mass action within the brain has been a controversy of long standing. The reasons for the persistence of this controversy are numerous: Some are biological—the data just do not seem to be conclusive; others are conceptual or logical—we neither have a very good taxonomy of mental processes to localize nor is there yet an adequate mathematical means of analyzing highly interacting systems. In this section, I consider some of these conceptual and biological difficulties that are encountered when one tries to validate either form of localization theory or to substitute the network concept for both.

a. *Poor Definition of Psychological Constructs*

In Chapter 4, I attempted to provide a working description of the various psychological processes that collectively make up that aspect of organic activity that we call *mind*. The strategy followed was one based upon a relatively practical consideration, namely, the processes that are objects of study in the laboratories of experimental psychologists. Hopefully, it was made clear that this overly

---

[1]I am indebted to my colleague Charles M. Butter whose astute comments helped clarify some of the points made in this section.

practical approach is itself fraught with difficulties. Not only is any analysis based upon current research interests unlikely to be all-inclusive (it often reflects accidents of available technology and instrumentation rather than the true biology of the system), but it was also indicated that there was a great deal of confusion concerning the taxonomy of the various psychological processes. We really do not yet know whether or not there are separable mental processes or, to the contrary, whether each construct is only a different aspect of some sort of a unified mental activity. Thus all current categorizations of mental processes are inadequate including my own attempt in Chapter 4. We have no completely satisfactory theoretical analysis or taxonomy of mind at the present, and the search for a locus for such ill-defined processes becomes extremely difficult.

This difficulty is reflected in the localization literature in a number of ways. The processes that various investigators seek to localize in the brain are themselves enormously diversified. Some search for a locus for "emotional" behavior, others for "memory," others for "form perception," and others for such narrowly defined laboratory operations as "delayed responses." The problem of brain loci of such nebulously defined psychological processes must itself be intrinsically nebulous. When there is not even a good agreement on the nature of the functions for which a locus is sought, the problem is inevitably going to be a tangle from the outset.

b.   Poor Definition of Neural Units

Surprisingly, there is also a comparable difficulty on the neuroanatomical side of the problem of localization. As was pointed out previously in Chapter 3, the lines of anatomic demarcation between the various portions of the central nervous system are not easy to determine definitively. It often requires special staining and microscopic techniques to establish the boundaries of the various centers of the central nervous system. Frequently these techniques involve physiological changes that differentially tag nervous tissue with radioactive or fluorescent substances. At least some of the relevant neural structures are defined in part by their functional, rather than solely by their gross anatomical, characteristics, to add a further note of circularity and difficulty.

A question must also be raised, therefore, concerning the criteria that are used to define the geographical limits of a proposed neural locus. Although the more or less directly observable gross anatomy of brain structure can be used in some cases—distinguishing between the cerebral cortices and the brain stem, for example, is fairly direct—subtle cytoarchitectonic characteristics must often be used to distinguish among the many different anatomical regions of the cerebral cortex or the nuclei of the thalamus, to take two obvious examples.

Other criteria, such as the common origin of afferent input connections or the common destination of efferent output connections, can be used. But the anatomist, just as the psychologist, is constantly faced with the difficulty of distinguishing between what is merely a convenient artifact of nomenclature or taxonomy and what is, in fact, the actual anatomical organization of the brain.

To make this point more clear, let us consider the problem of "centers" within the cerebral cortex. Obviously, one means of organizing the various "centers" of the cortex is simply to look at the surface of the cortex as a map upon which can be plotted the various functional loci determined by stimulation-evoked potential or ablation procedures. However, as we have seen, cytoarchitectonic differences among the regions of the cortex have also been influential in defining its organization. The reader should refer back to Figs. 3-36 and 5-2, which show the cytoarchitectonically defined Brodmann areas. But there are other criteria that might be used as well.

The surface of the cortex, for example, is divided by a set of highly obvious lines of demarcation—the fissures that divide the cortex into physical sulci. I have already noted that the fissures and sulci are, very possibly, only a fortuitous result of mechanical buckling due to the extraordinary growth of the cerebral mantle during individual maturation. Any apparent functional distinctions that occur between adjacent gyri may be due to this buckling, because the adjacent gyri are actually topologically quite distant from each other, rather than the fact that the gyrus has any intrinsic functional significance. (See Fig. 3-34 and the discussion, in Chapter 3, of the work of Richman, Stewart, Hutchinson, & Caviness, 1975.) Harry Jerison, probably the outstanding modern authority on paleopsychobiology, himself questions the concept that the sulci and gyri are necessarily significant correlates of physiology and mental function. (See, for example, Jerison, 1973, p. 296.)

The point being made by this digression is that there are a number of different means of establishing maps of the different cerebral regions. Unfortunately, there is as yet no full agreement between the cytoarchitectonic, the postablation behavioral, the degeneration, and the macroanatomic criteria for mapping the cortex. Until one or the other of the sets of criterion proves to be uniquely valid, psychobiology will have to accept the fact that brain structures are, to a significant degree, equally as poorly identified as the psychological processes. If it turns out that the brain regions defined by the different criteria are very inconsistent, then a major new conceptual difficulty will exist that exacerbates the problem of localization of function even further. In that case, we would simply not have a good definition of what consititued a demarcatable locus.

Similarly, there remains the general problem of the appropriate level or size of the neural unit that best corresponds to a given mental function. There are many alternative ways of defining unit areas in the brain (the Brodmann approach, the sulcus approach, etc.). The problem is which structural unit can be linked to which functional unit, and what is the appropriate unit size for specific levels of analysis. The cerebral cortex may be appropriate for some purposes, but a single cell or nucleus may be appropriate for others. The problem is especially severe when the different techniques give rise to boundaries that do not coincide.

Another aspect of the lack of precision concerning the identification of anatomic regions should also be noted. There is another form of organization within the brain that is not as obvious as its surface topography. Upon microscopic examination, the cortex, in particular (and many other brain structures also), is seen to be arranged as a series of layers or lamina. These multiple layers are organized vertically and thus add another form of structural complexity to the multiple horizontal organization defined by the criteria we have already mentioned. There are, therefore, anatomical subdivisions in addition to surface topography that deserve attention and that may be expressions of structural, as well as functional, differentiation.

Obviously, many of the questions raised here are only questions and have not yet been fully answered. Until they are resolved, the specification of what neural units are and what constitutes the appropriate neural unit must remain a major difficulty in our quest to determine whatever degree of localization of mental process actually occurs in the nervous system.

c. Variable Data from Humans

Of all of the experimental animals that one might seek to use for studies of localization of mental function, the most useful should be man himself. Yet the human is the one animal on which controlled experiments concerning brain localization of psychological function can only rarely be carried out. This is the case for the best and noble of legal and ethical reasons. The ethical constraints, obvious enough not to need detailing here, dictate that all human brain localization studies must be carried out in situations in which accident, war, or degenerative brain disorders have led to the need for some kind of explorative or therapeutic surgery, on the one hand, or postmortem examination of brain tissue, on the other. Yet these situations are all instances in which either the resulting lesions of the brain are poorly defined or in which the experimenter is denied simultaneous comparison of structure and function. Thus, in most human studies, lesions are not properly placed from the point of view of theory-oriented research, are ill-defined in terms of their extent, or are carried out on patients in whom brain pathologies may be simultaneously present. The data obtained from humans, therefore, are intrinsically highly variable and idiosyncratic, despite the huge mass of war and traffic wounds to which the people of the earth have so tragically been exposed during the past century. With few exceptions, the sample of well-defined injuries that provide information about any particular locus or condition is surprisingly small.

To make this point clear, consider the following. A number of years ago, I had the opportunity to visit the laboratory of a distinguished neurosurgeon. A very large room was filled with records of neurosurgical operations and of electroencephalographic recordings taken from deep within the human brain from a very large number of patients. Although the total mass of the records was large, it very quickly became clear that almost every record was unique. Each patient's record was an astonishing anecdote—a novel and almost unique piece of data. Sadly, there seemed to be almost no way to either synthesize the data into a comprehensive statement of what any part of the brain did, nor was there even any way, in most of the cases, that any individual "experiment" could be replicated. The enormous body of knowledge represented by these records, therefore, was almost useless to the scientist whose demands for systemization and synthesis transcend the mere accumulation of unrelated data. No matter how interesting these records are individually, they contribute little to our ability to predict the effects of particular lesions, except in the most general way.

The conceptual problem that this variable human data creates concerns the interpretation of the fact that brain injuries result in very diverse behavioral deficits. The experimenter is always faced with the question: Is the variability due to the variability of the lesion, to actual variability in the locus of the function, or to uncontrolled pre- and post-operative experiential factors?

Another difficulty with research on humans in the study of localization is that the situations in which the living brain is actually exposed for stimulation or recording are exactly those situations that are the least propitious for the time-consuming application of well-controlled and statistically well-designed tests of mental function. It would be a most unusual situation, indeed, in which a psychologist might be free to apply some well-standardized laboratory test of human performance in the amphitheater of the brain surgeon. Thus psychobiology is, in the main, denied high-quality versions of the most relevant and most desirable form of data on localization of psychological function and must turn to use of experimental animals as models.

Perhaps the current utility of clinical data can be best summed up by quoting the words of Alexander Luria (1966b), the international grand master of the effects of brain lesions on human performance:

> The clinical evidence shows that any complex behavioral function (perception, action, speech, writing, reading, calculation) is never lost in a patient with a lesion of only one circumscribed area of the cortex, but it may be impaired in lesions of widely different areas of the brain, sometimes far distant from each other. At the same time, a lesion of one circumscribed area of the brain never leads to the isolated loss of any one complex behavioral function, but causes a group of disturbances which, although they always possess some common link, is reflected in the normal course of what are apparently diverse functions [p. 69].

Luria's clinical data has also led him to the belief that, although there is no sharp localization or mass action, the brain is acting as a system in which many differentiated structures are involved in even the simplest form of mental action. Whether this perspective is supported or not by his findings depends in large part upon the quality of the human data on which his perspective is based. Although my bias is to agree with Luria's point of view in general (and there are few more eloquent or intelligent statements of the problem of localization than his), the possibility must at least be considered that a network concept of brain action, like Luria's, may have been too heavily influenced by the very variable human data.

d. Only Deficits Can Be Localized

Just as in statistics, where it is only possible to reject a hypothesis and not to prove one, there is a logical constraint on exactly what can be validly localized in an ablation experiment. Indeed, if one considers the matter carefully, it becomes clear that normal psychological functions themselves cannot be localized by lesion studies; only the produced deficits in or deviations from normal functions produced by a lesion can be evaluated. No experimental design could ever completely establish that a function was uniquely localized in some center; for example, ablation experiments are capable only of saying that a given center is involved to some degree in the processing of a certain function.

To go beyond this level of putative association between locus and deficit, a researcher would be required to carry out an almost impossible series of multiple disassociation experiments. For each and every pair of areas, one would have to show that ablation of Area 1 led to a disruption of Function 1 but not of Function 2 and that ablation of Area 2 led to a disruption of Function 2 but not Function 1. Only in this way could a series of experiments on the localizations of deficits, perhaps, be interpreted in terms of precise localization of some function. Clearly this is an idealistic experimental paradigm that probably would never be carried out because it is certain that not pairs, but many sites of the brain are involved in any particular psychological process.

e. The High Level of Interconnectivity of the Central
Nervous System

As we saw in Chapter 3, the various nuclei of the central nervous system of mammals are very highly interconnected. Almost every day, a new pathway is reported in the literature. Both gross and microscopic anatomical results speak to the fact that there are almost as many interconnecting channels among the various centers of the brain as can be imagined. Indeed, almost everything seems to be, at least, indirectly connected in most mammals' brains to almost everything else. These anatomical data reveal that the brain is not likely to be operating, even to a first approximation, as an aggregate of relatively independent nuclei. Rather, it must be organized in such a way that the action of one nucleus affects the action of many other nuclei, and, in turn, each nucleus is acted upon by a number of others. In such an interconnected system, the analogy of the linked chain becomes a totally inadequate representation of the facts, and another type of model is required. A more appropriate model is a cybernetic (or feedback) network composed of a number of nodes, richly interconnected by both feedforward and feedbackward links. Such a network was illustrated in Fig. 3-71.

Theoretical psychobiologists like Arbib (1972) tell us that the important and relevant point about networks of this sort is that they are very difficult to understand by a process of successive partitioning. Depending upon the nature of the links, whether they are inhibitory or excitatory, the action of the network may be very peculiarly affected by the ablation of any one of the nodes. Theoretically at least, it is probably not too strong to say that the ablation of any node may affect the action of any other and that the resulting effects may be of any polarity given a suitable interconnecting network.

Thus, assuming for the moment that this form of network organization is a true characterization of brain organization, the removal of any given nucleus would lead to a rather drastic disruption of almost any output, i.e., behavioral, function even though the nucleus removed was only remotely involved in the direct representation of the behavior. Such a result would be a compelling reason for any investigator, unaware of the true organization, to assume that the ablated center was directly responsible for mediating the particular function that was disrupted. Yet, the facts of the matter might be that the ablated nucleus only indirectly affected the essential one.

The interactions that can occur between nodes in some hypothetical system, or between nuclei in the brain, can be very deceptive in spite of relatively simple forms of interconnection. For example, it is possible for one nucleus (A) to *increase* the activity in another (C), even though all interconnections are inhibitory, through the mediation of the reduction in the activity of a third nucleus (B), which is located between the two. This process, known as disinhibition, is illustrated in Fig. 5-5. For example, if nucleus C is inhibited by nucleus B, the inhibitory action of nucleus A on nucleus B would result in the decrease of inhibition on nucleus C, and thus a net increase in its activity.

A similar interactive process that may result in misleading conclusions concerning the localization of a mental process is based on an exclusively excitatory process. Suppose that a given nucleus D functioned only when it received a facili-

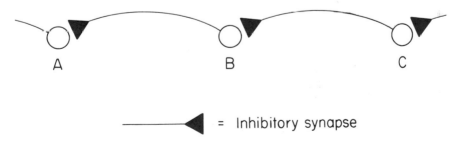

FIG. 5-5   Diagram illustrating the nature of disinhibition — the increase in activity in neuron C because of the inhibition by A of the inhibition exerted by B on C. (From Uttal, 1975b.)

tory input from some other nucleus E. Suppose further that the facilitating nucleus E was ablated from the brain and that the behavior exhibited some sort of deficit. The initial assumption might be that nucleus E is the locus of the process. In fact, this would be an erroneous conclusion, for nucleus E only exerted some sort of facilitory or arousing influence on the true locus of the function—nucleus D. The important point is that although this proto-"motivational" role of nucleus E is important in this interacting net, it should not be identified as the true transactional locus of the process under study.

Exactly analogous to the difficulty of excitation and inhibition and resulting in quite similar effects would be situations in which some previously infrequently observed response occurred more frequently as a result of an ablation. Such a result may only be interpreted in terms of a release from inhibition. In this case, the logical difficulty is less severe because the nature of the interaction that produced the effect is more obvious. As noted previously, multiple stages of this sort of inhibitory and facilitory interaction in a network could produce an extremely complicated response pattern that is not amenable to the conventional tools of mathematical analysis.

The behavioral effects of such network interactions in the brain can be amazing and surprising. For example, Sherman (1974) has shown that the destruction of portions of visual cortex can actually lead to an improvement in some previously degraded visual processes (perimetric measurements) when the deficit had originally been produced by depriving a cat of visual experience in one eye. Apparently, the destruction of the cortex led to the release from inhibition of some sort of visual space perception process mediated by an alternative visual pathway passing through the superior colliculus.

As another example, Fonberg (1975) has reported that deficits produced by dorsal amygdalar ablations on the eating behavior and instrumental performance of dogs could be reversed if a further ablation was made in the lateral region of the amygdala. The amygdala, therefore, must be composed of at least two interacting nuclei, but it cannot be said that one is the site of the eating behavior and the other inhibits it. Even after the destruction of the eating "center," the removal of the inhibitory lateral region led to recovery of the "missing" function.

Finally, we may note a sensory study in this genre carried out on rats by Vom Saal, Hamilton, and Gandelman (1975) in which performance on an olfactory discrimination task was enhanced by ablating a portion of the septum. Although this is a clearer case of a release from inhibition than the two previous studies, the same point is made by all of these experiments, namely, that removing tissue can improve performance in certain instances.

Experiments of this sort, in which previously lost functions are recovered or normal performance is enhanced as a result of additional ablation, are perhaps the best exemplars of the conceptual difficulties that are engendered in even the most simple and direct localization studies by complex feedback loops.

f. Information Communication Versus Information Processing

When one is dealing with the peripheral sensory systems, it is usually quite easy to distinguish between the communication aspects of the afferent pathways, on the one hand, and the integrative or information processing aspects of the central neural structures, on the other. Few researchers would, for example, assume that the isolated retina or the cochlea are themselves capable of conscious experience. Rather, it is almost universally assumed that the peripheral sensory channels serve mainly to communicate information to the brain. At some higher level, information is represented as a pattern of neural impulses that must be identifiable with the perceived experience. Although the peripheral structural mechanisms may perform some preliminary processing, such as contour enhancement, their main role is to serve as transmission lines to the higher centers at which the essential interpretive processing occurs.

However, when one is studying those portions of a sensory system within the brain, it is not always so obvious exactly which parts should be considered as part of the communication mechanisms and which are parts of the interpretive mechanisms. As one specific example, consider the following question: Is the occipital cerebral cortex of Brodmann's Area 17 really the "locus" of visual perception, or is it merely a more central portion of the transmission system that communicates information to some more fundamental interpretive region? Certainly, lesions of Area 17 do lead to highly specific scotomata (blindspots) in the visual field. But it is not clear whether this should be considered a result of the ablation of the perceptual interpretive mechanism or simply a break in the line that communicates this portion of the visual field elsewhere.

Psychobiologists have generally assumed, without an adequate empirical foundation, that the coded signals at the level of Area 17 are identifiable with perception. However, there is a significant body of data that suggests that visual perception deals with symbolic aspects of the stimulus in ways and at more central levels that transcend the isomorphic representations observed at the more peripheral neural levels of the occipital cortex. If true, then the effects of Area 17 ablations should be interpreted in quite a different way than they often have been. Alternatively, it might reasonably be suggested that the coded or symbolic levels of the nervous system at which the interpretive processes identifiable with perception actually occur have simply been cut off from their necessary inputs. The observed deficits in visual function, according to this analysis, should be described as a communication, rather than as an interpretive breakdown. Thus the occipital cortex would be serving mainly as a communication link rather than in the integrative role usually associated with it in current theory.

Obviously, this is a very complex issue and, until we know more about just what parts of the brain are directly associated with perceptual experience, it may be very difficult to resolve it. The residual doubts about the communicative or interpretive role of a given center remain, nevertheless, a potential obstacle to the full understanding of the localization of psychological processes.

g. Redundancy—Multiple Nuclei Serving a Single Function

Another difficulty encountered by the student of localization is the problem of redundancy. It is entirely possible and indeed appears to be the case on the basis of a considerable amount of data, that most mental functions are multiply represented in the central nervous system. Thus, even though the ablation of a given nucleus may produce no observable behavioral deficit, this nucleus may be intimately enough involved with a certain psychological process to the extent that it alone is *sufficient*, even though not *necessary*, for the mediation of that process. Such multiply localized functions would be extremely difficult to pin down to specific anatomical regions, because multiple ablations would be required to demonstrate adequately the roles of the redundant loci. Although this may not seem to be too difficult a task, the reader should consider the scientific "sociology" of the situation. Psychobiological experiments of this genre are usually stimulated when some clue fortuitously suggests that a given neural center may be involved in a certain psychological process. If multiple and redundant localization exists, then any such potential clue would always be hidden by the fact that accidental ablations of the individual centers will produce little in the way of an observable deficit. Redundancy would mask the deficit and, therefore, the relevant experiments simply will never be stimulated into existence.

h. Multiple Functions of Single Nuclei

A related barrier to the correct interpretation of the data of localization studies lies in the biological fact that most central nervous system nuclei are not uniquely associated with a single function. Just as there may be redundant nuclei subserving a single function, there also may be multiple functions served by a given nucleus. Thus ablation of a given neural structure may lead to the alteration of several functions, and only the most obvious deficit may be assigned to that particular center. A gross underestimate of the broader role of the center would thereby result.

i. Recovery of Function

Another major difficulty in the study of localization of function is due to the repeatedly observed fact that the behavioral deficit is not constant; it may change or apparently may even be completely eliminated with the passage of time. Thus, to the degree that behavioral functions do reappear, the possibility is raised that the surgically destroyed locus may not have been uniquely related to the observed deficit.

Furthermore, explaining why recovery of function occurs in particular cases is especially difficult. Following the recovery of a function initially impaired by some more or less extensive lesion of brain tissue, the investigator is faced with at least five possible alternative explanations of the recovery:

1. The deficit was caused not by the direct action of the ablation of the "center" but by the general shock and disorganizing effect of the surgery. Even "sham," i.e., control-lesioned operations, do not necessarily exclude this possibility, because the shock effect of removing some centers may be greater on some behaviors than on others.

2. Some other center has been gradually brought into action that provides an alternative mechanism for mediating the process that had been affected by the surgery. This explanation would essentially assume that there is no rigid localization of function but that there is sufficient plasticity or potential for reorganization in the nervous system to allow several combinations of nuclei to perform the same function if needed.

3. The recovery of function is due to the regeneration of the ablated tissue. Although the regeneration of central nervous tissue in mammals is known to be restricted, there is always the possibility that some small portion of regenerated tissue, sufficient to replicate the function, may have repaired at least a portion of the ablated tissue.

4. The recovered function is, in fact, not identical to the originally lost function. Rather, some new response mode has been substituted for the original one but so successfully as to completely simulate the original process.

5. Another possibility has been raised by LeVere (1975). He suggests that any recovery of function following a lesion is unrelated to regrowth or reorganization, but on the other hand, is always produced by spared tissue. LeVere is thus implicitly suggesting that the extent of the region that may be presumed to be associated with the particular behavior is actually larger and less localized than it is usually thought to be. Therefore, localization is a poor model of the neural-mental relationship, in general, according to LeVere.

Another line of evidence that supports the notion that a simplistic measure of the amount and locus of tissue ablation is not an adequate model of the behavior deficit or recovery following localized ablation lies in the fact that the amount of deficit and the course of the recovery is closely linked to the time sequence in which the lesions are made. If the ablated tissue is removed in one operation, deficits are usually produced that may recover after a period of time. However, if the same amount of tissue is removed in several serial operations, and if a deficit is produced by this ablation, a number of investigators [see Finger, Walbran, & Stein (1973) for a recent review of serial sparing] have shown that recovery from the deficit may not occur. Patrissi and Stein (1975) have carried out a systematic study of the effects of interoperation intervals and have shown that short interoperative intervals (10) days led to substantially greater decrements and poorer recovery of function than did intervals of 20 and 30 days, even though great care was taken in assuring that the tissue removed was alike for both long- and short-interval treated rats. Thus any explanation of recovery based simply on the amount and/or locus of tissue removed alone must be incomplete.

Clearly, it is very difficult experimentally to disentangle these alternative explanations, and indeed, it may even be difficult to do so from some logical point of view. Recovery of function is an extraordinarily serious contraindication to any arguments that champion radical localization theories.

j. Miscellaneous Data Difficulties

Finally, I can refer to a grab bag of miscellaneous difficulties for supporters of localization theory that arise out of the nature of the empirical results themselves. There is a considerable amount of data that indicates, without very much controversy, that sharp and precise localization of complex mental functions does not occur in the nervous system. The classic example is the conclusion that Lashley (1950) reached after years of searching for the location of the memory trace. Reluctantly, he was finally forced to conclude on the basis of a long series of experiments that memory processes were actually widely distributed throughout the brain—no specific locus for memory storage could ever be found for most kinds of learning. Although there is some recent evidence that learning is regulated to some extent by nuclei such as the hippocampus of the limbic system (see Isaacson, 1974), there still seems to be little or no evidence for localized storage of memories. Many workers, most notably Karl Pribram (Pribram, 1969) and E. Roy John (John, 1972), now look to distributed mechanisms to explain memory functions.

Similarly, in recent years, considerable evidence has accumulated that suggests that some of the areas previously considered to be exclusively motor or sensory now must be considered to contain both sensory and motor neurons. The notion of polysensory areas into which auditory, visual, and somatosensory afferents all seem to project has also come to be generally accepted.

All of this data suggest that simplistic notions of neat boundaries, exclusive representation, and complete differentiation of function associated with a radical theory of localization must fall victim to a newer approach in which some compromise between the ideas of radical localization and radical mass action will have to be achieved. It is my belief that this compromise will ultimately be found in the form of an interacting network theory.

Having completed a discussion of the conceptual and biological difficulties inherent in localization research, I now review the history of the concept that mental functions can be more or less precisely localized in the neural centers of the brain. I then present a modern view, from this historical perspective, of current localization data and theory.

3.   History of Localization Theory[2]

The question of the possible localization of mental processes in anatomical structures and substructures is of great antiquity. Indeed, it may be considered to be
one of the great historical issues of science, and, from some points of view, the
classic embodiment of the mind-body problem. Although we do not know who
the man was who first inquired into the possibility of a specific localized relationship between some parts of his body and particular aspects of his thoughts,
the first recorded consideration of the problem in a serious scientific or philosophical manner is usually attributed to the classic Greek philosophers during the
500 years prior to the birth of Christ.

From that time until the present, there has been a more or less overlapping
and parallel growth of a number of proposed solutions to the problem. Although
it is interesting to note that the elements of both radical mass action and radical
localization theory are to be found in the various Greek philosophies, we should
also remember that the cryptic comments from the historic past are prone to
overinterpretation. The poetic thoughts of a Greek philosopher, relayed to us
through medieval transcribers, are, like Nostradamus' predictions, open-ended
enough for almost anything to be read into them. Therefore, intellectual "precedents" of this sort should be taken with a grain of salt.

As one surveys the total history of the localization issue, however, it quickly
becomes clear that there are five distinct stages in the history of this subaspect
of the mind-body problem. The first period, lasting from about 500 B.C. to 200
A.D., was the Classic epoch dominated by the teachings of Greek philosophers.
At that time, the main controversy revolved around the issue of which major
organ (i.e., the heart, the liver, or the brain) was the receptacle of the fluid "mind
stuff."

The second, and most amazingly persistent, historical period (it lasted from
the second century to about the sixteenth century) was a time in which a localization theory was supported that was based upon the assumption that the
mind was embodied in the fluids of the brain and that the vesicles or cavities of
the brain were the significant repositories of those mind fluids. The teachings
of Galen (129-200 A.D.), in particular, reigned supreme during the latter parts of
that entire period.

A third period occurred when, along with the Medieval cultural renaissance,
there also emerged a scientific renaissance in the sixteenth century. During this
period, thinking about the localization issue began to change, and attention began to be directed at the semisolid portions of the nervous system rather than
the fluid-filled cavities. Scientists who were clearly the intellectual antecedents
of contemporary psychobiologists began to speculate that the various parts of

---

[2]In this historical section, I have followed the tradition of indicating the birth and death
dates of the earlier workers.

the brain, which were apparent even in gross dissection, might have different functions.

Theories of the fourth period in the history of the localization problem began to take specific form in the nineteenth century as a combined result of developments in "faculty" psychology, on the one hand, and some important anatomical discoveries, on the other. The faculty psychologists assumed that mental traits were distinct and separate to an extreme degree. For example, the early faculty psychologists assumed that psychological functions such as acquisitiveness and musical ability were independent and separate processes. The anatomical discoveries of this same period also seemed to suggest that a similar sort of specialization was present among the parts of the brain, with the most extreme differentiation being exhibited by portions of the cerebral cortex. The impulse toward a union of these two developments was overwhelming, and indeed the concept that emerged—separate psychological functions mediated by differentiated brain structures—has remained the dominant theme of psychobiology throughout most of the twentieth century. It has only recently begun to be superceded.

The fifth and most modern period is both a reflection of newer observations of the dynamic interactions that occur between the various processes and centers and a reflection of more modern empirical data that suggest that the effects of narrowly circumscribed lesions and electrical stimulation of particular brain regions are far more complex than some of the earlier workers had thought. The processes of interaction, inhibition, facilitation, and complex feedback loops play a much more important role in current theory now than they did even a decade or so ago.

In the following parts of this section, I survey in greater detail the concepts and contributors who have kept this issue of localization of mental process in the forefront of the mind-brain problem for almost 2500 years. Although this history is necessarily brief, more detailed discussions of the role of localization theory in the development of modern psychobiology can be found in Polyak (1957), Wolstenholme and O'Connor (1958), Fulton and Wilson (1966), Penfield and Roberts (1959), Brazier (1959), and Luria (1966a). These are the major sources that have served as my guide in preparing this brief summary. In addition, since writing this section, I have encountered an elegant consideration of the nineteenth century developments in localization theory by Robert W. Young (Young, 1970), which I particularly call to the interested reader's attention.

a. The Classic Greek Philosophical Period — The Foundation Stones

Although Plato (428-347 B.C.) and Aristotle (384-322 B.C.) remain the best known of the Greek philosophers, many of their most relevant ideas concerning mind and brain had been anticipated by over a hundred years. Indeed, it was among their predecessors in the sixth and fifth centuries B.C. that the first organized concepts concerning the function of the brain began to be discussed and recorded. Although the record of these pre—Platonic philosophers is for the most part lost, we do know, across the millenia, of such personalities as Alcmaeon of Croton (?550-500 B.C.?), who, in about 520 B.C., suggested the relatively sophisticated notion (for that time) that the brain was the most important organ of the body in terms of both its sensory and motor functions as well as in terms of the integrative or thought processes that related these input and output functions. Such a description of the role of the brain sounds surprisingly modern, and may be considered as the earliest antecedent of the information processing or cybernetic models so popular in contemporary psychobiology.

Approximately one hundred years later, Hippocrates of Cos (460-380 B.C.)— he of the medical oath—asserted that the brain was exclusively the organ of mind. But Philolaus of Croton, a contemporary Greek philsopher-physician whose birth and death dates are unknown, suggested (perhaps formally for the first time) that the brain was only the seat of rational (i.e., intellectual) functions, and the heart accounted for the more primitive functions of sensation and emotions. This idea has persisted in popular language, if not in the theories of contemporary workers, up until the present day.

Most historians agree that by this period the Greek physicians were certainly carrying out elaborate dissections of the brain and had a pretty fair knowledge of its general structure. It seems likely that these early physicians must have realized almost at once that the brain was intimately involved with the networks of nerves that ran through the body and must have more or less come to the conclusion that these networks were directly related to mental function.

However, the roles of the heart and the brain were thoroughly confused by the Greeks in a most unfortunate way that persisted for almost two thousand years. Even William Harvey (1578-1657), the great anatomist who discovered the circulation of the blood, still assumed, much as did Aristotle almost two thousand years earlier, that the circulatory system was in some way directly associated with mental process. Aristotle, whose philosophy and teachings were to be so influential for so many centuries, differed from Plato in this key regard. Plato's theory of localization of mental processes was much more in the tradition of modern times, because he assigned mental functions directly to the nervous system rather than to the circulatory system.

How is it that the circulatory system played such an overly important role in localization theory for so many centuries? There are several reasons, but among the most important was the general theoretical perspective that dominated so much of scientific thinking during prerenaissance times. Hydraulics and pneumatics were the physical sciences that were dominant prior to the discovery of electricity. As one traces the history of the mind-body problem, one of the most persistent themes is that, whatever the contemporary model, it is usually an extrapolation of the currently dominant physical theory. Hydraulics played this role during the Classic and Medieval periods, then electricity after its discovery, followed by the telephone system during its day, and finally by the computer—

the latter model gradually to be superceded by the healthier neurophysiological-reductionistic theory that is predominant today.

Another reason for the persistence of the circulatory theory of mind is the empirical fact that the heart does become active—very obviously so—when a person becomes emotional. Furthermore, the spurious correlation between the cessation of consciousness and the cessation of the pulse is also a compelling argument for a central role of the heart in the absence of other knowledge. The brain, on the other hand, lies silently in its vault and could have been, as was suggested by Aristotle, merely a cooling mechanism for the blood.

Although Plato's classification of mental processes was also quite different than those of contemporary psychology, it is he who probably deserves the credit for the first specific localization of mental functions within different regions of the nervous system. In particular Plato assigned "mind" to the brain, "passion" to the upper levels of the spinal cord, and what he called the "lower drives" to the more caudal portions of the spinal cord. In his localization theory, the heart and the liver also played important roles. The more rostral portions of the spinal cord, in which the passions were localized, was thought to interact closely with the heart (again the heart is involved in the emotions—an "obvious" association derived from the considerations mentioned above), and the liver, interacting with the caudal portion of the spinal cord, was responsible for urogenital delights of various kinds.

Plato thus explicitly assumed that there were three different kinds of mental process or, in virtually synonymous terms, three kinds of soul. The next question that must naturally evolve from this point of view was: What links these mental processes and the relevant parts of the body? However, the answer to this question, the next step forward in localization theory, did not occur until almost five hundred years later in the thoughts of a Greek physician who lived in Rome.

b.   The Galenic Period—The Hydraulic Theory

Galen, one of the most remarkable teachers of biology in human history, led a colorful and widely traveled life after his birth in the Greek city of Pergamum. The majority of his most important works, however, were carried out in Rome after he had completed his education in Greece and Alexandria. By Galen's time, the theory of mind that had the widest general acceptance among the protopsychobiologists of the Mediterranean world was a hydraulic one. Fluids and vapors of one kind or another were supposed to be closely associated, in fact identifiable, with mental processes. "Vital spirits" flowed where thoughts did, according to the reductionism of the times, and it was certainly true that the early anatomists and physicians had found fluids of many different kinds coursing about through the body. The early anatomical studies of the brain also turned up another important and seemingly relevant fact. The brain was not a solid mass but rather contained several fluid-filled cavities or ventricles. The obvious conclusion to be drawn under the press of the hydraulic theories and the presence of these ventricles in the very center of the brain was that they were also at the very center of human psychological experience.

The ventricles and their contents, themselves, thus became in Galen's view the specific correlates of mental process. Galen's theory asserted that the ventricles were the repositories or storage units of the fluids that constituted mind. However, because there appeared to be more than a single ventricle, even to the anatomists of Galen's time, additional subdivision or localization of functions was assumed. Galen believed, as did Plato, in a trichotomy of mental process; mind was made up of input or sensory processes, output or motor processes, and an integrating or linking set of processes that he called reason interposed between input and output processes.

Galen's theoretical schema was a step forward from the ideas of his predecessors based on the analogy that could be drawn from the fact that there were the three known ventricles and the classic Greek concept of three different kinds of mental process. Specifically, he assumed a form of localization in which the anterior ventricle and sensory experience, the middle ventricle and reason, and the posterior ventricle and the control of responses were respectively linked. It was, therefore, a brain theory of the localization of mind rather than a spinal or cardiac theory. However, from another perspective, it should also be noted that Galen's model was something of a retrogression back from the basic idea that mind was a brain function that had been implicit in the work of some of his predecessors. Although the three brain ventricles stored the fluids that were the stuff of the mind, Galen attributed the origin of the "vital" fluids to other of the internal organs of the body, such as the liver and heart, thus misemphasizing the role of the viscera in the mental process. Galen's physiology did, however, extend the previously vague hydraulic theories to a highly specific model. He speculated that all of the fluids of the body moved about from one organ to another and that in each place they were transformed from one type of substance to another.

Although Galen's theory was predominantly hydraulic and dealt mainly with fluid-filled cavities, he also considered the role of the solid tissues of the brain. He suggested that the anterior portions of the brain, those surrounding the first venticle, were primarily sensory and that those surrounding the posterior ventricle mainly controlled movement. In this subdued and secondary portion of his theory, Galen thus also began to lay the foundation stone of the theory of localization that predominated until very recently, namely, that different functions reside in different solid portions of the brain.

Galen's hydraulic theory persisted almost completely unchallenged and unchanged for about 14 centuries. The notion that fluid-filled cavities were at the root of mental process was still current in the sixteenth century as evidence by the drawing shown in Fig. 5-6.

FIG. 5-6   A sixteenth-century model of the brain attributed to Dryander. (From Magoun, 1958, with the permission of The Ciba Foundation, London.)

One other major innovation of the utmost importance that was introduced by the Galenic tradition and that was even more persistent was the concept of a nervous *system*. Medieval interpretations of this concept are shown in Figs. 5-7 and 5-8. These two early figures display the brain as a system of nodes connected by interconnecting transmission links. Although the nodes are fluid-filled cavities and the links are presumably tubes in each of these drawings, the basic concept of a *system of interacting units* is implicit in Galen's theory. The notion of a system of interconnected parts plays a key role in the historical development of theories of the nervous system, and it is to Galen and his followers that this idea must be originally attributed, regardless of the fact that the nature of the communicated material, the nodes, and the transmission links, all happen to have been incorrectly chosen.

Implicit in Galen's writing (as well as in that of his Greek predecessors) is also the important concept of the triple nature of brain and mind. Both the anatomical structures and the sensory input, motor output, and associative processes were thought of as triumvirates. This input-central-processing-output trichotomy is quite modern, being the essence of modern information theory models of both neuroanatomy and psychological process as noted earlier.

The notion of central integrative or association regions intermediary and communicating, in particular, between the input sensory and the output motor mechanisms has also played an enormously influential role in contemporary

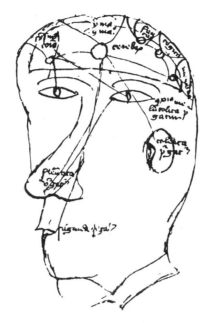

FIG. 5-7 A thirteenth century model of the brain attributed to Roger Bacon. (From Magoun, 1958, with the permission of The Ciba Foundation, London.)

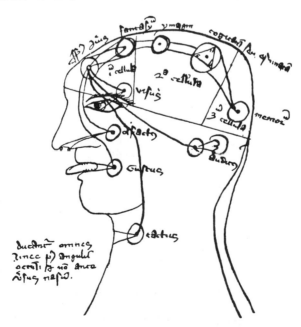

FIG. 5-8 A fourteenth century model of the brain. The artist-author is unknown. (From Magoun, 1958, with the permission of The Ciba Foundation, London.)

neuroscience and psychology. Although we are becoming aware that the so-called association areas of the brain are not simply regions for meshing sensory and motor activity, the importance of the concept of association in the last century has been extraordinary, particularly for psychological theory and our concept of the nonsensory and motor regions of the cerebral cortex.

An interesting historical sidelight is that 200 years after Galen, at about 390, a Syrian Christian bishop, Nemesius of Emesa, proposed a modification of Galen's model that anticipated thoughts that were to emerge in full flower only many years later. Nemesius was among the first to suggest the existence of a number of relatively independent psychological faculties, including memory, perception, and thought. It was these faculties that he associated with each of the three ventricles. In so doing, though perpetuating an incorrect model of the brain, he did help to set the stage for the phrenological and faculty psychology developments of the nineteenth century.

The intellectual lacuna of the Dark Ages then overcame Europe, and philosophic and scientific inquiry almost completely disappeared from the face of the continent. It was only in the Asian countries and, more relevantly for western thought, among the Arab physicians that the study of relationships between the brain and the mind continued. Polyak (1957) has described some of the extraordinarily important Arabic work on the nervous system. Although his main interest was in Arabic ophthamology and visual system neuroanatomy, Polyak notes that the theories of the Arabian physicians also included a rapidly changing role for the brain. Figure 5-9, for example, depicts the visual system from a book that was written in the eleventh century. The gross anatomy in this drawing is not too dissimilar from that to be found in modern texts, and the relationship of the nerves and the brain that is depicted is more or less consistent with modern views. Most important of all, in the context of localization theory, is the idea implicit in the fact that the visual receptors are connected by specific tracts to a particular portion of the brain. The Arab physicians, however, were limited by their Moslem religion from performing dissections on the human body, and much of their science in this area, therefore, was directly derived from translation of the work of Galen. Their contributions were significant, though, and the role they played in preserving European knowledge during the Dark Ages with its destruction of literally countless numbers of priceless libraries was exceedingly important.

c. The Middle Period—The Function of the Solid Portions Of the Nervous System

About 1500 A.D., science, as well as art, began to wake from its European torpor. A number of important developments occurred about this time that had a direct influence on the problems of mind and brain. One of the most important was the reawakening of interest in anatomy. Andreas Vesalius (1514-1564),

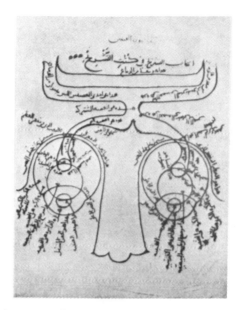

ΓIG. 5-9   An eleventh century diagram of the visual nervous system attributed to Ibn-al Haitham. (From Polyak, 1957, with the permission of The University of Chicago Press.)

for example, artfully depicted the structure of the human brain, based upon his personal dissections. An example of one of his etchings of the brain is shown in Fig. 5-10. Vesalius also planted the seed for the rejection of the hydraulic theories that had been so persistent for so many years when he reported his inability to detect the cavities within nerves through which the vital spirits or fluids were supposed to be transported.

Another influential scientist of the time was Jean Fernel (1497-1558), an exceptionally versatile polymath, who contributed both to the physical and biological sciences as well as to philosophy. Fernel's work was important in a number of neurological areas, but, in particular, he was one of the first to express another fundamental premise of localization theory by suggesting that different nerves had different functions. A most important contribution lay in his suggestion that some nerves had sensory functions and others had motor functions.

Even the great Leonardo Da Vinci (1452-1519) had apparently dissected human brains. In the Galenic spirit, he had directed his enormous talents toward the determination of the shape of the cerebral ventricles. He accomplished this tour de force by filling the ventricles with melted wax (a direct adaptation of the "lost wax" technique used in jewelery making) and then dissecting away the rest of the brain. The remaining congealed wax thus revealed the exact shape of the ventricles. Figure 5-11 displays the results of this virtuoso combination of art and science.

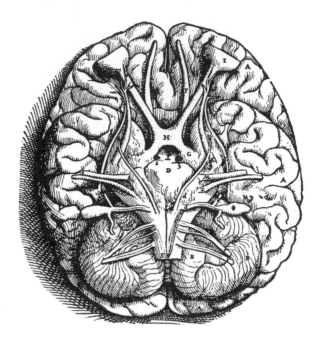

FIG. 5-10   The base of the brain as drawn by Vesalius. This is the forty-eighth plate from the fourth book of Vesalius' masterpiece, *De Humani Corporis Fabrica.*

At about this same time, other important theoretical developments began to occur as the traditional Galenic teachings came under scrutiny and attack for the first time in any serious way. Some scientists were beginning to pay increasing attention to the solid parts of the brain. For example, Magnus Hundt (1449-1519), in his 1501 encyclopedia, called attention to the "layers of the brain" as possible participants in mental processes. The anatomy of the cranial nerves was also becoming well-understood, and, a most important conceptual addition, the fact that the different nerves served different sensory functions also came to be appreciated. The observation that the different sensory pathways each coursed to its own portion of the brain was a strong argument for the rapidly strengthening conviction that separate portions of the brain might serve different mental functions.

During the latter part of the sixteenth and the early part of the seventeenth century, however, brain research appears to have been relatively unproductive. The period was characterized, on the one hand, by research that sought to localize the seat of the soul or the mind (e.g., René Descartes, 1596-1650), who assigned this role to the pineal gland) and, on the other, by a last burst of enthusiasm with regard to Galenic hydraulic theories [e.g., André Du Laurens,(1558-1609)]. The two traditions, one favoring the view that the solid parts of the brain were the most important and the other that the vital spirits or fluids were

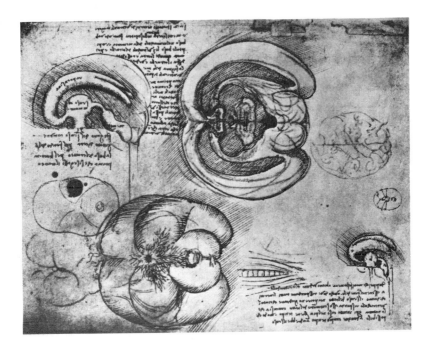

FIG. 5-11   Leonardo da Vinci's drawing of the ventricles of the brain as determined with a lost wax method. (From Polyak, 1957, with the permission of The University of Chicago Press.)

of prime significance, coexisted along with consensual agreement that the brain was of general importance as an undifferentiated receiver of signals from all of the senses. The brain was, in the terms of the times, an unspecialized "sensus communis," into which all sensory information flowed — a theoretical view quite antithetical to the idea of differentiated localization.

In 1664, Thomas Willis (1621-1675) published a book on the anatomy of the brain that must be considered another milestone in the history of localization theory. This book marks the beginning of a period in which knowledge of the gross anatomy of the brain was, for all practical purposes, modern. Although Willis himself was still a believer in the Galenic hydraulic theory, his work, which showed conclusively that there were no cavities in the various major nerves through which the "vital spirits" could flow, was, in fact, a damning criticism of any simplistic hydraulic theory.

Writers like Nicholas Stensen (1638-1686) also began to vigorously criticise the hydraulic theories and reject the notion that fluids were transmitted within hollow nerves. The stage was thus set for a total commitment to the notion that the solid parts of the brain were the critical portions responsible for the representation of mental processes.

Willis' work was critically important in another regard. It provided the conceptual foundation for the workers who were specifically interested in the functions of the nerves that entered and left the spinal cord and brain stem. Other scientists also contributed to this sequence of ideas. Robert Whytt (1714-1766) established in 1751 that the reflexes of the body were mediated by spinal mechanisms. Georgius Prochaska (1749-1820) followed with the next important contribution in 1780, when he suggested that the brain itself was a mechanism for reflecting back along nerves that were exclusively output pathways, modifications of the information that had been inserted along nerves that were exclusively input pathways. In other words, he stressed the idea that all human behavior may be considered to be a hierarchy of more or less high-level reflexes.

The concepts implicit in Prochaska's physiology and Willis's anatomy led to another great step in the development of the concept of neural localization of function. The spinal nerves were known to be anatomically divided into two groups—those emerging from a set of ventral roots and those emerging from a set of dorsal roots. Not only were the two sets of nerve roots anatomically separate, but also the dorsal and ventral roots looked different. The dorsal root had a noticeable swelling near its junction with the spinal cord; the ventral roots were essentially of constant diameter. The discussions of the prior century concerning the possibility that nerves were separated according to input and output functions led quickly to the notion that the anatomical dichotomy might be parallel to the functional one. In 1809, based entirely on logical considerations such as this, exactly that conclusion was drawn by Alexander Walker (1779-1852). Unfortunately, Walker's approach was entirely nonphysiological and his guess, though ingenious, was wrong. He incorrectly proposed that the dorsal roots were motor and the ventral roots were sensory.

The matter was correctly resolved within the context of a nasty priority dispute between Charles Bell (1774-1842) and Francois Magendie (1783-1855), revolving around papers they had published in 1811 and 1822 respectively. Bell had definitively shown that mechanical stimulation of the ventral roots produced muscular responses. Thus, he was correct in noting that they were at least in part motor in function. However, in his original paper, Bell had not mentioned the associated idea that the dorsal roots might be exclusively sensory. When Magendie published his research eleven years later, he correctly and completely spelled out the total division of function between the two sets of spinal roots. Bell, however, claimed priority and apparently altered reprinted editions of his original paper in a way that would support his claim. Although this important and basic law of neural localization is now referred to as the Bell-Magendie Law, most historians now agree that it was Francois Magendie who first formulated it in its full form and who deserves the credit of priority, for whatever it may be worth.

The line of research aimed at specifying the functions of the anatomically distinct peripheral nerves continued to be a main task of neuroanatomy and neurophysiology for the remainder of the nineteenth century. The next step was a consideration of the great cerebral mantle—a structure of obviously great structural and functional differentiation but, up to then, perhaps the most mysterious organ of the body.

d. Faculty Psychology and Cerebral Localization

Although the enthusiastic search for the function of the peripheral nerves represented one major thrust in neurophysiology at the beginning of the nineteenth century, other workers were also becoming concerned at about this time with the possible differentiation of function within the central nervous system itself. Actual experimental work was relatively modest, however, at least in part because of the enormous implications that such studies might have on the religious institutions of the time. Another difficulty, which may have been even more of a hindrance, lay in the fact that experimental work on the brain was exceedingly difficult to carry out for purely technical reasons. Operated animals typically went into a state of shock and then, most uncooperatively, characteristically died shortly after surgical intrusions into their skulls.

Prior to 1800, therefore, only a few workers had concerned themselves with experimental studies of specialized function of particular regions of the central nervous system. The absence of an adequate base of empirical knowledge and the difficulty in evaluating the confused results of the few experiments that were performed led to a great deal of controversy concerning the fundamental nature of the brain itself. Some workers suggested that the brain was an undifferentiated mass into which the sensory impulses fed. (I have already referred to the notion of the *sensus communis*.) Others suggested that the brain was instead made up of separate centers or "little organs" that had evolved to handle separate mental and behavioral functions. At the turn of the nineteenth century, however, it would be fair to say that the dominant theory was that the brain was a homogeneous mass that functioned as a unit with much the same functions being performed in any of its subregions. Albrect von Haller (1708-1777), who many consider to be the dean of eighteenth century physiologists, placed his enormous prestige behind this theory of brain homogeneity. Indeed, this theory of radical homogeneity of brain function persisted well into the nineteenth century, as evidenced by the adherence to its basic premise by such important neurologists as Pierre Flourens (1794-1867).

Late in the eighteenth century, however, some experimental work began to be reported that challenged the theory of homogeneity. Polyak (1957, p. 122) reports that some of the early French neurologists of that period had discovered a respiratory center in the medulla and apparently were also aware that the fore and hind limbs of the dog were activated by different regions of the cortex.

In 1808, however, Franz Gall (1758-1828) and Johan Spurzheim (1776-1832) published a paper that can be considered the first serious exposition of a comprehensive theory of localization in which specific mental processes were asserted to be the particular function of restricted cortical regions. Unfortunately, their approach to cerebral localization was so extreme for its time (as well as our own), that the "phrenological theory," as it was called, was not taken seriously by contemporary neurologists, except as an object of ridicule, or, even worse, as a popular cult-like fad. The functions that Gall localized in the cortex were not the simple sensory and motor functions that previous workers hinted at but such complex psychological processes as "cleverness" and "courage," Furthermore, Gall exascerbated the situation when he expanded his theory in a way that made it almost totally ridiculous. He suggested that the external bumps on the skull were external signs of the brain loci that handled these complex functions, and that by examining these external bumps, estimates of the personality of the subject could be obtained. It took little more than the observation that the bumps on the outside of the skull did not correspond to the bumps on the brain's surface to make his idea acceptable only in the halls of charlatans and cultists. Figure 5-12, for example, is one of Gall's maps of the localization of psychological functions that he believed could be measured on the outside of the skull.

Nevertheless, Gall's work is important because it concretized the emerging notion that there was some sort of differentiation and specificity of brain structures. During the years that followed, a wide variety of experiments were reported that attested to this side of the equipotentiality-localization controversy. There were three strands to this research effort that were of special consequence: One dealt with the notion of localization of speech, one with the localization of motor functions, and one with the localization of the visual function.

First, let us consider the history of studies in which the location of speech centers was studied. As early as 1825, Jean Bouillaud (1796-1881), working with postmortem material, mistakenly reported that there was a frequent association between difficulties in speech and lesions of the anterior portion of the frontal lobes. Only a few years later, this particular localization of speech function was determined to be incorrect. In 1861, Pierre Broca (1824-1880) discovered, also using postmortem material, that a speech center was more probably localized in only the posterior portion of the frontal lobe. Shortly thereafter, in 1874, Carl Wernicke (1848-1905) reported another quite distinct cerebral region that was also involved in speech on the temporal lobe of the cortex. Since then, many other regions of the cortex have also been nominated for involvement in speech processes. In fact, some workers now believe that damage to any part of the so-called speech hemisphere (more about that later) will produce some sort of speech deficit. I elaborate the current view later in this Chapter.

The determination of the motor centers of the brain is an easier and more direct research task than the identification of the speech or sensory regions for a simple reason. An indicator of a neural response—the actual movement—is built

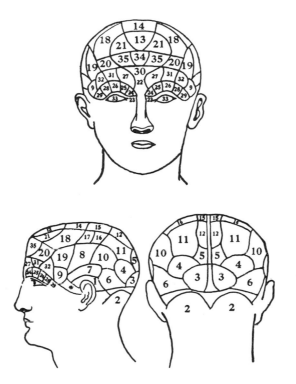

FIG. 5-12   A phrenological map showing the regions of the skull purported to be associated with specific psychological faculties. Some of the imaginative associations between brain loci and psychological processes are 17 (hope); 7 (secretiveness); and 21 (imitation). (From Boring, ©1950, after Spurzheim, 1834, with the permission of Mrs. E. G. Boring.)

into the preparation itself! When a motor region of the brain is stimulated, there is a concomitant and tell-tale twitch of some portion of the body of the animal.

Although some workers (Polyak, 1957, p. 122, cites the French neurosurgeon Saucerotte as being among the earliest) had been stimulating the cortex of experimental animals and arguing that there was a difference in motor response produced by different loci as early as 1768, it was not until the work of Gustav Fritsch (1838-1891) and Edward Hitzig (1838-1907) in 1870 that the concept of a specific area of the cortex with exclusively motor function crystallized. Fritsch and Hitzig (1870) showed that the sulcus in front of the central fissure of the dog's cerebral cortex was most likely to elicit motor actions when stimulated and, furthermore, that the foci for individual muscle groups were relatively small and seemed to be separate from each other. More precise mappings of the motor cortex were subsequently carried out by David Ferrier (1843-1928) in 1873 and 1876 and most completely by Charles Edward Beevor (1854-1908) and Victor

Horsley (1857-1916) in 1894. From that point on, a relatively modern concep-tualization of the topographic mapping of the motor cortex was available to those involved in the brain localization problem.

An important breakthrough was made when the Russian neuroanatomist Vladimir Betz (1834-1894) observed in 1874 that the cells in the prefrontal region, then becoming accepted as the motor cortex, was populated by the con-spicuously large pyramidal cells of which I have already spoken in Chapter 3. Thus the region was observed to be cytoarchitectonically, as well as functionally, distinct from its neighbors.

The major breakthrough in mapping the motor areas in later years resulted from the work done on conscious humans, usually in the course of surgery for the control of epilepsy. This extraordinary type of surgery was first performed by Harvey Cushing (1869-1939) in 1908 and subsequently, and more completely, by Wilder Penfield and his colleagues (for an extended summary, see Penfield & Roberts, 1959).

Although it was technically easier to determine when a motor cortical region was being stimulated, progress was also being made during this same period on the localization of sensory function on the surface of the cerebral cortex. The earliest recorded association of the correct brain region as a sensory projection area—the occipital lobe with vision—has been attributed by Polyak (1957) to Bartolomeo Panizza (1785-1867) who in 1855 worked both with experimental animals and with clinical cases and autopsies.

Ferrier had also been interested in the problem of the localization of visual function as well as localization within the motor regions for which he is better known. Unfortunately, in the case of the visual area, with its greater conceptual and technical difficulties, he badly mislocated what he considered to be the visual region and incorrectly asserted that the occipital lobes could be ablated without any effect on vision.

The person to whom the correct experimental localization of the primary visual cortex can be atributed is Hermann Munk (1821-1894). In 1879, Munk was able to correlate a substantial amount of clinical and experimental evidence and definitely assign visual functions to the occipital regions. Munk also correctly explained the role of the crossover of visual neurons at the optic chiasm and was probably the first to make explicit the topographic mapping of the retinal image on the occipital cortex. Many of these ideas are depicted in his drawing (shown in Fig. 5-13), which is almost up-to-date in its general form.

In addition to Munk, other of his contemporaries had also zeroed in on the occipital cortex as the probable main projection region of visual information. On a purely anatomical basis (his discovery of the laminar arrangement of the "striate" cortex of the occipital lobe), Theodor Meynert (1833-1892) had suggested in 1869 that this region had a special relationship to the visual fibers that he ob-served terminating there. Herman Wilbrand (1851-1935) came to the same con-clusion in 1881 on the basis of postmortem examinations of a substantial number of patients known to have visual difficulties who were also shown to have occipi-

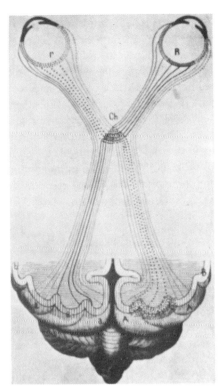

FIG. 5-13 Munk's 1879 diagram of the organization of the optic pathways. Note particularly that his idea of the function of the optic chiasm is for all purposes quite up-to-date. (From Polyak, 1957, with the permission of The University of Chicago Press.)

tal lobe lesions. Other neurophysiologists also supported this localization after observing infants who were born both congenitally blind and without occipital lobes. Observations of the relationship between the extent of visual field and restricted tumors of the occipital lobe also helped to confirm the fact that this region was heavily involved in the visual process.

In sum, by the turn of the twentieth century, there was an almost complete acceptance of the fact that the brain was not homogeneous, or equipotential but that different areas seemed to be particularly involved in specific behaviors. The work on the sensory, motor, and speech centers was exceedingly compelling, and the older ideas of homogeneity or equipotentiality, supported by such distinguished eighteenth century scientists as von Haller and Flourens, simply were no longer tenable.

However, one major conceptual difficulty still remained. Although the sensory, motor, and speech functions did seem to be localized in relatively well-defined areas, a large number of other psychological processes (or faculties, as they were popularly called during the nineteenth century) were not such clear-cut functional entities and could not be equally well localized. What, for example, is intelligence or cowardice, and if we cannot say what they are, how can we find a place in which to localize them? In spite of this definitional difficulty, many, who might nowadays choose to call themselves psychobiologists, sought out specific cortical loci in which to localize these nebulous functions.

The search went on into the twentieth century and reached a high, but perhaps not terminal, point in the history of radical localization theory, with the publication of Karl Kleist's (1879-1960) drawings in a famous 1934 monograph. A sample of one of his localization charts is presented in Fig. 5-14. Since then, however, radical theories of strict localization have begun to be tempered by experimental fact and by the addition of some more moderate views. In the next section, I explore the contemporary theoretical response to the question of localization of psychological functions in the brain.

4.   A Contemporary Approach to Localization Theory

Although it now seems universally agreed that the brain is not homogeneous and that we must accept the fact that there is a considerable amount of differentiation between different regions, most modern workers now agree that no theory of radical localization can be accepted either. As discussed previously, the brain appears to exhibit at least two especially important properties that are antithetical to naive notions of radical localization. First, it is now universally agreed that the brain is a highly interconnected network of subregions; no nucleus operates independently. Second, in many instances, particularly when one is considering higher mental functions that go beyond simple sensory or motor processes, there often seems to be an extraordinary propensity for recovery of function that stretches the credibility of any explanation based on central neural regrowth. Thus both anatomical evidence of extensive interconnectivity and physiological and behavioral evidence of recovery of function have compellingly directed the attention of contemporary psychobiologists toward a resolution of the localization problem on a basis of probabilistic concepts that are considerably deviant from the ideas held by the nineteenth-century psychobiologists and neuroanatomists.

What is meant by a "statistical" or "probabilistic" approach to localization of function in the brain? An emerging point of view among contemporary psychobiologists tends to more and more often assume that any given portion of the brain, rather than being uniquely associated with or completely disassociated from any given mental function, is better described as simply being more or less likely to produce a deficit when damaged. This holds for all except the most immediately communicative areas and pathways; i.e., for all brain regions except the primary sensory projection regions and final common motor areas and their respective pathways. Thus, probabilistic statements about the potential involvement of a particular locale in any given function may be more appropriate than statements of precise localization.

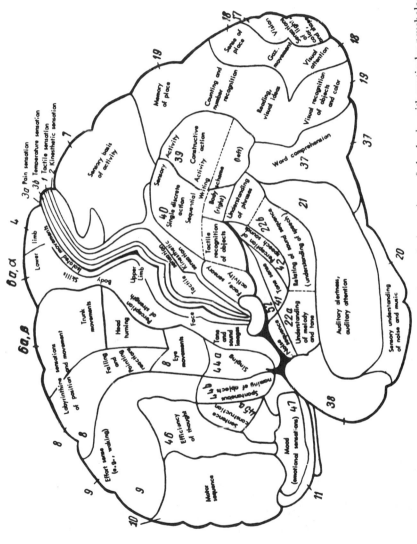

FIG. 5-14   Another relatively modern (1934) chart associating particular regions of the brain with particular psychological functions. (From Luria, ©1966a, after Kleist, 1934, with the permission of Consultants Bureau and Basic Books.)

As new anatomical and physiological knowledge has accumulated and an appreciation of the clinical and postmortem human data has become clarified, the view has emerged, therefore, that the brain is operating in a much more complex fashion than most psychobiologists of the first half of the twentieth century envisaged. Even highly localized lesions in humans seem to produce a variety of behavioral symptoms, and almost any area seems to be able to produce some deficit in such general and complex behaviors as speech. In animals, areas that had previously been considered to be exclusively sensory have been shown to have motor functions and vice versa; regions once supposed to be exclusively the domain of a single sense have now been shown to be polysensory. In general, there has been a blurring of the role of even those regions that had been considered only a few years ago to possess relatively sharply defined function. There has been a general diffusion of the notion of a "center" as well as in the boundaries ascribed to regions of localized function.

It is also important in setting the stage for an exposition of the contemporary point of view to reiterate the distinction between the parts of the cortex that primarily serve a communication function and those that primarily serve an integrative function. The primary sensory projection regions and the region from which motor signals emanate do seem to be more permanently affected by lesions, to have more sharply defined boundaries, and to possess at least topologically constant topographic representations of the external world. Establishment of the limits of a circumscribed "speech" center or, worse yet, of a "courage" center, however, is far less easily achieved.

Is it possible that this difference between the sensory or motor regions and the other more nebulously defined centers reflects a more fundamental distinction? Should the regions that have commonly been called sensory projection regions more properly be considered as a part of the peripheral nervous communication pathways that convey information to and from the brain, rather than among those regions that directly mediate perception or cognition?

These are important questions for the very reason that the role usually assigned to these primary projection centers by many contemporary psychobiological theorists is one in which it is taken to be almost axiomatic that these regions are the areas in which "perception" actually occurs. Those workers who feel that single neuron responses are the unique concomitants of perceptual processes speak, with few exceptions these days, of pontifical neurons (neurons whose activation is tantamount to perception) that are to be found in the parietal-somatosensory or occipital-visual areas, for example. It is possible, however, that these regions are not the loci of the neurophysiological correlates of conscious perceptual experience, but that they only represent a part of the afferent communication system? Even though they are capable of some preliminary preprocessing (such as contour intensification and feature selection), these regions, an alternative theoretical view would suggest, are only carrying topographically encoded information to some more central sites where the neural processes identifiable with perceptual experiences actually occur. If these regions are only playing a communication role and not an interpretive one, and if the dichotomy is a valid one, then the notion of a pontifical neuron is a serious and profound misinterpretation of an important body of neurophysiological data that deals with the function of neurons in these regions. I speak more of this problem of representation in Chapters 6 and 7.

I have already spoken of the distinction between symbolic and isomorphic representation. It is also desirable to keep in mind, in the context of the distinction between communication and representation, the fact that whereas communication systems should work best when isomorphy is maintained, the interpretive aspects of brain function should be much more heavily characterized by processes that depend on the symbolic aspects of stimuli.

It should also be remembered that there is a fundamental difference between the encoding characteristics of the occipital and parietal primary projection areas and the interpretative characteristics of perception. The projection regions mentioned are topographically organized; perceptual processes are greatly influenced by symbolic as well as geometric properties of the stimulus. This difference adds further credence to the suggestion that the primary projection areas are not the actual locus of the perceptual experience, but merely more central portions of the afferent communication system.

What are the basic premises on which the emerging modern view of brain localization of psychological function are based? A partial answer to this question can be found in the thoughts of some contemporary psychobiologists. For example, speaking about the data obtained from clinical studies with human beings, the eminent Russian psychobiologist Alexander Luria (1966b) sums up the clinical data in the following words:

> Numerous observations made by neurosurgeons on patients with gunshot wounds and tumors of the brain have shown that a disturbance of a particular complex function does not in fact arise in association with a narrowly circumscribed lesion of one part of the cortex, but is observed, as a rule, in patients with lesions of several different parts of the brain [p. 12].

Luria goes on to more completely express his views in another important book (Luria, 1966a):

> The higher mental functions may be disturbed by a lesion of one of the many different links of the functional system; nevertheless, they will be disturbed differently by lesions of different links [p. 71].

> A lesion of a single, circumscribed area of the cerebral cortex often leads to the development, not of an isolated symptom, but of a group of disturbances, apparently far removed from each other [p. 74].

> A generalized disturbance in the dynamics of the nervous processes must make its effect felt primarily on those forms of cortical activity with the most complex organization [p. 76].

A distinguished American physiological psychologist, Elliott Stellar, spoke to the problem of localization of motivational function, paying particular attention to the concept of a "center" in an important essay (Stellar, 1954):

> Throughout this discussion the terms "neural center" and "hypothalamic center" have been used. "Center" is a useful and convenient term, but it is also a dangerous one, for it may carry with it the implication of strict localization of function within isolated anatomical entities. Actually this implication is not intended, for it is recognized that localization is a relative matter and that no neural mechanism operates in isolation. Furthermore, it is also possible that there may be no discoverable localization of the neural mechanisms governing some types of motivated behavior. The theory simply states at the moment that the best general hypothesis is that some degree of localization of the mechanisms controlling motivation can be found in the hypothalamus [p. 15-16].

The consensus that appears to be replacing the radical localization theories of the earlier parts of the twentieth century can thus be seen to be based on the concept of systems, interactions, variability, and probability. Certain areas of the brain, it is accepted, are more involved with certain functions than are others, and many leading contemporary psychobiologists seem to agree that if a certain area of the brain is damaged, there is a higher probability that a particular kind of function will be affected than some other kind. But, the notion of singular centers mediating specific functions is rapidly being phased out.

In spite of this trend toward a modification of contemporary dogma, research attention in the past few years is still almost always based on the concept that particular portions of the nervous system are particularly closely associated with certain major psychological functions. We of the psychobiological community are very much children of our past, in spite of the dynamic state of theory in the psychobiological sciences. It seems to be enormously difficult for many of us to throw off our scientific heritage, even if the problem were not further compounded, in this particular case, by the fact that the interpretation of experimental findings regarding brain function without the crutch of some form of localization theory is extremely difficult.

One of the reasons for this conservatism is a purely pragmatic one. Psychobiology still has not developed a research paradigm that is suitable for the study of interacting systems of nuclei! Our major research tool to deal with the problem of functional localization in the brain is that of ablative surgery. But this is a tool that has implicit in it a theoretical superstructure more closely associated with radical localization theory. The study of large numbers of nuclei, organized into interacting networks, has no equally highly evolved research methodology, and there is a significant probability that such techniques will not be available in the foreseeable future. Partitioning of systems to understand their function, as I have noted earlier, is a very peculiar and intrinsically self-defeating procedure that is unlikely to produce a general solution to the problems of networks even in relatively simple systems. The point of these comments is that the reader should be forewarned that there is in fact a discrepancy between what the psychobiologist intuitively feels is a currently accurate model of brain organization and the greater part of the data base, which is mainly a product of a research paradigm that is in large part obsolescent.

In the sections that make up the remainder of this chapter, I present discussions of the roles played by those brain regions that have been most closely linked to particular psychological functions. Although these discussions necessarily will be heavily loaded with data that suggest a more radical form of localization theory (for the reason just mentioned), it should be emphasized at this point that this is to a degree misleading. The main emphasis should be on systems of and interactions among nuclei of the brain. This is the intended emphasis of the material that follows in this chapter even though the discussion is constrained by the limits of the conventional research paradigm in some cases to what appears to be a more radical concept of brain localization.

There is another practical difficulty that is encountered and is necessarily handled in a way that is not completely satisfactory. In the discussion of each topic, it is manifestly impossible to survey all of the published research that is now available. In place of an exhaustive and encyclopedic survey, I present what I believe are only the most important or the most useful illustrations of the point being made. The reader is directed, wherever possible, to a more comprehensive source for further details and discussions.

This expedient is made necessary by the breadth of this book. It should not pass unremarked that what is usually presented as the complete content of a conventional text of physiological psychology is, in fact, only an expanded version of the material presented in this single chapter. On the other hand, localization, which is seen by many as the main theme of this field, is presented in this volume as only one of the many tasks confronting psychobiology. Our discussion, therefore, must be an abbreviated one stressing general principles and sample experiments.

5.   A Brief Comment on Method

Although I discussed methodology extensively in Chapter 3, it might be desirable to briefly point out some special methodological problems that are encountered in research on the problem of localization. It is possible to attack the problem of localization in the simpler portions of the sensory and motor regions of the brain by any one of the many degeneration, evoked gross potential, or microelectrode recording techniques that are available to the anatomist and electrophysiologist. We can, for example, define the regions of the cortex to which the optic nerves project and make the reasonable assumption that this region is probably more involved in vision than is an area that does not receive such direct connections. We can stimulate with sounds, record evoked potentials from the cerebral cortex, and assume that the regions which produce the maximum responses are more likely to be the sites of auditory functions than those that produce lesser responses. We can even put microelectrodes into what are assumed to be the motor regions and record potentials that are consistently produced prior to a motor response and thereby associate these areas with motor control functions.

However, for the most part, these are not the techniques that are used by localization theorists who are studying higher mental processes. Rather, the technique of choice in this case is more frequently the ablation or extirpation (the physical removal) of chunks of tissue from the brain or the transection of pathways that communicate between the centers of the brain. But even the simplest of the ablation techniques requires that relatively massive surgery be performed on the animal. The skull must be opened and the brain must be mutilated. Sometimes overlying regions must be damaged to get to the intended site of the lesion. The general effects of such a massive intrusion into the skull, independent of the specific effects of the ablation of a specific region of the brain, must always be considered. A major control required in all experiments of this sort, therefore, is the "sham" or control operation that produces a surgical insult equivalent in general magnitude to the experimental operation but without the actual removal of the specific nervous tissue under study.

Ablation may be carried out by undercutting with a scalpel or scooping with a spatula, but brain tissue in most animals is soft enough that it can often be aspirated by suction. Some newer techniques can be used to produce equivalent results without actual tissue removal. Drugs can be used to destroy a portion of the brain, or low temperatures can be used to temporarily block or permanently destroy a particular region. Cryogenic techniques are particularly useful when the lesion to be produced lies deep within the innermost portions of the brain.

A never-to-be-underestimated problem, regardless of the technique of choice, however, is the determination of the exact location and extent of an ablation. Such a determination is always difficult given the substantial amounts of individual variability and the lack of exact control with cutting or freezing procedures. Not only are the boundaries of a lesion usually not sharp, but destruction of blood vessels in one place can cause neural damage due to ischemia in regions far removed from the point of the actual incision.

Another technical aspect of localization research concerns the repertoire of methods that are used to assay the extent of any behavioral deficit that may or may not have been produced by one of the ablation procedures described in the previous paragraph. It is completely out of the question to review the enormous variety of behavioral techniques in use today. They range from something as relatively simple as a perimetric test of the regions of the visual field that remain after cortical ablation to assays of as relatively complex a cognitive task as mental arithmetic. Nevertheless, a word of caution is in order. There is, implicit in any behavioral assay technique, a further major conceptual and logical difficulty. It is not always easy to determine just exactly what is being measured by a particular procedure. For example, what fundamental psychological or biological process (or constellation of processes) is measured by a test as complicated as a delayed response test, or what is really meant by an aberration in the ability of a human to "make long-term plans." The ill-defined nature of some of the behavioral assay procedures themselves, therefore, makes it difficult to fit behavioral deficit data into a general scheme of functional localization.

Furthermore, all too rarely are the inadequately defined behavioral processes sufficiently analyzed into units that come even close to possessing the time scales of the neural processes to which they are compared. For example, only a few workers have attempted to break the complex of behaviors incorporated into a complex behavior like eating into subprocesses that make sense in the time domain of neurophysiological units. One psychobiologist who has is H. Philip Zeigler (Zeigler, 1976), whose analysis of the eating behavior of birds is almost unique in this field. Figure 5-15, for example, shows the analysis of the various stages of eating (peck, manipulate, swallow) that Zeigler feels are reasonable candidates for neurophysiological comparisons. It is only in terms of such a detailed analysis that precise neural and behavioral correlations become possible.

To conclude this introduction to the problem of brain localization of psychological function, it should be noted that localization of function may be either relatively static and even genetically determined, or dynamic and determined by

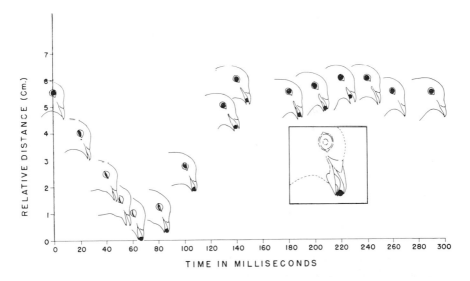

FIG. 5-15 Graph showing the time course of the various components of the pecking behavior of a pigeon. (From Zeigler, ©1976, with the permission of Academic Press.)

either the developmental stages or experiences of the organism during its matura-tion. The data on recovery of function (for example, see Lennenberg, 1974) and some of the extraordinary clinical records of patients who were born with-out a portion of the brain only to lead relatively normal lives, suggest that local-ization, even if it exists in the normal, highly differentiated, adult animal, may not exist in rigidly predetermined form in the infant.

The difficulties in disentangling the genetic and environmental aspects of any complex psychobiological process are immense. Prudence suggests that I should not try to resolve the nature-nurture problem here, even within the narrow arena of localization of function. It simply would amount to another book. Thus, emphasis in the discussion to follow is aimed at the mature animal in its relative-ly normal state. Let me simply note, very briefly in passing, that it is entirely possible that whatever degree of localization that does exist may differ from one animal to the next as a result of its experiences and variations in its development. The notion of a genetically prescripted allocation of particular functions to par-ticular loci in the brain would, in light of such a concept, be badly in need of some revision. Clearly this and related conceptual issues are of such magnitude that revisions in our perspective concerning them could change much of what we now accept to be fundamental "laws" of psychobiology.

Finally, it should also be noted that there is an overlap in the discussion that follows in this chapter and the discussions of coding in Chapters 6 and 7. Local-ization is, in fact, just another name for one of the most important coding di-mensions—place. Thus there is a direct relation between any discussion of neural coding and any discussion of localization of function in the nervous system. Unfortunately, I have not been successful in either integrating or disentangling the two concepts. Therefore, the conceptual model of psychobiology that I propose in this book is, in this regard, incomplete and unparsimonious.

B.   ON THE LOCALIZATION OF VISUAL FUNCTIONS IN THE BRAIN—PERCEPTUAL PSYCHOBIOLOGY

Because of the relative simplicity of the sensory projection areas of the brain and brain stem, and because exploration of the functions of these areas is anchored to well-controlled physical parameters such as time of occurrence, place of occurrence, amplitude and quality, we have a very complete set of information concerning the relationship between sensory functions and brain localization. Indeed, the abundance of the literature on the various senses is staggering, and it is necessary to abstract merely a small portion of it to present general principles.

Thus, I limit the discussion to a single sensory modality. Because the best data base is available for the visual system, I concentrate attention on sensory inputs to the brain from the eyes. The results on the visual system are, in most ways, sufficiently similar to the conclusions that may be drawn concerning any of the other senses, that discussion of the visual modality is adequate to make the conceptual points clear for all modalities. This is particularly so if adequate care is made to compare truly equivalent properties of vision and audition, for example. If the reader wishes more detail about the other senses, he might consider reading either Somjen (1972) or Uttal (1973).

In this section, I only briefly mention the regions of the brain that are currently assumed to be the relevant projection areas for the other modalities. Figure 5-16, for example, depicts the organization of the primary and secondary sensory areas (as well as the several motor areas) observed on the surface of the human cerebral cortex by Penfield and Roberts (1959). One of the most important facts immediately stressed by this diagram is that there are always multiple projection areas for each modality. For example, there are primary, supplementary, and secondary somatosensory regions indicated on this drawing. I discuss later in this section the role played by the multiple visual regions as an example of the differentiation of function among the projection regions.

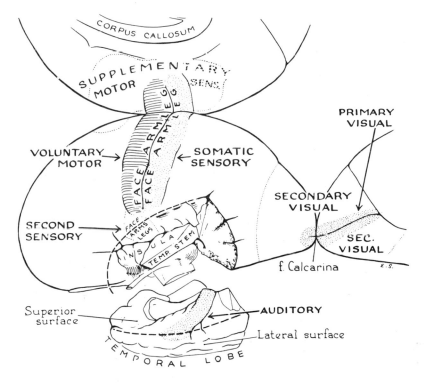

FIG. 5-16 The sensory and motor regions of the human cortex. Primary motor regions are lined; primary sensory regions are stipled. Secondary and supplementary areas are also shown. (From Penfield & Roberts, ©1959, with the permission of the literary executors of W. Penfield and The Princeton University Press.)

The regions of the human cerebral cortex that are not identified as either sensory or motor are relatively large. These nonsensory and nonmotor regions have conventionally been called *association regions,* although this term is now considered to be more or less a vestigial misnomer from earlier theories of brain organization and will be replaced, for reasons mentioned later, by *intrinsic regions.* On the surface of the cerebral cortex in other nonhuman mammals, the amount of uncommitted "association" cortex is much smaller. Figure 5-17, for example, is a drawing of the surface of the cerebrum of the cat, showing by comparison with Fig. 5-16 that a much larger proportion of the cortex is taken up by the sensory and motor areas in cat than in man. However, it should be noted that in the cat, too, there are multiple sensory and motor regions represented on the cortical surface.

Both the conventionally designated somatosensory area, posterior to the large central fissure (the postcentral sensory cortex), and the conventionally designated motor area, anterior to it (the precentral motor cortex), are laid out in a highly

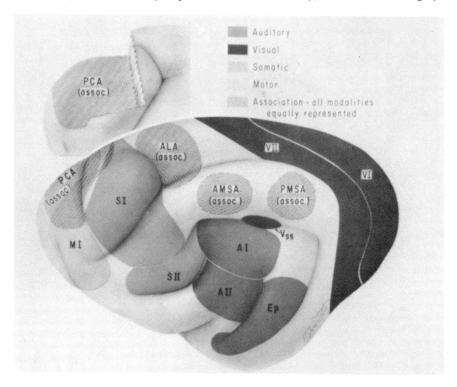

FIG. 5-17   A map of the surface of the cat's cerebral cortex showing the various sensory, motor, and intrinsic (association) area regions as mapped with the evoked potential technique. Abbreviations indicated are: VI, VII, VIII, Vss = visual areas; AI, AII, Ep = auditory areas; SI, SII, MI = sensory-motor areas; and PCA, ALA, AMSA PMSA = association response areas. (From Thompson, Johnson, & Hoopes, ©1963, with the permission of The American Physiological Society.)

organized form that reproduces, in a topologically precise and constant manner, the arrangement of afferent projections from the body surface (Fig. 5-18). In general, the relative amount of cortical tissue devoted to representing any portion of the body in either the motor or sensory areas is always seen to be related to the sensory acuity or precision of motor use of that particular organ; in other words, to its innervation density or motor unit size. For example, the fingers are seen to have much larger areas assigned to them than does the back in both the motor and sensory representation of this cerebral "homunculus." Details of the somatosensory projections to the cortex of various animals may be found in the work of Benjamin and Welker (1957) and Woolsey (1952).

It is interesting to note in passing that this topographic representation of body parts also holds at lower levels of the brain than the cerebral cortex. Campbell, Parker, and Welker (1974), for example, have studied the somatosensory projections in the external cuneate nucleus of the rat's medulla. There too, stimulation of various muscle groups seem to produce selective responses in different lobes of this small nucleus. Figure 5-19 shows the location of the external cuneate nucleus in the medulla and the locations to which various muscle groups project.

For readers who wish to pursue the problem of the organization of the somatosensory system in greater detail, one of the best discussions of the principles of organization of one major relay station, the ventrobasal complex of nuclei, can be found in a brilliant paper by Wally Welker of the University of Wisconsin (Welker, 1973). This paper spells out in great detail the function of these important sensory relay nuclei and, in particular, emphasizes their interaction with the rest of the central nervous system. In particular, the reader may wish to study Welker's Figure 19 (not reproduced here), which depicts the circuit interconnections among the many involved nuclei. Presumably a similar kind of topographic localization occurs at all levels of this complex system.

The details of organization of the cerebral cortical auditory areas have also been studied by Clinton Woolsey and his colleagues at the University of Wisconsin for many years (see, for example, Woolsey, 1961). They have shown that the auditory areas are also laid out on a topographic basis. But the map, in this case, does not represent the body but rather the distance along the basilar membrane which relates to the frequency and amplitude of tonal stimuli—the critical parameters of the auditory space. Figure 3-6 has already displayed an example of this sort of mapping observed on the auditory cortex of a dog.

Although the somatosensory, visual, and auditory primary projection areas on the cerebral cortex are well known, much less is known of the projection of the chemical senses, such as olfaction and gustation and the vestibular receptors to the cortex. Fibers activated by chemical stimulation of the tongue do terminate in the general region of the somatosensory areas of the tongue, and this may be considered to be a taste projection region. Olfactory signals project to the amygdala and the olfactory tubercule and to the thalamus (Heimer, 1972). However, no surface area of the cortex is known to serve as a primary olfactory projection

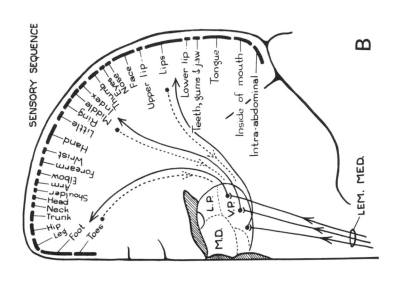

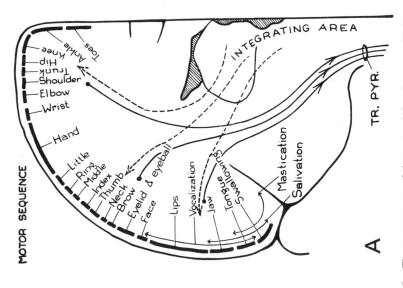

FIG. 5-18   The arrangement of the motor (A) and sensory (B) homunculi on the post-central and precentral sulci of the human brain, respectively. The figures emphasize the regular somatotopic order preserved in these regions but do not support any theory of discrete, nonoverlapping localization. (From Penfield & Jasper, ©1954, with the permission of Little, Brown, and Company.)

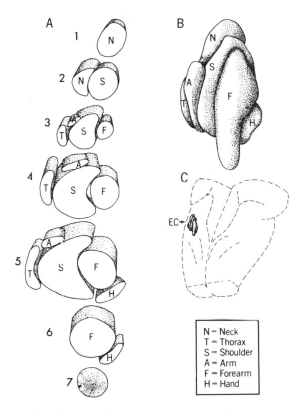

FIG. 5-19   The map of the body on the somatosensory cerebral cortex has an analog in the external cuneate nucleus of the rat. This figure shows the somatotopic localization of various portions of the body in this small nucleus as well as its location in the brain stem. (From Campbell, Parker, & Welker, ©1974, with the permission of Elsevier/North-Holland Biomedical Press.)

area. A small vestibular cortical region has been identified by Andersson and Gernandt (1954).

With this brief background review of the other sensory and motor areas in hand, I can now turn to the visual system. The visual system, as noted, has been chosen because it is the best known and because the aspects of visual perception with which we shall be most concerned are well-grounded in the dimensions of the physical stimuli. Vision, therefore, presents the best opportunity to make explicit the general concepts of perceptual localization that are implicit in modern sensory theories.

1. Anatomy of the Visual Brain

Perhaps the first point to be stressed about the organization of the visual system is that it is multiple, not only in terms of cortical projection areas but also in terms of the number of pathways that course from the eye to the brain. It is now well-established that, in addition to the "classical" and well-known pathway from the retina through the lateral geniculate body of the thalamus to the striate regions of the cerebral cortex (the retinal-geniculo-striate pathway), there is also, in mammals, one other well-validated major visual pathway that projects from the retinae to the superior colliculus, or tectum (roof), of the brain stem. This extrageniculate or collicular pathway seems to perform functions associated with general visual orientation, in at least some animals, rather than precise pattern vision (Schneider, 1969; Trevarthen, 1968). A third visual pathway has also recently been suggested by Graybiel (1974) that passes from the retina to the cortex via the pretectal region of the brain stem. At this point, little is known of the possible function of this third visual pathway. Figure 5-20 diagrammatically plots one theory about the relationship among these three pathways.

For readers who are interested in a comparative analysis of the interconnections of the various brain nuclei in the visual systems of the various vertebrate classes, by far the best analysis is that presented by Ebbesson (1970). His diagrams, in particular, are rich fonts of understanding of the organization of this complex of multiple nuclei that mediates vision in vertebrates. Recent discussion with colleagues such as Glenn Northcutt and Steven Easter of the University of Michigan, who are far more expert than I with the anatomy of the vertebrate visual system, suggest that Ebbeson's diagrams only show the major visual pathways. In such animals as the frog, as many as a dozen distinguishable pathways may actually exist.

I have already noted the existence of the multiple visual projection areas on the surface of the mammalian cortex. It seems fairly certain that the occipital pole of the cortex is the primary projection area of the visual cortex for the geniculo-striate pathway in primates and many other mammals. This occipital Visual Area 1, which shall be referred to as V1, is, in turn, surrounded by a peristriate region known as Visual Area 2 or V2. The inferotemporal (lower portion of the temporal lobe) cortex has also been known to be an important area for the processing of visual information.

In recent years, many additional regions previously assumed to be association area cortex have either been demonstrated to serve important visual functions through evoked potential and single unit procedures or to be structurally linked to the visual pathways by means of degeneration techniques. It is now thought that there are possibly as many as a dozen visual areas on the surface of the primate cerebral cortex. For example, Allman and Kaas have extensively studied visual projections to the cortex in the owl monkey and have discovered, in addition to the three "classic visual areas" (V1, V2, and inferotemporal cortex), an additional visual area in the posterior portion of the temporal lobe (Allman and Kaas, 1971) and a crescent-shaped "middle temporal" visual area located between the peristriate region and the root of the temporal lobe (Allman, Kaas, Lane, &

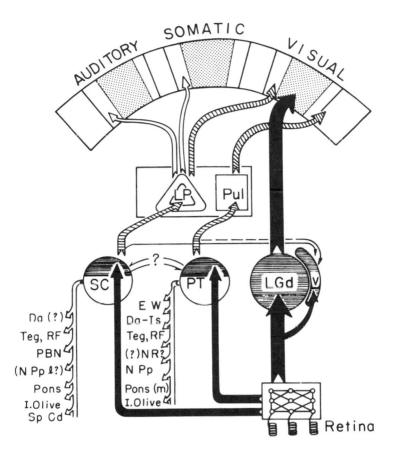

FIG. 5-20   One theory of the organization of the visual system emphasizing three different visual pathways. The right side shows the classic retino-geniculo-striate pathway; the left side depicts the tectal and pretectal channels. Abbreviations indicated are: SC = superior colliculus; PT = pretectal region; LGd, v = dorsal and ventral nuclei of lateral geniculate body; LP = nucleus lateralis posterior; Pul = pulvinar; EW = nucleus of Edinger-Westphal; Da = nucleus of Darkschewitsch; Is = nucleus interstitialis of Cajal; Teg-RF = tegmentum, reticular formation; NR = nucleus ruber, perirubral fields; NP_p = nucleus papilioformis; Sp Cd = spinal cord; and I. olive = inferior olive. (Figure and abbreviations from Graybiel, ©1974, with the permission of The M.I.T. Press.)

Miezin, 1973). In addition to (or perhaps instead of) these areas, by employing degeneration techniques, Zeki (1971) has shown that the peristriate area (V2) of old world monkeys projects to other regions, which, although they do not maintain the retinal topographic organization, also appear to serve comparable visual functions. These supplemental visual areas are now referred to as V4, V4a, V5, and PSTS (the posterior superior temporal sulcus) by Zeki. In addition, V2 itself, he believes, may actually be two separate regions designated as V2 and V3.

The interconnections of these cortical and subcortical centers is at least partially summarized for old world monkeys in Fig. 5-21. This figure indicates that some of the signals initiated in the retina project directly to the striate cortex and then pass to the peristriate (or circumstriate) cortex. The next step in this pathway conducts to the multiple visual cortical regions, described by Zeki, and from there to the inferotemporal cortex. This diagram also indicates one of the possible extrageniculate pathways from the retina to the superior colliculus and then to the pulvinar from where paths have been tracked to the cortex. Although this diagram differs slightly from the one shown in Fig. 5-20, both are included to indicate two different modern theories of visual neuroanatomy. Another similar "theory" of mammalian visual system organization is embodied in Figure 6 of Ebbesson (1970).

According to Charles Gross and his colleagues (Gross, Bender, & Rocha-Miranda, 1974), visual pathways from the inferotemporal cortex then pass to both the frontal lobes of the brain and to subcortical centers of the brain stem, including those especially interesting ones of the limbic system. Obviously, in most mammals, a very large portion of the brain is potentially involved in visual function according to current anatomical evidence. A much more realistic diagram of the organization of the visual system of a typical primate is shown in Fig. 5-22.

In the remaining portions of this section, I review the available data that indicate the particular roles played by the more important of these brain loci in visual behavior.

2. The Role of Visual Areas 1, 2, and 3— The Striate Cortex and the Peristriate Cortex

It would be most satisfying if a simple answer could be given to the question: What happens to visual behavior when a particular visual area of the cortex is ablated? However, the history of this question is enormously complicated both by the anatomical and surgical complexities, on the one hand, and the difficulties in assessing behavioral changes with more or less arbitrary measures, on the other.

Among the earliest modern studies of the effects of ablation of the striate cortex (V1) were the reports from the laboratory of Klüver (1941). Klüver removed what he believed to be V1 and concluded, on the basis of tests of visual form discrimination, that the operated animals seemed to have lost all pattern vision. His experimental animals were unable to detect the difference between triangles and squares, for example, and exhibited a marked deficiency in moving about in an obstruction-filled field. In other words, the animals appeared to be blind to everything except the overall brightness of the visual environment.

However, in recent years, a number of workers, most notably Lawrence Weiskrantz (as summarized in Weiskrantz, 1974), have suggested that the conclusions

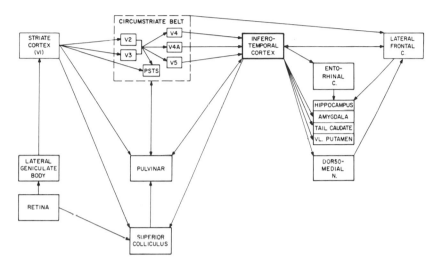

FIG. 5-21 Another possible theory of the organization of the primate visual system. (From Gross, Bender, & Rocha-Miranda, ©1974, with the permission of The M.I.T. Press.)

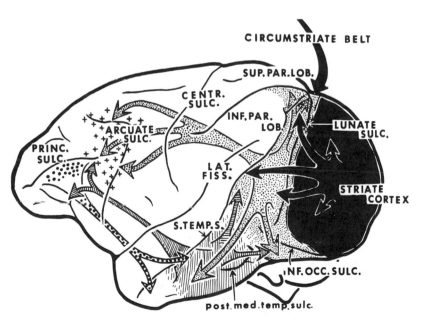

FIG. 5-22 A more realistic depiction of the visual pathways in the primate brain. (From Kuypers et al., ©1965, with the permission of Academic Press.)

drawn by Klüver from his ablation experiments may be in need of considerable modification. Weiskrantz believes that animals that have total destruction of V1 (including the inevitable retrograde degeneration of the lateral geniculate nucleus) can still discriminate patterns (Pasik & Pasik, 1971; Weiskrantz, 1972), although less well than normal animals. Weiskrantz also believes that his results indicate the striate cortex is actually a region in which detailed pattern discrimination is mediated, but only to the extent that it is particularly dependent upon fine spatial discriminations. He thus suggests that the animal without V1 is behaving more or less as if it were only suffering from a gross diminution of its spatial acuity, but that many other visual tasks involving form, localization, and brightness are still adequately handled.

Weiskrantz (1974) goes on to report that when the peristriate cortex (V2 and V3) is ablated, in *addition* to V1, only then does the animal behave as if it was totally incapable of processing any information about visual form. However, when only the peristriate cortex is ablated, the results are far more subtle. The effects seem to be restricted to very complex sorts of visual information processing such as spatial relations among objects; on most simple visual tasks, the animals seem to do fairly well.

A specific explanation of how this residual form perception remaining after ablation of V1 may be mediated has been suggested by Dalby, Meyer, and Meyer (1970), who carried out V1 ablations on cats and also observed that some primitive pattern vision is maintained. In their experiments they used stimuli such as visual cliffs and checkerboards that varied in the length of their constituent visual contours. On the basis of the results, they suggested that the residual visual form perception was actually functionally related to cumulative differences in the length of the constituent visual contours.

This explanation would thus relegate "residual form perception" to the cumulative amount of optic nerve activity rather than any stimulus structural sensitivity per se. This makes sense because activity is known to be associated with contour length as a result of lateral interactions within the retina. Because of a dimensional transformation, form would therefore have been coded as amplitude!

Unfortunately for this simple explanation of what had been a rather perplexing observation, Dalby and the Meyers also observed that even when flux differences and contours were carefully balanced in displays composed of squares or circles, there was still some residual discriminability on the basis of form alone. Whether another form-to-intensity transformation was occurring or not could not be ascertained. Nevertheless, their work does suggest that it is possible for what appears to be a residual form discrimination ability to be explained in terms of a quasi-intensive code rather than one directly reflecting the geometry of the situation.

It is obvious that the complexity of the problem of what functions the visual areas of the cortex perform is great, and the technical difficulties are profound. There still is no general agreement as to even the basic questions. Ablating two areas does not lead to a simple summation of the effects of the two independent surgical extirpations. Nevertheless, it is clear that these portions of the cortex— V1, V2, and V3—are more likely to produce a visual deficit involving form perception than any other behavioral deficit yet observed.

However, discrepancies are far easier to find than generalities, because, as laboratory research has accumulated on animals other than primates, it has become clear that the regions that correspond in other mammals to V1, V2, and V3 in primates can be ablated with a remarkably small amount of pattern discrimination deficit being generated. If any generality is forthcoming, it is that in primates the finest form discriminations based on best acuity seem to be more closely associated with these visual projection areas than they are with other parts of the visual brain.

3. The Inferotemporal Cortex

Another region of the cerebral cortical mantle that has been shown to be intimately involved in visual learning is the inferotemporal cortex—the lower or caudal portion of the temporal lobe. The anatomy of the inferotemporal lobe, as observed both electrophysiologically and with degeneration techniques, reveals that its main inputs come from the striate cortex (V1) via the peristriate areas (V2 and V3) possibly by way of V4, V4a, and V5. However, it has become increasingly clear in recent years that this region must also receive inputs from the collicular and pulvinar pathways, as shown in Fig. 5-22.

Originally all of the temporal lobe was thought to be generally involved in producing visual deficits (Klüver & Bucy, 1937, 1938). However, in later years, Mishkin (1954, 1966) demonstrated that it was only the lower or inferior portion of the temporal lobe that was responsible for the visual defects that had been observed by Klüver and Bucy. Microelectrode recordings from the neurons of the inferotemporal area seem to be exclusively responsive to visual inputs (Gross, Schiller, Wells, & Gerstein, 1967; Gross, Bender, and Rocha-Miranda, 1969), adding further credence to the concept that it is almost uniquely a part of the visual brain.

The type of visual effects observed after the ablations of the inferotemporal cortex are extremely subtle. They are exhibited most often in experiments in which the animal under study is required to perform some kind of visual learning task. However, not all visual learning tasks are equally effected, and ablations of different portions of the inferotemporal lobe produce different types of learning deficits. For example, consider Fig. 5-23, which depicts the effects of ablations of several different regions on different types of learning. The effects obtained when only a single discrimination is required in each trial can be inconsequential. However, if the experimental task is only slightly complicated, for example, by having several discriminations concurrently present in each trial, massive performance deficits can be produced. According to Weiskrantz (1974), the posterior

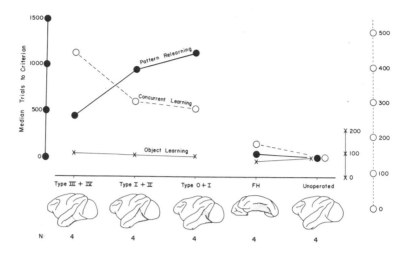

FIG. 5-23   Graph showing the effects of different lesions on three different learning tasks (pattern relationship, concurrent learning, and object learning). The horizontal axis indicates the region of the lesion in the experimental and control animals. The extent of the lesion is indicated both in the drawing and by the arbitrary Roman numerals. The three vertical co-ordinate scales are necessary because of the different rates of learning of the three learning tasks. Abbreviations indicated are: N = number of animals in each group; and FH = a sham operated control group in which the hippocampus lobe was lesioned. (From Mishkin, ©1972, with the permission of Springer-Verlag, Inc.)

region of the inferotemporal cortex is involved in the selection of, and attention to, visual cues, but the anterior portion may possibly be more closely associated with visual memorization. Clearly, though, these terms are mere shorthand for mental processes that are complex enough to evade adequate explication at present.

Two general facts emerge from this type of analysis. First, it seems clear that the inferotemporal cortex performs functions that are subsequent to or of a higher order than those performed by the earlier portions of the visual system. Thus, while the striate cortex seems to be necessary for fine-grain form perception, the inferotemporal cortex is much more intimately related to visual learning processes that are harder to define precisely. Lesions of inferotemporal cortex may have profound effects on even simple visual learning tasks. Yet, according to Gross (1973), previously learned information is not forgotten after inferotemporal lesions, and it seems almost certain that none of the more basic visual functions such as form or brightness discrimination are affected at all by inferotemporal lesions. Thus the inferotemporal lobe is certainly neither the storage unit (if there is any) for the acquired memories, nor is it required for the discrimination of form. Rather, its role seems to be more involved in controlling the acquisition, rather than in the actual storage, of visual information.

Meyer (1972) believes that the function of the inferotemporal cortex is even more specific. Noting that animals tend to learn how to learn, that is to develop what Harlow (1949) called *learning sets,* Meyer has suggested, on the basis of extensive experimentation in which especially careful control was made of the tasks required of the experimental monkeys, that the deficits produced by inferotemporal lobe lesions were entirely explained in terms of a reduction in the ability to develop the learning set. Tasks that involved only short-term retention or single stimuli appeared to be totally unaffected even by very extensive inferotemporal lesions.

This then brings us back to the other main observation concerning the role of the inferotemporal cortex—it is responsive only to visual stimuli. Because this region receives inputs from at least two, and possibly three, independent visual pathways and seems to be heavily involved in learning, it might be regarded as a region specialized for the integration of information from multiple inputs.

The integrative role of the inferotemporal cortex may, thus, be one in which links are established between coverging inputs from the collicular and the geniculostriate visual pathways. As we have seen, fine pattern discrimination seems to be mediated in the latter, and, as we shall see in the next section, the collicular pathways seem to be more concerned with orientation and localization. The function that may best describe the role of the inferotemporal cortex is the merging and integrating of these two sources of visual input information prior to the selection of appropriate responses.

However, there is an argument against even this role. Recent microelectrode studies (e.g., Rocha-Miranda, Bender, Gross & Mishkin, 1975) have suggested that the visual responses of the inferotemporal cortex are totally abolished if the striate cortex is ablated. The visual input to the inferotemporal region, therefore, may be exclusively through connectives that come from the geniculo-striate pathway either directly or through the forebrain commissures and may not directly involve the collicular inputs. This issue of the role of the inferotemporal cortex is yet to be resolved.

A useful and comprehensive review of the problem of inferotemporal lesions and their behavioral effects has been published by Dean (1976). He concludes that all of the inferotemporal lesion experiments are explicable in terms of either deficits in the ability "(a) to categorize visual stimuli or (b) to form associations with them [p. 41]." Clearly, at this point the difficulty inherent in such vague definitions of the relevant psychological constructs become dominant.

4. The Superior Colliculus

In the late 1960s, a considerable amount of interest in the visual functions of the region known as the *superior colliculus* (or *tectum*) of the brain stem was generated by the work of a number of psychobiologists. We have already seen how the tectum and, perhaps, also the pretectal areas are now considered to be independent pathways of visual information flow[3] from the peripheral retinae to the central nervous system. However, another role has been suggested for the superior colliculi that stresses an independent contribution that they may make to visual perception. Among others, Schneider (1969) has hypothesized that the collicular system, rather than being just another means of getting visual information to the cortex, may actually represent an independent and sufficient visual interpretive system. For example, in lower vertebrates, such as amphibia, the tectum is believed to be the main visual projection; and frogs, for example, which do not possess a cerebral visual cortex (see Ebbesson, 1970), perform quite well in their visual environments.

Anatomical and ecological clues, like this one from lower vertebrates, led Schneider to study mammals to determine the respective roles of each of their constituent visual systems. Working originally with hamsters, Schneider noted that specimens in which bilateral undercutting of the colliculi was performed seemed to have a considerable amount of difficulty in orienting toward stimuli. Upon initial examination, the animals appeared to be functionally blind; they stumbled about and were unable to direct their gaze at food objects. But more detailed testing showed that these animals could indeed "see" fairly well. They were, for example, able to discriminate among patterns.

On the basis of such evidence, Schneider assumed that the two visual systems —the geniculostriate and the collicular pathways—are respectively responsible for what may be broadly considered to be two different kinds of vision. He supported the concept that the geniculostriate system is responsible mainly for discriminating among forms and shapes mainly mediated by the high acuity region of the retina—the fovea, and added the idea that the collicular system is more involved in localization and orientation over the entire visual field but seems to be incapable of independent form recognition. The collicular system, Schneider proposed, acts to bring biologically significant stimuli into the foveal field of view for detailed examination and should, therefore, be closely associated with the musculature that controls eye movement and head position. It would thus be expected to have large receptor fields for its visually sensitive neurons.

---

[3]Although I stress the visual function of the superior colliculus in this section, it is important to note that it also has other sensory functions. Dräger and Hubel (1975) have shown that single neuron responses can be elicited from this area in the mouse by acoustic and tactual stimuli as well as by the visual ones. The more general function of the superior colliculus, they suggest, is to represent the geographical environment of the animal whether the information is forthcoming from his eyes, ears, or whiskers. It is also possible, considering that the neural responses lead the ocular muscle contraction, that it also plays a motor role in eye movements.

A great deal of subsequent research has tended to reinforce the concept that the colliculus or tectum is involved mainly in aspects of visual perception that involve spatial localization and orientation. Some workers, such as Schiller and Koerner (1971) and Wurtz and Goldberg (1972), have convincingly shown that the collicular visual system is implicated in the control of eye movements. Schiller and Koerner have specifically shown that activation of the collicular system does bring a visual stimulus that may fall initially on the peripheral portion of the retina into the foveal field of view where the pattern perception mechanisms of the geniculostriate system may contribute to the recognition of the stimulus.

Just how collicular neurons may be involved in eye movements is demonstrated in Fig. 5-24. This graph, from Schiller and Koerner (1971), shows the direction and magnitude of a large number of saccades (eye movements). The open circles, randomly distributed across the field of this figure, are those in which

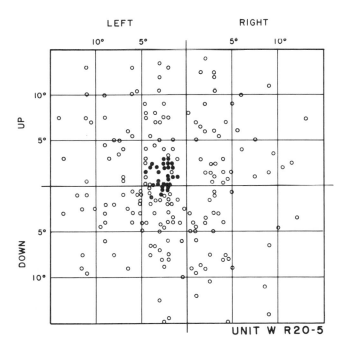

FIG. 5-24   In this figure, the results of an experiment are displayed in which a microelectrode was inserted into a single collicular neuron. Each time a saccadic eye movement occurred, a dot or circle was plotted on the graph to indicate direction and size of the saccade. If the cell emitted a burst of activity prior to the saccade, a dot was plotted; if the cell was quiet, an open circle was plotted. The results of this experiment indicate that the cell impaled was associated with a very sharply defined range of saccadic movements. (From Schiller & Koerner, ©1971, with the permission of The American Physiological Society.)

there was an eye movement but no response from an extracellular microelectrode located close to a certain group of neurons in the deeper layers of the superior colliculus. However, the black dots indicate a set of saccades of a particular size and in a particular direction that was always preceded by activity in the neurons near the microelectrode. The important fact in this record is that the neurons from which the signals came seemed to be associated with a particular direction and magnitude of movement.

The implication of this result is that the neurons in the deeper layers of the colliculus are very deeply involved in the control of eye movements. A further insight into the nature of this control lies in the fact that the saccades indicated with black dots were not all initiated from the same point. Rather, the neurons seemed to emit control signals that specified a size and direction of the saccade that was independent of its initial point. The superior colliculus, therefore, is presumed to send out signals that participate in the control of what must essentially be considered ballistic[4] eye movements that tend to bring stimuli into the foveal view, based on the low acuity but general orientation information of the visual inputs it receives from the peripheral field of view.

There is one warning that should be introduced into this discussion, however, in the spirit of the critical analysis that I have been carrying out for this material. There is still some residual doubt whether these recorded neuronal responses are, in fact, the output of motor units. It is possible, quite to the contrary, that these are not motor neurons directly controlling eye movements but sensory neurons reflecting feedback signals from muscle receptors. This could be the case, even if the electrophysiological response led the observed motor response in time because of the inertial characteristics of the mechanical aspects of the oculomotor system. Whatever the role of these deeply situated neurons, they do seem to be involved in some aspect of motor activity.

When the electrodes were not thrust as deeply into the colliculus, Schiller and Koerner found a different pattern of results. In the superficial collicular layers, neurons seemed to display a purely visual sensory function. However, neurons located there failed to exhibit any of the sensitivities to the pattern, shape, or direction of movement that are so characteristic of the neurons in the striate and peristriate cortices. Rather, the neurons of these superficial layers of the superior colliculus are much more likely to have both large receptive fields and high sensitivity to such general factors as the size than to the movement or shape of the stimulus.

---

[4]A ballistic motion is one in which the trajectory is mainly determined by the forces exerted at the time of projection. There is no "course correction" or guidance subsequent to release of the missile.

In sum, the superior colliculus in mammals appears to act as an initial early-warning system that acquires visual stimuli and then contributes to the orientation of the animal, or its eyes, to bring the stimulus into the foveal retinal areas that the cerebral pattern perception mechanisms depend upon for their function. The proximity of the superficial sensory layers and the deeper motor layers suggests an integrative role for the colliculus in which sensory inputs are linked to fairly specific motor outputs.

5.   Subcortical Mechanisms in Visual Perception

It is obvious that other subcortical centers as well as the superior colliculus, including the basal ganglia and the thalamus, may be involved in perceptual processing. Some human clinical observations summarized by Riklan and Levita (1969, chap. 5) lend substantial support to the notion that basal ganglia pathologies that produce symptoms of Parkinson's disease also produce associated perceptual difficulties, as evidenced in responses to drawing-type tests like the Bender Gestalt, or unstructured interpretive tests like the Rorschach. Riklan and Levita suggest that one of the more important roles played by the basal ganglia is in the integration of postural and visual afferent signals to determine the perceived vertical in a tilted-chair experiment. Proctor, Riklan, Cooper, and Teuber (1964) discovered that after therapeutic surgery of the basal ganglia for Parkinsonism, patients made many more errors in determining vertical alignment than did normal controls.

However, as I have already noted, most human clinical data are very variable and difficult to interpret, and, unfortunately, there has been relatively little work done on perceptual deficits produced by experimental lesions of the basal ganglia in experimental animals with which to compare these human data.

However, a considerable amount of work has been done on rats, cats, and, in at least one important study, monkeys with regard to brain stem involvement in visual information processing and learning. Thompson and Myers (1971), in an important experimental study of the monkey's brain stem have also reviewed a considerable amount of the material on perceptual effects produced by similar lesions in rats and cats. They note that research on rats and cats has pointed to three different areas of the brain stem that seem to impair visual learning and discrimination. Specifically they state:

> There are at least three circumscribed areas of the brain stem which may play an important role in visually guided behavior. One of these lies in the vicinity of the pretectum. In the rat, the critical pretectal focus appears to occupy the anterior half of the nucleus posterior thalami (Breen, 1965; McNew & Thompson, 1966; Thompson & Rich, 1961). In the cat, the results of one study (Thompson, Lesse, & Rich, 1963) suggest that the critical focus lies within the posterolateral portion of the pretectal area and the subjacent nucleus posterior thalami.

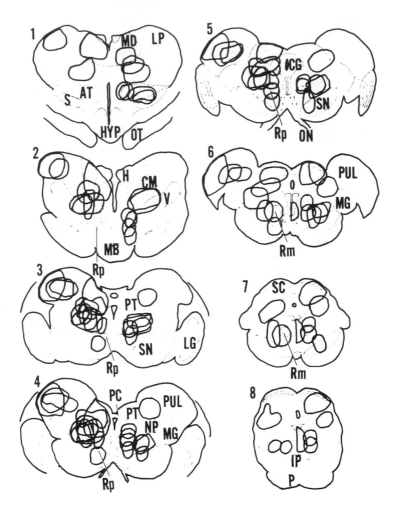

FIG. 5-25 Maps of eight different levels of the brain stem. The animal was trained in a visual discrimination task, and then the lesions (indicated by circles) were made. Those on the left-hand side of each figure were effective in reducing the performance following recovery; those on the right-hand side were not. Obviously visual memory is influenced by almost all levels of the brain. Abbreviations indicated are: AT = area tegmentalis; CG = central gray; CM = centre medial; H = habenula; HYP = hypothalamus; IP = interpeduncular nucleus; LG = lateral geniculate nucleus; LP = lateral posterior nucleus; MB = mammillary bodies; MD = medial dorsal nucleus; MG = medial geniculate nucleus; NP = nucleus posterior; ON = oculomotor nerve; OT = optic tract; P = pons; PC = posterior commissure; PT = pretectal region; PUL = pulvinar; Rm = magnocellular division of red nucleus; Rp = parvocellular division of red nucleus; S = subthalamic nucleus; SC = superior colliculus; SN = substantia nigra; and V = ventral nucleus. (Figure and abbreviations from Thompson & Myers, ©1971, with the permission of The American Psychological Association.)

A second area of the brain stem critical to visual discrimination performance in lower forms is located within the ventromedial midbrain, particularly in the region of the red nucleus. Bilateral destruction of this area has repeatedly been found to impair the execution of a visual discriminative response in rats (McNew, 1968; Thompson, 1969; Thompson, Lukaszewska, Schweigerdt, & McNew, 1967) and markedly diminishes responsiveness to visual cues in cats (Myers, 1964; Sprague, Levitt, Robson, Liu, Stellar, & Chambers, 1963).

The third area of the brain stem supporting normal visual discrimination performance is located in a zone between the pretectal region and the red nucleus. In the rat, this area lies immediately lateral to the rostral extension of the central gray substance and descends caudally in close conjunction with the habenulopeduncular tract (Thompson, 1969; Thorne, 1970). Although less intensively investigated in the cat, this area seems to include the deep subcollicular region, the lateral portion of the central gray substance, and the subjacent tegmentum (Myers, 1964) [Thompson and Myers, 1971, p. 480].

Thompson and Myers (1971) then report the results of their experimental studies of visual effects when lesions were produced at various levels of the monkey's brain stem. In each level, they assayed the visual effects of the lesion by using a simple discrimination task in which the monkey had to choose between different objects that might cover a piece of banana.

Figure 5-25 summarizes the results of their study. This figure shows the extent of the lesions that were created at eight different levels of the brain stem, as determined with post-mortem histology. The lesions drawn on the left side of the figures indicate those areas that did produce a deficit; the ones on the right indicate areas that when damaged did not interfere with the kind of visual performance tested. In general, Thompson and Myers found that only two brain stem regions consistently produced a deficit—the pulvinar nucleus and a region composed of the posterior thalamic and pretectal nuclei. A number of other nuclei produced inconsistent interference with this type of visual discriminative task.

An important finding from this work was Thompson and Myers' discovery that the deficits produced by these brain stem lesions were the same as those produced by inferotemporal lesions. Thus they were led to suggest that the role in visual learning that had been ascribed solely to the inferotemporal cortex might, in fact, be mediated by a vertically organized system of interacting structures rather than that cortical region alone. Much of what has been said so far about the inferotemporal cortex may, therefore, be applicable more appropriately to this vertically organized system in general.

There are, however, some caveats concerning this work that should be mentioned. Because of the complexity of the behavioral processes that were assayed in Thompson and Myers' study, it is entirely possible that the interference was produced by means other than a direct effect on visual discrimination per se.

Lesions in the thalamus, for example, may simply have interfered with the flow of visual information to the brain. Furthermore, some of the lesions led to "a severe and relatively permanent paralysis of downward gaze" (Thompson & Myers, 1971, p. 504). Inability of the animal to normally scan the visual scene may, therefore, also have played a role in decrementing the performance in a way that was unrelated to discriminative or memorial functions.

Nevertheless, although there may be some question about the exact details of Thompson and Myers' work, it is particularly significant in stressing that no one "center" exclusively controls visual discrimination and learning. Rather, the same general picture emerges here as in most other studies of central nervous system localization: Each mental process is the result of the interaction of a system of constituent nuclei. The idea of a unique center will die hard, but it will die as this type of data becomes more widely appreciated.

6.   Some Comments on Microlocalization

So far in our discussion of localization in the visual system, we have only considered localization with regard to the brain macrostructure—the lobes and grossly demarcatable regions. There is another level at which the problem of localization can also be attacked, however, that is of much more minute dimensions. The various regions, themselves, are not homogeneous. If one switches research techniques, dropping the paradigmatic approach in which the behavioral effects of ablations are examined and adopting the recording microelectrode as one's main research tool, a whole new set of data and dimensions concerning the localization problem becomes available.

The extra- or intracellular microelectrode (often less than one micron in diameter) serves as the exploring tip of an electrophysiological recording system that is capable of detecting the responses of individual neurons. Almost all conceivable dimensions of the visual stimulus, including brightness, color, and spatial and temporal pattern, have been shown to elicit and/or modulate activity in one or another part of the visual nervous system. Variations in these dimensions are transformed or encoded into patterns of neurophysiological response in different regions that may be selectively sensitive to one or more of the trigger dimensions I have mentioned. Which particular neuron in which particular place will respond to which particular stimulus dimension is a question that is the microscopic place coding analog of the macroscopic localization issue.

Unfortunately, there is also no general answer to the question of microscopic place coding. Rather, there are a number of issues that are involved in the search for the coding parameters of sensory neurons that are not usually considered from the point of view of localization theory. Complicating the matter is the fact that a single neuron may often respond differentially to a number of different parameters of the visual stimulus. Thus a single neuron may be found to be varying its frequency of firing as the color, place, and intensity of the visual stimulus vary. There is no unique place code, or microscopic localization, therefore, at this level; rather, other dimensions (than where a neuron is located) are responsible for conveying information about these aspects of the stimulus to particular neurons in particular places. The reader interested in the problem of sensory coding is referred to Chapters 6 and 7 in this book or, for a more complete discussion, to my earlier work (Uttal, 1973).

What does occur within some of the visual areas, however, is a sort of localization or, more properly, place encoding of the spatial arrangement of the visual field. It is well-established that in the early portions of the visual pathway, up to and including V1, V2, V3, and probably V4, retinotopic (i.e., a spatially isomorphic or map-like) representation of the external world is maintained. However, as one proceeds further to the higher-level regions, such as the frontal or inferotemporal cortices, there is a breakdown in this form of localization; no evidence of an isomorphic retinotopic localization can be observed. Thus a kind of microlocalizational, topological mapping of the environment, is present but only within some of the more peripheral brain areas assigned to visual processing.

We may conclude that there does appear to be a certain degree of differentiation of function observable among different areas at both the macro- and micro-levels of the visual nervous system. Localization, or place encoding, as some would call it, is an important aspect within the visual process just as place is an important code for sensory modality. But it is a form of localization that involves more than a single visual center; it is a system of interacting component centers, each of which depends for its function upon the integrity of others, and each of which may be heavily interconnected with other portions of the brain and brain stem.

This then completes our brief survey of the ways in which visual perception is localized in the central nervous system. I now turn to a consideration of systems of components of the brain that seem to be heavily concerned with some more complex cognitive processes.

C. ON THE LOCALIZATION OF THOUGHT PROCESSES IN THE BRAIN—THE PSYCHOBIOLOGY OF THINKING AND SPEECH

1. On the Anatomy of the Intrinsic Areas

The psychological processes that I consider in this section are among the most elusive to define in an exact fashion. I use the rubric of "thinking" to include such diverse mental functions as those behind language behavior, on the one hand, and highly structured and abstracted laboratory tests of decision making, on the other, to emphasize the most extreme examples. The breadth of this topic should become clear as readers progress through the later parts of this section.

For the moment, however, let us consider the anatomy of the neural structures within which modern research suggests that these complex cognitive processes may, to a certain extent, be localized. For the most part, I deal in this section with the parts of the brain that have classically been called the *association areas of the cerebral cortex*. There are a number of experiments that suggest that some of the subcortical centers of the brain and brain stem may also be involved to some extent in the processes considered, but most of the relevant research has been carried out on the cortical association areas (the nonsensory or motor regions—the "uncommitted" regions) that were shown in Fig. 5-16.

The regions with which I am now concerned have been referred to as association areas for some compelling historical reasons. The early psychobiologists thought that these nonsensory and nonmotor regions were literally responsible for the "association" of sensory input signals with the appropriate motor outputs and that the brain operated as a giant switchboard. It was assumed that sensory signals flowed first into the primary projection areas and then were routed to the association areas where they were linked together with appropriate responses. The molar process of learning was the external behavior that many of the nineteenth-century associationists thought reflected the formation of these neural links. After suitable experience, specific stimuli came to be associated with particular responses. The stimulus-association-response concept of human behavior was the predominant psychological tradition during this period.

We now have a somewhat different view of the role and nature of the so-called association areas of the cortex. It is clear that almost all of these areas also receive direct signals from the sensory systems. Indeed, it is often possible to cut the connectives from the sensory projection areas to the association areas, without producing major deficits in behavior. It now seems that the many connections that run between the different association areas themselves may be more important than the pathways between the primary sensory projection regions and the association regions.

Because of these and related considerations, Pribram (1960) has urged us to call these areas the "intrinsic" areas rather than use the archiac term "association" areas. From this point on and for the reasons he suggests, I follow this revised nomenclature, which stresses an entirely different role for these important areas.

The detailed anatomy of the intrinsic areas and their interconnections is extremely complicated. Very little is known of their cellular architectonics. We simply do not have adequate conceptual anchors to use in an analysis of intrinsic area function comparable to the well-ordered stimulus dimensions, the simple input pathways, and topographic layout of the primary sensory projection areas. Furthermore, there seem to be an abundance of interconnections between and among the various intrinsic areas. It must be remembered that, except for the thin shell of the cerebral mantle and the other subcortical nuclei, most of the cerebral hemispheres are made up of myelinated nerve fibers interconnecting the various nuclei of the cortex.

It is patently impossible to adequately review the many anatomic studies of the interconnecting tracts in this important part of the brain, but the reader may wish to look again at one of the very good neuroanatomic texts such as Crosby, Humphrey, and Lauer (1962) or Carpenter (1976) to review this material.

2.   The Frontal Lobes and Time Binding

It has been known for almost a century that the effects of frontal lobe injuries or ablations produced subtle behavioral effects, but the appreciation of exactly what these effects were proved to be extremely elusive, in spite of a considerable amount of research on animals and on humans. The classic case of Phineas Gage, often described in elementary textbooks, still serves as an excellent illustration of the subtle but important psychological processes that seemed to be associated with these regions of the brain. Mr. Gage, after recovering from the initial trauma produced by having a crowbar thrust through his eye and out the top of his head in a way that essentially amputated his frontal lobes, led a relatively normal life. The exceptions to his complete recovery were behaviorally delicate and difficult to precisely define. He seemed to have lost ambition, judgment, and his "organizational" abilities, all of which were important personality attributes for the job he held as a railroad construction foreman prior to his injury.

Unfortunately, in this oft-told tale, we are left with only these extremely vague measures of Mr. Gage's personality changes. It is not exactly clear from the critical point of view of the empirically oriented laboratory psychobiologist just what such vague dimensions of behavior as "judgment" or "organizational ability" are. They sound all too much like phrenological faculties. The search for some more specific behavior deficit has thus led to the use of some highly abstract laboratory tests of performance that can be quantified in a way that the term "ambition" cannot be.

Stemming from many other more modern studies, reported by such distinguished neuropsychologists as Luria (1966a), is the discovery that the frontal lobe seems to be intimately involved in complex behaviors that have to do with organization of sequences or complexes of responses. According to Luria, lesions in this region typically produce a deficit in the ability of patients to evaluate the subsequent effect of their present behavior. As suggestive as this notion is, these deficits are still relatively poorly defined.

In animals, much more carefully controlled research procedures, of course, can be used; and similar lesions produce symptoms that seem to be very much in this same category. Behavioral processes that require the organization of responses into sequences or that might be involved in the evaluation of the future effect of those responses are also degraded in experimental animals. The typical effect of amputation of the frontal lobes in a dog or monkey is the generation of a difficulty in locating food that is placed in the field of view contralateral to the amputated frontal lobe. The animal seems not to be blind in any sense; discrimination tests make it clear that the animal is capable of discriminating between forms. Rather, the animal seems to simply neglect the visual stimulus, to not appreciate the fact that this stimulus is a potential satisfier of hunger. Furthermore, the deficit exists only for a period of a few weeks following the surgery. After that, the animal recovers its attentiveness to food, and the effect of the ablation disappears. If the other frontal lobe is then ablated, the process simply repeats—the animal at first disregards or neglects a visual food stimulus in the contralateral field of view and then recovers what appears to be near normal behavior.

By far the most unusual laboratory test used in the study of behavioral destruction following frontal lobe ablation is the delayed response test in which an animal is prevented from responding immediately following the presentation of a stimulus (Jacobsen, 1935). In its most familiar form, the delayed response task is carried out in the following way. The stimulus object is exposed to the animal for a period of time. It is then removed (or obscured), and a second period of time passes prior to the exposure of the manipulandum that the animal must use to make his response. The duration of this second interval between the stimulus and the presentation of the manipulandum is usually the independent variable in experiments of this sort.

A host of experiments using the delayed response task have shown it to be particularly sensitive to frontal lobe ablations (see, for example, Butter, 1964; and Chapter 8). The dorsolateral regions of the frontal lobe seem to be particularly effective in producing this delayed response deficit according to Butter's and related work.

In humans, the effects of frontal lobe injury are more complicated. Luria (1966a) discusses disturbances in voluntary motor patterns, including a disintegration of serial sequences of motor responses, a tendency toward perserverance (such as might be evidenced by an inability to reverse a motor or verbal response in accord with a sequence of alternating verbal instructions) as well as some more complex speech and visual replication difficulties. Luria also characterizes the general change in personality often observed as a loss of goal directedness in the afflicted humans.

The general picture that emerges from this brief discussion of the effects of frontal lobe ablations and injuries is that these effects are, in large part, associated with what some have called *time binding*. All of the deficits, whether they are delayed responses in monkeys or a loss of sequence control or even "ambition" (whatever that is) in humans, are linked by this common thread. Each exhibits a behavioral change that is in some way associated with events that are spread over an extended period of time. The frontal lobe deficit seems most likely to involve an inability to string sequential events together or to appreciate the subsequent effects of some currently emitted response.

Pribram (1973), in summing up the proceedings of an important congress, suggested that the weight of the data concerning frontal lobe injury led him to the idea that the frontal lobes act to inhibit mutual interference that would otherwise occur among a series of near simultaneous brain events. This concept is nearly synonymous with the notion of a time sequencer expressed in the preceding paragraph, because once interference is reduced, the opportunities for the serial ordering of sequential events and the determination of the subsequent biological value of earlier events would necessarily be enhanced. In Pribram's terms, the "ability to resist novelty" (Pribram, 1973, p. 306) is also a function of the frontal lobes. One of the other effects often noticed with frontal lesions, he notes, is that the operated animals do not normally habituate to repeated stimuli. Rather, they continue to respond as if the stimulus was fresh and new far longer than do normal animals.

In sum, the notion of time binding, the linkage of a sense of mental state into a smoothly flowing stream of consciousness and behavior, permeates almost all of the literature that describes behavioral changes due to frontal lobe lesions.

3. The Left Hemisphere and Speech

Even though language production has often been considered one of the most clear-cut examples of a relatively discretely localized psychological function, a close examination of the recent literature suggests that speech is no better localized than any other function we have discussed so far. Two of the preeminent psychobiologists who have studied the brain localization of speech mechanisms (Penfield & Roberts, 1959) have emphatically stated: "No discrete localization of lesions producing various types of agnosia and apraxia has been found. It seems as *Jackson* (1931) stated, that any acute lesion to any gross part of the left hemisphere will produce some disturbance in speech [p. 78]."

The late Eric Lennenberg (1974) also put the problem of localization of speech functions into perspective when he noted:

In many aphasiologists' opinion, the exact anatomical substrate for language remains elusive, especially for the cognitive side of language. If one compares the various aggregate maps of cortical lesions prepared, for example, by Conrad (1954), Penfield and Roberts (1959), Russell and Espir (1961), or Luria (1970, 1972), there do not seem to be sharply delimited or structurally well defined areas that are alone responsible for the appearance of specific clinical language deficits. In other words, specific aphasic symptoms are not pathognomonic for destruction of one, and no other, cortical area. Instead there are gradients of probability for the occurrence of a symptom complex that may appear in connection with a lesion in a given area [p. 524].

These points of view are stressed at the outset of our discussion because it is all too easy to infer from a first reading of the literature that the opposite conclusion, namely that a high degree of localization of speech function does occur, is actually the true state of affairs.

However, it is also important to note as we begin this discussion that some of the most active workers in the field of brain localization of speech functions still adhere to the general theme of the theory of radical localization originally proposed by Carl Wernicke one hundred years ago. Geschwind (1970), for example, still feels that Wernicke's (1874) classic hypothesis of precise cerebral localization of the various speech functions is the most useful contemporary theory and that the functions assigned by Wernicke and his predecessor Broca to particular centers of the brain still hold. Masland (1971) is another contemporary worker who feels that there is a great deal to be said for rather specific localization of speech function on the surface of the cerebral mantle. We must recognize, therefore, that there still is a great deal of controversy concerning the localization of speech function.

I begin the discussion by considering the value of speech itself. It is a truism that speech is an especially important, and perhaps unique, human function, binding individuals and people together in time and providing the necessary basis for cultural progress. Until recently, it was thought that symbolic language, such as speech and writing, was exclusively a human process. In recent years, however, several workers (Gardner & Gardner, 1969; Premack, 1971) have shown that it is possible to train chimpanzees to use signs in symbolic ways that are difficult to distinguish from the vocalizations of human speech. This extraordinary and exciting act of animal training would be just a trick if it were not for the fact that it emphasizes an extremely important theoretical point: Language is not a single process or act but is a complex of a number of different sensory, response, and integrative functions.

Language, according to this point of view, may best be thought of as including three different sets of subprocesses. One set includes the actual motor processes that control the production of the speech sounds or phonemes. A second set corresponds to the processes that form the sequence of appropriate speech terms in accord with the rules of grammar. Linguists would refer to this aspect of speech as syntax generation. A third set concerns the processes that regulate the semantic context or meaning of the spoken or written sentences.

Could these three aspects of language behavior reflect three different aspects of brain anatomy? Certainly some of the early workers in the field thought so. There was already an elaborate taxonomy of the various kinds of aphasias that could result from specifically placed brain lesions by the middle of the nineteenth century. The generally accepted theory was that different forms of these aphasias reflected inabilities to form speech sounds, to sequence words in accord with the rules of grammar, or to process the symbolic meaning of the respective speech sounds. Table 5-1 tabulates some of the better-known speech difficulties in accordance with these three classifications.

TABLE 5.1

Disorders of Symbolic Communication

A. Disorders of articulation and hearing
  1. Aphonia—Inability to speak due to vocal organ damage
  2. Apraxia—Inability to speak due to loss of motor control
  3. Anarthia—Inability to form or articulate speech sounds
  4. Deafness—Inability to hear for mechnical or neural reasons

B. Disorders of syntax
  1. Conduction aphasia—Aphasia in which words are skipped or repeated

C. Disorders of semantics
  1. Semantic Aphasia—Inability to understand meaning of words
  2. Agnosia—Inability to recognize meaning or spatial and temporal relations of objects
  3. Alexia—Inability to understand meaning of written words
  4. Anomia—Inability to name objects
  5. Apractognosia—Inability to handle spatial relations
  6. Asymbolia or asemia—Inability to understand significance of symbols
  7. Finger agnosia—Inability to recognize one's own finger
  8. Acalculia—Inability to do simple arithmetic
  9. Agraphia—Inability to write
  10. Aphemia — Inability to express meaningful words

What can presently be said with assurance about the localization of these speech disorders in the brain? One of the points on which all contemporary workers currently agree is the fact that the two cerebral hemispheres are not exactly symmetrical. Depending to some degree but not entirely upon the handedness of the person, one or the other hemisphere is found to be dominant for processing speech and writing. It is only in unusual circumstances (such as congenital or early damage to the corpus callosum) that the dominant hemisphere will not be the one contralateral to the dominant hand. Given that most people are right-handed (the cited figures vary from 70 to 90% from different sources), the left hemisphere is the one in which the dominant speech centers are said to be most often located. Damage to the right hemisphere can be remarkably extensive without any deficit being produced in verbal behavior. (But, note also the relevance of and the caveats within the discussion on the split brain preparation later in this chapter.)

Since the time of Broca, there have been assumed to be well-defined regions within the confines of the dominant (usually left) cerebral hemisphere that, when damaged, will produce particular types of aphasic deficits. I have already alluded to the early studies in our historical survey, but to be more specific, I should note that Wernicke himself assumed that the area known as Broca's Area (indicated on Fig. 5-26) was primarily involved in the organization of the syntactical relations between items in a sequence of speech sounds, and that portion

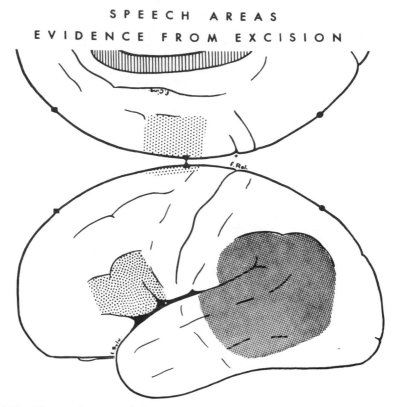

SPEECH AREAS

EVIDENCE FROM EXCISION

FIG. 5-26   Three major areas of the brain believed by many to be associated with speech function. The posterior area stippled with many small dots is known as Wernicke's area, the anterior area stippled with irregularly placed larger dots is Broca's area, and the regularly spaced dots denote an area (on the inside of the hemispheric fissure) known as the supplementary motor area. The extent of each area indicated on this diagram is only approximate. (From Penfield & Roberts, ©1959, with the permission of the literary executors of W. Penfield and The Princeton University Press.)

known as Wernicke's Area (also seen in Fig. 5-26) seemed to be more closely related to the symbolic, representational, or semantic processing of the meaning of speech.

The other aspect of speech, motor control, has typically been assumed to be controlled by the classical motor areas that are located on the most caudal portion of the motor cortex quite near Broca's Area. The proximity of these two regions has often produced difficulty in distinguishing between the motor and syntactical aspects of speech.

Other workers have shown that lesions of the supplementary motor regions on the top of the cerebral hemisphere also produce speech disturbances very much like those produced by lesions in Broca's Area. This area is also shown on Fig. 5-26.

Geschwind (1970) has also suggested that there is a special role played by the band of axons—the Arcuate Fasciculus—connecting Wernicke's and Broca's Areas. When transmission of information along this band is disrupted, he asserts that there is a characteristic kind of speech difficulty produced that is referred to as *conduction aphasia*. Conduction aphasia is most typically characterized by the patient's inability to repeat words spoken to him, even though other aspects of his speech might be nearly normal.

At the risk of misleading the reader into accepting the concept of the localization of speech function with greater credulity than is justified, Fig. 5-27, from Penfield and Roberts (1959), is presented as a summary of several of the historic theoretical positions. This chart depicts the regions of the left hemisphere that were assumed for many years to be associated with a number of the different kinds of specific aphasic conditions. As one studies this figure, it is particularly important to keep in mind the fact that modern theories postulate a much less specific form of localization of function than is suggested there.

One source of confusion that led to the formularization of this somewhat misleading map lies in the fact that true syntactic or semantic aphasia is a con-

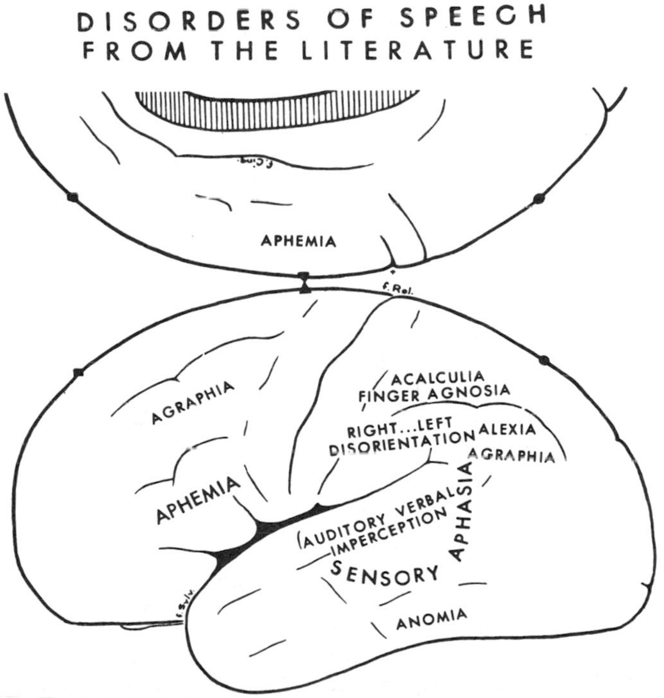

FIG. 5-27   Penfield and Robert's summary of the areas of the brain that seem to be associated with particular forms of speech disorder. (From Penfield & Roberts, ©1959, with the permission of the literary executors of W. Penfield and The Princeton University Press.)

dition that can be closely imitated by much simpler sensory or motor difficulties that have little to do directly with the interpretive and symbolic aspects of speech. Another difficulty with any theory of sharp localization of speech function is the fact that there is a great deal of recovery of function in almost all cases of traumatic aphasia. Although almost any damage to the left hemisphere will produce some sort of speech deficit, there is practically no area that will produce a permanent speech deficit when injured. Even the extreme speech deficits produced by lesions of Broca's or Wernicke's Areas are often transitory; speech function usually recovers except in cases in which a progressive neural degeneration is induced. Furthermore, the younger the patient is, the better the chances of recovery of full speech capabilities.

Clinical reports of the recovery of perfectly normal speech function after total destruction of the classic Wernicke and Broca Areas continue to be forthcoming (see Lennenberg, 1974, p. 525 for a summary of recent studies). Because clinical data are the only source of information concerning brain localization of the uniquely human ability to speak, it is of the utmost importance that even exceptional and anecdotal evidence be carefully considered, even though it is often "noisy" by conventional laboratory standards.

If strict localization of speech function, in the sense originally proposed by Wernicke, is no longer tenable, what organizing theorem can we use to guide future research and therapy? What we must turn to instead is another expression of the general theory that asserts that a number of brain centers must interact to produce any complex mental function. Indeed, the notion that it is possible to separate the articulatory, syntactical, and semantic aspects of speech from each other may be just as fallacious as the attempt to assign these functions to separate parts of the brain.

Once again, it is Eric Lennenberg (1974) who best summed up the contemporary view:

> Very many parts of the brain must contribute to the proper function of a behavior that is as inseparable from perception, memory, concept formation, and every other cognitive process as is language. The anatomy of gross and microscopic connections of the brain may as easily be cited in support of the notion that language is the product of many different physiologically interacting parts of the brain as in support of a speech-centers-with-connections model—perhaps more reasonably so. Locke stressed that cortical areas that have been called "language centers" are probably merely regions with certain physiological functions such that, when impaired, they disturb the smooth interaction and harmonious interplay among various suborgans of the brain. Some such disturbances are evidently more injurious to certain types of capacities (say language) than others. In short, my point of view denies that types of behavior have their own specialized and autonomous centers; rather, it proposes that every differentiated part of the brain makes its own physiological contribution to widespread activity patterns, resulting from interactions of different parts of the brain, and that these activity patterns are the proper correlates of such behavior as language.

While it is likely that no connection in the brain is random and that there is an orderly relation between fields of cells in the cortex, for example, and correlated areas in the retinae, the skin, the skeletal muscles, or in subcortical nuclei, this does not lend credence to the notion of centers with principal control over any particular kind of circumscribed behavior. The brain is not a loose aggregate of autonomous organs, but a single organ. Its anatomical subdivisions undoubtedly have their own specific physiological functions, contributing to various types of behavior in different ways. But, so far, we know of no behavioral entity that is the exclusive product of just one brain region alone [pp. 627-629].

4. Asymmetry of the Cerebral Hemispheres

It now appears that there is a good argument to support the hypothesis that the two cerebral hemispheres do not serve identical roles with regard to their sensory, integrative, and motor functions. The primary sensory projection regions of the cerebral mantle are typically arranged with at least some degree, and in some cases, a complete, crossover of this ascending and descending neural pathway. It is well-known, for example, that the postcentral somatosensory regions and the prefrontal motor regions are mainly crossed so that the left hemisphere predominantly receives signals from the somatosensory receptors on the contralateral side of the body and, with some exceptions, sends motor signals back to the contralateral side of the body. Similarly, the visual system, because of the crossover of the nasal portions of the visual field at the optic chiasm, is organized so that the left cerebral hemisphere receives signals from the left nasal and the right temporal hemiretinae, and the right hemisphere receives signals from the right nasal and left temporal hemiretinae (see Figs. 5-9 and 5-12). Many auditory fibers also cross over.

It is clear, therefore, that the two hemispheres of the brain are not functionally or anatomically identical even at the level of these relatively low-level sensory input and motor output regions. The question we face now, however, does not concern these communication areas; rather it is concerned with the nature of the functional dissimilarities that may occur between the intrinsic areas of the brain, which are more likely than the other regions to be involved in higher cognitive functions. The intrinsic areas of the left (usually) hemisphere appear to be more involved in the mediation of several different kinds of speech processes in the normal human than are those of the right hemisphere. The question now arises: What role is played by the extensive intrinsic regions of the right hemisphere, which have previously gone unmentioned?

During the last twenty years, considerable progress has been made in the study of the lateralization of the functions of the intrinsic cortical regions using a remarkable surgical technique based upon an unusual anatomical fact. The two cerebral hemispheres are structurally separate from each other and can communicate at the cerebral level only through two bundles of heavily myelinated fibers. The main cross-connective is the great corpus callosum shown in Fig. 5-28.

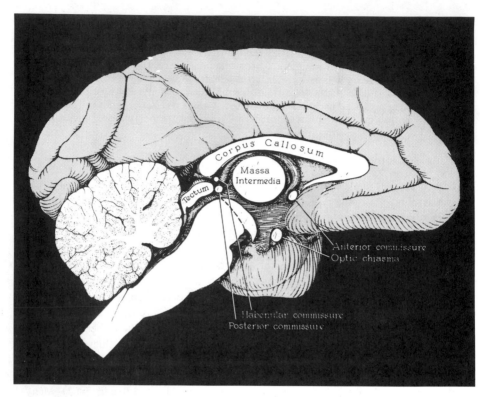

FIG. 5-28   A ventral dorsal section of the brain showing the important midline connecting links between the hemispheres of the brain. (From Sperry, ©1967, with the permission of The Rockefeller University Press.)

This band of neurons constitutes by far the largest number of interconnecting neural pathways, although there are a few other and considerably smaller commissures directly caudal to the corpus callosum. The posterior and the habenular commissures are, in fact, cross-connectives at the level of the diencephalon rather than the telencephalic cerebrum. The anterior commissure, on the other hand, which is truly a connective between the two cerebral hemispheres, is so intimately linked with the corpus callosum that surgical transection of the latter almost always includes the former.

The main function of the corpus callosum is to interconnect all of the regions of the two hemispheres, with the exception of the inferotemporal lobes. The anterior commissure is responsible for the transmission of signals between the two inferotemporal lobes. The details of this arrangement are shown in the diagrammatic representation of Fig. 5-29. In sum, surgical transection of just the anterior commissure and the corpus callosum abolish all direct interhemispheric communication, sparing only those indirect links that flow through the lower centers of the brain.

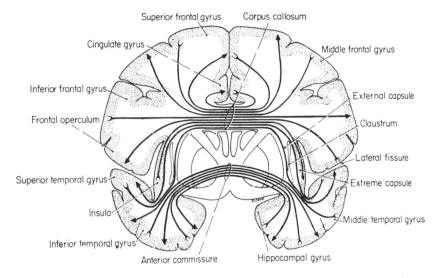

FIG. 5-29   Cross section of the brain showing the general pathways of the cerebral commissures and the regions interconnected by each. (From Crosby, Humphrey, & Lauer, ©1962, with the permission of Macmillan Publishing Company.)

If the corpus callosum of an experimental animal is transected (such a relatively simple operation is called a *commissurectomy*), there is practically no difficulty in keeping the animal alive. None of the life-sustaining homeostatic processes, generally controlled by the lower brain stem centers, are affected to any substantial degree. Rather, the commissurectomized animal is generally normal in all except the most subtle ways. Indeed, even humans who have had their corpus callosum transected, either through unfortunate accident or in some therapeutic surgical procedure, appear to be almost entirely normal except under the most highly controlled test conditions. In such highly structured test conditions, great care is taken to prevent indirect communication between hemispheres (for example, eye movement might allow both hemispheres to receive the same stimuli). Both animal and human studies have resulted in the demonstration of some extraordinary effects of commissurectomies.

These effects may vary from an inability on the part of an operated animal to transfer a task learned with one hemisphere to the other (Myers & Sperry, 1953) to what appears to be the emergence of two relatively independent conscious personalities (Sperry, 1966) within the skull of a single human. The determination of just what functions can be performed by each of the separated hemispheres has become one of the most important targets of contemporary psychobiological research.

Sperry and his colleagues (for summaries, see Gazzaniga, 1970; 1975) have shown that in commissurectomized humans the two hemispheres can operate independently to perceive and learn in those situations in which the inputs are carefully restricted so that only those from one side of the body, or one visual field, reach each hemisphere. This can be accomplished most easily for visual inputs by tachistoscopic exposures and proper placement of stimuli in the field of view of each hemisphere. When stimuli are carefully restricted in this manner, the two hemispheres each function as if there were no communication of the learned or perceived information between them.

In the course of these early experiments, which have demonstrated a not-too-surprising absence of communication (given that all known interhemispheric connections have been transected), it was also observed that the mental capabilities of the two hemispheres were not symmetrical. Each hemisphere appeared to display demonstrably different capabilities. For example, the left speech hemisphere (for a right-handed subject) was better able to recognize an object and verbally respond by naming the object, either orally or written—an act of symbolic language processing. However, when the same object was placed in the field of view restricted to the other hemisphere, the patient was unable to name the object. Nevertheless, even though the object cannot be named, the patient was able to recognize it and process information about the object in appropriate and often complex ways. For example, if an object, like a screwdriver or a cup, was put into the left hand of a normally right-handed person, the signals transmitted to the right hemisphere produced appropriate manipulation of the object; the right hemisphere, therefore, was said to be capable of *stereognosis*. This manipulative skill indicated that the patient was able to process some sensory information in a meaningful, cognitive fashion, in spite of the fact that he was unable to name the object either verbally or in writing.

The right hemisphere in this case was, therefore, assumed not to be unconscious, imperceptive, inattentive, or incapable of cognitive function. It was simply asserted to be less capable with specific regard to its ability to assign language symbols to perceived objects! Sperry and his collaborators showed in these early experiments that the right hemisphere of the brain was just as capable as the left in the processing of two- and three-dimensional spatial information, but lacking the ability to verbalize the ongoing mental processes. As shown later in this section, however, the hypothesis of a mute right hemisphere is no longer so strongly held.

The extraordinary phenomenon of the emergence of two almost independent personalities in humans with split brains can lead to some curious situations. Sperry (1966) discusses situations in which one hand of a patient actively tried to prevent the other hand from performing routine tasks, like putting on the patient's pants! Anecdotes such as this should be read, of course, with a great deal of caution. It is almost impossible to interpret exactly what is implied by these conflicts between two "separate" personalities. A great deal of research is yet to be done on split brain preparations to exploit this very important discovery in order to interpret its full impact on theories of brain localization and psychological function.

To emphasize the preliminary nature of theories of lateral hemispheric specialization, however, it should also be noted that very recently one of Sperry's colleagues (Zaidel, 1973; 1974) has demonstrated that substantial verbal ability does appear to exist in the right hemisphere of commissurectomized patients when the appropriate experiments are carried out using a special optical system (Zaidel, 1975). Although this verbal ability seems to be limited to short phrases or single words, it is now clear that speech information can be received and interpreted to at least some degree by the right hemisphere. Thus it is not quite as profoundly deaf and mute symbolically as had first been thought.

As a final caveat, however, it is extremely important for the reader to remember that the split brain preparation is critical in carrying out any analysis of differential functioning of the two hemispheres. A large number of studies that purport to study the function of the separate hemispheres are carried out on normal subjects without commissurectomies. These experiments supposedly take advantage of the fact that portions of the visual pathway go initially to a single side of the brain or that right-eared and left-eared auditory performance differs. Unfortunately the cross-connections between the two hemispheres in the normal subject make any such analysis in the normal subject spurious. It is not possible to state where the mental processes have occurred. It is totally inappropriate, therefore, to suggest that without a comissurectomy, the effects of a single hemisphere are assayed by a visual task, even if the stimulus had been positioned so that it was sent originally to only one hemisphere (as was done by Patterson & Bradshaw, 1975)—or that difference in left-ear and right-ear performance indicated difference in auditory hemispheric capability (as was claimed by Bever & Chiarello, 1974). In addition to the possible cross-connectives through the corpus callosum and the other commissures, it should also be noted that the auditory system sends signals to both hemispheres from either ear with crossover occurring as low as the medulla. Not only should an auditory experiment not be used in the normal patient to study this problem, but it would be an inappropriate stimulus to use in dealing with all except the most deeply split brain preparations!

In sum, it is now clear that there is some asymmetry in the function of the two cerebral hemispheres, particularly with regard to symbolic language processes. But there is considerable flux in the interpretation of the available data. One way to sum up the hypothetical details of this asymmetry is to present Fig. 5-30, prepared by Sperry (1970b), to graphically portray his findings as they were understood at that time.

In the last few years, however, there has been considerable change in the theory of localization of the processes indicated in this figure, as well as in its

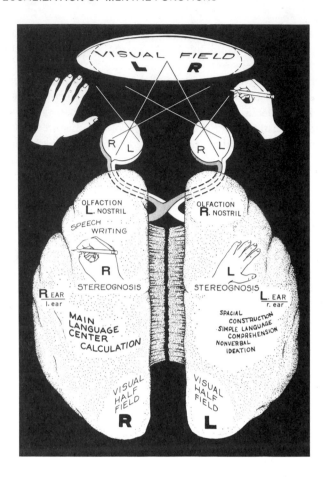

FIG. 5-30   Sperry's theoretical attribution of the functions mediated by each of the cerebral hemispheres. (From Sperry, ©1970b, with the permission of The Association for Research in Nervous and Mental Disease.)

general concept. This figure, therefore, is somewhat misleading in stressing a more complete differentiation of cerebral function than is now thought to be the actual case. Needless to say, the technique of split brains is exceedingly important but has not yet been thoroughly exploited in the analysis of the localization of cerebral function.

D.   AROUSAL AND ATTENTION

In 1975, two papers on the psychobiology of arousal and attention were published by two authors from somewhat divergent portions of the psychological community. One of the authors, Michael Posner (Posner, 1975), has been primarily trained in the field of human performance; the other, Karl Pribram (Pribram & McGuinness, 1975), came to psychobiology from medical neurology. Both of these highly respected contemporary scientists have converged on a research problem of extreme complexity—that of arousal and attention. Both have become interested in elucidating the brain mechanisms that are involved in the determination of that state of an organism that has to do with the responsiveness to and selection of particular stimuli.

Although it seems that neither Posner nor Pribram was aware of the work of the other (there are no citations of the other's work in either of the two papers), there is an important overlap in the two papers that may be extremely instructive in helping us to understand exactly what is meant by the terms *arousal* and *attention*. It is an extraordinary example of convergent scientific thought that both Posner and Pribram attempt to define attention in terms of a tripartite classification. By comparing their two attempts at definition, we should be able to determine if there is a common base of agreement in their approaches from which we can draw a single, unified view that is prototypical of the term *attention* among contemporary researchers in the field.

Posner's (1975) tripartite classification of attentional acts is based mainly upon psychological considerations; he indicates three "senses" of the word attention:

> 1. One sense of the word attention is called alertness and concerns the study of an organismic state which affects general receptivity to input information.
> 2. The second sense of attention involves selection of some information from the available signals for special treatment.
> 3. Finally there is a sense of attention related to the degree of conscious effort which a person invests [pp. 443-444].

Pribram's analogous approach to the problem is based upon his long experience with the neurological and physiological aspects of arousal and attention research. Nevertheless, Pribram, in the Pribram and McGuinness (1975) paper also comes up with three kinds of attentional processes:

> 1. One regulates arousal resulting from input. ... arousal, which is defined in terms of phasic physiological responses to input.
> 2. ... a second controls the preparatory activation of response mechanisms. ... activation, which is defined in terms of tonic physiological readiness to response.
> 3. A third operates to coordinate arousal and activation. ... This coordinating effort is defined as demanding effort [p. 116].

Or, in a more succinct fashion, later in their paper:

> Three neurally distinct and separate attentional systems—arousal, activation, and effort—operate upon the information processing mechanism. The presumed operation of these control systems is perhaps best illustrated as follows: The orienting reaction involves arousal but no activation; vigilant readiness involves activation

but no arousal; the defense reaction involves both arousal and activation; when neither arousal nor activation is present, behavior is automatic, that is, stimulus-response contingencies are direct without the intervention of any of the control mechanisms of attention [p. 133].

Are the two definitions of attentional processes similar? In fact, there appears to be a remarkable correspondence between these two approaches to the definition of the term. Posner and Pribram, along with the latter's colleague McGuinness, all agree that their first process is concerned with the "general receptivity" or "regulation of arousal" to incoming stimuli. Likewise, there is a near synonymity of the notion of stimulus selection, on the one hand (Posner), and the notion of activation of a particular response mechanism, on the other (Pribram & McGuinness). With regard to the third point, the words are virtually the same—both note the importance of *effort* in regulating the balance between the two processes or the stimuli to which attention shall be directed.

Thus, despite their separate intellectual origins, the definitions developed by both Posner and Pribram are in essential agreement as to just what psychological processes are being dealt with when one studies attention. Whether the approach is psychophysical or physiological, the notions of receptivity, selectivity, and effort, permeate the study of what is today known as *attention* and *arousal*.

One of the most important of the brain structures involved in arousing an animal and readying it to attend to and select among stimuli appears to be the brain stem reticular activating system shown in Fig. 5-31. The reticular activating system consists of a very complex network or reticulum of neurons in the central core of the upper spinal cord and the brain stem. It is anatomically characterized by containing some of the largest single neurons of the central nervous system. Figure 5-32, for example, depicts only a part of the axonal arborization of one reticular cell. According to Scheibel and Scheibel (1958), this extensive collateral arborization is displayed along the entire course of all neurons of the ascending reticular system.

Even if the detailed cytological structure is very difficult to describe because of cytological size and complexity, the general functional arrangement of the ascending reticular activating system has been relatively simply conceptualized. The most important fact of reticular function is that it receives collateral inputs from all of the primary sensory pathways as they pass from the periphery to the sensory projection regions of the cerebral cortex. The ascending reticular system has multiple inputs and is thus universally polysensory. After a considerable amount of integrative interaction among these individual sensory inputs, a generalized, nonspecific output, elicited by any one or all of the inputs, is sent from the reticular system to many portions of the cerebral cortex—sensory projection, motor, and intrinsic areas alike. Thus visual inputs will actually produce nonspecific reticular output signals to most of the areas of the cerebrum in addition to the specific signals to the visual areas.

This general distribution of sensory information from the reticular system is thought to be necessary for the general arousal of cortical response. Indeed, we

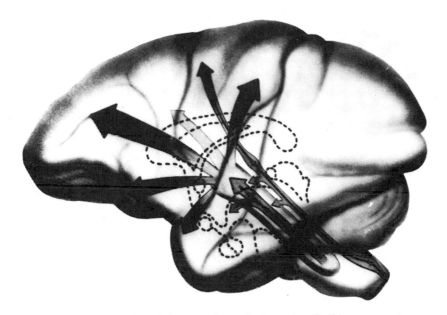

FIG. 5-31 The organization of the ascending reticular system. In this case, somatosensory afferents are seen to enter the spinal cord. Signals from these afferents are thought to be distributed to almost all portions of the cerebral mantle through the reticular system. (From Magoun, ©1954, with the permission of Blackwell Scientific Publications.)

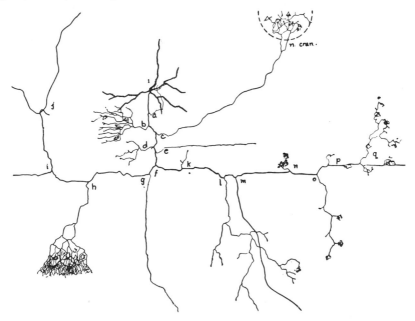

FIG. 5-32 A fairly typical multibranched neuron of the ascending reticular system of the brain. (From Scheibel & Scheibel, ©1958, with the permission of Henry Ford Hospital.)

know that (Libet, Alberts, Wright, & Feinstein, 1967; Uttal & Cook, 1964) both the specific sensory signals and the nonspecific signal propagated along the reticular activating system seem to be jointly necessary for conscious awareness of a stimulus. This important fact has been determined because of a convenient difference between the conduction velocities of the specific and the nonspecific signals to the cortex. The evoked potential produced in the sensory specific projection regions appears at about 50 msec. following a stimulus; the nonspecific reticular signal, recordable over the entire head, occurs much later—about 200 or 300 msec. after the stimulus. A series of evoked brain potentials of this sort is shown in Fig. 5-33. Note that when a subject goes to sleep, there is virtually no change in the early signal from the primary projection area, but there is a nearly complete diminution in the late nonspecific signals. The conclusion to be drawn from this observation is that both the specific sensory signal to the primary projection region and the nonspecific generalized activation that passes through the reticular activating system are necessary for perception, awareness, and attention, although neither alone appears to be sufficient.

The ascending reticular activating pathway was originally observed 70 years ago during some of the early anatomical studies of the brain stem (for a fairly up-to-date discussion of the cytoarchitecture of the reticular system see Olszewski, 1954). About 40 years later, Bremer (1935, 1937) observed that transection of the reticular system produced animals that seemed to be chronically asleep. A little more than a decade later, the results of some extraordinary experiments by Moruzzi and Magoun (1949) demonstrated that electrical stimulation of the reticular system produced EEG responses that were identical to those observed in animals that were normally aroused, alerted, or awake. The notion that the reticular system was an activating system, therefore, became immediately apparent, and, within a few years, a considerable amount of anatomical and physiological evidence was filling in the details of the function of this portion of the brain stem. There now seems to be a fairly strong body of evidence that supports this concept that the reticular system is particularly involved in arousing and maintaining readiness for stimuli. Without the reticular system, an experimental animal sleeps, and electrical stimulation of the reticular system produces both behavioral and physiological states (such as EEG patterns and pupil diameter changes) characteristic of an alert, aroused, and attentive animal.

But is the reticular activating system really necessary and sufficient for the maintenance of arousal? A considerable difference of opinion has emerged with regard to this question in recent years. Unfortunately, as in so many other situations in brain research, it has turned out that there was considerable recovery of the arousal function following some cases of reticular transection. Use of the Bremer technique (total reticular transection in small steps) resulted in animals that often spontaneously awakened after a few weeks. As usual, when one discusses the problem of localization, the story is not as simple as it may have seemed in the early 60s. The reticular system probably is not alone in controlling

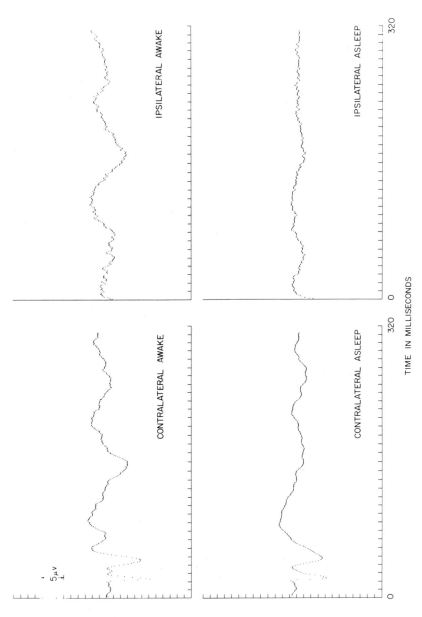

FIG. 5.33 The effects of sleep on the averaged evoked potential showing the change in the trailing edge of the N wave and the decrease in amplitude of the O wave when subject is asleep. The N and O wave nomenclature is now obsolete. (From Uttal & Cook, 1964.)

arousal. Nevertheless, it seems certain that the reticular system is involved in arousal as is at least part of the necessary neural system.

What are the other contributing nuclei? Thompson (1975) extensively reviews the role of such other brain loci as the medial thalamus, which appears to produce an inhibitory effect on arousal, an effect originally described by Magoun (1963); the frontal lobe, which, when ablated, produces an increase in the general level of activity in primates (French, 1959); the hippocampus, which will also produce hyperactivity when damaged (Kim et al., 1971). Furthermore, a number of other brain stem nuclei, other than the reticular formation, have also been shown to be involved in the control of sleeping and waking. Examples, Thompson notes, of these other brain stem sleep centers are Jouvet's (1967) raphé nucleus and the nucleus known as the *locus caeruleus*.

By far the most elaborate and specific theory of the role of the brain loci (other than the reticular activating system) involved in arousal and attention, however, is to be found in the paper by Pribram and McGuinness (1975) that I have already discussed. Figure 5-34 depicts their view of the multiple brain loci that they feel are involved in the control of arousal and attentional processes. Pribram and McGuinness go far beyond a simplistic theory based only on reticular system function to spell out a comprehensive theory in which specific neural centers are associated with the arousal, activation, and effort aspects of attention, respectively. They speculate (on the basis of a considerable amount of cited experimental and anatomical evidence not necessary to repeat here) that the amygdala may be the main center for accepting the neural inputs from the ascending reticular system, and furthermore, that the amygdala is specifically an intermediary in the production of the general, overall level of arousal that they refer to as *phasic* and which is associated with heightened autonomic responses. However, the amygdala in their theory is thought to be under the control of two neocortical regions that exert mutual inhibitory and excitatory influences on it. On the one hand, the orbitofrontal portion of the cortex acts to inhibit amygdala arousal; damage to this region will produce a hyperaroused and extremely active animal. On the other hand, the frontolateral portion of the cortex, in their theory, acts to excite the amygdala's response, and damage to it will reduce autonomic responses such as the generalized electrodermal responses that would have otherwise been produced by stimulation of the amygdala.

Pribram and McGuinness go on to pinpoint the basal ganglia as the especially relevant loci for the mediation of the part of the arousal process they call *activation*. Furthermore, they assert that the hippocampus and those centers that interact with it are associated, in particular, with the attentional aspect they call *effort*. This region, they believe, serves to coordinate the arousal and activation processes mediated by the amygdala and the basal ganglia, respectively.

It would be well to emphasize at this point that, although many of the individual interactive links shown in Fig. 5-34 are fairly well known, the scheme proposed by Pribram and McGuinness is, in its entirety, quite speculative. The

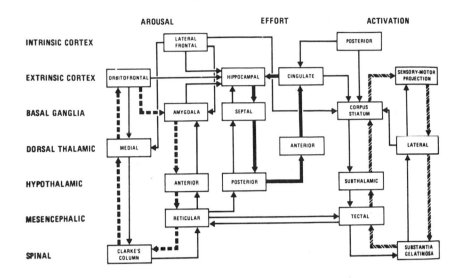

FIG. 5.34   Probram and McGuinness's model of the organization of the "attention" system. See text for details. Dotted lines indicate inhibition; solid lines indicate excitation. (From Pribram & McGuinness, ©1975, with the permission of The American Psychological Association.)

associations they make between structure and function are often based on indirect clues and, of course, are always biased by the relatively artificial definitions of the psychological processes that may be involved. Nevertheless, Pribram and McGuinness have made a major contribution by synthesizing a large body of information into a well-structured model. Whether or not this particular model subsequently turns out to be correct in every detail, it undoubtedly could play a major role in coordinating research efforts in this field and in serving as a foundation on which some future, more accurately descriptive theory will ultimately be built.

Pribram and McGuinness' model, unlike its predecessor theory of a unique reticular role, emphasizes the very important fact of the variety of neurostructures involved and the complexity of interactions that must certainly occur among them to mediate arousal.

E.   THE LIMBIC SYSTEM AND EMOTION

Developing an adequate definition of emotion is particularly difficult due to a gross failure of a satisfactory behavioral taxonomic analysis. We still do not have good definitions of emotions. Furthermore, as with any other mental process, the experience of emotion remains intrapersonal and can be, at best, only inadequately suggested by verbal or other behavioral means or measured by physiological indicators that are assumed, on the basis of a very mixed bag of data, to be associated with the emotional experiences. The very abundance of indicators of emotion itself can create a problem. It is usually very difficult to distinguish between changes in the evoked motor response and the underlying motivating states, and this can lead to major misinterpretations of the role of some lesioned nuclei. Furthermore, the use of autonomic or other physiological indicators as measures of emotion also raises an important additional conceptual problem. Although the premise that certain of these physiological indicators are equivalent to emotional states seems implicit in the writings of some contemporary psychobiologists (for example, many psychophysiologists imply that the electrodermal response is equivalent to emotional "arousal"), it must be remembered that there is not necessarily any direct association (in the sense of coding or psychoneural identity relationships) between such electrophysiological responses as the EKG or changes in the skin resistance, on the one hand, and the psychological states we call *attention* or *arousal,* on the other hand. Or, for that matter, is there any direct correspondence between these electrophysiological signals and any other mental process? Although there is considerable evidence that the two domains of response, the electrophysiological and the mental, are often *correlated,* it is absolutely essential for the reader to keep in mind that it is possible to disassociate autonomic responses and emotional mental states. This is one of the striking and important implications that is to be gleaned from the extensive current efforts on the conditioning of autonomic responses, which is usually understood to speak to other issues. In other words, autonomic response can be conditioned without conscious awareness. This repeatedly demonstrated but usually overlooked disassociation is a compelling argument against any idea of a direct correspondence between autonomic response and the intrapersonally private emotional mental states.

Clearly, this is a point of considerable import in today's world of pop psychobiology, commercially available (to the public) biofeedback training devices, and the quasilegal status of commercial lie detection services. It is also important in those formal laboratory studies of "emotion" in which localized electrophysiological activation and some autonomic responses have been used as stimuli and responses, respectively, and in which the autonomic response is dealt with as if it were tantamount to emotion. The persistent possibility of this conceptual confusion should be kept in mind in the following discussion.

Emotion, though it may not be any more precisely definable than a perceived color and is far less well anchored to specific physical referents, may be best understood in relation to the affective states that are popularly described by such words as "love" and "pleasure," at one end of the continuum, and "rage," "hatred," "pain," and "displeasure," at the other. The intrapersonal experiences that fall along the emotional continuum are very often associated with either approach or avoidance behavior, depending upon the valence of the affect or the pleasure-displeasure balance in an ambivalent stimulus. It is clear then that even these intrapersonally private dimensions of emotional response are necessarily going to be very closely associated with other brain and mental processes that might, at first glance, seem to be quite independent. Fear, rage, or anger and love or pleasure are all referenced to some particular stimulus object. Only in pathological states is rage not object-directed. Thus emotional responses must necessarily be closely interrelated to sensory processes. Similarly, the state of arousal of the organism usually will also play a very important role in its emotional response as will any previous cognitive experiences that it has had with regard to the referenced object. Therefore, many of the anatomical structures that are believed to be more involved in sensory, attentional, or learning acts must also be involved to at least some degree in the action of the emotional mechanisms.

We can fairly ask, however, what brain mechanisms seem to be most intimately involved in controlling emotional behavior, even if it is conceptually inappropriate to regard them as the unique locus of the emotional process. As we look back over the history of theories of emotion, we see that there has been a well-ordered sequence in the development of psychobiological theories of the localization of emotion. One of the earliest of the modern neurologically oriented theories of emotion was the one proposed by William James (1842-1910) that has become known as the James-Lange Theory of Emotion. The James-Lange Theory was based upon a fact well-known since antiquity, namely that the automomically driven structures of the circulatory system and the viscera are actively involved in many emotional reactions. James proposed that the experiences that we refer to as emotions are, in fact, sensory experiences produced by afferent signals fed back from the viscera. He assumed that the viscera were themselves excited by efferent signals from the central nervous system, but that interoreceptors within the viscera lay at the "heart" (if the reader will excuse the pun) of emotional experience. To James, therefore, emotion was simply sensory awareness of visceral states. The key neural structure in the James-Lange Theory, therefore, is the cerebral cortex itself, which receives and interprets these visceral sensory signals.

The next stage in the development of psychobiological theories of emotion emerged when it became apparent that there was usually a time discrepancy between the physiological visceral response and the psychological emotional response, and that the psychological response occurred even if the viscera were disconnected from the rest of the body. In light of this sort of discrepancy, the James-Lange Theory was no longer tenable, and subsequent workers like Walter B. Cannon (1871-1945) turned to subcortical centers in their search for the locus of the emotional experience. Cannon (1927), for example, proposed that emotional experiences occurred when the dorsal regions of the thalamus were activated and, furthermore, that the hypothalamus controlled the emission of appropriate motor, visceral, and secretive responses.

However, both the James-Lange Theory of visceral sensation and the Cannon thalamic-hypothalamic theory subsequently fell victim to newer developments in neuroanatomy and clinical medicine. In 1937, an exceedingly influential paper (Papez, 1937) was published by James V. Papez in which he described the anatomical and functional organization of a coordinated set of neural structures of the diencephalon and the basal portions of the telencephalon. He believed that these portions of the brain were specifically involved in the control of emotional experience and responses. The system of centers that Papez described contained structures that had previously been collectively referred to as the *rhinencephalon,* due to the fact that they had long been thought to be part of the olfactory portion of the brain. This system is now referred to as the limbic[5] system and has already been depicted in Figs. 3-38 and 3-39.

Papez suggested, in his original paper, that a particular subset of the limbic structures formed a discrete neural circuit within this complex of interacting centers, and that the functioning of this circuit was essential for the elicitation of emotional experience and response. It is of some historical interest to consider the specific details of "Papez' emotional circuit" at this point. Papez proposed that afferent sensory signals, in addition to being projected to the primary sensory cortex, were also directed to the hypothalamus. Signals from the hypothalamus were sent back along the mammillothalamic tract to certain anterior nuclei of the thalamus. Signals from the thalamus were then projected to the cingulate lobe of the cerebral cortex. It was this cortical locus that Papez presumed to be the seat of the emotional experience, itself. From this locus, signals were sent along the cingulate tract to the hippocampus and from there, via the fornix, to another large conduction tract, to return to the hypothalamus where visceral responses were controlled. This pathway can be picked out in the diagrams of Fig. 3-38 or 3-39.

It now appears to be the case that this famous "Papez Circuit" (as well as the theory of emotion that it embodies) is only part of a much more extensive complex of interacting loci and pathways within the limbic system and other parts of the brain stem that have been found to be involved in the regulation and control of those psychological processes we call *emotion.* I shall now briefly consider the role of the various components of the brain in the control of emotional experience and behavior, according to the best contemporary judgments. It is fortunate that we have, as a guide for the limbic aspects of this complex story, an important and insightful new book (Isaacson, 1974) devoted entirely to the anatomy and function of the limbic system. Another useful review (Clemente & Chase, 1973) of limbic system function in aggressive or antagonistic behavior will also be of special value to the reader who prefers a more detailed discussion than is possible here.

Some of the most significant early studies of the roles of the various brain structures in emotion were carried out by Bard and his collaborators (see, for

[5]Limbus means edge, and these structures are found along the inner edge of the cerebral hemisphere.

example, Bard, 1934; Bard & Mountcastle, 1947). In an extensive series of experiments, Bard and his co-workers showed that there was a progressive change in emotional behavior as the surgeon descended deeper into the nervous system with a progression of transecting cuts. The general effect of the removal of the cerebral neocortex was to produce an animal that had a very low threshold for extreme emotional responses—the classic rage reaction. Typically, however, such animals were not able to direct the evoked rage toward a particular stimulus object. On the basis of this kind of data, Bard suggested that the cortex mainly served as an inhibitor of emotional centers deeper in the brain and as a director of the rage response.

When progressive surgical transections were made below the level of the thalamus and hypothalamus, however, Bard observed that there was a gradual decrease in the variety of the components of the emotional response that could be obtained. The deeper the cut, the fewer the number of constituent emotional responses that could be emitted by the animal.

Bard's major contribution—the suggestion that the hypothalamus was the unique nervous center for emotion—though no longer acceptable today, was based on this pattern of results. However, as we now know and as was pointed out by Papez in his classic 1937 paper, the hypothalamus is only one part of the limbic system, and it is to this complex of structures rather than the hypothalamus alone that more recent workers have looked for a more complete explanation of the neural basis of emotional behavior.

The exploration of the functions of the nuclei of the limbic system has generally revolved around the effects of stimulation or ablation of one or more of the various centers on some particular emotional response, such as a rageful reaction. If I were to summarize, in a few words, the conventionally hypothesized role of the involved limbic nuclei, I would have to say that the hypothalamus is thought to play a rather special and central role in its ability to elicit emotional responses, and the other nuclei seem to be better described in terms that characterize their ability to modulate hypothalamic activities. A detailed review of work in the last twenty years on elicitation of aggressive behavior by hypothalmic stimulation can be found in Berntson (1972).

An example of the central role played by the hypothalamus in emotion lies in the fact that it seems to contain centers of affect that are so compelling as to deserve the designation of "pleasure" or "pain" centers. Electrical stimulation of the lateral hypothalamic nuclei produces the powerful form of the self-stimulation response made famous by the fortuitous observation of Olds and Milner (1954). In this germinal report, these workers originally showed that animals in instrumental conditioning paradigms would repetitively stimulate themselves (occasionally to the point of exhaustion and even death) by depressing a lever that applied electrical currents to those portions of the limbic system. It is now thought by James Olds (Olds, 1962) that the most powerful of these "pleasure" centers are located in the region of the lateral hypothalamus. Furthermore, the hypothalamus is also thought to contain analogous regions that are equally powerful elicitors of avoidance behavior, presumably because activation of these centers produces such a painful or unpleasant affect.

As important as the Olds and Milner discoveries have been to physiological theories of behavior in the last two decades, I should not omit another important caveat at this point. As we see in the next section on motivation, it now appears that many of the hypothalamic effects on feeding and drinking are mediated not by hypothalamic nuclei but rather by interruption of the sensory-motor signals conveyed by fiber tracts that pass in close proximity to these nuclei. A similar situation might also exist in the case of those "pleasure centers." There has never been an adequate proof given that the self-stimulation responses were produced exclusively by the neurons of the hypothalamic nuclei and not by stimulation of these nearby sensory or motor fiber tracts. The specific idea of a localized pleasure center, although appealing to classical ideas of the localization of mental phenomena, still requires a considerable amount of further research for its validation.

The hypothalamus is also thought to be deeply involved in the direct control of aggressive and defensive behavior. In another comprehensive review of the role of the hypothalamus in antagonistic behavior, Kaada (1967) concludes that a considerable amount of response-specific differentiation occurs among the constituent nuclei. An animal that is stimulated in the lateral hypothalamus will tend to attack some emotion-producing object, but an animal that is stimulated in the ventromedial portion will exhibit defensive behavior, and an animal that is stimulated in the dorsal hypothalamic nuclei will flee from the same threatening object.

Berntson and Beattie (1975) have shown that these hypothalamic nuclei are not totally independent of each other, however. Rather, there is, quite to the contrary, a considerable amount of overlap between regions that produce attack and/or simply threatening behavior. Again the organization that is suggested is one in which certain nuclei are more likely to produce one or another behavior but not one in which they are divided into mutually exclusive subfunctions.

It cannot be overemphasized, however, that even though the hypothalamus may be a dominant central command unit for emotional behavior, it is subject to strong inhibitory and excitatory influences from other of the structures that make up the limbic system, as well as from other neocortical centers. The hippocampus, for example, seems to exert a general inhibitory sort of function on hypothalamic nuclei. Removal of the hippocampus, rather than decortication in general, probably was the specific cause of Bard's original observations that decorticated animals tended to be hyperemotional and to display a very low threshold for rage reactions.

The amygdala, quite to the contrary, seems to produce either inhibition or excitation of hypothalamically driven emotional behavior, depending upon which of two of its subregions are stimulated. The lateral and basal regions of the amygdala, when activated, tend to increase fear and avoidance behavior, but activation of the medial region tends to damp out such emotional behavior.

It should not be forgotten, however, that the amygdala is actually a constellation of about a dozen nuclei and is no more a homogeneous unit than is the thalamus. Yet most lesion research on this area produces very large regions of damage. It is quite understandable why the results from such experiments are sometimes inconsistent and self-contradictory.

The septal regions of the limbic system also seem to be deeply involved in the control of emotional behavior. In the first days immediately following septal damage, animals display a classic hyperemotional, antagonistic behavior pattern known as *septal rage*. Such septal animals can be extremely dangerous in the first days following the operation; they display vicious attack and aggressive behavior and generally make very bad house pets. It is a curious paradox, however, that the animal will exhibit an increased tendency to flee from fear-producing objects over time and appear much more "cowardly" than would a normal animal. In general, animals with septal lesions tend to become eventually much tamer than normal animals.

However, the septum, too, is not homogeneous, and a number of studies [for a recent example, see Golda, Nováková, & Sterc (1975), which also reviews the problems of septal differentiation in detail] have shown that lesions in different portions of the septum may produce distinguishable behavioral effects. Golda and his colleagues, for example, have shown that laterobasal septal lesions produce a reduced tendency to aggressive reactions, but dorsal and mediobasal lesions do not seem to interfere with these reactions to the same degree. Electrical stimulation of the septum, on the other hand, does not produce a stable pattern of responses but produces results that are highly dependent upon the species of the animal and its current emotional state.

The reader who feels the urge for greater detail of this important series of experiments concerning the limbic system and emotion should refer to Isaacson (1974) or Clemente and Chase (1973), or, for a particularly clear discussion, to Valenstein (1973).

It should also be appreciated that psychobiologists now generally accept the notion that other nonlimbic systems are also deeply involved in the control of aggressive behaviors. In an important study that clarifies the role of sublimbic systems in attack and threat behavior, Berntson has shown (Berntson, 1973) that stimulation of the pons can produce attack and threat behavior of complex kinds as well as a more docile grooming response. In another paper (Berntson, 1972) he has also shown that lesions of midbrain tegmentum can drastically alter the responses that are produced by hypothalamic stimulation. Medial tegmentum lesions inhibited the release of hypothalamically stimulated aggressive behavior, suggesting that this medial region normally exerted an excitatory influence on the hypothalamus and that lesions of the lateral tegmentum allowed attack behavior to spontaneously erupt, suggesting that this lateral region normally exerted an inhibitory influence on it.

Berntson's studies, therefore, are important in providing evidence that the control of emotional behavior is not limited to the hypothalamic regions or even to the limbic system. His findings once again stress the important generalization that almost all complex behaviors can be affected by almost any part of the brain and that the sort of localization that occurs must be interpreted more in the form of a system of interconnecting nuclei than in terms of any theory of sharply demarcated functions of single "centers." His findings specifically suggest the presence of a vertically organized system of nuclei that is involved in the control of emotions. Coupled with what we know of the involvement of other sensory and limbic centers in emotional behavior, it is clear that a major portion of the brain is actually involved in the regulation of emotional behavior.

As this section comes to an end, it should be pointed out that the data obtained from experiments that explore the effects of either stimulation or ablations in the limbic system and related nuclei are intrinsically difficult to conceptualize. The responses that are used as behavioral indicators of limbic activity are very often complex patterns of behavior themselves (e.g., a generalized attack behavior pattern) rather than discrete events occurring at single instants in time. Subtle changes in the behavior of an operated animal could occur and be invisible to almost any particular behavioral assay technique that might be used. There is, in addition, a particular difficulty in controlling all of the relevant variables when one is studying emotional behavior. The effect of stimulation to or ablation of almost any portion of the vertically organized system to which I have alluded can be modulated by activity in almost any other region. Both the present environment and the past history of the animal can also dramatically alter the results produced by the manipulation of any independent variable. Furthermore, results of stimulation or ablation change over time; ablation of a specific region may initially lead to enhancement of emotional activity but then later to a reduction, or vice versa.

The point being made by raising these complications in the interpretation of lesion- or stimulation-produced emotional behavior is that the current description of the role of the various centers of the system that controls emotional behavior is, at best, incomplete and inadequate and, in some cases, must certainly be misleading.

Perhaps this difficulty has been best summed up by Alberto Zanchetti (Zanchetti, 1967), who, speaking only of the limbic system, said:

> A host of ablation and stimulation experiments have shown that emotional behavior can be altered, in either direction, by manipulation of various portions of the limbic system. Unfortunately, there is still no definite agreement on the part played by each structure. Although I do not intend to enter into details of this highly controversial subject, I shall cite the opposite effects of amygdalectomy described by Bard and Mountcastle (1947), who obtained increased susceptibility to rage behavior, and by Klüver and Bucy (1938), who observed placidity as a typical feature of their classical temporal lobe syndrome [p. 607].

About the most meaningful comment I can make, therefore, is that we are at the very beginning of an understanding of the complex interactions that occur within the emotional controlling system and how they relate to emotion. At present, the main conclusion with which I most comfortably end this section is that there does seem to be a vertically organized system in the brain, which includes the limbic system and particularly the hypothalamus, that more directly controls emotional behavior than do most other portions of the brain. This does not mean that the other portions of the brain are entirely excluded from a role in emotional response. Many of the nuclei I have mentioned are also heavily interconnected with other regions of the brain. On the other side of the coin, it should also be remembered that neither the limbic system nor any of the other nuclei I have mentioned are exclusively involved in the control of emotions. For example, the limbic system, as one would expect considering the close relationship between emotional and appetitive drive states (motivation), is also involved in eating, drinking, mating, and maternal behavior, and, indeed, in some problem-solving behavior (see Thomas, 1968).

The associations described in this section can only be my best guess based on some information that is variable, incomplete, and inconsistent. We simply do not know everything that should be known concerning the function of this complicated emotion-controlling system.

Indeed, in light of the totally inadequate taxonomy of mental processes and behaviors, which is, perhaps, more blatant in the field of emotion than in any other area of psychology, it may be that many of the questions concerning this mental process that we are asking in the psychobiological laboratory are not only unanswered but also essentially meaningless.

F.   MOTIVATIONAL PROCESSES

It is quite clear that the emotional or affective responses that I described in the previous section must necessarily be closely linked to the motivational state of the organism. Animals tend to strive for those things that are pleasant and to avoid those things that are painful. Thus the drive to approach some particular object or to avoid some other is inextricably associated with the affective or emotional experience produced when the goal object is encountered.

Because of this obvious amalgamation of mental process and, as we shall see, at least a partial overlap in involvement of the particular structures of the brain, emotional and motivational states can be distinguished only with difficulty. Motivation is particularly elusive of definition because it is not so much reflected in a cluster of observable and specific responses, as for example rage and fear, as much as it is merely a state of the organism—a set of tendencies or weighting factors toward producing a variety of overt responses, any of which can achieve the goal of staisfying some specific need. Motives or drives may thus be better considered as propensities toward action rather than actions themselves. Localizing a "tendency" of this sort thus becomes a most elusive task, perhaps a non-sensical one.

Another problem is that motivation, as evidenced by the overall behavior of the animal, is very strongly affected by the environment. The specific responses that are elicited by stimulation of particular nuclei of the hypothalamus are highly dependent on the external sensory stimuli the animal is momentarily experiencing. A typical example of this sensory impact is to be observed in the fact that, although certain hypothalamic nuclei were classically thought to be involved in the control of lactation, the secretory process is highly dependent upon the stimulation provided by a suckling infant. Sexual and food appetites are also directed at specific objects and require specific motor responses. Clearly, the electrophysiological states of the so-called emotional brain centers are not entirely definitive of the motivational states of the organism. Sensory and motor systems also contribute to their control.

What, then, are the motivational processes for which we should search for a neural correlate? Generally, the appetitive drives, as they are often called, are those tendencies, or propensities, of the organism that impel it toward the execution of certain responses that tend to satisfy some of the physiological requirements for the maintenance or perpetuation of life processes within a relatively stable or homeostatic range. I only mention in passing the more complex drive states acquired through experience for the acquisition of certain objects that are not directly relevant to physiological maintenance. For example, such drives as the urge for "power" or "glory" or "wealth" are totally beyond the scope of this book. Thus the ingestion of food or water, the consummation of sexual activity, breathing, temperature regulation, sleep, lactation, and excretion, are all responses toward which the organism is impelled by drive states created within the body by some centrally detected imbalance in the internal chemical, mechanical, or thermal condition of the organism.

Motivational drives, therefore, in addition to their necessarily close linkage to external sensory stimuli (the target or the goal object) and to effector mechanisms (through which the drives are consummated), must also be closely linked to brain sensory mechanisms that are sensitive to the internal state of the organism. Internal receptors must be able to determine the deficiency or superabundance of some substance, such as oxygen, glucose, water, or hormones in the blood stream, a shift from optimal body temperature, or a pressure in the lower intestine. There is a considerable amount of evidence which indicates that sensory receptors exist in the hypothalamus that are specifically sensitive to the chemistry of the blood and are able to detect the concentration of nutrients, salinity, CO_2, and oxygen, as well as blood temperature.

The findings of the last five years, in particular, have not only argued strongly against the conventional behavioral taxonomy of motivation as a family of specific behaviors, but have also stressed the fact that no single center or group of nuclei has exclusive control over the generalized behavioral tendencies that we call *motivations*. Prior to this last five-year period, a classic hypothalamic theory of motivation was almost universally accepted. It was generally assumed that motivated behavior like drinking, eating, and sex were controlled by specific hypothalamic nuclei. For example, destruction of certain hypothalamic regions was thought to specifically enhance drinking, and other ablations specifically inhibit drinking. Other nearby nuclei regulated eating or sex in a similar antagonistic manner. It appears now that this classic theory is a gross oversimplification of the true state of affairs. Not only are many other nuclei of the central nervous system now known to produce similar motivational effects, but there is at least some suggestion that transection of nearby bundles of axons to interfere with sensory motor processes may have been a more important influence on the behavioral change than the actual destruction of hypothalamic nuclei.

The purpose of this section is both to review the classic point of view and to consider some of the more recent studies that argue against the notion that hypothalamic nuclei are specific centers for the control of motivated behavior.

The classic view was that a key role was played by hypothalamic centers in motivated behaviors. The general role of these hypothalamic nuclei was thought to be to maintain a homeostatic balance. As an example of this classic theoretical viewpoint, consider the proposed role of hypothalamic nuclei in the control of drinking behavior. Drinking behaviors are necessary for the replenishment of fluids within the body. Serious cellular damage can occur when the extracellular water level is depleted. As the relative salt concentration of the extracellular fluids increases, a discrepancy between the elevated external salt concentration and the normal intracellular salt concentration is produced. There is, therefore, a strong osmotic tendency for fluids to be transported from the inside of the cells to the outside. This can quickly lead to the disruption of the life-sustaining electrophysiological processes that are dependent upon ionic concentration differences being held between certain narrow limits.

How does an animal's nervous system know that body fluids are depleted? What causes a motivational state to be created that can lead to behavior that will correct this deficiency? In addition to any indirect sensory channels for the communication of information—the dry feeling in the mouth that must be mediated by somatosensory receptors, for example—there are probably receptors in the hypothalamus itself that detect the water balance within the body. Andersson and McCann (1955) have shown that high concentrations of salt solutions applied directly to nuclei located in the lateral regions of the hypothalamus can serve as an effective stimulation for excessive drinking. Bilateral removal of these lateral nuclei of the hypothalamus, it has been shown, produced adipsia (a total absence of drinking behavior). However, it is now thought that other centers of the limbic system are also specifically and primarily involved in controlling drinking behavior. When either the major portions or posterior regions of the septum are ablated, the animal becomes hyperdipsic and enormously overdrinks (Anand & Brobeck, 1951; Epstein & Teitelbaum, 1960; Harvey & Hunt, 1965; Lubar &

Wolf, 1964). Such results suggest that there is a system of excitatory and inhibitory, or start-drinking and stop-drinking, centers that operate as antagonists to produce drinking or nondrinking behavior, depending upon which center is momentarily dominant.

Another important characteristic of the classic theory of the function of many of the hypothalamic nuclei was that the nuclei seemed to be especially sensitive to the most minute amounts of certain hormones. Some of these supereffective hormones, such as angiotensin, are produced in other portions of the body as a function of reduced water levels. Therefore, it was realized early that there are other means of communication, in this case, the circulatory system, present in addition to the direct neural regulation of the state of the various anagonistic hypothalamic nuclei.

The classic view also proposed that the hypothalamic nuclei that control eating were either the same as or located nearby those involved in drinking. There also appeared to be two distinct eating centers that operated in an antagonistic fashion just as there were in the control of drinking. One group, the lateral hypothalamic nuclei, if destroyed, seemed to selectively produce an animal that does not eat at all (Anand & Brobeck, 1951); it is said to be aphagic. On the other hand, if the ventromedial regions of the hypothalamus are damaged, the animal will become hyperphagic; it will continue to eat indiscriminately, far beyond its physiological needs, and may become grossly obese (Hetherington & Ranson, 1942).

The beginning of apostasy from this classic theory might be found in a line of evidence which indicates that the adipsic and aphagic behaviors that are produced by lesions of the hypothalamus are generally only transitory. Teitelbaum and Epstein (1962) found that there is a remarkably orderly sequence of recovery of normal eating and drinking functions following lateral hypothalamic lesions, as shown in Fig. 5-35. Although an animal might not eat or drink at all immediately after the lesioning operation, it will progress from this first stage into a second stage in which it will eat small amounts of particularly palatable, moist foods. The recovering animal then progresses into a third stage in which it will eat almost everything that is wet. As time goes by, the animal will then pass to a fourth stage in which it will eat and drink normally. As one psychobiologist put it, it is almost as if the animal with lateral hypothalamic lesions progressed through the normal developmental stages of the maturing animal, learning or relearning this behavior anew. This progressive recovery of ingestive function began to suggest the very important possibility that the role of each of the hypothalamic nuclei may be acquired and differentiated from that of its neighbors on the basis of certain maturational and experiential factors that transcend any predetermined neural interconnections. If this is the case, then the proposed role of any of these nuclei as unique loci for motivational control becomes highly equivocal.

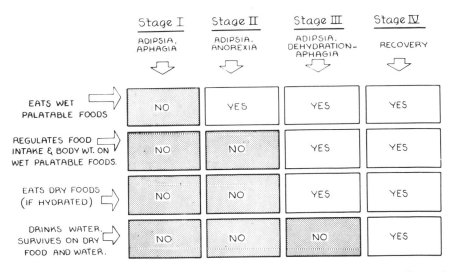

	Stage I ADIPSIA, APHAGIA	Stage II ADIPSIA, ANOREXIA	Stage III ADIPSIA, DEHYDRATION- APHAGIA	Stage IV RECOVERY
EATS WET PALATABLE FOODS	NO	YES	YES	YES
REGULATES FOOD INTAKE & BODY WT. ON WET PALATABLE FOODS.	NO	NO	YES	YES
EATS DRY FOODS (IF HYDRATED)	NO	NO	YES	YES
DRINKS WATER. SURVIVES ON DRY FOOD AND WATER.	NO	NO	NO	YES

FIG. 5.35 Diagram showing the stages in the recovery from the adipsic, aphagic effects of surgical ablation of the lateral hypothalamus. (From Teitelbaum & Epstein, ©1962, with the permission of The American Psychological Association.)

Other regions that produce eating and drinking deficits have been repeatedly demonstrated. Specific evidence of the involvement of the basal ganglia of the cerebrum, for example, has been presented by Neill and Linn (1975). They found feeding deficits in rats that were comparable to those produced by lateral hypothalamic lesions produced by surgical insults to the corpus striatum and the globus pallidus. Marshall, Richardson, and Teitelbaum (1974) have also found similar effects when other points of the pathway between the substantia nigra in the brain stem and the basal ganglia were interrupted by injections of G-hydroxydopamine. These findings led both groups of investigators to suggest that the feeding deficits produced by the lateral hypothalamic lesion were in no way unique to the hypothalamus but actually represented only one of many possible lesions that could interrupt this elaborate system of nuclei and tracts that run from the mesencephalon to the telencephalon.

To complicate matters further, it also has been demonstrated that the cerebral cortex itself and particularly the frontal lobes are also involved in the control of eating behavior. Rice and Campbell (1973) chronically implanted stimulating electrodes in the lateral hypothalamus of rats. Electrodes placed in these nuclei will normally produce eating behavior when electricity is passed through them. However, this evoked-eating could be markedly reduced and the thresholds for electrically elicited-eating could be markedly increased if major portions of the frontal lobes of the rat were removed. This suggests an interaction between the frontal cortex and the lateral hypothalamus such that the frontal cortex facilitates the hypothalamically driven hyperphagia.

Braun (1975) has also shown similar disruptions in normal eating behavior following various kinds of neocortical lesions. Rats with complete decortication showed a shorter but qualitatively similar course of the deficit in eating and drinking behavior as did the hypothalamic animals.

This sort of data makes it quite clear that, though the hypothalamus may play some role in initiating or terminating eating and drinking behavior, it is by no means sufficient to control the entire process. This idea is further supported when viewed in the light of other observations that indicate that driven hypothalamic eating behavior is always directed at *reasonable* food objects. The idea of hypothalamic triggering (GO) or terminating (STOP) mechanisms that themselves are heavily influenced by nonhypothalamic centers may be a much more realistic model of their role than is the theory that a single omnipotent hypothalamic "eating" or "drinking" center exists.

An alternative view of the role of the hypothalamus is that it determines a "set point" for body weight. The set point hypothesis assumes that the ingestive and metabolic resources of the organism will be mobilized to achieve a prescribed weight. Some factor other than food intake will be used by the body to regulate the motivated level of hunger. This other factor may be the amount of fatty tissue or the blood glucose level, or for that matter almost any one of a number of more or less indirect stimuli to continue eating long past the time the nutritional needs of the organism have been fulfilled. Overeating (hyperphagia) results, according to this view, from a missetting of the hypothalamically controlled set point rather than from an induced hyperphagia per se.

If this view is correct, the role of the hypothalamus as a sensory center of the internal milieu may be more important than the alternative role as an "eating" or "GO-STOP" triggering center. The concept of the set point has been eloquently summarized by Keesey and Powley (1975).

A sobering further reminder of the fragility of any model that assumes that the control of specific eating-drinking behaviors is localized in certain areas of the brain has been presented by Gazzaniga, Szer, and Crane (1974). They carried out the classic lateral hypothalamic lesion in rats and found, as expected, that these animals were greatly deficient in their drinking behavior. However, Gazzaniga and his colleagues also noted that the rats used in their experiments displayed an increased propensity to run as a result of the lesion. Greatly increased drinking rates could be elicited from these animals, however, if the opportunities for running were made contingent upon prerequisite drinking behavior. Gazzaniga and his colleagues proposed that these results should make us very careful about localizing drinking behavior in a specific hypothalamic center. They suggest, on the other hand, that the ability to regulate this complex motivation is dependent upon "the entire cerebrum" as well as subcortical centers.

Clearly the interactions suggested in this section and the result of such contingent experiments should make us wary of localizing any functions too sharply and further prepare us for thinking about the nervous system as a closely coupled set of interacting structures rather than as a system of independent functions.

The hypothalamus does seem to play an important, if equally nonunique, role in several other forms of motivational behavior. Sexual behavior, the powerful and compelling means of satisfying the urge for somatosensory delights, has been assumed to be both directly and indirectly controlled by a number of hypothalamic components. The indirect route—a chemical one—is supported by findings that the hypothalamus regulates the production of the hormones estrogen and androgen and also displays a high level of chemical sensitivity to these hormones within several of its constituent nuclei.

The nuclei of the anterior hypothalamus may also be involved in direct neural control of sexual development and mating behavior. If the anterior nuclei of a female rat are ablated, she will not go through the normal estrous cycle; however, she will ovulate. If the female's ventromedial nuclei are destroyed, there is a degeneration of the ovaries and a resulting reduction in ovulation. In the male, erections and ejaculations can be produced by direct electrical or chemical stimulation of various portions of the hypothalamus as well as other portions of the limbic system. However, these responses can also be produced by spinal stimulation in animals with transected spinal cords, and thus the hypothalamus may only play a triggering or modulating role in these male sexual behaviors.

A considerable amount of direct and indirect evidence, however, now indicates that many different portions of the nervous system are involved in the regulation of sexual activity. Almost every new journal brings a new demonstration of the role of some other center. For example, Clark, Caggiula, McConnell, and Antelman (1975) have just demonstrated that an area in the mesencephalon of a rat increases sexual activity after it is lesioned. This excitatory function is probably mediated by releasing other nuclei from inhibitory controls but once again illustrates the complex interactions between a number of centers that may influence such motivational processes. But obviously, here too, we are only at the beginning of an understanding of how particular brain nuclei exert their influence on sexual behavior.

In conclusion we can see that the classic model of the hypothalamus as an essential and unique center for the control of motivated behavior is under strong attack these days. Many other brain regions other than the hypothalamus have been shown to have effects on eating, drinking, and sex, and there are strong interactions between the various nuclei. There is, therefore, an emerging consensus that the concept of the hypothalamus as a unique motivation "center" is totally incorrect. At best, it is only one of a number of important regions in a much more complex system than had hitherto been appreciated. At worst, some recent psychobiological theories have suggested that the role of the hypothalamus in motivation has been completely misrepresented and that it is more likely that "hypothalamic" lesions produce their effects because sensory and motor fibers passing near this region are damaged during the classic operations. Grossman (1975) in particular has proposed a strong argument for a model in which the hypothalamus plays only a minor role in motivation, and the alterations in eating behavior usually attributable to it are, in fact, due to sensory motor dysfunction produced by the interruption of nearby transmission systems. Zeigler and Karten (1973) and Zeigler (1974) have specifically implicated the trigeminal pathways as the possible sensory tracts that may produce the apparently misnamed "lateral hypothalamic syndrome" in pigeons.

Obviously, we have a highly fluid theoretical situation at the present time. Even though the classic notion of the hypothalamus as a region uniquely specialized for motivational control is being discarded, the new theories are in a state of flux and no new general perspective prevails. If any single concept seems to characterize the essence of these new views, however, it is that the motivational systems are more likely to be controlled by widely diffuse systems of nuclei with heavy sensory-motor influence than by any single master "center." This emerging point of view is entirely consistent with the interacting systems viewpoint championed here to explain most other mental functions.

G. MOTOR CONTROL

This section contains a very brief mention of the neural mechanisms involved in the control of the musculature of the body. I have already mentioned the cortical motor areas on which topographic maps of excitability may be drawn (as shown in Fig. 5-18a). I have also already mentioned in Chapter 3 the two systems of descending fibers from the motor cortex to the spinal motor neurons.

The first efferent motor system, the pyramidal system, sends fibers to the spinal cord without synaptic interruption. Most of these fibers are arranged so that they cross over and control muscles on the opposite side of the body; however, a few pyramidal fibers descend without crossing. The second descending motor system—the extrapyramidal system—is much more complex. Efferent fibers from the cortex synaptically terminate in many centers of the basal ganglia and the brain stem. From their relay points, they send secondary motor efferents to such structures as the pons (and thence to the cerebellum), the substantia nigra, the caudate nucleus, and others. From these nuclei, motor fibers may descend directly to the spinal or cranial motor roots where they are communicated to the effectors. A partial diagram of the descending motor systems, including both direct pyramidal pathways and indirect extrapyramidal fibers, is shown in Fig. 5-36.

The cerebellum is mainly associated with the coordination of integrated patterns of motor movements, although it also mediates some reflex activity, is important in maintaining a general level of muscular tonus, and may be involved in other more complex behaviors (see Chapter 3). The spinal cord, in addition to its role as the major communication pathway between the central

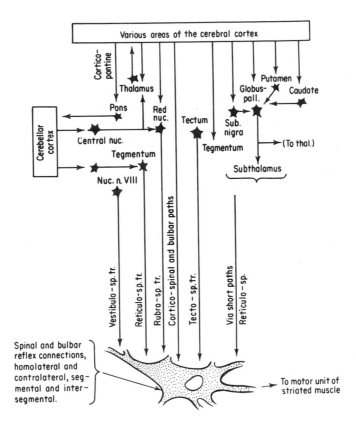

FIG. 5.36 The multiple pathways from the motor regions of the cortex to the typical motor neuron. (From Thompson, ©1967, after Ranson & Clark, 1959, with the permission of W. B. Saunders Company.)

nervous system and the periphery of the body, is also a major integrative center for relatively simple and direct reflex activities. Defects in the function of the substantia nigra has been particularly implicated in such neuromuscular disorders as Parkinson's disease. Not indicated on Fig. 5-36 are additional interconnections with sensory systems. Obviously, the cerebellar inputs that maintain general posture do have interconnections with the visual system and the somatosensory receptors, as well as inputs from the vestibular system.

The cerebral hemispheres, according to the prevailing views, exert a generalized inhibitory control over the brain stem portions of the motor system to prevent a massive tonic contraction of the musculature in addition to the general regulatory control with both inhibitory and excitatory efferent signals. This is most dramatically exhibited by the fact that a condition known as *decerebrate rigidity* occurs if the cerebral hemispheres are surgically or traumatically disconnected from the rest of the lower centers. Less severe forms of motor disorders, such as cerebral palsy, occur as a result of defects in the interaction of the cortical and brain stem components of the motor system.

In conclusion, it is clear that, as we examine the motor system we once again observe the action of an integrated system of centers, each of which contributes in many different ways to the overall control of muscular responses. In no sense of the word is there a single locus for motor control that operates exclusively and in isolation to regulate the individual muscular contractions, despite the dramatic and highly regular somatotopic mapping on the prefrontal cortical surface.

H.   AN INTERIM SUMMARY

In this chapter, I have considered several problems concerning the localization of various psychological functions in the nervous system. The problem has been a central one throughout the classic philosophical and modern scientific periods of the mind-body problem. The idea that parts of the mind may be localized in particular parts of the brain is a natural evolutionary conceptual development because both mind and brain have been traditionally analyzed into subcomponents. However, the localization question is also thought by some contemporary psychobiologists to be conceptually confusing and inadequate.

For the past 200 years, students of the mind-body problem have believed the brain to be the unique part of the body for mediating mental processes. There have been two divergent schools of thought that have repeatedly emerged with regard to the question of the way in which the brain performs this function. The first—radical localization theory—asserted that specific mental processes were sharply localized in specific neural centers in the brain. The other—radical homogeneity theory—asserted that the brain acted en masse as a unified and equipotential organ to mediate mental processes. In recent years, another view, somewhat intermediary between these two radical positions, has emerged that is based on the concept that the brain is organized as a system of subcomponents that have differentiated, but interacting, functions in each psychological process. It is only with the greatest difficulty that the components of a system can be separated from each other and the details of the circuitry interconnecting the components unraveled without losing the essential nature of the brain's functioning.

It has been repeatedly emphasized in this chapter that the available data that speak directly to the question of localization are exceedingly complex and "noisy" and that there are a number of conceptual, logical, and biological difficulties that make a simple and precise answer to the question of localization elusive. Thus, the general points of view of the brain localization or homogeneity must be considered to be theories rather than statements of "empirical fact." This is true, to an even greater degree, when one considers the function of specific nuclei within the brain. There is even a considerable amount of disagreement among various workers as to the exact nature of the data in what, at first glance, might seem to be well-defined and carefully designed experimental inquiries. In this chapter in every instance that a particular nucleus or group of nuclei was associated in a particular way with a given psychological function, a statement of principle was made that was highly interpretive, hypothetical, and theoretical, as well as being subject to repeated review and reinterpretation as new data and new perspectives are brought to bear on the problem.

Psychobiology simply does not yet have solid answers to many of the subtle questions concerning brain localization with which it deals. In this chapter, I have even mentioned a number of instances in which two investigators have obtained diametrically opposed answers to the same question. Furthermore, the dynamic and variable effects of brain surgery have also made the temporal course of ablation-caused deficits a source of considerable confusion in the search for a solution to the problem of localization of function.

In this chapter I have tried to emphasize a modern theoretical view that stresses the concept that no nucleus acts in isolation to mediate any single psychological process. Multiple nuclei are always found to be involved in any single psychological function, and each individual nucleus seems to be involved in many different psychological functions. The reader should especially recall how many different roles were mentioned for the system of nuclei that we call the *hypothalamus,* for example, in the course of the several sections of this chapter, as well as how many other nuclei have already been shown to produce effects similar to hypothalamically induced ones.

It must be further remembered that the actual testing of the potential role of any particular structure in any psychological function requires that some sort of an initial hypothesis be proposed concerning its involvement. This hypothesis may be based on some chance observation of an accidentally produced behavioral deficit or on a clue provided by some related anatomical or psychological observation. Once a given structure is implicated as having a potential functional role, it is necessary to apply specific and complex tests to assay its contribution to that function. No matter how careful or ingenious the experimenter may be, however, it is impossible for him to claim that a particular structure is *not involved* in the psychological process under study. This is so for two reasons. First, the assessment techniques employed simply may not have been sensitive to some subtle deficit that was produced by a given lesion. Second, the candidacy of a particular center simply may not have been tested in a way that excludes redundancy of function. There is, therefore, a strong paradigmatic and even social (i.e., in the society of scientists) influence on even the empirical data in this esoteric area of psychobiology.

The figures that have been selected to illustrate the organization of the neural systems involved in each of the psychological processes described in the several subsections of this chapter have often overlapped considerably. In that regard, they also tend to divert support away from a theory of radical localization by showing that individual nuclei are involved in several functions. The general nature of these systems charts also strongly emphasizes the emerging modern perspective that any psychological function, no matter how simple, is regulated by an interacting system of nuclei in which there are complex lines of inhibitory and excitatory feedforward and feedback rather than by singular centers of control. No pretense is being made that we have as yet unraveled the details of any of these systems nor that any of these diagrams is complete or accurate. Rather, they have been presented to emphasize the concept of interacting systems and the premise of nonunique localization of each psychological function. What we can only say, beyond expressing the general view that we are more likely to observe complex system interactions than exclusivity of regional representation, is that some regions are more involved in some processes than others. It also appears that there is a considerable degree of differentiation of function of the various areas of the brain and the brain stem; that is, they are not equipotential.

The fundamental conceptual problem of defining exactly what we are trying to localize is another significant source of difficulty obstructing simplistic solutions to the localization problem. In many cases, the psychological process for which a representational locus is sought is conceptually very nebulous. In some cases, the process may only be a specific motor pattern. In other cases, it may be a generalized tendency, and in still other cases, it may be a task based on criteria of convenience in the laboratory or of experimental method that have little or no ecological validity in the natural life of the organism.

In concluding this summary, it is most important to stress again the point that however strong the notion of radical localization may be in contemporary research and in currently popular textboods, the actual facts of the matter appear on close scrutiny to be otherwise. Perhaps the current situation can best be summed up by quoting the words of two distinguished contemporary psychobiologists, Elliott Valenstein and Alexander Luria.

> It has yet to be demonstrated that electrical or chemical stimulation of any region of the brain can modify one and only one specific behavior tendency [Valenstein, 1973, p. 32].

> Mental functions, as complex functional systems, cannot be localized in narrow zones of the cortex or in isolated cell groups, but must be organized in systems of concertedly working zones, each of which performs its role in [a] complex functional system, and which may be located in completely different and often far distant areas of the brain [Luria, 1973, p. 31].

This theoretical perspective is subtantially different from either of the classic antagonistic positions taken by the radical homogeneists or the radical localizationists respectively.

6

Representation and Coding:
the Background

A.   THE ISSUES

1.   What is Meant by Representation and Coding?

In the previous chapter I dealt mainly with the brain in terms of its gross structures when I asked which regions of the brain mediate which psychological functions. In the present chapter[1] the discussion descends to a considerably more microscopic level. The comparisons now to be drawn between the neural structures and behavior will deal with the characteristics of and interactions among individual neurons rather than with larger portions of the brain.

The basic axiom of this book should be restated explicitly at this point; it is that the nervous system provides the immediate, necessary and sufficient mechanisms for the embodiment of all mental processes. The corollary of this axiom germane to our present discussion is that the key to the particular ways in which mental processes are encoded and represented lies in the function, arrangement, and interaction of neurons, the constituent building blocks of the nervous system.

If I were to propose a prototypical question that would best characterize the problem posed in this chapter, it would probably be similar to the following: How do the actions of individual or relatively small groups of neurons contribute to the ensemble networks that serve as the physiological equivalents of psychological processes?

---

[1]The material discussed in Chapters 6 and 7 has been the author's main research interest for the last two decades. Therefore, certain portions of this chapter have been adopted from previously written materials. It is hoped that continuity and currency have been achieved by substantial editing, cutting, and linking with new material.

Admittedly, even this restricted form of the prototypical question is complicated and can be asked in a number of different ways depending upon the viewpoint of the individual psychobiologist. He or she might ask, for example: Do the characteristic responses of single neurons in the nervous system map in some direct way onto the domain of psychological responses? Alternatively, he or she might ask: What is the relationship between single cell responses and psychological functions? Some contemporary psychobiologists have phrased the question in slightly different ways that are limited to their own field of interest. Because of their relative simplicity, initial isomorphism of stimulus and receptor response, and primarily undirectional flow of information, questions of the representation of psychological responses have been asked most often in the domain of sensory or perceptual systems. Thus, for example, Naomi Weisstein (1969) asks what is essentially the basic and prototypical question, although restricted to the processes of visual perception, when she queries: "Are there 'property analyzers' in the human visual system, and, if so, what properties do they analyze for, and how [p. 157]?" As does Stuart Anstis (1975), who asks: "What does visual perception tell us about visual coding [p. 269]?"

Nevertheless, all of these questions, regardless of the domain or specific formulation, are virtually synonymous in basic concept. Each asks the same fundamental question. Each is based on the single premise that the proper level of neurophysiology at which to study the problems of the representation of psychological function is that of the action and interaction of individual neuronal responses. Regardless of the particular viewpoint or the specific research topic or the technological approach, all psychobiologists are tackling the same problem when they consider this aspect of the mind-brain question. That problem is the one that we have brought together in this chapter under the rubric of *representation* or *transactional coding*. In this chapter either of these two terms (or the abbreviation, coding) can be used interchangeably to classify the processes by which neural responses become equivalent to or identifiable with (in Feigl's terms) mental processes. I elaborate later a more formal definition of what is meant by these terms. Briefly, however, there is a subtle distinction that should be mentioned. The terms *representation*, or *transactional coding*, represent the general process by which neural signals come to be the physical equivalent of mental processes. The word code, however, is more specific and refers to the symbols and rules used by that process.

The essence of the study of representation or coding is the comparison of the functions of individual neurons, encoded as they are in their own particular symbols of graded or all-or-none electrochemical activity, and psychological processes. This is the main issue developed in Chapters 6 and 7.

To begin the search for a solution to this problem of representation, we must start by being explicit about exactly what the terms "representation" and "coding" mean. The science of language and meaning, or as it has been called—*semiotic*—by such workers as Charles Morris (1955), is an excellent model to help us understand what is meant by these terms. The problem of the representation of thought processes by language—one particular set of symbols and the syntactical rules for their use—is identical to the problem of representation of mental processes by neural activity patterns or states—another set of symbols subject to its own set of syntactical rules. Both neural representational codes and written or spoken languages deal with the assigned associations between the constituent symbols and certain concepts. In each case, the essential problem is how different coding systems can be interconverted to each other.

Perhaps the issue of neural representation can be clarified by a few simple analogies taken from semiotic. Imagine a line of speakers, each of whom is only able to translate the information presented to him in one language into a different language. Each speaker then passes the information on to the next person in the chain. The communicated idea can usually be regenerated, barring linguistic anomalies, into the original language at the end of the chain by an appropriate final translator. At the end of the chain, however, the exact sentence structure probably will not have been maintained. Furthermore, there is always the possibility that mistranslation or misinterpretations, either intentional or accidental, may have occurred. (This sort of "noise" is a constant byproduct of all but the most perfect of communication systems.) But, with a bit of good luck, the meaning of the communicated idea will be more or less reproduced, even though it has been represented by several different languages at several different stages of the communication process.

Languages are the analogs of codes in the lexicon of the sensory-coding theorist. Words are the analogs of neurophysiological signals. Grammatical rules are the analogs of the rules of transformation and encoding. On the other hand, it is often not so easy to discern the analog of the message in the case of neural coding and representation. We may assume either that the physical geometry and timing pattern of the stimulus initially define a message, or perhaps more properly, that the dimensions of sensory experience are the real components of the message. As is well-known, the two do not always directly correspond. Outright hallucinations and illusions produced by conflicting cues are both common experiences in which there is a patent lack of correspondence between the percept and the stimulus.

An important implication of the allegorical chain of translators is the virtual impossibility of determining which languages have been used at intermediary stages of the chain, if the translators have done a good job. It is only in the most unusual instances that the final translation will contain some clues as to the intermediary languages in which the message may have been encoded. This fact raises an important question concerning whether or not the neural codes studied in psychobiology may be decoded by behavioral research alone. I assert that they cannot. For example, neither the subjective experience of variable brightness nor differing behavioral responses to a fluctuating visual stimulus need necessarily contain any information regarding the internal neural encoding. A simple numerosity code reflecting neuronal recruitment, a frequency code, or even a spatial code are all equally good candidates to represent stimulus intensity. In the same way, the person who listens to a telephone or radio cannot tell whether or not the message had been communicated by a frequency or amplitude modulation system or even by one of the new, more exotic, pulse-coded communication systems used for economizing channel width.

What, then, is a formal definition of a representational or transactional code? I formally define a code as a set of symbols that can be used to represent message concepts and meanings (patterns or organization) *and* the set of rules that governs the selection and use of these symbols. For example, the representation of the amplitude of a stimulus or of a sensory magnitude (the message) by a train of nerve impulses (the symbols), whose frequency is related to the stimulus magnitude by a logarithmic compression law (the transformation rule), is a fairly complete statement of at least one coding situation.

Armed with this definition I can now consider some of the implications and the general background of the problem of representation and coding. Although language provides a useful allegory, because its terms are more familiar than those of neural representation, it would be inappropriate to recapitulate much linguistic theory here to elaborate the notion of coding and representation. It is germane, however, to note simply that much of the analysis of how language could represent meaning is directly relevant to the problem of how neural activities can do so. Ernst Cassirer (1874-1945) eloquently stated the case for language as a system for the representation of ideas in a way that may be directly analogized to the case of neural representation and coding. Cassirer (1953) said:

> In analyzing language, art, myth, our first problem is: how can a finite and particular sensory content be made into the vehicle of a general spiritual "meaning"? If we content ourselves with considering the material aspect of the cultural forms, with describing the physical properties of the signs they employ, then their ultimate, basic elements seem to consist in an aggregate of particular sensations, in simple qualities of sight, hearing, or touch. But then a miracle occurs. Through the manner in which it is contemplated, this simple sensory material takes on a new and varied life. When the physical sound, distinguished as such only by pitch and intensity and quality, is formed into a word, it becomes an expression of the finest intellectual and emotional distinctions. What it immediately is, is thrust into the background by what it accomplishes with its mediation, by what it "means." The concrete particular elements in a work of art also disclose this basic relation. No work of art can be understood as the simple *sum* of these elements, for in it a definite law, a specific principle of aesthetic formation are at work. The synthesis by which the consciousness combines a series of tones into the unity of a melody, would seem to be totally different from the synthesis by which a number of syllables is articulated into the unity of a "sentence." But they have one thing in common, that in both cases the sensory particulars do not stand by themselves; they are articulated into a conscious *whole*, from which they take their qualitative meaning [pp. 93-94].

This elegant passage of insightful prose is full of relevance to the problems of the neural representation of mental process discussed in this chapter. Strongly emphasized in this passage is the notion that different sets of symbols are equally suitable for the representation of a single idea or concept. Indeed this is one of the basic notions of representation theory, i.e., there is no one unique code, but rather there are many codes, perhaps strung end-to-end like the line of previously described translators converting a simple message from one language to another. As mentioned, this concept of multiple equivalent representations speaks directly to an important aspect of the problem of neural representation of psychological processes. It asserts that many different codes may be used at intermediate stages to represent a communicated message without leaving any residual clue that the message had at one time or another been in any particular code. Thus, psychophysical data cannot tell us what kind of neural code may have been used internally, and there is no best code.

Another important concept that is implicit in Cassirer's paragraph is his idea of wholes, or conceptual "sentences," or more generally in modern psychobiological terms, of "ensembles." As Cassirer says for language, the individual sound (and by this I believe he means both phoneme and word) means little in isolation. Only when it is in the context of a "sentence" does it acquire meaning from the configuration of the entire string of elements of which it is but a part. In an analogous sense, neural coding is also virtually meaningless to the student of representation when he looks only at the individual neuron (even though few neurophysiologists would admit it). The global, molar or holistic behavioral state must be defined not by the behavior of any single "pontifical" (decision-making) neuron but rather by the aggregate state of a large group of interacting neurons within some organized network. In particular, the relative aspects of their individual responses must be evaluated to determine the message carried by each neuron.

This perspective, of course, is in strong conflict with the philosophy underlying much of the single cell representational theory that has such wide currency in contemporary psychobiology. It is interesting to note, however, the defensive position to which this single-cell perspective leads. For example, Naomi Weisstein (1970), an active modern proponent of single-cell correlates of perception, is forced to fall back on hypothetical neurons that encode "symbolic" properties such as "in back of." Stuart Anstis (1975), also a strong believer in single neuron models, after reviewing many of the associations that have been drawn between psychophysical and neurophysiological research, is also forced to conclude that for many classes of perceptual phenomena: "It is clear that the higher perceptual processes exemplified here cannot be explained by any kind of edge extraction of spatial filtering, or any known type of physiological mechanisms. They are of a different logical type [p. 316]."

There is, thus, a break appearing in the relatively strong support for contemporary theories of neural representation that assert that single neurons are themselves capable of representing psychological processes. The newly emerging opinion is one that asserts that networks of neurons and their interactions are closer correspondents to behavior and thought than are single neurons or classes of neurons. I believe that there is a powerful and compelling analogy between Cassirer's concept of "wholes" and the idea of a network. Obviously, many psychobiologists are now becoming increasingly ready to accept this relationship, even if they have not yet fully ascribed to it.

2.   Isomorphism—A False Clue; An Unnecessary Code!

In raising the possibility of different "logical types" of relationships between neurophysiological mechanisms and psychophysical processes, Anstis clearly opens a Pandora's box of further conceptual problems. Assuming there are at least two conceivable classes of representational relationship, one dependent upon the direct representation of mental processes by patterns of single neuronal responses that are spatially or temporally isomorphic to the stimulus, and the other dependent upon symbolic or nonisomorphic representations, where should the boundary between the two be placed? Given the validity of symbolic representation in at least some cases, could not the concept of isomorphic representation and equivalence so frequently championed in contemporary literature merely be an artifact of the analogy existing between neurophysiological and psychophysical data? Have we in some way overextended our theories from what are essentially peripheral communication processes to much more complex integrative processes? Is it possible, instead, that the processing carried out by individual neurons is actually only symbolically rather than isomorphically related to the psychophysical process? Have we been seduced, because of some superficial sort of similarity that exists between responses in the psychophysical and neural domains, to see identity where only analogy actually exists? In Chapter 7 I discuss some evidence that suggests that this is exactly what has happened in at least some cases.

The same criticisms implicit in these questions are also explicit in Cassirer's paragraph. He also notes a condition in which the symbols of the language of the code need bear no isomorphic equivalence to the symbols of the external or internal worlds. When Cassirer suggests (somewhat incorrectly[2]) that pitch and intensity can be encoded into "intellectual and emotional distinctions" he is also obviously aware of the assertion that there is no need for dimensional isomorphism between the stimulus and the percept. Yet the propensity to glorify apparently isomorphic data (even though it may be illusory) is ubiquitous in modern psychobiology. It is assumed implicitly by too many psychobiologists that any dimensionally similar responses and codes are likely to be representa-

---

[2]Cassirer's error is not germane to the discussion of this section but is important. Physical stimuli have no pitch, subjective amplitude, or quality. These latter psychological dimensions are attributed to the neural representations of the stimulus by the observer. The acoustic physical stimulus has only amplitude of pneumatic pressure and frequency of oscillation. Sound, a subjective experience, has pitch and loudness.

tions of each other. More often, and, perhaps, more fundamentally erroneous, it is misassumed that dimensionally nonequivalent stimuli and representations are, a priori, not equivalent from a coding point of view.

Both of these assumptions are demonstrably incorrect! The basic axiom of coding theory is that it is not necessary to have dimensional equivalence or isomorphism for one set of symbols in one language to represent a concept in another no matter how complex the concept may be. This holds true for both peripheral sensory and central cognitive representations. Logically it is no more necessary for isomorphic coding to occur in the sensory mechanisms than centrally where the symbolic relationship is more blatant. That peripheral mechanisms, in fact, are often isomorphically coded does not detract from this statement. Isomorphism is easily engendered early in an information processing system and is progressively reduced as information passes onward in that system.

This logical assertion is a direct corollary of one of the major axioms of modern mathematical and computer theories. Any concept, no matter how complicated, can be represented by a sufficiently long sequence of binary digits. A further corollary of this idea is that any concept can be represented in any language, although it is likely to be encoded less efficiently in some than in others. These mathematical and linguistic theorems may be extended to the psychobiological sphere and assert what is clearly the basic premise of this chapter.

Any psychological concept or percept, no matter how complicated, can be represented by a wide variety of different neural response patterns. No one pattern, isomorphic or not, is, a priori, any better than any other. The neural representation may be totally nonisomorphic, for that matter, and still faithfully encode the mental process, whatever it may be.

3. The Concept of the Neural State

This brings us to another basic point more obliquely referred to in Cassirer's paragraph—the idea of neural state. It was fashionable in the past to ask: "Who reads neural codes?" (see Bullock, 1961; and Perkel & Bullock, 1968, p. 285). The implication of this question is that the message communicated from receptor organs to the central nervous system had to be decoded or interpreted by some central mechanism. The four main possible answers proposed by Perkel and Bullock to this question as late as 1968 are:

1. Single "pontifical decision making" neurons
2. The effector mechanisms such as muscles and glands
3. A large "pool of neurons acting as a unit"
4. A system of parallel pathways that converge, but not to a single unit, with decisions made at the "narrowest part of the funnel" [pp. 285-286].

I believe, however, that the question of who or what "reads neural codes" is itself fallacious and invalid. It is simply the modern myth of the homunculus restated in the terminology of coding therapy. A more correct resolution of the issue would be to assert that nothing and/or no one reads the neural code. Rather, after a series of neural processing stages, a certain state of the involved neurons is established. This state itself is, in fact, the equivalent of the psychological experience. The state is not "interpreted" or "read" in any sense of the term; it simply *is*. The homunculus, like Louis XIV, must say, "L'Etat c'est moi."

In this regard it is important to note that the representation approach itself, in general, and in its currently most highly developed aspect—sensory coding theory—in particular, represent an important escape hatch for many of the paradoxes and perplexities of mind-brain philosophical controversies of the past. Relationships that had been sought by classical mind-brain theorists are explicit and quantifiable in coding theory. Many of the more nebulous aspects of the problem, by definition, cease to be issues. The psychobiologist no longer must search exclusively for isomorphic mappings, because he can now accept the idea of encoded and symbolic representations by the state of a neural net. This is a vitally important difference between classic and contemporary research in this area that simplifies and restates the mind-brain problem in a very significant manner.

4. Are Compound- or Single-Cell Action Potentials the Key Codes?

Finally, it should be noted that there are two main ways to measure the action of individual neurons and the ensembles they form. One way is to use a microelectrode technology to observe and record the response patterns of individual neurons. The functions of a neural ensemble could then be determined by repeated observations of many individual neurons and thence by inductive synthesis of these observations into theories of ensemble action.

An alternative approach would be to use a statistical measuring instrument that itself performs the synthesis of the aggregate response profile into a single molar measure. Macroelectrodes tuned to detect low-frequency compound responses are examples of this overall response approach. Just as cumulative gas pressure measurements indicate the collective response of an ensemble of individual gas molecules, compound potentials give us insights into the collective or statistical behavior of the ensemble of neurons. However, the compound action potential obscures, as does the gas pressure meter, the details of individual unit activity.

Although the choice of macro- or microelectrodes is fundamentally a technical issue pertinent to the goals of each experiment, an important conceptual perplexity arises from the presence of these two alternative means for studying neuronal processes. Which one is the more fundamental in the representation of psychological processes? Is mind more a reflection of the action of individual neurons or is mind a statistical process more akin to the compound potential that reflects the mixed activity of many neurons?

A vigorous controversy surrounds this question in contemporary psychobiology. Single-cell theorists often assert that compound potentials are as meaningless as the voltages that might be measured with a similar technology on the outside of a computer. The adherents of compound potential theories point out that the activity of an individual neuron would be equally meaningless in the sea of twinkling neurons in which it is embedded. What system, they ask, could possibly allow the state of any one neuron, or even any one kind of neuron, to predominate or "pontificate" in the specification of the dimensions of the psychological process? They note also that the temporal dimensions of psychological processes are more similar to those of the compound action potential than to those of single neuronal responses. Mental processes typically occur in tenths of seconds, like compound-cell action potentials, not in milliseconds like single-cell action potentials.

In this chapter I consider the conceptual basis of both of these technical means of examining the action of neuronal ensembles—the approach based upon the study of the response of single neurons *and* the approach based upon the study of compound potentials because this perplexity has not been resolved. The discussion of neural compound-cell action potentials to be presented should not be misunderstood, however, as an argument for some type of "field" theory of mental action. The compound-cell potential is simply a convenient way to determine what groups of neurons are doing, in which the statistical processing is done by the electrode rather than the experimenter.

These thoughts conclude my introduction to the conceptual foundations of the representation problem. In the remainder of this chapter, I have strived to provide the historical, methodological, and conceptual basis of fields of psychobiology that seek to relate electrophysiological signals to behavioral events. The discussions of single neuron and compound action potentials is followed by a specific analysis of the problem of sensory coding as an example of the representation problem. I have chosen this area on which to concentrate simply because it is by far the best developed, but it should not be misunderstood that this is the only area in which the problems of representation and coding exist. Ultimately psychobiology will have to come to grips with the more complicated codes for problem solving, emotions, and all of the other psychological processes. In Chapter 7 I consider the specific empirical data that have been obtained relevant to the problem of representation.

B.   A BRIEF HISTORY OF ELECTROPHYSIOLOGY[3]

Unlike the problem of localization of psychological processes within the nuclei of the brain, the problem of representation of psychological processes at the neuronal level is of very recent vintage, and its history is, therefore, brief. The

[3]Some of this section has been excerpted from Uttal, 1975b (*Cellular Neurophysiology and Integration*), with the kind permission of the publisher, Lawrence Erlbaum Associates, Inc.

reasons for this historical difference between the two problems are obvious. Whereas localization theory dealt with processes and material entities that were of the same macroscopic scale as that of the human observer and his intuition, the processes and entities of representation take place at a microscopic level whose existence was only guessed at until the invention of the high-power microscope in the sixteenth and seventeenth centuries. Even then the full significance of the roles played by the tiny neurons and their ultrafine parts did not become evident until the application in the past few years of high power electron micrographs and intracellular microelectrodes. Indeed, the very manner in which neurons carried out their biological function was not understood until the fact that they were essentially electrochemical machines was appreciated. That detailed understanding of membrane electrochemistry did not even begin to emerge until about the beginning of the twentieth century. The availability of the electronic and microscopic technology that was necessary for the study of individual neurons actually occurred within the lifetime of most current neurophysiologists. How very recent this is compared to the speculations of Alcmeon, the Greek philosopher, concerning which part of the body was associated with which mental processes!

The understanding of the fact that neurons were electrochemical in function and the development of the microelectrode recording technique were two major breakthroughs in cellular neurophysiology. The discovery of compound electrical signals from the brain and the development of the percutaneous evoked potential technique were other important technical developments. The major events in the development of these ideas is the topic of the remainder of this section.

1.   The Origin of the Idea of the Electrical Basis of Nervous Action

Neurophysiology and physics are extraordinarily intertwined from the late eighteenth century on. Discoveries in physiology stimulated findings in physics, which in turn provided impetus for new areas of physiological research. The apex of these exciting times occurred in 1791, when Luigi Galvani (1737-1798) published his observations on a series of experiments carried out on a neuromuscular preparation from the frog. Galvani showed that preparations, consisting only of amputated frog legs and the attendant stumps of the severed nerves, could be made to respond to electrical stimuli that were produced in any number of different ways. Electricity was manipulated (if not completely understood) well enough by this time that it could be produced from electrostatic generators, stored in Leyden jars (the early capacitor), or acquired from lightning rods.

Figure 6-1 shows one of Galvani's experiments. Clearly the electrical stimulus produced by lightning was the direct antecedent of the observed action in the frog legs; although this did not necessarily establish electrical action *in* the

FIG. 6.1 Etching of one of Galvani's experiments in which the nerves of a frog's leg were stimulated by atmospheric lightning. (From Green's 1953 translation of Galvani's original work.)

nerves (that discovery would have to wait until the tiny neuronal responses could be electronically amplified and displayed a century later), it was a minuscule logical step to the assumption that the physical energetics of the neuron were the same as the stimulus. In fact we now know that this logical leap is not necessarily valid. The modern view of sensory transduction is based upon the premise that the physical energy of the stimulus is converted to other forms of physical energy in the nervous system. Indeed, the variety of stimulus energies to which the receptors are normally sensitive should have warned against such a deduction.

Nevertheless, the twitch of Galvani's frog legs signaled an end to hydraulic theories of nervous action and a beginning of the electrical theories, versions of which have persisted until our time. It is now understood that the electricity of the nervous system does not function in the same way as the electricity in a metallic conductor. Although both are electrical and can be described by the same mathematical functions, in each case the carriers are different. Electrons and "holes" convey charge in metals, and ions convey charge in the neuron. In addition, the properties of the conductors are different. Metals have low resistances, and neurons exhibit mixed resistive and capacitive impedances of appreciable magnitude. The capacitive and resistive aspects of neural membranes and the nature of the charge carrier specify that conduction velocities will be far slower in biological tissues than in a wire. Furthermore, the neuron is a metabolic system that, in many instances, produces its own power from energy sources located within the cell itself. This is quite unlike the metallic conductor, which must be powered by an external power source.

As noted earlier, Galvani's observations were also extremely influential in the development of the physical science of electricity. One experiment carried out by Galvani involved the stimulation of a frog's nerve-leg preparation by hanging it on a metal railing. The source of the electricity in this case was initially obscure, but a contemporary of Galvani, Allessandro Volta (1745-1827), correctly suggested that the source of the electrical stimulus was the junction between the two different metals of the hook and the railing. Stimulated by Galvani's biological data, Volta went on to invent the bimetallic battery, a device that provided a steady electrochemical source of electricity. This invention led to the many discoveries and technological advances in electricity of the next two centuries, eventually culminating in, among other innovations, a modern neurophysiology that is based on the use of electronic instruments. Thus the circle of interaction between electrophysiology and electrotechnology was completed.

By the middle of the nineteenth century there was little remaining controversy regarding the electrical concomitant of nervous action. Most researchers had accepted the notion without argument and went on to special problems of their own interest. However, we now know that electricity is a byproduct of electrochemical reactions. Even then, some workers suggested roles for electricity in nerve action that sound surprisingly modern. Among the most notable of these was Johannes Muller (1801-1858), the formulator of the *law of specific energies of nerves*. According to Brazier (1959), Muller was also one of the first to suggest specifically that electricity "was an artificial excitant that had no part in natural excitation." Nevertheless, the notion of electricity as an easily recordable and universal correlate of nervous action was firmly established in the science of neurophysiology by this time. As it turned out, the view of electricity as fundamental was to be modified by a continuing series of developments in biochemistry in the twentieth century. But as an indicant of biochemical processes, which themselves are difficult to measure, the electrical changes associated with neural activity still reign supreme. Much of the future development of neurophysiology depended upon the development of electrical instrumentation.

2.   Stimulators and Recorders

Once the electrical activity of the neuron was discovered, investigators began a search for the perfect stimulator with which to activate neural tissues. This search continues to this day. Electricity is so easily controlled compared to other forms of physical energy, and it is so effective in giving the experimenter control over the stimulus pattern whether or not it is an "artificial" stimulant, that the technology of electrical stimulation is still under active development today.

Indeed, the history of electrical stimulators is highly correlated with the history of neurophysiology even when it was not so intended. It is amusing to note that one of the earliest recorded nerve stimulators was thought by its inventor in the seventeenth century to be purely mechanical, but, may very well have been electrical. This early work was carried out by a young student at the University of Leyden by the name of Jan Swammerdam (1637-1680). Although the results of his experiments were not published for over 100 years, it seems fairly certain that in the year 1660, Swammerdam was unwittingly stimulating nerves with what was most probably an electrical stimulus. His "mechanical" stimulator is best described by his own words:

> If, instead of the heart, we should chuse [sic] to make use of some other muscle, we may proceed in the manner represented in the eighth figure [see Fig. 6-2], where the glass siphon, *a*, contains within its hollow the muscle, *b*, and the nerve hanging from the muscle is fastened, without being cut or bruised to a slender twisted silver wire, *c*, that runs at the other end, an eye made in a piece of brass wire, soldered to the embolus or piston of the siphon, *d*. Things being thus made ready, a drop of water, *e*, must be let into the slender tube of the siphon by a very fine funnel. Now, if after this, the silver wire be cautiously drawn with a leisurely hand *f* through the ring or eye of the brass wire, till the nerve is irritated by the compression, it must by this means undergo, the muscle will contract itself in the same manner with the inflated heart, whose alterations, upon a similar occasion, I have already described, even the drop of water will in some measure sink, though afterwards it never rises again [Swammerdam, cited in Fulton & Wilson, 1966, p. 212].

There is a catch, however, in this description. The astute reader will have noticed that the muscle hung on a silver wire, which was in turn passed through a brass eye. The necessary conditions for electrical stimulation with current from a bimetallic battery were therefore present, and it certainly seems that Swammerdam may have inadvertently stumbled upon an electrical stimulus 100 years before Galvani. Nevertheless, because the concept of the existence of electricity had not yet been established in the seventeenth century, there was no way in which this could have made sense to him.

Another electrical stimulator used over 100 years later was simply another animal. Galvani himself used the spinal cord or the crushed end of a frog's leg nerve to produce muscular contractions in a second frog's leg. These experiments were especially important because they showed that the signals involved in the electrical action of nerves had nothing intrinsically to do with the metals of some bimetallic battery or other parts of the stimulating mechanism. Rather, they suggested that the mechanism of the electrical stimulus was also intrinsic to the nerve and occurred even though no wire, bimetal junction, or lightning was present.

The conceptual link between electricity and nerve action having been made, the design of electrical stimulators became more specifically directed. After

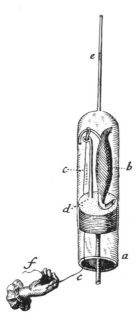

FIG. 6.2 Etching of one of Swammerdam's experiments in which he may have inadvertently stimulated the nerve with an electrical voltage produced by a bimetallic contact. Abbreviations indicated are: c = silver wire; d = brass support. (From Swammerdam's book, *Biblia Naturae*, published in 1737, as reproduced by Fulton & Wilson, 1966.)

Volta's description of the bimetallic battery effect, Claude Bernard (1813-1878) developed some small units especially suitable for stimulating nerves. A drawing of one of his battery stimulators is shown in Fig. 6-3.

The next important development in stimulator technology occurred as a result of the rapidly evolving physical science of electromagnetism. The transformer, a voltage magnifier consisting simply of two coils of wire wrapped around the same core, came into general neurophysiological use in the form of the induction coil introduced by Emil du Bois-Reymond (1818-1896) in the nineteenth century. The idea of the induction coil is simple. A circuit containing a relatively low-voltage source, typically a battery and a coil of wire wound with relatively few turns, could be interrupted with a simple switch. During the turn-off and turn-on times (the periods in which the flow of current through the first coil is varying), a fluctuating magnetic field is produced. That magnetic field is capable of inducing a much larger voltage (though a smaller current) in a second coil with a larger number of turns wound concentrically with the first. Because the switched interruptions could be controlled by mechanical rotators, the time sequence of a pattern of electrical stimuli could also be varied. Figure 6-4 is a sketch of one of du Bois-Reymond's induction coils.

The induction coil was used as the main electrophysiological stimulator well into the twentieth century, when it was finally replaced by all-electronic stimulators that allowed much better control over the amplitude, wave form, and timing of the stimulus. The earliest units were constructed from vacuum tubes, but

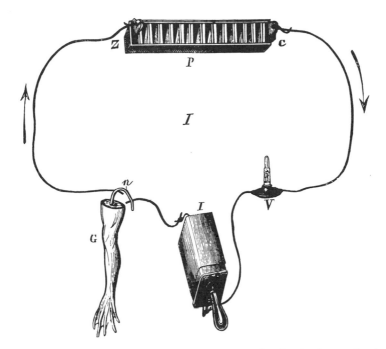

FIG. 6.3 Etching of one of Claude Bernard's voltaic pile electric stimulators, showing the switch (I = interrupter), the voltaic pile (P), and the frog's leg preparation (G). (From Bernard, 1858.)

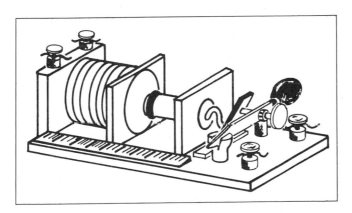

FIG. 6.4 Drawing of one of du Bois-Reymond's early induction coil stimulators, c. 1848. (Courtesy of Grass Instrument Company, Quincy, Mass.)

this technology ultimately gave way to one based on transistor technology that became available in the 1960s. In recent years such luxuries as constant-current and voltage-isolated features have come to be routinely included in even the least expensive stimulators.

Although stimulating instrumentation has changed greatly in appearance, and its convenience has increased enormously, there is little fundamental difference between the action of the earliest induction-coil stimulators and the most modern integrated circuit designs, and none as far as the biological preparation is concerned. Both types of stimulators are means of exciting nervous action by the production of appropriate electrical driving forces.

On the output end of the experiment—the amplification, display, and recording of faint signals from neurons—the situation is entirely different. Recording and display equipment has progressed to a level of such complexity and utility that a truly qualitative change has occurred in the neurophysiologist's ability to see and conceptualize what is happening.

The earliest recording devices were, once again, other organic units. The muscle twitch induced in the frog's leg was the very first indicator of neural activity. Credit for the initial application of this organic "scope" must be attributed either to Swammerdam or to his contemporary, Thomas Willis (1621-1675).

The next major step in recording technology was the subsequent invention of the electrometer, a simple device composed of two leaves of thin metal foil suspended in a glass jar from a metallic bulb, as shown in Fig. 6-5. Electrometers act as detectors of electricity because of the repulsive forces generated by like electrostatic charges. When the bulb at the top of the jar is charged, the two foil leaves become identically charged to the same potential because they are electrically interconnected to the bulb. The electrostatic repulsion between equally charged objects, even if slight in amplitude, is sufficient to force the delicate leaves apart. Similarly, a charged electrometer (and thus one in which the leaves were spread apart) would be discharged in the presence of any appropriate conductive pathway that allows the electrometer's stored charge to leak away. Unfortunately, neither the frog's leg nor the electrometer could respond rapidly enough to keep up with the speed of a neural response, nor could they give a quantitative measure for the magnitude of the signal. Neurophysiologists thus eagerly capitalized on the development of a new instrument, the moving coil galvanometer in 1882 by Arsene d'Arsonval (1851-1940). A sketch of one of his instruments is shown in Fig. 6-6.

The moving coil galvanometer is essentially a small motor consisting of a smaller coil of wire mounted between the poles of a permanent magnet. When the current from a voltage source, such as a neurophysiological preparation, passes through the smaller coil, it turns it into a small electromagnet. The interaction of the two electromagnetic fields is sufficient to produce a mechanical force, and if the small magnet is free to rotate (restrained only by a light spring)

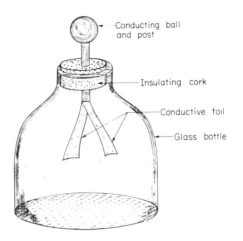

Conducting ball
and post

Insulating cork

Conductive foil

Glass bottle

FIG. 6.5 Drawing of a simple electrometer. This device primarily measures electric charge but can be used to detect the presence of ionization or radiation due to their effect on charge accumulations.

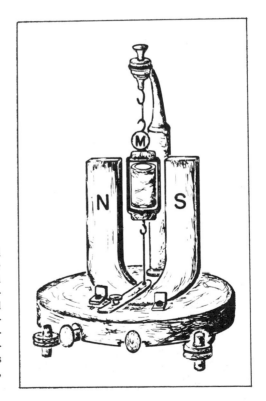

FIG. 6.6 An early D'Arsonval galvanometer used to measure weak electrical currents. M is a small mirror, attached to the rotor, that is used to detect the small rotations created by the interaction of the induced electromagnetic field with the permanent magnetic field. (Courtesy of Grass Instrument Company, Quincy, Mass.)

and has a pointer attached to it, the rotation of the coil produced by the tiny neuropotential can be measured. Moving coil galvanometers were used until the electronic instrumentation revolution began in the 1930s.

Other forms of galvanometers and electrometers have also been developed. The general effort in each case was to reduce the mass of the moving coil to the minimum so that the speed of response of the system would be improved. In 1897, W.D.B. Duddell made a step in this direction by reducing the coil to a single loop of wire. The ultimate in moving coil galvanometers, however, was the development in 1901 by Willem Einthoven (1860-1927) of the string galvanometer in which the coil was replaced by an ultrafine metalized quartz fiber that had to be observed through a microscope.

The moving coil galvanometer also can be modified so that it operates in a "ballistic" fashion. In the ballistic galvanometer, the maximum deflection of the coil is proportional to the total amount of current that has flowed through the coil. The peak of the deflection is, therefore, a time integral of all the current produced by the driving voltage.

Another innovative device, invented in 1873, was the capillary electrometer, a sketch of which is shown in Fig. 6-7. This device is essentially a modern analog of the old leaf electrometers. In the case of the capillary electrometer, however, the moving component was a tiny bubble of sulfuric acid in a column of mercury. The position of the bubble in the capillary tube was also proportional to the applied voltage. Capillary electrometers rivaled in sensitivity some of the string galvanometers and were particularly useful in neurophysiological research because of the small mass of the bubble.

Nevertheless, the major problem inherent in any electromechanical device is the considerable mass of the moving element no matter how lightly it is constructed. Because there is always inertia associated with bodies of any mass, or viscosity of the medium through which even a bubble moves, a substantial amount of energy was required to accelerate the pointers of the early measuring instruments. This is so even if the mass of the pointer is only as slight as a small piece of metal or the viscosity as low as that of air. There was a great need, therefore, to develop instruments of little mass and low inertia, that moved in vacuums and that, therefore, could move fast enough to keep up with the low-powered electrochemical processes of neurons.

This problem was not solved until the twentieth century, with the development of electronic measuring and display instruments. A. Forbes and C. Thatcher (1920) first used a vacuum tube amplifier to extend the range of a string galvanometer. The major innovation, however, was the cathode ray tube, an engineering achievement that resulted in the development of recording instruments (oscilloscopes) with nearly instantaneous response time because the moving element—a beam of electrons—had neglible mass. The first application of cathode ray oscilloscopes to neurophysiological recording is usually attributed to Joseph Erlanger (1874-1965) and Herbert Gasser (1888-1963) in 1924 who studied

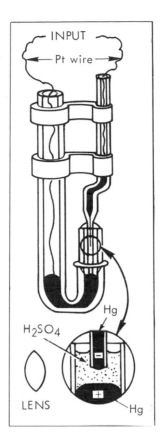

FIG. 6.7 A drawing of one of Lippmann's capillary electrometers for the measurement of weak electrical voltages. The observer views the position of the meniscus of the column of mercury that varies in height as a function of the voltage. (Courtesy of Grass Instrument Company, Quincy, Mass.)

compound (multifiber) responses in the phrenic and sciatic nerves of the cat. Erlanger and Gasser took advantage of a newly developed electronic technology to make some extraordinary neurophysiological discoveries. In the years that have followed, the general recording and display techniques they pioneered have become universally used in this kind of research. Today there is a substantial industry providing not only these recording instruments but also the electrodes and other elements needed to run a complete laboratory. Where once the recording of the simplest neural potential was a technical *tour de force*, now even undergraduate students make use of equipment and procedures that would have astounded senior investigators only a decade or two ago.

Certainly there are new developments on the horizon, and not all that is to be done has yet been accomplished. Perhaps no single technological development is needed so badly, or is so imminent in the neurophysiological laboratory, as the use of the small digital computer to process information acquired by amplifiers, thus producing more convenient and meaningful displays of data summaries. Only minimal beginnings in the use of this important tool have yet been reported.

The histories of the computer and of neurophysiological research in the past 20 or 30 years are also curiously intermingled, continuing the trend of parallel development in electrical technology and neurobiology. In the 1940s and 1950s there was a tendency for computer scientists and neurophysiologists to compare what appeared to be many common features of computers and nervous tissue. Today, however, it is clear that the digital computer, as it currently exists, is a poor model of even the simplest brain. Nevertheless, there is no question that the computer will have a profound impact on neurophysiology as it becomes more widely used as a data processing and display device and as a generator of stimulus patterns. The many powerful ways in which the digital computer can analyze and display summaries of large amounts of data promise to be particularly important in future studies of the interactions of large numbers of neurons.

3. Intracellular Techniques

Antoni van Leeuwenhoek's (1632-1723) development of the first high-power simple microscope in 1682 opened a window into the microscopic world that was to revolutionize all of biology. Although his best models consisted of only a single lens (see Fig. 6-8) and had magnifying power of only about 275, the world they opened to scientists was amazing in both its beauty and complexity. By the early 1800s, higher-power compound microscopes consisting of multiple lens elements[4] had evolved to the point where they provided a level of magnification sufficient for observation of the microstructure of animal tissues. It became obvious to nineteenth century investigators that nerves, which previously were believed to be relatively homogenous tissues, were actually multiple cables of smaller fibers. In fact, the microstructure of the axonal filament of a single neuron was beginning to be understood by that time. Theodore Schwann (1810-1882), among others, had observed the outer fatty covering, the myelin sheath, of the axon formed from those specialized nonneural cells that now bear his name.

As the nineteenth century passed, the concept that the really important processes occur at the cellular level grew stronger, along with what must have been enormous frustration. Although researchers knew that they should be looking at single cell responses, these single cells were simply too small to be investigated individually with the techniques then available.

In the twentieth century, with the development of oscilloscopes and high-gain and noise-free amplifiers, the task of recording neural activity from within single cells became a major but continually elusive goal of many neurophysiologists. A few investigators in the 1930s were able to dissect a small bundle con-

---

[4]Surprisingly, *low-power* compound microscopes were originally developed by Janssen in 1590, and were in common use by such scientists as Schemer in 1628, and Hooke in 1660, prior to the Leeuwenhoek development of a high-power simple microscope.

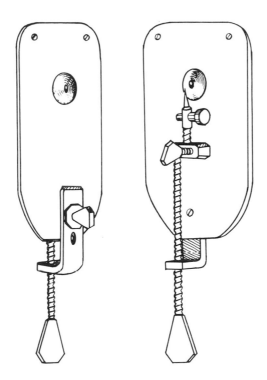

FIG. 6.8   A drawing of one of Leeuwenhoek's 2-inch long, simple (single spherical lens) microscopes showing the screw arrangement that was the antecedent of the modern mechanical stage. This type of microscope had a maximum magnification of about 275X. (From Bradbury, ©1967, with the permission of Pergamon Press.)

taining only a single active fiber, free from a compound nerve, and by laying it across some large electrode (e.g., a saline-soaked cotton wick), were able to pick up extracellular action potentials from single cells. But extracellular potentials are only weak and distorted (by the external media) reflections of what is actually going on across the cell membrane. Most workers in the field realized that neurochemical theory would have to remain speculative until it became possible to record potentials across cell membranes, and that meant placing an electrode inside the neuron.

The task was finally accomplished because of an anatomical freak. J.A. Young (1936) described a most unusual neuron, a giant cell in the squid nervous system, which had an axon as large as 1 mm in diameter. This axon was sufficiently macroscopic that even a relatively large glass tube could be inserted into the intracellular space. If this tube contained a salt solution, it could act as the necessary internal electrode. Tubular electrodes were used to record transmembrane, intracellular potentials by two groups almost simultaneously (Curtis &

Cole, 1942; Hodgkin & Huxley, 1939). The experimental procedure is sufficiently important to warrant quoting their description (Hodgkin & Huxley, 1939) in its entirety:

> A 500 μ axon was partially dissected from the first stellar nerve and cut half through with sharp scissors. A fine cannula was pushed through the cut and tied into the axon with a thread of silk. The cannula was mounted with the axon hanging from it in sea water. The upper part of the axon was illuminated from behind and could be observed from the front and side by means of a system of mirrors and a microscope; the lower part was insulated by oil and could be stimulated electrically. Action potentials were recorded by connecting one amplifier lead to the sea water outside the axon and the other to a microelectrode which was lowered through the cannula into the intact nerve beneath it. The microelectrode consisted of a glass tube about 100 μm. in diameter and 10-20 mm. in length; the end of the tube was filled with sea water, and electrical contact with this was made by a 20 μm. silver wire which was coated with silver chloride at the tip. . . . A small action potential was recorded from the upper end of the axon and this gradually increased as the electrode was lowered, until it reached a constant amplitude of 80-95 mv. at a distance of about 10 mm. from the cannula. In this region the axon appeared to be in a completely normal condition, for it survived and transmitted impulses for several hours [p. 710].

This technique was astonishingly influential in its impact on theory, for virtually the first observation—that the electrical potential across the membrane went positive rather than simply retreating to zero during the production of a spike action potential—necessitated a drastic reformulation of the contemporary theory of membrane action.

As productive as the procedure was, this sort of intracellular recording required a freak neuron; the study of neurophysiology could advance only if a procedure for the intracellular recording of neuronal action potentials of broader applicability could be developed. The important step of nondestructive penetration of a cell by an electrode was accomplished by Ralph W. Gerard (1900-1974) and his colleagues (Graham & Gerard, 1946; Ling & Gerard, 1949) on muscle fibers, but the technique is identical to that currently used on neurons. Their procedure involved the use of a tiny fluid-filled glass tube. These tiny tubes were made by a process in which tubes of soft glass were heated and then pulled evenly from both ends until they thinned and broke in the middle. The fluid characteristics of molten glass act as a "demagnifier" to produce a replica of the original tube with the same shaped cross section but at a greatly reduced size. These microelectrodes, or *micropipettes* as they are often called, are so tiny that they may be literally pushed through the membrane of even a very small neuron without destroying it. The membrane forms a seal around the micropipette, like a self-sealing tire; this seal is sufficiently robust to allow the neuron to continue operating for hours, or even days, after being impaled. Modern micropipettes may be smaller than 1/10 of a μm (one ten-millionth of a meter).

Again, the technique is of sufficient importance that excerpts from an early Ling and Gerard (1949) publication are still, after a quarter century, extremely interesting:

> We have pushed in the direction of drawing and filling microelectrodes of well under 1 μ tip diameter and properly tapered and were rewarded by obtaining highly constant membrane potentials.
>
> The making of the microelectrodes was critical. Extensive trial led to a tip tapering over a terminal millimeter from a diameter of 25 μ to a few tenths at the opened end. This is stiff enough to handle and to obtain easy penetration and slender enough so that deep insertion does no further damage and that the electrode is still usable after the extreme tip is lost.
>
> Electrodes are drawn from capillary tubing of .5 to .7 mm. o.d. (Schaar and Co.). Instead of a microburner, the flame of an air-gas blow torch is used. The capillary is gradually moved in from the side toward the flame and pulled abruptly when sufficiently soft. With some practice, two good needles, separated and with open ends, are obtained fairly regularly. The needle is bent at 90°, with the aid of forceps, and about 30 at a time are mounted for filling on a glass plate with cotton thread wound on it; other materials produce sediment which clogs the needles.
>
> Filling is easily achieved by boiling vigorously in KCl solution under slight intermittent back pressure. The holder is placed in half isotonic KCl in a porcelain evaporating dish of 12" diameter to which another, of 10" diameter, serves as cover. The dish is heated with the blow torch for about half an hour, by which time the volume is reduced to half and the air in the needles replaced by vapor. Cool isotonic KCl is then added and the needles promptly fill. This treatment, associated with building up and sudden release (as the lid lifts at intervals) of some pressure, leaves all the needles completely filled with approximately isotonic KCl.
>
> Each tip is then examined for shape and for absence of bubbles under the microscope and is tested for resistance (normally 100 megohms, usually falling with use but still satisfactory at 20 megohms) on the amplifier in a convenient holder [Ling & Gerard, 1949, pp. 383-385].

This description is sufficiently detailed to be used as a manual for contemporary microelectrode production. A more detailed discussion of microelectrodes of several modern kinds is given later in this chapter.

4. The Membrane Theory of Neuronal Action

From a purely historical perspective, it is astonishing how quickly new knowledge accumulated and new theories developed in the twentieth century regarding the cellular and biochemical basis of nervous action. The general framework of contemporary theory was spelled out by Bernstein in 1902 when he suggested that the basis of neural action was the selective passage of various ions through the semipermeable plasma membrane of the neuron. However insightful this notion, it was based on what were then some very flimsy ideas. Even the existence of an intracellular fluid filled with mobile ions was not firmly established until R. Hober's work (1910; 1912) on the red blood cell. Although there was some suggestive evidence for the existence of the membrane itself, its physical properties were not measured until the mid-1920s by Fricke. He was the first to suggest that the membrane is only a molecule or two thick and to estimate (correctly, as it turned out) its electrical capacitance. Direct viewing of the cell membrane with an electron microscope has been possible only since the mid-1940s.

Once routine entry of the cell with micropipettes was possible, many speculations of the past were opened to direct experimental inquiry. Hodgkin and Huxley (1939), as we have noted, quickly demonstrated the voltage overshoot; on the basis of impedance measurements, they were able to show that the whole course of the spike action potential could be explained solely on the basis of variations in membrane permeability and the resulting flow of particular ions. This series of ideas still forms the basis for most contemporary theory, although a number of details are still topics of active investigation. For example, the nature of the channels through which the ions flow, and the nature of the active pumping processes that produce the electrochemical driving forces, are not entirely understood yet.

5.   The Discovery of the Compound Action Potentials

Although the measurement of the transmembrane potential did not become commonplace until the second half of the twentieth century, the discovery of the brain's gross electrical activity occurred much earlier. In 1875, Richard Caton (1842-1926), a young physiologist at the Liverpool Royal Infirmary School of Medicine, discovered that electrical signals could be picked up from the exposed surface of the brain of rabbits and monkeys. The signals he detected were of two kinds.

The first, now known as the electroencephalogram (EEG), is characterized by a more or less spontaneous and continuous oscillation. When these signals were also discovered to be present in man by Hans Berger (1873-1941) in 1925, it was determined that the EEG was at maximum amplitude when the subject was mentally inactive. In this state the neural activity underlying the EEG is thought by some to be more or less idling, allowing a high degree of synchronization of the individual cellular responses. The synchrony of response of many neurons presumably produces the large differences between the high peaks and low valleys of the recording. When the subject becomes mentally active (e.g., by doing mental arithmetic or looking at a picture), the characteristic result is a diminution in the EEG. This reduction in the amplitude of the waves is thought to be associated with the desynchronization of the individual cellular responses and not a reduction in the overall level of neural activity.

The EEG has traditionally been frequency analyzed into sinusoidal components (Fourier analysis) to quantify the characteristics of any given record. The strongest (most energetic) sinusoidal component of these human brain potentials typically has a nominal frequency of 10 Hz, although both faster and slower signals are regularly observed. A sample of a typical EEG and its frequency analysis are shown in Fig. 6-9.[5] For a more complete story of the intriguing history of the discovery of the EEG, the reader is referred to Brazier (1961).

The second class of signals that Caton observed were transients produced in a particular region of the brain when a specific stimulus was applied to one of the normal sensory receptors. These signals are now commonly referred to as *evoked brain potentials*. The evoked brain potential differs from the EEG in that it is neither spontaneous nor continuous. It is, rather, a brief transient that follows a specific time course after the application of a particular stimulus. The typical evoked potential consists of two parts. The first is a rapid component that appears to reflect the arrival of the signal at the specific cortical projection area following its passage up the primary sensory pathway. The second component is much longer and probably reflects the nonspecific response produced by passage of the signal along the ascending reticular system. The somatosensory evoked brain potential, for example, consists of a rapid signal from the postcentral cortex and a later more diffuse response recordable virtually any place on the surface of the skull.

A major development in evoked brain potentials occurred when techniques were developed for recording them through the intact skull in humans. Previously this sort of mapping of the brain had been restricted to situations in which the brain was surgically exposed by reflecting a portion of the skull. Through the use of computer averaging techniques, however, even the tiny component of the evoked potential present on the skull's surface can be detected. This development was based on World War II developments in radar signal analysis that depended on the photographic superimposition of multiple images of noisy echoes.

In 1947, G. D. Dawson suggested that similar superimposition techniques could be used to detect the small evoked potentials from the human brain. (He also pointed out that the technique, like the radar solution, was functionally identical to the idea used by Francis Galton (1822-1911) in 1883 to enhance the similarities among a collection of facial portraits.) Dawson's contribution to the

---

[5]It should be remembered that the fact that a complex signal is analyzable by Fourier analysis into a family of sinusoidal signals does not mean that the brain is actually generating sinusoids. The mathematical processes inherent in Fourier analysis are very general and will produce the sinusoidal *equivalents* of any signal no matter what form the original generating functions may have taken.

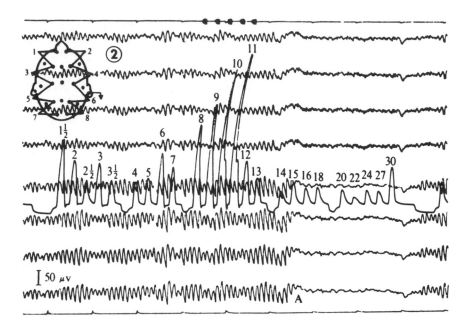

FIG. 6.9   A frequency analysis of an electroencephalographic trace. The spectral plot (frequency analysis) is drawn on top of the more usual representation of the EEG. The alpha rhythm (10-12 cps. component) is suppressed in this set of records at *A* by the subject's having opened his eyes. (From Hughes, ©1961, with the permission of Wright & Sons Medical Publishers.)

sciences of brain and behavioral physiology has been most influential. His techniques created an almost unprecedented opportunity for electrophysiological studies of the awake and intact human. Although Dawson's first photographic superimposition techniques are primitive compared to the sophisticated real-time computer averaging techniques used today, the general nature of the concept is identical.

Dawson (1954) also developed what was perhaps the earliest electrical device actually to perform a pseudo-averaging function, a commutator-driven bank of capacitors, each of which charged to a level corresponding to a weighted algebraic sum of the signals at a given time after the stimulus. Figure 6-10a and b are sample records from Dawson's original photographic superimposition technique and from the electromechanical device he subsequently invented. For comparison, Fig. 6-10c is a plot of an averaged brain potential generated by one of today's general-purpose digital computers.

This, then, is a brief glimpse of the past. In the following section I summarize the current status of cellular neurophysiological data and theory to which these historical precedents have contributed so much.

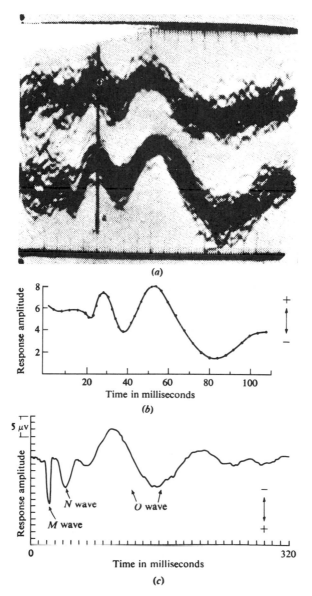

(a)

(b)

N wave

O wave

M wave

(c)

FIG. 6.10 The development of the averaged evoked potential technique has been consider-able since it was first suggested by Dawson. (A) An evoked potential produced by repetitive tracing on a cathode ray tube. This is a 75-msec long sample from two electrodes on either side of the central fissure of the brain. (From Dawson, ©1950, with the permission of the Medical Department, The British Council, London.) (B) A 100-msec plot of an evoked brain potential produced on the electromechanical mechanism developed by Dawson. (From Dawson, ©1954, with the permission of Elsevier/North-Holland Biomedical Press.) (C) An averaged evoked potential produced by a general-purpose digital computer for a longer period of time following the stimulus (320 msec). (From Uttal & Cook, 1964.)

C. THE NEUROPHYSIOLOGY AND TECHNIQUES OF
SINGLE NEURONS[6]

1. Principles of Cellular Neurophysiology and Integration

The study of the physiology of individual neurons and of their interaction at the specialized communication junctions called *synapses* has become a major endeavor in the biological sciences in the last few decades. Unfortunately, a full discussion of cellular neurophysiology cannot be included in this chapter without making it cumbersomely long. There are a number of introductory texts, however, that concentrate specialized attention on this body of knowledge. The reader is referred to any of the following for a more complete discussion: Aidley (1971), Hodgkin (1964), Katz (1966), Ochs (1965), Schmidt (1975), Stevens (1966), and Uttal (1975b).

In place of a full discussion of cellular neurophysiology, some of the more important principles are simply highlighted here to provide a partial foundation for understanding the material to follow. These summary statements have been condensed and adapted from the concluding chapter of my earlier work on the subject (Uttal, 1975b). A full discussion of the background behind each of these summary statements can be found in that text. It is hoped this list will provide a brief recapitulation and review for those readers who are acquainted with this material and that, coupled with the neuroanatomy described in Chapter 3, it will be sufficient to make the detailed discussions of neural representation theory that follow in later chapters understandable.

1. Modern neuron theory assumes a system of discrete cells that are not protoplasmically interconnected by that interact through specific points of contact known as *synapses.*

2. Neurons are specialized cells characterized by an exceptionally high degree of electrochemical reactivitity. Their function in the nervous system is primarily communication and integration of information patterns, but it is becoming increasingly evident that many neurons also play a secretory role.

3. Neurons carry out their communication and integration functions by means of electrochemical reactions. The flow and concentration of a few ions (sodium, potassium, and chloride) mainly define the direction and magnitude of the voltages measured during any neural response.

4. Neurons respond in a number of different ways. Both regenerative spike action potentials and graded potentials are to be found at different points on the cell. Some of these responses are activated by mechanisms intrinsic to the cell (e.g., spontaneous or pacemaker action potentials), and others are produced by outside stimulation (e.g., receptor or post-synaptic action potentials).

---

[6]Some of this section is adapted from Uttal, 1975b, and is used with the permission of the publisher, Lawrence Erlbaum Associates, Inc.

5. The category of "action potential" (contrary to popular usage) includes responses other than the spike action potential. In fact, any deviation from the potential level of the resting membrane that is not related to the metabolic or homeostatic processes of the membrane may be considered to be an information-bearing action potential. Specifically included in the category of action potentials, in addition to the spike, are nonregenerative graded potentials.

6. The electrical signals picked up from neurons are correlates of the dynamic and steady-state distributions of the involved ions. The electrical signal, however, should not be considered the primary aspect of neural activity. We are learning now that the electrochemical action of the neuron is more chemical than electrical. Our fascination with the electrical concomitants is largely due to the procedural fact that our recording technology is more highly developed to measure volts than ion concentrations.

7. The electrochemical events underlying nervous action are currently assumed to be most directly mediated by the mechanisms and processes of the neuronal or plasma membrane. This general assumption is the key premise of what has come to be called *membrane theory*. In particular, variations in the impedance of the membrane to the passive flow of sodium, potassium, and chloride ions seem to explain much of what we know of neural processes. Active transport or pumping actions also play critically important roles.

8. Neurons exhibit a wide variety of anatomic forms, depending upon their particular function. Neurons specialized to transmit signals over long distances possess elongated axons, whereas neurons specialized to integrate information from general inputs more often display extensive arborization of the dendritic trees. Receptor neurons may or may not have elongated axons. However, generalizations about the anatomic form of neurons usually turn out to have many exceptions, particularly when particular associations are made between form and function.

9. Transmission neurons can actually conduct in both orthodromic (normal) and antidromic (opposite to normal) directions. Synapses are not, however, in general, bidirectional.[7] Synaptic rectification, therefore, is the main basis of directional information flow in the nervous system. The refractory period following a spike response also helps to make the nervous system directional by preventing retrofiring.

10. Transmission neurons often are covered with a myelin sheath composed of multiple layers of Schwann cell membranes. This myelin sheath acts to produce a rapid form of neural transmission by allowing the ionic currents to skip between the nodes of Ranvier—the periodic discontinuities along the length of the sheath.

11. The plasma or cell membrane of a neuron is a region of demarcation between the inside and the outside of the cell. Because the membrane can just be resolved at the limits of electron microscopy, there is no consensus concerning

---

[7]We see in Chapter 9, however, that some electrical synapses do seem to be bidirectional.

its structure. A number of competing theories of membrane structure currently exist. They all involve a combination of lipid and protein molecules, most likely arranged as a bilayer of lipid molecules penetrated by protein molecules.

12. The most generally accepted theory of membrane action asserts that an ionic concentration equilibrium is established across the membrane by a metabolically driven pumping action operating in a direction opposite to the passive forces of diffusion, osmosis, and potential driving. The establishment of ion concentration difference by the "pump" is hypothesized to produce a resting potential characteristic of the unactivated neuron.

13. The exact nature of the "pump" itself is not yet fully understood, but it does appear to pump out of the neuron at least two ions of sodium (creating a potassium ion surplus inside the cell). Chloride ion concentrations seem to follow more or less passively and are determined by the final resting potential, although the existence of a separate chloride pump has also been suggested.

14. The transmembrane channels, through which sodium and potassium ions flow, appear to be different, because it is possible to selectively block one or the other with various pharmacological agents.

15. All deviations from the resting potential are the direct result of ion concentration shifts caused by changes in the permeability of the membrane or by active pumping action.

16. Neural transmission may occur by either of two processes. The first is a passive, decremental spread of electrical signals by ionic currents. This process is suitable only for transmission over short distances. The second is the propagation of regenerative spike action potentials. This is a nondecremental process, suitable for communication over long distances.

17. Spike action potentials are produced by a sequential but independent breakdown in the membrane's permeability, first to sodium, and then a millisecond or so later to potassium. These breakdowns occur in successive patches along the length of an axon. The increase in sodium flow, according to the generally accepted Hodgkin-Huxley (1952) theory, accounts for the leading edge of the spike, and the increase in potassium flow accounts for the rapid recovery of the spike back to almost the resting potential level.

18. Long-term recovery of ion concentrations to resting potential levels, however, appears to be dependent upon an extended period of sodium and potassium pumping.

19. The triggering of the breakdown in membrane permeability that leads to a spike is a threshold phenomenon. Once a local depolarization has achieved that threshold, the remainder of the process is spontaneous and requires no further introduction of extracellular energy. Because the process produces larger electropotentials than those needed to trigger it, the spike is able to propagate to distant locations without decrement.

20. The amplitude of a spike is independent of the stimulus; it is a function only of the state of the neuron. This fact is known as the *all-or-none law.*

21. The speed of spike propagation is a function of the size and degree of myelinization of the neuron as well as of its general metabolic state.

22. Both electrical and chemical means of synaptic transmission are known. The two types of synapse differ in the spacing between the involved neurons, the rapidity of synaptic transmission, the degree of electrical coupling, and the relative sizes of the pre- and postsynaptic regions.

23. Chemically mediated synapses work by diffusion of transmitter molecules secreted by the presynaptic region to receptor sites on the postsynaptic neuron.

24. A single neuron does not produce more than a single kind of transmitter substance. This fact is known as *Dale's principle*.

25. A single transmitter substance may produce either inhibitory or excitatory responses, depending upon the nature of the postsynaptic receptor sites.

26. The transmitter substance appears to be bundled into packets of several hundred molecules each and produces quantal miniature postsynaptic responses associated with the arrival of the contents of individual packets at the receptor sites. These miniature quantal responses, however, may sum with each other to produce postsynaptic potentials of virtually continuously graded amplitude.

27. Excitatory postsynaptic responses always appear to be depolarizations, but inhibitory potentials may be either hyper- or depolarizing, depending on the level of the resting potential. In the vertebrate retina, however, some excitatory potentials are hyperpolarizing; in invertebrates, photoreceptor potentials are depolarizing. Therefore, no simple relationship exists between excitatory and inhibitory responses, on the one hand, and hyperpolarizing or depolarizing membrane potentials, on the other.

28. Inhibitory postsynaptic responses generally seem to involve an increase in the membrane's permeability to potassium and chloride ions. Excitatory postsynaptic responses seem to involve changes in the permeability of the membrane to sodium and potassium ions, changes which are similar to those occurring in other membrane actions. However, there are notable differences between the neurochemical and neuroelectric actions of synapses and axons. Synapses, for example, cannot sustain spike action potentials and can communicate only by chemical transmitter substances and graded electropotentials.

29. Neural integration, occurring primarily at synaptic junctions, represents what is perhaps the most significant neurobiological process. It is the basis of all network functions, thus all selective interconnections, adaptive behavior, and ultimately, of all cognitive functions. Neural integration is defined as the cumulative effect of multiple inputs such that the conducted information pattern is modified in an adaptive manner.

30. Integration is a property of most neurons, including receptors and motor units that receive multiple inputs, as well as interneurons, the latter being defined as "neurons that connect neurons to neurons"; i.e., all neurons except receptors and the final effector units.

31. A number of processes that tend to modulate the flow of information occur within the neuron. The major integrative factors modulating information flow, however, occur at the synapses.

2. The Techniques of Cellular Neurophysiology[8]

Earlier in this chapter, I briefly discussed the origins of the techniques that have been used to explore the function of individual microscopic neurons. The abundance of information that has been forthcoming using these techniques has been utterly staggering. A plethora of journals publish innumerable articles on a wide variety of neurophysiological topics. This flood of information would challenge and strain anyone's ability to integrate these data into a reasonably comprehensive theory of mind-brain relationships. Yet virtually every recent psychobiological theory of perception, learning, or general cognitive function is derived from these cellular physiological findings, and thus virtually all psychobiological theory is a direct outcome of the recording, analyzing, calculating, integrating, and display capabilities of the available instrumentation. In the long run, therefore, our instruments dictate both our theoretical constructs and general views as much as they determine which measurements will be made.

In light of this fundamental role of instrumentation in theory construction, the purpose of this section is to provide a more complete discussion of the techniques of single-cell neurophysiology than has been presented so far. Because so much of the material presented in the rest of this book is derived from experiments in which recordings were made of the responses of single neurons, it seems appropriate at this point to make a purely methodological and technical digression. I review the techniques that are used to detect, record, and analyze single-cell electropotentials. Figure 6-11 is a block diagram of a typical electrophysiological research system that could be used to examine neuronal function. The most important, indeed the essential, component of this system is the tiny microelectrode that acts as the interface between the bioelectric and electronic components of the combined system. This electrode must be mounted on a mechanical electrode manipulator that, in turn, is supported by a rigid stand also holding a preamplifier that is designed to detect the bioelectric signals picked up by the electrode, but draining only microscopic amounts of current from the neural elements. Even slight amounts of current drain could greatly distort the displayed signal. The main, or power, amplifier is responsible for production of the high-power signals necessary to drive the display units, the devices that convert the detected temporal voltage patterns into readable formats.

In any neurophysiological recording system, the functions of two or more of these devices shown in Fig. 6-11 may be combined into a single physical unit.

---

[8]Some of this section is adapted from Uttal, 1975b, and is used with the permission of the publisher, Lawrence Erlbaum Associates, Inc.

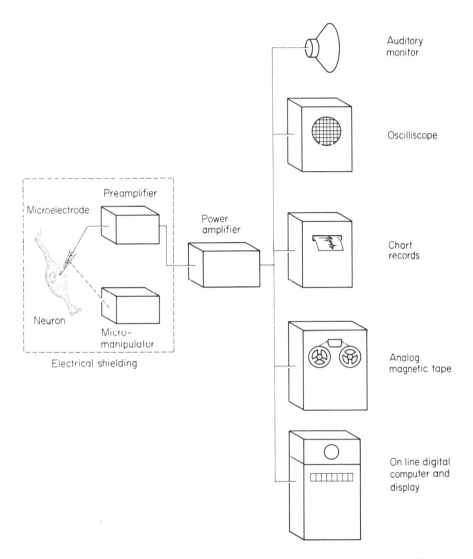

FIG. 6.11   Diagram of the components of a typical electrophysiological recording system. (From Uttal, 1975b.)

Although this combination may result in a reduced number of separate physical boxes, each of the devices indicated in Fig. 6-11 must be accounted for at one place or another in the system.

A further stage of instrumentation that is becoming increasingly important, as noted earlier, in electrophysiological experiments is also shown in Fig. 6-11: an on-line computer that may be used either to produce simple or complex stimulus patterns or to analyze and display the results of an experiment. I now consider each of the devices shown in this typical neurophysiological research system in detail.

a. Electrophysiological Recording Electrodes

The problem of interconnection between electrical measuring equipment and organic tissue became a major one as soon as it was understood that there is something electrical about nervous activity. The earliest electrodes were simple pieces of metal. For many years, however, the signal distortion from the nerves caused by these primitive junctions between metals and biological tissues was not apparent because all of the available display devices were inadequate. With the advent of good electronic amplifiers and cathode ray tube oscillographic displays, the distortion became obvious. Modern electrophysiological electrodes reduce the distortion of the signal in a number of ways that are enumerated in the following discussion.

The present section can best be organized by dividing electrodes into categories on the basis of their size. *Macroelectrodes* include the relatively large contacts best suited for detecting neural signals that are generated by many different cells, are distributed over a wide region, or come from neurons that can be isolated from their neighbors. *Microelectrodes*, on the other hand, are small enough (only a fraction of a micron in diameter, at their smallest) that the responses of individual neurons can be selectively detected.

Macroelectrodes.   The signals generated by the brain (electroencephalogram) or the heart (electrocardiogram) are typical of signals that are best recorded by macroelectrodes. Depending upon the size of the macroelectrode, these macrosignals summate the activities of a relatively large number of individual voltage sources distributed over a relatively wide area. However, some workers have been able to routinely record single-cell responses by simply inserting the cut-off end of a relatively thick, insulated wire into brain tissue (e.g., Ito and Olds, 1971) and using it as a macroelectrode. In other instances, when cells can be physically isolated from one another, as in a teased nerve preparation, the separated neuron may simply be laid on top of a macroelectrode (see Hartline, Wagner, & Ratliff, 1956; Uttal & Kasprzak, 1962) to record single cell potentials.

A macroelectrode can be as simple as a wad of cotton soaked in an appropriate solution, a metal hook, or a metallic button pasted to the skin or immersed in a conducting solution. In the latter case, the electrolytic solution has the function of reducing the resistance of the interface between the tissue and the electrode; thus most of the biologically generated voltage will be developed across the electrode rather than lost across the interface resistance.

The electrolytic solution also performs another important function in electrodes exposed to moderately high-current densities or prolonged immersion. Most metallic electrodes (especially metals like silver and zinc) *polarize* under conditions in which electrical currents are sustained in a single direction. Polarization is a phenomenon similar to the normal action of a battery in that a constant electrochemical voltage is maintained by the electrode itself on the basis of changes occurring on its surface. Polarized electrodes selectively exhibit relatively high impedance to low frequencies and also have an intrinsic reverse potential opposing the biologically generated current. This results in a differentiated representation of the actual form of the signal along with a strong D.C. bias. These distorting actions are thus produced when the electrode takes on significant electrical properties of its own rather than remaining an inert detector of neural action potentials. Polarization is due in part to changes in the surface of the metal electrode and in part to the electrolysis of the fluids in which the electrode is immersed. Gas bubbles formed from the electrolytic breakdown of the solution can gather on the electrode and contribute to the battery action, as well as increase the interface resistance.

The depletion of ions from the active region of the electrodes may also be a factor in creating electrode polarization. When carriers of electrical charge are removed in any manner, the effect is to increase the internal resistance of the interface between the electrode and the specimen. For those applications in which electrodes are used for stimulation rather than recording, polarization is not a significant problem, because the stimulating currents are very large compared to the polarization potentials. However, when tiny potentials are recorded from a nerve cell, polarization potentials can be equal to, or greater than, the signals themselves. The increased resistance, coupled with even the small capacitance of the electrode-preamplifier wiring, can reduce the overall frequency response of the electronic system by substantial amounts (i.e., the range of electrical frequencies that will pass through the amplifier is reduced).

Polarization is prevented by coating the electrode with one of its own salts or by isolating the metal from the fluid by a salt-solution bridge. The reader is referred to Silver's (1958) sterling article on electrodes in Donaldson's (1958) book on bioelectric recording technique for a more detailed review of the chemistry and prevention of polarization on electrodes.

Microelectrodes. The second type of electrophysiological electrode, the microelectrode, mentioned earlier in the historical section of this chapter, is designed to be small enough to penetrate the interior of the neuron without affecting its function. A microelectrode can record the potential difference, therefore, between the inside and the outside of a single cell if a reference electrode is placed in the extracellular environment. Eventually cells punctured with these tiny electrodes become less responsive, but a skilled electrophysiologist can often keep a microelectrode-penetrated cell alive for up to 48 hours. Apparently the initial puncture does less harm than the subsequent tissue movements around the electrode tip. These movements may enlarge the puncture wound to a size preventing the cell's self-healing properties from working.

The earliest microelectrodes (see the historical discussion of Ling and Gerard's work earlier in this chapter) were fine glass tubes drawn by hand to submicron diameters after being heated to the temperature at which glass becomes viscous. The fine glass tube, or *micropipette*, is not actually the electrode itself, as glass is a good insulator. The micropipette must be filled with an electrolytic salt solution, which serves as the true electrical conductor making contact with the intraneuronal juices through the tiny hole at the end of the micropipette.

The electrolyte-filled glass microelectrode is still the best choice in many intracellular recording situations. However, for extracellular recording, metallic microelectrodes are used increasingly because of their rugged durability. One way to construct a metallic electrode is to fill a glass micropipette with a low melting-point metal such as indium. An alternative method is to sharpen electrolytically a relatively coarse wire by passing an electric current through it while it is suspended in an etching solution. By regulating the amount of current, it is possible to control the sharpness and gradient of taper of the tip. Hubel (1957), Parker, Strachan, and Welker (1973), and Spinelli, Bridgeman, and Owens (1970) are among the many who have discussed techniques for sharpening tungsten. Electrolytically sharpened electrodes of platinum and its alloys have also been successfully used. These kinds of electrodes are then usually insulated with a plastic or varnish except at the recording tip to restrict the region from which signals will be picked up.

New electrodes have been designed that are specific to the action of a single ion species. For example, Neild and Thomas (1973) describe a chloride-sensitive microelectrode constructed from a glass-insulated, chlorided silver wire, which can be used intracellularly. Thomas (1970) describes a similar, sodium-sensitive glass electrode specific to that ion. Figure 6-12 shows several types of microelectrodes, including one of an ingenious multiple-barrel design.

b.   *Preamplifiers*

The purpose of the electrode-amplifier-display chain is to reproduce and record the amplitude and time course of the neuroelectric signal under investigation, with as high fidelity as possible. But connecting electronic equipment to the delicate neuronal electrical source without distorting the waveform is not simple. In this section several possible sources of distortion are discussed that can be produced by the preamplifier and the electrode-preamplifier interface. We also consider ways in which this sort of distortion can be minimized.

Microelectrodes have considerable internal impedances. A microelectrode with a tip diameter of 1 micron may have an internal resistance on the order of 10 to 20 million ohms, and smaller electrodes may have internal resistances as high as 10^8 ohms. The internal resistance of the electrode and the input resistance of the preamplifier to which it is connected, along with the unavoidable

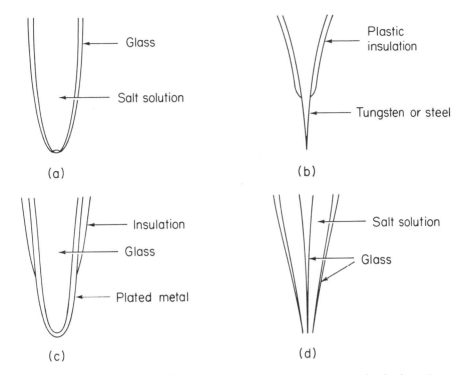

FIG. 6.12   Drawing of four different kinds of microelectrodes: (A) a simple glass micro-pipette that might be filled with a conducting saltwater solution; (B) an insulated metal microelectrode that has been electrolytically sharpened; (C) an insulated metal micro-electrode that has been formed by electroplating a metal on a glass substrate; and (D) a complex multibarrel microelectrode drawn simultaneously from two glass tubes. (From Uttal, 1975b.)

stray capacitance of the wiring, form a resistance-capacitance voltage divider as shown in Fig. 6-13.

Two difficulties are created as a result of this implicit voltage division. The first difficulty is due to the internal resistive component of the electrode itself. The entire neuronal potential under study is effectively applied across the two ends (marked A and B) of the voltage divider shown in Fig. 6-13. But only a small portion of this voltage may be detected. This occurs because the part v of the total applied voltage V that is sensed across a resistor in such a series cir-cuit is proportional to the ratio of the individual resistance value r and the total resistance R, a relation that may be expressed as

$$v = \frac{r}{R} \ V$$

(Equation 6-1)

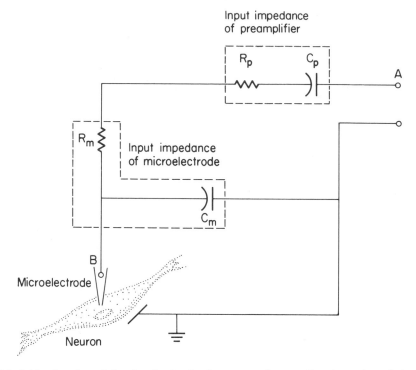

FIG. 6.13   Drawing of the electric circuit of a neuron, the recording electrode, and the re-cording preamplifier. (From Uttal, 1975b.)

where (in Fig. 6-13)

$$r = R_p$$
$$R = R_p + R_m$$

Therefore, if the input resistance of the preamplifier is smaller or even com-parable in magnitude to that of the electrode, only a portion of the total neu-rally generated voltage will be "seen" by the amplifier. Because neural potentials are so small compared to the ambient electronic noise levels, this can be a serious handicap. In order to sense a large portion of the neural signal, the input impe-dance of the preamplifier should be very high compared to that of the electrode.

Preamplifiers with input impedances as large as thousands of millions of ohms (gigohms) are now commercially available. Such units develop most of the signal voltage across their inputs rather than across the electrode even when they are attached to relatively high-resistance microelectrodes. High-input impedance pre-amplifiers were originally constructed with vacuum tube cathode-follower inputs or special high-input impedance electrometer tubes; now that high impedance semiconductor devices have become available, all-solid-state, high-input impedance preamplifiers are commercially available from a large number of manufacturers. These solid-state preamplifiers often use field effect transistors (FET), a form of transistor that is wired much like one of these special vacuum tubes and that has the same unusually high input resistance.

Another advantage of high preamplifier input impedances is the small current drawn by the electrode-preamplifier circuit. If it were larger, it could interfere with the normal physiologic processes of the cell and thus artifactually distort recorded data.

The second difficulty associated with input impedance arises from the combination of the resistive and capacitive components of the electrode and preamplifier impedance, as also shown in Fig. 6-13. Even a small input capacitance, when combined with the typically huge input resistance of a good preamplifier, can produce an electrical circuit with a long resistance-capacitance (RC) time constant. This long time constant results in the reduction of the high frequency sensitivity of the amplifying system. Therefore, the recorded biopotential will be seriously distorted by the inability of the preamplifier to follow the rapidly changing components of the signal. Rise times will be artifactually elongated, and rapidly changing signals will not be passed at all by the electrode-preamplifier circuitry. Thus, many preamplifiers in addition to being designed for high-input impedance, also contain special circuits to reduce the time constant by minimizing input capacitance.

Older amplifiers accomplished the reduction in RC time constant by laboriously minimizing the actual input capacitance, either by placing the first stage of the amplifier very close to the tip, or by elaborate shielding. Amatniek (1958) has described an ingenious method, however, for reducing the effective input capacitance of a preamplifier in an entirely different manner. He suggested that the input capacitance be neutralized by balancing it with an equal but opposite capacitive effect. In such a device, the input signal is simply inverted by an amplifier with a grain of 1. This inverted signal is applied to a second capacitor, which is adjusted by the experimenter to be equal to the input capacitance of the preamplifier. Thus there are two capacitors, equal in size and connected in parallel, but with opposite polarities of applied voltage. The net result is that the *effect* of the input capacitance is reduced to a vanishingly small value even though the capacitance is still present. The advantages of input capacitance neutralization are offset, in part, by an increase in the noise level of the output signal. However, this is not a serious impediment, considering the relatively large signals produced by high-impedance intracellular electrodes of the sort requiring input capacity neutralization. Extracellular electrodes may generate only 100 *micro*volts; intracellular signals may be as large as 100 *milli*volts.

In certain cases it is useful to design preamplifiers to have differential or bipolar inputs rather than a single-ended input. The need for the differential input arrangement is dictated by the fact that some biopotentials cannot be referenced to any external ground or common potential level but exist only as voltage differences between two different parts of the tissue. A good differential input amplifier also possesses good *common mode rejection*, that is, the ability to reject signals that are common to both of the input electrodes. Satisfactory common mode rejection, however, requires balanced inputs and thus is not generally available with the idiosyncratic microelectrodes. If common mode rejection is good, a differential preamplifier will not pass any significant amount of the 60-Hz voltages, for example, that might be picked up from overhead lighting and other electrical equipment. If this "pick-up" is too great, metal screens or sheets can be used to shield specimen materials from most sources of interference.

Preamplifiers usually do not have substantial voltage gain. They are primarily impedance matching devices coupling the high impedance of the electrode to the low-input impedances of the main power amplifiers, in order to maximize power transfer from one to the other. They may thus produce an output signal only slightly larger in voltage magnitude than the original signal but many times more powerful in current driving capacity. This low-level voltage capability means that many preamplifiers can be entirely battery operated, another feature that can contribute to the reduction of noise injected into the neurophysiological record by the electronic system.

Amplifiers in general can be separated into two types on the basis of the kind of coupling that exists between successive stages. The first type of amplifier is said to be *direct current* (DC) coupled from one amplifier stage to the next. This simply means that no series capacitors are used in the interstage circuitry, and constant voltages will thus pass as easily throughout the system as changing ones. These slow signals may include such biopotentials as the resting potential of a cell membrane, potentials defined by the position of the eye, slow surface changes on the brain, and similar signals of long or continuous duration. These signals require the use of DC amplifiers, but spurious voltages with similar low-frequency characteristics may also be present that can distort or obscure the desired signal. Thus a number of problems are associated with the design of DC amplifiers simply because they allow constant and slowly changing signals to pass.

Interfering voltages to which DC amplifiers are sensitive include amplifier base-line drift and electrode polarization effects, in addition to spurious electrophysiological signals. Base-line drift results from the amplification of tiny, gradual, long-term fluctuations in the values of component parts of the amplifier. In a DC-coupled amplifier, a slight change in a resistor's value as a result of temperature can produce a minute voltage shift early in the train of amplifying stages that can be amplified at the output to a substantial voltage fluctuation. Such interference may completely obscure a low-frequency neural signal. Similarly, slight fluctuations in the characteristics of the electrode, such as the smallest amounts of polarization, can be amplified and result in large constant output signals.

The second type of *alternating current* (AC) coupled amplifiers is usually used for the study of signals that are relatively brief transients, such as spike action potentials, electrocardiograms, and evoked potentials, rather than for examining constant or long-duration voltage shifts. AC-coupled amplifiers have capacitive circuits inserted between the several amplifying stages. These capacitors, by virtue of their high impedance to low-frequency signals, tend to block steady voltages and pass only signals that vary to some degree. By placing a bank of capacitors and resistors of various sizes on a ganged multiple position switch, it is possible to select the band-pass characteristics of the amplifier, because the resistance-capacitance combination determines which frequencies will be passed. AC-coupled amplifiers thus have the advantage of allowing the investigator to select the optimum frequency range for the particular signals under investigation. It is possible to adjust the lower bound of the band-pass range to reject low-frequency shifts due to electrode shifts, for example, or the upper bound to reject signals due to high-frequency noise in the preamplifier. For 1-millisecond-long spike action potentials, a band pass from 300 to 2000 Hz would be desirable. For evoked brain potentials, a range of 3 to 300 Hz would be preferred.

c. *Stimulators*

All the equipment discussed so far is designed to detect, amplify, and display the tiny electrophysiological voltages generated by neurons. However, many experimental situations also require some sort of stimulating apparatus to elicit a neural response under controlled conditions. Over the years a substantial change has occurred in the sort of stimulators used in neurophysiological experiments. In the early days almost all stimulators were impulsive types; i.e., they were designed to produce the briefest possible stimulus. Each stimulus transient, click, flash, or tap could vary only in amplitude. The impulse was considered to be instantaneous, and little consideration was given to the stimulus pattern in either space or time. One distinguished scientist, H. L. Teuber of M.I.T., is reputed to have referred to this as the "flash of lightning and burst of thunder" school of stimulation. The stimuli used to elicit neural responses were flashes of lights produced by stroboscopes or shutters, clicks of sound, mechanical taps to the skin, and impulsive electrical stimuli—that almost universal stimulus—applied to any place in the nervous system.

Over the years, substantial changes in the philosophy of neurophysiological research have affected the design of stimulators for the various modalities. Perhaps the most important single milestone occurred in the late 1950s when Hubel and Wiesel (1959) and Lettvin, Maturana, McCulloch, and Pitts (1959) discovered that stimuli with various features in time and/or space (e.g., dots, lines, corners, and edges moving in particular directions at particular speeds) were much more effective than simple impulses in eliciting neural responses in the visual system. This was so even when the patterned stimuli were less energetic than the impulsive ones.

As this trend toward more elaborately patterned stimuli continued, stimulator technology changed in some unusual ways. At first there seemed to be a tendency toward simplification. The flashers and clickers of the past were not replaced by more elaborate stimulators but by less complex ones. In their many distinguished studies (e.g., Hubel & Wiesel, 1962, 1965), Hubel and Wiesel have used a simple light source projecting an appropriately shaped image that was moved about manually within the visual field of the animal. The work of Lettvin's group was done with an ingenious though equally simple stimulator using magnets to move a similar visual stimulus about on an aluminum sphere placed in a frog's field of view.

In recent years, however, a number of investigators have been forced to turn to more elaborate apparatus by the increasing complexity of their experiments. Some have used computers (e.g., Spinelli, 1967; Uttal, 1969; and Gourlay, Uttal, & Powers, 1974) to generate elaborate patterns of visual stimuli.

A full discussion of the variety of photic, mechanical, acoustical, and chemical stimulation procedures used in electrophysiological research is beyond the scope of this book. The interested reader may find a more complete discussion of various means of stimulating neural activity in another book of mine (Uttal, 1973, chap. 2).

In this section only the electrical pulse stimulator is discussed for two reasons. First, electricity is the most general stimulus used to activate the nervous system. It is the one stimulus that allows the neurophysiologist to bypass the receptor, thus generating a known pattern of neural responses rather than one defined by the receptor's transductive mechanisms. This is possible because electrical stimuli can produce one spike action potential for each electrical stimulus pulse when applied to axons. Second, the use of electrical stimuli complicates the use of the sensitive amplifying and recording equipment already discussed in this chapter. It is necessary, therefore, to understand how some of these complications can be overcome.

The major difficulty in simultaneously using electrical stimulation and high-gain preamplifiers in the same system is a result of the discrepancy between the amplitudes of the electrical stimulus and the neuroelectric potentials. Stimulator voltage outputs, typically applied through macroelectrodes, may be as high as 100 *volts* before they can be effective in eliciting neural responses. However, the preamplifier is tuned to pick up intracellular signals that are, at best, measured in units of millivolts and often (with extracellular electrodes) only in microvolts. Thus the preamplifier is exposed during each stimulus pulse to a very much larger voltage than that level to which it is tuned to respond. Under these conditions most amplifiers overload, and their ability to pass any input low-level signals is momentarily blocked. Blockage of this sort is enhanced when the stimulus voltage and the neuroelectric signal are closely "coupled" to each other electrically; i.e., when they are referenced to the same common or ground potential.

This problem can be overcome if the two potentials are decoupled, or *isolated* from each other. Potential isolation can be achieved in a number of ways, all of which involve an electrical transmission from a grounded to a "floating" (ungrounded) circuit. Simple transformers can be used as the simplest expedient, but they do not have good isolation or waveform preservation properties. Two more recent developments have improved the degree of isolation that can be obtained. One innovation is a radio frequency system, developed by Schmitt and Dubbert (1949), which makes use of a small radio transmitter that sends a signal across a small air gap to an equally small, tuned receiver. The net effect of the signal transmission across the gap is to provide a voltage on the receiver side that is free of any reference to ground except for leaking through parasitic (stray) capacitances that occur when two wires simply run near each other. The more recent use of optical isolators achieves an even greater degree of isolation. These systems substitute a voltage-controlled light source and a light-sensitive variable resistor for the transformer or radio frequency transmitter-receiver. When an input signal activates the unit, the light source (usually a photodiode) glows. The light activates a photodetector, changing resistance in a way that controls the magnitude of the current passing through the output circuit. The net effect of this optical transmission, once again, is to isolate the stimulus from ground reference.

The second major difficulty encountered with electrical stimuli revolves around the fact that the resistive and capacitive properties of the stimulated tissue can so distort the stimulus that a very constant voltage will produce a very nonconstant current. This effect is mainly due to the charging of the capacitive components of the tissue in such a way that the applied voltage waveform is differentiated. Only the rise and fall (high-frequency components) of the waveform are passed when a current is so differentiated. The distortion can result in an actual stimulus current waveform like that shown in Fig. 6-14, even though the applied voltage stimulus is rectangularly shaped.

Special electronic circuitry is used to overcome this difficulty. Circuits can be designed that produce constant current stimuli rather than constant voltage outputs. In a constant current stimulator, the voltage applied to the tissue is not constant but varies to maintain a constant current through the tissue. Because most investigators believe the applied current is a more satisfactory stimulus amplitude measure than the voltage, this is a desirable feature. In any event, a constant current can be quantified more precisely than a varying voltage.

I have now considered a number of the important technical procedures and instruments important to cellular neurophysiological research. This equipment, as noted at the outset of this chapter, not only constrains and limits the phenomena investigated, but also directly influences the concepts and theories used to describe findings. Nevertheless, the fruitfulness of these instruments has been

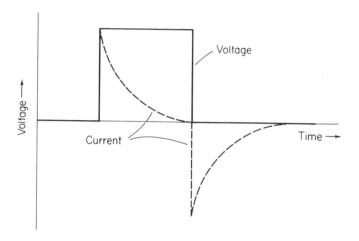

FIG. 6.14   Diagram showing the effect of applying a constant voltage current to a load (e.g., the skin) with substantial capacitive impedance. The generated current is essentially the derivative of the applied voltage. (From Uttal, 1973.)

so great in the last 20 years that at least tentative answers can now be given to some of the very important questions concerning the actions of individual and microscopic neurons.

D.   THE NEUROPHYSIOLOGY AND TECHNIQUES OF COMPOUND ACTION POTENTIALS[9]

As the number of neuronal spike or graded action potentials increases, the individual spikes may not be discernible on an oscilloscope trace. Rather, the voltages generated by each individual neuron may combine to produce a cumulative signal, which is the arithmetic sum of the single neuron responses, in accord with the usual laws of voltage addition. As the number of individual spike action potentials increases, pooled potentials show increasing numbers of complex spike forms resulting from the superposition of individual spikes. These voltage mixtures can usually be identified by extra bumps and notches on the otherwise smooth rise and fall of the spike; but occasionally deceptively simple, perfectly synchronized responses occur. In the central nervous system, almost any electrode not positioned intracellularly, except ones that are fortuitously highly selective, will pick up such multiple responses because of the dense neuronal packing.

[9]Some of the material in this section has been adapted from Uttal, 1975b, and is used with the permission of the publisher, Lawrence Erlbaum Associates, Inc.

If the electrode is unselective and has a relatively large field of action, the response will reflect the cumulative response of thousands or even millions of both graded and spike action potentials. Under such conditions, no vestige of an individual response is retained, and the potential picked up by the electrode exhibits very different properties than those of individual spikes. For example, it may last for very long periods of time—up to seconds or even longer in some free-running signals such as the electroencephalogram. Furthermore, compound action potentials of this sort always exhibit graded properties as the quantal nature of the contributing signals is obscured by the very large numbers involved.

Compound action potentials represent another important candidate for the representation of mental processes. They are particularly interesting because they have time dimensions quite close to those of psychological processes and also because they may be able to represent aggregate neural coding patterns where the individual spikes cannot. They thus represent an important possibility as a medium for encoding the collective action or statistical properties of large numbers of neurons.

If all the neurons are artificially synchronized by an electrical stimulus, pseudocompound action potentials can be recorded from preparations in which the normal coding process is actually more fairly represented by a different type of record. Figure 6-15 shows sample compound action potentials recorded from the human ulnar nerve by placing a rather large (3/16-inch diameter) electrode on the skin and recording the signal through it. Although this response looks similar to a single spike action potential, the dependence of its amplitude on stimulus intensity (a relationship that is not shown in Fig. 6-15) indicates that it is not. A single-cell response follows an all-or-none law. This compound signal is clearly the sum of a large number of spikes all occurring at nearly the same time, and its amplitude may vary over wide ranges. Yet the duration of the response is almost as brief as an individual spike, indicating a high degree of synchrony indeed. Very simple, brief compound action potentials of this kind can be recorded with a technique originally developed by Dawson and Scott (1949), which allows such signals to be picked up through the skin percutaneously with-

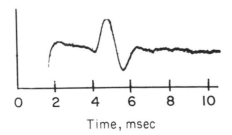

Time, msec

FIG. 6.15   A sample record of a compound electrical potential evoked at the superficial portion of the ulnar nerve at the elbow by a brief (.5 msec) electrical stimulus applied to the superficial portion of the nerve at the wrist. (From Uttal, 1959.)

out surgery. As stimulus strength decreases, the signal gradually fades away until it can no longer be detected. Individual cellular responses, therefore, are not detectable with this technique, which can only be used with the relatively massive compound responses produced by the electrical stimulus.

The general technique of electrical stimulation and compound action potential recording with large electrodes was first developed by Gasser (see, e.g., Gasser, 1938) almost 40 years ago for use on animals on whom experimental surgery could be performed. When the saphenous nerve of a cat was dissected free and cleared of its outer sheath, simple hook electrodes were able to record a more elaborate response pattern than that observed with the Dawson technique used percutaneously on humans. Erlanger and Gasser (1937) showed that the compound action potential recorded in this situation is composed of several sequential components that conduct at different velocities. A major result of this difference in conduction velocity is observed when the action potential is recorded at increasingly greater distances. The further the recording electrodes are from the stimulating electrodes, the more dispersed the various components of the signal become. Figure 6-16 shows the difference in shape of a typical response recorded at different distances from the site of stimulation.

It has been possible to reconstruct the shape of a compound action potential of this sort by algebraic summation of the individual spike action potentials that are assumed to be produced by axons having diameters distributed in accord with anatomical measurements. The compound action potential in this case seems to be produced by a simple voltage addition of the individual spike action potentials from the family of neurons of varying diameter found in peripheral nerves.

Although these peripheral nerve action potentials are relatively large (approximating 100 or 200 millivolts), evoked brain potentials are relatively small (usually less than 200 microvolts or so). To be seen at all, an evoked brain potential must be processed by a computer to extract it from the severe electrical noise conditions produced by interfering electroencephalographic and electromyographic signals, as well as simple electrical "shot noise" (i.e., random fluctuations) in the recording electronics. Even so, this tiny evoked response is the cumulation of the potentials of a large number of individual membrane responses. Its properties are not the same as the peripheral compound action potential previously described, because it is obviously much longer in duration and exhibits a much more complex form than that peripheral nerve mimic of the classic single neuron spike waveform. In the next sections I consider the evoked brain potential in detail. Its use also raises certain important conceptual issues—the most important being the need to distinguish between what I call *signs* and *codes*.

1.   Detection of Evoked Brain Potentials

Investigations of the evoked brain potential are beset with a classic signal-to-noise problem. As I just noted, the signal is typically so small, particularly when

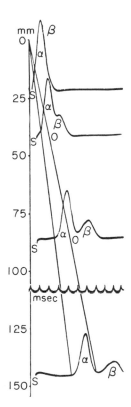

FIG. 6.16   Records showing the dispersion of a single compound action potential into multipeaked waves at various distances as a function of conduction time. The effect is due to the different conduction velocities of the fibers contributing to each peak. *S* indicates the occurrence of the stimulus. (From Patton, 1965, after Erlanger & Gasser, with the permission of The American Physiological Society.)

it is being recorded through the intact skull and scalp of the animal, that it is hidden in the ongoing noise. One might find, for example, that many important components of the evoked potential from the human somatosensory system are only 15 microvolts in amplitude, whereas the amplitude of the usual electro-encephalographic activity may be as great as 1/2 millivolt. The problem facing the investigator then is to extract the tiny evoked potentials from the other interfering signals. Such a procedure is possible because of the evoked potentials' synchronization with the impulsive stimulus that generates them. In contrast, the noise is, by definition, activity unrelated to the stimulus. Therefore, at any given delay following a series of stimuli, the amplitude of the unstimulated activity or noise tends to be randomly distributed. When averaged, the randomly fluctuating signal will tend to converge on the value zero. On the other hand, when one averages a signal that is synchronized or time-locked to the stimulus, the average value at each delay following the stimulus will converge toward some representative nonzero value. A mixture of the two types of signal, synchronized and random, will tend upon repetitive averaging to reproduce the waveform of the smaller timelocked activity.

Averaging may be formally defined by an equation of the following form:

$$E_t = \frac{1}{N} \sum_{n=1}^{N} E_t^n$$

(Equation 6-2)

In this equation, E_t is the average value of the signal at a given time, t, following the stimulus; N is the number of sequential responses averaged; and E_t^n is the voltage at time t for the nth record. The equation represents but one point on the averaged curve for a particular time t after the stimulus. The variable t must be varied systematically to plot out the entire time function. In practice, the preparation of an average response requires the presentation of a repetitive number (N) of stimuli. For digital computer averaging, each evoked potential is then digitized by means of an analog-to-digital converter at a rate sufficient to provide an adequate density of sample points. A large number of averages, equivalent to the family of t's, is then computed with the use of Eq. (6-2), and the values of the family of averages are plotted or displayed on some appropriate output device to represent the average time course of the response.

In the most sophisticated digital computer averages, a true division by N is made with each successive stimulus presentation. Performing a division, however, is a complicated logical operation that may be avoided by a simple expedient. Thus, many commercial special-purpose averagers do not actually average but are serial accumulators. Each time a stimulus is presented, an analog-to-digital converter samples the data, as described above. These coded values may be summed according to Eq. (6-2), but the division by N is never accomplished. Instead, the cumulative value in the register corresponding to

$$\sum_{n=1}^{N} E_t^n$$

(Equation 6-3)

that is corresponding to a single t, increases throughout the entire experiment. In this manner, the values accumulated in each of the registers gradually increase in magnitude up to the maximum capacity of the storage registers.

Because there is as much likelihood that an unsynchronized signal will be above the mean value as below, after any given number of stimuli, once again the contents of each register tend toward some mean value. In this case, however, an increasingly nonzero mean value will be produced as the number of stimulus presentations increases. The division by N, therefore, simply acts as a scaling factor to normalize the amplitude of the signal for any N. It is here that the price is paid for eliminating the arithmetic circuitry necessary to accomplish the division. Because the scale of the oscilloscope display is usually set to display the final reading properly, it is not possible to visualize the unaveraged results of a single sweep during the early states of the averaging process because the summed values are just too small. Only after a considerable number of stimuli have been presented do the characteristics of the signal begin to enlarge sufficiently to become visible to the observer.

2.   The Origin of the Compound Action Potentials of the Brain

An important general question that arises in dealing with compound action potentials concerns the relation of this waveform to the individual neuronal action potentials. For each compound response, we would like to know as much as possible about the contributing neuronal population and how their individual responses were summated. The problem of the peripheral nerve compound action potential is relatively straightfoward. The calculated sums of the individual spike action potentials have proven to be adequate in predicting the shape of the compound nerve response. However, for such compound action potentials as the evoked brain potential and the electroencephalogram, there is a great deal of controversy among different authorities as to the origin of the potential.

The major controversial issue concerning compound evoked brain potentials is in regard to their cellular origins. Purpura (1959) comprehensively reviewed theories of the genesis of cortical potentials and stated that the early models stressing the contribution of spike action potentials, which were invoked to explain slow brain potentials, could no longer be accepted, principally because spike activity could not be associated experimentally with slow potentials. These models, he further stated, have been replaced by newer ideas in which slower dendritic and synaptic potentials are hypothesized as the basic subunits that are summated to produce the slow electrocortical potentials.

Amassian, Waller, and Macy (1964) expressed this same point of view in one of the first symposia on sensory evoked response in man. For a number of reasons, including the apparent ability of experiments to disassociate spike and slow activity and mathematical considerations of the volume-recording technique, they also concluded that spike action potentials do not contribute directly to the compound evoked brain potential recorded from the surface of the head. They also stated that the slow potentials already known to exist, such as the postsynaptic and the various postspike after-potentials, are more likely added together to produce the waveform.

The problem of the origin of the compound potentials and their relations to cellular responses was also reviewed in detail by John (1967). He also reported the prevailing view that compound evoked potentials were almost universally considered to be the summation of postsynaptic potentials, slow transmembrane potentials, and long duration after-potentials following spikes. But, he did also suggest that it was only in some statistical sense that any correspondence could be detected between the spike action potential pattern and the compound potentials. This idea was based on an important experiment that had been carried out by Fox and O'Brien a couple of years earlier. Fox and O'Brien (1965) used a combination of computer analysis techniques to demonstrate a very high correlation between the latency histograms of spikes from a single cortical cell, as recorded with a high frequency band-pass preamplifier through an extracellular microelectrode, and the averaged compound evoked brain potential, recorded through the same electrode but with an amplifier passing lower-frequency signals. The correlation between these two measures is great enough when the sample size is large enough (see Fig. 6-17) to suggest that spike action potentials may have been prematurely rejected as major contributors to the production of compound potentials. Fox and O'Brien's work suggests that the compound-evoked brain potential is a direct correlate of the *probability* of spike firing, and thus they may have demonstrated the missing relation between spike activity and the compound evoked brain potential.

For the time being, it is sufficient to state that the genesis of the compound evoked brain potential is still being vigorously debated; whereas some feel it is a

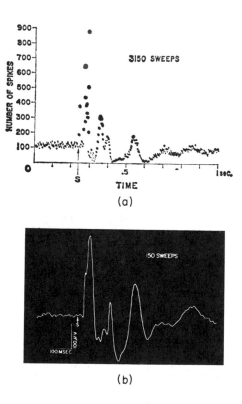

(a)

(b)

FIG. 6.17   Two records showing the high degree of correspondence between the probability of firing of a single cell (A) and the locally generated evoked brain potentials (B) recorded from the visual cortex of a cat. (From Fox & O'Brien, ©1965, with the permission of The American Association for the Advancement of Science.)

direct reflection of synaptic and dendritic graded activity, others argue strongly for direct spike action potential contributions to the compound evoked brain potential.

Fox and Norman (1968) expanded the earlier notions of the relationship between the spike and the compound evoked brain potential by proposing a new measure they call *congruence.* Congruence is a measure that describes in a quantitative fashion how typical an individual cell's pattern of response is of the total sample of cells contributing to a particular compound evoked potential. The activity of the single cell and of a microelectroencephalogram were recorded in the manner previously described by means of one electrode and two amplifiers with differing band-pass characteristics.

Fox and Norman formed three functions from these recorded data. The first function was the distribution of amplitudes of the microelectroencephalogram recorded with the low band-pass amplifier. A digital-to-analog converter sampled the amplitude of this continuously varying slow potential every millisecond and made an entry into one of 256 amplitude categories each time the amplitude of the signal was within its range. In this way, an amplitude histogram was formed that showed the number of occurrences of each amplitude value. An example of this type of histogram is seen in Fig. 6-18a.

The second function was based upon the occurrences of the spike action potential from a single cell, as detected with the high band-pass amplifier. Every time the cell fired a spike, it would trigger the computer to determine in which of the 256 amplitude levels the slow potential currently resided. Another computer analysis program then developed a second amplitude histogram based upon the number of times a spike occurred for each of the 256 amplitude levels. An example of this type of histogram is shown in Fig. 6-18b.

So far, this procedure is a relatively straightforward process in which two simple amplitude histograms are developed. Now consider that some of the amplitudes of the slow potential occur more frequently than others. The extreme values, of course, occur relatively infrequently, and the mid-values occur relatively frequently. The frequency of the spikes shown in the second histogram is strongly biased because there are many more mid-value amplitudes of the slow potential than there are extreme-value amplitudes. It is, therefore, necessary to normalize these data by dividing the distribution of spike occurrence by the distribution of amplitude occurrence. By carrying out this simple calculation, Fox and Norman controlled for unequal numbers of the slow potential amplitudes. The results of this normalization form a third histogram, shown in Fig. 6-18c, which plots a function that is essentially equivalent to the number of times a spike occurred at each amplitude value of the slow potential. This characteristic histogram of spike occurrence is, therefore, normalized for the number of times each slow potential amplitude value occurred.

If we carefully study the three histograms, a most important fact emerges. Even though there is an almost normal, i.e., an almost random distribution of the first two functions, there turns out to be a very high degree of correlation

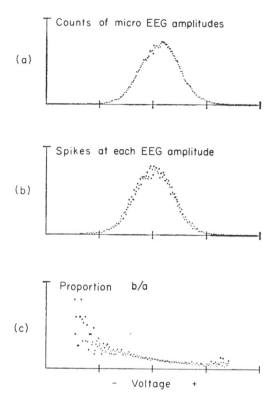

FIG. 6.18   Three distributions that show the close relation between the probability of a spike action potential and the local electroencephalogram (EEG). (A) Histogram of the amplitudes of the micro EEG at various times. (B) A histogram of the number of spikes produced at each EEG amplitude. (C) A new distribution produced by dividing (B) by (A), displaying a high statistical correlation. (From Fox & Norman, ©1968, with the permission of The American Association for the Advancement of Science.)

between the microelectroencephalogram amplitudes and spike occurrence. This is indicated by the nearly straight line that is obtained when the data are normalized and plotted.

The specific numerical value of the correlation between the activity of a given single cell and the microelectroencephalogram can be computed and was found by Fox and Norman to vary from experiment to experiment. This fact in itself is a very significant result, because it confirms the notion that the microelectroencephalogram recorded locally is not a measure of activity of any single cell but rather represents the action of a large population of cells. Thus, if the single-cell activity varies in its congruence with respect to the microelectroencephalogram, it indicates that other cells in the neighborhood are also contributing to the overall potential. If the single-cell recording had always correlated with the microelectroencephalogram, it would have raised the ever-present specter that the microelectroencephalogram is something quite different from that recorded in a more conventional manner with very large electrodes.

If the notion of congruence is a reasonable one, it should also be expected that when the sensory system into which the electrodes have been placed is driven by an appropriate stimulus, the correlation between spike count and the amplitude of the microelectroencephalogram would increase. This is exactly the result obtained for those cells in the visual cortex of the cat that respond to light flashes. (The visual cortex does, of course, include other cells that are not directly and simply activated by a light stimulus alone, and for these cells the congruence was seen to decrease.)

In summary, Fox and Norman presented a valuable new measure for the estimation of the "coordination" or congruence of a group of cortical cells. This measure has a number of important implications. First, the high degree of correlation with single-cell activity tells us that the microelectroencephalogram, if it is not a direct product of the spikes themselves, is certainly derived from processes that also underlie spike generation. The two are essentially analogs of each other and may be considered to be at least informationally equivalent if not representationally identical. Second, the microelectroencephalogram gives us a measure that is a cumulative index of the activity of many cells in the region surrounding the recording electrode rather than a measure of the activity of a single cell. Such a measure may be the only plausible way of investigating the action of ensembles of neurons—and ensembles may be the "name of the game." Third, congruence is a direct estimate of the degree to which the activity of a single cell represents the mean biological activity of all the cells in the region contributing to the slow potential. Congruence should, therefore, prove in future years to be an important measure of brain activity and contribute greatly to an understanding of how it is that the activity of single cells are pooled into compound responses.

Another way in which the relationship between cellular and compound action potentials can be made is through the medium of a conceptual drawing based on experiments carried out by Verzeano (1963). His drawing has taken on the status of a classic as a provocative model of the process of compound potential production. Verzeano believes that the shape of the evoked potential or of the electroencephalogram is due directly to the summation of spike action potentials. His drawing also emphasizes the point that shape of the compound potential is determined by the statistics of very large numbers of individual spike action potentials. These cellular responses may be either highly synchronized or completely desynchronized. When the cellular spikes occur at the same time, there is a tendency to produce high-amplitude compound potentials even though the same average amount of spike activity would produce no compound potential if it were completely desynchronized.

Figure 6-19 illustrates Verzeano's reasoning. In this thought experiment, four electrodes are inserted into closely adjacent regions of some neural tissue. Figure 6-19a shows a considerable amount of neural activity, but that activity is totally unsynchronized among the four electrodes. The resultant compound potential is very small. In Figs. 6-19b, c, and d, there is a progressively higher degree of synchronization of the activity at each electrode and a progressively larger amplitude of the compound potential. It is interesting to recall in this context that the unsynchronized activity is associated with a high degree of mental activity, whereas the synchronized activity is generally associated with an "idling" mental state. This, indeed, is the one classic and unequivocal electroencephalographic conclusion.

One final point should be made with regard to the possible origins of the compound potentials that can be recorded from the brain. As we learn more about glial cells, the supporting units found between neurons, it is becoming clear that they, too, produce bioelectric potentials. Some of these voltages may be produced under the indirect influence of the neurons that are embedded among the glial cells. In some cases (e.g., the Muller cells—retinal glial cells), the time course of the glial and neuronal cells' response may be nearly the same. Thus, it is possible that even though they are not involved in representative information processing as discussed previously, glial responses may be correlated with responses to stimuli or psychological processes. It has been further suggested that the direct cause of glial depolarization is the increased potassium concentration in the extracellular space as a result of neuronal activity. This possibility has been considered in detail by Orkand, Nicholls, and Kuffler (1966) and in an extensive review by Kuffler and Nicholls (1966). The simple fact that such glial action potentials exist raises the possibility that they may contribute to the production of compound action potentials.

In any event, there is as yet no complete agreement as to an explanation of the origins of electroencephalographic or evoked brain potentials; any or all of the voltage sources mentioned so far may contribute to those compound action potentials. Hopefully, the problem can be resolved in the not-too-distant future, but frankly, there is considerable reason to believe that the problem will be very refractory. What we do know, without doubt, is that they can be detected, and because they do come from the brain, it is obvious that many will inquire into their relationship to mental processes. This is the topic of the next section.

FIG. 6.19 (*Opposite page*) Verzeano's conceptualization of how spike activity may lead to compound waves like the EEG (GW). If the spikes are all firing randomly, the amplitude of the EEG is low. As the synchronization increases, however, the peak-to-trough amplitude of the EEG increases even though no more spikes may be firing than previously. In this figure, the model has been drawn in two different ways. On the left-hand side, the signals from four electrodes are shown as serial temporal records. On the right-hand side, a snap shot in time has presented the spatial pattern at different stages of synchronization. (From Verzeano, ©1963, with the permission of *Acta Neurologica Latinamerica.*)

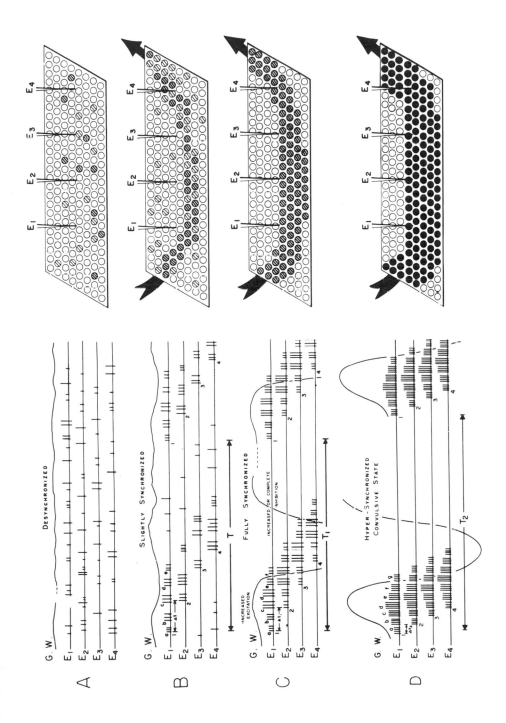

3. Are Compound Action Potentials Codes of Psychological Processes?[10]

Because the recording technology of the compound evoked brain potentials is so straightforward, it is sometimes assumed without adequate justification that these electrical signals from the brain directly reflect the essential brain activities that may be identifiable with psychological processes. However, the issue is far more complicated, and such an inference of identification is not justifiable without considerable further attention being directed at the logical and empirical aspects of the putative association.

To summarize a widely current view, many psychobiologists explicitly and implicitly suggest that evoked brain potentials, obviously coming from the brain and often apparently correlated with psychological and stimulus dimensions, are indeed the transactional equivalents of mental processes measured under similar circumstances. In this section I have tried to show that the determination that such a potential, even though it may come from the brain, is a true transactional or representational equivalent requires far more stringent tests of necessity and sufficiency than are usually applied. I assert that a far more correct view is that no matter how high the correlation between some parameter of the evoked brain potential and a psychophysical function, the assumption of equivalence is not, a priori, acceptable. The simple, logical fact is thoroughly obscured by the large number of studies purporting to demonstrate an association between certain components of the evoked brain potentials and various aspects of behavior. Although it would be impossible to completely review all of this material, the reader is referred to Cobb and Morocutti (1967), Donchin and Lindsley (1969), MacKay (1969), and Regan (1972), as well as the last 20 years of the journal *EEG and Clinical Neurophysiology* to satisfy his or her urge for a detailed data base. These sources provide abundant evidence of the effort that has been expended on the search for compound evoked potential correlates of psychological processes. Whether this search has actually been fruitful in contributing to the solution of the mind-brain problem is another matter.

In general, a typical sensory evoked potential such as that depicted in Fig. 5-33 can be considered made up of several major components. The first component is a short latency (20-50 msec) signal that is most probably a manifestation of the activity in the primary sensory cortical projection area. This early component is mainly restricted to the portion of the skull directly over the appropriate primary projection area, and its properties directly depend upon the physical properties of the stimulus. Later components (250-500 msec), however, are more general, can be detected over wide portions of the scalp, and seem much more closely related to the "mental" state of the subject and/or the symbolic or meaningful aspects of the signal. It is these later signals that are most affected by the state of consciousness of the subject and that also seem to de-

----

[10]Some of this material is adopted from Uttal, 1967, and is used with the permission of the University of Chicago Press.

pend upon such factors as the significance or ecological relevance of the stimulus. Experimenters have observed that these latter components of the evoked potential are sensitive to such factors as uncertainty (Sutton, Braren, Zubin, & John, 1965), decision making (Squires, Squires, & Hillyard, 1975), degree of learning (Jenness, 1972), attention (Picton & Hillyard, 1974), and even to the different meaning of two alternative interpretations of an ambiguous stimuli (e.g., Johnston & Chesney, 1974).

In spite of these many correlative results, the question of whether or not these evoked potentials are truly the transactional equivalent (in the sense of a psychoneural identity relationship) of a psychological process remains unclear.

Much of the data reported in experiments using evoked potentials is based upon small differences produced by alternative conditions of the independent variable and only one particular portion of the total waveform. Not all portions of the signal perform in the same way, and not all differences are reliable from one laboratory to another. There is, therefore, a great deal of controversy over both interpretations and the empirical facts, themselves. For example, Galbraith and Gliddon (1975) strongly criticize Johnston and Chesney's (1974) paper on the basis of a vocalization artifact. Johnston and Chesney's (1975) rebuttal is only partially satisfactory in meeting this criticism. Another example is a highly interpretive and thoroughly opaque controversy between Donchin (1975) and Stowell (1975) on the one hand, and Begleiter and Porjesz (1975b) on the other, over interpretation of data in an earlier paper by Begleiter and Porjesz (1975a) concerning decision-making effects on the evoked brain potential. Again, both sides have strong arguments and no clear resolution is apparent.

As one looks over the history of this field, it seems in general that the level of disagreement is very high. There seems to be more of these critiques and rebuttals in the evoked brain potential field than is usual in science, and this controversy may reflect a lack of crispness in the data base.

A more fundamental difficulty, however, lies in the conceptualization of the relationship between the evoked brain potentials (if they do ultimately turn out to correlate satisfactorily) and the psychological responses. This difficulty lies in the fact that it is not always easy to determine whether a neural signal is a code or a sign; that is, whether the neural signal is the true underlying equivalent of the psychological process or simply a correlated concomitant. This important distinction between these two categories of neural response is now elaborated.

Earlier in this chapter I offered a general definition of a *code* as a set of symbols and transformation rules that allows an economical representation of a body of information. For the special problem I am discussing here, it is also necessary that the code actually become the equivalent, at some stage, of a mental process. A representation that is not so utilized but is lost at a more central level of information processing is, in this context, a *sign*. A sign may be useful to an external observer who may decode it or measure its properties as an indication of the current state of the stimulus environment or of the neural communication system. However, within the behavioral framework with which we are most concerned, such fluctuations represent little more than concomitant variations of lesser interest.

For example, in some central nervous tissue, there are cells in which a high degree of correlation exists between the variance of the intervals between successive action potentials and stimulus amplitude. Under conditions of minimal external stimulation, the intervals are widely spaced and considerably varied. On the other hand, when high amplitude stimulus levels are imposed, the intervals shorten and decrease in variability about their new mean value as demonstrated by Poggio and Viernstein (1964). The change in variability has been shown to exist, but its effect on behavior is what must ultimately identify such variability as either a code or a sign. If fluctuations of interval variability affect subsequent levels in such a way that they differentially influence some behavioral or mental function, then the fluctuation itself is a true *code* for that process. If, on the other hand, the influence of the neural fluctuations is lost and cannot be shown to affect any behavior or thought, such fluctuation is only a *sign* of the external environment.

In addition, it is useful to distinguish between two kinds of signs. The first category includes those signs that are completely stimulus-determined but which lose their influence because of the insensitivity of some subsequent portion of the nervous system to their particular kind of fluctuation. I refer to these as *stimulus signs.* On the other hand, *systemic signs* include those fluctuations that are introduced into neural signals by factors other than external stimuli but which still do not affect all subsequent levels of the nervous system. An example of such a systemic sign is a change in the amplitude of an evoked potential caused by a metabolic deficit which, though altering the signal, does not affect the behavior.

It should be noted that there can also be *systemic codes.* Systemic codes include stimulus-unrelated fluctuations in the neural state that affect behavior. The neural mechanism underlying memory is a good example of a systemic code, affecting perception as it does in a way that is unrelated to the current stimulus impact. In a discussion of evoked brain potentials, a careful distinction between the two kinds of signs is as important as the distinction between a sign and a code.

In peripheral sensory nerves, the distinction between a sign and a code can be more easily conceptualized. In the context of peripheral nerves and their action potentials, an adequate demonstration of the psychophysical *discrimination* of a given signal fluctuation is operationally sufficient to define it as some sort of a code, because discrimination indicates a sensitivity equivalent to interpretation. But, whereas the family of potential signals in peripheral nerves can be easily categorized, the complex interactions of the net of neurons constituting the central nervous system are much less well understood. In each case, however, the sufficiency test for a code is the same. It requires that we use the entire efferent action—a complex and multi-influenced process that has been generally called *behavior*—as the measuring instrument.

This point is emphasized to make clear that no neurophysiological measurement, no matter how sophisticated, no matter at what high level of the nervous system it is carried out, and no matter how highly correlated, can substitute for a behavioral test to distinguish a sign from a code. Therefore, the psychobiologist must consider the behavioral response as the ultimate test of whether or not some complex neural process actually is the basis of some mental awareness or experience.

With the evoked brain response, we are dealing with an integrated electrical potential in which much of the microscopic details of the states of the individual neurons in the system have been lost. It is a mathematical truism, as I have noted previously, that such composite waveforms can be formed by an almost infinite number of combinations of subcomponents. On the other hand, does the central nervous system process these components of the evoked brain potential in a statistical way which is so similar to that exploited by the electrophysiological recording techniques that, in fact, they can be considered codes? Of course, this is another way of stating the same essential question.

There is an argument that the use of the terminology and the approach of the compound evoked potential may be the most realistic way of answering the fundamental question of representation asked at the beginning of this chapter. It is possible that an analysis of mind and/or behavior to the level of the individual neurons and synapses, on a strictly deterministic basis, may be just as difficult as describing the behavior of a box of gas on the basis of the dynamics of the individual molecules constituting the gas. This is not only due to the practical difficulties of the quality of individual measurements (as limited by the Heisenberg uncertainty principle) but also to the mathematical-conceptual problem defined by the fact that an infinite number of combinations of individual-gas-molecule dynamics could lead to the same gross behavior. Thus, the issue of the compound evoked potential may not only be a useful adjunct but, because it is intrinsically a statistical process, may represent a set of techniques that are the only conceivable means of asking the important questions about the representation of mind's action by brain's structure. This may be so in spite of the fact that the brain is microscopically orderly and not a "mess of porridge" or a homogeneous gel.

I repeat, this approach is a possibility and a plausibility; but it is also important to note that there is as yet inadequate justification for acceptance of this concept of the evoked potential as a *coded* statistical representation of mind. Much progress has to be made in the laboratory and the study before such an idea can gain consensual acceptance.

The discussion of the distinction between signs and codes in the context of the compound evoked potential also holds true within the domain of individual neurons, the other possible major level at which we could expect to find codes for mental processes. In turning to the problem of sensory coding in the next section, our attention is, thus, redirected to this world of the individual neuron. It is important to remember, however, that even though it is in the realm of sensory processes that so many of our data have become available concerning the specifics of neural representation, this is only a portion of the problem of coding and representation. Ultimately, all other mental processes must be subject to a similar analysis.

E.   SENSORY CODING[11]

Because of the anchor provided by the metrics of the physical stimulus and the relative simplicity and directionality of the sensory pathways, the study of representation at the cellular level has reached its highest state in modern research on the problem of sensory coding. The general question of representation is constrained in this case to ask only—How are the percepts that are the results of impinging patterns of stimuli and the information that is communicated along the afferent pathways encoded? Although psychobiology can take pride in the substantial progress that has been made in studies of sensory coding, it must also acknowledge that the profession is only at the beginning of any systematic knowledge about the coding of cognitive processes. Indeed, most current experiments, even though carried out on nonsensory or nonmotor portions of the cerebral cortex (the intrinsic regions), are in the sensory paradigm.

It is true, therefore, that although simple sensory communication mechanisms do serve as a partial model for more complex central integrative functions, there is only an imperfect analogy between the two domains of research. In at least one regard, they are fundamentally different. As I have noted previously, the criteria of excellence of the nervous system's communication aspects are based upon the fidelity of information transmission. It is at this level that a closer approximation to isomorphic representation of the communicated information may be found and be useful, even though it is no more necessary here, in some logical sense, than more centrally. It is clear, on the other hand, that the representation of central cognitive processes maintains little semblance of such isomorphic mapping. The central cognitive or symbolic coding of a concept or a percept may be in dimensions bearing no geometrical relationship to the original stimulus pattern. What research there is on the topic suggests a gradual progression away from geometrical congruent representations in the periphery to increasingly less "mappable" representations more centrally. The central symbolic processes, therefore, allow considerable "patching" to be done to the relatively poor sensory information that does make its way to the intrinsic areas. Holes may be filled in, clues interpreted, past experience introduced, and judgments made about relationships that differ considerably from the simple geometric or temporal characteristics of the original stimulus. The criteria of excellence of integrative mechanisms are, therefore, based on the richness of the mixture of information and the deviation from, rather than fidelity to, simple reproduction of

[11]Some of this section of the chapter is adapted from Uttal, 1973, and is used with the permission of the publisher, Harper & Row, Inc.

the input stimulus pattern. It will probably turn out, therefore, that sensory coding theory is a fairly poor model for cognitive coding theory.

Another important point should be made here with regard to sensory coding in particular. The general problem of sensory coding is a much more complex and multifaceted one than the singular determination of the functional relationship between stimulus intensity on the one hand, and nerve impulse frequency on the other hand. In the past, this single task had often been presented as "the" sensory-coding problem. Although such an oversimplification is not as frequent as it was, there still is a tendency to emphasize this single aspect of sensory coding in the current literature.

It is easy to understand the reasons for this misemphasis. The dramatic size and explosiveness of the propagated spike potential make it a far more visible and interesting signal than the more delicate graded synaptic and receptor potentials. But these latter neural signals are also candidate codes. In addition, the usual technology in a single-cell electrophysiological experiment involves the use of a micropipette and an oscilloscope. For all their virtues, these instruments are limited in scope. The micropipette responds to events at but a single place, and the oscilloscope (at least until some of the recent developments of some highly ingenious spatial display techniques) usually was used as a simple plotter of time functions. Experiments based on this particular methodology, therefore, tend to overemphasize the importance of time functions at a particular point in space. It was not realized until recently that many other possible neural codes of equal importance even existed. This is certainly an example of the tremendous constraining influence on one's perspective that can be produced by one's technology.

Similarly, psychophysicists have concentrated on the psychological problem of judged magnitudes or intensities. The search for "the" psychophysical law has, in large part, been a search for relationships between perceived magnitude and stimulus dimensions. But here, too, magnitude is only a portion of the total span of dimensions that are involved in the sensory coding problem. Quality, temporal, and spatial parameters also must be encoded by neural signals, and the elucidation of their codes is also a part of the sensory coding problem.

In the following pages I spell out a view of the coding problem that is based upon the correlation of two groups of dimensions rather than only magnitude and action potential frequency. The first group of dimensions describes messages. The second describes the neural responses. We must separately ask: What is the pattern of the information (the message) that is carried along the neural communication pathways, and what are the parameters of the neural response in which that information is encoded?

1. The Common Sensory Dimensions; the Message

There is a certain amount of ambiguity in defining the conveyed information, because there are two perspectives from which the characteristics of the message may be discussed. One way is to assume that the key reference is, in fact, the physical stimulus and that it is sufficient to merely talk about physical stimulus dimensions. After all, that is the original source of the message.

On the other hand, our knowledge of the transductive processes should have forewarned us that physical dimensions may be very quickly reencoded into entirely different neural dimensions even within the receptor itself. A temporal dimension might be converted into one of magnitude, and a spatial one might become a temporal one under the appropriate conditions. An alternative scheme in which such conversions could be accounted for is to be much desired.

An eminently feasible alternative is to base our discussion on the aspects of perception rather than the dimensions of the physical stimulus. This alternative set of dimensions might well be called the *set of discriminable dimensions* of the physical stimulus, or alternatively, the *set of common sensory dimensions*. This latter nomenclature emphasizes the fact that this schema is modality independent. The same set of common sensory dimensions can be used to describe patterns as well in one sense as in any other. Thus perceived magnitude, or subjective intensity, is a term that can be used for visual brightness, auditory loudness, or even olfactory smelliness. Such an approach has the additional advantage of biasing the experimenter toward searches for those coding factors that are common to all of the senses and biasing the theorist toward the development of a general, rather than a modality specific, theory of sensory coding.

The relationship between the stimulus, the neural code, and the common sensory dimension can be made somewhat more concrete by a specific example. Consider the auditory sense. A stimulus with a certain physical intensity produces, at a given level of the ascending pathway, a neural fluctuation along some dimension. This neural fluctuation, or code, is interpreted by the nervous system in such a way that in a psychophysical experiment, subjects may report that the stimulus was associated with a certain loudness or perceived magnitude. It is also important to realize that the relationship between the subjective experience and the neural fluctuation is the key problem that must be unraveled in coding theory. It is not the relationship between either the stimulus and the neural fluctuation or the stimulus and perceived magnitude. This fact is usually hard to grasp, because all three domains—the physical, external environment and the stimuli it generates; the neurally encoded pattern of signals; and the psychophysical responses—are involved in the process. Perhaps the reader will find some balm for this perplexity by looking once again at Fig. 2-10, which provides some order for these various interacting variables.

This discussion of a schema of sensory dimensions also reminds us of another fact. If a stimulus dimension can be varied without producing any mental or behavioral effect in either the short run or the long run, for all practical purposes, it is not a dimension of interest to students of the psychobiology of sensory coding. An example of such an indistinguishable dimension change would be a shift in wavelength of the emitted radiation from an infrared or ultraviolet source. Although there is a great change in the characteristics of the physical energy, this change simply would be undetected by the sensory mechanism. Fluctuations within the differential threshold or beyond the absolute thresholds would also presumably fall outside of our category of discriminable physical stimuli. From this psychobiological point of view, two stimulus patterns that are not discriminated by the organism as being different are identical even if they produce disimilar neural responses.

2.   The Candidate Codes—The Neural Language

Once having defined the common sensory dimensions, the second part of this task is to identify the relevant neural coding dimensions. In an earlier presentation of this conceptual model (Uttal & Krissoff, 1968), the words "possible dimensions of the neural code" were used to catch the intended flavor of this plan. A preferable phrase has come into use since the publication of that paper. Perkel and Bullock (1968) refer to the possible neural dimensions as "candidate neural codes," which may be defined as any neural signals that have been observed to vary concomitantly with some variation in a physical stimulus dimension. As I noted earlier in the discussion of compound evoked potentials, the neural signal need not be demonstrably associated with any mental or behavioral dimension to be a candidate. Only after it has passed certain tests of necessity and sufficiency (not usually carried out in neurophysiological experiments) can a candidate code be accepted as a true code. Nevertheless, additions to the list of candidate codes lie purely in the domain of the neurophysiologist. Interestingly, the concept of testing to confirm a candidate as a true code has now been expanded to the field of neurochemistry. Putative neurotransmitters must be similarly tested to convincingly enter lists of "true" neurotransmitters.

It is important to remember that there is a dual air of uncertainty concerning the dimensions that are to be entered on the list of candidate codes. First, there can never be any assurance that such a list is complete. New dimensions of variation are constantly being discovered and added to the list of candidate codes. For example, only in the last decade have we become aware that not only the conventional mean frequency dimension of nerve impulse trains is a candidate code, but that the independent higher-order statistics of interpulse interval might also be candidate codes. Other possible additions to the list might also be lurking just offstage, awaiting the development of some new measuring instrument or an insightful investigation by some ingenious experimenter.

The second element of uncertainty concerning dimensions entered on the list of candidate codes lies in the fact that certain dimensions, which have single metrics in some external measuring system, may have alternative and independent ways in which they might be decoded. For example, frequency is an ambiguous dimension—it may be decoded by either measuring the average interval between two impulses or by counting the number of intervals in some integrating period. In this case, also, we must wait for some further experimenter to resolve how the influence of a particular dimensional variation is exerted.

3. Discriminable Dimensions of the Physical Stimulus (The Common Sensory Dimensions)

a. *Perceived Quantity*

The sensed intensity or magnitude of a physical stimulus has long been an area of concern to the psychophysical cryptographer. Although psychobiologists might have initially considered referring subjective magnitude solely to stimulus intensity, it is clear that this is not the thing to do. Whereas all subjective magnitudes vary with stimulus intensity to a major degree, there are also any number of other secondary means by which they can be influenced. For example, consider that the brightness of a photic stimulus varies not only with the number of photons but also with the wavelength of the spectrum of the stimulus. Similarly, it is equally well-known that the loudness of a sound is dependent on the acoustic frequency as well as the sound pressure level. Pairs of electrical pulse stimuli applied to the peripheral nerves (Uttal, 1959) produce sensations of varying amplitudes as the interpulse interval varies even though the total amount of current remains constant. Thus, in general, stimulus intensity is not the only correlate of sensory magnitude. Conversely, stimulus intensity variations are not always sensed purely as sensory magnitude shifts. Increasing stimulus intensity beyond certain limits can produce substantial quality changes—in hue, in saturation, in pitch, or even in the production of pain. Sensory magnitude, therefore, seems to be a more appropriate dimension for the coding problem than stimulus intensity.

b. *Perceived Quality*

The kind or quality of a sensory experience is, of course, the other classic area of sensory research. Yet, there is also an ambiguity in the interpretation of this term or of its closely related biological equivalent, sensory modality. At its most gross level, the problem of modality is trivial. It is clear that the receptor organs make an initial analysis of incident physical energies by virtue of a lowered threshold to one kind of physical stimulus. There is no question that the human eye is best able to detect radiant energy between 400 and 800 nm., or that, among the sense organs, the ear responds maximally to pneumatic pressure fluctuations within the range of 30 to 15,000 Hz. This is the "adequate stimulus" basis of gross "place" coding of the senses.

The second part of this dual interpretation is not trivial and has been the major point of attack of sensory theoreticians for the past century. The problem in this case concerns those different kinds of qualities discriminable within a given modality. The nature of color vision and pitch perception, each representing families of micromodalities within vision and hearing, respectively, are problems at this level.

Another problem encountered in the study of quality coding is that in some of the sense modalities neither the stimulus properties nor the sensory experiences are adequately defined. In vision and hearing research, for example, the specifications of the physical stimulus are very highly developed. We have a single physical dimension in each case that can be systematically varied to alter the microquality of the visual or auditory sensation. However, when one deals with senses such as somesthesis, olfaction, and gustation, another complication arises. The separation of the various modalities into their families of micromodalities is based upon popular, historic, and nonscientific traditions. The complexities of subjective quality in the cutaneous senses are probably not adequately described by a statement mentioning only the classic categories of touch, pain, pressure, warmth, cold, and an open-ended group of "derived" sensations. The electrical stimulation of the skin, for example, gives rise to sensations, some of which mimic some of these qualities and some for which these older classification schemes have no descriptive term.

It is surprisingly difficult to give a good definition of quality. It might well be defined as the discriminable changes that are left over after one has accounted for the magnitude, temporal, and spatial differences between stimuli. The best I can do here is a statement that hopefully leaves the reader with the notion of discriminable differences between *kinds* of stimuli of the same modality.

c. *Temporal Discriminations*

There appear to be many different kinds of temporal discrimination, and these may be interpreted in manners common to several modalities. For very long durations and intervals, the temporal judgments made by an observer may be considered to be modality independent, because the stimulus events merely serve to delimit some other internal timing process. A click, a flash, or a tap can be used equally well to beat out a rhythm. On the other hand, specific timing considerations for very short times within a modality are critical. For example, the ability of the nervous system to use a frequency code for intensity is bounded at the high-frequency end of the spectrum by the refractory period of neurons. At the low-frequency end, theoretically there is no bound, but practically, as interpulse intervals increase, there arrives an interval beyond which the neuronal circuitry can no longer wait to do its counting.

Fraisse (1966) has recently published an important volume dealing with the perception of time. It remains the best survey of temporal psychological processing available. Beyond the scholarly presentation of a wealth of studies of temporal discrimination, Fraisse's main contribution is an elucidation of the complexity of the family of time senses. A summary of his categorization of temporal skills includes the following discriminative abilities.

Relative temporal order.   The ability to determine which of two different stimuli arrived first is of a high level of biological significance. This parameter of the stimulus may be dealt with in purely temporal terms by the observer, but, surprisingly, it is more often interpreted spatially particularly when the interstimulus interval is small. One of the most familiar of this latter class of discriminative abilities is the auditory system's use of differential time of arrival (and for higher-frequency tones—relative intensity) to localize a sound source in space. The timing precision of binaural localization is astonishingly high, corresponding to only a few microseconds of asynchrony in the arrival times.

Relative temporal order of two spatially disparate stimuli can also be a major determinant of the spatial localization of the resultant combined thermal, tactile, and gustatory sensation. Von Békésy (e.g., 1963) has demonstrated many instances of such effects and has shown that very slight differences in the relative temporal order of the two stimuli can substantially change the apparent position of the fused sensation in audition, somatosensation, and even gustatory localization.

Temporal acuity.   Temporal acuity is defined as the ability to distinguish two identical stimulus events, sequential in time, as being separate rather than a single event. Temporal acuity is, of course, directly related to the relative temporal order sense, because to specify one stimulus as having preceded another, they must have been distinguished as separate events temporally. Yet it seems certain that these two capabilities are distinguishable from each other, because the former capability requires an ordinal judgment in addition to the more primitive resolution capability of temporal acuity. Hirsh and Sherrick (1961) demonstrated just such a distinction between simultaneity and order in their classic study of the time senses by demonstrating situations in which it was possible to precisely state that two events had occurred even though the subject was confused about relative temporal order.

Duration or interval.   Another temporal sense involves the ability to replicate the sustained duration of an event or the interval between two events. This sense requires the organism to be capable of clocking time. How this is accomplished is a problem of much current speculation, because so many biological rhythms, which could serve as bases for the clocking operations, have been discovered. It is clear that there is probably no reason to distinguish between a marked interval and a continuous event, because the true stimulus information is only that included in the initiation and termination of the interval or event.

All three of these temporal discriminative abilities probably play an important role in what might be called *complex temporal pattern recognition.* Whether there are other temporal abilities that must be added to fully describe all aspects of temporal discrimination is yet to be determined.

d. *Spatial Discriminations*

The seminal visual research of Hubel and Wiesel (1959), Lettvin, Maturana, McCulloch, and Pitts (1959), and of Barlow and Hill (1963), among others, has emphasized the importance of special codes for spatial stimulus parameters. In each case, stimuli were shown to produce different nerve messages when the stimulus pattern differed geometrically, even though all other stimulus dimensions were held constant. On a simpler level, it is clear that spatial localization of stimuli applied to different points of the receptor fields must be accounted for, and although we have a good deal of evidence to suggest that this is carried out by a corresponding place code (topographic representation) at least in the more peripheral portions of a sensory channel, there still remain two other major problems. First, how does one explain the pseudolocations made of interacting patterns, such as those summarized in von Békésy's (1958) paper on funneling on the skin? Second, how does the mapping of spatial localization by a topographic code overlap with those theories of quality coding or of other stimulus dimensions that also require spatially distributed codes?

In the study of interactions between different spatial areas, a great deal of progress has been made. Ratliff (1965) has reviewed the work of the last century, not only describing the spatial codes for contours, but also giving a detailed electrophysiological analysis of the transformation processes, which lead from the original spatial stimulus pattern to the evoked pattern of neural signals. We must, furthermore, determine how it is that different stimulus locations are discriminated from each other. We must determine what the neural codes are that allow us to discriminate size differences and enhance contours or even see textures.

These, then, are among the most prominent of the common sensory dimensions that we know to be discriminable and that must be accounted for in any attempt to define the complete neural code. I next consider the possible dimensions of the nervous activities—the candidate codes—which might provide symbols for the representation of these sensory variables.

4. Possible Dimensions of the Neural Code
    (The Candidate Codes)

To associate common sensory dimensions accurately with neural response dimensions, one must be cognizant of as many of the likely neural dimensions as possible. The purpose of this section is to list and describe the more important of these dimensions without resorting either to a meaningless class inclusive of all classes, such as "the spatio-temporal pattern," or to biologically unlikely possibilities.

There are, however, two important cautions, which should be noted before we consider the items in this list. First of all, the list has its origins primarily in the observed dimensions of neuroelectrical signals. It should be remembered, as noted earlier, that many of these electrical signals may not be themselves the essential agents; rather, they may only be indicators of chemical processes, for example, which are more directly involved in the information flow.

For example, at the synapse, the information flow is signaled by the amplitude of both the graded presynaptic and postsynaptic potentials. The actual synaptic transmission, on the other hand, is mediated by the number of packets of transmitter substance that migrate across the synaptic cleft. Both of these types of representation, the amount of the transmitter substance and the amplitude of the synaptic potentials, are presumably related, and each is a continuous function of input signal magnitude. Nevertheless, the code actually read by the postsynaptic tissue is not usually an electrical one, but a chemical one. That electrical signals generally are only indicators of more basic chemical processes elsewhere is rapidly becoming a prime tenet of modern neurophysiology.

However, from the point of view of the network hypothesis, which has gradually been evolving in the book, neither of these means of communication of information, electrical or chemical, is really the essence of the relationship between the nervous system and the mind. Rather, the essential aspect of the nervous system is the arrangement of the neurons in the net, regardless of what "technology," chemical, electrical, or what have you, is used to implement the interconnections.

The second important caveat, already alluded to, is that this list of potential information-carrying neural signals is necessarily incomplete, and new items are being added to it almost every year as new candidate codes are uncovered by neurophysiologists. New instruments, new experiments, and, perhaps most important, new insights all suggest new candidate codes, which must be fit into this scheme. By accentuating the dimensionality of the signals rather than their specific physics, however, a considerable amount of generality and flexibility is achieved, and the list remains open-ended.

It should also be reiterated here that the compilation of the list of candidate codes at this stage has nothing whatsoever to do with the psychophysical dimensions. It is, rather, a task that must be carried out by the neurophysiologist and, as such, is independent of any perceptual significance that the candidate code might later be shown to possess. Once a code has been identified as a candidate, then its relationship to perceptual dimensions must be separately assayed by persons who are best operating in the field of science I have referred to as psychobiology.

a. *Place*

The particular location or place activated by an incoming signal is one very important means of representing some attribute of the input signal. There are several different kinds of spatial codes so far suggested. One of the most common is referred to as the *labeled line*. In neuronal communication systems, the mere fact that a given nerve is activated by virtue of the specific characteristics of the transducer is tantamount to a candidate code. There are many conceivable ways in which one particular neuron or group of neurons might be selected for the transmission of information by an incident stimulus. Lowered thresholds to particular types of physical energy or specific temporal pattern sensitivities are among the most interesting possibilities.

Johannes Muller's theory (Muller, 1840) of the specific energy of nerves is a formal statement of place coding, which seems to hold true in a gross way for the representation of sensory quality. Activation of the optic nerve, for example, by any stimulus, no matter of what form, always produces a visual sensation. In a more microscopic sense, however, the coding of microquality (hue, pitch, and so on) by place codes seems to break down and depend more on some relative temporal code (see subsequent discussion). Individual fibers are not uniquely associated with a particular microquality, and therefore Muller's law does not hold at this level.

b.   Number of Activated Units

Another possible dimension of neural coding is, simply, the number of activated fibers or cells in a given nerve tract or ganglion. Magnitude is the sensory dimension most often considered to be mapped, at least in part, by the number of responding neural elements. Because an increase in the number of responding units also means that more places must have been activated, strong interactions might be expected between stimulus dimensions coded by place and those coded by number. But this is not necessarily so. If there is an increase in activity in some regions and a decrease in others as a result of an increase in stimulus intensity, the resulting change in total number of activated units may, in fact, be zero!

In addition to the number of fibers that fire, we may also consider that the number of times that a given fiber fires or the duration of a burst may be codes in some instances. Thus the number of activated units may be really a subclass of a more general candidate code—the number of impulsive responses occurring in a given volume in a given period of time.

c.   Neural Event Amplitude

The discovery of the all-or-none law effectively removed the amplitude of the response of a single axonal spike potential from the list of candidate coding dimensions. It now seems certain that the all-or-none law is valid for axonal spikes and that the amplitude of the individual nerve impulse is related only to the metabolic state of the axon and not to any characteristic of the stimulus once the spike threshold is exceeded. However, it should be remembered that in other parts of the neuron, it has been equally clearly established that slow potentials of graded amplitude and prolonged duration are the significant information symbols.

The amplitude of the neural signal appears as an important information-carrying code in many different contexts. Two of the most important examples are: the receptor-generator potential and the potentials that are recorded from post-synaptic tissues.

In another context, we must also consider that some of the amplitude measures recorded from peripheral nerve compound action potentials may be closely associated with one or another discriminable stimulus dimension. Very often, however, differences in such compound neuroelectric amplitudes merely reflect more fundamental processes. For example, the compound action potential recorded from peripheral nerves is most probably a cumulative index of the number of constituent axons that are responding in an all-or-nothing fashion.

d. *Temporal Pattern*

Naming "temporal pattern" as one of the candidates for neural coding is almost as weak a statement as falling back on a coding category of "spatio-temporal patterns"; each notion is so vague as to be almost meaningless. In the following paragraphs, I strive for more precision by specifying exactly what temporal dimensions are under consideration.

Graded potential time functions—the shape of the response.   Graded potentials of all kinds, receptor-generator potentials, compound action potentials from peripheral nerves, evoked brain potentials, and even free-running electroencephalographic recordings, all can be described as having certain shapes. Shape is a vague term, of course, and what is usually meant by shape is a function or set of measures that describes the amplitude fluctuation of the graded potential as a function of time. Some of these parameters are relatively straightforward. For example, the simple latency pattern of the various amplitude deviations following the presentation of a stimulus can be used as a first approximation to shape. But superimposed on these simple latency measures can also be descriptions of the characteristics of the rise of the waveform. Does it abruptly appear, or does it rise gradually in either a linear or exponential fashion? We have to answer precisely this kind of question in any attempt to use shape as a descriptor of the initial portion of a graded response.

Another class of time function dimensions, which has often been of importance in the representation of sensory phenomena, deals with the steady-state or quasi-steady-state portion of the response. For example, one might want to know: Does the stimulus maintain a constant amount of activity, or is there a significant amount of adaptation or neural accommodation over the time course of a constant stimulus? For those signals, such as the free-running electroencephalogram, which are varying spontaneously (the word "spontaneously" must, of course, be read in this case as "under the influence of unknown stimuli"), such shape parameters as the rate of change, the frequency spectrum, and the rise and fall pattern of specific waveforms, all must be considered as candidate codes.

The following temporal candidate codes are descriptors of the pattern of regenerative spike action potentials. Here, in accord with the all-or-none law, there is no suggestion that the amplitude of an individual spike can carry any useful information. Spike amplitude merely reflects local metabolic conditions perhaps modulated by conditions of previous response. The temporal parameters of importance are, therefore, only those that describe the pulse frequency modulation characteristics of groups of spike potentials.

Frequency of firing.   Although place and the number of activated neural elements are relatively unambiguous measures, which can be evaluated without confusion (even though the technical details may be cumbersome), frequency is an ambiguous dimension of neural activity. Frequency, or the number of responses per unit time, may be evaluated in one of two different ways by a subsequent decoding mechanism. The first way is one in which time measurements are made of the intervals between each pair of sequential responses. The alternative form of decoding possible for frequency is one in which a count is made of the number of neural events occurring within some basic integrating unit of time. As Anatol Rapoport (1962) pointed out, the interval-sensitive procedure would be essentially an analog process, because the range over which the interval varied could be continuous. On the other hand, the counting procedure is essentially a digital process dealing only with integral values of the number of events.

Macrofluctuations in frequency pattern.   Wall and Cronly-Dillon (1960) suggested that a specific code for somatosensory quality, at certain levels, might be the macropattern of the frequency of neural discharge in afferent pathways. Thus a frequency pattern in which the nerve impulse rate goes from a minimum frequency to a higher frequency very rapidly and then slowly diminishes would be perceived differently than a signal in the same pathway and with the same average frequency but whose frequency pattern slowly increases and then rapidly diminishes. These macrofluctuations are regularly observed in many types of neurophysiological recordings from single cells and might be of significance in the encoding of stimulus dimensions other than quality.

Microfluctuations in frequency pattern.   An important related question is whether or not the nervous system is able to detect microfluctuations in frequency and whether such an arhythmia is a candidate neural code. A microfluctuation would be defined as a transient change in the frequency pattern. A missed pulse, an extra pulse, or a momentary gap in the train of spikes, all might be codes for one or another common sensory dimensions.

Temporal comparisons between two or more places.   Another important class of candidate codes includes those situations in which comparisons are made in some neural center between temporal patterns that arrive on spatially separate channels. The auditory system, for example, certainly operates in some fashion that takes into account the phase and amplitude differences of neural responses to the synchronized stimuli applied to the two cochlea. Mountcastle, Poggio, and Werner (1963) have reported a similar temporal comparison process in position indicators in the cat's somatosensory thalamus. Furthermore, Pfaffmann (1959) has suggested that a similar kind of relative activity detection process might underlie gustatory quality coding. A related idea is the volley principle (Wever, 1949), which has been invoked to explain high-frequency following by the auditory system. According to this principle, spatially separate neural structures are capable of cooperatively conveying a frequency that exceeds the capacity of any individual neural structure. Such a process would require a high degree of synchronization detection ability on the part of the neurons involved and a precise comparison of their firing rates—an ability that somewhat surprisingly does seem to occur. In any of these cases, the important fact is that the critical information is not absolutely contained in a single channel of information; rather it depends upon comparison of relative amounts of activity in parallel channels. This is the basic idea of what are generally called *pattern, crossneuron pattern*, or *ratio theories of sensory quality.*

Derived statistical measures. When I spoke of macrofluctuations, I was referring to relatively continuous changes in the frequency pattern. When I spoke of microfluctuations, I was referring to transient changes in the frequency pattern. There is, however, another possibility. There may be long-term fluctuations in the statistics of the pulse pattern that depend upon an evaluation of the microtemporal fluctuations but in a summarized fashion over long periods of time. Thus, the standard deviation and the range of the interval histogram of individual units in the cochlear nucleus of the cat have been shown to exhibit a specific signature by Rodieck, Kiang, and Gerstein (1962). Mountcastle, Poggio, and Werner (1963) have also shown similar effects in thalamic cells representing joint position and have given an interesting analysis of how this information could be used as a code.

Furthermore, other derived statistical measures are common descriptors in statistics. In addition to the mean frequency and the variance (or standard deviation) of the interval pattern, higher-order moments can also be calculated, which can be used to compute such characteristics as the skewness or kurtosis of an interval histogram. These derived statistical measures may also conceivably play a role in neural coding. Unfortunately, there have been no attempts to determine if these derivatives of the higher moments actually vary systematically with stimuli. Thus no progress has been made in testing their role as candidate codes, much less in determining how they might be associated with common sensory dimensions.

5. Cautions in the Association of Sensory Dimensions and Candidate Codes

From the vantage point provided by the preceding discussion, it should be apparent that the general solution of the sensory-coding problem contains a number of substeps. First, the dimensions of sensory experiences must be elucidated by psychophysical experiments on man and animals. Second, the neurophysiologist must identify dimensions of neural activity for inclusion in the list of candidate codes by determining which dimensions are functions of stimulus variations. Third, preliminary associations can be made between common sensory dimensions and candidate codes at various levels of the ascending pathway.

These associations, however, are at best only tentative. There are a number of conceptual constraints, which make final confirmation of the association—the fourth step—very elusive indeed. These constraints place limits on the assurance with which we can accept any sensory-coding association. In the following paragraphs I point out some of these potential conceptual and technical pitfalls, which impede final confirmation of tentative associations between candidate codes and common sensory dimensions.

a. The Sign-Code Distinction Revisited

Every point made in the discussion of the relevance of the distinction between signs and codes for evoked brain potentials earlier in this chapter is also germane at the level of the single-cell responses more typically encountered in the sensory-coding problem. There simply is no way of guaranteeing that any observed fluctuation in any neural response, no matter how closely it correlates with stimulus properties, is truly a code unless certain tests of necessity and sufficiency are carried out. A full discussion of this important problem in the domain of cellular responses and an example of an analytical test of a code are presented in Uttal (1973) in my discussion of spike action potential interval irregularity.

b. Dimension Alterations

It must be expected from what we already know of the coding of sensory information that there will be very drastic changes in the coded form of a stimulus pattern at various levels of the afferent nervous system. For example, the most current theory of auditory encoding assumes that there is a transduction from temporal (frequency) stimulus patterns to a spatial code by a hydraulically mediated cochlear place localization of different frequencies. It is not too surprising, therefore, to learn of other specific neural structures that respond spatially to a specific temporal pattern of stimulus input. The existence of temporal "keys"—particular temporal patterns capable of activating specific loci, thus converting time to space—has been suggested by recent results (see, for example, Segundo & Perkel, 1969). On the psychophysical side of the ledger, MacKay (1961) has also reported several instances of spatial patterns that give rise to flickering changes in the visual field, suggesting the conversion of spatial to temporal patterns. Presumably, these affects are related to eye movements. Thus we should expect spatial-to-temporal, as well as temporal-to-spatial, transformations.

The caution inherent in these results is that we should not demand dimensional constancy throughout the afferent pathways and that codes at one level need not be identical nor even of the same dimensional category as codes at another level. All that is required is that the information pattern be represented in one way or another at all levels. Thus a stimulus pattern might be represented at one level by a temporal code, at another by a spatial code, and at another by an amplitude code. As I have repeatedly said, no topographic or isomorphic consistency is really necessary, nor is there any need for linear (or nonlinear) representation of functions that appear to the perceiver to be linear (or nonlinear). All that is required is some representational scheme that transmits the critical information of the input pattern in some available language. (The metaphorical line of speech translators discussed early in this chapter is the best way to concretize this important concept.)

For these reasons, it is important to avoid the narrowing of perspective, which would arise from the false requirement that temporal stimulus patterns be represented by temporal candidate codes and from other similar but equally incorrect isomorphisms. A most important corollary is that there is no one coding scheme that can be identified for each dimension of each sense but only local definitions of codes at specifically defined levels.

c. *Boundary Condition Results*

Another caution relates to the fact that many results are significant only in the sense that they represent limiting cases or boundary conditions. The determination of a threshold in a psychophysical or a neurophysiological experiment is a case in point. The threshold may impose a limit on the availability of a certain dimension to serve in some particular coding operation, but it does not necessarily completely define the functional variability of such a dimension as the corresponding stimulus dimension is varied. Different coding mechanisms may come into play at different stimulus amplitudes, for example.

d. *Multiple and Overlapping Coding in Two or More Dimensions*

The old phrase "spatio-temporal pattern," naive and virtually meaningless as it was, did reflect a certain problem. Many complex stimulus patterns are not unidimensional, and it is sometimes misleading to expect a given stimulus dimension to be associated with only one candidate code. In fact, such a separation may not be possible without considering interdimensional interaction, because some dimensions may act to modify some other dimensions. It is probably misleading to presume a one-to-one relationship between all stimulus dimensions and a single candidate code. As we see later, there appear to be many multiple codes used in the nervous system.

There are two quite different ways in which multiple coding may be exhibited. The first way might be best called *redundant coding*. In this situation, the variation of a single stimulus dimension may lead to the simultaneous variation of two or more candidate codes. An example of such a phenomenon is the now well-known simultaneous variation of mean frequency and variance of a spike action potential pattern as stimulus amplitude is varied.

The second way in which multiple coding may be exhibited might best be called *overlapping coding*. In this situation, two or more stimulus dimensions may be capable of altering a single dimension of neural coding. For example, both the intensity and wavelength of a photic stimulus are known to affect the rate of firing of a ganglion cell axon in the optic nerve. Of course, in this case of a single neuron, such overlapping coding would lead to an ambiguous situation, because the change in wavelength could always be compensated for by a change in intensity. This ambiguity can be resolved only on the basis of other parallel neural communication lines that convey similarly coded information but with slightly different coding characteristics. In fact, this is probably the basis of color coding and perhaps of quality coding in general.

A related matter of concern is produced by the very high degree of convergence within the nervous system. Signals at higher levels may not reflect the influence of a single input alone. Rather, such a higher-level signal may be the result of the integration and processing of patterns of inputs from several sources. The matter is further complicated by the fact that feedback signals from more central portions of the nervous system can also alter the pattern of activity at peripheral levels. This and related kinds of centrifugal (information flow from the central to the peripheral nervous system) effects often lead to responses of great complexity, because input-output relations now become subject to both regenerative and degenerative effects of positive and negative feedback. The difficulties and surprises of signal tracing encountered in systems with elaborate feedback loops are well-known to electrical engineers.

e. Species and Intraindividual Variability

Whereas ideally we would like to be able to generalize as much as possible to keep sensory theories as simple as possible, it is probably also important to keep in mind the fact that not all organisms, either within or among species, operate in exactly the same fashion. Furthermore, there is also the possibility of what Perkel and Bullock (1968) refer to as "labile coding." At different times in the organism's development, it is conceivable that different coding mechanisms underlie a single function. Analogous differences in coding mechanisms may be expected to exist at different stages of the evolutionary scale.

f. Attentional Limits on Our Perspective

I have, several times in the course of this book, referred to the fact that the attention of the scientific community is directed to small portions of the total problem by accidents of technology and of paradigm. The overemphasis on the frequency factors of spike action potentials as codes for intensity has been the classic example. The development of the more general notion of the coding problem was inhibited until new instruments and new experimental paradigms widened our perspective. A very complete study of the general problem of paradigms of consensus and the ways in which revolutions in scientific perspectives occur has been made by Kuhn (1970) and may be of interest to the more philosophically oriented reader.

F. AN INTERIM SUMMARY

It should now be clear what we mean by a theory of sensory coding in particular and neural representation in general. Although there are a number of cautions that have to be observed, the general task involved in the unraveling of the codes of the nervous system is the precise definition of the association between percepts, experiences, and thoughts and the candidate neural dimensions. For the sensory domain, we might consider this task to be one in which we are required to fill in the entries on a correlation matrix such as that shown in Table 6-1.

A table such as this will have to be developed for each level of afferent neural coding. This means that there may be several different levels of coding even within a single cell and many within the entire course of the ascending pathway. This need for a multiplication of coding matrices would be somewhat discouraging if it were not for the fact that we may also expect to find some common features at equivalent levels as comparisons are made across the senses. This places the severe requirement on the sensory-coding theory to be sure that all of the comparisons being made are between truly comparable levels of encoding.

It is not too difficult to be led astray and to make false comparisons between levels that are actually nonequivalent in this search for a general theory. A classic example has been the oft-repeated statement that the frequency discrimination of the skin is far poorer than that of the ear. In fact, however, the frequency discrimination capability of the ear, from a neural coding point of view, is more comparable to spatial discrimination capability on the skin than to its frequency sensitivity. The analysis of acoustic frequencies into spatial patterns on the cochlea confuses the issue and illustrates some of the problems that can develop when one depends too much on the potential physical stimulus as a referent. On the other hand, when the acoustic nerve is driven electrically (Simmons et al., 1965), comparisons of the frequency discrimination capabilities of the ear and the skin turn out to be very similar.

This brings me to my final point. The concept of representation or coding has intrinsic within it a major theoretical perspective that could reorganize much of our thinking in experimental psychology. If represented information, regardless of the dimensions of the specific neural code, may be transformed into percepts with other, and perhaps different, dimensions, then it follows that the interpretation of any coded afferent signal may be quite variable depending upon the circumstances of its surround or the previous experience of the perceiver. This variability in percept, it is important to note, is possible without a corresponding distortion in the particular afferent pattern of neural signals. Thus

TABLE 6.1

A sample of a correlation matrix that must be filled out for each level of sensory coding. (From Uttal, 1973.)

		Neural Response Dimensions (The Candidate Codes)				Temporal Parameters			
Common Sensory Dimensions		Place	Topographic Pattern	Number of Activated Units	Neural Event Amplitude	Frequency	Frequency Macrofluctuations	Frequency Microfluctuations	Derived Statistical Measures	Temporal Comparison Between Two Places
Temporal Parameters	Quality									
	Quantity									
	Relative Temporal Order									
	Temporal Acuity									
	Duration									
Spatial Parameters	Spatial Localization									
	Spatial Interaction and Patterns									

431

stimuli in this new light become flexible clues to solution of a perceptual problem rather than specific triggers to the automatic elicitation of equally specific perceptual responses.

Perhaps the clearest example to make this important idea concrete can be found in the literature of human stereopsic vision. Psychologists almost universally assert (see Kaufman, 1974, p. 278 for a discussion of theories of stereopsis) that the visual images conveyed from the two eyes must either be "fused" or that one must be "suppressed" to create a single three-dimensional percept.

The theory of neural coding or representations suggests, however, that we can look at this problem in a completely different way. The two images, according to this alternative point of view, are neither "fused" nor "suppressed," but instead the incoming barrage of neural data from each eye may be thought of as contributing to a common pool of information that leads to the emergence of a percept of a single object in depth. It is the total aggregate of incoming information from both eyes that gives rise to the impression of a single object in space rather than any fusion or suppression of two (nonexistent) monoptic perceptual images. The stereoscopic image has its own qualities and its own properties and does not represent some processed version of the two monoptic images. It exists instead of, rather than because of the fusion or suppression of, the monoptic images.

This is but one example of an important generalization. A theory of coded and nonisomorphic representations allows us to think in an entirely different way about the relationship between the external physical environment and mental states. The two are not in direct correspondence with each other at any point beyond the retinal mapping. There are really no very good maps, geometrically congruent with the outside, inside the head. Rather, there is a system of communication of ideas and percepts by a correlated system of clues and codes. Only a portion of the total stimulus information is ever available, and that information may exert its impact on the mind in highly variable ways. Illusions, misperceptions, and all of the other incongruities between the physical stimulus and percepts become directly understandable in a new way from this revised perspective. The search for isomorphic neural correlates of many perceptual processes thus becomes a search for a chimera!

This then completes what is essentially a conceptual, methodological, and preparatory excursion to set the stage for the next chapter. I have elaborated in this chapter the fundamental concepts and techniques that are required to unravel the problem of representation that itself is a subclass of the mind-brain perplexity. However, I have only briefly mentioned the actual state of knowledge of the field today.

In Chapter 7, as an illustrative example of the empirical problems associated with the study of representation, I consider whether or not it is really reasonable to argue back and forth between the languages of visual perception and behavior, on the one hand, and neurophysiology, on the other. In attending to the data of vision, however, it should be kept in mind that it (and related sensory issues) is but one small portion of the general problem of representation at the neural level. The process of representation is obviously fundamental to all aspects of mental life. In the ultimate analysis, everything that we are mentally must be explicable in terms of the states of networks of neurons that operate in similar ways. The hope, of course, is that the knowledge gained from the study of sensory systems is transferable to that of other cognitive processes.

7
Representation and Coding:
Methods, Findings, and Theories

A. INTRODUCTION

In Chapter 6, I discussed many of the conceptual issues and prerequisite materials that are involved in achieving an understanding of the manner in which individual neuronal responses represent or encode psychological functions. In this chapter I concentrate on the actual data base that has been obtained from extensive laboratory investigations in this area. I also delve deeper into the extremely perplexing question of whether or not the activity of single neurons or classes of neurons is detectable in a direct and simple way in the molar behavior of the organism.

As I do so, I must reiterate that there are two critically important ideas that must be kept continuously in mind and not lost in the noise of individual experiments:

1. Representation is a very general concept that deals with other aspects of the mind-body problem than sensory coding. All psychological processes must be represented some place in the brain.

2. The application of the simplistic ideas of isomorphic sensory coding to more complex perceptual or integrative processes is probably one of the most serious conceptual errors in modern psychobiological theory. Neither the data nor simple logic supports much of the theory that is presently proposed by psychobiologists to explain certain kinds of perception.

I stress these points at the outset because the problem of representation has often been exclusively approached in the laboratory from a point of view that has only emphasized the need for determination of trigger features of a stimulus that are most effective in eliciting activity in single sensory neurons. Without doubt, the discovery of the selectivity of sensory neurons to particular spatio-temporal features of stimuli was one of the most important breakthroughs in neurophysiology. An emphasis on feature selectivity is particularly appropriate when one is dealing with the more peripheral stages of sensory processing where the geometry of the stimulus is still isomorphically encoded or represented.

However, an emphasis on isomorphic coding has very often been misapplied to neurons in areas of the brain that are not the primary sensory projection regions. I feel that it is probably the case that the most important functions performed by neurons of the brain are *not* spatio-temporal feature selections but rather are integrative and response-oriented processes that are more remote from stimulus geometry than are the intrinsically simpler and more peripheral communication processes. Studies like those of Ranck and Mountcastle on nonsensory aspects of representation (to be described later in this chapter) represent a fundamentally new paradigm, for the study of representation of these more centrally mediated processes, that is quite independent of any need for isomorphic coding.

For practical reasons (most of the available data base concerned with representation is concentrated in visual studies), I have to concentrate on the sensory literature (and vision in particular) in the discussion of representation to be presented in this chapter. In doing so, however, I hope the reader will not forget that representation is not solely a sensory problem and that isomorphic relations between the neural codes and stimulus inputs are not a necessary prerequisite of representation theory.

Some of this chapter is adapted from my earlier book (Uttal, 1973) on sensory coding. I have substantially updated this older material and introduced a number of topics not dealt with in that volume. The greatest lacuna in this chapter is a discussion of the specific details of what is known of the coding of sensory quality, magnitude, and spatial and temporal variables in the more peripheral parts of the sensory systems. It is the material that is best known in the field of representation but also the material that was covered in fullest detail in that earlier work.

It is with reluctance that I leave it out, but I have such a sense of closure on that material that any further exercise of it would be superfluous.

B.   REPRESENTATION IN THE VISUAL SYSTEM

1.   Some Basic Mechanisms[1]

Later in this chapter, when I discuss the potential mechanisms of representation in the visual nervous system, I often consider rather complex feature selecting, extracting or filtering mechanisms. It is important to mention at the outset of this discussion that these feature processing characteristics must be assumed to be the result of a few kinds of simple interactions occurring between individual

[1]Parts of this section are adapted from Uttal, 1975b.

neurons. Even though we may observe some complex process such as a specific feature selectivity in the response pattern of a single neuron, it is almost certain that the neuron's actions reflect the contribution of a myriad of interacting neurons at earlier stages of the nervous pathway rather than its own selective filtering. Later, after discussing the properties of some of these visual nervous system neurons, I give a specific example of how the basic mechanisms can lead to spatio-temporal feature selectivity in the rabbit retina.

The general point to be made here is that the basic interactions that can occur between individual neurons must be considered the primitive operations that ultimately lead to the selectivity, feature filtering, or trigger sensitivity of high-order neurons as well as all other neural information processing. In this section I briefly describe some of these primitive types of interactions that can occur among neurons as prerequisites to the emergence of the more involved pattern processing properties.

a.   Spatial Convergence and Divergence

There is probably not a single case within the nervous system of any animal in which a neuron possesses only a single synaptic input and a single synaptic output. All neurons and neuron nets have several inputs and several outputs. This basic fact implies that, to a considerable degree, all neuronal activity is integrative in that the response of any single cell necessarily results from the mixing of multiple samples of encoded incident information.

The idea of multiple origins and multiple destinations have been formalized in neurophysiology by the terms *spatial divergence* and *spatial convergence*. In a divergent system, information moving along a single axon is spatially replicated by being distributed in several collateral pathways as shown in Fig. 7-1b. This divergence amplifies the neural signals' impact by increasing the number of neurons activated at subsequent levels of the network. Neural convergence, the opposite process, is depicted in Fig. 7-1a. In a convergent system, information moving along several inputs is brought together to affect a single neuron. Convergence is also an amplifying process but one that increases the activity in a single neuron by pooling the activity of several other neurons in a single channel.

More importantly, spatial convergence leads directly to the possibility of integrative interactions among multiple spatially disparate inputs. This is particularly significant for the graded action potentials that represent the main media of coding and communication at the synapse. The ability of a neuron to integrate graded potentials is, from many points of view, the most important single aspect of nervous activity.

Spatial convergence can produce a number of different kinds of logical integrative operations depending upon the number and polarity (i.e., whether they are inhibitory or excitatory) of the input signals. In the simplest case of spatial convergence, two separate synapses, which terminate in close proximity, might jointly produce a postsynaptic potential sufficiently strong to exceed the threshold for the elicitation of a spike in cases where neither synapse could alone.

Logicians and computer designers call such an integrative process a logical "and" operator; in this case both inputs are required to produce an output signal.

On the other hand, spatially convergent neural interactions may be more complicated than simple summation. For example, some synaptic contacts can be inhibitory such that the effects of excitatory synapses can be completely or partially cancelled. A neuron that will fire only when no inhibitory inputs are activated implements a logical function that is called "and not."

(a) Spatial convergence

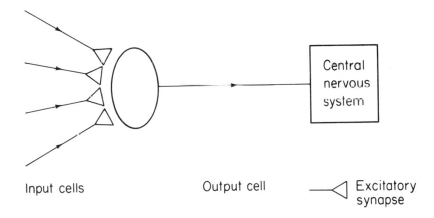

(b) Spatial and temporal divergence

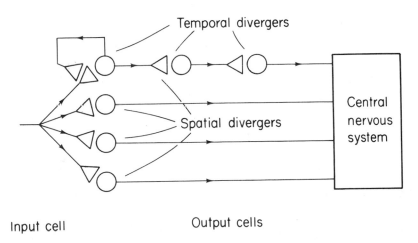

FIG. 7.1 Diagram illustrating the nature of (a) spatial convergence and (b) spatial and temporal divergence. (From Uttal, 1975b.)

A third logical possibility arising from spatial convergence is somewhat more complex. Given our knowledge of the summative nature of interactive synaptic actions, "majority" logical processes could occur in which the output was determined by the relative weighting of several simultaneous inhibitory and excitatory inputs. Thus a postsynaptic neuron might fire only if the sum of the incident excitatory inputs exceeded the sum of the incident inhibitory inputs.

A fourth possible form of convergent network organizational logic also exists. If any one of the inputs of a convergent neural network is capable of eliciting a postsynaptic response, then the circuit functions as an "or" logical unit.[2] If two or more inputs occur, the result is the same as if any one occurred.

All four of these forms of convergent spatial interaction are alternate means of processing neural information in a systematic and meaningful manner. Such primitive integrative logical processes provide the means by which incoming patterns of information are transformed to other patterns—some simpler and some more complex. Such neural transformations are not trivial; they ultimately underly the rich diversity of behavioral variability that results in all that is worthwhile in human life.

Spatial convergence also leads more directly to another measurable property of a neuron—the receptive field—that is of relevance to our discussion of sensory, and in particular, visual mechanisms. The receptive field, a property of an individual neuron, is defined as the area in the external environment in which a stimulus will elicit activity in that neuron. Because each visual neuron, for example, probably receives inputs from a number of preceding neurons, and the initial ones are the retinal receptors, the array of receptors that can produce activity in the higher-level visual neurons will be distributed over some substantial retinal area. Thus each central neuron that is driven by photic stimulation always has a field of view representing the receptive areas of a relatively large number of photoreceptors. It should be remembered, however, that the criterion for the definition of a receptive field is the external stimulus field and not the retinal area. Receptive fields of individual neurons at all levels of the nervous system vary in shape, in size, and in their dynamic and temporal properties. Thus they exhibit temporal-spatial feature filtering capabilities. In all cases, however, these properties are a direct result of the primitive spatial convergence of the activity of many peripheral receptors on a single more central neuron. Figure 7-1a, in picturing spatial convergence, thus is also a model of the neural arrangement leading to the existence of receptive fields.

[2] It is interesting to note that in computer theory only an "and" and an "or," or either an "and" or an "or" together with an inverting circuit (capable of changing a positive to a negative signal, or vice versa), is required to form the "simplest set." A simplest set refers to the smallest set of logical units capable of implementing any logical process no matter how complicated. Although use of the simplest set is uneconomical in terms of the total number of units required to produce any particular logical circuit when one is dealing with computers, the use of such a simplest set might be plausible in a system like the brain in which units are extremely abundant.

b. Lateral Inhibitory and Excitatory Interactions

Spatial convergence and divergence stress the longitudinal organization and integrative capability of the nervous system. Lateral interactions among neurons at the same level, however, also play an important role in information processing within single levels of the nervous system. Lateral interactions among the receptor units of vertebrates and invertebrates is now a widely accepted concept. Hartline and his co-workers were the first to demonstrate reciprocal interactions between neighboring receptors of the compound eye of the horseshoe crab. The concept of antagonistic inhibition and excitation has been extended to the vertebrate eye by Kuffler (1953) and Barlow and Levick (1965). It is now widely accepted that lateral interactions in the periphery are fundamental to such important perceptual processes as the intensification of contours.

In the horseshoe crab eye, Hartline and his collaborators (e.g., Hartline, Wagner, & Ratliff, 1956; Hartline & Ratliff, 1957) have demonstrated that the receptor neurons are interconnected in a purely inhibitory fashion. Activity in one neuron inhibits activity in a neighboring one as a function of (a) the distance between the two neurons, and (b) the amount of activity in the inhibitor. The action is reciprocal in that interconnected receptors inhibit each other. Thus simultaneous stimulation of two receptors leads to a much smaller amount of activity in each than when they are separately stimulated. Figure 7-2 demonstrates this basic form of inhibitory interaction.

Kuffler has shown that a somewhat different interactive organization appears to characterize the vertebrate eye. Receptors located in concentric and antagonistic portions of a receptive field of a single central neuron commonly interact in excitatory as well as inhibitory modes. Thus, in some cases, activation of some receptors can lead to an increased activity and in others to inhibition in the central neuron. Figure 7-3 depicts the result of this form of bivalent lateral interaction in the vertebrate eye. Figure 7-4 graphically diagrams the difference in the pattern of interaction between neurons in the receptive fields of invertebrates and vertebrates respectively.

Can inhibitory interactions also occur between levels of the visual system as well as at the same level? Fuortes and Simon (1974) have shown that a similar form of inhibition is, indeed, produced by a feedback process from the horizontal cells to the photoreceptors in the turtle eye. Thus, though I have stressed lateral (within level) inhibition in these comments, it seems highly likely that inhibitory interaction is also to be found between neural levels.

c. Temporal Interactive Processes

The interactions just described illustrate integrative mechanisms that operate to combine spatially disparate information. All responses were implicitly assumed to be functionally simultaneous in the preceding discussion. It is possible, however, that in addition to spatial integration of this sort, a sequence of signals

(A)

(B)

FIG. 7.2 Sample records showing the reduction in activity in one neuron (A) as a result of lateral inhibitory interaction from a second one (B). (From Hartline, Wagner, & Ratliff, ©1956, with the permission of The Rockefeller University Press.)

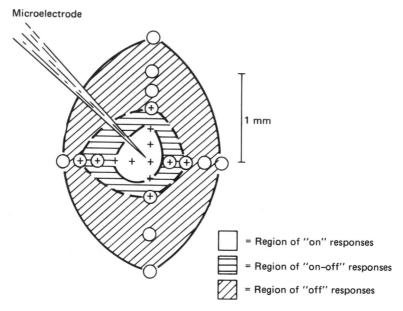

Microelectrode

1 mm

☐ = Region of "on" responses

▤ = Region of "on–off" responses

▨ = Region of "off" responses

FIG. 7.3 Organization of a receptive field in the cat's retina. In this particular ganglion cell's receptive field, a center region capable of only producing "on" responses is surrounded by a middle ring of "on–off" sensitivity and then a larger annulus of purely "off" responses. (From Kuffler, ©1953, with the permission of The American Physiological Society.)

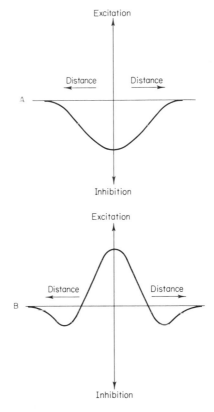

FIG. 7.4 Two diagrams showing the nature of the interaction between the receptor cells in invertebrate and vertebrate visual organs. In the upper figure, the invertebrate pattern of interaction is seen to be entirely inhibitory and typically drops off with distance. In the lower picture, the typical vertebrate pattern is displayed — a center-surround type of interaction. In the particular case shown, there is an excitatory summation within the central region but a ring of inhibition surrounding the central region.

appearing at a single neuron might interact over a period of time to alter, for example, the postsynaptic information pattern. This interaction of temporally dispersed signals is referred to as *temporal summation* (or *inhibition*). This concept usually connotes the ability of an excitatory signal to cumulate its effects in such a way that a temporal series of subthreshold signals in concert can achieve something that a single input signal cannot.

Temporal summation of inhibitory or excitatory influences does not simply increase or decrease the probability of a response. It can also have profound effects on what information is passed on by a neuron and may act in highly selective ways to specify the decoding capabilities of a given synapse. For example, the effect of a presynaptic volley of stimuli can be either excitatory or inhibitory in the same postsynaptic neuron, depending upon the frequency of impulses in that volley (Wachtel & Kandel, 1967). Obviously, the temporal characteristic of an integrative synapse is also a powerful means of controlling the information transmitted.

It is also possible to amplify temporally the effects of a single presynaptic impulse by means of a "repeater" action produced by a simple feedback circuit. For example, Fig. 7-5 shows a recurrent feedback loop in which the output of the postsynaptic neuron functions to delay and then reproduce an input to the presynaptic neuron. In this manner, a single presynaptic pulse may be recirculated so that it is extended into a train of pulses. Of course, this simple circuit would continue to recirculate a simple input until the animal died, unless it were terminated by some inhibitory mechanism. Presumably, this sort of recurrent process could only work satisfactorily if it were part of a more complex net that also has some kind of an effective turn-off mechanism.

These basic mechanisms of neural interaction have been observed in various preparations. The details of their operation are not, however, at the level of greatest interest in the context of this chapter. In the subsequent sections of this chapter, I consider the next level of neuronal information processing, which arises from these basic interactive processes—the spatio-temporal trigger or feature sensitivities, which are thought by some to be the direct neural equivalents of certain psychological processes. The important point of this preceding material is that these basic mechanisms of neuronal interaction are the basis of these selective properties exhibited in the records from individual neurons at higher levels. The "feature filtering" *neurons,* therefore, should more properly be considered indicators of the processes going on in feature filtering *networks.*

2.   A Germinal Study—"What the Frog's Eye Tells the Frog's Brain"[3]

Prior to the 1960s, the typical stimulus used in many neurophysiological experiments was an impulsive (i.e., brief transient) click or flash of light (or, as H. L. Teuber put it, "bolts of lightning and crashes of thunder") with little complex structure and no temporal or spatial patterning. In 1959, Lettvin, Maturana, McCulloch, and Pitts published a very important paper that was to influence research for the next two decades. The major impact of this paper lay in its suggestion that because the stimuli with which the organism usually deal are not simple impulsive stimuli, there is no reason to assume that the neural organization had evolved to deal with impulsive stimuli either. Rather, they suggested that more natural properties might be especially effective.

Lettvin and his colleagues' paper concerned the responses recorded from single fibers of the optic nerve or their terminal branches in the superior colliculus (the tectum) of the frog. Most insightfully, they entitled their paper "What the Frog's Eye Tells the Frog's Brain," a whimsically anthropomorphic title that emphasizes the notion of complex processing in the periphery rather than merely passive mosaic reproduction and transmission of the stimulus patterns. This work has stimulated an enormous amount of research in which the

[3]Parts of the next two sections are adapted from Uttal, 1973.

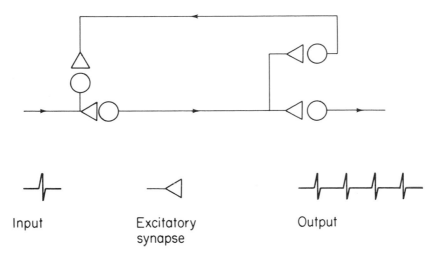

Input   Excitatory   Output
               synapse

FIG. 7.5   Diagram illustrating the nature of reverberation produced by positive feedback in neural nets. (From Uttal, 1975b.)

temporal and spatial pattern of a stimulus came to be considered as important as, if not more important than, its intensity, extent, or its onset and offset times. There is no question as to the fundamental importance of this new idea. Their own simple and clear statement of the sort of thinking that led these investigators to this most significant conceptual breakthrough is well worth quoting here:

> The assumption has been that the eye mainly senses light, whose local distribution is transmitted to the brain in a kind of copy by a mosaic of impulses. Suppose we held otherwise, that the nervous apparatus in the eye is itself devoted to detecting certain patterns of light and their changes, corresponding to particular relations in the visible world. If this should be the case, the laws found by using small spots of light on the retina may be true and yet, in a sense, be misleading [Lettvin, Maturana, McCulloch, & Pitts, 1959, p. 1942].

This paper by Lettvin and his colleagues initiated an era in which neurophysiologists for the first time adequately took into account several important facts. First, peripheral neurons are capable of responding differentially to complex stimulus patterns in a manner transcending simple registration and transmission. Second, complex stimulus patterns may produce responses that are not predictable on the basis of a mosaic-like replication of the spatial pattern. Third, the types of responses that are recorded in the frog's visual system (and probably in all neural nets) are associated in a meaningful way with the environmental challenges faced by the animal. The frog does not live in a world of static spots of light or of diffuse fields of undifferentiated stimuli. It lives in a patterned world containing flies and dragonflies and, for that matter, snakes and hawks. These complex stimuli are better modeled by moving spots, or moving convex edges (in other words, by complex spatio-temporal patterns), than by stationary dots or forms. One of the most surprising results emerging from this seminal work, and that of other laboratories exploring similar processes, is that specific pattern detection mechanisms occur as peripherally as the retina in at least some species.

Lettvin and his colleagues made other important conceptual contributions in that important and germinal paper. At the time it was published, the statement that different anatomical types of retinal neurons could be associated with specific classes of behavioral responses seemed improbable. Yet, as we see from the following, evidence is accumulating that this is exactly the case. Specifically, the key idea is that the different anatomical types of the ganglion cell are functionally differentiated by the differing spatial distributions of their dendritic trees. Such differences in the extent and nature of the arborization allow various manners of interconnection to the more peripheral neural levels, which include the bipolar and amacrine cells of the frog's retina; this means that each type can selectively receive and emphasize a different specific spatio-temporal distribution of excitation and inhibition from the more peripheral neurons.

The unique contribution of Lettvin, Maturana, McCulloch, and Pitts depended upon their realization that the older stimulus paradigms were incomplete from both adaptive behavioral and neurophysiological viewpoints. To make more realistic visual stimuli, they developed a 14-in. aluminum hemisphere upon which small dots, rectangles, and other stimulus shapes could be attached and moved by external magnets. Figure 7-6 is a drawing of the stimulus arrangement, showing the hemisphere upon which the stimulus was placed and the arrangement of the apparatus, which held the platinum-black-coated metal electrodes inserted into the optic nerve or the superior colliculus through a hole in the frog's skull.

By examining the effects of a variety of stimulus patterns, four different classes of optic nerve fibers emanating from the ganglion cells were found. First, they discovered a certain group of unmyelinated fibers, which was responsive to contrast, per se. A difference in the brightness of two portions of the visual field led to continuous firing of this type of cell. These "sustained contrast" cells had the additional property of being able to maintain activity for over a minute after the stimulus was removed. Furthermore, the output of these cells saturated at low stimulus intensity and did not vary with further increases in stimulus intensity.

The second type of unmyelinated fiber, which Lettvin and his colleagues referred to as the "net convexity detectors," responded only to small moving spots (a fly?) but not to large moving objects unless they entered the receptive field of the cell corner first. Dotted or checked patterns, even though containing small units, were not able to activate these fibers. The particular adaptive utility of such a fiber was best expressed by the authors:

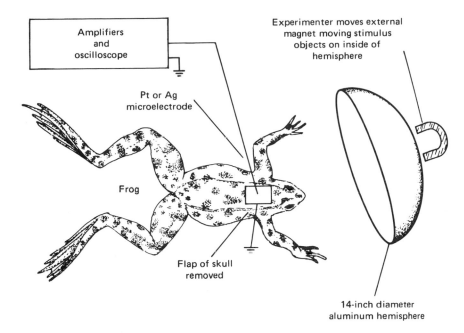

FIG. 7.6   The experimental arrangement used in the Lettvin, Maturana, McCulloch, and Pitts (1959) experiment. (From Uttal, 1973.)

A delightful exhibit uses a large color photograph of the natural habitat of a frog from a frog's eye view, flowers and grass. We can move this photograph through the receptive field of such a fiber, waving it around at a seven inch distance: there is no response. If we perch with a magnet a fly-sized object 1° large on the part of the picture seen by the receptive field and move only the object, we get an excellent response. If the object is fixed to the picture in about the same place and the whole moved about, then there is none [Lettvin, Maturana, McCulloch, & Pitts, 1959, p. 1945].

A third class, but in this case made up of neurons with myelinated fibers, was solely responsive to moving edges. A stationary edge, though of exactly the same shape, was totally ineffective in activating members of this third class of neuron. Is this the correlate of a dragonfly?

The fourth type included myelinated fibers that responded to any overall dimming of the field. This cell type, with its characteristically large receptive field, also possessed the fastest conducting axons. Is this fourth neuronal type behaviorally associated with the detection of predators? Whatever the evolutionary history of such a mechanism, it is a highly useful feature of the frog's neural mechanism, because it appears to be associated with some sort of a danger signal—such as the darkening of the sky as a hawk moves in for the kill—and an emitted escape response.

The four sets of neuronal axons observed in the optic nerve by Lettvin, Maturana, McCulloch, and Pitts sort out at the level of the superior colliculus or tectum. Each type projected to one of the four tectal layers, and each layer seemed to represent topologically the layout of the whole retinal mosaic. Thus the retinal image is represented four times in different layers, each of which is particularly responsive to a different class of features of the stimulus pattern.

Lettvin and his colleagues have suggested that the remarkable ability of the optic nerve (ganglion cell) fibers to respond to specific aspects of the spatio-temporal stimulus patterns is due to the fact that the differently shaped dendritic trees of the four types of ganglion cells sample a variety of different inputs from the bipolar and receptor layers of the retina. They used Cajal's (1911) classic microanatomy to link the associated neuron types with each trigger feature. Figure 7-7 shows the four types of ganglion cells that Lettvin's group interpreted from Cajal's work as prototypical of the frog's retina, identified on the basis of their neurophysiological behavior. Lettvin and his colleagues associated the sustained contrast detector with the constricted field ganglion cell, the convexity detector sensitive to small moving spots with the E type of ganglion cell, the moving edge detector with the H type, and the dimming detector with the broad tree.

Recently, Pomeranz and Chung (1970) reported a developmental study demonstrating that the four types of ganglion cells do not all appear at the same time in the metamorphic development of the tadpole. They also found that the adaptive significance of these cell types suggested by Lettvin and his colleagues was

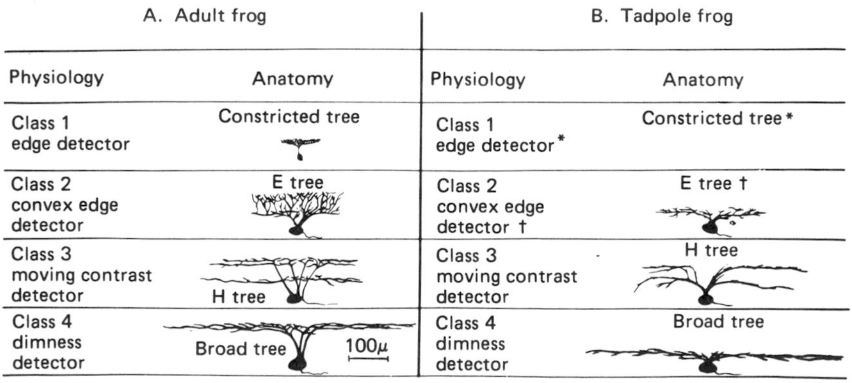

A. Adult frog		B. Tadpole frog	
Physiology	Anatomy	Physiology	Anatomy
Class 1 edge detector	Constricted tree	Class 1 edge detector*	Constricted tree*
Class 2 convex edge detector	E tree	Class 2 convex edge detector †	E tree †
Class 3 moving contrast detector	H tree	Class 3 moving contrast detector	H tree
Class 4 dimness detector	Broad tree 100μ	Class 4 dimness detector	Broad tree

FIG. 7.7   The four types of ganglion cell dendritic arborizations found in the adult frog and in the tadpole and the associated spatio-temporal specificities suggested by Lettvin and his colleagues. (*) Absent from tadpole; (+) absent from tadpole's retinal periphery. (From Pomeranz & Chung, ©1970, with the permission of The American Association for the Advancement of Science.)

supported when the presence or absence of a specific neuron type was compared with the relative ability of the tadpole or adult frog's retina to produce one of the prototypical feature-specific responses. Pomeranz and Chung found with microscopic examination that during the tadpole stage of the frog's development, the restricted field ganglion cell is totally absent, and the "E tree" ganglion cells are absent from the retinal periphery. These anatomical findings are also summarized in Fig. 7-7. Their electrophysiological recordings showed, correspondingly, that the "sustained contrast" type of response pattern was totally absent in the tadpole and that the "small spot convexity" detection process could not be observed in its peripheral retina. This correlation between microanatomy and process adds substantial support to the earlier speculations of Lettvin's group, which related specific cellular anatomy and physiologic response pattern on an intuitive rather than empirical basis.

Not all students of retinal physiology agree with this analysis, however. Rodieck (1973), for example, strongly criticizes these structural-functional associations made by Lettvin's group mostly on the historical grounds that the original associations drawn by them did not agree with the original fivefold cellular classification proposed by Cajal. Once again, theory, hypothesis, and controversy seem to take the place of simple "direct" empirical conclusions.

3. Another Germinal Research Program—Hubel and Wiesel's Cortical Bar Detector

a. The Concept of Cortical Columns

About the same time that the work just described was going on in Lettvin's laboratory, two other researchers were beginning to report what was to be a most remarkable series of studies of the organization and specific sensitivities of visual cells in the mammalian nervous system. Hubel and Wiesel had quickly moved to take advantage of a very sturdy new tungsten electrode developed earlier by one of them (Hubel, 1957) that allowed very long and stable periods of recording from single neurons in the central nervous system. The papers, which have been forthcoming from the continued collaboration of these two investigators, have compellingly established the fact that mammalian visual neurons also are sensitive to the spatio-temporal pattern of visual stimuli rather than simply to the quality of light.

In the first application of the new electrode, Hubel (1959) observed a specific sensitivity of neurons of the cat's visual cortex to the spatio-temporal features of stimulus patterns similar to the response patterns Lettvin and his colleagues had discovered in the frog's optic nerve and tectum. Recording from the striate cortex of unrestrained cats, Hubel had found large numbers of neurons that were unaffected by the general level of retinal illumination but that produced large amounts of spike activity when a small spot of light was moved across the retina. Not only was movement necessary, but those neurons also seemed to respond maximally to a specific direction of movement. In a paper later that year, Hubel and Wiesel (1959) mapped out the shape and polarity of the receptive fields of these neurons and showed that these fields were organized somewhat differently than those observed earlier in the retina of cats by Kuffler (1953). Rather than concentric rings of inhibition and disinhibition, the antagonistic regions in the cortex were usually arranged in side-by-side linear patterns.

Although all of the cortical neurons mapped did not require movement to elicit responses, the responses were enhanced from most neurons when the stimulus was an oriented line or an edge moving broadside at right angles to the long axis of the neuron's receptive field, as shown in Fig. 7-8. The responses of many of these neurons seemed to be dependent not only upon movement and a preferential direction but also upon the shape of the moving stimulus. Whereas bars of light were effective for some neurons, dark bars or moving edges were found to be the best stimuli for others. Presumably, the effectiveness of these rectangular stimuli is associated with the shape of the receptive field and the adjacent elongated regions of inhibition and excitation.

It is important in the following discussion to keep the distinction between *orientation* sensitivity and *direction of movement* sensitivity separate. For most of the cortical elements discussed, the most important property is their selectivity to stimulus patterns that are *oriented* at a particular angle rather than to

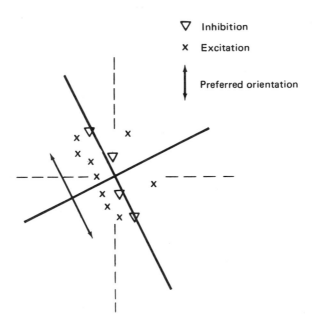

FIG. 7.8   A typical linearly arranged receptive field of a cat's visual cortex neuron with side-by-side antagonistic excitatory and inhibitory regions. (From Hubel & Wiesel, ©1959, with the permission of the *Journal of Physiology*.)

movement in a particular direction. The issue is sometimes confounded because one of the best ways to provide intermittent oriented stimuli is to move them across the receptive field of a central neuron.

Hubel and Wiesel (1962; 1963) made another important discovery about the cortical organization of the moving bar detectors; they were organized into vertical columns. Suggestions had previously come from electrophysiological work in some of the other senses (e.g., see Mountcastle, 1957, for a discussion of the column organization of the somatosensory cortex), as well as from anatomical studies showing such vertical patterns of organization (see Chapter 3). The cells of the primary projection areas of the sensory cortex seem to be in general arranged in functional as well as structural columns oriented normal to the surface of the brain. Columnar organization of a similar kind also seems to be characteristic in intrinsic regions of the brain (see Mountcastle, Lynch, Georgopoulos, Sakata, & Acuna, 1975).

Hubel and Wiesel showed that as a microelectrode penetrated into the successive layers of a single vertical, cortical column, the experimenter would pick up spike trains from a succession of individual cells, all of which behaved in the same way. An important observation was that each cell in the penetration series was specifically sensitive to movement of a line stimulus in the same orientation with respect to the receptive field. Of course, it was not always possible to keep the microelectrode within one column in their experiments; it seemed, however, in these early studies when the microelectrode emerged from one column and entered another, the preferential direction of activation almost randomly changed to any new orientation and remained so oriented until the electrode entered another column. Figure 7-9 shows the results for a penetration in which the electrode had fortuitously remained in a single column during the entire course of its penetration and for a penetration in which it did not.

Recently, however, Hubel and Wiesel (1974) (and Wiesel & Hubel, 1974) have changed their view concerning the arrangement of the orientation sensitive columns. They have conducted an extensive series of investigations that suggest that the columns are not randomly ordered on the surface of the cortex, as they had originally thought, but rather are organized in a highly systematic fashion. The key procedural trick that clarified this important issue was that the microelectrode penetrations were intentionally made, in this case, at oblique orientations to the surface of the cortex. In their earlier experiments, every effort had been made to make the penetrations perpendicular to the surface of the cortex to maximally elucidate the role of the individual vertical columns. In this case, the goal of the experiment, however, was to determine the relationship between adjacent columns.

The results of one of Hubel and Wiesel's penetrations are illustrated by the graph shown in Fig. 7-10. As the microelectrode was advanced, it encountered a systematic variation in the preferred orientation of the neurons that were sequentially sampled. This particular record shows a sequence of orientation sensitivities that, at first, is progressively more clockwise and then, at a penetration

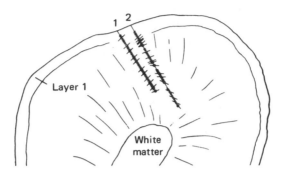

FIG. 7.9   Two parallel pathways of microelectrodes into the cat's visual cortex. One of the tracks apparently has slid down a column in which all of the cells have specific sensitivities in the same direction (1). The other track (2) crosses from column to column hitting many cells with different directional sensitivities (as indicated by the small cross lines) in sequence. (From Hubel & Wiesel, ©1963, with the permission of the *Journal of Physiology*.)

distance of about 1mm, reverses so that the neurons subsequently encountered are oriented progressively more counterclockwise. There is, therefore, contrary to their early interpretations, apparently a high degree of order observed as the electrode advances.

This change in opinion regarding the organization of the cortical columns is more than just a trivial empirical matter. It is fundamental and strikes at the very foundation of the whole theory of cortical organization that I have discussed so far in this section and in Chapter 3. The issue involves no less than the very existence of the cortical columns themselves. In an important analysis of the problem, Arnold Towe (Towe, 1975) has considered some of the theoretical implications and practical predictions of the hypothesis of columnar organization. He notes that the columnar hypothesis (a theory of discrete organization) is the antagonist of a continuous, or analog, hypothesis of topographic arrangement that asserts the alternative interpretation that the properties of the neurons of the cerebral cortex are simply less and less alike the further apart they are. Of the several implications of the cortical columnar hypothesis, the most distinctive and distinguishing corollary is the proposition that the boundaries between adjacent columns of differing properties are sharply demarcated and that adjacent columns should differ greatly in their preferred orientation sensitivity. In fact, Towe notes that this idea of sharp boundaries is the essential and unique premise of the columnar hypothesis. Without sharp boundaries and irregular order of columnar sensitivities, the topographic and columnar hypotheses simply fade into each other and cannot be distinguished. Towe also questions the ability of the current electrophysical research instrumentation to measure the columns

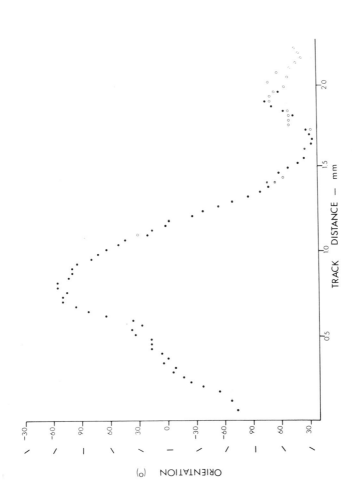

FIG. 7.10 This graph shows the extremely regular transition in preferred orientation angle of single cells in the monkey's visual cortex as an electrode is driven obliquely through this part of the brain. Open circles indicate responses driven by the contralateral eye; closed circles indicate responses driven by the ipsilateral eye. (From Hubel & Wiesel, ©1974, with the permission of the Wistar Press.)

precisely, even if they do exist. He thus has raised a question concerning the validity of a concept that has become almost axiomatic in contemporary neurophysiology.

Even though Towe, himself, says that this matter cannot be resolved now, it is important to keep the fundamental question of the existence of the columns in mind. More generally, it is important to remind ourselves that even the most "empirical" observation, such as columnar organization, in the final analysis, is really a neurophysiological or anatomical hypothesis or "theory" rather than an "established fact."

b.   Neuronal Feature Sensitivity

Hubel and Wiesel (1965) have discovered that the spatio-temporal specificity of the cells in the mammalian cortex involves at least four different kinds of cellular feature extractors. Some cells displayed the simple shape, orientation, and direction of movement specificity that I have already discussed. The three other classes, however, seemed to include cells that responded to more complex features than did this primitive simple type of cell. In fact, there appeared to be a hierarchy of complexity—simple, complex, lower-order hypercomplex and higher-order hypercomplex—in which each cell type had a progressively more complex set of criteria for activation. Some (the simplest ones) responded only to stimuli in a particular location and at a particular orientation; others (the more complicated ones) responded to multiple positions and directions but still required a particular movement, direction, and shape for their optimal activation. The specific sensitivities of each of the four types are presented in Table 7-1, which has been summarized from Hubel and Wiesel (1965).

The fact that some of the more complex cells seem to possess properties that could possibly be explained by the convergence of the outputs of a number of neurons of the more simple levels suggests a hierarchical organization of these cortical cells. The sensitivity of more complex neurons, it was suggested, could be produced by the integration of inputs from several simpler types. Thus, at first it was thought that the more complex neurons were located further along the visual pathway. Now however, it seems clear that neurons of all levels of complexity are to be found in the visual area 17, the first receiving area of the thalamic cortical pathway. Thus, to survive at all, the notion of a hierarchy of complexity detectors had to be maintained in a somewhat altered form in which the progression in complexity was from one vertical lamina of a given region of the visual cortex to another, rather than from one visual region to another. Even this modified form of the hierarchical hypothesis, however, does not seem to fit the available data too well, as we now see as I discuss the work of Kelly and Van Essen.

The very existence of feature detectors does suggest, however, that there may be structural explanation of the functional differences observed between the different kinds of neurons. Two particularly interesting experimental studies of the

TABLE 7.1

Cortical cell types sensitive to specific aspects of the temporal-spatial pattern of visual stimuli. (Adapted from the discussion in Hubel & Wiesel, 1965.)

Cortical cell type	Best stimulus shape	Other stimulus conditions	Possible mechanism
Simple	Edges, bars, slits, all with preferred orientation of movement	Critically dependent on location within receptive field	Interaction of inhibitory and excitatory influences of receptive fields
Complex	Edges, bars, slits, all with preferred orientation of movement	Independent of location within receptive field	Integration of the output of a number of simple cells
Lower-order hypercomplex	Edges, corners, tongues, and angles of particular sizes	Specific to length of stimulus. Some cells required a stimulus exactly the width of receptive field. Others required one that ended (a tongue) within the field. Stimulus must not extend beyond a certain point.	Integration of the output of both inhibitory and excitatory complex cells
Upper-order hypercomplex	Edges, corners, tongues, and angles of particular size	Similar to lower-order hypercomplex. But in addition, cells of this group responded in two preferred directions 90° apart.	Integration of the output of two or more lower-order hypercomplex cells

anatomical and the biochemical properties that underlie the different kinds of visual cortical neurons are especially relevant and also contribute to our understanding of what sort of hierarchical organization may actually be present in these visual cortical neurons.

In one of these studies, Kelly and Van Essen (1974) directly compared, using an ingenious technique, the anatomical structure of visual cortical neurons and their electrophysiological sensitivities. They used a glass micropipette as an electrode to record the neurons' intracellular electropotentials. In this regard, their technique was more or less routine, even though the more common procedure for recording from cortical neurons had been to use an extracellular, electrolytically polished metal microelectrode. The glass microelectrode, in addition to containing the conductive electrolyte, also contained a portion of the fluorescent dye Procion yellow, which was iontophoretically injected into the cell after the electrophysiological potentials were recorded. The tissue was subsequently prepared for fluorescence microscopy in the usual way. A substantial portion of the cells that had been both electrophysiologically analyzed and filled with the Procion yellow dye were found when postmortem tissue was subsequently examined under an ultraviolet microscope. A definitive pattern of association was observed between the anatomically defined types of cortical neurons (see Chapter 3) and the functional categories proposed by Hubel and Wiesel.

Although the correlation of anatomical structure and physiological type was not perfect, it did turn out that most simple cells examined by Kelly and Van Essen were stellate cells of layer IV. On the other hand, complex cells most often seemed to be pyramidal cells in either the more superficial or in the deeper layers of the cortex. This anatomical separation of the simple and complex neurons is roughly in accord with what we know about the serial progression of information from layer IV, where sensory afferents from the lateral geniculate nuclei enter, to both the more superficial and deeper layers of the cortex. It thus provides some support for a simplistic theory of hierarchical organization in which simple cells feed information to complex cells.

Unfortunately, for any such hierarchical theory that suggests that hypercomplex sensitivites are subsequently produced by multiple inputs from complex cells, the hypercomplex and complex cells seemed to be distributed in the "wrong" way. Complex cells were found not only in layers II and III but also in layers V and VI, whereas the hypercomplex cells were found only in layers II and III. What an appealing hierarchical theory might have been supported if the hypercomplex cells had been found only in the most superficial and deepest layers (I and VI) and if the complex neurons had been found only in layers II, III, and IV. Unfortunately for this elegant theory, this appears not to be the case, and there now appears to be little support for a general hierarchical hypothesis. Instead, we are left only with the alternative hypothesis that the several different types of complex cells represent different concatenations of inputs from simple cells and that the level of complexity simply represents differences in qualitative sensitivities rather than an orderly hierarchy.

If the data obtained by Kelly and Van Essen are true reflections of the distribution of these neuron types, then factors other than anatomical hierarchy must be invoked to explain the distinctions between the different cell categories. One obvious alternative candidate is the actual pattern of interconnection of the neural network that impinges upon each kind of neuron. Some workers have suggested that inhibitory connections are responsible, in large part, for determining the specific spatio-temporal trigger properties of these visual cortical neurons. This theory has received considerable support from work such as that of Pettigrew and Daniels (1973). They utilized the properties of a remarkable chemical known as *bicuculline,* an akaloid derived from plants. Bicuculline is a strong antagonist of GABA (γ-aminobutyric acid), a substance that has been convincingly demonstrated to be a potent inhibitory synaptic transmitter substance (see Chapter 9).

Bicuculline, when administered intravenously in large doses, produces convulsions. These convulsions are thought to result from the reduction of the normal and necessary general inhibitory interaction that stabilizes brain function. The immediate source of these convulsions is usually attributed to the fact that bicuculline destroys the efficacy of the GABA-sensitive inhibitory synapses either by inactivating the GABA or its postsynaptic receptor sites.

Pettigrew and Daniels took advantage of bicuculline's ability to reduce the GABA-driven inhibitory signals to study the chemical sensitivity of the neural networks that may be responsible for the special feature sensitivities of the various categories of cortical neurons that Hubel and Wiesel had observed. Bicuculline was administered in doses that were insufficient to produce convulsions but that were sufficient to produce changes in the cortical neuron's response properties. The important result of their study was that the changes they observed in each of the three major categories of neurons (simple, complex, and hypercomplex) were different. For example, the simple neurons were affected least. There were no changes in their orientation or directional sensitivity. The only significant change in simple neuron behavior was diminishment in the general level of their activity.[4]

Complex neurons, on the other hand, showed marked changes particularly in the stimulus features that would selectively activate them. They also exhibited a substantial increase in their overall level of activity indicating a reduced level of inhibition. After the injection of bicuculline, complex neurons also seemed to lose their high degree of line orientation selectivity.

For hypercomplex neurons, the observed changes seemed to be similar to those observed in bicuculline-drugged complex cells. Unfortunately, the entire population of hypercomplex neurons studied consisted of only two cells. Nevertheless, the drugged sensitivities of these two cells were identical. Lines previously too long to produce a good response now became effective stimuli. This change implies that the inhibitory regions on the flanks of the hypercomplex receptive field had also been substantially diminished.

A summary of the changes occurring in each of these three types of neurons is shown in Fig. 7-11. This figure also illustrates the major result of the Kelly and Van Essen study just described. Simple cells are usually stellate cells in Layer IV, and complex and hypercomplex cells are typically pyramidal cells of other layers.

---

[4]In a more recent and much more extensive study, Sillito (1975), using the same technique, did report significant changes in the response pattern of simple neurons as a result of the iontophoretic injection of bicuculline. The changes, however, did differ from those observed in complex neurons, and the general argument, therefore, still holds.

The interpretation given to these results by Pettigrew and Daniels is that bicuculline specifically affects the pattern of inhibitory interactions that determines the sensitivity of each type of cortical cell. It is the particular pattern of inhibitory connections to which they attribute the specific feature-sensitive response characteristics of the various types of neurons rather than hierarchical convergence from one level of complexity to the next.

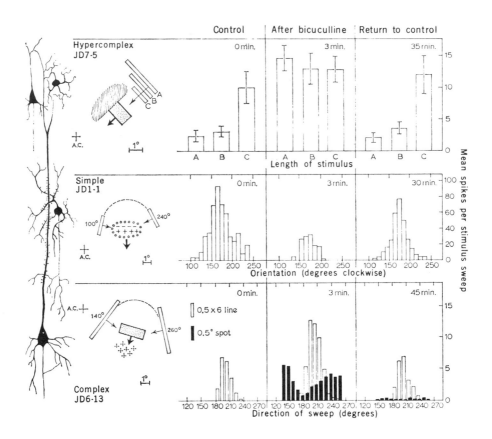

FIG. 7.11   This rather complex figure shows the effect of bicuculline on three different neurons in the cat's visual cortex. The results are indicated for simple, complex, and hypercomplex cells. In each case, the response sensitivity prior to the administration, during a period in which it is affected, and after a long-term recovery period are shown. The hypercomplex cell loses its ability to discriminate between stimuli of different lengths, the simple cell is reduced in sensitivity to a line oriented in the appropriate direction, and the complex cell increases its sensitivity to both a spot and the best line. In each case, the effect of the bicuculline is to alter the spatio-temporal sensitivity of each cell. Because bicuculline is known to act on inhibitory synapses, the selectivity sensitivity can be attributed to the pattern of inhibitory connections. (From Pettigrew & Daniels, ©1973, with the permission of The American Association for the Advancement of Science.)

This is an important idea, and it may be generalized to the following hypothesis: The characteristic behavior of any neuron is a function of its individual interneural connection pattern. It is remarkable, however, how little empirical justification this almost universally accepted hypothesis has. We still know little about the specific details of the patterns of synaptic interconnections among mammalian neurons. Each neuron is exceedingly complex and is typically examined anatomically or electrophysiologically only once, thence to be lost forever. It is probably not too much of an exaggeration to say that we do not know any of the details on interconnection of any particular mammalian neuron. Only such general facts as the relationship between the class of bipolars and the class of ganglion cells in the retina, as one example, or that inhibitory connections are responsible for feature selectivity, for another, are known. Even more important, however, is our almost total ignorance of the interactions that occur between functional assemblies of neurons such as the cortical columns just described. These functional assemblies and their interactions may be much closer to being the transactional equivalents (or codes) of mental processes than the individual neurons and their interactions. The latter simpler structures and processes may correspond, on the other hand, more closely to the basic functional mechanisms I discussed at the beginning of this chapter.

In invertebrate preparations, however, the neurons are large and occur reliably from one preparation to the next, and the network is simple enough so that we are beginning to unravel some of the details of their synaptic interconnections. Identified and named cells, particularly in arthropods and mollusks, have been studied in detail, and many of the facts of their individual synaptic arrangement have been worked out. For a complete discussion of this topic, the reader is directed to Chapter 8 or to Uttal (1975b, Chap. 11). Unfortunately, it is not at all clear that these invertebrate models of learning or perception are directly extrapolatable to neural explanations of analogous mammalian porcesses for reasons I have already discussed.

c.   Ocular Dominance

To return to the present context, however, there is another form of microscopic neural specialization to be observed in the primary striate and peristriate visual cortex of mammals that has also been elegantly elucidated by the continuing work of Hubel and Wiesel. They have recently made another important discovery (Hubel & Wiesel, 1968; 1972) using an anterograde degeneration technique in which selected lesions were made in the lateral geniculate body as well as electrophysiological recording procedures. A second pattern of spatial arrangement of neurons (in addition to the cortical columns oriented perpendicularly to the cortical surface) was discovered to exist in the occipital cortex. Hubel and Wiesel's studies indicated that occular dominance neurons (neurons preferentially activated by one eye or the other) were laid out over the cortex in alternating bands. This arrangement is shown in Fig. 7-12.

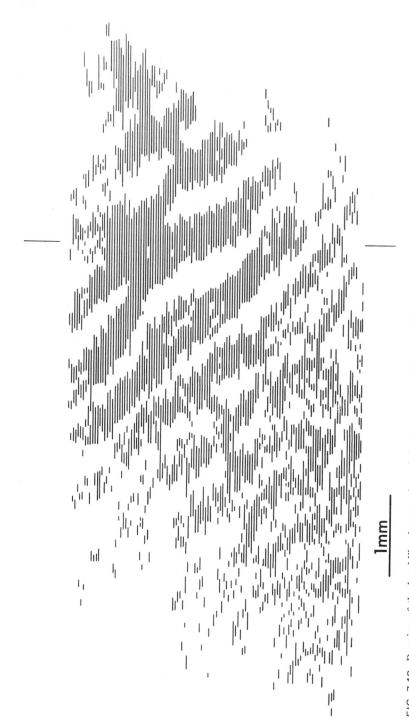

1mm

FIG. 7.12 Drawing of the band-like degeneration of the visual cortex following lesions of the lateral geniculate body of the thalamus. See text for details of the experiment and its significance. The two vertical lines indicate the point of sharpest curvature on the brain of the monkey. (From Hubel & Wiesel, ©1972, with the permission of The Wistar Press.)

The occular dominance bands themselves were also observed to be subdivided, depending upon which layer of the visual cortex was examined. Layer IV, the cortical layer in which the afferent axons that originate in the lateral geniculate terminate, was found to be populated by neurons that were exclusively driven by either one eye or the other. Deeper (Layers V or VI) or more superficial layers (Layers I, II, or III) were populated by neurons that were driven by a combination of left and right eye inputs with one or the other eye often dominant. This layering effect—and the differences in the function of the neurons at each of the levels—represents another form of microlocalization of function within the occipital lobe of the cortex.

The general arrangement of the two interwoven sets of orientation-sensitive columns and ocular dominance bands envisaged by Hubel and Wiesel is shown in Fig. 7-13. Although the columns may not exist in the randomly ordered form originally suggested by them, there is clearly a different role played by different portions of the cortex at this microanatomic level that is analogous to the more macroscopic differentiation of function to be observed in the macroanatomy of the cerebrum. This additional example of differentiation of function within adjacent microregions strongly attests to the fact that the brain is not acting as if it were a completely homogeneous unit and clearly illustrates how the problems of localization and representation fuse into each other at this microscopic level.

d. Feature Detection in the Inferotemporal Cortex

One further interesting example of just how specific individual neuronal representation of symbolic stimuli can be is found in a report by Gross, Rocha-Miranda, and Bender (1972). These psychobiologists studied the properties of cells in the inferotemporal cortex. Many neurons in this region display relatively large receptive fields and are sensitive to some of the same trigger features (e.g., shape and direction of movement) as the neurons found in the occipital cortex.

A few of the inferotemporal neurons they sampled, however, seemed to be selectively responsive to highly specific geometrical stimuli. One of the neurons, for example, was triggered to respond maximally by a pattern that looked like the monkey's own hand. Stimuli varying progressively from that ideal "trigger" shape evoked a progressively smaller response. Figure 7-14 shows an array of stimuli used by Gross and his colleagues to test the sensitivity of this cell.

It is moot just how far this notion of single units, specifically sensitive to particular geometrical forms, can be used to explain the phenomenological aspects of visual perception. The idea that each possible visual image has associated with it a particular "pontifical" neuron, individually and selectively sensitive to a "grandmother" or a "yellow Volkswagen," is neither empirically supported nor aesthetically pleasing. Curiosities like this "monkey's hand" neuron will continue to attract wide attention, but they may possibly be completely misleading in terms of the emphasis they place on a single neuron's response to particular patterns of stimuli, rather than on what I consider to be the much more appropriate consideration of the action of ensembles of neurons.

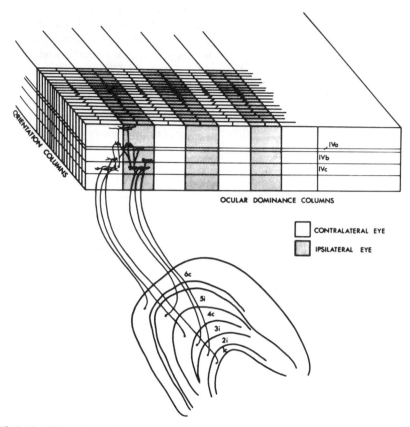

FIG. 7.13   This schematic drawing shows Hubel and Wiesel's conceptualization of the arrangement of the cortical columns and the ocular dominance columns in the monkey's visual cortex. Columns of cells mainly driven by one eye or the other alternate with each other. Running perpendicular to these columns is another organized set of columns that are selectively sensitive to a particular orientation of a line stimulus (as indicated by the small lines). The ocular dominance columns are driven by alternate layers of the lateral geniculate body of the thalamus as indicated. (From Hubel & Wiesel, ©1972, with the permission of The Wistar Press.)

4.   Spatio-Temporal Sensitivity in the Other Visual Centers of Mammals

The work of Lettvin, Maturana, McCulloch, and Pitts and that of Hubel and Wiesel has stimulated many other investigators to examine other centers of the ascending visual pathways for evidence of their representational mechanisms. Several investigators have found evidence of similar directionally sensitive cells at all other levels of the visual system, although with some curious species differences.

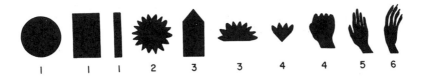

FIG. 7.14   A sequence of shapes progressively more capable of eliciting a response from a neuron in the monkey's inferotemporal visual cortex. This neuron seemed to be tuned to respond maximally to a stimulus approximating the shape of the monkey's hand. (From Gross, Rocha-Miranda, & Bender, ©1972, with the permission of The American Physiological Society.)

Arden (1963) was examining the receptive fields of lateral geniculate cells of the rabbit when he, too, discovered that small spots of light, which were relatively ineffectual stimuli when immobile, became remarkably effective when they were moved about in the receptive field. Not only was the movement of the spot necessary for the effective elicitation of responses, but many cells seemed to exhibit preferential sensitivity to movement in a given direction.

Kozak, Rodieck, and Bishop (1965) reported a comprehensive study of the effect of moving stimuli in the lateral geniculate body of the cat. They found directionally sensitive units but without the same narrow range of specificity reported by Hubel and Wiesel in the cat's cortex. However, when this work was extended to the cat's retina (Rodieck & Stone, 1965), they found that, although the center-surround arrangement was present and the responses were sensitive to such factors as size, shape, contrast, and speed of movement of stimulus objects, retinal cells were, in fact, not directionally sensitive![5] This finding is in sharp contrast to the observation of directional sensitivity in the retina of the pigeon (Maturana & Frenk, 1963) or of the rabbit (Barlow & Hill, 1963), as well as several other animals.

How can directional sensitivity arise out of the interaction of simple neurons, which are not themselves directionally sensitive? Perhaps the most instructive answer to this important question, using the rabbit retina as a model system, has been presented by Barlow, Hill, and Levick (1964). First, I discuss the details of their experimental procedure and some of their findings, and then I consider their neural model of directional sensitivity based upon the basic interactive mechanisms discussed earlier in this chapter.

Fine tungsten electrodes were inserted directly through the rabbit's sclera into the retina by Barlow, Hill, and Levick to obtain their recordings. Extracellular ganglion cell spikes are recorded in this manner, and this means, of course, that the responses observed reflect the integrative activity of at least two

[5]It now appears (Stone & Hoffman, 1972) that directionally sensitive neurons are present in the cat's retina but that they are relatively rare.

preceding synaptic levels and probably several other horizontal interactions. Barlow, Hill, and Levick report the presence of ganglion cells organized with antagonistic center-surround receptive fields, as well as ganglion cells that seemed to be activated solely on an "on" and "off" basis without the antagonistic surround arrangement. These latter cells, in particular, seemed to have specific sensitivities not only to the direction but also to the speed of the moving spot. Figure 7-15 (adapted from Barlow, Hill, & Levick, 1964) shows the differential sensitivity to direction of movement of a particular center-surround type of cell. It can be clearly seen that this cell is maximally sensitive when the stimulus is moving upward and declines in sensitivity to virtually zero response levels when the stimulus is moving downward. Intermediate directions of movement produce intermediate numbers of spike action potentials.

Barlow, Hill, and Levick also observed two other types of cells in the rabbit retina, in which the speed rather than the direction of a moving stimulus was critical in determining the amount of induced spike activity. One type had a rather large receptive field and proved to be maximally activated by rapidly

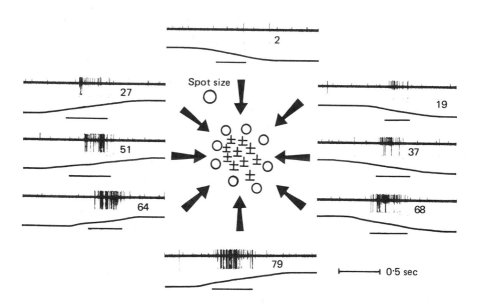

FIG. 7.15   Directional sensitivity in the ganglion cell of the rabbit retina, showing the response of a cell that is maximally sensitive to upward-moving stimuli and minimally sensitive to downward-moving stimuli. Numbers indicate spike count, and ± marks indicate the size of the receptive field in which both "on" and "off" responses were elicited by stationary spots. Curved lines indicate movement of stimulus; straight lines indicate periods of stimulus illumination. (From Barlow, Hill, & Levick, ©1964, with the permission of the *Journal of Physiology*.)

moving stimuli as shown in Fig. 7-16. On the other hand, there were also ganglion cells present, which had very small fields and were maximally activated by very slow-moving stimuli—a most unusual sort of specific sensitivity for which the adaptive utility is not immediately obvious. Such a response pattern is shown in Fig. 7-17.

Barlow and Levick (1965) have also shown that retinal direction sensitivity in the rabbit is primarily due to the sequence in which various portions of the receptive field have been stimulated. If a sequence is presented in the opposite order, then the effect of the stimulus would be nil or, in some cases, might even inhibit the level of spontaneous activity. They believe that some sort of *inhibitory* lateral interaction must be the basis of the sequence detection process.

That the interaction is inhibitory is not a conclusion that can be drawn a priori, because there are two complementary mechanisms—one excitatory and one inhibitory—which could produce exactly the same sort of directional sensitivity. Other tests must be made to determine whether an excitatory or inhibitory process accounts for this particular feature-detection process.

Perhaps the distinction between the two possible mechanisms can be made more clearly by considering two possible logical systems, as Barlow and Levick have done, each of which is capable of producing a response only when the stimulus is moving in a preferred direction. Figure 7-18 shows the two hypothetical nerve nets. One operates on the basis of an excitatory interaction; the output, indicative of movement in the preferred direction, occurs only when the stimulus activates a given receptor *and* the receptor that preceded it, in that order and at a particular interval. The other possible mechanism is based upon an inhibitory process; an output will occur if a stimulus activates a given receptor, but

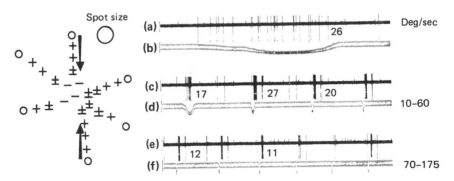

FIG. 7.16   Response of a cell with a large receptive field. This cell responds best to movements that are moderately rapid. (a), (c), and (e) are the spike responses resulting from the movement shown in (b), (d), and (f), which are photoelectric traces of the stimulating light (also showing considerable 50-Hz ripple from the power source). The small numbers indicate the number of spikes in the preceding burst. This cell obviously responds best to intermediate speeds of movement. Symbols as in Figure 7-15. (From Barlow, Hill, & Levick, ©1964, with the permission of the *Journal of Physiology*.)

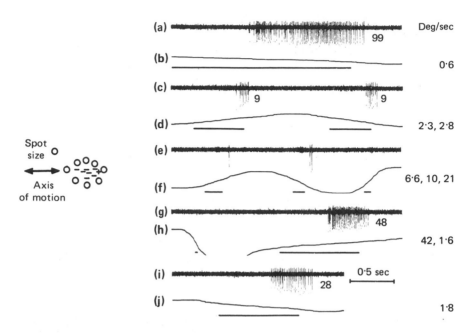

FIG. 7-17   Response of a cell with a small receptive field. This cell type responds best, sur-prisingly, to very slowly moving stimuli as indicated by the small number of spikes to rapid-ly moving stimuli and the large number evoked by slowly moving stimuli. Symbols as in Figure 7-15. (From Barlow, Hill, & Levick, ©1964, with the permission of the *Journal of Physiology*.)

only if the prior receptor has *not* been activated in the period defined by the time delay. In this case, the directional-sensitive mechansim is one based on the inhibition of a response that otherwise would have occurred. In the former case, a response can occur only if gated, or allowed, by an appropriately timed excita-tory response.

Barlow and Levick carried out experiments that showed that two spatially disparate stimuli activated in sequence produced a smaller number of spike ac-tion potentials than when the two were presented separately. This suggested to them that the mechanism for the sequence detection, and thus the directional sensitivity, was more likely to be an inhibitory mechanism than an excitatory one. To complete the story, some correlation must be shown between the hypo-thetical logical mechanisms and the known anatomy of the rabbit's retina. Fig-ure 7-19 is Barlow and Levick's schematic diagram of the anatomy of the rabbit retina. The function of the logical "and" units (the gating or allowing function) is performed by the bipolar cell, such that no output will occur unless both of the inputs are activated. Inputs from the horizontal cells are assumed to be main-ly inhibitory and able to prevent the bipolars from firing if a group of cells has already been activated at an appropriate prior interval. The conduction time of

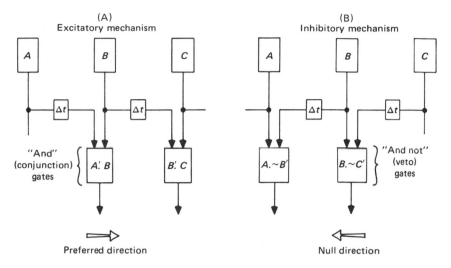

FIG. 7.18 Two equivalent logical circuits, both of which may display directional sensitivity, but which are based on (A) summation and (B) inhibition mechanisms, respectively. Δt is a time delay unit, which delays the signal from a preceding receptor sufficiently to allow either synchrony (thus enabling the "and" gate) or dysynchrony (thus enabling the "veto" gate) of inputs from adjacent receptor units. (From Barlow & Levick, ©1965, with the permission of the *Journal of Physiology*.)

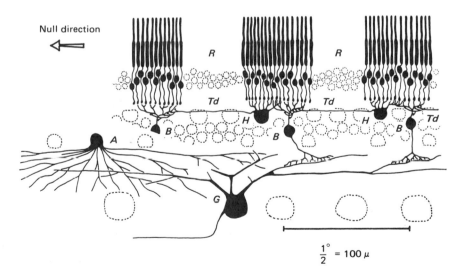

FIG. 7.19 A more anatomically reasonable model of the inhibitory circuit that, Barlow and Levick, feel, shows how certain known structures could fill the role of the logical unit shown in Figure 7.18. The indicated abbreviations are: R = receptor layer; Td = teleodendria of the horizontal cells; H = bipolar cells; A = amacrine cells; and G = ganglion cells. The ganglion cells act as the logical veto cells of Figure 7-18, and the horizontal cells serve to insert the time delay. (From Barlow & Levick, ©1965, with the permission of the *Journal of Physiology*.)

the horizontal cells is supposed to be identifiable with the time delays indicated in Fig. 7-18. As Barlow and Levick (1965) note: "The strength of the proposed scheme arises from the fact that a function can naturally be assigned to the neural elements that are known to exist without making esoteric or revolutionary assumptions about how they work [p. 497]." For the purposes of the present discussion, this model represents a sample of the sort of neural interaction that will probably have to be invoked to explain the action of feature-sensitive cells of varying degrees of complexity and hypercomplexity at all levels of the nervous system.

Specific physiological evidence of the inhibitory interconnection of the rabbit's retina, which underly this directional sensitivity, has been provided by Wyatt and Daw (1975). Similar directional sensitivity seems to be widespread throughout many vertebrates, both in the retina of rabbits, the ground squirrel (Michael, 1967; 1968), and goldfish (Wartzok & Marks, 1973), and at other levels of the nervous system as evidenced by the work of Hubel and Wiesel that I have already discussed.

It would be impossible to adequately review the abundant literature that has so definitively established that there are neurons in all levels of the visual nervous system of many different vertebrates that are selectively activated by particular temporal-spatial patterns of photic stimuli. Fortunately, there are excellent summaries of this research literature. For the retina, the work has been summarized best by Rodieck (1973) in what clearly is one of the most significant books in sensory neurophysiology to be published in this decade. The reader is referred to his chapters on the horizontal and bipolar layers (chap. XIV) and on the amacrine and ganglion cells (chap. XVI) in particular. For the central nervous system, the reader is referred to *The Handbook of Sensory Physiology* (1973) (Volume VII/3 part B) for excellent summary discussions; chapter 18 (Freund, 1973) deals with the neurophysiology of single neurons in the lateral geniculate body, and chapter 21 (Brooks & Jung, 1973) deals with the comparable results for neurons of the visual cortex of the cerebral hemispheres. Table 7-2 summarizes the trigger features for a number of vertebrate visual systems.

5.   On the Plasticity of Feature-Specific Neurons

The specific issue of the plasticity of the feature-specific neurons from which recordings are made at the several levels of the visual system has become of special interest in recent years to workers interested in perceptual representation. The problem is: Are the feature-sensitive properties and the receptive field organization of visual neurons affected by an animal's early experience? There are two possible answers to this query. One is that the feature sensitivity is dependent, in whole or in part, on the visual stimuli experienced in the animal's early development. The alternative answer asserts that the various kinds of feature specificity are essentially predetermined when the circuits are constructed during development and are the result of the animal's genetic heritage. The problem is complex and now beset by conflicting data. In this section, I bring the reader up to date on this important topic.

In 1970, two pairs of psychobiologists (Hirsch & Spinelli, 1970, 1971; and Blakemore & Cooper, 1970) reported results that they believed supported the contention that the orientation and form specificity of visual cortical neurons depends to a substantial degree upon the early experience of the experimental animal. Hirsch and Spinelli (1970; 1971), for example, demonstrated that if a cat was reared in such a way that one eye was exposed only to vertical lines and the other only to horizontal lines, subsequent tests of the receptive fields of monocularly activated cortical neurons from these animals showed them to be selectively sensitive to the orientation with which the eye had early experience. Cells that were driven by the eye that had seen only vertical lines had receptive fields with the axes oriented vertically. The cells driven by the eye that had seen only horizontal lines were characterized by a horizontal orientation of their receptive fields. Blakemore and Cooper (1970) and Blakemore and Mitchell (1973) produced essentially identical data. Figure 7-20 depicts this reputed selective effect of experience.

This was, if true, an extraordinary discovery. An important implication of this result was that the findings of the previous decade, from the laboratories of such workers as Hubel and Wiesel, on the shape of receptive fields were strongly determined by the environment in which their animals had been raised. It is entirely possible that the "biologically innate" receptive field organizations originally observed and thought to be only impaired by an absence of stimulation were at least partially environmentally determined.[6] Indeed, in retrospect, the fact that straight line sensitivity occurred so often when individual neurons were mapped should always have seemed to be something of a curiosity. Why should neural receptive fields exhibit that particular type of sensitivity to what is more often than not a man-made geometry? Of what adaptive utility would hypersensitivity to straight lines be to an animal that had evolved in a world that had few, if any, linear contours? Although the world may seem, at first glance, to be composed of straight lines (blades of grass and tree trunks), these contours usually are curved or irregular, and real linear segments are quite rare in nature except in the microcosm of crystal structure. A satisfying answer to these perplexing questions lies in the possibility that the receptive fields observed in lab-reared

[6]In the following discussion I deal mainly with the plasticity of the receptive fields of cortical visual neurons reared in visual environments with restricted orientation. A related but not identical problem concerns the impairment of visual neuron functions as a result of a *totally* deprived visual environment. This issue is not discussed in detail. There seems far less doubt about this latter issue. Many investigators have shown impaired function of neurons in animals that have been deprived of all visual stimulation. The reported effects include receptive field shape deficits (Ganz, Fitch, & Satterburg, 1968, Hubel & Wiesel, 1970, Shaw, Yinon, & Auerbach, 1974, and Wiesel & Hubel, 1963); as well as in binocular effectiveness (Blake & Hirsch, 1975).

TABLE 7.2

Trigger features of single neurons at the indicated level of the nervous systems of several species.
(Adapted from Barlow, Narasimhan, & Rosenfeld, ©1972 by the American Association for the Advancement of Science.)

Anatomical location	Trigger feature	Anatomical location	Trigger feature
	Goldfish		*Cat*
Retina	Local redness or greenness	Retina	Local brightening and dimming
	Directed movement	Lateral geniculate	Local brightening and dimming
	Frog	Visual cortex area 17	Simple cells: moving, slits, bars, edges with specific orientation
Retina	Convex edge		Complex cells: combinations of simple cell outputs of same orientation.
	Sustained edge		
	Changing contrast	Visual cortex area 18	Hypercomplex I cells: ends of lines
	Dimming		Hypercomplex II cells: line segments and corners
	Dark		
Optic tectum	Newness		
	Sameness		
	Binocularity		
	Pigeon		
Retina	Directed movement		
	Oriented edges		

Ground squirrel

Retina	Local brightening or dimming
	Local blueness or greenness
	Directed movement
Lateral geniculate body	Color coded units
Optic tectum	Directional units
	Oriented slits or bars
	Complex units

Rabbit

Retina	Local brightening or dimming
	Directed movement
	Fast or slow movement
	Edge detectors
	Oriented slits or bars
	Uniformity detectors
Lateral geniculate	Greater directional selectivity
Tectum	Habituating units

Infrequent types in cat

Retina	Directed movement
	Uniformity detectors
Lateral geniculate	Local blueness or greenness
	Binocular, directional, and orientational units
Optic tectum	Directed movement
	Complex units

Monkey

Retina	Local brightening or dimming
Lateral geniculate	Local redness, greenness, or blueness
	Various forms of color coding
Cortex	Similar to cat; some color coded
Inferotemporal cortex	Very complex; possible hand detector

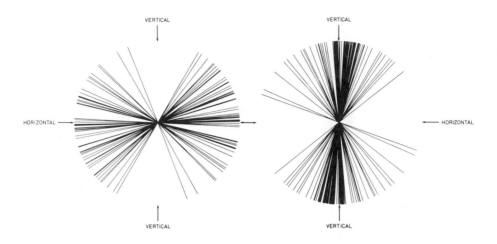

FIG. 7.20   Two polar histograms showing the purported results of an experiment in which kittens were reared in environments of only vertical or only horizontal lines, respectively. The authors believe that this restricted environment led to a shift in the distribution of orientation sensitivities as shown here. The left-hand figure shows the reported orientation preferences of visual cortex neurons obtained from an animal that had been reared in an environment of horizontal lines; the right-hand figure is the same sort of data for an animal reared in an environment composed only of vertical lines. However, see Figure 7-22 for an alternative set of data concerning this same problem. (From Blakemore & Cooper, ©1970, with the permission of Macmillan Journals Ltd.)

cats were the product of the man-made environment of straight lines with which they interacted during their upbringing.

The purported plasticity of cortical neurons is so important to theories of perceptual representation that the question of its validity became extremely pertinent. A number of workers even believe that the phenomena of neural plasticity is even more prevalent than originally thought. It has been reported not to be limited solely to single straight lines alone. Spinelli, Hirsch, Phelps, and Metzler (1972) report neurons that display sensitivity to much more elaborate properties of the training patterns. Some animals, brought up in an environment that contained three parallel lines, were shown to possess neurons that exhibited receptive fields. shaped like three parallel lines. Figure 7-21 shows an example of such a receptive field structure.

Furthermore, if a young kitten is brought up in an environment with no straight lines, or for that matter, no structure at all (e.g., a featureless white field), Pettigrew and Freeman (1973) have reported that there will be no linear structure to the cortical receptive fields. Rather, the cortical neurons seemed to

FIG. 7.21 These 12 computer-generated plots show the responsiveness of neurons in the visual cortex of cats that had been raised in an environment in which one eye had been exposed only to three vertical bars and one eye to three horizontal bars. Rows 1 and 2 are from a cell that responded best to a left-to-right movement of a small black dot. Rows 3 and 4 are from a cell that responded best to the right-to-left movement of the small black dot. Rows 1 and 3 indicate the positions in the receptive field at which the cell responded once to the moving dot; Rows 2 and 4 indicate the less dense positions at which the cell responded twice or more. The three columns represent the conditions in which both eyes (BE), the vertically experienced eye (VE), and the horizontally experienced eye (HE) were stimulated, respectively. There is suggestive evidence that the receptive field of the neuron studied in this case has been affected by the experience to display a three-lined pattern. (From Spinelli, Hirsch, Phelps, & Metzler, ©1972, with the permission of Springer-Verlag, Inc.)

them to typically display round receptive fields that are more sensitive to spots than to lines. These results also suggested that the linear nature of the receptive fields observed by Hubel and Wiesel and others may be due in large part to the experienced environment and should not be interpreted as necessarily having any special biological significance.

There has even been some suggestion that receptive field plasticity is not limited to early experience in kittens but may also be present in the adult cat. Creutzfeldt and Heggelund (1975) have reported that normal adult cats who were kept in the dark for 2 weeks (except for 1 hour each day in an environment of vertical lines) displayed a disproportionate number of cortical neurons that displayed vertically aligned orientation sensitivity. If this report is correct, rapid and continued adaptive plasticity of receptive field shape would be possible even in mature animals.

Unfortunately, there has been considerable controversy surrounding the findings of receptive field plasticity. [The reader is referred to Grobstein and Chow (1975) for an intelligent discussion of the issues involved.] Representational flexibility on the part of the receptive fields of the neurons of the visual cortex, although an exciting and desirable property, does not seem to be supported by as unequivocal a data base now (1976) as had been originally thought 6 years ago.

Two recent papers, in particular, challenge the general concept of receptive field plasticity in visual cortical neurons. Leventhal and Hirsch (1975) report an experiment in which kittens were reared in environments that selectively contained only diagonal or horizontal and vertical lines. Neurons with receptive fields that were oriented horizontally or vertically in the cortex of animals who had been raised in diagonal environments were relatively normal in performance and abundance. However, neurons that displayed receptive fields with preferred diagonal orientations occurred only when the animal was reared in an environment that contained some diagonal lines and not in those animals reared with only horizontal or vertical environments. Thus Levinthal and Hirsch suggest that there is some kind of a difference between horizontally and vertically oriented neurons, on the one hand, and diagonally oriented receptive fields, on the other. The former seem to be essentially innate and refractory to experimental effects, although the latter must be "recruited from a population uncommitted initially, whose orientation specificity is affected by the animal's early existence" (Leventhal & Hirsch, 1975, p. 904).

A much more serious discrepancy in the data, however, is to be found in the work of Stryker and Sherk (1975). They used a "blind" experimental design in which they did not know which group of kittens had been reared in a horizontally lined environment and which in a vertically lined environment. The electrophysiological recordings were also carried out with great care to sample from an adequately large region to avoid any biased sampling based on a differential distribution of orientation sensitivities across the surface of the cortex. With these careful controls, Stryker and Sherk were unable to measure any deviation from a random distribution of orientation specificities in animals with restricted early environments. Figure 7-22 shows the orientation sensitivities from seven cats; four had been reared in a horizontal environment and three in a vertical environment. The absence of any effect is clear, and the possibility that the entire story of plastic receptive fields was based on some sort of sampling error or scientific "illusion" is, therefore, upon us.

There is an important general methodological point to be made, and, although very important, it will be offensive to many neurophysiologists. If it does turn out that the story of receptive field plasticity is not valid, the error can, in large part be attributed to the generally sloppy research design typical of neurophysiological research. Unlike psychology, which has always been forced to use carefully sampled "blind" or "double blind" experimental designs because of the more obvious multivariate and subjective influences on their experiments, neurophysiology until recently has not had this tradition.

It may be a serious weakness in just the kind of research discussed here, and it may lead more frequently than is appreciated to situations in which the neurophysiologist sees what he wants to see or what is consistent with the contemporary scientific paradigm. The problem has now come to a head because of the increasing complexity of the problems being studied and the increased potential

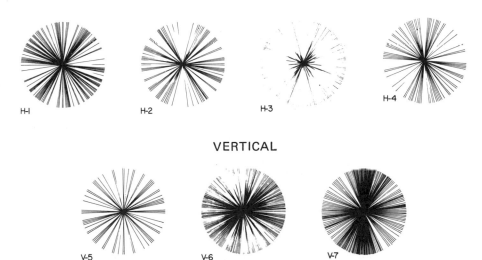

HORIZONTAL

H-1   H-2   H-3   H-4

VERTICAL

V-5   V-6   V-7

FIG. 7.22   Polar histograms, similar to those of Figure 7.20 but obtained using a double blind procedure. No effect of the rearing procedure is apparent in these experimental data. (From Stryker & Sherk, ©1975, with the permission of The American Association for the Advancement of Science.)

for erroneous sampling to lead to misleading conclusions. Neurophysiology may be greatly in need of the sophisticated sampling theories and rigorous controls that have characterized psychological research for the last half century.

6.   Fourier Analyzers in the Visual System— A Brief Comment

Analogy between different levels of scientific discourse, history, available mathematical and electronic equipment, and contemporary fad, all contribute to the evolution of scientific theories as we have seen in the several historical sections of this book. It is, therefore, not surprising that the concept of feature-specific visual mechanisms should be extended to other features than the simple types described in the previous sections. Rather, as mathematical tools for the analysis of spatial patterns have evolved, a number of mathematically trained psychobiologists have suggested new forms of visual information processing mechanisms that might also represent or encode visual stimuli.

One of the most influential of the contemporary alternative models of visual function is based upon the notion of Fourier spatial analysis. It is well-known that one-dimensional temporal patterns, e.g., speech sounds, are apparently frequency-analyzed by the auditory mechanisms. It was not well appreciated until the last decade or so, however, that two-dimensional integral mathematics of a similar kind are also applicable to spatial patterns, e.g., the stimuli encountered by the visual system.

In the remainder of this section, I consider the spatial frequency analyzer theory of visual perception in some detail. The reader is forewarned, however, that this discussion is severely critical of the hypothesis of Fourier channels in the visual system. My conclusion is that the theory of spatial frequency analyzers now appears to many psychobiologists to have been an interesting idea but one that was fundamentally erroneous in its physiological premises.

The general idea in one-dimensional frequency analysis is that any pattern no matter how complex can be analyzed into a family of sinusoidal (or any other orthogonal set) functions. In the acoustic domain high-frequency sinusoids represent regions of rapid change of acoustic pressure, and low frequencies represent regions of slow change of acoustic pressure. The analogy to the one-dimensional acoustic stimulus in visual space would be the two-dimensional spatial stimulus pattern. When a spatial pattern is Fourier analyzed, it is not decomposed into a family of pure sinusoidal time fluctuations but into pure spatial frequencies measured in cycles of brightness and darkness per degree of visual angle.

In this two-dimensional space, regions of rapid spatial change in brightness that occur over short distances are represented by high spatial frequencies. Regions in which the brightness only gradually changes are represented by low spatial frequencies. Application of the same sort of mathematical logic on which

Fourier analysis is based (but in two dimensions rather than one) produces a new pattern which is the Fourier transform of the original stimulus. Figure 7-23b, for example, illustrates an optical Fourier analysis of the simple geometrical pattern shown in Fig. 7-23a.

Much of the current discussion of optical image processing is framed in similar mathematical terms. The use of optical Fourier analysis and image processing to filter out particular properties of patterns using the interaction of wavefronts of coherent light has become a powerful approach to image processing. Diffraction patterns produced by passing coherent light through transparencies (Lendaris & Stanley, 1970) are also a closely allied transform. Indeed, diffraction patterns in general can be considered nothing more than spatial Fourier transforms of the original stimulus pattern, and this analogy may have substantially contributed to the emergence of the theory.

It was within the context of this highly useful and totally unassailable application of modern mathematical optics that in 1968 Campbell and Robson suggested that at threshold the visual system was composed of a number of nearly independent *neurological* mechanisms that could be considered two-dimensional Fourier spatial frequency filters. They suggested further that these mechanisms or channels were relatively narrowly tuned so that each conveyed information only when the spatial frequency of a part of the stimulus was within rather narrow limits. To illustrate this point more clearly, Fig. 7-24 shows several sample stimulus patterns that vary only in their spatial frequency. Imagine a hypothetical neuron that varies in its responsiveness to the different spatial frequency stimuli.

Campbell and Robson and others have presented both psychophysical and neurophysiological evidence that they believed showed that at threshold the various channels were more or less independent and did not interact—the two essential criteria of their hypothetical spatial frequency analyzers. For example, in some of the experimental studies, gratings of particular frequencies were used to selectively fatigue, desensitize, or adapt what was presumed to be a narrowly tuned portion of the Fourier analyzing visual system. The response of the visual system to other stimuli with varying spatial frequencies appeared not to be affected to the same degree as stimuli of the conditioning frequency by this selective adaptation (Blakemore & Campbell, 1969). In related experiments, other visual psychobiologists (e.g., Kulikowski & King-Smith, 1973) have purported to show that a summatory interaction between two near threshold gratings occurred only when the two were rather close in spatial frequency. Indeed, this sort of procedure was used to measure the *bandwidth* of a particular "channel" by defining the bandwidth as the range of spatial frequencies that would summatively interact within a single channel to lower the detection threshold for a grating.

This sort of approach also led to a wide variety of other experiments based upon the premise that narrowly tuned spatial frequency-specific channels are

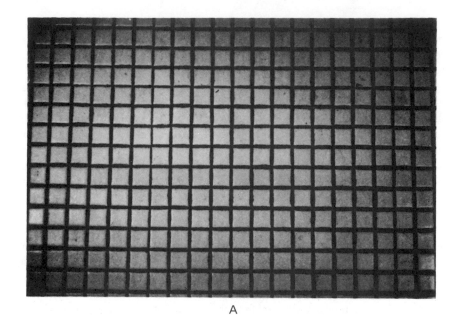

A

B

FIG. 7.23 (A) A grid of black lines on a white background that produces a strong illusion of diagonal lines. (B) A two-dimensional optical Fourier transform of (A) showing the complete absence of any diagonal line components. This comparison disassociates spatial frequency channels from the psychophysical result in a way that severely challenges the Fourier model. (From Schachar, ©1976, with the permission of The American Association for the Advancement of Science.)

476

present in the visual system. Electrophysiological studies included reports by Campbell, Cooper, and Enroth-Cugell, (1969); Campbell, Cooper, Robson, and Sachs, (1969); Campbell and Maffei, (1970); Enroth-Cugell and Robson, (1966). Psychophysical experiments of relevance included the work of Blakemore, Nachmias, and Sutton, (1970); Campbell, Nachmias, and Jukes, (1970); Campbell and Robson, (1968); Gilinsky, (1968); King-Smith and Kulikowski, (1975); Kulikowski and King-Smith, (1973); Sachs, Nachmias, and Robson, (1971); Stromeyer and Julesz, (1972); and Weisstein and Bisaha, (1972).

Furthermore, Pollen, Lee, and Taylor (1971) proposed a theory that assumes that the striate cortex is a massive Fourier analyzer in which strips of the visual field are processed by neurons sensitive to linear patterns. Ginsburg (1971) and Ginsburg, Carl, Kabrisky, Hall, and Gill (1976) have also shown a number of correspondences between the digital computer Fourier analysis of simulated stimuli and the human observer's perceptual responses to the same stimuli.

As suggested earlier, however, I believe there are a number of problems with this Fourier spatial analysis approach. First, it must be remembered that the whole concept of Fourier or frequency analysis, whether it be in the single-dimensional temporal domain, or in the two-dimensional spatial domain, is based upon the powerful generality of the procedure. Any pattern, the original theorem states, no matter how complex can be represented by a superimposition of a group of components such as a family of sine waves, square waves, or even triangular waves. Thus whatever aspect of two-dimensional visual space is being considered, whether it be the stimulus itself, the projected retinal pattern, or some higher neural representation, it is theoretically possible to represent the encoded pattern as a Fourier analyzed family of spatial frequencies even if there is no neural analyzer selectively sensitive to spatial frequencies actually present. The

FIG. 7.24 Three square wave gratings with differing spatial frequencies.

very generality of the approach, therefore, makes spatial frequency-tuned channels suspect as a specific theory of neural implementation within the visual system.

The specific *neurological* implication of Campbell and Robson's hypothesis, however, is exactly that the spatial channels do actually exist and, furthermore, that they are relatively narrowly tuned. These axioms of their theory are quite specific and amenable to experimental test. Unfortunately for anyone who wishes to obtain a positive answer to this question of the validity of the Fourier channel hypothesis, and in spite of the enthusiastic reception of their suggestion and the widespread popularity that has accrued to it, a pair of papers have now appeared that show that the channels probably do not exist in the physiological form proposed by Campbell and Robson.

Specifically, Stromeyer and Klein (1975) demonstrated that the detectability of a complex frequency modulated grating, such as that shown in Fig. 7-25a, cannot be accounted for by channels with narrow bandwidths. The spatial frequency components of such a signal are shown in Fig. 7-25b. Sufficient contrast to allow detection of this complex grating cannot be achieved by summation of any narrowly grouped adjacent set of those components. Rather, a channel having a bandwidth of at least an octave would be required for detection. Yet, subjects can make this detection. Thus it is unlikely that the Campbell and Robson "channels" are as narrowly tuned as they assert.

Another premise of the Campbell and Robson theory, as noted previously, is that the hypothetical spatial channels possess substantially different spatial frequencies and are functionally independent of each other. They should only weakly interact according to their theory. Specifically, they hypothesized that one grating should not be able to mask another unless the spatial frequency tuning curves of the two are close together. Henning, Hertz, and Broadbent (1975) have shown to the contrary, however, that masking interactions could occur in situations in which the spatial frequencies of gratings were as far apart as two octaves. Thus it is unlikely that the Campbell and Robson "channels" are noninteracting.

Another compelling suggestion that suggests that the Fourier analysis model of visual pattern perception is not as easily acceptable as some would hope has recently been published by Schachar (1976). He points out that there is a strong illusion produced when a grid such as that shown in Fig. 7-23 is presented to a subject. The impression of diagonal lines in this display is very powerful, especially when the grid is rotated 45 degrees. However, he points out that when an optical Fourier analysis is performed on the grid, the resulting transform (see Fig. 7-25b) shows no indication of the diagonal lines. The implication, therefore, is that the Fourier description does not adequately model the perceptual response. The disassociation of the theory and the percept, in at least this one case, suggests that the association in other cases may just be fortuitous and a result of the generality of the Fourier model rather than because there are real Fourier "channels" in the nervous system. Such specific failures of the theory of Fourier channels, if true, are probably lethal to the general idea of frequency-tuned channels although it may take a long time to get the idea out of contemporary thinking.

If these three new studies are correct in principle and execution, they strongly suggest that the spatial frequency-selective channels that were hypothesized by Campbell and Robson are neither narrowly tuned nor noninteracting and therefore may not exist in any real physiological sense. The basic premises of their hypothesis are, to a degree, challenged, and the general theory of the representation of visual form by specific spatial frequency-sensitive neural channels appears to be highly questionable.

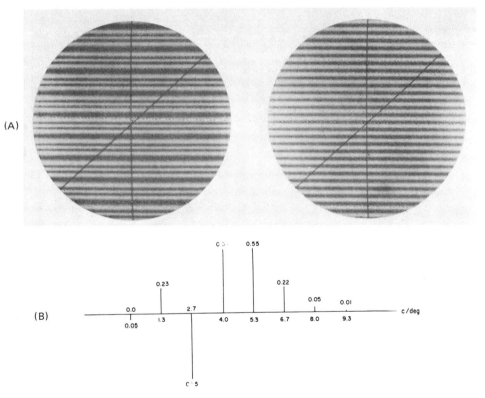

FIG. 7.25 One way to challenge the Fourier model is to show that regular and irregular patterns are equally discriminable. Such a result would severely challenge the idea that the channels are narrowly tuned. In this experiment, Stromeyer and Klein have demonstrated just that effect. They compared the detectability of pure sinusoidal patterns with sinusoidally modulated sinusoids (as shown in A on the right and left, respectively). The two were equally detectable in spite of the fact that the spectrum of the sinusoidally modulated sinusoid is as shown in B instead of the single line of the pure sinusoid. (From Stromeyer & Klein, ©1975, with the permission of Pergamon Press.)

It is important and fair, however, to indicate that the argument against the Fourier theory of visual perception is equally as tenuous as the one for it. Recently, a counter-criticism has been published by Graham and Rogowitz (1976), which specifically attacks the argument made by Stromeyer and Klein (1975), and a critique of Schachar's demonstration by Ginsburg is also said to be in press in *Science.* *

Even more fundamental is the fact that there are aspects of the Fourier model that are consistent with the generally emerging view that pattern perception processes may be mediated by neural mechanisms that are widely distributed throughout the brain. Indeed, later in this chapter I present my own personal favorite, the autocorrelation model, which is in agreement with this distribution corollary of the Fourier model. The autocorrelation theory differs from the Fourier model in its rejection of the notion of independent feature selecting channels (the weakest aspect of the Fourier model), in favor of a network of unspecialized and interacting neurons. What, hopefully, will be agreed upon someday is the idea that whatever spatial analysis is being performed by the brain is not based on independent and selective subcomponents (whether they be single cells or Fourier "channels") but on a more distributed process within the neural network that makes up the brain.

7. A Summary of Representation in the Central Visual Nervous System

In the preceding sections I have dealt only with a few specific examples of representative mechanisms in the visual nervous system. There are many other aspects that have been glossed over that are also extremely important, however. Fortunately, a brief tabular summary has been made of this material by Brooks and Jung (1973) that is particularly useful. Their tabulation of the important landmarks in this field is so succinct and inclusive that with their permission I have taken the liberty of making a modest number of modifications and reproducing it here in full.

Historical Landmarks of Neurophysiology Research on Visual Cortex Neurons (Adapted from a compilation by Brooks and Jung, 1973)

1. The first *extracellular neuronal recordings* in the cat's visual cortex (v. Baumgarten & Jung, 1952; Jung, v. Baumgarten, & Baumgartner, 1952). Half of the cortical neuronal population did *not respond to diffuse illumination,* in contrast to retinal neurons, all of which did (Jung & Baumgartner, 1955).

---

*(Note added in proof.) Indeed, it now appears that Schachar's argument is totally invalid as indicated by a triple-barreled critique on pp. 960–962 in the December 2, 1977, issue of *Science.*

2. *Convergence of specific and nonspecific afferent input* was first investigated by Creutzfeldt, Baumgartner, and co-workers (Akimoto & Creutzfeldt, 1957/1958; Baumgartner & Jung, 1956; Creutzfeldt & Akimoto, 1957/1958; Creutzfeldt & Baumgartner, 1955).

3. *Direction-specific movement responses* of visual cortical neurons were first recorded by Hubel (1958) in freely moving cats.

4. *Specific "receptive-field-axis-orientation" and "columnar organization"* was discovered by Hubel and Wiesel (1959) and investigated with detailed histological controls (Hubel & Wiesel, 1962; 1963).

5. *Microelectrophoretic studies of synaptic transmission* were made in 1958-1962: Following experiments by Grusser with acetylcholine electrophoresis, mentioned in 1958 (Jung, 1958), Spehlmann made systematic studies with multibarreled microelectrodes on visual cortical neurons (Spehlmann, 1963; Spehlmann & Kapp, 1961) since 1961.

6. *Multisensory convergence of vestibular, acoustic, and somatosensory input* at visual cortical neurons was first described by Grusser et al. (Grusser & Grusser-Cornehls, 1960; Grusser, Grusser-Cornehls, & Saur, 1959) and studies in detail by Kornhuber, Murata, and co-workers in the cat (Jung, Kornhuber, & da Fonseca, 1963; Kornhuber & da Fonseca, 1961; Murata & Kameda, 1963; Murata, Cramer, & Bach-Y-Rita, 1965), and by Lomo and Mollica in the rabbit (Lomo & Mollica, 1959; 1962).

7. *Intracellular recordings of postsynaptic potentials.* Li and co-workers in 1960 obtained the first convincing registrations of EPSPs and IPSPs (Li, Oritz-Golvin, Chou, & Howard, 1960) from visual cortical neurons. These were followed by Creutzfeldt's method of "quasi-intracellular" recordings from visual neurons initiated in 1965 (Fuster, Creutzfeldt, & Straschill, 1965).

8. *Plasticity and conditioning in visual cortex neurons.* In 1960, Morrell (1960) and Jasper and co-workers (Jasper, Ricci, & Doane, 1960) published neuronal changes in the visual cortex during conditioned responses, and several Russian authors studied neuronal conditioning (Skrebitsky, 1969; Sokolov, Polyansky, & Bagdonas, 1970; Vinogradova & Lindsley, 1964) in the following years.

9. *Complex and hypercomplex receptive field characteristics of higher-order neurons in area 17* were described by Hubel and Wiesel (Hubel & Wiesel, 1962).

10. *Color coding in cortical neurons of monkeys* was first studied by Lennox-Buchthal (1962) and Motokawa and co-workers (Motoakawa, Taira, & Okuda, 1962).

11. *Influences of visual experience on the maintenance of innate receptive field properties* were first investigated by Wiesel and Hubel (Hubel & Wiesel, 1963; Wiesel & Hubel, 1963; 1965a; 1965b).

12. *Special hypercomplex and higher-order receptive fields in the peristriate cortex (areas 18 and 19)* were reported by Hubel and Wiesel (1965).

13. *Receptive field disparity between the two eyes and its relation to binocular depth mechanisms* were first investigated by Barlow, Blakemore, and Pettigrew

(1967) and since then extensively by Bishop and co-workers (Pettigrew, Nikara, & Bishop, 1968).

14. *Neuronal activity during normal eye movements* was first studied in area 17 of monkeys by Wurtz (1968; 1969a; 1969b; 1969c) and by Noda et al. in the cat (Noda, Creutzfeldt, & Freeman, 1971; Noda, Freeman, Gies, & Creutzfeldt, 1971).

15. *Morphological correlates for ocular dominance in columns of the monkey's visual cortex* were found by Hubel and Wiesel (1969).

16. *Effects of controlled and specific visual experience on receptive field organization* were described by Hirsch and Spinelli (1970; 1971) and Blakemore and Cooper (1970; 1971).

C. REPRESENTATION IN THE INTRINSIC AREAS OF THE CORTEX

Our understanding of neural representation and coding has, as repeatedly noted, advanced farthest for the visual sensory projection pathways. The clearly defined stimulus parameters and the conceptual anchor they provide, the highly ordered anatomy, the (at least initially) isomorphic representation, and finally the mainly monodirectional (afferent) information flow in the sensory pathways, all contribute to this understanding. Once the primary projection areas of the cortex are left and the integrative intrinsic areas are entered, however, the problem becomes far more complex, because most of these stimulus-response technical controls and conceptual simplicities are absent. No longer can the psychobiologist control the situation as completely as he might have in a purely visual experiment. For example, where a highly defined stimulus pattern might be used to evoke a correlated and, perhaps more important, a timelocked neurological response in the projection pathways, the representation of mental processes in the intrinsic areas is much more complex. The psychobiologist is faced not only with the problem of identifying the relevant neural response but also the stimulus and/or the behavior with which it may be related.

The difficulty of the problem increases in light of the fact that the mental processes that are represented in the intrinsic areas are the end-products of extended sequences of integrative interactions and not the direct resultant of precisely defined antecedent stimuli. The neuronal responses are not only due to the signals coursing along the main sensory pathway, because information coming from the other sensory modalities, the internal state of the animal, and of course, previously stored experience and inbuilt response tendencies, all contribute to the definition of the neural state or the creation of some mental experience.

For these biological, practical, and organizational reasons, there is a much less abundant literature on representation in the intrinsic regions of the cortex. We do, however, know quite a bit and are now aware of some of the general properties of these regions. I stress these general properties by discussing a few examples of pertinent research.

As befits regions of the brain that are thought to be more integrative in function than communicative, the intrinsic areas of the cerebral cortex are characterized by many neurons that seem to be polymodal, i.e., to be responsive to more than a single sensory modality. In fact, it is now agreed that in many areas of the cerebral cortex, two-thirds or more of the neurons from which electrophysiological responses are recorded are polysensory in that they respond to visual, auditory, and somatosensory inputs. Amassian (1954), in one of the germinal papers in this field, has shown that both evoked and single-cell recordings from the intrinsic areas display this polysensory responsiveness. Although it has been more recently shown that some of the neurons in particular portions of the intrinsic regions may preferentially respond more to one kind of sensory input than others, it seems that in many areas most neurons (half or more) are almost equally activated by any sensory inputs. Even in those neurons that are differentially sensitive to one modality, there is usually secondary sensitivity to other stimulus modalities. For example, Dubner and Rutledge (1964), when working with neurons of the suprasylvian gyrus considered to be primarily "photic association" cells, found that these neurons were also sensitive, although to a lesser degree, to auditory and somatosensory stimuli.

What I say about the special properties of intrinsic area neurons in the following discussion should not be interpreted to mean that the coding mechanisms observed in the more peripheral sensory specific areas of the cortex are never to be found in these more central intrinsic areas. This is not the case! For example, Dow and Dubner (1969; 1971) have shown that some of those predominantly visual neurons in the anterior portion of the middle supersylvian gyrus display characteristic receptive fields and feature selectivity much like those of the neurons of the primary projection areas 17 and 18. Nevertheless, the intrinsic area neurons that are sensory do typically respond to more than one input modality and to aspects of the stimulus that seem to transcend its simpler physical and geometrical properties.

It must be appreciated, however, that Dow and Dubner's studies of the neurons of the suprasylvian gyrus and others of that genre were carried out very much in the tradition of the paradigm of the earlier sensory studies. Conventional visual stimulus patterns were used, and these investigators almost certainly looked upon their experiments as simply further steps in the tracing of the visual signals.

There may be a serious misemphasis, however, built into experiments that do seek to demonstrate some sensory or motor characteristic of the neurons of the intrinsic cortex. The problem arises because there are many other neurons that are not at all sensory (or motor) in the classical sense but that alternatively represent or encode quite different processes. Mountcastle, Lynch, Georgopoulos,

Sakata, and Acuna (1975), for example, note that many of the neurons of the parietal area of the monkey are not sensory or motor but are related to such psychological functions as the command to explore the space about the animal with the hands or the eyes. Such representational mechanisms are of a completely different sort than those of the primary sensory projection regions. It is possible, therefore, that the uncritical extension of the research paradigm suitable for the projection regions to the intrinsic regions may be a collosal strategic error.

1.   Neurons Coding Complex Behavior

An excellent example of what appears to be a more meaningful way to approach the problem of coding or representation in the intrinsic areas is exemplified by some extraordinarily interesting studies by James Ranck and his collaborators at the University of Michigan. Some of the difficulties encountered in this work also demonstrate the increased complexity that is encountered as one progresses from the sensory to the intrinsic areas and the inappropriateness of the sensory paradigm for studies in those regions.

Ranck (1973) and Feder and Ranck (1973) were interested in the problem of how one would study representation in neurons that are associated with thoughts and overt behaviors that are not clearly tied to the convenient stimulus dimensions of the sensory domain. As noted earlier, without that fixed reference, experimenters are faced with enormously difficult conceptual and technological obstacles. That difficulty is the absence of experimental control of the relevant antecedent condition evoking a particular neural activity. Although there is no greater technical difficulty in recording from hippocampal or septal cells than from the visual cortex, Ranck was faced with an enormous procedural difficulty. How was he to know which aspects of the animal's behavior were to be correlated with the recorded neuronal responses? The anchor provided by the reliable association of stimuli and their synchronized evoked responses was simply no longer present.

Another relatively simple technical difficulty (compared to the difficulty of establishing the behavioral correlates) was that the single cell recordings had to be obtained in situations in which the animal was moving about freely in its environment. To solve this problem, Ranck developed a recording technique that did not involve the cumbersome stereotaxic instruments usually used in single cell recording. Instead, he mounted a small screw-operated microelectrode holder on the skull of the animal itself whereby the microelectrode, an etched tungsten wire, could be moved up and down with a simple but stable screw mechanism. Thus the rats used in Ranck's experiments were free to move about more or less normally and could even be handled, in most cases, without any loss of the responses from the neuron. Figure 7-26 shows the special microelectrode holder.

After the response of a suitable neuron was isolated by the advancing electrode and its basic response characteristics determined, Ranck put the animal through a highly proscribed series of tests involving both sensory stimulation and situationally induced behavior. The sensory stimuli were not the parametrically controlled kinds usually used in sensory electrophysiological studies but included naturalistic stimuli such as "patting" the rat. Such stimuli could easily be repeated from animal to animal and fron one test session to another. However, to induce more complex consummatory behavior that could be correlated with the observed cellular responses, Ranck deprived the animal of food and water for specific periods. His experimental rats would then typically head directly for the food and water when introduced into the experimental cubicle; this stereotypical behavior could be repeatedly compared with the recorded neuronal responses on trial after trial.

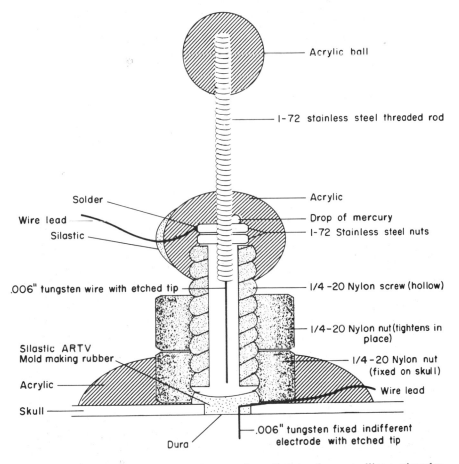

FIG. 7.26   Schematic drawing of head-mounted manipulator for controlling a microelectrode in a freely moving rat. (From Ranck, ©1973, with the permission of C. C. Thomas Publisher.)

The series of tests used by Ranck was designed to assay as many different behavioral correlates of the neuronal response patterns as possible in a brief test period. The best way to describe his protocol is simply to reproduce the list of the response states observed in Ranck's (1973) own words:

The running protocol was: (a) The rat is in slow-wave sleep. (b) The rat is in paradoxical sleep. The relation of phasic episodes of paradoxical sleep to cell firing was determined in two ways: during a run the cell was listened to and the rat, especially his vibrissae, was watched; and eye movements were recorded on a polygraph and were later correlated with photographic records of the cell. (c) The rat is in quiet arousal. (d) The rat smells amyl acetate, or camphor, or turpentine, or wintergreen on a Q-tip. Usually only two of these were tested. (e) The experimenter moves his hand in front of the rat's face, flashes a flashlight, and moves the light across the rat's visual field. (f) The experimenter snaps a cricket (aversive), and bangs cans or claps hands (this startles the rat). (g) The experimenter touches all parts of the rat's skin. This is done in the form of petting him. (h) The rat grooms his face, legs and body, and genitalia. (i) Eating behavior: The rat approaches a 1-2 g food pellet, picks up the pellet, carries the pellet across the cage, eats, explores the floor after finishing the pellet, and follows a pellet as it is moved in the experimenter's fingers. On continuous reinforcement, the rat bar-presses for 45-mg food pellets delivered by a chute. (j) Response to novel nonnutritive objects (paper, wood, pencils, etc.) is observed. (k) Drinking behavior: The rat approaches the water bottle, explores the water bottle, drinks, and explores the water hole after removal of water bottle. This is compared with drinking from a small cup and lapping up drops of water on the floor. The rat bar-presses for water or continuous reinforcement, drinking from a dipper. (l) The experimenter interrupts the rat's eating or drinking by putting his hand in cage, and, if necessary, making noise. (m) The rat explores the cage, including sniffing at the floor and sniffing while standing on his hind feet, i.e., sniffing when there is no apparent object to sniff. (n) The rat is picked up in experimenter's hand. (o) The experimenter blows on the rat. Rats try to escape from this. (p) The experimenter pinches rat's tail. This causes vocalization and escape. After his tail has been pinched once or twice, when his tail is picked up the rat runs off (avoids). (q) Passive avoidance: The rat has been trained so that he drank immediately and almost continuously during the few brief periods when the water bottle was present. The waterspout is then hooked to a 0.27-ma 60-Hz current and the grid floor of the cage grounded so that the rat is shocked when he drinks [pp. 468-469].

Ranck found that the neurons from which he was able to record responses in the hippocampal and septal regions had certain properties that hindered rapid progress on this research. Many of these neurons were silent and displayed no spontaneous activity until the behavior with which they were subsequently associated occurred. Thus the initial acquisition of neurons that potentially might be associated with some specific behavior was difficult. The process, as Ranck carefully points out, had to be essentially circular. He was forced to seek neurons that responded in a particular situation and then to draw the conclusion of an association between the response of that neuron and a particular behavior on the basis of that original observation. At best, this must be an adaptive and convergent process and, at worst, the results may be strongly biased by the initial assumptions of the investigator.

Regardless of these difficulties, Ranck was able to classify the obtained neural responses into either one of two broad categories. One category, which he refers to as the "Theta cell group," was characterized by neurons that never emitted more than a single spike action potential whenever it responded. The other class, which Ranck designated the "Complex Spike cell group," was characterized by neurons that always responded with a group (perhaps six or seven) of spikes with progressively declining amplitude in quick succession as shown in Fig. 7-27.

These two neuronal response types were associated with two distinct types of behavior. The theta cells were most active when the rats were in certain sleep stages and least active when they were involved in what Ranck calls "automatic" or "well-learned" response patterns, e.g., eating, drinking, and bar-pressing. On the other hand, activity in the complex spike neurons seemed to be associated with four distinct kinds of behavior defining four different kinds of complex spike neurons. The first kind of behavior Ranck associates with an "approach-consummate" neuron. This type of complex spike neuron was most active when the animal behaved in a way that "successfully" satisfied some bodily need,

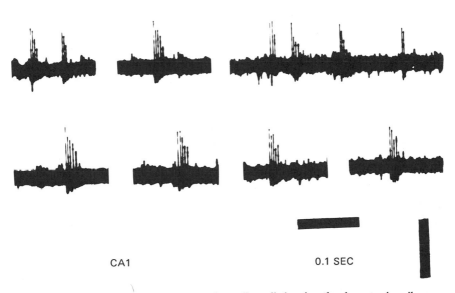

CA1   0.1 SEC

FIG. 7.27   Several responses from a complex spike cell showing the decrease in spike amplitude during the burst. Vertical calibration is equal to 360 μvolts. (From Ranck, ©1973, with the permission of Academic Press.)

for example, eating. The second kind of behavior, Ranck felt, characterized an "approach-consummate-mismatch" type of neuron. In addition to firing at the same time as the "approach-consummate" neuron, this type would also respond if the food object was not available when the animal approached the usual site of feeding. The third kind of behavior was associated with a kind of neuron that Ranck refers to as an "appetitive" neuron. It was active while the rat approached a goal object but not during the consummatory behavior. The one exception to this generality was that an "appetitive" neuron typically became active during sleep—a process that actually may be considered also to be a form of consummatory behavior. The final category of behavior produced activity in a fourth class of neurons only during orienting movements.

Obviously, these behavioral-neuronal associations are based on what are, to a certain degree, subjective judgments by the experimenter. Ranck judges the adaptive relevance of the rat's actions at the moment a neuron fires. This is a substantially different way of estimating the behavioral role of a neuron than is determining the relationship between a visual stimulus and the highly reliable synchronized neuronal response which it clearly evokes. Although Ranck's achievements make clear the possiblity of meaningful progress using this subjective approach, there is obviously a great deal more "theorizing and hypothesizing" of the neural-behavioral association implicit in this approach than in sensory studies. In the long run, one must hope that these almost naturalistic observations will converge upon suitable explanations and adequate models of the representation of these appetitive and consummatory behaviors. Because the investigator is always going to be biased by his previous research and educational experiences, much more in this case than in simpler experimental designs, he may be especially susceptible to misinterpretations. This is so, in spite of the fact that as Ranck (1973) notes "The behavior of the neuron shapes the behavior of the experimenter [p. 463]." Nevertheless, the expectation is that this approach must be guided by the biological reality of the situation. In any event, it represents one of the only conceptually fertile routes to understanding the representational role of neurons in the intrinsic regions of the brain.

2. Neurons That Count

In an interesting study by Thompson, Mayers, Robertson, and Patterson (1970), another important point was made concerning representation in the intrinsic cortex. Thompson and his colleagues had shown that certain neurons of the cortex of cats respond selectively to the *number* of input stimuli. Such neurons seem to count sequential stimuli. For example, it produces a spike action potential only after seven (no more, no less) sequential stimuli occurred. The really significant aspect of this otherwise only modestly relevant result was that these neurons counted out sequential stimuli regardless of the interstimulus interval, the sensory channel along which the signal came, or the intensity of the stimulus. The "counting" neurons, therefore, are abstracting a common symbolic property (numerosity) from a stimulus train rather than responding to any of their physical, temporal, or geometrical properties. Indeed, the representational properties of these interesting neurons seem to contrast sharply with the usual sensory coding properties of the feature-sensitive neurons where almost completely opposite criteria seem to have held.

The ability to encode symbolic aspects of the message, independent of its physical attributes, is a most attractive neural property and may constitute a major function of the association or integrative neurons of the intrinsic areas of the brain as opposed to the isomorphic encoding required in the afferent systems. If this is the case, it suggests that those studies that simply shift the simpler sensory paradigm to the intrinsic regions of the brain (e.g., Dow & Dubner, 1969; 1971) may be fundamentally inadequate to test more complex hypotheses regarding the functional and representative role of neurons in these regions.

3. Neurons That Command

In addition to these two examples, there has been a gradually increasing interest in electrophysiological studies of single neurons in various regions of the intrinsic cortex in the 1970s as reflected in other studies. Among the most notable of these is the work of Kubota and Niki (1971), Desiraju (1972), Sakata, Takaoka, Kawarasaki, and Shibutani (1973), Hyvärinen and Poranen (1974), and, perhaps most notably, the work of Mountcastle, Lynch, Georgopoulos, Sakata, and Acuna (1975) to which I have already alluded. This latter study, carried out on the parietal cortex, led Mountcastle and his colleagues to hypothesize the existence of neurons whose activity seems to initiate generalized soultions to problems of manual and visual search rather than specific motor responses.

The important distinction between the parietal neurons this group studied and ordinary motor region neurons is that the activity in these cells seemed to be associated with the general process of search rather than with specific motor sequences. The "command" function of the neurons thus hypothesized by this group is an analog of a "volitional state," in the words of Mountcastle and his colleagues; its activity seems to say "achieve some goal" rather than "move some muscle." Such an association is, of course, exceedingly difficult to precisely define, but Mountcastle and his colleagues make a compelling case for the generalized role of these neurons and their representation of this highly integrative, complex cognitive, and symbolic act.

It is probably too early to accept the conceptual argument being made by Mountcastle and his collegues in its entirety. The possibility of some subtle feedback is still present, and the emphasis on the single cell may be invalid in a science that is moving toward network ideas; but clearly this is an important piece of work that may provide a significant new insight into representational processes for cognitive processes.

The work of Mountcastle, Ranck, and Thompson, and their collaborators, it should be observed, are models of neurophysiological coding that stress the "symbolic" aspects of representation rather than the isomorphic or geometrical aspects. This emphasis on symbolic representation may more appropriately describe the essential function of the intrinsic regions than does the older paradigm of "associations" between sensory and motor function.

Another empirical approach, which also emphasizes the symbolic role of these regions, uses the compound evoked potential rather than single neuronal response as an electrophysiological indicator. Psychobiologists who have studied such processes as task relevance, stimulus uncertainty (e.g., Sutton, Braren, Zubin, & John, 1965), or stimulus novelty (e.g., Courchesne, Hillyard, & Galambos, 1975) on the evoked brain potential may be more correctly emphasizing the main role played by the association areas of the brain, even though these compound signals are unlikely to be the true transactional coded equivalents of these mental processes (see Chapter 6).

In spite of the empirical and theoretical criticisms of the evoked potential techniques presented in Chapter 6, an enormous amount of research is currently carried out using these techniques. The ethics of human experimentation have always been a sufficiently compelling argument to pursue any technique that promises to tell us anything about the activity of the brain without surgery, even if there are some residual doubts of its validity. Although I have grave doubts about the compound evoked potential approach, as indicated in Chapters 6 and 8, the reader may want to look at a review by Beck (1975) for a more supportive, as well as more comprehensive, discussion of relevance of the compound evoked potential to the associative, symbolic and cognitive processes that characterize intrinsic area function.

D. THE REPRESENTATION OF PERCEPTION— A PSYCHOBIOLOGICAL COMPARISON[7]

1. Some Difficulties

Having discussed some of the neurophysiological studies pertinent to the problem of representation, I can turn at this point to another aspect of the problem. I now consider some of the psychophysical contributions to the problem of how perception, in particular, is encoded by neural activity. In doing so I also hope to develop some general conceptual difficulties in theories based on association of single neuronal responses and psychological processes.

[7]Much of this section is adapted from Uttal, 1973.

A vitally important point to remember before this discussion begins is the fact that contemporary neurophysiological explanations of psychological responses are, in their entirety, *theories* and *speculative interpretations* of the relationship between the two domains that are, at best, supported only by indirect clues. Perhaps the point has never been made more eloquently than in the words of Charles S. Harris of the Bell Telephone Laboratories, when he said at a recent scientific meeting *"Some people forget that when neurophysiological data are used as explanations of psychological phenomena, they then become neurophysiological theories."*

The point Harris is making is that there is no direct empirical link between the two domains, but, instead, there is a host of vague correlations and analogies. The associations that have been drawn, more or less competently, by so many psychobiologists are dependent, in large part, upon analogs and superficial similarities between the data of the two domains.

It would be unfair to the reader of this section not to admit that the position that I champion in the following pages is a minority view. Many thoughtful psychobiologists have been strongly influenced by the work of such distinguished neurophysiologists as Hubel and Wiesel or Hartline and Ratliff to assume that the answer to the question of whether or not perceptual reflections of single-cell activity are directly measurable has been answered in the affirmative. Weisstein, Ozog, and Szoc (1975) and Breitmeyer and Ganz (1976) are only among the most recent to postulate lateral inhibitory interaction models of visual masking and, as we have seen, a host of studies purport to support the spatial frequency analyzer hypothesis as an explanation of the psychophysical responses to grating-like stimuli. The analysis presented in some (but not all) of these models, however, seems to me to ignore many of the fundamental conceptual and empirical discrepancies that suggest that there is rarely the fundamental agreement between the data from the two domains to support a definitive association. In other cases, the similarities between neurophysiological and psychophysical responses are often simply analogs of each other or are based on spurious correspondences arising out of the generality of the mathematical models.

It is further interesting to note that in recent years many of the neural models of perception have evolved away from hypothetical single-cell correlates of perception to more complex "channels" or antagonistic interactions between two lateral inhibitory processes that differ only in their time constants. (See Weisstein, Ozog & Szoc, 1975, and Breitmeyer & Ganz, 1976, for discussion of such dual channel models.) This development in many contemporary models moves such theories into a context in which the neural mechanisms themselves are not directly observed and, perhaps are not observable entities either; they now are much more like the mathematical descriptions than the empirically observed cellular neurophysiological data originally proposed as explanatory concepts.

It is also important to realize in this regard that the two-channel or dual-process hypothesis is, in fact, a direct spin-off of the need to explain the nonmonotonic functions so often obtained in the metacontrast type of experiment.

It is a mathematical truism that an equation with only a single degree of freedom or of linear order cannot model such a process. To simulate a U-shaped curve, one is forced to develop a model that has incorporated two separate processes or that is of the second order. The ability of such mathematical functions with two degrees of freedom to simulate the U-shaped metacontrast curves is not, therefore, tantamount to a proof that two laterally interacting channels of visual information processing are really present; that is a separate physiological assumption that transcends the descriptive mathematics. An equally plausible case could be made that the U-shape curves result from a single process that changes in some manner over the course of the interval between a stimulus and a mask or from a stable single process that was functionally dependent on the square of the interval in some manner.

The conceptual difficulties engendered by any inferential approach that seeks to associate single neuron responses and molar behavior are therefore varied and include those described in the following paragraphs. In the following section, however, I do not directly challenge each and every single neuron model of perception. Only the general concept is discussed, and a few counter-examples of the most obvious disagreements and discrepancies are given.

a.   Time Constant Incompatibility

Time course similarities between perceptual and neurophysiological processes are not as common as often asserted by psychobiological theorists. In fact, usually single neuron processes display much more rapid time constants than are observed in what are suggested to be corresponding psychological processes. Only in rare cases are the time constants of the two domains comparable. One of the few recent experiments showing them to be nearly equivalent is to be found in a study reported by Maffei, Fiorentini, and Bisti (1973). These workers found neurons in the visual cortex of the cat that responded to exposure to gratings with a prolonged inhibition of response with a time course comparable to that of a similar human psychophysical experiment. In this experiment, the assay of the adaptive effect produced by the prolonged exposure was performed by determining the threshold of a brief test grating of a lower contrast than the preadapting grating. Both the human psychophysical phenomenon and the neurophysiological findings in the cat show a reduced response following preadaptation that was of approximately the same duration. Figure 7-28 displays the results of the response of a neuron to a test stimulus prior to and following adaptation and after recovery from the 30-second-long inhibited period to the stimuli shown.

Maffei, Fiorentini, and Bisti's study is important primarily because it is an exception to the generalization that the time constants of neurophysiological and perceptual phenomena differ. In many other experiments that purport to show temporal correspondence, it should be noted that there is a great deal of

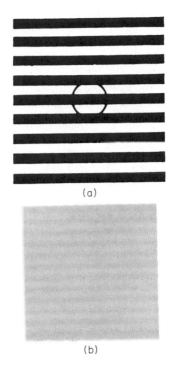

(a)

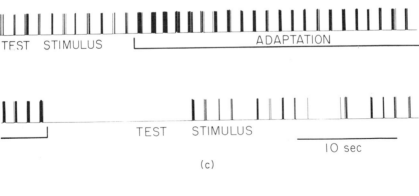

(b)

TEST STIMULUS | ADAPTATION

TEST STIMULUS

10 sec

(c)

10—10

FIG. 7.28 A possible neurophysiological correlate of visual perception: (a) the adapting stimulus, (b) the test stimulus, (c) the record of the neural response of a cat's striate cortex neuron sensitive to the frequency of the adapting grating stimulus. Following the adapting stimulus, both the neural response in the cat's brain and the human perceptual sensitivity to the test grating are reduced. The time course of each process is roughly the same. (From Maffei, Fiorentini, & Bisti, © 1973, with the permission of The American Association for the Advancement of Science.)

difficulty in determining if the psychological and neurophysiological time constants are indeed the same because of the problems inherent in actually measuring
the duration of a percept. In many cases in which it can be done, the differences
seem to be totally out of accord.

For example, consider the example of the colossal discrepancy between a
perceptual time course and the neural process to which it is usually attributed as
reported by Jones and Holding (1975). The well-known McCullough Effect
(McCullough, 1965) consists of a contrasting red or green and tilted negative
after-response to an achromatic and vertical test grating following the prolonged
observation of a green or red grating tilted in the opposite direction. This phenomenon is usually attributed to an adaptation or fatigue of the neurons in the
visual system. Jones and Holding, however, have shown that the McCullough Effect can last for as long as 6 months if the effect is not tested during that period.
This time constant incompatibility between the perceptual and neurophysiological processes makes any neuronal fatigue explanation of the McCullough
Effect patently absurd and places it in a learning or cognitive domain quite
different from the early explanation.

b.   Errors in Explanatory Levels

Another frequently encountered problem with psychobiological theories
is that errors may be made in the attribution of the cause of some psychological
phenomena to an incorrect neural level. For example, what is actually a central
process may be attributed to the periphery, or vice versa. The main reason for
this kind of error is that the associations that are drawn between the two domains—the psychological and the neurophysiological—are almost always based
upon similarities or analogies in the course of the phenomena and proposed
neural correlate. This error of analogy is often compounded by an apparent reluctance to properly weigh the significance of simple first-approximation descriptions of the psychological phenomena by observers. In Uttal (1973) I described
one example of this error of levels in the explanation of the simultaneous contrast illusion. For the moment, I say only that many investigators have attributed
this illusion to simple contour interactions in the periphery. In doing so, they
ignore the weak correspondence between the global aspects of the illusion as
described by observers and the properties of the peripheral nervous system
explanation. I also described in that book (Uttal, 1973) the impact of form similarity on metacontrast illusions (masking by suceeding stimuli), also usually attributed to peripheral neural mechanisms by many contemporary psychobiologists.
The fact that form recognition is a prerequisite for metacontrast seems to me to
be a strong first-approximation argument that the effect is actually mediated by
mechanisms much more central in locale than the retina.

The difficulty in each of these examples is common. Misinterpretations of
available data and an overly zealous commitment to a particular theoretical
orientation have led, in some cases, to a gross mislocalization of the responsible

mechanism, when in fact they are more likely to be the result of much more complex and central mechanisms.

c. The Perils of Modeling

Whenever a psychobiologist uses a theoretical model to study some aspect of the mind-brain problem, he injects certain potential conceptual difficulties into his analysis. The use of model preparations (infrahuman species) for reasons of convenience, ethics, or simplicity, in a search for understanding of human mental process, may also often mislead the reductionistically oriented theoretician. We have a considerable amount of information about neurophysiological mechanisms in animals such as the crayfish, the leech, the cockroach, and the sea hare. Some of these data describe processes that appear to exhibit many of the functional properties of psychological processes such as learning or perception. Although all of this material has been stimulating and suggestive, it must be continually kept in mind that *similar processes* (analogies) do not necessarily imply *identical mechanisms* (homologies). The modifications in synaptic conductivity that accompany experience in *Aplysia*—the sea hare—for example, may not be homologous with the neural processes that mediate human learning. Nevertheless, model preparations play an important role in the understanding of representational processes in psychobiology. The interested reader may wish to explore the problems and advantages of some of the more common model preparations in an interesting paper by Ingle and Shein (1975).

Mathematical modeling also can be misleading in certain instances. The power of mathematics arises from the fundamental flexibility of the algebraic notation; a symbol may represent almost any process without saying anything about the nature of the mechanical device that carries out that process. Mathematical models, best considered as descriptive analogs, are often erroneously accepted as specifying the physical implementation or mechanism of the process they model. Experience with analog computation helps to dispel this misconception. In an analog computer laboratory, it is constantly made clear that certain processes (such as oscillation) can be described or represented by any one of many different mathematical or physical mechanisms. The charging or discharging of capacitors, or the swinging of a pendulum bob, both trace analogous oscillatory processes as does the common solution to several different differential equations. In both of the mechanical analogs, the same mathematical description is valid, and the two forms of oscillation may be properly considered to be process analogs of each other. The physical implementation in each case, however, is entirely different.

To further make this point, consider the use of list processing languages in modeling cognitive processes among practitioners of the esoteric art of artificial intelligence. Similarities of meaning are modeled or analogized by propinquity in the list structure. Nevertheless, the kind of neurophysiological representation and reductionism with which we are presently concerned in this chapter is not to be found anywhere in the model. Similarly, list structures are not likely to be found embodied in neural nets in the head. The levels of discourse are different, and any attempt to neurophysiologize a list model can be seriously misleading.

d.   Misidentification of Stimulus Dimensions

Another pitfall facing the psychobiologist who attempts to show a correspondence between psychophysical and apparently similar neurophysiological processes is the misinterpretation that the respective stimuli are the same when, in fact, they are quite different. One of the most blatant examples of such a misidentification has been identified by Wasserman and Kong (1974) in a paper that suggests that some such psychoneural correlations are outright "illusions." These psychobiologists were interested in almost unanimously accepted association between the apparent brightness enhancement of a short light flash (the Broca-Sulzer effect) and the after-discharge of a neural response to the onset of a similar flash. The time courses of the two processes are, indeed, very similar, as shown diagrammatically in Fig. 7-29. However, Wasserman and Kong point out that the two stimulus conditions that produce these two response functions are actually quite dissimilar! The psychophysical result is functionally dependent on the duration of the stimulus, whereas the neurophysiological result is purely a function of the time after the onset of the stimulus. When the stimulus dimension that produced the Broca-Sulzer effect (the duration of the stimulus) was varied in an ingenious neurophysiological experiment using the horseshoe crab's eye as a model preparation, there was no corresponding enhancement of the neural activity. The original analogy that had been drawn had, thus, been based on the spurious association of analogous responses produced by quite different stimuli. When the same stimuli were used, the analogous functions were not obtained.

Similar misidentifications of stimulus conditions have led a number of psychobiologists to mistakenly conclude that simultaneous contrast and interactions between small, nearby stimuli are examples of the same phenomena when, in fact, a more cautious examination of the stimulus conditions (and, as we have seen, also the distinctive characteristics of the respective responses) suggests that the two phenomena are quite different.

In concluding these introductory comments, I can answer the questions with which I opened Chapter 6 (i.e., "What does visual perception tell us about visual coding?"; "Are the functions of property analyzers observable in molar behavior?"; "Do single-cell properties such as adaptation and lateral interaction adequately model human visual perception?") by noting that there is little direct evidence for an affirmative answer in each case. Rather there are some suggestive similarities and some ingenious speculation about analogous properties. What the neural hypotheses do provide to psychobiology is a useful means of theorizing about some potential mechanisms of representation, although this approach is fraught with certain conceptual pitfalls. Simply put, we still do not know very

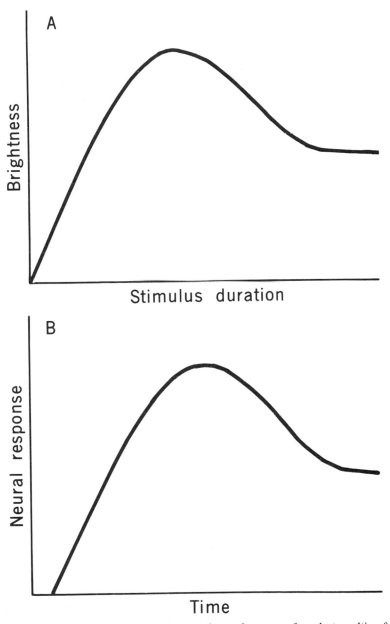

FIG. 7.29 Two curves showing an obvious analogy of response form but resulting from totally different stimulus dimensions. If stimulus duration is used to evoke the neural response, the analogy is no longer apparent. See text for complete discussion. This suggests that a superficial similarity between response forms has been overextended to generate a spurious theory of this aspect of visual perception. (From Wasserman & Kong, ©1974, with the permission of The American Association for the Advancement of Science.)

much about the relationship between neuronal activity and psychological process. Anyone who thinks that the link has been definitively established is seriously fooling himself as I try to establish in the rest of this chapter.

In the following sections I describe some specific discrepancies and difficulties with contemporary psychobiological theories of certain perceptual phenomena that specifically assert that the behavior of individual cells at specific levels of the nervous system is observable in the molar behavior of the entire organsim.

2.   Some Discrepancies[8]

a.   Missing Parts

The representational hypothesis that the operations of simple feature-filtering networks are reflected in molar behavior has a necessary corollary; i.e., that the features to be detected must be present. This axiom might be said to be "syntactical," because it deals with the specific geometrical placement and structure of the parts of the pattern. From the perspective of a feature-filtering theory, the meaning or significance (semantic content) should not be an effective variable if a feature-filtering model is correct. Some recent experiments, however, in which the critical stimulus material is actually missing suggest that some kinds of form perception may be influenced more by general organization and context than by the presence or absence of specific features or the simple geometrical information content of this stimulus pattern.

Warren (1970) reports the results of an extremely interesting experiment in which a masking sound (such as a cough or a tone) is used to completely replace a speech sound in a recorded sentence. Because of the sequential redundancy, as expected, listeners in this situation have no difficulty in reproducing the sentence, including the missing sound. Surprisingly, however, they also report actually hearing the missing speech sound. The redundancy built into the recorded sentence is not only sufficient, therefore, to convey the meaning but also to allow the listener to "perceive" the missing speech sound, even though it is not physically present. Most interestingly, Warren also shows that if the missing speech sound is not replaced with an extraneous noise but simply clipped out of the recording, it is easy to detect and locate the gap.

This auditory study is an analog of a number of visual phenomena. Our inability to deal with lacunae, as lacunae, is a striking phenomenon, which has been too infrequently studied. The minimum thresholds for visual temporal gap detection (Uttal & Hieronymus, 1970), the general inability to detect the "blind spot" of the eye, and other similar phenomena all speak to this point. Leeper's (1935)

---

[8]Parts of this section are adapted from Uttal, 1973.

classic studies of the perception of fractured figures also clearly show the perception of form to be heavily influenced by overall organizational factors other than specific features. The general significance of the remaining portions of partial figures becomes instantly clear when appropriate clues of meaning are given in a way that could hardly be considered to be due to the action of simple neural feature filters.

Man's perceptual repertroire is filled with many such instances in which missing parts are filled in, disjoint parts connected or incongruous parts ignored by the perceiver. An example is Fig. 7-30. This drawing evokes a complex and well organized perception from a series of fractured components. The overall shape and form of the assemblage of parts is more influential in defining the perception features or components, each of which is quite irrelevant to the overall form. Indeed, it is only when a detailed inspection is forced that the individual fractured features (which are comparable in size to the receptive fields of some central neurons) become important.

FIG. 7.30   A sample of a fractured figure emphasizing the importance of the overall configuration rather than local features in the determination of the perceived form. (From Leeper, 1935, after Street's Gestalt Completion Test.)

The visual system also has a profound ability to create percepts that are suggested rather than stimulated by specific physical energies patterns. Figure 7-31, for example, shows a figure which produces a subjective contour—i.e., the percept of a contour that is not actually there.

There is a strong argument implicit in such demonstrations that speaks against the simpler peripheral neurophysiological models of such interactive processes that have such wide currency these days. This is not to say, of course, that there is no neural correlate of the illusory contour—it must be represented in the state of the nervous system somehow—but rather to emphasize the fact that the explanations of these phenomena may have been misplaced into the periphery when, in fact, more central (and possibly nonisomorphically encoded) neural processes truly represent the corresponding psychological functions.

The important general point that is made by all of these missing-part experiments is that features must be there to be detected if one is depending entirely on feature-detecting mechanisms. If percepts can be completed when major portions of the physical stimuli are absent, it becomes much more likely that some sort of mechanism not dependent upon local features but more dependent upon the overall pattern or Gestalt is the real explanation of our pattern perception abilities.

An elegant example especially supportive of the notion that features are not sufficient to account for pattern perception is H. L. Teuber's[9] report at the 1976 International Congress of Psychology that certain brain-damaged subjects would not recognize faces drawn as that shown in Fig. 7-32. They would say instead, "Ah, that is an apple, but it is rotten. I can see the gash near the bottom and in the middle and the two worm holes at the top." Obviously, even though the features were "detected" the form was not recognized. Form perception, at the least, is more than feature-detection models can begin to explain.

Experiments (Uttal, 1970; 1971) in which dot patterns are used as targets to be detected in interfering dotted "visual noise" also are examples of stimuli with missing parts. See Fig. 7-33 for a sample stimulus embedded in the masking dots. No continuous features are actually present in such a stimulus—only arrangements of dots. Thus the "features" are only suggested by the geometrical relations of the dots, and any explanatory model of these phenomena based on feature analysis alone would have to involve higher-level statistical or global evaluation of the cumulative response of individual local receptive areas.

One of the initial results of these studies (Uttal, 1969) was that not all characters were identified with equal ease. At very high noise levels, at which most characters could not be detected with any greater success than chance levels, the four characters I, K, L, and X were still surprisingly recognizable. The character X was on this list because of a rather curious artifact. In the font used in that experiment, X unlike all other characters of the special alphabet, had no long

---

[9]Sadly, as this book went into press, the psychobiological community learned of the death of Luke Teuber, one of the leading contributors to this field. His loss will be deeply felt by all of us.

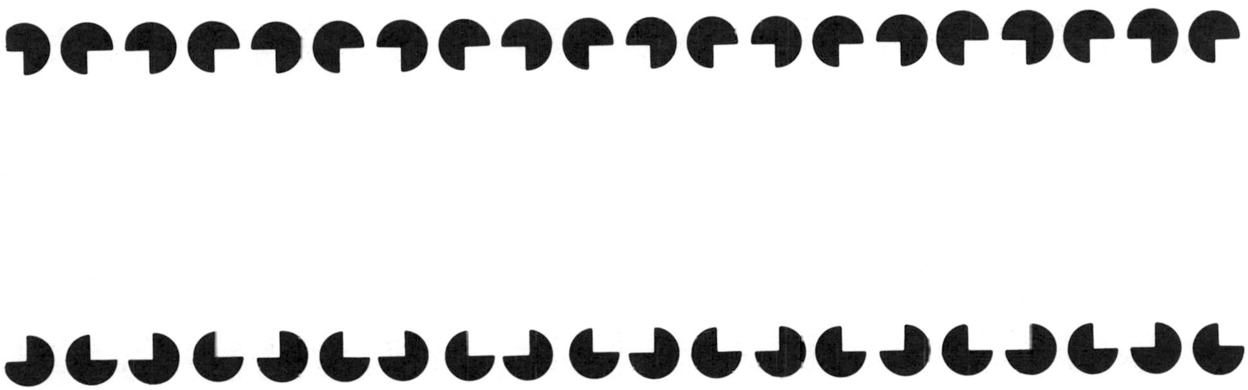

FIG. 7.31 A subjective grating that can produce the same kind of masking (of a test grating) that is produced by a real grating with the same spatial frequencies. This effect of the subjective grating occurs even though none of the spatial frequency components necessary to fatigue a "channel" are present. (From Weisstein, Matthews, & Berbaum, 1974.)

FIG. 7.32   A drawing used by H. L. Teuber to demonstrate that even though features may be detected, there may be no holistic pattern recognition. This shape was reported by a brain-damaged human subject to be a rotten apple with a gash at the bottom and three cuts near the top. Is feature detection an adequate base for a theory of global form recognition?

straight lines of dots and was, therefore, almost invisible even at moderate noise levels. The subjects learned early that when they saw nothing at all, they had probably been presented with an X and thus reported that character. Quite artifactually, therefore, the "recognition score for X" was elevated. The characters I, K, and L, however, were recognized at supernormal levels for two different reasons. First, their confusion with other members of the alphabet stimulus set was lower than that of the other characters; second, they contained long straight dotted lines, which uniquely defined these three characters. Long lines of dots appeared to be more easily detected than the shorter fragments that provided the distinguishing criteria for many of the other characters. When other members of the character set containing long lines of dots received low recognition scores, it was usually due to the difficulty of detecting the shorter line segments that were critically necessary to define which of several confusable characters was actually presented.

These preliminary experiments led the way to a more comprehensive study (Uttal, 1975a) of the factors of line segment and polygonal organization on detectability of dot patterns other than the strongly over-learned alphabetic characters. The effect of variation of several different dimensions of pattern was evaluated in a series of psychophysical experiments. Specifically, the effect of each of the following dimensions of the dotted targets were considered with the results indicated:

1. Dot numerosity—more dots, more detectable
2. Line orientation—no effect
3. Deformation of straight lines into curves and angles—more deformation, less detectable
4. Colinear dot-spacing irregularity—more irregular, less detectable
5. Transverse dot-spacing irregularity—more irregular, less detectable
6. Missing parts in triangles—sides were more important than corners
7. Polygonal orientation—no effect

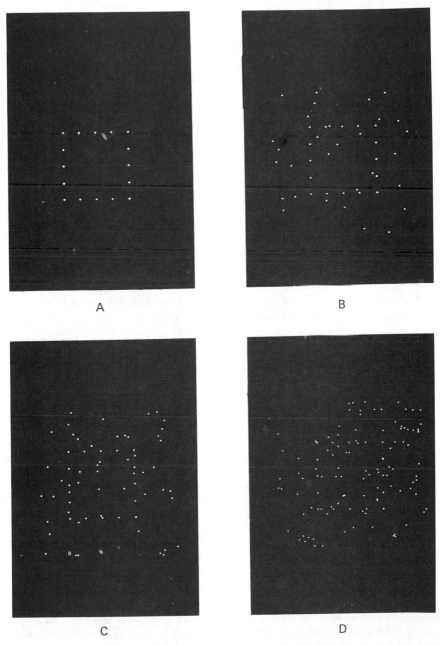

FIG. 7.33 A dotted square presented in four different levels of random dotted noise: (A) no masking dots, (B) 30 masking dots, (C) 50 masking dots, and (D) 100 masking dots. Note the progressive decline in the detectability of the target square as the number of masking dots increases. (From Uttal, 1975a.)

8. Distortions of squares into parallelograms—more distortion, less detectability
9. Organized straight line patterns versus "pick up stix" patterns composed of the same lines—more organized, more detectable
10. Distortions of squares and triangles by misplacing one or more corners—more distortion, less detectable
11. Figural goodness—no effect

This psychophysical data base was then compared to the results of a computer simulation model based upon an autocorrelation transformation that operated on simulated samples of the stimuli. The autocorrelation model was formalized by the following equation:

$$A(\Delta x, \Delta y) = \iint f(x, y) \cdot f(x + \Delta x, y + \Delta y)\, dy\, dx \qquad \text{(Equation 7-1)}$$

where Δx and Δy are shifts in the positions of the stimulus pattern $f(x, y)$. A family of $A(\Delta x, \Delta y)$ values is then computed to fill the autocorrelation spaces. An example of a set of simulated stimul and computer plots of their autocorrelations are shown in Fig. 7-34.

The autocorrelational transformed stimulus is seen in this figure to be made up of a number of peaks distributed in the Δx, Δy space. By applying the following empirical expression:

$$F_m = \frac{\displaystyle\sum_{i=1}^{I} \sum_{n=1}^{N} \frac{A_i \cdot A_n}{D}}{N} \quad (i \neq n) \qquad \text{(Equation 7-2)}$$

a single numerical "figure of merit" (F_m) can be generated for each autocorrelation. In this expression, A_i and A_n are the amplitudes of peaks taken pairwise, D is the distance between the two peaks, and N is the number of peaks. This figure of merit, it is hypothesized, should be associated with the detectability of the figure measured psychophysically. In Fig. 7-34, the four-digit numerals represent the figure of merit for the four autocorrelations.

The order of detectability of the patterns in each of the experiments was compared with the order of the figures of merit from the simulation. In almost every case, the two rank orders were in agreement.

The proposed autocorrelation model is a specific alternative to any model that emphasizes highly specific feature-sensitive single neurons. The autocorrelation process is able to mimic a considerable amount of the psychophysical data obtained in these and related studies on the basis of information processing by a purely homogeneous network of undifferentiated neurons such as that shown in Fig. 7-35 rather than by tuned or feature-sensitive neurons or channels. This is not to say that single neurons, selectively responsive to various parameters of shape and time, are not to be found in the nervous system; the basic neurophysiological observations by Hubel and Wiesel have been too often replicated to challenge their essential message. It may be appropriate, however, to reexamine what these neuronal response sensitivities actually mean. Instead of playing the role of feature-filtering *mechanisms* of the form detection process itself, these single-neuron responses may reflect the output of some other distributed network type of detection mechanism. They may be, in a certain sense, indicators of the function of some more fundamental algorithmic processing mechanism such as a neural autocorrelator. In some way, they may be more like the figure of merit expression than feature filters.

It is evident how a theoretical perspective drastically changes as the emphasis shifts from the one approach to another—from a restrictive theory that concentrates on single neurons as feature filters to one that encompasses the action of an ensemble of neurons acting as a collective parallel information processor in an algorithmic fashion. A contribution to this change in emphasis is the most important outcome of the dot pattern detection experiments and the autocorrelation model. Purely on grounds of intuition and parsimony, it is aesthetically difficult to assign priority for perceptual representation to one neuron, or small set of neurons, in a network made up of many millions. Such a difficulty is an inescapable concomitant of any theory that is based on the selectivity of specialized single neurons. Such an approach leads to such illogical absurdities as the presence of "grandmother"-sensitive neurons. Even the simplest perceptual phenomena, all would agree, must alternatively be based on the concatenated action of many millions of neurons. A priori, network theories involving many homogeneous neurons seem to be more authentic descriptions of what is actually going on in the brain than those based on single-neuron or neuron class functions.

b.   Some Other Psychophysical Data

The missing-part experiments are only one subset of a much larger group of psychophysical experiments suggesting that the obtained psychophysical results do not concur with microtheories based on the action of simple nerve nets. In my earlier work on sensory coding (Uttal, 1973) I extensively reviewed some of the data that suggests that such processes as simultaneous contrast and meta-contrast should not be attributed to the same peripheral neural mechanisms as the contour intensification effects discussed earlier. The reader is directed there for a more complete analysis of the problem. In particular he should read pages 447 to 455 if interested. The following material is added as a supplement to update that discussion.

Some of the most interesting new data deal with the effects of subjective stimuli. It turns out that they can produce just as strong perceptual effects by suggesting the stimuli as do their real counterparts. The implication of this type of data is that there need be no isomorphic neural representation for many of the geometric masking effects to occur nor do the phenomena seem to be results of simple feature detection mechanisms.

For example, Weisstein, Matthews, and Berbaum (1974) have recently shown that it is possible to mask a grating with other gratings that do not in fact exist! For example, Fig. 7-31 is a drawing of a grating that exists only in the eye of the

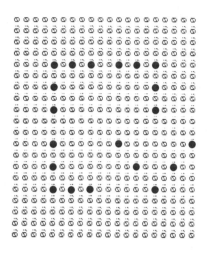

10202

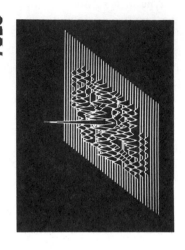

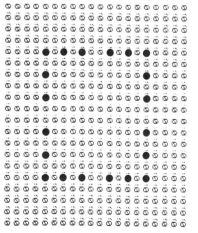

7328

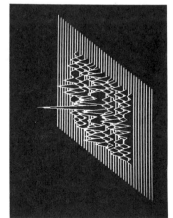

A

B

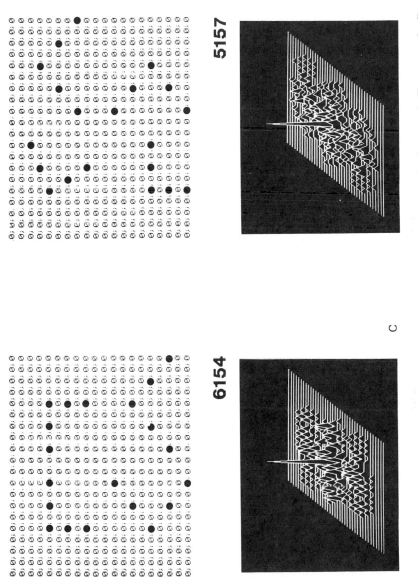

FIG. 7.34 Four autocorrelations showing the effect of disorganizing the corners of a square on the figure merit. The greater the disorganization, the lower the merit. (From Utta, 1975a.)

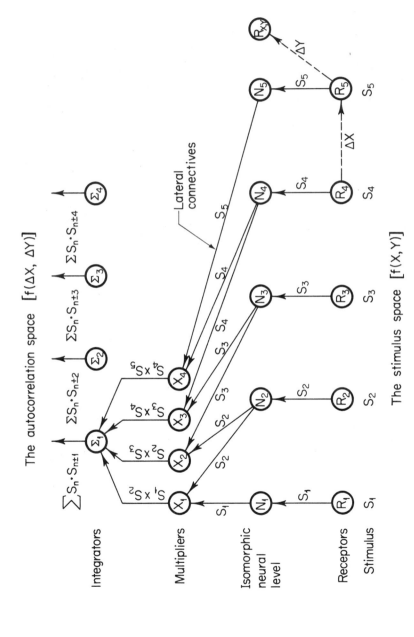

FIG. 7.35 A plausible neural network that could accomplish an autocorrelation transform. (From Uttal, 1975a.)

508

beholder. However, if the eye is preconditioned with this pattern, its ability to detect test gratings with the same spatial frequency is substantially degraded.

Kaniza's (1976) demonstrations of other subjective contour effects also make the point more directly. For example, consider the several diagrams of Fig. 7-36. Optical illusions can be produced by illusory subjective contours as shown in Fig. 7-36a and b. Furthermore, subjective contours can have entirely different orientations and degrees of curvature than do the lines that produce them, as shown in Fig. 7-36c, or can even be produced by the simplest dot-like suggestion, as shown in Fig. 7-36d. All of these demonstrations clearly argue against any simplistic theory of single-cell line detectors as satisfactory explanatory models of visual perception. Rather, the role they do play must be in terms of whatever contribution the individual cell makes to the operation of a much more complex network of neurons.

There are a number of other psychophysical studies, some of which I have already mentioned in various places in this book and others which I have not, that make the same point. Jones and Holding's (1975) work showing the extremely long persistence of the McCullough Effect, Hogben and Di Lollo's (1976) study showing strong practice effects in the metacontrast experiment (and that the effect is barely increased by having two rather than one adjacent masker rectangle), and Fehrer and Raab's (1962) study showing that reaction times do not decrease with metacontrasted brightness decreases as they do with real stimulus intensity decreases, as well as many other uncited but comparable experiments, all make the same general point; the simple peripheral neuronal models of perceptual phenomena invoking lateral inhibitory interactions or feature-sensitive neurons do not, even to a first approximation, begin to explain the multifaceted complexity of human visual perception. The tendency to peripheralize and to lean on single-cell data is strong, but it seems on the basis of much psychophysical evidence that visual perception is, in much larger part than usually asserted, mediated by exceedingly complex neural mechanisms that encode symbolic meaning more than they do isomorphic geometry.

c. A Few Discrepant Neurophysiological Data

Specific attempts to demonstrate the identity of neurophysiological data and certain perceptual phenomena have also led to some data that contradict the notion that the operation of simple neural net mechanisms is satisfactory explanatory models for some of the perceptual phenomena we have discussed. This is a rare category of evidence, however, because experiments that do not produce positive results are often not reported.

One line of research dealing with visual sequential interference has been pursued very effectively by Peter Schiller. Distinguishing among three different kinds of sequential masking—masking in which a bright diffuse light reduces the likelihood of detection of a dimmer smaller light, masking of complex patterns that

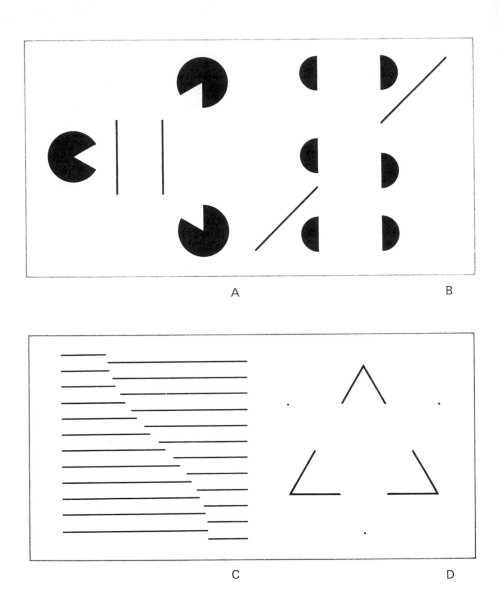

FIG. 7.36 Four examples of the powerful role that subjective contours play in visual perception. The important point made by these examples is that they are as effective in producing percepts as are real contours. A question thus arises of the relationship between the real contours and their purported neural and perceptual responses. See text for details of the significance of each of these four figures. (From Kanizsa, ©1976, with the permission of *Scientific American*.)

overlap, and metacontrast, where the stimuli do not overlap—Schiller (1968; 1969) has shown that it is only when stimuli of the first two categories are used that the single cells of the lateral geniculate body and cortex exhibit any analogous interactive effects. The metacontrast situation, which has so often been subject to a quasiphysiological kind of theorizing that attributes it to peripheral magnitude effects shows no lateral geniculate cellular response analogs that might be so correlated. Schiller (1968) goes on to say, "metacontrast is a complex phenomenon, which may depend on levels in the visual system above the LGN (lateral geniculate nucleus) [p. 865]."

In related work, Fehmi, Adkins, and Lindsley (1969) find very peripheral suppression of the neural response but only when the stimuli overlap in the same manner as the first two categories of the Schiller experiments.

DeValois and Pease (1971) have shown, furthermore, that single-cell responses from lateral geniculate neurons definitely separate stimultaneous contrast and the border effects leading to such phenomenon as the Mach band into two separate and distinct processes just as suggested by the psychophysical data. Comparable lateral interactions among these cells were observed when stimuli, which led to psychophysical contour enhancement, were used. However, there was no evidence of any suppression of the neural response when the stimulus was similar to that producing the simultaneous contrast effect described earlier. DeValois and Pease conclude that these latter data are compelling arguments for much more complicated and more central cortical mechanisms for simultaneous contrast. The implication is that the geometry of the situation is not critical, and therefore mechanisms such as lateral inhibitory interaction and center-surround organization probably play a small, if any, role in such phenomena.

I have already mentioned the insightful study of Wasserman and Kong (1974), which is also a good example of a discrepant neurophysiological result.

E.   CONCLUSIONS

It is important to explicitly express a critically important caveat at this point to avoid what could be a colossal misunderstanding. The following concluding comment in my discussion of coding and representation is not intended to suggest that the fundamental monistic philosophy underlying modern psychobiology should be rejected or that the neurophysiological data showing spatial-temporal feature selectivity of individual neurons are, in any way, less than fully valid within their own realm. Rather, this section is intended to stress the idea that neurophysiological reductionism for the particular theories of visual perceptual representation discussed in the preceding section may be somewhat premature. The general question of whether or not aspects of single-cell activity can be detected at the molar psychological level is critically important but still unanswered.

This concluding section raises the more specific question of whether or not these very particular perceptual phenomena can be meaningfully ascribed to lateral inhibitory interaction, feature filtering, or cortical column forms of representation at the present time in light of recent psychological and physiological evidence. Although the issue of representation is common to all levels of the nervous system and all levels of psychological function, I have constrained the discussion to the domain of perception because of the simple fact that this is the area in which most of the data and specific models are to be found. The general question is reopened later when I discuss the representation of learning.

Someday psychobiologists may consider this current trend in single-neuron feature filtering "explanations" of representational processes exactly as we now look upon the computer models, the telephonic models, or even more ancient hydraulic and pneumatic models of brain function of the past—as simply the subsequent stage in a series of reductionistic fads. It is entirely possible that they will also make some judgments about reductionism itself, which may not differ too drastically from those judgments made by physicists in the field of gas dynamics. Few physicists would consider a microscopic analysis of the dynamics of individual gas atoms as a possible and practical means of predicting the overall behavior of a container of gas. Instead, they use the external metrics of pressure, volume, and temperature—statistical estimates of the central tendencies of the individual particles.

Psychobiologists may in the not-too-distant future also come to the same sort of conclusion—that complex mental activities, though admittedly represented by the pooled statistical properties of ensembles of individual cells, still cannot in any practical sense be explained in terms of the individual behavior of these microscopic structural units.

This may be more obvious in some areas of psychobiological investigation than in others. The communication of information patterns through the ascending pathways seems amenable to some type of single-cell analysis. The explanation of most perceptual phenomena, however, lies at a level of network complexity with which no current neurophysiological technology can yet deal, just as the more macroscopic problem of networks of nuclei described in Chapter 5 is impeded by an absence of an appropriate methodology. It is also true that we have a very difficult time distinguishing between processes that superficially seem closely related by experimental designs but that may have quite different underlying mechanisms.

At the outset of this chapter and several times within it, I have reiterated the important concept that analogies of process should not be mistaken for homologies of structure. This is essentially a negative comment. It would be appropriate to end this chapter on a more positive note of enormous good sense with regard to this issue. Eric Kandel, a distinguished modern neurophysiologist who works mainly on the gastropod *Aplysia,* made some comments at a recent meeting on the biological basis of learning. Although he was talking specifically about learning, his attitude toward the general problem of representation is particularly significant as a summary of the point of view presented in this chapter. The ideas expressed also provide a stepping stone to the next chapter, on the nurophysiological basis of learning. His thoughts have been summarized by the meeting's organizers as follows:

> The vocabulary used to describe the alterations seen at a cellular level should be distinguished from the vocabulary used to describe alterations in the behavior of an intact organism. Even if a cellular response showed all the features associated with behavioral habituation, Kandel argued the cellular alteration is not habituation and should not be called that. Rather the cellular changes should be referred to by its mechanisms or its properties: excitatory synaptic decrement, inhibitory recruitment, etc. This would avoid the difficulties inherent in (incorrectly) applying behavioral terms to physiological processes. Habituation is an animal process much like walking and talking. One would certainly not say that a cellular change is walking. Why then should it be habituating? The fact that we sometimes speak *colloquially* about the "behavior" of cells should not mislead us into thinking that this is logically equivalent to the "behavior" of an organism. Unless the definition of behavior is to become meaningless, it should be restricted to the movement of muscles, secretion of glands, etc.
>
> The tendency to apply behavioral terms to cellular processes is unfortunate even when the behavioral function of the cell is known. It is worse, as is usually the case, when there is no demonstrable relationship between overt behavior and cellular processes being examined. Here one could be in the position of calling a synaptic change "habituation at the cellular level" without knowing what the cell actually contributes (if anything) to the behavior or its habituation. Thus, it is possible that a change called habituation at the cellular level might ultimately be shown to be directly involved in producing reflex sensitization! It was Kandel's contention that the rational development of behavioral psychology and neurobiology and their merger require that critical distinctions at different levels of discourse be maintained [from Teyler, Baum, & Patterson, 1975, p. 67].

In other words, Kandel is presenting us with the equally valid converse of Harris's statement quoted on page 491. The application of behavioral observations to physiological observations is an act of theorizing, just as is applying a neural explanation to behavioral processes. The direct linking of the microscopic physiological and molar behavioral levels—the problem *of representation*—is a complex task that is both different and more difficult than that of the tasks of either neurophysiology or psychology. One cannot assume that the conceptual linkage has been established simply on the basis of a similarity in the form or time course of the process. Far more evidence is required to establish the actual coded representation of any mental act by a network of neurons, and that evidence is yet to be forthcoming in almost every case.

8

Neural Correlates of Learning: Basic Concepts and Findings

A. INTRODUCTION

In this chapter I turn to another aspect of the problems of representation and localization—the issue of the physiological bases of learning. The study of learning has been one of the main streams of psychology in this century. The reason for the enormous interest in learning was best summed up by Sigmund Koch in his article on behaviorism in the 1968 edition of the *Encyclopedia Britannica,* when he said:

> Traditional psychology had approached learning as subsidiary to sensory and perceptual problems. But an S-R psychology, by sidestepping perception, is prone to place central emphasis on learning. Moreover by 1913 learning had proved to be a field eminently open to objective study—whether the task was reception of Morse code by man or escape from problem boxes by animals. Behaviourism became primarily a learning psychology and remained so throughout its history [p. 400].

When one is unable to explain the basic mechanisms of such an elusive phenomenon as mind, as the behaviorists claim we cannot, how very satisfying it is at least to be able to study the dynamics of change in that phenomenon. That portion of the problem that is not understood is at least held constant, and that part (the dynamics of variation) that is measurable becomes preeminent. Furthermore, learning per se has enormous intrinsic interest. It represented (incorrectly as it turned out) to early twentieth century psychologists one of the main features that distinguishes man from the lower species. Knowledge about learning behavior also possesses enormous practical implications considering the huge investment of time and money in education made by all societies, primitive or modern.

It was not until the emergence of what Koch refers to as the Neobehaviorism of the 1950s and 1960s therefore, that a renaissance of theoretical, introspective, and physiological reductionistic traditions in experimental psychology stimulated a resurgence of interest in perception, mental phenomena, and, most germane to the present discussion, a physiological approach to the study of learning.

Why is the study of the neural basis of learning conceptually important? It is important because the dynamics of the neural network are a strong clue to the network's nature. It is often only in the changes that occur among the inter-connections that we are able to discern the relevant aspects of network organization. It is as if the static states are camouflaged by the enormous complexity of which they are a part until they change. Thus the study of neural plasticity can act as a window to a better understanding of the more general nature of representation of mental processes by neurons and help to clarify the nature of the missing logical link between single cells and molar behavior. It is that not-yet-understood link, probably mediated by the concatenated action of networks of neurons, that remains the greatest puzzle in representation theory.

The study of the neural basis of learning is also important because of the biological significance to the organism of rapid behavioral responses to environmental challenges. Without plastic synapses, the entire evolutionary development of animal species would be greatly retarded. Fewer animals would be able to survive long enough to be sorted out by natural selection and pass on their strengths and abilities to the next generation. Although the existence of plants, which do not learn, may seem to be a counter-example to this concept, animals face different challenges than do plants because their activity and mobility places them in self-generated and active, rather than passive, interaction with their environment.

In spite of its importance, as we see in this chapter, there is still no definitive theory of the cellular basis of learning. Those cellular studies that have concentrated on neuronal changes as a result of experience often result in an unsatisfactory and logically frail linkage of the neural and behavioral data.

In spite of a diversity of theoretical opinion and weakness in the logical foundation of contemporary theories of learning, a number of complementary hypotheses have emerged describing one or another aspect of the many plausible changes in neural networks that must be correlated with the adaptive behavioral changes we call *learning*. The general appreciation that there are multiple neural basis of learning is, itself, important. It implies, as Elliott Valenstein (1970) has pointed out, that there is "no compelling reason to maintain that only one mechanism underlies the stability and plasticity of all behaving organisms [p. 20] ."

The multiple viewpoints, theories, descriptions, and models of learning probably truly reflect the fact that there are multiple neural mechanisms serving as the neural substrates of a wide variety of the dynamic and plastic processes referred to as *learned behavior*. Furthermore, the different points of view resulting from the experiments carried out in behavioral, neurophysiological, or biochemical laboratories also reflect the technical and conceptual complexity of the problem of establishing acceptable neural explanations of learning.

The problems of definitively establishing that some neural process is a true transactional or coded equivalent of some adaptive behavioral response is identical in principle to the problem of determining whether a candidate sensory code is a true code. Because of the more complex nature of the learning problem, however, the possible opportunities for misidentifying plastic responses and adaptive behavior are more numerous there than in the sensory problem. Indirect feedback effects, similar temporal courses of learned responses and the actual plastic neuronal change, changes in posture, and confusion of control and storage functions, all can contribute to spurious misidentifications of what are otherwise unequivocally sound neurophysiological data with the information storage process itself. I develop some of these obstacles to understanding the neural basis of learning in the discussion to follow.

But what is learning? It is with this question that my discussion must begin. In the next section I provide one possible definition of this important complex of mental processes.

1. Toward a Definition of Learning

Behavioral plasticity, or learning, is certainly one of the most useful biological capabilities of organisms. Learning permits appropriate high-speed adaptive response to immediate environmental challenges, just as organic evolution provides a longer-term means of accommodating the organism's behavior and structure to environmental pressures. It is not yet certain exactly where in the animal kingdom true learning can actually first be observed or, for that matter, if there is any lower limit; even protozoans have been reported to learn. We do know that as one ascends the phylogenetic tree, there is a gradual increase in the complexity of abilities on the part of animals to rapidly modify their behavior as a result of previous experience. In the culminant case of man, this behavioral plasticity, and the memory of past experience that it embodies, has been complemented by the time-binding provided by the memories stored in libraries, archives, architecture, and all other artifacts of what is called *culture*. The process of teaching, through either oral or written means, is the process that links the past to the future by guiding the student to appropriate material in the cultural storehouse. Because, as most evolutionists agree, experience does not directly affect genetic coding, rapid behavioral plasticity is the unique medium through which experience can cumulate as each generation builds upon the cultural foundation provided by previous ones.

Curiously, in spite of its preeminent role in the life of advanced animals, a satisfactory formal definition of learning has not been forthcoming. A typical dictionary says only that learning is the "acquisition of knowledge," and much of modern experimental psychology still is directed at nothing more than an elaboration of this simple definition. Perhaps this deficiency is a result of the scope of the problem and the multiple interpretations the word learning has in so many aspects of human existence. The definition usually given in elementary psychology textbooks of learning as a "change in behavior as a function of experience" is obviously too vague and but a poor paraphrase of the dictionary definition. The psychological definition is too simplistic because it is all too easy to mistakenly include behavioral changes within this broad rubric that most psychobiologists and lay observers would agree should not be called learning. Behavior could directly change as a direct result of an experience that damaged some part of the behaving organisms response mechanism; yet that obviously is not what is generally meant by learning. Similarly, there are many processes that produce changes in behavior over a period of time closely related to the experiences of the organisms that should also not be called learning. Berlucchi and Buchtel (1975), for example, exclude the following processes from any definition of learning: "growth, maturation, aging, fatigue, receptor adaptation, changes in arousal, attention, motivation, and obviously disease [p. 481]." The distinction between processes such as development and aging, on the one hand, and learning, on the other, in particular, represents the most serious empirical difficulty in research in this area. Because development and experience are always going on simultaneously, the experimental difficulties involved in determining which is the causal agent in altered behavior are often profound. Careful control of developmental change during what are ostensibly extended studies of learning is not always possible, and, therefore, a considerable literature has grown up concerning what is usually referred to as the nature-nurture issue.

Definitions of learning based on exclusion of other processes, particularly when they too are ill-defined, do not satisfy, however, and a more precise means of defining what I discuss later is required. Although it is possible to define learning on exclusively operational bases, I prefer a definition that stresses the general conceptual similarities of the many forms of learning.

One approach to a conceptual, rather than an operational, definition of learning is to add some criterion to the general notion of behavioral change that includes the appropriate processes rather than excludes the inappropriate ones. One such criterion is the *specificity* of the learned change. This criterion has the desirable property of providing a definition of learning based on conceptual inclusion rather than exhaustive exclusion.

A thoughtful and concise definition of learning stressing the idea of specificity (although restricted to conditioning types of learning paradigms) has been presented by Neil Miller (1967). His definition meets many of the desiderata of crispness and exclusiveness to which I have alluded. Miller (1967) asserts that: "Learning is a relatively permanent increase in response strength that is based on previous reinforcement and that can be made specific to one out of two or more arbitrarily selected stimulus situations [p. 644]." He then expands upon the key terms of the definition in more specific terms:

1. "Relatively permanent" means that the change lasts for days or months rather than seconds or minutes. Perhaps some of the physical processes involved in learning are transient, but under normal circumstances the final product of the entire sequence should be relatively permanent.

2. "Increase in response strength" means an increase in the prepotency of the response; in other words, in its ability to occur in competition with other responses. If the strength of the competing responses remains equal, there is an increase in the probability that the response will occur. But learning can also result in a decrease in the probability that a specific response will occur. It is obvious that such decrements are frequently the product of learning new responses that are incompatible with the one that is becoming less probable; we are *tentatively* assuming this is the case with all learned decreases in the probability of response occurrence.

3. "Reinforcement" involves association by temporal contiguity and can be produced in two ways:

a) In *classical conditioning* a conditioned stimulus (CS) is reinforced when it is followed promptly by an unconditioned stimulus (UCS) that elicits the response to be learned.

b) In *instrumental learning* (also called trial-and-error learning, type II conditioning, or operant conditioning), a response is reinforced when it is promptly followed by a reward.

4. The final criterion—that a learned response can be made specific to an arbitrarily selected stimulus—is believed to be the most fundamental one. When the response is not, initially, reasonably specific to the arbitrarily selected stimulus, it can be made so by trials on which it is reinforced to that one stimulus and not to others.

Miller (1967) concludes:

As far as I know, phenomena that will meet the foregoing test of criterion 4 also will be found to satisfy all of the other criteria. This increases our confidence that we are dealing with a fundamental aspect of nature rather than with a purely arbitrary and relatively useless definition. Criteria 1 and 2 are necessary but not sufficient; criterion 3 may also be used as a test of learning. Actually, all of the laws of learning are a part of its definition, and the more of these a particular example is known to satisfy the more confident we can be that it actually is Grade-A Certified Learning [p. 644].

Miller then notes that these criteria specifically exclude from the rubric of learning such phenomena as fatigue, increases in performance capability as a result of higher level of physical fitness, some forms of habituation (a decrease in response strength to familiar stimuli), and unreinforced response increases such as sensitization or pseudoconditioning.

I believe that Miller's definition of learning is vastly superior to any other so far proposed. But it is clear, after reading his commentary, that Miller has restricted his definition to a relatively narrowly defined class of laboratory learning situations. Those are the ones that are commonly referred to as *conditioning.* An important aspect of the "neobehaviorism" of recent years has been the expansion of the domain of psychological research into a number of other topics collectively called *cognitive learning*. No longer do the association models of learning (which assert that a link is established between a stimulus and a response because of simple contiguity or instrumental reward) satisfy the learning researcher, nor do models of learning that assert that the more complex forms of learning are produced by concatenations of simple conditioned "reflexes" into complex cognitive learning. Thus the idea that classical and instrumental conditioning encompass all of the important aspects of learning is clearly much too restrictive.

As admirable as Miller's definition is, it creates a number of difficulties in light of the broad scope of contemporary learning research and this drift away from theories that assume that complex learning is nothing more than a concatenation of simpler forms of conditioning. Miller's definition is deficient particularly with regard to his first and third points but because of too limited scope rather than any basic conceptual error.

It is clear that Miller's first point, concerning the relative permanence of anything that might be called learning, is obsolescent in light of the wide variety of short-term storage processes now encompassed within the learning rubric. Although a distinction may be made between different kinds of learning based mainly on the duration of persistence of the memory trace (as we see in greater detail later in this chapter), there is little to justify the exclusion of the shorter-term behavior changes from the general category of learning as Miller would suggest. Furthermore, even classical conditioning can be quickly extinguished and thus is reversible and not "relatively permanent." This observation alone is sufficient to invalidate the universality of Miller's first point.

The essence of the criticism of Miller's third point is simply that his attention is limited in this aspect to only two of the many different research paradigms of learning of current theoretical interest and does not incorporate studies of more complex forms of cognitive learning.

In spite of the constrained context and exclusion of cognitive and short-term memory, Miller's definition still stands as the best available general definition of learning. This is mainly because of his insightful emphasis of the powerful principle of specificity elaborated in his fourth point. The essence of his definition, as he says, is that specificity is both the necessary and sufficient criterion of learning.

To end this initial attempt to define learning and provide a common vocabulary, let us consider a number of interrelated terms that play an important role in the subsequent discussions of this chapter. Although everyone will not agree with all aspects of these definitions, the following paragraphs indicate how I use the words.

Memory: If learning is the process by which behavioral changes occur, then memory is the mechanism within which the acquired patterns of information are stored. An alternative definition of memory is that it is the stored information itself. The nature of the memory *mechanism* as well as the nature of the learning *process* are both essential aspects of the psychobiological problem of the neural basis of behavioral plasticity.

Consolidation: Most experimental studies of learning have shown that there is a period following the initial training or experience during which information is highly labile. Subsequently it becomes more permanently recorded in the memory. The process of conversion from labile short-term storage to a permanent long-term storage is referred to as *consolidation.*

Forgetting: Reduction in learned response strength is usually referred to as *forgetting.* Determination of the actual mechanism involved (forgetting could be due to competing responses, trace decay, unlearning, or some interference between new and old experiences, to mention only a few examples) is an area of active inquiry in many psychological laboratories. Forgetting may be essentially passive and occur simply as a result of the passage of time (although this is, like the general nature-nurture question, difficult to definitely establish) or essentially active, as evidenced by such processes as controlled extinction, and may require the actual learning of competing responses or unlearning of old ones.

Reinforcement: Reinforcement is a general term used to describe the procedure by which stimulus salience and thus response selectivity is achieved. In the most general sense, reinforcement is the establishment of the biological significance or symbolic meaning of a stimulus that seems to be required to effectively (and some would say meaningfully) link a particular stimulus with a particular response pattern. In a classical conditioning experiment, reinforcement is merely the near simultaneous presentation of the stimulus that naturally evokes the particular response and the initially ineffective stimulus that is to be associated as a result of the training with that response. As the simplistic associationist theories of the origin of more complex forms of learning have declined in popularity, reinforcement has taken on a more cognitive meaning. A stimulus is reinforcing to the extent that it creates some affective state that either exascerbates or satisfies some biological need. Reinforcement in either the classic or more modern sense may be negative or positive, increasing or decreasing the responses produced by a particular stimulus.

Now that a general definition of learning and some of the more important related terms have been approached, if not completely clarified, I can move on to the next step—an attempt to produce a classification of the various kinds of learning.

2. Two Classifications of Learning

Dynamic response processes that are initiated by experience and meet the criterion of selectivity incorporated into Miller's definition are to be found in a wide variety of animal behavior. In this section, two schemes of classification that bring order to our otherwise bewildering variety of empirical studies are considered. In presenting these two classifications, the reader should be forewarned of the patent impossibility of adequately reviewing the full scope of learning research in the few pages allotted to the topic here. The scope of both theory and data in the field, to put it simply, are overwhelming and often not particularly germane to the psychobiological goals of this book. For more detailed discussions of the specifics of psychological technique and data, the reader is referred to such excellent sources as Adams (1976), Murdock (1974), and Kintsch (1970).

The two ways in which learning are classified are based on completely different criteria. The first and somewhat obsolescent approach is a scheme based mainly upon the types of procedures used in laboratory studies of learning. This classification covers the full spectrum of learning processes by an exhaustive listing of empirical operations but does not emphasize the common features of learning exhibited among the various paradigms. This scheme, nevertheless, embodies sufficient useful information to justify its consideration at this point.

The second approach to classification of learning processes stresses certain common biological characteristics that transcend the particular methodologies. It is based upon the temporal properties of the several different kinds of learning. Learning in this schema is primarily classified according to measures of the persistence of the memory trace.

a. A Classification of Learning Based on Experimental Paradigms

This section presents a classification scheme of learning types based upon the experimental paradigms used in psychology laboratories. Included are the types of learning referred to as *habituation, classical conditioning, instrumental conditioning, latent learning, verbal and cognitive learning,* and *motor skill learning.* The following paragraphs elaborate upon the meaning and significance of each of these categories.

Habituation. Habituation is the progressive reduction in the amplitude of a response to repeated presentations of a stimulus although all salient dimensions are kept constant. Habituation can be distinguished from fatigue mainly because it is quickly reversible (dishabituation) when some aspect of the stimulus is changed. Habituation and dishabituation, therefore, are more closely related to the novelty of a stimulus than to any aspect of metabolic breakdown or depletion of available energy stores.

Although the mechanisms may be obscure, habituation and dishabituation are clearly forms of learning in which there is a transient, rather than a semipermanent, reorganization of the neural apparatus as a result of experience. Indeed, habituated responses also recover as a result of the passage of time as well as through dishabituation. An opposite effect, a progressive increase in response strength as a result of repeated stimulation, known as *sensitization,* or *pseudoconditioning,* is also frequently observed and is a regular artifact in many types of learning experiments.

Classical or Pavlovian conditioning. Probably the best known form of learning is classical conditioning, the result of a now almost ritualized procedural design made famous by the work of Ivan Pavlov (1849-1936) in the nineteenth century. Pavlovian conditioning is a highly circumscribed procedure in which a conditioned stimulus (CS), which previously was incapable of eliciting a response that is naturally (or through prior training) evoked by an unconditioned stimulus (UCS), acquires the ability to trigger that response. The medium of reinforcement for the production of this form of learning is the nearly simultaneous presentation (pairing) of the CS and UCS. It has been repeatedly shown that a half-second asynchrony of the two stimuli is optimal for most forms of classical conditioning. Simple effector responses such as a foot lift, eyelid twitch, or salivation are the typical responses used in this type of experiment.

Early learning theories often asserted that a simple conditioned association of a CS and a response was the prototype of all other forms of learning. More complex learning, it was hypothesized, simply resulted from a concatenation of myriads of simple, classically conditioned associations. Although such a concatenation theory is possible in some mathematical sense, such an approach is generally not accepted by modern psychological theorists as plausible. As we see later, however, most neuronal explanations of learning are, in fact, relatively restricted models of classical conditioning.

Instrumental or operant conditioning.   Instrumental conditioning, as commonly practiced in the laboratory, requires the uncontrolled emmission of spontaneous responses that are not originally under the experimenter's control. Typically, an animal is placed in an environment and allowed to explore and manipulate the objects in it. The experimental subject is rewarded when it "accidentally" performs all or some portion of a desired response. In the simplest case, within the context of the prototypical "Skinner Box" (a device containing a response mechanism and a means of providing reinforcement), a hungry or thirsty monkey, for example, might be afforded the opportunity to press a lever. In exploring the interior of the box, seemingly more or less fortuitously, the monkey may occasionally so respond. At that point a reinforcement, such as a pellet of food or a few drops of water might be presented. As in classical conditioning, the key factor in reinforcement seems to be that the emitted response and the reinforcement occur in sufficiently close temporal proximity to become "associated" with each other. Figure 8-1 shows an elaborate Skinner box controlled by a digital computer and designed to determine a monkey's audiogram.

Instrumental conditioning was made especially famous by both the laboratory work (Skinner, 1938; 1966) and the social commentary (Skinner, 1971) of B. F. Skinner. Simple instrumental conditioning, as classical conditioning had been a few years ago, is now thought by some contemporary authors to be prototypical of many of the more complex cognitive and linguistic forms of human learning. However, the analogy between complex verbal and cognitive learning and simple laboratory paradigms of instrumental learning also appears to be a superficial one at best.

Instrumental conditioning is both more interesting and more difficult to explain than classical conditioning, because many of the relevant stimuli, particularly those leading to the evocation of the exploratory responses, are ill-defined or unknown. Indeed, it is uncertain which aspect of the original exploratory response is the key aspect in the learning process, and many training trials are usually required to "shape" the desired behavior.

Because of the lack of crisply defined antecedent conditions, studies that attempt to establish the neural correlates of instrumental learning are beset by a fundamental problem; successful conditioning of a neuronal or brain response, such as modulation of an electroencephalograph, may result from causes only indirectly relevant to the actual learning mechanism thought to be under examination.

Latent learning. It is entirely possible for a subject to learn on the basis of stimuli of which he is unaware. Awareness or attentiveness seem not to be an absolute necessity for some kinds of learning. Animals as well as humans can learn as a result of having passively experienced a particular evironmental situation. This may be achieved without any specific reinforcement for the particular responses emitted or explicit awareness of the stimuli from that environment. Such learning is referred to as *latent learning* and is considered by many to underlie many learning activities in humans.

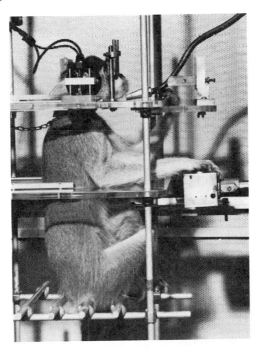

FIG. 8.1 A sophisticated operant conditioning apparatus for testing the audiogram of monkeys. Note the monkey's paw on the response lever and the tube conveying liquid reinforcement to him. This entire apparatus is under computer control. (From Stebbins, Clark, Pearson, & Weiland, ©1973, with the permission of S. Karger AG, Basel.)

In the laboratory, however, there is a much more specific meaning to the term. The prototypical experiment of Tolman and Honzik (1930) showed that rats that had simply spent some time wandering about in a maze learned the correct pathway in subsequent reinforced test trials faster than rats that had no experience with the maze. Obviously such a form of learning ignores the possible presence of implicit reinforcing factors such as the opportunity to explore, the pleasure of creeping along a wall, or the delights of simply living in a complex environment. These intangible reinforcements, although difficult to quantify and control, might well have contributed to a form of learning akin to those of real life situations.

Latent learning thus serves as an important link to other forms of human learning stressing the cognitive or symbolic aspects of experience that may have nothing to do with explicit reinforcements. It is possible, of course, to describe such a state as "knowing one's way around" as implicitly reinforcing, but the highly specific notion of reinforcement usually accepted begins to blur and disappear in such a context.

An important conceptual problem is suggested by the study of latent learning. Learning paradigms such as classical conditioning may omit some essential parts of the total complex composing human learning processes. Although it is useful, of course, to fraction out some microcomponent of a complex process for careful conceptual analysis, there may be a fatal difficulty introduced by such abstracted experiments if one's goal is actually the understanding of the more macroscopic aspects of learning. The repeated failure of attempts throughout the history of psychology to synthesize complex learning from simpler forms attests to the magnitude of this difficulty. The point is that learning, even in its simplest forms, may actually be far more complex than such categories as "classical" or "instrumental" conditioning suggest.

Motor skill learning. Another major class of learning research includes the acquisition of complex and coordinated motor responses. In general, the learning of motor skills is a self-guided process in which the "reinforcements" result directly from the acts themselves. Riding a bicycle, shooting baskets or following a moving dot in a laboratory pursuit task are all skills that are mainly self-tutoring. The reinforcement is implicit in the successful consummation of the motor act rather than in any immediate affective or appetitive pay off. It is difficult to specify the specific stimuli that are utilized, the individual motor unit responses that are learned, or the nature of the complex motor patterning that is produced. Indeed, the individual motor acts may differ greatly for two subjects performing the same task. Interestingly, the cerebellum, the portion of the brain most involved in coordinated motor control, is at once the center of the brain with the greatest number of neurons (see Chapter 3) and (with the exception of the peripheral portions of the sensory nervous system) characterized by the most simple and repetitive structural organization. It is possible to think of the cerebellum in terms of a simple switchboard model to a greater degree than any other portion of the brain. It is not surprising, in addition, to note that learned motor skills remain remarkably resistant to forgetting.

Verbal and cognitive learning. Finally, we come in this first classification scheme to the enormously complex, and as yet neurophysiologically obscure, kinds of learning that are associated with words and other symbolic pattens. Verbal learning is, without question, the epitome of human learning capacities and perhaps the most specific single criterion distinguishing the human species from its relatives.

Prior to the last decade, verbal learning had been studied in such highly simplified and abstracted forms that this distinction had been lost. Typical of verbal learning paradigms was the use of nonsense syllable lists as a "pure" verbal stimulus form uncontaminated by the associations that real words might have with some cognitive (and thus, possibly, highly reinforcing) experience. A considerable amount of work was done with regard to the serial position of items in a list, the pacing of the learning experience, and a number of other variables thought to be essential descriptors of human verbal learning capacities. Other factors such as the relevance of the material or "chunking" strategies (in which material was implicitly organized into subdivisions for easier learning), were thought to only contaminate the "essential" aspects of verbal learning.

In recent years, however, there has been a gradual realization that these "contaminants" were, in fact, the essential aspects of verbal learning. All of the careful efforts to reduce the semantic and cognitive content of the subject matter, or to block strategic "chunking," had hindered the development of understanding about how people actually learn really important things. In retrospect, as is usually the case, the hints were always there that affirmed this misdirection. No successful teacher ever used classical conditioning as a tutoring method; and anyone with a minimum of classroom experience knew that learning proceeded faster with meaningful than with meaningless materials. Whatever the influence of such simple parameters as the massing of trials or the order of study, it was greatly outweighed by the much stronger cognitive and semantic variables.

Now the main thrust in verbal learning research is toward these same cognitive parameters that were once considered to be contaminants. Cognitive learning in humans, rather than classical conditioning of animals, is now the most active area in experimental psychology learning laboratories. A whole new spectrum of research problems that stress the cognitive aspects of learning have become the dominant themes in modern verbal learning research. For example, a typical issue (August 1975) of the *Journal of Verbal Learning and Verbal Behavior* consisted of the following titles:

1. Speech Recoding in Reading
2. On the Acquisition of a Semantic System
3. Conceptual Complexity and Imagery in Comprehension and Memory

4. A Test of Confusion Theory of Encoding Specificity
5. Output Editing for Lexical Status in Artifically Elicited Slips of the Tongue
6. Within Word Structure in the Tip-of-the-Tongue Phenomenon
7. Rehearsal Strategy Effects in Children's Discrimination Learning: Confronting the Crucible
8. State-Dependent Accessibility of Retrieval Cues in the Retention of a Categorized List
9. Memory for Serial Position
10. Storage and Retrieval Changes that Occur in the Development and Release of PI

Only the ninth article in this list appears to be a vestige of the older tradition, and even this paper contains a new procedural twist that distinguishes it from the earlier and narrower studies of nonsense syllable acquisition. Thus there has been a substantial shift in the content of laboratory studies of verbal learning toward paradigms in which the meaning and significance of words are stressed.

In changing its content, however, contemporary learning research has moved away from any possible psychobiological explanation. This is a critically important point that must be reiterated here. It is a basic feature of all of the ensuing discussion that there is absolutely no physiological theory that even begins to suggest mechanisms that could mediate learning of the more complex cognitive types I have just discussed. Although neural mechanisms have been conceived that mimic to a certain degree the classical or instrumental conditioning paradigm and although compound brain potentials concomitantly vary with certain cognitive aspects of stimuli, there is not even a glimmer of understanding of the neural bases of even the simplest aspect of cognitive learning. This does not mean that the basic concept of a network state modulated by synaptic plasticity is invalid as an explanation of behavioral change or that it is not generally applicable in some ultimate theoretical sense. Rather, the point is that no link has yet been established between the coded transactional processes formed of a concatenation of myriads of elemental neural processes and these more complex mental processes. To summarize, in contrast to simpler forms of learning for which speculative theories have been proposed, no psychobiology of cognition or cognitive learning yet exists.

b.   A Classification of Learning Based on Temporal Properties

In this section I consider an alternative means of classifying various learning processes that is based on the measured temporal properties of the memory traces rather than one based on the experimenters' paradigm of research. The classification scheme generated on the basis of such temporal cirterion has widespread popularity today and, like the one presented in the previous section, encompasses a wide variety of learning phenomena.

The major premise of this approach is that there exists a hierarchy of learning mechanisms with different time constants that are differentially reflected in a variety of human behavioral experiments. Each of the mechanisms in this hierarchy is characterized by a particular duration of persistence of its form of the memory trace. Adherents to this temporal hierarchical theory, both implicitly and explicitly, make the assertion that the family of assumed mechanisms are separately assayable by approrpiate experimental procedures.

Among memory-hierarchy theorists, however, there is no universal agreement on the number of stages that should be included in the theory. Originally, writers like D. E. Broadbent (1958) suggested a simple dichotomy of short- and long-term memory. In recent years, as the technical approaches have proliferated, additional categories of learning have been proposed. At the present time, at a minimum, the following memory mechanisms are usually included in any hierarchical theory of memory:

1. After-Images and Iconic Memory—The Sensory Store
2. Short-Term Memory
3. Intermediate-Term Memory
4. Long-Term Memory

After-images and iconic memory — The sensory store.   At the first level of the hierarchy (in terms of the brevity of their persistence) are two forms of very short-term sensory memory—after-images and "icons." These forms of storage are characterized by rapidly fading images that maintain the pictographic aspects of the original stimulus in an almost photographic fashion. Until very recently, it was thought that simple visual persistence—after-images—explained everything about the initial short-term availability of information following the cessation of a stimulus; that is, most workers viewed after-images and icons as essentially the same thing. Recently, however, Barbara Sakitt of Stanford University has suggested that the primitive after-image, presumably due to simple photochemical persistences, exhibits significantly different characteristics than does the process that has come to be called *iconic storage* by such workers as Ulric Neisser (1967). The conventional after-image is generally produced by much higher stimulus energy than is required to establish iconic storage. Furthermore, the classic after-image lasts for many seconds, whereas it has been repeatedly demonstrated that the relatively low-stimulus-energy driven, visual icon lasts for only a few tenths of a second.

Nevertheless, Sakitt (1975; 1976) has presented convincing experimental evidence that the visual icon is, however, like the after-image, also a retinal and not a centrally mediated phenomena. In this regard, these two processes are probably quite different from other memory storage mechanisms that are almost certainly mediated centrally.

Iconic sensory storage was originally brought into prominence by the work of Sperling (1960) and Averbach and Coriell (1961). These workers showed that the visual icon of sensory store lasted for approximately 150 milliseconds and that information (in the form of random alphabetic characters) could be read out at the rate of one alphabetic character every 10 milliseconds.

In large part, therefore, iconic memory seems to behave as if it was another form of simple temporal persistence or spread of the original brief stimulus.[1] Thus brief physical stimuli are thought to be prolonged by the temporal "spread function" of the peripheral visual system. A large number of visual phenomena dealing with the short-term interaction of sequential stimuli are therefore encompassed by this same explanation. Such diverse phenomena as the critical duration for visual thresholds (the time in which two subthreshold stimuli can summate to produce a suprathreshold response), critical flicker fusion experiments, and the phenomena associated with what has been called the *psychological moment* [i.e., the time in which events are perceived as simultaneous, as defined by Stroud (1955)], all seem to be within the scope of this form of sensory storage.

Short-term memory.   For about 20 or 30 seconds following the presentation of almost any stimulus, there is a retention of the incoming information that is referred to as *short-term memory*. The storage of information at this level seems also to be independent of the cognitive or semantic content of the material and dependent only upon its phonemic or geometrical form. Nonsense syllables, for example, have been satisfactorily used to explore the persistence of short-term memory (e.g., Peterson & Peterson, 1959).

Short-term memory seems to act as a buffer that allows immediately useful information to be retained in a quickly usable and unencoded form. It also maintains the incoming information long enough for it to be transcribed (consolidated) into longer-term memories. Another use for the short-term buffer has been proposed by Atkinson and Shiffrin (1968; 1971). They suggest that short-term memory serves as the bidirectional interface between the environment and longer-term memories. They additionally suggest that after previous registration in the long-term memory, symbolically encoded information is returned to and possibly decoded in the short-term memory prior to its actual use. According to them (Atkinson & Shiffrin, 1971), this essentially equates the: "short term store with consciousness, that is, the thoughts and information of which we are currently aware can be considered part of the contents of the short term store [p. 83]."

Another special characteristic of short-term memory is its limited size or capacity. It is obvious, with its proposed link to awareness, that the capacity of short-

---

[1]Although simple temporal spread explanations are generally quite useful, there is at least one case in which they do not work. This problem occurs in a particular kind of masking experiment in which dichoptic and binocular observation procedures are compared. Masking experiments in which the mask is presented to one eye and the target to the other and the mask leads the target (forward masking) produce no masking. If, in the same viewing situation, the mask follows the target, then substantial masking occurs. But, if forward masking is done so that the same eye receives both mask and target, then masking is effective. For a full explanation of this perplexing empirical anomaly, the reader is referred to Uttal (1975a, pp. 81-88).

term memory must be much smaller than that of the longer-term memories. In fact, many learning theorists suggest that short-term memory acts as if it were similarly organized to the "push-down-and-out" mechanisms found in some modern computers. New information can be entered only at the expense of older information that is pushed out of this modest capacity storage unit.

Intermediate-term memory. Some psychologists have also suggested that there is also a memory of intermediate persistence. Ervin and Anders (1970), for example, have postulated a memory with a storage capacity that is larger and more persistent than that of short-term memory but less persistent and smaller than that of the very large capacity long-term memory. They assume, on the basis of experiments such as those of Baddeley and Dale (1966), that intermediate-term memory also differs from short-term memory in terms of the way in which the stored information has been processed. The phonemic, geometrical, and isomorphic aspects of the stimulus that predominated in sensory and short-term memories are superceded by symbolic reconstructions. Thus information is rearranged into meaningful "chunks" or groups and recoded into a symbolic representation that might have no relation to the original physical arrangement of the stimuli.

Long-term memory. Finally, current theory suggests that the information stored in intermediate-term memory is "consolidated" into a nearly permanent memory. Long-term memory seems to be characterized by both enormous capacity, very long persistence, and the ability to have the information it contains be accessed by probes or cues that operate on the basis of meaning or content, rather than stored location. This type of memory is referred to as *content addressable or associative store.* Surprisingly, long-term memory also seems to have relatively rapid access times and retrieval mechanisms that can be triggered by simple cues. We can rapidly call up recollections of a rich variety of experiences on the basis of the simplest of hints or clues; a flower's aroma may recall a complex of past experiences.

McGaugh (1968) has presented a useful diagram to conceptualize the major differences among the several different kinds of memories, which is reproduced in Fig. 8-2. The buffer referred to in his diagram was probably meant to be equivalent to a composite of after-images and the icon. The other three forms of learning correspond closely to the classification scheme presented in the preceding paragraphs. An important general characteristic of the four kinds of memory, of course, is that the rapidity with which the particular kinds of memory can be loaded corresponds, in each case, to the persistence of the trace. Memories that load quickly are of short persistence; those that load slowly are of long persistence.

Table 8-1 (originally prepared by Ervin & Anders, 1970) summarizes the charactersitics of the various types of memory included in the temporal hierarchy categorization scheme. This table, and the classification it embodies, represent

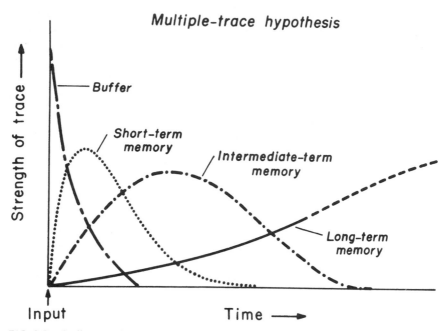

FIG. 8.2   A diagram showing the time courses of the several different kinds of memory. Note that the more persistent the memory is, the longer it takes to be loaded with information. (From McGaugh, ©1968, with the permission of Academia Nazionale dei Lincei.)

a relatively new approach to the problem of classifying memory types. It is more fertile than the classification scheme characterized by experimental methods in providing a conceptual basis for the integration of a wide variety of physiological data into a more universal and contemporary theory of learning and memory.

The notion of a hierarchy of memories of varying persistence, however, is not universally accepted. Melton (1970), for one, argues that it is actually exceedingly difficult to distinguish between a continuous process passing through successive stages, on the one hand, and a truly discrete system embodying the hierarchy presented here, on the other. Indeed, on the basis of behavioral evidence alone, it is not certain whether we are actually dealing with the single trace, dual trace, or multiple trace models shown in Fig. 8-3. The similarity of this argument to Towe's discussion of cortical columns in Chapter 7 may be of special interest to some of my readers.

One appealing alternative to the temporal hierarchical model of learning was detailed by William Whitten of the University of Michigan in an informal communication. He notes that the hierarchical memory model has been strongly challenged recently by models of learning that alternatively stress progressive and continuous cognitive reorganization or recoding of the material to be learned. This succession of reorganization might be carried out within a single memory

TABLE 8.1

Characteristics of the various kinds of human memory. (From Ervir & Anders, ©1970, with the permission of Rockefeller University Press.)

	Storage System				
	Sensory Memory	Short-term Memory	Intermediate-term Memory	Long-term Memory
Capacity	Limited by amount transmitted by receptor (?)	The 7 ± 2 of the memory span	Very large (no adequate estimate)	Very large (no adequate estimate)
Duration	Fractions of a second	Several seconds	Several minutes to several years	May be permanent
Entry into storage	Automatic with perception	Verbal recoding	Rehearsal	Overlearning
Organization	Reflects physical stimulus	Temporal sequence	Semantic and relational	?
Accessibility of traces	Limited only by speed of read out	Very rapid access	Relatively slow	Very rapid access
Types of information	Sensory	Verbal (at least)	All	All
Types of forgetting	Decay and erasure	New information replaces old	Interference: retroactive and proactive inhibition	May be none

531

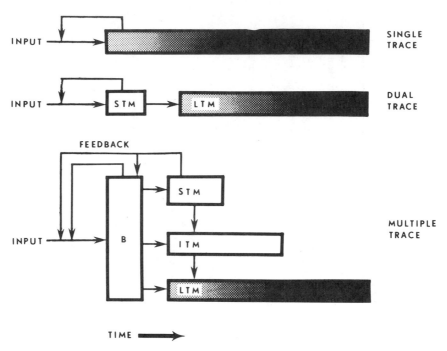

FIG. 8.3   Three possible models of the organization of the memory system proposed by McGaugh. In this drawing, the three models are contrasted against each other not only in terms of their differential time constants but also in terms of the flow of information between them. Abbreviations indicated are: STM = short-term memory; ITM = intermediate-term memory; LTM = long-term memory; and B = Buffer. (From McGaugh, ©1969, with the permission of Plenum Publishing.)

mechanism rather than in the anatomically discrete memory centers implicit in the hierarchical model. In support of this recoding hypothesis, Whitten points out the wide variability in measurements of short-term memory storage capacity and persistence. He also directs attention to the many kinds of implicit rehearsal processes now known to be occurring in learning that are not adequately represented in the hierarchical models. Whitten's suggestion is analogous to a computer *programming* alternative to the *hardware* solution implicit in the hierarchical model.

Clearly, at the black box level at which psychologists work, neither the hierarchical nor the recoding models can be fully "proven." They are but two of many possible theories explaining memory function. The hierarchical model, nevertheless, is a useful heuristic for contemplating possible physiological mechanisms. Furthermore, as we see later, some physiological investigations also support the hypothesis of several memories distinguishable on the basis of varying persistence.

The hierarchical hypothesis is also supported by the fact that the temporal dimension, along which these memories are classified, is a parsimonious and practical link between the physiological and psychological data and theoretical bases. Thus different stages in the psychological hierarchy are often found to be associated with physiological processes with distinctive temporal properties. Whether this is merely accidental or is a real equivalence of physiological and psychological processes with comparable time constants is the main point discussed later in this chapter.

Blocking experiments. The highly specific action of various blocking agents on particular forms of memory is also a strong argument in favor of a hierarchical system of memories. Experiments featuring controlled and selective blocking of particular stages of the learning process have been frequently reported in the last few years. In addition to the more classical psychological blocking procedures, such as interspersed recitation or rehearsal of irrelevant materials, and the few useful clinical cases of post-traumatic amnesia in human experiments, some more physiologically strenuous blocking procedures have been utilized in animal learning experiments. Electroconvulsive (Zornetzer & McGaugh, 1970), chemical or thermal shocks (Riccio, Hodges, & Randall, 1968), injections of antibiotics (Agranoff, 1967) or other chemicals that block protein synthesis, anesthetics, carbon dioxide (Lovell & Eisenstein, 1973), and other chemical poisons [particularly those that affect acetylcholine metabolism (Kety, 1970)], all produce effects supporting the general idea that several different forms of memory with varying time constants are simultaneously providing the basis for binding our past to our present. The reader is direct to Agranoff, Springer, and Quarton (1976) for a complete discussion of this topic.

In general, the agents blocking the synthesis of protein seem to selectively prevent the consolidation of short- and intermediate-term memory into long-term memory; agents that disrupt the electrical activity of the brain, such as electroconvulsive shock, seem to affect short- and intermediate-term memory but not long-term memory once acquired; and anesthetics seem to selectively inhibit medium-term memory.

Atkinson and Shiffrin's model. Psychologists have incorporated the hypothesis of a hierarchy of memory stores in some highly specific descriptions of possible and plausible organizations of the memorial elements and the information flow between them. A popular contemporary model of learning is the information-processing theory proposed by Atkinson and Shiffrin (1968) and Shiffrin and Atkinson (1969). Figure 8-4, a block diagram of their concept of the organization of the different types of memory, reveals its intellectual roots in the information-processing and computer technologies that have been so influential in guiding both theory and empirical strategies in psychology during the last three decades.

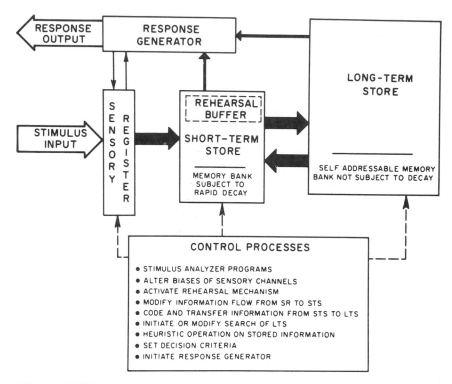

FIG. 8.4   Shiffrin and Atkinson's model of human memory. (From Shiffrin & Atkinson, ©1969, with the permission of The American Psychological Association.)

There are several essential elements to the Atkinson and Shiffrin theory that should be made explicit. One major contribution of their model is a specific hypothesis concerning the paths along which information is transmitted from one stage in the memory hierarchy to the next. Although the flow lines are procedural and do not represent particular anatomical pathways in their thinking, this formalization has been exceedingly useful in concretizing some psychobiological research strategies. Specifically, they suggest that information is passively transmitted from the sensory icon to the short-term store. Within the short-term store, information is processed by a reverbatory recycling that they refer to as "rehearsal." During the rehearsal stage, previously acquired information may enter short-term memory from long-term memory and become associated with the newly arriving information.

Another exceedingly important premise of the Atkinson and Shiffrin model is that the phonemic and geometric information in short-term memory is not represented isomorphically in long-term memory but rather is encoded into symbolic representations.

A further element to which I have already alluded is their emphasis on the central role played by short-term memory as the single interface between the subject and the external environment. Information entering through short-term memory, and subsequently stored in long-term memory, can produce appropriate responses only when it is decoded and restored into short-memory. In other words, short-term memory acts very much like an input-output channel in a typical digital computer. All information communication to or from the environment is controlled by the short-term memory even though that information may be either permanently or temporarily stored elsewhere.

Atkinson and Shiffrin propose that long-term memory, on the other hand, is capable of only highly specialized and limited interactions with the environment and internal transformations of the stored formation. Once information has been encoded and entered into long-term memory, it is unavailable until decoded and restored to the short-term memory. One task that long-term memory does effectively, and perhaps uniquely, is retrieval of information by "associative" recall procedures that depend upon the content of the stored information. These content-oriented recall strategies are remarkable feats of information processing themselves.

Rehearsal plays a highly important role in the Atkinson and Shiffrin model. Items are effectively transferred to long-term memory as a direct function of the time that they are rehearsed. This simple functional relationship thus accounts in their model for the well-known advantage that is possessed in recall by items presented either early or late in the training sequence.

It is in this emphasis on the critical importance of rehearsal, however, that the Atkinson and Shiffrin model displays its main weakness. The degree to which information will be successfully entered into long-term memory is obviously more a function of the nature of the information that simply of the number of times material has been rehearsed. We know that meaningful material is more accurately and longer remembered than is meaningless material. Significant information will be remembered after a single learning trial even though it is totally unrehearsed. Although some form of hypothetical implicit rehearsal may itself be related to meaningfulness, Atkinson and Shiffrin's model is clearly far too mechanical. Alternative approaches are needed that concentrate more upon the semantic content of stimulus information. Atkinson and Shiffrin's theory is best considered a model for rote learning of relatively meaningless information; the computer analogy that it embodies is appropriate only with respect to these highly constrained types of information processing. At a modest level of ecological validity, however, the model fails completely.

However, these are models of learning that do stress the semantic content of the information in ways that more realistically portray human memory. In recent years there has been a gradual fusion of the techniques and theories of "cognitive" and "learning" psychology. Words like "plans," "intentions," and

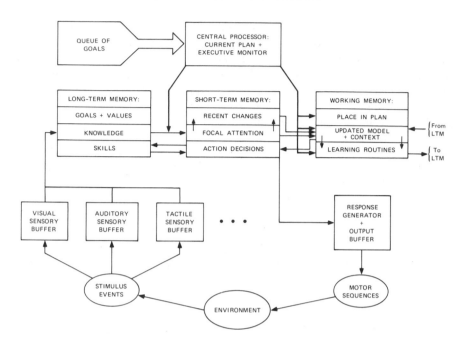

FIG. 8.5   Bower's model of the cognitive system involving both memorial and perceptual functions. Note the introduction of such terms as *goals* and *plans*. This kind of description of mental processes is not amenable to any conceivable psychobiological theorizing at the present time. (From Bower, ©1975, with the permission of Lawrence Erlbaum Associates.)

"meaning" are now to be found in discussions of memory and learning. Hypothetical processes such as "coding" and "chunking" characterize the work of the most recent learning theorists. A good introduction to this new approach is the volume edited by Estes (1975).

Anderson and Bower (1973) have proposed a new model of the organization of memory and learning that is significantly more complicated and inclusive than that proposed by Atkinson and Shiffrin, as well as far less dependent on simple mechanical processes such as rehearsal. The postulates of that theory are couched in contemporary linguistic terms and involve such heady topics as the "organization of knowledge." As one example, consider Bower's (1975) update of the Atkinson and Shiffrin model, as shown in Fig. 8-5. This newer model goes far beyond the computer-like information flow stressed by the older model. Bower obviously is talking about something quite different than rehearsal when he incorporates into memory and perception systems such terms as "goals," "values," and the "place in [the] plans."

Clearly, contemporary psychology has moved beyond the simple hierarchical model that was emphasized earlier in this section and beyond psychobiology's ability to speculate about the physiological underpinnings of many of the newly incorporated processes. Thus this new theory of learning, however accurate as a description of the relevant psychological processes, remains beyond the subject matter of this book. Simply put, there is no way yet to capture the "meaning" of a "cognitive plan" on the tip of the electrode.

3. Foundations of Contemporary Theory

In the following sections of this chapter, a sample of highly technical psychobiological data is reviewed. In this section I concentrate on some of the conceptual foundations of this data base by considering briefly the thoughts of two of the most important learning psychobiologists—Karl Lashley and E. Roy John.

At this point it is also appropriate to reiterate that there is, as yet, no universally accepted physiological explanation of the learning process and few robust proofs of most theories. Almost everything to be said in terms of reductionistic explanation is, at best, informed speculation based on considerations of reasonableness and exclusion of biological absurdities.

Why should the development of a solid psychobiological theory of learning be so difficult and progress so limited? The answer to this question is simple enough. The contemporary philosophy of and technology behind the study of neuronal function and process localization is largely misleading with regard to the study of learning! The main thrust in contemporary neurophysiology has been toward the development of techniques for the study of individual neurons. The main thrust in the ablative psychobiology has been to determine the function of specific nuclei. Yet if there is anything that is agreed upon by almost all psychobiologists when learning is considered, it is two points that are totally antithetical to these two thrusts. First, it is generally agreed, as I subsequently show, that all complex forms of learning must be the result of the change of state of networks of very large numbers of neurons rather than attributable to single neurons or synapses. Second, it is also agreed that learning is not a process that can be localized in any particular portion of the nervous system but is much more likely to be distributed widely throughout all levels of the brain and possibly even the spinal cord.

a. Lashley's Contribution

The general acceptance of the concept that memory is widely distributed in the central nervous system is traceable to what is probably the most celebrated of all papers in the field of the psychobiology of learning—Karl Lashley's (1950) classic discussion entitled "In Search of the Engram."

The engram in Lashley's terms is the biological, anatomical, or physiological means by which information is stored—the actual physical trace of the experience. It is analogous to the direction of magnetization of a magnetic core, or the hole punched in a paper card, in computer terminology. The concept of the engram, which Lashley has bequeathed us, does not describe the stored information itself but the mechanism by which that information is stored. It is a pattern presumably of minute biochemical changes. The organization and arrangement of that pattern are codes for the experiences in which the organism has participated in the past. One can legitimately search for the engram—it is a system of physical changes—but when one finds it, one will only observe variations in something like synaptic conductivity or membrane resistance, not the experience itself. The engram, like the neural action potential pattern in sensory systems, is a coded representation of mental processes and is, thus, subject to all of the conceptual pitfalls concerning sensory coding that I discussed in Chapter 6.

Lashley (1890-1958), still a preeminent figure in the psychobiology of learning, spent a lifetime applying brain ablation techniques in search of the nature of the engram that was laid down as a result of experience and the region or regions of the brain in which it might reside. After decades of work, he summed up his conclusions about the nature and locus of the engram in the following excerpts:

1. It seems certain that the theory of well-defined conditioned reflex paths from sense organ via association areas to the motor cortex is false. The motor areas are not necessary for the retention of sensory-motor habits or even of skilled manipulative patterns.

2. It is not possible to demonstrate the isolated localization of a memory trace anywhere within the nervous system. Limited regions may be essential for learning or retention of a particular activity, but within such regions the parts are functionally equivalent. The engram is represented throughout the region.

3. The so-called associative areas are not storehouses for specific memories. They seem to be concerned with modes of organization and with general facilitation or maintenance of the level of vigilance. The defects which occur after their destruction are not amnesias but difficulties in the performance of tasks which involve abstraction and generalization, or conflict of purposes. . . .

4. The trace of any activity is not an isolated connextion between sensory and motor elements. It is tied in with the whole complex of spatial and temporal axes of nervous activity which forms a constant substratum of behaviour. Each association is oriented with respect to space and time. Only by long practice under varying conditions does it become generalized or disassociated from these specific coordinates . . .

5. The equivalence of different regions of the cortex for retention of memories points to multiple representation. [2] Somehow, equivalent traces are established throughout the functional area. Analysis of the sensory and motor aspects of habits shows that they are reducible only to relations among components which have no constant position with respect to structural elements. This means, I believe, that within a functional area the cells throughout the area acquire the capacity to react

[2]Lashley might also have pointed to the problem of incorrect, misidentified, or misplaced lesions in this regard. The interplay between those errors of methodology and a true biology of multiple representation may be profound.

in certain definite patterns, which may have any distribution within the area. I have elsewhere proposed a possible mechanism to account for this multiple representation. Briefly, the characteristics of the nervous network are such that, when it is subject to any pattern of excitation, it may develop a pattern of activity, reduplicated throughout an entire functional area by spread of excitations, much as the surface of a liquid develops an interference pattern of spreading waves when it is disturbed at several points (Lashley, 1942). This means that, within a functional area, the neurons must be sensitized to react in certain combinations, perhaps in complex patterns of reverberatory circuits, reduplicated throughout the area.

6. Consideration of the numerical relations of sensory and other cells in the brain makes it certain, I believe, that all of the cells of the brain must be in almost constant activity, either firing or actively inhibited. There is no great excess of cells which can be reserved as the seat of special memories. The complexity of the functions involved in reproductive memory implies that every instance of recall requires the activity of literally millions of neurons. The same neurons which retain the memory traces of one experience must also participate in countless other activities [Lashley, 1950, pp. 478-479].

The truly remarkable thing about these excerpts from his paper is that a quarter of a century later, most of the general points made by Lashley could well serve as the credo for the most modern psychobiological learning theory. To emphasize his insight and the contemporary validity of his argument, let us abstract the essential aspects of Lashley's comments:

1. A simple linking or "connectionistic" role of the "association" cortex is denied.

2. Memory is not specifically localized but is found within widely dispersed regions of the brain or major centers.

3. Memories are not stored solely in the association regions.

4. Memory is not a simple link between sensory inputs and motor outputs.

5. Memory is multiply represented and may be encoded by waves of activity akin to interference patterns.

6. The engram is represented at the cellular level by changes in the statistical state of the neural network as mediated by synaptic plasticity.

How elegantly simple, persuasive, and persistent are the ideas expressed in this brief abstract of Lashley's conclusions after a life's work. Amazingly, the general theme expressed in this brief list is not inconsistent with most current psychobiological theorizing (with the exception of the hypothesis of interference patterns, which is as yet not accepted by a majority of current theorists), although a few of us see it as a convenient metaphor for the action of a distributed neuron net.

Lashley's perspective, however, is predominantly a negative one. Points 1, 2, 3, and 4 are statements of what memory is not, and points 5 and 6 champion a hypothesis of ensemble aggregation that, for the most part, is not testable by contemporary neurophysiological techniques. In spite of the inherent negativism of Lashley's conclusion, his ideas must be considered as the foundation of most work in the field and to have at least defined the limits of contemporary thinking. The principles he ennuciated are still the touchstones of modern theory, although they have been embellished with a considerable amount of empirical data in recent years. Contemporary workers such as Roy John, with his statistical theory of learning, and Karl Pribram, with his holographic hypothesis, have contributed to the further specification and a more positive exposition of Lashley's principles. To a considerable degree, however, they still base their theoretical orientation on the perspective Lashley so insightfully created. What these and other psychobiologists have done is to add substance and specific mechanism to the suggestions made by Lashley.

To sum up this discussion, let me propose three major hypotheses characteristic of modern theories of the neural basis of learning that also summarize the most persistent aspects of Lashley's work:

Hypothesis 1:   The engram for a learned response is distributed throughout much of the central nervous system.

Hypothesis 2:   The engram, like all other mental processes, is encoded by the pattern of organization (or state) of a network composed of a large ensemble of neurons.

Hypothesis 3:   Changes that occur in the network's state are direct functions of cellular changes that occur, most likely, at the synapse.

The first of these hypothesese is but a restatement of support for the conclusion drawn by Lashley that memories seem not to be localizable in any particular center of the brain. As we see later in this chapter, although certain nuclei of the brain seem to play an important role in the control of learning, there is still no empirical support for the suggestion that any particular portion of the brain is a specific repository of memory.

The second hypothesis is the essence of the message of representation and is discussed in detail in the next section of this chapter.

The third hypothesis asserts that, of all the nervous system's parts and processes, the only plausible candidate to encode the highly adaptive and informationally rich properties of behavioral learning is synaptic plasticity. Only the synapse possesses the rich and widespread integrative capacity.[3] Although synaptic plasticity has been the object of research attention for many years, the synaptic effects studied, without exception, are proposed as analogs of only the simpler forms of learning, such as classical conditioning, rather than of cognitive learning. This is an important constraint, for the synaptic hypothesis must transcend an enormous conceptual gap at this point to be linked to more complex mental processes. To transcend that gap one must establish that all learning

[3]Interestingly, the hypothesis of synaptic plasticity is quite antique and was not a de novo creation by Lashley. It was probably first proposed by Tanzi (1893) in the nineteenth century.

(as well as other mental processes), no matter how complex, is the result of the concatenation of simple and elemental neural processes into molar behavior patterns. This is most certainly the case, but we still do not know the nature of that concatenation.

In the absence of a specifically understood link between cellular plasticity and learning, the generalization of the synaptic hypothesis must depend upon the logical assertion that any concept, no matter how complicated, can be represented by a sufficiently large number of elemental and discrete processes. This assertion is a major theorem of modern mathematics, but in the brain it still represents a statement of faith that in some fundamental way runs counter to the current rejection of the idea of concatenated conditioned reflexes in atoms of learning. That a serious dilemma is thus generated is obvious. That there are, yet, no resolutions to this dilemma is also undeniable.

b. John's Contribution

What general notion can one turn to when faced with the constraints of Hypothesis 1 and Hypothesis 3 (the engram is "nowhere and everywhere," and the ultimate atom of learning is the plastic synapse) as a unifying theme of the neural basis of learning? The answer to this question is implicit in Hypothesis 2—the concept of the network state, which has been developed in its most coherent and explicit form by E. Roy John of the New York Medical College in a book (John, 1967) and in a paper (John, 1972) specifically concerned with learning. The concept is much more broadly interpretable, of course, as a model of the neural basis of all mental activities.

The fundamental premise of the network state, as emphasized in John's statistical theory, has implicitly permeated every chapter of this present book. That is, all behavior must in the ultimate analysis be attributable to the action and interaction of large numbers of neurons rather than to the response of any single unit or class of neurons. Each expression of behavior at the molar level is the direct result of the manner in which many millions of neurons are collectively performing at any given moment. The network of interacting neurons, some active and some inactive at any instant, momentarily defines a highly complex state of the nervous system. Each mental and behavioral process must correspond to some such state. Changes in behavior (learning) are the direct result of changes in the network state due to plastic mechanisms at the cellular level.

The idea of a network state and of a statistical theory of learning is different from simple associative or switchboard theories in a number of ways, as has been eloquently pointed out by John. First, there is no implicit need in a network state for specific synaptic connections. Conditions must be similar only in the average statistical sense for two network states to be functionally identical.

Another essential characteristic of the network-state hypothesis, which differs from the specific connectionistic approach, is the fact that an individual neuron may perform several different functions in overlapping neural networks. Conversely, any particular statistical, behavioral, or molar state may be encoded by many anatomically distinct but functionally equivalent systems of neurons that individually serve other functions in other states as well. Permeating all of this thinking is a viewpoint that also argues strongly against the notion of specific pontifical neurons or classes of neurons in the nervous system as I have in Chapter 7.

The evolution of a system that allows even single synapses to serve multiple functions would be a highly useful logistic adaptation in nervous function. Even though the number of synapses available is quite large (possibly as many as 10^{16} synapses are to found in the human brain), the fact that complex concepts may require very large numbers of synapses to be adequately represented suggests that without multiple usage there could be a shortage of plastic synapses as the number of stored memories increased. If each synapse could participate in the recording of more than one memory, there would be an increase in the available storage capacity by many orders of magnitude.

To further clarify some of the ideas, the following excerpt from John's (1972) seminal paper is presented. Although his emphasis in this excerpt is on the temporal aspects (the common mode of activity) of the network state, the general concept of a statistical network state is eloquently presented.

These considerations and related data led me to propose (John, 1967) an alternative to switchboard theories: the statistical configuration theory. The critical event in learning is envisaged as the establishment of representational systems of large numbers of neurons in different parts of the brain, whose activity has been affected in a coordinated way by the spatiotemporal characteristics of the stimuli present during a learning experience. The coherent pattern of discharge of neurons in these regions spreads to numerous other regions of the brain. Sustained transactions of activity between participating cells permit rapid interaction among all regions affected by the incoming sequence of stimuli as well as the subsequent spread. This initiates the development of a *common mode of activity,* a temporal pattern which is coherent across those various regions and specific for that stimulus complex. As this common mode of activity is sustained, certain changes are presumed to take place in the participating neuronal populations, which are thereby established as a representational system. Whether such changes are alterations of "synaptic efficiency" or not, it is assumed that the critical feature of these changes is to increase the probability of recurrence of that coherent pattern in the network. Certain types of preexisting neuronal *transactions* become more probable, but no new connections are assumed to be formed.

This theory is statistical, in that the informational significance of an event is represented by the average behavior of a responsive neural ensemble rather than by the exclusive behavior of any specifiable neuron in the ensemble. The same ensemble can represent many different items, each with a different coherent pattern of deviation from randomness or from its baseline pattern. The theory is configurational in that new responses are based upon the establishment of new temporal patterns of ensemble activity, rather than upon the elaboration of new pathways or connections. Learning increases the probability that particular temporal patterns of orderly activity will occur in coupled ensembles of neurons. By this process, the representational system acquires the capability of releasing the specified common mode of activity as a whole if some significant portion of the system enters the appropriate mode.

It should be emphasized that this is not a "field" theory, nor does it deny the highly organzied structure of the brain. The firing pattern of neural ensembles undoubtedly depends upon connections between neurons. Configurations of activity in representational systems are presumed to become established by modification of interneuronal relationships, perhaps by changes located at the synapse although other alternatives are conceivable. However, in this laboratory we doubt that memory is based upon the establishment of new connections rather than upon the modification of existing relationships. We consider representation of information by statistical features of temporal patterns of ensemble behavior more likely than by the localized activity of specific cells [pp. 853-854].

Although many contemporary psychobiologists would disagree with John's presentation in a number of particular details concerning the mechanisms by which the network state is achieved, this eloquent statement effectively expresses John's view of the statistical nature of neuronal network function, a contribution that seems currently to be the most plausible basis of all mental activity, including learning.

Clearly, the notion of the network state is fundamental to all of contemporary psychobiology and to all reasonably plausible theories of the neural basis of mental activity. John's hypotheses and assumptions are central to the development of the material in the rest of this chapter in particular but also to all of the topics discussed in this book. It is not the only approach, however, to the study of the neuronal basis of learning. In the following section, however, it will become clear that, in spite of a diversity of perspective, relatively little intrinsic incompatibility exists between any of the proposed theories.

c. Rationalization of Diverse Theories

As one scans the theoretical and empirical learning literature, it becomes obvious that the direct object of research attack by most empirically oriented psychobiologists is not the concept of the neural network state just described. In fact, for only a few of them is the network state of focal interest. It is exceedingly difficult to assay the complex interactions of a distributed network of neurons that, by their collective action, is encoding molar states in a presumably statistical manner. Even Roy John, the champion of this statistical approach, usually turns to the evoked compound potential or the electroencephalogram to pursue his attack on this problem. This indirect attack on the problem may reflect either a fundamental or technological limit of the network hypothesis: Tests of it may, of necessity, have to be approached from some molar electrophysiological or behavioral point of view. Of course, many researchers feel that the problem can only be approached with the tip of the microelectrode. In doing so, however, their attention is necessarily directed to the responses of individual units or clusters that are smaller than those most likely to be involved in the representation of even the simplest aspects of human learning.

These electrophysiological approaches are not the only means being employed to study learning. Other workers are tracing out the time course of the consolidation process by interrupting the transfer from short-term to long-term memory with various agents. Some researchers approach the problem of memory from a point of view that emphasizes biochemical or neuroanatomical features of neural plasticity, whereas some others have even sought to attribute the storage of memories to the configuration of the atoms in macromolecules rather than to the state of the nervous network. Nor should we overlook the molar behavioral or gross anatomical approaches using either intact animals or animals that have been subjected to some sort of surgical ablation of brain tissue.

Each of these empirical approaches has added to the accumulation of a body of data and has stimulated the growth of theoretical explanations of the learning process. With one significant exception, however, it is the thesis of this section that all of these theories are complementary to each other and are not fundamentally antagonistic or contradictory to the three primary hypotheses of the neural basis of learning mentioned on page 540. The reason for this is that the various theories attack the problem at complementary, not contradictory, levels. All actually agree that the network is the key neural level of analysis of mind.

Psychological theories of learning are descriptions of the way in which the learning processes are organized and how neural plasticity is exhibited at the molar level. No assertions are made about the neural mechanisms themselves.

Theories based on data, in which the main measure is a compound neural action potential, stress the necessity of using these compound potentials as global indicators of the statistical properties of the neuron ensemble that is involved in the relevant network. Even in the most extreme field theories, the basic idea of the interaction of individual neurons in a network is not rejected.

Theories based upon studies of single neuron responses utilize information about the components of the network and occasionally provide some insight into the local interactions within these simple networks.

As one descends further into the microcosm to studies of synaptic plasticity, assumptions are often made about the possible locus of the membrane dynamics that are responsible for the alterations in the neural network state. The basic idea of neuronal concatenation, however, is still preeminent.

Finally, many theories emphasizing the effects of biochemicals, and particularly RNA (ribonucleic acid) involvement, provide explanations about the possible mechanisms regulating growth and/or change at the synaptic junction. They do not reject the notion of the neural net either; they merely suggest ways in which the interconnections might be made.

All of these experimental paradigms and reductionistic theories and models are thus consistent in the final analysis with the proposition that mind is encoded by a network state. Each simply represents a different level of inquiry into a problem involving multiple levels of explanation.

Incidentally, this analysis may also be the basis of the resolution of the dilemma proposed by Kety's allegory in Chapter 1 (pp. 11-13). The most appropriate level of neuro-reductive analysis of mental activity according to this perspective, is that of the network state. Although neurophysiological and biochemical studies at more microscopic levels are interesting, in fact they are irrelevant in the same way that the paper on which a book is printed is irrelevant to its content. Although the nature of the paper or the printing process may create certain constraints, only the pattern of information-organization is essential. The essence of pattern is found at the level of the words and sentences that are used in a book or the patterned arrangement and interconnections in the neural network.

There is one significant exception to this broad-based agreement, however. For the past 90 years, a group of psychobiologists including Ribot (1881), Semon (1904), Katz and Halstead (1950), Hydén (1959), McConnell (1962), and Ungar (1966) have repeatedly suggested that the memory trace or engram is not stored in the dynamic or static state of the network of neurons but rather in the organization and pattern of atomic arrangement in macromolecules. These atomic patterns, they have proposed, are generated as a direct result of the experiences undergone by the organism. In other words, molecular theories of the engram incorporate as an alternative hypothesis to neural or cellular network organization the idea that molecular structures encode memory.

There are a number of difficulties with this theory, not the least of which is the considerable disagreement with regard to the empirical facts obtained in the kinds of experiments that are used to support the molecular storage hypothesis. Experiments in which some learned task is transferred by extraction of some chemical from a trained animal and injection of it into an untrained subject (McConnell, 1962; and Ungar & Oceguera-Navarro, 1965) have been severely challenged into recent years (Byrne et al., 1966; and Gross & Carey, 1965). From a theoretical point of view, however, perhaps the most serious problem is the absence of any acceptable explanation of how information that might conceivably have been encoded in some macromolecular structure could ever be read out at the speeds typical of most recall behavior. Interestingly, the readout time for molecular information is more typically measured in the time constants of growth processes rather than in the small fractions of a second typical of reaction times. This difficulty is a lethal argument against any theory of engram storage in molecular structure.

It is important to point out, however, that many biochemical studies that do show the involvement of particular chemicals do not embody the hypotheses of molecular storage and should not be mistakenly discarded along with the transfer experiments. A number of investigators (e.g., Agranoff, Davis, & Brink, 1965; Hydén, 1967; Flexner, Flexner, Roberts, & de la Haba, 1964; and Barondes & Cohen, 1966) have been stimulated by the developments in theoretical genetics and the dramatic unraveling of the genetic code during the 1950s and 1960s (and, perhaps, also by the transparent weaknesses of the macromolecular storage hypothesis) to suggest that specific chemicals such as transfer ribonucleic acid (RNA_t) and the enzyme that deactivates it, ribonuclease, were involved not only in genetic memory but also in individual memory in some other way. Although the role of these substances in the learning process is not yet understood exactly, it seems likely from a wide variety of studies that they are involved in learning. RNA_t and ribonuclease are both known to be intimately involved in the growth of proteinaceous membranes. It is therefore reasonable to assume that these chemicals may play quite an important role in learning even though the direct information storage role, suggested as an explanation for the reputed transfer studies, is not tenable. RNA_t is likely to be involved in any growth process in which proteins are formed. Thus the introduction of ribonuclease or puromycin, an antibiotic that inhibits protein production, is likely to inhibit membrane growth. This quite different involvement brings these chemicals into the domain of network state theory by assigning them an important role in the production of new or enlarged synapses and thus in guiding changes in the organization of the network.

In sum, although there are many different approaches to understanding the biological basis of learning, it is likely that there is no great inconsistency or antagonism between any of them, with the possible exception of the macromolecular storage theories. Rather, the abundance of various theories simply reflects the wide variety of methods of investigating the dynamic state of either an individual neuron or an ensemble of neurons. I expand upon this idea of a consensus in learning theory in the concluding discussion of Chapter 9.

B.   ON THE LOCALIZATION OF LEARNING MECHANISMS IN THE BRAIN

In Chapter 5 I dealt with the general problem of localization of mental functions and noted some of the difficulties involved in the assignment of a particular mental process to a specific location in the brain. When dealing with learning, the problem becomes even more complicated. Even the simplest form of learning involves sensory, motor, and integrative mechanisms and processes that are difficult to isolate from the specific dynamics of neural plasticity or behavioral change. Furthermore, as I have noted, a considerable tradition has grown up over the years, in large part based upon Lashley'a work that suggests that learning, in particular, is not a process localizable to any particular "center" or unique group of nuclei in the brain. Rather, the plasticity underlying learning may represent a general capability of all neural tissue. In the most extreme form of this tradition, all areas of the brain are assumed to be equipotential in their information storage capacity. As we see later, neurophysiological recordings from many brain levels seem to support the general conclusion that candidate plastic mechanisms are widespread throughout the brain if not ubiquitous.

Incorporated within the premise of equipotentiality was the specific hypothesis that declines in learned performance for many skills were often solely simple functions of the amount, or mass, of tissue removed, quite irrespective of its locale. Although maze learning is especially sensitive to this law of mass action, probably because it involves several different senses, the fact that other skills show less extreme forms of learning deficits when tissues from apparently irrelevant regions of the brain are ablated is another argument for at least a partial degree of neural specialization. Learning paradigms involving tasks heavily dependent upon a single sense modality, for example, displayed more specific deficits and greater deviation from a simple law of mass action. As a general rule, the more inclusive of diverse motor and sensory processes, the more closely the data will reflect a simple mass action law.

If one were to describe the contemporary consensus concerning the localization of learning and memory functions, it would probably have to be framed in terms much like those used by Lashley 30 and 40 years ago. It is still true that no specific locus has been discovered that is a unique and specific repository of memory, nor has any brain center been shown to be completely uninvolved in at least some form of behavioral plasticity. Indeed, as unequivocal success has been achieved in recent years in the conditioning of spinal mechanisms, it appears that even this most peripheral portion of the central nervous system is capable of the rudiments of plastic adaptation to experience. Similarly, in the sections of this chapter to follow, we see ample evidence, both in single neuron responses and compound action potential recordings, that almost all levels of the nervous system can exhibit at least a rudiment of neuronal plasticity. In this light, learning and memory seem to be a generalized property of almost all nervous tissue.

Another important generalization somewhat contrary to the conclusion of distribution and/or equipotentiality is that a number of nuclei have been shown to be particularly important in the regulation and control of certain aspects of the learning process and thus may, indeed, have specialized functions in learning. These neural mechanisms are often found in the limbic system, the brain subsystem that is composed of centers often intimately involved in motivation, emotion, and attention—organismic states that certainly could affect the progress of learning in indirect manners.

In this section I consider two topics in detail. First, spinal conditioning is examined to exemplify the widespread capability of all nervous tissue to adapt to experience, and second, the specific role of certain nuclei in learning is discussed.

1. Spinal Conditioning

There seems to be no lower limit to the complexity of nervous systems capable of learning. As noted, the lowliest protozoans and most primitive metazoans of the animal kingdom seem to some investigators, at least, to exhibit behavioral changes fitting within the learning rubric.[4] Therefore, another approach has come into prominence in the past 30 years. The question of the minimum nervous system exhibiting learning can be asked within the context of a single vertebrate species by pursuing a strategy in which portions of the central nervous system are sequentially isolated. The experimenter then determines in each case whether behavioral change is possible in the resulting reduced systems. Specifically, the issue has been particularized by posing the question: Is it possible to condition the legs of a vertebrate that has had its spinal cord disconnected from the brain?

The classic experiments concerning this question of "spinal" conditioning were carried out by Shurrager and Culler (1940) and by Kellogg (1947). The two papers terminated in completely opposite conclusions, however. Shurrager and Culler (using a technique that involved acutely prepared animals and excised muscles) reported spinal conditioning, whereas Kellogg (who used chronic animals that were intact except for the spinal cut) reported none!

In more recent times, the tide has turned in Shurrager and Culler's favor. Patterson, Cegavske, and Thompson (1973), for example, feel sure they have unequivocally demonstrated classical conditioning in cats. Horn (1970) cites a large number of other earlier studies that also purported to have successfully achieved classical conditioning in spinal animals. Buerger and Fennessy (1971), furthermore, have demonstrated instrumental conditioning in an experiment in which a spinal animal learned to keep from lowering its leg onto an electrical shocking plate. Spinal habituation has also been clearly demonstrated by such workers as Thompson and Spencer (1966), and this behavior has even been tentatively related to certain specific synaptic effects (Groves, Glanzman, Patterson, & Thompson, 1970).

All in all, it is clear that some forms of learning can be mediated at the level of the spinal cord. Coupled with the data obtained from invertebrates (discussed later in this chapter), these findings add considerable support for the conclusion that learning is an ubiquitous feature of almost any nervous tissue, even regions such as the spinal cord that are more highly specialized for communication rather than complex integration.

2. The Controlling and Regulating Functions of Cerebral Nuclei in Complex Learning Tasks

Although the search for a particular nucleus of the brain in which information may actually be stored or for one that is exclusively a learning "center" has been unsuccessful, there clearly, are certain regions in the brain that are more invol-

---

[4]The interested reader may wish to look at the work on protozoans (Gelber, 1952), annelida (Ratner, 1962), octopi (Young, 1961), platyheminthes (McConnell, 1962), and arthoropoda (Horridge, 1962), as examples of learning in primitive organisms.

ved in the control and regulation of learning processes than are others. By far the most important regions of the cerebral mantle yet suggested to be heavily concerned with memory and learning are the frontal and temporal lobes of the brain. On the basis of varied lines of evidence, the hippocampal gyrus, a deeply buried portion of the temporal lobe, and other parts of the limbic system seem to be especially important in this regard. Evidence for this hypothesis has been forthcoming from studies by Douglas and Pribram (1966), Milner (1966), John (1967), Kimble (1968), and most recently by Thompson (1976), who particularly associates circulating patterns of neural responses in the hippocampus with short-term memory.

It is an interesting historical sidelight that a special role of the hippocampus in mediating temporal lobe effects had been suggested by the classic human open-brain experiments of Wilder Penfield (see Penfield & Roberts, 1959) several decades ago. Although Penfield and Roberts (1959) were clearly mistaken in their assertion that the hippocampus was the repository of memory, they were at least receptive to the alternative hypothesis proposing controlling function for this region when they said:

> When this stimulation of hippocampal gyrus was carried out, the hippocampal formation and amygdaloid nucleus were still intact. But the rest of the anterior half of the temporal lobe had been removed. The fact that stimulation could still produce a flashback of former experience would support the suggestion that comes from other evidence (Milner & Penfield, 1955) that the hippocampus of the two sides is, in fact, the repository of ganglionic patterns that preserve the record of the stream of consciousness. If not the repository, then each hippocampus plays an important role in the mechanism of re-activation of that record [p. 47].

A simple summary of the many studies attempting to determine the effect of particular brain lesions on memory and learning would be a most satisfying section to insert in the discussion at this point. Unfortunately, for reasons that should be quite obvious, most forms of cognitive learning seem to involve complicated interactions of multiple portions of the brain.

Perhaps the most comprehensive summary of the role of the cerebral cortex in learning is to be found in an article by Susan Iversen (1973) in an important recent compendium of diverse views on the physiological basis of memory (Deutsch, 1973). Iversen (1973) insightfully considers the current status of the problem of memory localization and sums up current knowledge by noting: "Lesion and anatomical studies suggest that both the hippocampus and frontal cortex are part of circuitry necessary if behavior is to be adjusted to a changing internal or external environment [p. 346]."

To emphasize the interacting role of these two centers in the governance of learning processes, Iversen prepared a tabular comparison of the effects produced by both frontal and hippocampal lesions. The message implicit in this comparison, shown in Table 8-2, is clearcut. The same effects on learning can and have been produced by lesions in either the frontal regions or the hippocampal gyrus

TABLE 8.2

The common effects of frontal and hippocampal lesions. (From Iversen, ©1973, with the permission of Academic Press.)
(The references cited here can be found in Iversen, 1973)

	Effect of lesion and behavioral measure	Frontal lesion	Hippocampal lesion
Increase	Locomotor activity	Gross, 1963	Douglas & Isaacson, 1964; Jarrard & Bunnell, 1968; Gotsick, 1969; Jarrard, 1968
Increase	Exploratory behavior	Lindsley, Weiskrantz, & Mingay, 1964	Kamback, 1967b; Leaton, 1968
Increase	Distractibility	Kamback, 1967a	Rogozea & Ungher, 1968
Change	Autonomic responses	Robinson & Mishkin, 1968	Votaw & Lauer, 1963
Impair	Spatial alternation or reversal	Jacobsen, 1936; Mishkin, 1964; Teitelbaum, 1964	Kimble & Kimble, 1965; Teitelbaum, 1964; Mahut & Cordeau, 1963
Impair	Delayed response	Jacobsen, 1936	Correll & Scoville, 1967
Impair	Alternation of two responses	Gross, Chorover, & Cohen, 1965	Gross, Chorover, & Cohen, 1965
Impair	Discrimination reversal	Gross, 1963; Teitelbaum, 1964; Harlow & Dagnon, 1942	Silverira & Kimble, 1968; Teitelbaum, 1961, 1964; Webster & Voneida, 1964

Impair	Maze learning		Kanda, Rasmussen, & Kveim, 1961; Jackson & Strong, 1969; Kimble, 1963
Impair	Shock avoidance	Pribram & Weiskrantz, 1957; Lichtenstein, 1950	Pribram & Weiskrantz, 1957; Isaacson & Wickelgren, 1962; Niki, 1962; Snyder & Isaacson, 1965
Impair	Go-No Go discrimination	Gross & Weiskrantz, 1962 Brutowski, Mishkin, & Rosvoid, 1967	McCleary, 1966
Impair	Matching to sample	Buffery, 1964; Glick, Goldfarb, & Jarrick, 1960	Drachman & Ommaya, 1964; Corell & Scoville, 1965
Disrupt	Extinction performance	Butter, Mishkin, & Rosvold, 1963	Douglas & Pribram, 1966; Jarrad, Isaacson, & Wickelgren, 1964; Niki, 1965; Peretz, 1965; Rabe & Haddad, 1968
Disrupt	Motivational control	Brutowski & Dabrowska, 1963; Brutowski, 1964	Schmaltz & Isaacson, 1966; Jarrad, 1965; Kimble & Coover, 1966; Pizzi & Lorens, 1967
Disrupt	Response control	Rosvold, 1970	Ellen & Wilson, 1963
Disrupt	Sequential responding	Pinto-Hamuy & Linck, 1965	Kimble & Pribram, 1963
Disrupt	Timing behavior	Stamm, 1963; Glickstein, Quigley, & Stebbing, 1964	Clark & Isaacson, 1965; Ellen & Powell, 1962

in almost every instance. Any attempt to localize a single aspect of the learning process in either region, therefore, would be spurious and misleading.

It is possible, however, to suggest a major role each of the involved centers might play in the interacting system. Let us consider first the hippocampus. In addition to the elicitation of memories as a result of hippocampal stimulation, retrograde amnesia can also be produced by electrical stimulation there (e.g., Sideroff, Bueno, Hirsch, Weyand & McGaugh, 1974). A more general effect of the hippocampus, as determined with lesion studies, on the other hand, seems to produce a general behavioral inhibition (for a complete discussion of this point, see Isaacson, 1974). It is not too surprising a fact, therefore, that when the hippocampus is lesioned, there often is an increase rather than a deficit in the performance of the animal on learning tasks, depending upon the specific task. This kind of task-dependent performance increase was demonstrated a number of years ago by Isaacson, Douglas, and Moore (1961). They showed that ablation of the hippocampus led to an increase in performance on avoidance tasks; but in tasks requiring response alternation, the same species showed deficits in performance. The strong tendency toward a general increase in overall activity and a tendency to perseverate in responses once initiated reflect the general inhibitory role played by that gyrus.

It also seems that the hippocampus may be deeply involved in the consolidation or transfer of information from short-term to longer-term memory. In human clinical cases, patients with lesions in the hippocampus typically have nearly normal behavior patterns, adequate short-term memory, and remembrance of events that occurred long ago. On the other hand, they do poorly at remembering the recent past and typically cannot recall events that occurred more than a few minutes previously. Because the hippocampal lesion does not interfere with the recall of information acquired prior to the lesion, the hippocampus is obviously not the storage medium itself. Rather, this type of clinical evidence supports the hypothesis that the hippocampus plays a regulating and controlling function in the conversion from short- to long-term memory. The mechanism by which this may occur is perhaps reflected in Thompson's (1976) work which shows that the hippocampus neurons fire in a temporal pattern that is a replica of the time course of the motor response of the nictitating membrane of a rabbit.

Other nearby centers of the brain also exhibit many of the same properties as does the hippocampus proper. Retrograde amnesia can also be produced when the amygdala (Kesner & Doty, 1968; Gold, Macri, & McGaugh, 1973) or the caudate-putamen complex (Wyers, Peeke, Williston, & Herz, 1968; Wyers & Deadwyler, 1971) are electrically stimulated in experimental animals.

Isaacson (1974), in his important monograph, also stresses that the amygdala and the septal regions of the limbic system may play an important role in controlling learning. Although he notes that the hippocampus acts as a generalized inhibitor of behavior (reducing maladaptive preservation of behavior that would interfere with learning) the amygdala in general seems to be an excitor. In drawing this generality, however, Isaacson points out that the specific effects of both hippocampal and amygdalar lesions, sometimes similar and sometimes directly opposite, are highly dependent upon the specific experimental task required of the animal. Much additional research will have to be done to explicate the reasons for these task dependent differences.

The frontal lobes have a less well-defined role in the learning process. The general role of the frontal lobes in time-binding behavior and in regulating motivation has already been discussed in Chapter 5. Any suggested role of the frontal lobes in learning has to be carefully controlled, therefore, for modulations in these sequencing and motivating variables. Reductions in the animal's motivational state, for example, could simulate an actual failure in the learning process. Yet such controls are quite difficult to insert into the complex experimental designs required to unravel the vaguely defined role of the frontal cortex in learning. About all that can be said with any degree of certainty now is that both the original suggestions by Jacobsen (1936), that the frontal lobes are the "repository" of short-term memory, and by Penfield, that the temporal lobe is the "repository" of consolidated long-term memory, cannot possibly be correct.

One plausible and interesting model has been developed by Douglas (1972) from a suggestion by Lynn (1966) concerning the general role of these regions of the brain that appear to contribute to the control and regulation of the learning process. Figure 8-6 depicts the main points of the Douglas-Lynn model. Although it is almost certain now that this diagram is incorrect both in detail and in its implication that those particular portions of the brain are involved only in the classical conditioning process, this flow chart serves as a useful exposition of the kinds of relationships that might occur in these portions of the nervous system that are most likely to be involved in learning. The theoretical model implicit in this flow chart does not suggest that any particular region serves as the actual repository of memory. The Douglas-Lynn model is a statement of process control and not of what the engram itself is or where it might be located. Furthermore, the control roles of the amygdala and the hippocampus are not defined directly in terms of memory and learning. Rather, their role is specified in terms of arousal and alertness—a not unlikely possibility. The role of these regions, Douglas asserts, may only be tangential to the learning process itself and may be better interpreted in terms of the creation and maintenance of an adequate internal environment in which learning can take place.

Although the Douglas-Lynn model is probably not correct in detail, it does illustrate a reasonable model of the roles of the mentioned brain nuclei in learning. A consensus seems to be emerging that the hippocampus and other limbic nuclei with which it is interconnected are involved in the regulation and control of the milieu that allows learning to occur. They time-bind and pace, they alert and arouse, they inhibit and excite; but only a few contemporary workers (e.g., Thompson, 1976) propose that they actually are the site of the engram for any of the four kinds of learning.

Kesner (1973) has recently proposed a somewhat different analysis of the brain structures that may be the main mediators of the various kinds of memory.

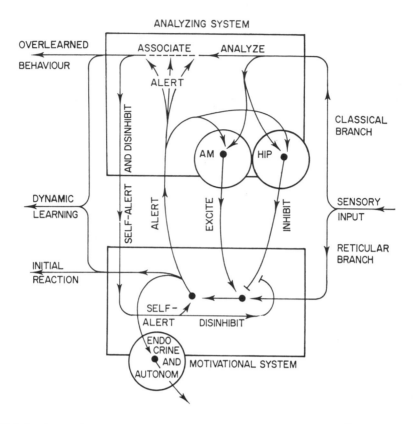

FIG. 8.6   A neural model of orienting and conditioning. (From Douglas, ©1972, with the permission of Academic Press.)

Surveying a very large body of information concerning the role of specific nuclei, he has suggested the involvement of other nuclei not usually thought to be involved in learning. Specifically, Kesner proposed that the midbrain reticular formation plays an important function in short-term memory (along with various intrinsic cortex regions). Nevertheless, his theory is conventional in most ways, and he concurs with the concept that the hippocampus has some sort of special function in the long-term memory consolidation process.

Kesner's classification system of the various memories is also somewhat different from the one presented here. He suggests that short-term memory is not a hierarchical precursor of long-term memory but rather that "information is transferred in parallel to short and long term memory systems [1973, p. 177]." Kesner's concept thus differs substantially from the Atkinson and Shiffrin theory in terms of the role attributed to short-term memory; his theory assigns it a much less central role. Kesner's theory is particularly well detailed, and the interested reader will find his review extremely interesting and informative.

Regardless of the durability or technical correctness of any of these theories, there is a theme of agreement among them. Each accepts the general concept that memory and learning are not functions of single portions of the brain. Each also accepts the fact that certain nuclei play more specific roles in the control and regulation of the learning process than do others. These two general points represent the essence of what can be concluded concerning the localization of these functions within the macroscopic portion of the human brain.

C. COMPOUND POTENTIALS AS INDICATORS OF LEARNING

Although it is not possible to find specific sites in the brain that are uniquely capable of storing information, it is possible to use electrophysiological signals as indicators of the learning process. Two approaches, one microscopic and one macroscopic, have been pursued in this search for electrical correlates of learning. One approach utilizes the compound evoked or spontaneous potentials from the brain (such as the EEG) recorded with macroelectrodes; the other approach searches for changes at the cellular level with microelectrodes. In this section I consider the compound potential approach and, in the next section, the cellular attack.

The general rationale behind the use of compound potentials to study learning is based upon the fundamental premise of network state theory that many neurons are involved in even the simplest forms of mental activity and that no single neuron can uniquely define the psychological state. The statistical characteristics of a large ensemble must be examined before any insight into the question of how neurons represent the learning process can be achieved.

The central idea behind the use of compound potentials, therefore, is that these potentials represent biological "statisticians" that carry out calculation of the "central tendencies" and "variability" of the population of cells contributing to a given compound potential, just as their collective action defines the mental response. Evidence like that collected by Fox and O'Brien (1965) and Fox and Norman (1968), discussed in Chapter 6, is strong support for the idea that many kinds of compound action potentials represent nothing less than a statistical description of a population consisting of many individual neuronal responses. Although we cannot be sure that all such compound action potentials encode relevant transactional information patterns (as we see in the following, there is considerable difficulty in interpreting their significance), some credence is added to the argument for their use in psychobiological research by the comparable temporal dimensions of many compound potentials and the molar learning processes.

Despite widespread criticism of the approach of attaching electrodes to the outside of the skull to observe compound potentials ("it is comparable to putting a voltmeter on the outside of a computer"), the application of these macro-electrophysiological techniques to the study of learning has become enormously widespread particularly in recent years. I assume in this section that this is the expression of some wisdom and not only stubborn folly.

A number of different compound potentials have been used in the study of learning. Slow potential changes recorded with D.C.-coupled amplifiers, transient evoked potentials driven by sensory stimulation, the Contingent Negative Variation (a potential closely associated with classical conditioning-like paradigms and recorded mostly from the vertex of the head), and fluctuations in the time course of the ongoing electroencephalogram, all have been used as electrophysiological indicators of learning. In the following sections I consider these potentials and their relation to learning in detail.

1.   D.C. Potentials

Very slowly changing electrical signals can be recorded from the brain. These signals have time constants of the order of minutes and, therefore, seem to be only slow fluctuations of potentials stable enough to be referred to as Direct Current (D.C.) voltages. D.C. potentials generally require the signal to be picked up by electrodes placed directly on or within the surface of the brain. The original technique for recording D.C. potentials from the brain was developed by Vernon Rowland (see, for example, Rowland & Goldstone, 1963), and the reader is directed there for technical details.

During classical conditioning experiments, widely separated regions of the brain have been found to produce slow potential changes that are highly correlated with the various stages of the conditioning process. For example, Irwin and Rebert (1970) have shown that the motor cortex, as well as the lateral hypothalamic region, produced slow potentials that were functionally related to progressive increases in the conditioning of a jaw movement in the cat. In each of these brain regions, the slow potential produced by an acoustic conditioned stimulus grew in amplitude as the strength of the conditioning increased. On the other hand, the reticular formation and the amygdala failed to show any corresponding change in slow potential as a result of this learning experience.

A typical D.C. potential produced by the acoustic conditioned stimulus after the animal was well trained is shown in Fig. 8-7. Note that the potential lasts for well over the 2-second epoch shown in this figure. (The large response at the beginning of the graph is a 100 microvolt calibration signal.)

In the following discussion, a question repeatedly reappears: Are the various compound signals actually encoded measures of the information transactions that are thought to be the actual coded equivalent of learning, or are they simply

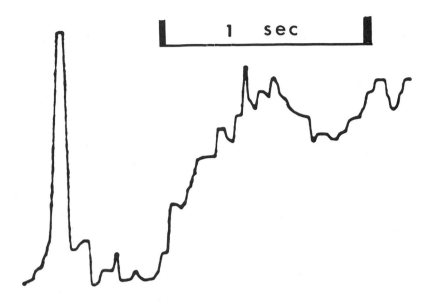

FIG. 8.7   A sample slow potential change (the longer-lasting later part of the signal) from the motor cortex of a classically conditioned cat. (From Irwin & Rebert, ©1970, with the permission of Elsevier/North-Holland Biomedical Press.)

reflections of the increased motor response amplitude or some other indirect mechanism with which the animal has been conditioned to respond? In the particular case of Irwin and Rebert's experiment, the question is most pertinent, because the D.C. amplitude increase occurred mainly in the motor cortex. This finding suggests that the recorded increase in D.C. potential amplitude may, indeed, have only been due to a conditioned increase in the motor response rather than to the learning process itself. As we see later, this same conceptual difficulty is recurrent throughout much of the following discussion of compound action potentials and learning.

2.   The Contingent Negative Variation

The contingent negative variation (CNV), a moderately rapid transient compound action potential first observed by W. Grey Walter (Walter, 1964), is recorded maximally from the vertex of the skull with electrodes that need not necessarily penetrate the skin of the scalp. Thus, the CNV may routinely be recorded from human subjects. The term CNV evolves from the fact that this potential is a surface negative potential whose amplitude seems to be closely related to the contingency or significance of the relationship between two successive stimuli. This particular signal typically grows in amplitude as the association or contingency between two stimuli is increased by a conditioning process. Roth, Kopell, Tinklenberg, Darley, Sikora, and Vesecky (1975), for example, have shown that the contingent negative variation depends upon the set size (i.e., the number of items in a trial) in what is called a *Sternberg memory task*. [Sternberg's (1966) paradigm involves the cued (by a pointer) recall of a single item from a tachistoscopically flashed row of alphabetic characters.] Roth and his co-workers suggest that the CNV reflects some aspect of the short-term storage of a brief visual display. Indeed, one of the most attractive features of this particular potential is that its behavior and temporal properties closely parallel psychophysical results in short-term memory experiments of this sort.

The contingent negative variation has much the same duration as the D.C. potential (it too lasts for several seconds), but unlike the D.C. potential, it is typically terminated abruptly by the presentation of the second stimulus. Its full time course, therefore, is not well defined because of the limits imposed by the experimental paradigm. Because of the percutaneous recording technique usually used, and the low level signals thus available, computer averaging techniques are required to extract the CNV from the electronic and physiological noise in which it is embedded. Figure 8-8 shows the time course of a typical CNV recording.

3. The Evoked Brain Potential

A briefer (than the CNV) evoked brain potential (EBP) can also be detected by computer averaging of responses elicited by sensory stimulation. The EBP displays sensitivity to the various dimensions of the stimulus, the response, and the particular stage of development of the conditioning process, as well as a number of other mental variables. For example, when dealing with the training of visual discrimination tasks, Spinelli and Pribram (1970) have shown that the compo-

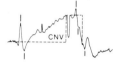

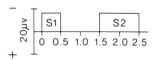

FIG. 8.8 Sample evoked brain potential showing the long negative (upward) swing referred to as the *contingent negative variation* (CNV). The calibration graph below shows the time relations of the two stimuli (S_1 and S_2) and the time base in sec. (From Roth, Kopell, Tinklenberg, Darley, Sikora, & Vesecky, ©1975, with the permission of Elsevier/North-Holland Biomedical Press.)

nents of the measured visual EBP reflect not only the nature of the stimulus but also the response made by the experimental animal, as well as the type of reinforcement. All three aspects of the response, however, are functionally dependent upon the stage of learning achieved by the animal. Figure 8-9, for example, shows the evoked potentials produced in several different conditions from one of the experiments in Spinnelli and Pribram's study. The shape of the evoked potentials differs following the presentation of a circle or of a group of parallel straight lines as shown in the first part of this figure. Thus the electrical response is dependent upon the shape of the discriminable stimuli. Evoked brain potentials can also be produced for the time period just prior to the response by maintaining a running record of the signal and then averaging backward from the response when it occurs. The second part of Fig. 8-9 shows that the evoked potential also is functionally related to which of two response levers was depressed by the animal. The third part of this figure shows that the shape of the evoked potential produced by the reinforcement is also dependent upon whether the reinforcement was rewarding a correct response or extinguishing an incorrect response.

In these three parts, the shape of the evoked potential that has been shown is for a relatively highly developed level of training. In general, Pribram and Spinelli found that the amplitude of the signal increased with training. This is not, however a universal observation. Other psychobiologists have shown that direction of the change in EBP amplitude may reverse not only as a function of the experimental paradigm but also as a function of the region of the brain from which the signals are recorded. Saito, Yamamoto, Iwai, and Nakahama (1973), for example, recording from the lateral geniculate body and the striate and parastriate cortices,

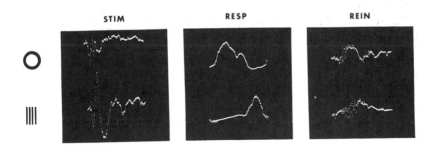

FIG. 8.9   Three photographs comparing the shape of the evoked brain potential responses to two different stimuli, for a positive and a negative response, and finally, as a function of the presence or absence of a reinforcement. The three sets of potentials were averaged out of the ongoing stream of neural activity at different epochs of the conditioning trial. The evoked brain potential is obviously sensitive to several aspects of the experimental situation. (From Spinelli & Pribram, ©1970, with the permission of Elsevier/North-Holland Biomedical Press.)

found that during the course of a similar visual discrimination training session only the potentials from the lateral geniculate were enhanced. Those from the primary visual cortices actually diminished in amplitude as behavioral proficiency for the task increased. Few psychobiologists would assert that the lateral geniculate body, a visual relay station, was the site of discrimination learning, yet the major positive effect on the amplitude of the evoked potential was observed there during learning.

The direction of change (growth or reduction) of the various evoked potential components, therefore, is not uniquely related to the process of learning. Selected components, including the earliest ones occurring in the 50 msec. following the stimulus (which had been thought to be associated with the responses of the primary sensory projection pathways), can be selectively either reduced or enhanced depending upon the nature of the reinforcement. These reversible bidirectional changes have been shown by Rudell and Fox (1972) (see Fig. 8-10).

Such data illustrate that the amplitude of the evoked potential is not a direct manifestation of learning per se. Rather, the evoked potential, and perhaps all of the other compound signals discussed, are more likely to be indirect measures of the learning process. It is possible that they are more closely related to the strength of the response than to the dynamic and plastic changes that occur within the nervous system. From this point of view, these compound action potentials may more properly be considered as responses themselves rather than as direct measures of the neural mechanisms underlying learning.

4.   The Electroencephalogram

The ongoing electroencephalogram (EEG) until recently has enjoyed great favor in the study of learning processes. During the last decade, however, the considerable development of improved techniques for the measurement of evoked brain potentials has made them preferred measures. Improved measurement techniques were only one factor in this shift of interest away from the EEG to the EBP, however. A number of biological considerations also were influential. For example, the time course of changes in the EEG usually extends over many seconds; this fact is inconsistent with more rapid and brief behavioral indicators of learning. Furthermore, even with the use of spectral analysis devices to provide a numerical metric, the direct relationship of the stimulus and changes in the EEG is not always clear, because subtle or short-term changes in its frequency components may not be apparent to the observer.

Another aspect of the biology of the EEG, however, was even more important in its decline from favor. The EEG is diminished, or attenuated, during the periods of the most intense psychological activity. This means that, in general, the ongoing signals are negatively correlated with mental activity and are at a maximum when nothing of significance is happening. Quite to the contrary, the EBP

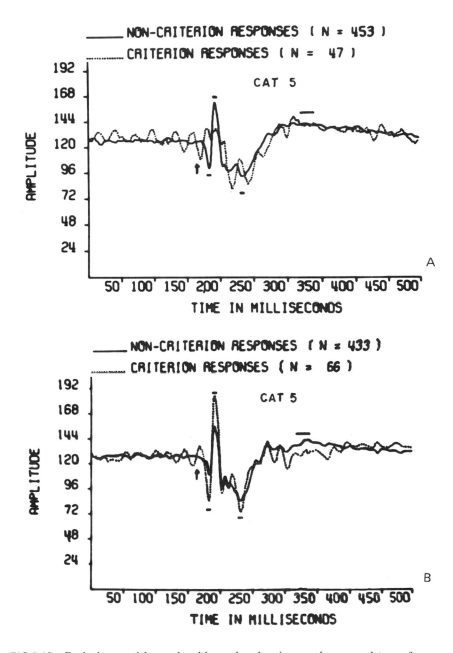

FIG 8.10 Evoked potentials can be either reduced or increased compared to a reference response. In (A), the evoked potential obtained from a cat has been "trained" to be smaller than the reference by positively reinforced small amplitudes. In (B), the evoked potential has been "trained" to be larger in amplitude than the reference by reinforcing large amplitudes. (From Rudell & Fox, ©1972, with the permission of The American Physiological Society.)

is highly correlated with many aspects of the stimulus as well as stiuational variables.

Adey (1966) presented one of the best summaries of the work done on EEG correlates of learning in the decade prior to 1965. Because little of interest in this field has been done since then, Adey's review is moderately up-to-date. He describes a number of instances in which classical conditioning and visual discrimination learning paradigms were used to modulate the electroencephalogram. Although a number of these experiments demonstrated the conditioned blocking of the ongoing EEG, a more interesting class of experiments has been carried out by Adey and Walter (1963). They showed that electroencephalograms recorded from the hippocampus with surgically implanted electrodes tend to be more synchronized later in the course of acquisition of a T-maze choice task than in the earlier trials. This increase in synchrony is shown in Fig. 8-11 with data obtained from sessions that occurred early in the training (July 7) and then again 3 weeks later (July 27). Records were obtained from both the right and left dorsal hippocampi. Early in the training sessions, when the animal was acquiring the discrimination that led him up the correct arm of a T-maze to a food reward, both of the hippocampal gyri seemed to produce very similar kinds of responses. When these signals were averaged for 20 runs, however, the resulting composite electroencephalogram displayed a very small amplitude. The reason for this low-level average EEG cannot be attributed to the fact that the signals themselves were of low amplitude; clearly, they are not. Rather the nearly flat curve is due to the poor synchronization of the individual EEGs. The averaging process, therefore, counterbalances the signals and spuriously suggests a small difference between the peaks and troughs when in fact there is a large difference.

On the other hand, 3 weeks later in the experiment and after substantial training, two important differences in the averaged data emerge. First, a substantial difference can be observed between the left and right hippocampal signals. This difference is attributable to a lesser degree of rhythmic firing in the left hippocampus. More germane to the present discussion, however, is the observation that the averaged electroencephalogram from the right hippocampus is considerably higher in amplitude than that from the left hippocampus. This difference is due mainly to a higher degree of synchronization in the recordings from the right hippocampus rather than to any increase in the magnitude of the individual response of the left. This increased synchrony in the right hemisphere appears to be caused by the animal's newly emerging ability to reset the phase angle of the EEG when the tone indicating the availability of the food is presented.

Thus the electroencephalogram and the other compound action potentials discussed so far can be conditioned or trained much in the same manner as a muscular response. However, the relationship between all of these compound potentials and the process of learning is not yet known. We still cannot say whether these signals reflect the representational processes that may be considered equivalent to learning, or whether they are merely signs, concomitants, or

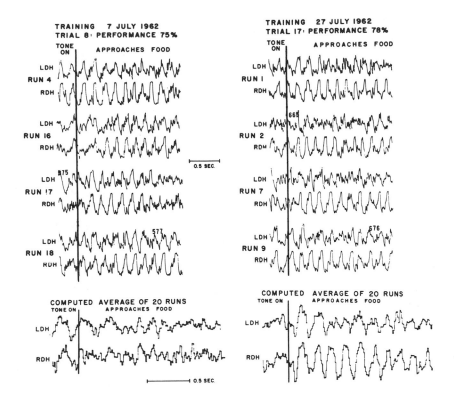

FIG. 8.11 EEGs from the hippocampus can be trained to occur in synchrony with a stimulus. On the left-hand side of this figure, the lack of synchronization leads to a very small averaged signal from both the RDH (right dorsal hippocampus) and the LDH (left dorsal hippocampus) even though the individual signals are uniformly quite large. These recordings were made early in the training. After substantial training, however, the averaged potentials show a substantial signal in the RDH (right dorsal hippocampus), because the phases of the various traces have been "trained" to be synchronous with the stimulus. (From Adey, ©1966, with the permission of Academic Press.)

epiphemona, only distantly related to the neural mechanisms actually undergoing the plastic changes.

It is essential to remember, no matter how high the correlation obtained between the behavioral data and the electrophysiological data, there is no assurance that the electrophysiological response is the necessary and sufficient transactional equivalent of behavior. Other tests are required (see Chapter 7) to prove that compound potentials are even statistically similar to the neural processes underlying learning. No one has yet come forth with such tests of necessity and sufficiency. Instead, the fact that researchers have been able to experimentally disassociate compound potentials and the behavior in a wide variety of situations is strong evidence that compound brain potentials are, at best, signs rather than codes and, at the least, irrelevant responses with no direct relationship to the behavioral learning.

D. VARIABILITY IN NEURONAL RESPONSES
AND LEARNING

The exact relationship between the compound potentials and learning continues to be elusive, partially because the conceptual link between the evoked potentials and their anatomical origins is yet to be established and partially because of the possible indirect feedback effects. There is a considerably more direct approach to the problem, however, when the psychobiologist is studying plasticity at the level of individual neurons. Although, here too, feedback effects cannot be totally excluded, at least the recorded potentials are localized to an individual unit.

A major conceptual problem related to single-cell studies of learning results from our inability as yet to provide a satisfactory explanation of the linking relationship between the responses observed at the cellular level and those at the molar behavior; i.e., we still do not know how the overall mental process arises from the activity of billions of individual cells. The hypothesis that a dynamic network, whose momentary state is modulated by changes at the synapses, is the neural equivalent of behavioral plasticity, although it may be quite plausible, is not tantamount to a rigorous proof of the link. No matter how often repeated, demonstrations of plastic changes in neurons do not prove that any of those cellular changes are the true physiological or transactional equivalent (i.e., the codes) of some form of short-term learning.

This logical difficulty is clearly expressed in the following statement by Irving Kupfermann (1975):

> There is an unfortunate tendency for some authors to utilize behavioral terms such as habituation to describe neurophysiological processes such as synaptic depression (e.g., Bruner & Kennedy, 1970; Zilber-Gachelin & Chartier, 1973), thereby blurring the distinction between studies of established behavioral significance with model studies that have only theoretical significance [p. 378].

Arnold Leiman and Clifford Christian (1973) express essentially the same point of view when they state:

> A related rationale for looking at neuronal analogs of learning is the general hypothesis that behavioral plasticity is mediated by analogous neuronal plasticity. The theory explains how two appropriately paired stimuli produced a conditioned behavioral response by proposing that the excitation of two input channels will produce a conditioned response at an individual neuron. The conditioned neuron then drives a command or motorneuron producing the behavioral response. Although this explanation

may have a prima facie appeal, there are a number of reasons why the behavior exhibited in learning paradigms places few constraints on the possible neuronal organization underlying it. In neuronal circuits with even a modicum of complexity, the properties of individual neurons are obscured in the operation of the system. Nor does the behavior of the system indicate the nature of its components or circuits [p. 151].

And a few pages later:

The attempts to find neuronal alterations during learning have been all too successful, for one is embarrassed with a superfluity of neurons changing their activity. There are single units at all levels of the mammalian central nervous system that exhibit changes in activity concomitant with behavioral conditioning. Most of these units probably have nothing more to do with producing a changed behavior in the animal than the activity of the muscles themselves; they are simply following altered input. To identify the neurons initiating these changes, it must be shown that the output of a neuron is altered while its input remains constant. This criterion of primary neuronal change has not yet been satisfied. Therefore, indirect measures, such as the correlation of neuronal activity with the conditioned response, provide the only evidence of the behavioral relevance and primacy of single unit modification [p. 158].

And finally, Eric Kandel and W. Alden Spencer (1968), his colleague, speak to the same point in summarizing their views of the relationship between single-cell plasticity and learning:

In conclusion, we believe that cellular neurophysiological approaches will prove increasingly important for the neural analysis of psychological processes. However, at these early stages of investigation the optimal growth of the independent but interrelated disciplines of experimental psychology and cellular neurophysiology can be best fostered by maintaining a healthy skepticism about proposed isomorphisms between behavioral and electrophysiological phenomena and between learning and analogs of learning [p. 124].

In spite of these caveats, there is an enormous interest in research on correlates of learning at the cellular level. Much of this work has been carried out without a clear expression of the conceptual basis of this work. This section, therefore, considers some of the more significant of published accounts of research on learning correlates at the neuron level and attempts to evaluate their significance in the emerging concept of the neural basis of mind. A thorough review of the mountain of literature forthcoming in this field obviously could not possibly be accomplished. The reader interested in more complete discussions of the neural correlates of learning is advised to turn to the comprehensive reviews by Jasper and Doane (1968), Kandel and Spencer (1968), Galeano (1972), Leiman and Christian (1973), Woody, Brown, Crow, and Knispel (1974), and Kupfermann (1975).

The following reviews results of only a few samples of the research correlating some aspect of neuronal plasticity with particular learning paradigms. Phenomena analogous to conditioning and habituation, observed in an invertebrate system, are considered in the first section. This topic is followed by a discussion of cellular plasticity as observed in a number of different mammalian nervous systems when classical conditioning paradigms are used. Next, operant conditioning of neural responses is considered. Finally, the possible neural correlate of a form of intermediate-term learning involving delayed responses is discussed.

One gap remains in this discussion. My readers should realize that there still is, at the electrophysiological level, no indication of any correlate of long-term memory. Yet long-term memory is perhaps the most important of all of the forms of storage in the hierarchy discussed earlier in this chapter. This omission itself may reflect an important biological fact. Long-term storage may not, indeed, be mediated by patterns of electrophysiological response but by more subtle and permanent structural changes in the organization of neural networks that are not detectable with microelectrodes. If so, the discussion presented in Chapter 9 of long-term changes in synaptic efficiency and anatomy may be far more relevant to long-term memory than to short-term memory, which seems more likely to have correlates in terms of dynamic patterns of activity.

1.   An Invertebrate Model of Habituation and Conditioning

One of the most extraordinarily useful invertebrate preparations for the study of learning has been the *Aplysia,* or sea hare, a gastropod mollusk of the subclass Opisthobrancia. This animal, which lives for about one year, grows rapidly and can be as long as 12 inches when fully mature. Although these factors are incidental, *Aplysia's* central role in neurophysiological studies of learning has been guaranteed by the fact that *Aplysia* (along with a number of other invertebrates) has a nervous system that is relatively so simple, in which the cells are so large, and for which there is such constancy from one preparation to the next, that individual neurons can actually be labeled and restudied in a sequential series of experiments carried out on different animals. The situation is quite unlike that found in the vertebrate's nervous system with its bewildering myriads of tiny neurons organized in patterns of almost unanalyzable complexity.

Aplysia has little commercial or aesthetic value to man. The great beauty and importance of the well-ordered neural nets that are involved in the simple behaviors of this otherwise unimportant animal is that *Aplysia* provides a simplified model of how networks of neurons may work together to produce behavior. Invertebrate preparations like *Aplysia* and a few others (the leech and the cockroach, for example), because of this intrinsic simplicity, can provide analyzable models that show great promise for helping us understand the general nature of the link between neural net responses and molar behavior.

An idea of the anatomic features of *Aplysia* and its system can be obtained from Fig. 8-12. Also shown in this figure is the manner in which one of the ganglia of *Aplysia's* nervous system, the bi-lobed abdominal ganglion, can be supported for electrophysiological recordings while simultaneously providing enough flexibility for the animal to respond with unimpeded motor movements.

Figure 8-13 shows the organization of the individual neurons in the abdominal ganglion as viewed from both the dorsal and the ventral aspects. This figure also shows that many of the individual neurons have been specifically named with a letter and number code. R10, for example, is a particular neuron in the right rostral quarter ganglion (RRQG). This cellular nomenclature shown holds in any *Aplysia,* as the stability of its anatomy is such that R10 and all other of the constituent neurons are interconnected in the same way and will serve the same function in all specimens. It is this extraordinary repeatability of structure that makes possible the detailed neuronal analysis of *Aplysia's* primitive ability to modify its behavior in a way that seems very close to what we call *learning*.

Kandel has considered an interesting complex of responses involving movements in three particular structures—the gill, the siphon, and the mantle shelf. The gill is a multilobed respiratory device; the siphon acts to funnel water through the mantle cavity and over the gills; and the mantle shelf is a flap of the mantle that covers the gills. These structures display three different kinds of normal reflexive withdrawal movement and one coordinated movement of interest to this discussion. The reflexive movements are:

1. A massive reflex withdrawal of all portions of the siphon, the gills, and the mantle shelf in a coordinated retraction is observed when the siphon or mantle shelf is stimulated with some object or an energetic flow of water.

2. A second form of reflex, involving only gill withdrawal, is elicted by stimulation of certain small restricted portions of the siphon or the mantle.

3. The third reflex action involves the individual lobes of the gill, which constrict when they are touched. However, this latter reflex seems to be mediated solely by local peripheral mechanisms (Peretz, 1970) that do not involve the central abdominal ganglia of the *Aplysia* as do the first two reflexes. Thus it is not discussed further in this section.

In addition to these three strictly reflexive patterns of response to peripheral stimuli, Kandel describes a fourth pattern of behavior as a coordinated and rhythmic contractions of many of the parts of the gill and mantle apparatus. This rhythmic response probably helps to cleanse the mantle cavity of sand and aerate the gills. The coordinated motion, according to an extensive series of studies by Kandel and his colleagues (Kupfermann & Kandel, 1969; Kupfermann, Carew & Kandel, 1974), seems to be initiated by central nervous system interneurons rather than by stimulation of a peripheral sensory receptor.

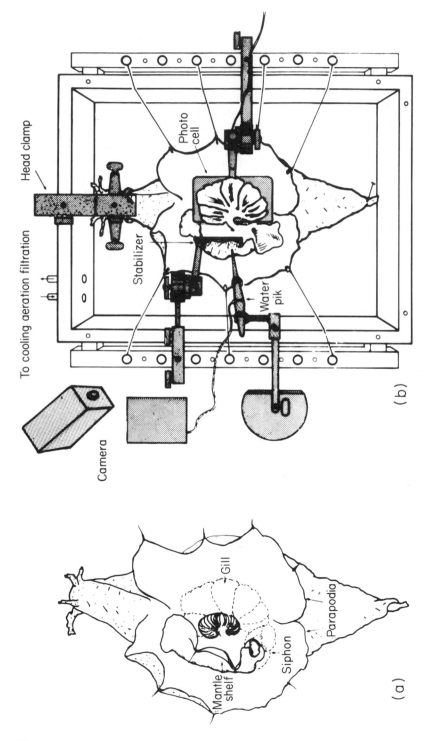

Head clamp

To cooling aeration filtration

Photo cell

Stabilizer

Water pik

Camera

(b)

Gill

Mantle shelf

Siphon

Parapodia

(a)

FIG. 8.12   Drawing of a nearly intact *Aplysia* (A) and a view of the apparatus used to restrain these animals for research on their nervous systems. (From Kandel, ©1974, after Castellucci, Pinsker, Kupfermann, & Kandel, 1970, with the permission of The M.I.T. Press.)

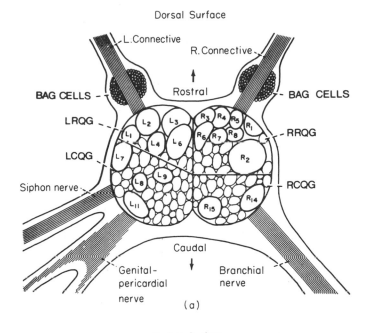

Dorsal Surface

L. Connective

R. Connective

BAG CELLS

Rostral

BAG CELLS

LRQG

L_2 L_3 R_3 R_4 R_5 R_1

RRQG

L_1 L_4 L_6 R_6 R_7 R_8

LCQG

L_7 R_2

Siphon nerve

L_8 L_9

L_{11} R_{15} R_{14}

RCQG

Caudal

Genital-
pericardial
nerve

Branchial
nerve

(a)

Ventral Surface

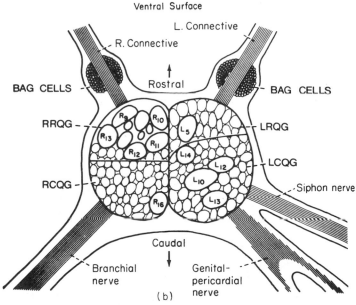

L. Connective

R. Connective

BAG CELLS

Rostral

BAG CELLS

RRQG

R_9 R_{10} L_5

LRQG

R_{13} R_{11} L_{14}

R_{12}

LCQG

RCQG

L_{12}

L_{10}

Siphon nerve

R_{16} L_{13}

Caudal

Branchial
nerve

Genital-
pericardial
nerve

(b)

FIG. 8.13   Enlarged views of the dorsal and ventral aspects of the abdominal ganglion of *Aplysia* showing the identified and numbered cells repeatedly present from one preparation to the next. RQC = rostral quarter ganglion; and CQG = caudal quarter ganglion. (From Frazier, Kandel, Kupfermann, Waziri, & Coggeshall, ©1967, with the permission of The American Physiological Society.)

The totally unusual and virtually unique aspect of the research I discuss here, however, is that Kandel's laboratory has been able to identify the exact details of the neural net that activates the three responses. Thus these simple animals become important models of both neural and behavioral plasticity. Surprisingly, all three response modes, the two reflexive ones and the centrally controlled rhythmic response, seem to be the result of the action of the same neural network. However, each particular response is controlled by a slightly different configuration that is the important and essential part of the discussion that follows.

Figure 8-14 shows the three different arrangements of the same network of neurons resulting in these three forms of behavior as analyzed by Kandel and his colleagues. Plate A shows the arrangement that produces the coordinated and rhythmic gill, mantle shelf and siphon movements that are useful in cleansing the mantle cavity or aerating the gills. This action according to Kandel, is initiated by an interneuron labelled *INT II*. At the time Kandel's work was published, no specific identification of *INT II* as any particular neuron of those shown in Fig. 8-13 was possible. Indeed, Kandel suggests that it is not unreasonable to assume that this functionally defined structure might actually be a group of closely related neurons rather than a single cell. Other neurons shown in Plate A of Fig. 8-14, however, are uniquely defined anatomic entities whose code numbers correspond to those identified in Fig. 8-13.

Plates B and C of Fig. 8-14 show the two other configurations of the same neurons that account for the two forms of reflexive withdrawal. Plate B depicts the network configuration that seems to account for the generalized defensive reflex withdrawal produced by a stimulus to an area of the mantle containing a hypothetical sensory cell labeled *Sensory N*. In this case, not only is there a direct excitement of all motor neurons, but there is also a feedback loop mediated by the group of excitatory neurons labeled *EXC INT* that amplifies the motor signals and thus accentuates the massive withdrawal reflex. It is only when a slower-acting group of inhibitory neurons (*INH INT*) begins to exert their influence that the massive contraction relaxes.

Plate C depicts the configuration of the network controlling the selective withdrawal of the gill when the siphon is stimulated. In this case, the motor signals to the siphon and mantle shelf have essentially been disconnected, and these structures do not respond. Plate C also indicates another important set of data. The small numbers (1-8) indicate possible sites of neural plasticity that might possibly modulate the overt response behaviors. I consider these possible synaptic and cellular loci of plasticity in greater detail in Chapter 9.

In the remainder of this section I delve further into forms of learning that Kandel and his colleagues feel have specific neural correlates in the nervous system of *Aplysia* in search of more understanding. First I consider a process analogous to mammalian habituation and its possible neural correlate. Then I consider an exceedingly plausible neural correlate of the classical conditioning paradigm.

CENTRAL COMMAND

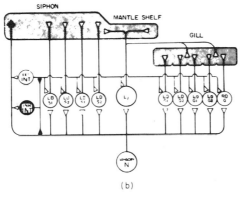

(a)

DEFENSIVE WITHDRAWAL REFLEX

(b)

GILL WITHDRAWAL REFLEX

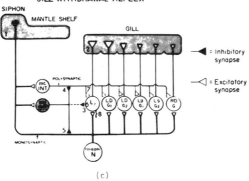

◀ = Inhibitory synapse

◁ = Excitatory synapse

(c)

FIG. 8.14 Proposed circuit diagrams of a dual-control mechanism for control of the *Aplysia's* siphon, mantle, and gill. Central commands allow coordinated movements of the structures for sand removal (for example) using one circuit arrangement (A), but the system may be switched into a massive reflex mode to allow rapid withdrawal of either the entire mass of soft tissue (B) or only the gill (C). (From Kandel, ©1974, with the permission of The M.I.T. Press.)

a.   Habituation in Aplysia and a Possible Neural Correlate[5]

Habituation, as I noted earlier in this chapter, is the progressive decline in response amplitude to repeated application of a more or less constant stimulus. It can be distinguished from fatigue by the fact that it seems to be reversible whenever novel stimuli are introduced. Thus if a new stimulus is presented, the old response may be as strong or even stronger than originally.

What is believed to be true habituation (and not simply some complicated form of fatigue) can be demonstrated in *Aplysia*. Kandel's group has also studied this problem, and they report (Pinsker, Kupfermann, Castellucci, & Kandel, 1970) that if the portion of the siphon that produces the selective gill withdrawal reflex is touched once every minute or so, the amplitude of the gill withdrawal will be reduced by about 70% after as few as 20 stimuli. When the same stimulus is applied to another portion of the siphon, however, "dishabituation" occurs, and the response magnitude is increased to nearly its original magnitude.

In addition to response recovery as a result of this kind of stimulus novelty, there is spontaneous recovery in response strength. Figure 8-15 shows the course of habituation for stimulus intervals of 1 and 3 minutes respectively. Each trace indicates the magnitude of the actual physical withdrawal as measured by the amount of gill interposed between a photocell and light source. Figure 8-15a shows the spontaneous recovery after a period of 2 hours. Figure 8-15b shows the immediate recovery of response strength produced as a result of simply moving the habituating stimulus to another location on the *Aplysia's* mantle—in this case, the simplest way of achieving novelty.

Having shown this behavior of habituation to be stable, Kandel and his colleagues then proceeded to accomplish what must certainly be considered a major tour de force in modern neurophysiology. They searched for, and found, the specific neurons in the *Aplysia's* abdominal ganglia responsible for the response habituation!

The way in which this was accomplished was a model of scientific detective work. Figure 8-14c made it clear that there are many places in the neural network mediating this behavior at which the neural plastic change could have occurred. Habituation could have been peripheral and merely involved a lessening of the effective stimulus strength impinging upon the sensory receptor. Alternately, there could have been a reduction in motor ability either at the neuromuscular junction or in the contracting muscle itself.

The specific experiments Kandel and his colleagues used to exclude these sensory and motor possibilities were elegant and simple. For example, Byrne, Castellucci, and Kandel (1974) showed that recordings from single afferent fibers displayed no decrement in any aspect of the signal as a result of repeated

---

[5]The following discussion of habituation has been summarized from Kandel's (1974) brilliant synthethis of the data and theory of habituation in *Aplysia*. The reader is referred to that review for more complete details.

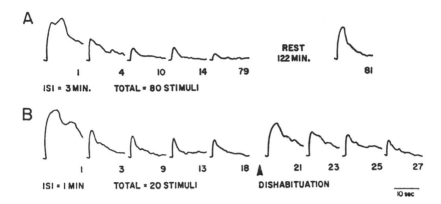

FIG. 8.15   Habituation, spontaneous recovery, and dishabituation exhibited in the magnitude of the *Aplysia's* gill withdrawal reflex. In (A), the response gradually habituates after 80 stimuli but following a rest of 2 hours is almost fully recovered in amplitude. The same degree of recovery, however, can be made to occur immediately by introducing a novel stimulus as shown in (B). Obviously, habituation is not simple fatigue. (From Pinsker, Kupfermann, Castellucci, & Kandel, ©1970, with the permission of The American Association for the Advancement of Science.)

mechanical stimulation. They also showed that electrical stimulation (with gross electrodes) of activity along these same fibers was able to elicit the original high level of action potential long into the habituation series. Similarly, electrical stimulation of the efferent fibers, which carried the motor signals to the muscles themselves, did not display evidence of a reduction in response strength following habituation. Thus both sensory and motor peripheral mechanisms were excluded as possible sites of the observed habituation.

It is necessary to attribute the critical aspect of neural plasticity, therefore, to the central neurons of the abdominal ganglion itself. Kandel's co-workers (e.g., Castellucci, Pinsker, Kupfermann, & Kandel, 1970; Kupfermann, Castellucci, Pinsker, & Kandel, 1970) attack the problem of how specific neurons were involved by inserting a microelectrode into them. Recordings were made of the excitatory postsynaptic potential (EPSP) from such neurons as L7, while simultaneously recording signals from sensory neurons and observing the muscular contractions of the gills. The sensory and motor neurons in this preparation were found to be directly connected by only a single synapse. Thus the preparation just described is essentially monosynaptic.

The main conclusion of these studies was that the habituation observed at this neurophysiological level, which is highly correlated with the motor responses of the gill mechanism, is exclusively due to plastic changes occurring directly at the single central synapse. Let us consider the main aspects of the neurophysiological findings that led to this conclusion. As with behavioral response strength, there was a gradual reduction in the strength of the excitatory postsynaptic potential (EPSP) generated at this synapse as a result of repeated presentations of an electrical stimulus to the presynaptic sensory neurons. The neural habituation effects "spontaneously" disappeared over a period of time with very much the same time course as the behaviorally measured habituation. Because of the monosynaptic nature of the preparation, the conclusion that the locus of the habituation is at the synapse itself is overwhelming. Because of the well-defined nature of the neural network and the correspondence of the temporal dimensions, Kandel and his colleagues felt secure in asserting that they had been observing the actual physiological mechanism of the behavioral response.

It was also important, however, to demonstrate that the effects observed were not attributable to simple fatigue in the postsynaptic neuron. A relatively simple control experiment confirmed that this was not the case. A novel stimulus situation was created by inserting the same electrical pulse that had been driving the habituated synapse along another of the nerve fibers that also activated the postsynaptic neuron into which the recording microelectrode was inserted. When this was done, the original EPSP reappeared with full-blown amplitude, and the behavioral contraction of the gills also reappeared at its original magnitude. The resultant dishabituated response had all the properties of the original unhabituated response. As final proof, this dishabituating electrical stimulus itself also was subject to a progressive reduction in its efficacy when it was sequentially repeated. This confirmed that the dishabituating mechanism did not involve some alternate mechanisms not subject to habituation. The fact that the original postsynaptic neuron was able to immediately respond at full strength to the dishabituating signal is also strong evidence for the conclusion that habituation, whatever its source, can only be a result of processes that occur at the synapse.

Castellucci, Pinsker, Kupfermann, and Kandel (1970) have proposed a theoretical model that evolved directly from these data to explain how these synaptic effects mediate the habituated response changes I have described. Figure 8-16 displays the essentials of their hypothesis. Specifically, they propose that the habituating system is made up of a receptor at the terminus of an axon (located in the siphon), which connects its own receptor cell body to the base of neuron L7. The junction between the sensory neuron and L7 is indicated as a crosshatched triangle. L7 is a motor neuron that is able to directly control a portion of the gill musculature. Another sensory neuron is shown with its receiving element buried in another portion of the animal's body—in this sample case, its head. However, it might also be a neuron that is located in close proximity to the first receptor in the region of the siphon. The model assumes that the secondary receptor possesses two collateral connections to L7 and the primary sensory receptor. One collateral proceeds directly to the L7 motor neuron, and the other passes to the synaptic junction between the primary sensory neuron and L7.

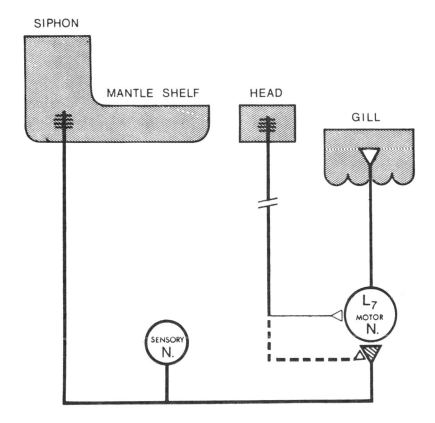

FIG. 8.16 A theory of neural organization underlying habituation and dishabituation in the *Aplysia* postualted by Kandel and his colleagues. (From Castellucci, Pinsker, Kupfermann, & Kandel, ©1970, with the permission of The American Association for the Advancement of Science.)

According to this model, habituation occurs when repeated stimulation of the primary sensory neuron, either via the primary receptor or (in the case of electrical stimulation) directly to its axon, results in a diminishment of the conductive efficiency of the crosshatched synapse. Although as late as 1973, Kandel could not state with certainty exactly what the membrane mechanisms were that accounted for this decrease in synaptic efficiency, they did speculate that it was largely due to reduced ability of the presynaptic cell to release the transmitter molecules may be associated with the actual depletion of the material, this seems unlikely because he also notes that it is possible to nearly instantaneously reactivate such a junction. We see in Chapter 9 that transmitter depletion is an unlikely candidate in general to explain synaptic plasticity. It therefore seems more likely that the junction is not physically depleted of transmitter substance as much as it is simply reduced in its capability to release its still available supply for reasons of membrane biochemistry that are not yet clear. The critical point is that this model asserts that habituation is definitely attributable to reduction in synaptic conductivity rather than any other portion of this simple network.

How, then, does the model account for dishabituation? Kandel and his colleagues suggest that dishabituation occurs when the "head" (or any other novel) receptor is activated. Although this secondary receptor has its own synaptic connection to L7 and can produce a response through that direct pathway, their electrophysiological evidence indicates that dishabituation is more likely to result from a direct increase in the conductivity of the habituated synapse through the axon indicated by the dashed line in Fig 8-16. This action of one synapse on another is presumed to suddenly revitalize the habituated synapse to nearly its original level of efficiency. Although the specific membrane mechanisms that produce the increase in the efficiency of the habituated synapse are not yet well understood either, they do seem to be associated with a restored ability to release the remaining large amount of available transmitter substance.

The key point in this analysis is that the changes in responsiveness of L7 (and all of its sister motor neurons) are accounted for in terms of changes in the conductivity of the synapses that it makes with other neurons rather than reverberating circuit effects, growth, or rearrangement of existing synapses. Whether or not this process is homologous or only similar to habituation mechanisms in higher animals is not known, but there seems to be little question that the behavioral change we call *habituation* in *Aplysia* is mediated by changes occurring at this particular synaptic junction. The important contribution of Kandel's group is that they have provided circumstantial evidence that analogous forms of behavior in higher animals may well be accounted for by the same sort of synaptic effects.

Concentration on this particular invertebrate study in my discussion of habituation should not mislead the reader to assume that no corresponding attempts have been made to explore the neural correlates of this simple form of learning in vertebrates. Groves, De Marco, and Thompson (1969), Segundo and Bell (1970), and O'Brien and Packham (1974) have studied the effects of habituation in mammalian brains and found essentially the same general results as those described for the invertebrate preparations. The essential difference between the two classes of research is the absence of detailed knowledge of the plastic changes in the neural net in the mammalian studies.

b. Classical Conditioning in Aplysia and a Possible Neural Correlate

In addition to simple habituation, *Aplysia* seems also to be capable of learning when subjected to the procedures of a classical conditioning paradigm. The simple anatomy and large neurons of *Aplysia's* abdominal ganglia have led to a highly specific hypothesis of a neural mechanism that may mediate the behavioral process. The neural mechanism involved has been referred to as *heterosynaptic facilitation*, which may be briefly defined as an increased responsiveness of a neuronal circuit to a previously ineffective stimulus as a result of the activation of an intermediary or alternative synaptic pathway by pairing the ineffective stimulus with a naturally effective stimulus.

To expand on this definition and as a brief introduction to the analogy that exists between classical conditioning and heterosynaptic facilitation, consider Fig. 8-17. The basic paradigm of classical conditioning, as seen in Fig. 8-17a, requires the synchronous pairing of a conditioned stimulus, which does not

(a) Classical conditioning

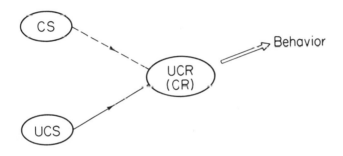

(b) Heterosynaptic facilitation

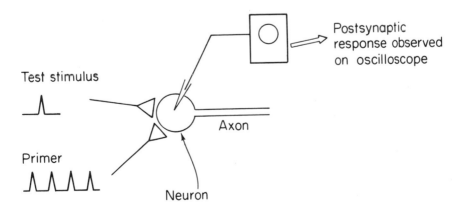

FIG. 8.17   Drawings of the paradigms of (A) classical conditioning and of (B) heterosynaptic facilitation. (From Uttal, 1975b.)

naturally produce a particular response, with an unconditioned stimulus that naturally elicits the same response. If the timing conditions are correct, the conditioned stimulus subsequently becomes "associated" with the unconditioned response and can independently elicit it.

Heterosynaptic facilitation, the analogous and possible homologous neurophysiological process, is depicted in Fig. 8-17b. Heterosynaptic facilitation is observed in neural nets in which a weak electrical stimulus (analogous to a conditioned stimulus) applied to a presynaptic neuron can be enhanced in its ability to evoke a postsynaptic potential. This enhancement is achieved by pairing the weak stimulus with a vigorous stimulus applied to another presynaptic neuron.

The distinction between heterosynaptic facilitation and post-tetanic potentiation (see Chapter 9) has not always been kept clear. Indeed, during the early work on the phenomenon of heterosynaptic facilitation, there was an assumption that it might simply be another version of post-tentanic facilitation. However, Tauc and Epstein (1967) and Epstein and Tauc (1970) clearly showed that the two were separate processes and that heterosynaptic facilitation occurred under conditions, such as low temperature or substitution of lithium for sodium in the bathing solutions, in which it was impossible to obtain post-tetanic potentiation. Even more important, work by these investigators showed that the heterosynaptic facilitory effect was not due to a mere change in the postsynaptic membrane but required the action of an intermediary neuron. Post-tetanic facilitation, on the other hand, is considered a homosynaptic effect, because it probably involves but one synapse.

To better understand the mechanism of heterosynaptic facilitation, consider Fig. 8-17b. In this model a stimulus is applied to one of the nerves feeding into the selected ganglion. The amplitude of this test stimulus is then adjusted to a relatively low value so that it produces only a small EPSP in a cell impaled with a recording microelectrode. This relatively weak *test stimulus* is then paired with another stronger stimulus applied to another of the nerves feeding into the ganglion. This second stimulus, usually referred to as the *priming stimulus* in the terminology originally suggested by Tauc and his co-workers, is adjusted so that it is just large enough to produce a vigorous response in the responding cell. If the test and the priming stimulus are paired repeatedly over approximately a 3-minute period, a subsequent presentation of the test stimulus alone will produce a greatly enhanced postsynaptic potential. The typical time course of the facilitation is shown in Fig. 8-18. As can be seen in this figure, the facilitation can last for over 15 minutes—an extraordinarily long time even in an invertebrate—and also, at its maximum, this facilitated response to the test stimulus closely approximates the response level of the original priming stimulus.

According to Kandel and Tauc (1964), only certain neurons found within the abdominal ganglion of *Aplysia* display heterosynaptic facilitation. Most neurons of the ganglion exhibit no change in response even with extensive pairing of the test and priming stimuli. In no case, however, did any neurons exhibit

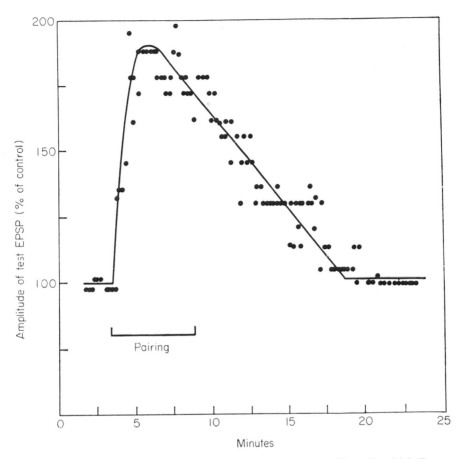

FIG. 8.18   Plot of the time course of heterosynaptic facilitation. (From Kandel & Tauc, ©1965a, with the permission of the *Journal of Physiology*.)

a facilitation without the actual pairing of test and priming stimuli. The fact that the facilitation could not be produced by the test stimulus alone, even when it was greatly enlarged and repeatedly presented, suggested that an intermediary synaptic mechanism must be involved in those instances in which pairing was effective. This led Kandel and Tauc to believe that the phenomenon of heterosynaptic facilitation is mediated by one of the other forms of presynaptic interaction shown in Figs. 8-19a and b.

In Fig. 8-19a, the presynaptic interaction is in the form of a direct facilitation. The neuron conveying the priming stimulus impinges directly on the presynaptic region of the junction between the neuron conducting the test stimulus (the test neuron) and the neuron in which the response occurs (the response neuron). By repeated activation with the priming stimulus, the synaptic junction between the test neuron and the response neuron acquires a heightened ability to produce postsynaptic potentials in the response cell when stimulated by the test stimulus alone.

Figure 8-19b diagrams a similar sort of neural circuit except that here an intermediary neuron is presumed to exist between the priming stimulus input and the presynaptic junction on the test neuron. Such an additional neuron in the circuit, Kandel and Tauc note, might have the advantage of maintaining the facilitory response over longer periods of time due to repetitive firing in this supplementary interneuron. Clearly this sort of plasticity in the nervous system is but one of many possible means of altering synaptic effectiveness and thus possibly mediating learning and memory behavior. Other plausible mechanisms are considered in Chapter 9.

Although presynaptic facilitory interconnections resulting from pairing can noticeably affect the response pattern of a single neuron, that single neuron's

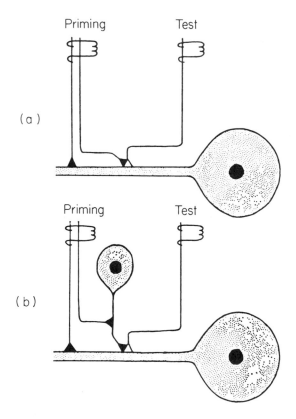

FIG. 8.19   Drawings of two possible circuits that might account for heterosynaptic facilitation: (A) does not but (B) does involve an intermediary neuron. (From Kandel & Tauc, ©1965b, with the permission of the *Journal of Physiology*.)

increased propensity to fire may have still other effects in a heavily interconnec-ted network. One such additional effect was reported by Kristan (1971), who showed that in the pleural ganglion of *Aplysia,* a marked increase in the syn-chrony of the signals from two impaled neurons is produced by a single stimulus when that stimulus is paired with a priming stimulus as described above and shown in Fig. 8-17b. This increase in synchrony is thought by Kristan to be mediated by the presence of an interneuron that, though originally ineffective, is activated to provide an additional indirect route for simultaneous driving of the two test neurons.

Here, then, are two examples of neural processes, a habituating mechanism and an analog of classical conditioning, that can be observed within the nervous system of *Aplysia.* Although we cannot be certain that these neural processes are actually identifiable with the mechanisms underlying the analogous behavior in higher vertebrates, these processes do represent an important kind of theoretical and heuristic model that has contributed greatly to our understanding of learn-ing.

Although I have restricted the discussion of invertebrate studies of learning to a single animal, *Aplysia,* studies of other invertebrate preparations have also con-tributed greatly to an understanding of the neural basis of learning. Notable among such studies are the work on the locust by Hoyle and Burrows (1973a; 1973b), on the cockroach (or more properly, the headless version of the animal) as studied by Horridge (1962), Nicholls and Purves' (1970) studies of the leech synapse, Maynard's (1972) work on the lobster's stomatogastric ganglion, and Krasne's (1969; 1973; and 1974) work on habituation in the crayfish.

I now consider mammalian nervous systems of much greater complexity than these invertebrates—systems for which there is no longer the remotest clue about the role of the individual neurons or of the detailed neuronal interactions. In giving up the anchor of direct cellular knowledge, however, we gain in its stead a much more elaborate repertoire of learning amenable to research inquiry.

2. Classical Conditioning of Individual Neurons in Mammals

Single-cell recording techniques have been applied in conjunction with various conditioning paradigms to study the plastic behavior of neurons in mammals as well as in other vertebrates and invertebrates. However similar these mammalian experiments may seem to the invertebrate studies just described, major differen-ces put this research in an entirely different conceptual class. In the study of the mammalian nervous system, there is no map of the involved neurons and no knowledge of which particular neurons are detected in any experimental trial. There is, furthermore, not the remotest likelihood that the same neuron will be detected in two different penetrations in the same animal much less in two dif-ferent animals. The individual neuron is found on the basis of chance alone and sends its message with profound anonymity. Furthermore, it is even possible that the whole concept of stable networks, repeated from one animal to another, may not hold in vertebrates. Different networks may mediate similar logical processes with entirely different populations of neurons from one situation to the next. The rich variety of vertebrate networks allows a dynamic variability to be conceived of, in a manner that is not possible in invertebrates with their relatively modest number of available neurons.

Thus although in *Aplysia* the conditioned or habituated changes were produced by changes in the synaptic junction, it is also possible that in more complex nets similar changes could be produced on the basis of circulating patterns of action potentials with little or no change in the synaptic structure per se. Circulating patterns of action potentials set up by conditioning procedures could easily produce alterations of the network state on the basis of timing fluctuations that perfectly simulate the conductivity changes observed in invertebrate preparations.

Furthermore, unlike the situation in most *Aplysia* experiments in which only a single synapse was known to be interposed between the axons that were stimulated and the neuron from which the postsynaptic potentials were recorded, it is highly unlikely that such a simple situation ever occurs in the mammalian brain. Only when electrophysiological studies are carried out at the level of the spinal cord or the neuromuscular junction can monosynaptic conditions be obtained. Indeed, it is not even certain, given the complexity of the mammalian central nervous system and the lack of detailed knowledge of the relevant neural circuits, just how few or how many synaptic relay steps may be involved in any given experiment. Feedback and feedforward loops may exist within the mammalian neural network. I have already shown how such interacting systems can complicate the observed input-output transactions.

There is, in addition, also a greater possibility that nonneural feedback loops may be involved in vertebrate than in invertebrate preparations. Muscular responses, and even glandular secretions, could produce dynamic changes in a neuron that did not exhibit any cellular plasticity itself. Thus the "learning" observed in neuronal nets, in which the synaptic connectivity is unknown, must very often remain equivocal with regard to the actual locus of the plastic change.

Another difficulty with mammalian studies is that the neural correlates of learning are not rare but rather are ubiquitous. The technical problem is often not to find a site that exhibits changes in cellular performance as a function of experimental manipulations but rather to find sites at which the cells are insensitive to them. Thus almost all portions of the brain respond to a greater or lesser extent to some aspect of the training paradigms. This diversity of responsiveness may reflect the fact that many of the supposed sites of learning suggested by various investigators may, in fact, be the result of feedback processes from responders.

The list of brain sites at which learning effects can be observed in single neuronal responses is long and even includes relatively peripheral portions of the sensory pathways. Halas, Beardsley, and Sandlie (1970), for example, searched for the neurophysiological effects of classical conditioning at a number of levels of the cat's auditory system and found units affected by the training in the medulla, the ascending reticular system, the thalamus, the cochlear nucleus, and the inferior colliculus, as well as in the auditory cortex. According to their results, therefore, learning affects neurons in the mammalian nervous system at all levels of the afferent pathway! In a study I consider in detail later, Olds, Disterhoft, Segal, Kornblith, and Hirsh (1972), using a very strict and constrained criterion of learning (latency brevity), found sites that they considered to be associated with learning in the rat's pontine reticular structure, ventral tegmentum, and thalamic nuclei, as well as in the CA3 field of the hippocampus and numerous other portions of the neocortical mantle. Fuster (1973) has found neural correlates of delayed response training, not unexpectedly, in the prefrontal cortex. And O'Brien and Fox (1969a; 1969b) have reported classical conditioning effects in the motor cortex of the cat.

Notwithstanding these caveats, the work done in studying the neuronal correlates of learning in mammals is intrinsically interesting and exciting. It is the purpose of this section to describe some of the more notable mammalian studies of neuronal plasticity reported in the recent literature and to critically analyze the logic of the proposed link between neuronal responsiveness and classical conditioning proposed in each case. I concentrate in particular on the work emanating from the laboratories of James Olds, Charles Woody, and James O'Brien.

a. *Olds' Studies of Classical Conditioning of Neurons in the Brain of the Rat*

Kandel's explorations into the neurophysiological mechanisms of learning in *Aplysia* were aimed at the elucidation of the role of particular neural networks and individual neurons. The simplicity of the preparation made it possible to attack the problem empirically and conceptually at this level. Direct and replicable identifications of individual neurons from preparation to preparation allowed specific statements to be made of the network organization and permitted Kandel and his colleagues to precisely identify plastic changes, which could have occurred at no other place than the synapse, as the likely equivalents of observed behavioral changes.

In the next studies I discuss, however, the anatomical facts of the situation preclude such a direct analytic approach. In this section I consider a series of studies in which the collected single-cell electrophysiological recordings are not used as a means of explicating the details of the neural net in which the microscopic neurons were involved. Rather, they are used as an indicator of the role of the macroscopic nucleus, of which the neuron is but one part, in learning. Thus in these experiments the main goal is more comparable to the localization studies discussed earlier than it is to the network analyses carried on with the *Aplysia* preparation. Nevertheless, a great deal of detailed information concerning the changing functions of individual neurons is implicit in the important studies reported from the laboratory of James Olds[6] that constitute the content of this section.

Even with this macroscopic orientation to the problem of neural correlates of learning, Olds' work is not, in any sense, a search for the site of the elusive engram, the actual repository of memory. He was more interested in a modern reformulation of the problem in which various other control and regulatory roles are emphasized rather than storage per se. The best expression of his research aim was expressed by Olds himself in one of his most important papers in this series (Olds et al., 1972): "The question of whether certain parts of the brain play an especially important role in processes related to learning and memory [p. 202]."

Clearly, although emphasizing the role of macroscopic structures, Olds and his colleagues were not rejecting the hypothesis of the essentially cellular nature of the problem or that synaptic plasticity probably played a key role in behavioral change. Immediately after stating their goal, they acknowledge the influence of the principles expressed much earlier by Burns (1957):

> Learning involves the rerouting of nerve impulses within the central nervous system . . . implying . . . that during learning the resistance of some synapses must change [as quoted in Olds, Disterhoft, Segal, Kornblith, & Hirsh, 1972, p. 202].

Although none of the data reported in this paper discriminates between synaptic "resistance" changes, on the one hand, and dynamic effects created by circulating patterns of nerve impulses, on the other, it is important to note that there is nothing inconsistent with any aspect of network state theory in this important work.

The essential criterion used by Olds and his colleagues for determining the relative importance of a given brain nucleus was a temporal one. They proposed that the earlier the effects of the conditioning were evidenced in the activity of one of its constituent cells, the more fundamental is the role of the nucleus in the learning process.

Unfortunately, it is difficult to accept this premise, the basis of all of Old's work, without reservation. Old's use of the temporal criterion is based upon a weak argument. He asserted that learning occurs when old responses are replaced by new responses and that the new excitation would initially follow the pathway of the old response. The responses are more likely to occur earlier, he further assumed, at the critical places at which the conditioning actually occurs (or is controlled) than at those points whose activity results from indirect feedback.

---

[6]As this manuscript was being sent to the publisher, news came of James Olds' unexpected death. Those of us who called him friend and colleague were deeply saddened by the loss. As one of the most creative and productive psychobiologists of the twentieth century, his contributions were enormous, his standards of the highest, and his dedication to the scientific enterprise a model for all of us and for all future students of this profession.

Other possibilities, including subtle, undetectable (with current technology) responses and contamination of the latency criterion by simple communication distance criteria, make this argument somewhat fragile.

This conceptual criticism, however, is not to be construed as criticisms of the actual electrophysiological results obtained in this study. Olds' work has been chosen for discussion in detail because it represents one of the more elegant and relevant bodies of data available in the area of the cellular basis of learning. Rather, the criticism is directed at the exceedingly complex biology of the situation and the limits of contemporary experimental techniques.

Olds chose to use freely moving rats as his experimental animal. A two-part training procedure was used throughout all of his experiments. For 1 or more days, the unconditioned and conditioned stimulus were presented unpaired, establishing a base line of the effects of habituation and pseudoconditioning. The artifactual changes in cellular responsiveness due to simple repetitive sensitization of the neuron would badly contaminate the interpretation of the results if a controlled base line was not established. These unpaired preliminary trials presented in this first part of the experiment also provided a means of establishing the base rate of the background activity over the period of the experiment. In the second part of the experiment, which might last for 1 or 2 days, the CS and the UCS were paired in the conditioning procedure. Delays between the CS and UCS were selected to maximize the magnitude of the conditioned neural response.

The most general of Olds' papers (Olds, Disterhoft, Segal Kornblith, & Hirsh, 1972) is a good example of the logic of his investigations. In this report these psychobiologists sought to determine the areas of the entire brain of the rat in which neural correlates of behavioral learning might be found. The UCS was the release of a food pellet by a relatively noisy mechanical mechanism into a receptacle in the testing chamber. The animals' response to this stimulus, grasping and eating the food, was well-defined as was entirely expected, because the rats had been food-deprived for many hours prior to the experiment. Two other stimuli were used; a 1-kHz tone and a 10-kHz tone. Either could be paired with activation of the food mechanism and thus serve as the conditioned stimulus (CS+), while the other tone (CS−) was unpaired and thus served as a second control to further establish the occurrence of true classical conditioning and not simply a sensory sensitization or subtle habituation effect.

The conditioned response in this experiment was actually the spike action potential pattern of a single neuron. In all of this work, Olds and his colleagues also observed the corresponding behavioral response, but the behavioral data were not essential. They merely served as another indicator of the development of the conditioned associations, and I do not consider them further here.

The measures used and the criteria established for terminating the conditioning trials are somewhat complex in this experiment. In a conventional classical conditioning experiment, results are usually displayed as a continuous plot of some measure of the magnitude or probability of the response as a function of the number of conditioning trials. In Olds, Disterhoft, Segal, Kornblith, and Hirsh's (1972) experiment, the single measure taken for each cell was the latency of the burst of spike action potentials measured at the end of the conditioning trials. The conditioning sequence was terminated by the achievement of one of two preset criteria: A response had appeared where none had occurred before, or a burst of spikes, which had occurred prior to the conditioning trials, now contained more than twice as many spikes as originally. Thus the latency of the conditioned spike burst after this criterion was achieved, a temporal measure, was the single number distilled from the elaborate experimental procedures.

Because the sole criterion for accepting the involvement of a given nucleus in mediating some aspect of the conditioning, according to Olds, was the brevity of the latencies of its constituent cells, all that had to be done was to replicate this procedure for a suitably large sample of neurons appropriately chosen from a large number of brain centers. The resulting latency measures could then be plotted on anatomical maps of the brain. Regions that had large numbers of short latency neurons would, ipso facto, be "centers" of learning. Unfortunately for any theory advocating that specific learning centers existed, Olds and his colleagues discovered that such short-latency cells (defined as those with latencies of 20 msec. or less) were scattered throughout virtually the entire brain of the rat. Although not all nuclei at all levels contained short-latency cells, there was no gross brain level from the medulla to the neocortex that did not contain at least some nuclei that possessed short-latency cells. An idea of the distribution of conditionable cells and their typical latency patterns following conditioning is shown in Figs. 8-20a, 8-20b, 8-20c, and 8-20d.

At any given level, however, it did appear that the short-latency neurons were to be found within certain relatively well circumscribed nuclei. The neurons were most common in the posterior nucleus of the thalamus and a few other thalamic nuclei (a surprising location considering the generally accepted proposition that the thalamus mainly functions as a sensory relay station), the pontine reticular formation and the ventral tegmentum. They were found in the CA3 but not in the CA1 region of the hippocampus as well as in a number of parts of the cerebral cortical mantle. It is to these regions, possessing short-latency neurons, that Olds specifically attributes a preeminent role in learning.

Thus the general thrust of these experimental results, when a temporal-latency criteria was utilized, was not to localize learning functions at particular levels as Olds had originally proposed. Rather, these data provide further support for the general thesis put forth many years before by Lashley; namely, the learning process and the resulting engram are not localizable to any single region of the brain but are to be found in widely distributed regions throughout the entire brain.

Olds and his colleagues, in a second part of this study, also used an additional criterion to analyze their data. They noted that the frequency of the spike action burst also varied differentially throughout the rat's brain. The magnitude of the conditioning was defined as the change in the spike rate from the original background rate, defined during the first day's unpaired pseudoconditioning trials, to the final rate following the completion of the training trials. It would be redundant to go into the details of the analysis of this data; it is sufficient to note that exactly the same sort of results were obtained with magnitude measures as with latency scores. Substantial changes in response rate were obtained at sites scattered throughout all levels of the rat's nervous system. In sum, both high levels of response magnitude and short latencies, Olds' two criteria for localizing sites he believed to be involved in learning, were found in the pons, midbrain, and at several different portions of the paleo- and neocortices.

This work is an important contribution to knowledge of the neural basis of learning as well as a technical tour de force. However, several comments about some interpretations are relevant. Olds' and his group's acceptance of widely scattered nuclei as sites for the storage of engrams or control of learning is inconsistent, in some ways, with both conventional thinking about the role of the particular regions they studied and reasonable estimates of the contribution to learning of nuclei that had not been previously supposed to play primarily integrative functions.

A number of other criticisms may be made, but most appropriately Olds and his colleagues are the ones who themselves point out some of the criticisms that might be made of their work. These criticisms are paraphrased from their report (Olds, Disterhoft, Segal Kornblith, & Hirsh, 1972) in the following list along with their proposed responses:

Criticism 1: The 10-msec. sampling precision was too gross. It obscured the temporal fine structure of sequential responses and thus confused the issue of localization.

Response 1: There was sufficient variability in the latency data to indicate that the list of centers with very short latency neurons was not all-inclusive. Thus, even if there was only modest precision, the data did seem to discriminate among different nuclei, and the main argument holds.

Criticism 2: The sampling of different regions could have been incomplete, and other centers with even shorter latencies undoubtedly remain to be discovered.

Response 2: The centers studied were mainly those assumed to be associated with some aspect of learning; the sample size was fairly large and, anyhow, there were few surprising results emerging in the later experiments of the series. This is essentially a question of sampling error. The data, however, suggests that the most important regions were covered.

Criticism 3: Neurons too small to be sampled adequately with the electrodes used might have exhibited very short latencies and have been very important in areas that seem to possess no short-latency neurons.

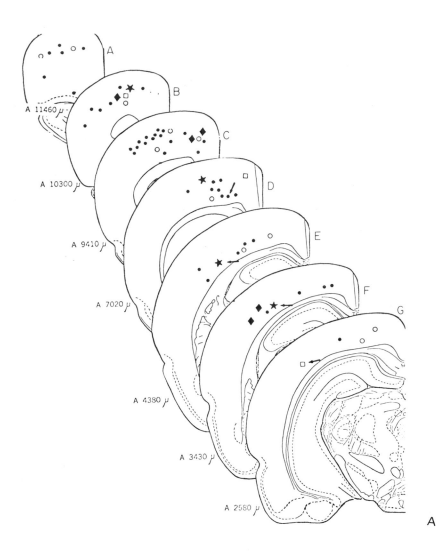

FIG. 8.20 The four plates of this figure show the variation in latency of single neurons obtained in the conditioning experiments of Olds et al. as described in the text. The main point of this figure is that short latency responses (indicative of "learning sites" according to Olds' criteria) are scattered throughout all levels of the brain. The four plates indicate the latencies obtained in the cortex, the hippocampus, the thalamus, and the midbrain respectively. The depth measurements are referenced either anterior (A) or posterior (P) to a stereotaxic "zero" reference point. Stars indicate 0-20 msec latency; diamonds 20-40 msec latency; squares 40-60 msec; and large circles 60-80 msec. Arrows indicate cells that may have had very brief (less than 10 msec) latencies. (From Olds, Disterhoft, Segal, Kornblith, & Hirsch, ©1972, with the permission of The American Physiological Society.)

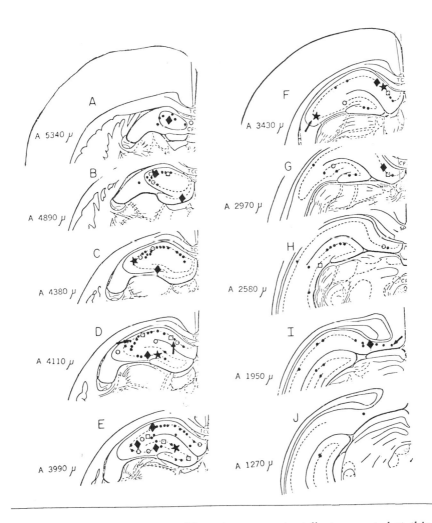

A 5340 µ
A 4890 µ
A 4380 µ
A 4110 µ
A 3990 µ
A 3430 µ
A 2970 µ
A 2580 µ
A 1950 µ
A 1270 µ

B

Response 3: Possibly true. There is no way to tell at present, but this is always a problem with any experimental tool.

Criticism 4: The effects observed may have been due to indirect sensory modulation due to postural changes by the animal that would affect optimum receptor organization.

Response 4: Olds and his colleagues interpreted this criticism as essentially based upon the response changes being produced by changes in stimulus effectiveness. They point out that the evoked signal strength in the inferior colliculus (a major relay station in the auditory pathway) did not change and that, therefore, the sensory effectiveness probably did not change either.

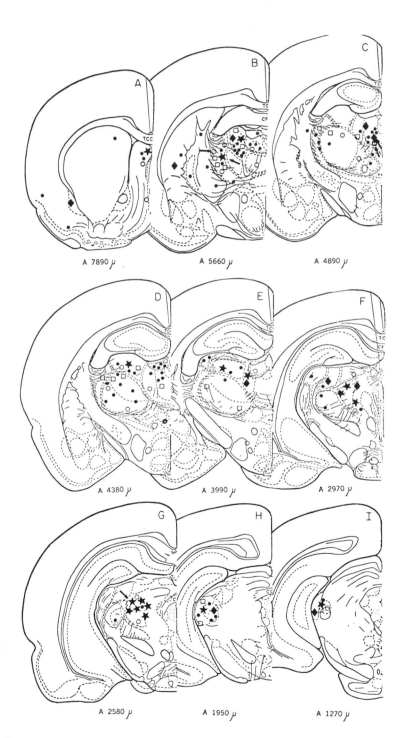

A 7890 μ   A 5660 μ   A 4890 μ

A 4380 μ   A 3990 μ   A 2970 μ

A 2580 μ   A 1950 μ   A 1270 μ

C

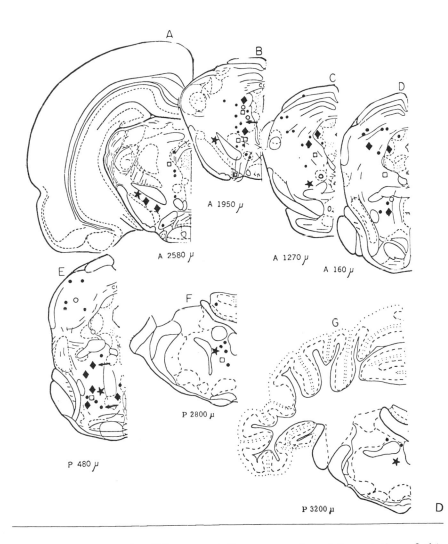

A 2580 μ

A 1950 μ

A 1270 μ

A 160 μ

P 480 μ

P 2800 μ

P 3200 μ

There is an entirely different and far more serious interpretation of this criticism that it appears Olds and his colleagues did not consider, however. It is possible the dynamic changes in responsiveness that Olds attributes to learning may be indirect sensory results of feedback signals from somesthetic receptors or even motor regions of the brain. Although it is true that the latency argument partially argues against this alternative interpretation of this criticism, it is possible that response changes could be observed at a particular site even though that site is not the locus of the relevant neural plasticity. The animal simply might be learning to place himself in a position or stance that optimizes his acquisition of the food reward. This change in musculature configuration could produce a proprioceptive sensory response that might be confused with a direct neural response to the CS.

Criticism 5: The effects may be due to changes in the arousal level of the animal rather than due to learning.

Response 5: The changes in arousal state presumably occurred on the first day during the pseudoconditioning trials. Therefore the effects seem to be directly associated with learning.

The reader and history will have to decide whether the criticisms they raise or the rebuttals they propose bear the greatest weight or whether other explanations of their data are more relevant. It is to Olds' credit that he and his colleagues were able to express the exceedingly complex issues raised in their experiments in such an even-handed manner.

A very serious additional challenge to Old's interpretation of his findings, however, arises out of a more fundamental problem that Olds and his colleagues did not explicitly mention—whether, in fact, they have used reasonable criteria to establish which brain nuclei are associated with learning. There is a substantial logical gap between the spatial idea of a site of learning and the temporal measure of short latency. The argument in their introduction, in which this association was initially made, leaves something to be desired in terms of closing that gap. This conceptual difficulty is both a function of the complexity of the problem and of an absence of suitable research strategies and techniques. Barring some new and unexpected technical development, such indirect approaches to the study of learning will be with us for a long time.

Either in spite of or because of these difficulties, it was clear that Olds' work clearly had to be extended to more detailed examinations of the individual centers that had been surveyed in this initial experiment. He and his group followed up the general survey of possible brain sites with a series of studies aimed at achieving more detailed information about the thalamus, cortex, and hippocampus, respectively. Thus Disterhoft and Olds (1972) compared the conditioning of a single neural units in the thalamus and in the cortex. The methods used were similar to those described in the previous study. Although the response was also defined as a change in the spike firing rate following the presentation of the conditioned stimulus, the reinforced tone, the data were tabulated in two different manners.

First, learning curves, functions of the number of training trials, that more graphically showed the progressive changes in responsiveness over the course of the conditioning trials were plotted. These curves were examined to determine at what point the neural responses became associated with CS+. Somewhat surprisingly, the neurons of the thalamus turned out to be conditioned in considerable fewer trials than those of the cortex. Thalamic neurons, in fact, seemed to be conditioned within as few as 30 or 40 trials, whereas cortical cells did not meet the criterion of a conditioned response until after 60 more successive pairings of the unconditioned and conditioned stimulus. This data is shown in Table 8-3. Note also, however, the reverse effect when background activity is measured.

The second means of tabulating these data was also in terms of response strength as defined in terms of the change from the base firing rate prior to conditioning to that observed after pairing. This data is shown in Fig. 8-21. Again, it should be noted that the cells of the thalamus seemed to condition to a greater degree than those of the cortex. That is, the pre- and postconditioning rates differ more than those of cortical neurons. Once again, it is the posterior nucleus of the thalamus that seem to display the greatest amplitude of response change as a result of the conditioning trials.

At first glance, and in accord with the simple criteria suggested by Disterhoft and Olds, the thalamus would have to be considered as the center more fundamental to the learning process. This, however, would be a disconcerting conclusion from other points of view. The thalamus is more usually considered a sensory relay station, as I have noted, rather than an integrative center. Disterhoft and Olds did implicitly acknowledge the possibility, however, that the implication that the thalamus is more important in the learning process than the cortex is spurious and that its apparent primacy may be due to feedback loops indirectly effecting the thalamic background activity. Specifically, they stated (Disterhoft & Olds, 1972):

> The data therefore reveal a possible correlation between background activity deceleration in the posterior cortex and in the posterior nucleus of the thalamus during a period of behavioral learning. This seems to suggest an excitatory connection between them, that is, a drop in posterior cortical background could have led to a drop in posterior thalamus background. Such a reduction in activity could have been importantly involved in preparing the posterior thalamus neurons for changed responsiveness to CS+ input of a more permanent nature [p. 677].

Nevertheless, they still felt that the major changes in the cortex and thalamus over the longer course of the entire conditioning sequence were relatively independently determined. This acceptance of at least one possible feedback interaction, however, represented the beginning of an important shift in their thinking. The question of whether or not the criteria of response latency and amplitude are appropriate designators of the actual sites in which the engram reposes or of the nuclei that control learning must again be raised in this context. Although this issue cannot be completely resolved at the present time, Olds' approach clearly leaves many unanswered questions.

Perhaps the uncertainty about the validity of the latency criterion and the role of feedback is most evident in his discussion of the comparable effects to be observed in the limbic system, in general, and the hippocampus, in particular. The hippocampus, as previously noted, for many independent reasons, has been thought to be intimately involved in learning. In a series of three papers (Segal &

TABLE 8.3

The initial point of learning and the initial point of background learning shift.
(From Disterhoft & Olds, ©1972, with the permission of
the American Physiological Society.)

	Initial Point of Learning			Initial Point of Background Firing Rate Shift		
		$\overline{X}$	SD		$\overline{X}$	SD
Frontal cortex	(18/23)[a]	7.38	6.43	(22/23)	3.62	3.09
Middle cortex	(24/30)	5.19	5.32	(29/30)	3.70	3.82
Posterior cortex	(12/13)	6.18	3.89	(13/13)	2.17	1.75
Cortex as a whole		6.15	5.43		3.37	3.26
Nonspecific thalamus	(29/31)	3.77	1.88	(29/31)	4.31	3.38
Dorsomedial nucleus	(14/19)	3.92	3.82	(18/19)	4.69	4.39
Ventral nucleus	(20/22)	4.15	2.96	(21/22)	4.19	5.38
Lateral nucleus	(12/13)	4.17	2.29	(13/13)	5.08	3.20
Posterior nucleus	(12/14)	3.33	1.87	(14/14)	3.46	3.70
Medial geniculate	(10/11)	5.12	1.55	(11/11)	4.78	4.38
Thalamus as a whole		4.01	2.49		4.39	4.07

[a]Number of animals from each group that was used in analysis (e.g., 18 of 23 for the first group).

Olds, 1972; Segal & Olds, 1973; and Segal, 1973), the role of the hippocampus and its constituent regions was examined using essentially the same techniques described previously. Once again, the constituent neurons of the various areas of the hippocampus were found to display considerable variability in both the number of trials required to develop a conditioned response and the amplitude of the resulting response. There was, however, a curious mixture of contradictions introduced in this case as to which hippocampal regions were more fundamental in the learning process when different criteria of conditioning were applied. Whereas the neurons of the dendate gyrus typically had longer latencies than those of the hippocampus, the dendate gyrus was the only area showing both an increase in activity to CS+ and a decrease to CS— during conditioning trials (Segal & Olds, 1973). On the other hand, during extinction trials, the dendate gyrus was the first to extinguish. Extinction occurred in serial order in a number of other hippocampal subcenters with the CA3 region extinguishing faster than CA1, which in turn extinguished faster than the ventral hippocampus (Segal, 1973).

Which area should then be considered as either the site or the master controller of the learning process in light of these conflicting criteria? Clearly, the

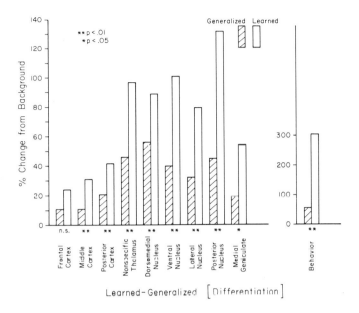

FIG. 8.21   Bar graphs comparing the change in neural firing rate for cells in various portions of the brain for the reinforced (learned) and unreinforced (generalized) stimulus conditions, respectively. The change in behavior as a result of the training is also shown. (From Disterhoft & Olds, ©1972, with the permission of The American Physiological Society.)

results forthcoming from Olds' laboratory hardly begin to answer these complex questions, and a considerable amount of doubt now is being raised that the particular criteria he chose actually point either to the sites that regulate the learning process or to those in which the engram may reside.

b.   Woody's Studies of Classical Conditioning of Neurons in the Motor Cortex of the Cat

Other workers have also studied the effect of classical conditioning on the responsiveness of single neurons in the mammalian brain. In another important approach, Charles Woody's group has drawn some conclusions about the actual changes in the neuronal membranes that may possibly lie behind the physiological indicators of neuronal plasticity.

It should be emphasized that unlike Olds, Woody was not interested in discovering the particular nuclei of the brain that might be especially involved in learning. Rather, his interest lay in determining what happened in the individual neurons during learning. Woody assumed that neurons of the motor cortex of the cat's brain are involved in the mediation of classical conditioning of facial responses such as eyeblinks and ear muscle twitches. The general procedure that he used was the classical conditioning of an eye blink response to a conditioned stimulus consisting of an auditory click. The unconditioned stimulus in Woody's experiments was typically a mechanical tap applied to the skin just above the root of the cat's nose. In some parts of his work, Woody used the evoked electromyogram (EMG) as the indicator of conditioning, but for all practical purposes both measures, the EMG and the unit neural responses, led to identical conclusions.

Woody studied the coronal-precruciate region of the brain, because the maximum compound evoked potential was produced in this region by a conditioned click stimulus during the training trials (Woody, 1970). Within this region, microelectrode probling of individual neurons had also indicated that the cells projecting directly to the eyelid were identical to those that modified their activity during conditioning. Furthermore, those same neurons also had the lowest threshold for activation when an electrical stimulus was applied through the microelectrode following conditioning (Woody, Vassilevsky, & Engle, Jr., 1970; Woody & Engle, 1972). Thus there were many clues that the coronal-precruciate area is intimately involved in the conditioned eyeblink response. Although these clues may be false (all of these criteria could also be true of a remote "response" region as well as the actual sites of plastic network reorganization), Woody's studies are interesting because of his attempt to establish a more direct link between a possible plastic change in the neuron and its physiological responsiveness.

The specific question Woody and his colleagues sought to answer concerned which mechanisms within the cell might possibly explain their change in responsiveness and in threshold sensitivity. The techniques used by Woody in his attack on this problem were multifaceted. In addition to conventional recording of EMGs through macroelectrodes and of single neuron spike action potentials through intracellular microelectrodes, Woody and Black-Cleworth (1973) also used the microelectrode to electrically stimulate individual neurons.

Conditioned cells showed substantial changes in both their absolute current thresholds and membrane resistance following conditioning. There was a substantial reduction during conditioning in the current required to excite a precruciate motor neuron that projected to the eyelid muscle being conditioned. In other words, the electrical threshold for spike elicitation was decreased. There was, simultaneously, a substantial increase in the selectively conditioned neuron's transmembrane resistance.

What do each of these changes mean, and what do they imply with regard to the possible cellular mechanisms of plasticity? Woody's analysis went as follows. The reduction in threshold current required to evoke spike potential might be caused by a partially depolarized resting membrane potential. Thus only a smaller driving voltage would be required to depolarize the cell to the point of regenerative depolarization and the production of a spike action potential. However, because microelectrode measurements of the resting membrane potential did not indicate any such partial depolarization, a depolarization of the membrane did not seem to be a likely explanation of the reduced electrical current threshold.

Assuming that the threshold voltage remained constant and that the resting potential did not change, what other possibility exists for making an electrical current stimulus more effective in its ability to bridge the gap between the resting potential and the threshold potential for the elicitation of a spike? To answer this question, Woody remembered the most fundamental law of electricity —ohm's law, which states that the voltage produced across a resistor is equal to the current passed through that resistor times its resistance—and on that basis proposed one possible answer. An increase in the membrane resistance would allow a smaller current to produce the necessary depolarizing threshold voltage. According to this hypothesis, the critical membrane factor in the changed responsiveness of these neurons was a change in the membrane resistance produced during the conditioning.

The identification of a membrane resistance change occurring during conditioning is a feasible explanation of the neuronal effects. Although it is not certain exactly where in the neuron the change actually occurs, it does seem most likely that this plastic neuronal effect of learning is actually occurring within the very same neuron that displayed the change in physiological responsiveness. This conclusion is further supported by the brevity of the latencies to the electrical stimulus as well as the fact that the currents required for evoking a spike action potential were very small and thus were unlikely to spread to nearby structures, according to Woody and Black-Cleworth.

The most important aspect of this conclusion is the inference that whatever the membrane and ionic changes are behind this kind of learning, they result from alterations on the postsynaptic side of a junction and not in the presynaptic portion. Although, as we see in Chapter 9, this conclusion need not be generalized to all hypothetical forms of neuronal plasticity, this linkage of membrane effects and neurophysiological response to the same postsynaptic neuron, in this case by Woody and Black-Cleworth, is a highly important contribution.

In conclusion, it is important to note that Woody's experiments do have one notable advantage over the work of Olds, for example. The actual response used by Woody—the eyeblink—is much more strictly controlled than are the instrumental responses of grasping and eating, which Olds used. Olds' consummatory response is far more complex and therefore much more difficult to analyze into its neural components. Woody's work has another advantage; there is a much closer link between the altered responsiveness of the neuron and a plastic change (increased membrane resistance) in that same neuron. Although all of the other possible caveats are applicable to some degree (feedback was possible, these were motor neurons, etc.), this association makes for a tighter argument that plastic changes associated with learning were actually occurring in these neurons.

c.   O'Brien's Studies of Single Cell Conditioning in the Cat Motor Cortex

Another important contributor to the study of neuronal conditioning in the vertebrate brain is James O'Brien of the University of Oregon. O'Brien's earlier work with Stephen Fox at the University of Iowa (O'Brien & Fox, 1969a) is quite similar in goals to some of the work I have already mentioned in this section. There are, however, several exceedingly interesting differences that should be highlighted here to round out the general picture of neuronal conditioning emerging from this discussion. In 1969, O'Brien and Fox (1969b) noted that the polysensory or multimodal neurons that responded to several different kinds of sensory stimuli in the unconditioned state seemed to be the ones that displayed the highest degree of adaptation to conditioning.

O'Brien has recently made another important contribution to our understanding of the involvement of single neurons in learning. He and a group of co-workers (O'Brien, Packham, & Brunnhoelzl, 1973) report that the changing pattern of background activity of conditioned neurons also seems to reflect the conditioning process just as does the stimulus evoked spike activity. This result emerged primarily because O'Brien and his colleagues had approached the problem of cellular plasticity with an experimental procedure that differed considerably from any of those yet described. Rather than measuring the mean frequency of the spike responses or their latency to a stimulus, they studied the temporal characteristics of the intervals between successive spikes in both driven and spontaneous conditions.

O'Brien's group recorded single neuron spike action potentials from the post-cruciate cortex with microelectrodes to study the variability of the intervals between spikes. The recorded signals were analyzed during a three-part 3.5-second-long epoch in which the initial second consisted entirely of unstimulated background activity; the next half-second consisted of the responses to a CS (a flash of light), and the remaining 2.0 seconds represented the response to the UCS (an electrical shock or puff of air). In the present discussion, only O'Brien's analysis of the initial period that was made up of unstimulated background activity is of concern.

The spike action potentials were fed into a small laboratory computer and analyzed by tabulating interstimulus interval (ISI) histograms. Samples of two ISI histograms of the background activity from two cells that differed somewhat in their statistical properties are shown in Fig. 8-22. In addition to the obvious difference in mean frequency of this background activity, there is also another characteristic difference between the activity patterns of these two cells.

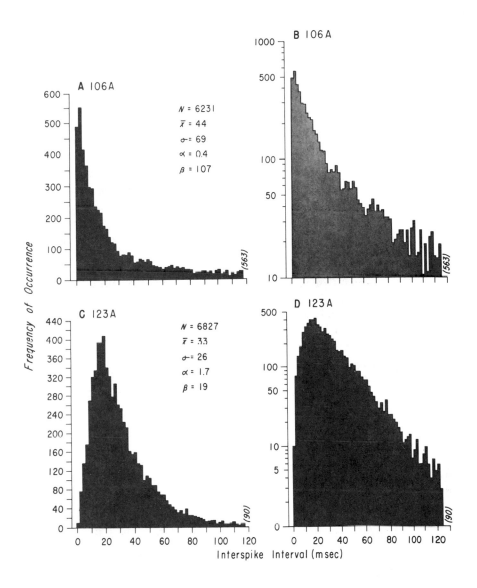

FIG. 8.22 The characteristic background activity "signatures" of two neurons plotted both on linear (A and C) and log (B and D) coordinates. To plot these characteristics, a histogram has been produced of the distribution of intervals between successive spikes. (From O'Brien, Packham, & Brunnhoelzl, ©1973, with the permission of The American Physiological Society.)

One cell (106A) showed an almost exponential fall-off in the size of the inter-spike intervals, and the other (123A) displayed a much less pronounced decrease in interval size as the intervals became longer. There is also a difference in the rate of increase in interval size at the short-interval end of the histogram. This difference is more clearly shown in plates B and D in which the data have been transformed to semilogarithmic plots.

To quantify the characteristics of these histograms and to provide simple metrics for their comparison, O'Brien and his colleagues defined a ratio β (beta) equal to the computed variance of the histogram divided by its mean frequency. Beta was only one of a number of similar metrics describing the histogram that they defined, but it was clearly the single one that proved to be the most infor-mative. Figure 8-23 shows a plot of the betas measured for four different kinds of neurons over the course of five stages of their conditioning experiment. The four kinds of neurons included those that conditioned well (High t), those that conditioned poorly (Low t), those that did not pseudocondition in control trials (Low t), and those that exhibit a pseudoconditioned change in their pattern of response as a result of unpaired presentations of the CS (High t). The five stages of the experiment indicated on this figure are: H—a habituation (or pseudo-conditioning) precursor block of 75 trials; C_1, C_2, and C_3—three conditioning blocks of 75 trials each; and E—75 extinction trials.

This figure illustrates the fact that β, which is purely a metric of the prop-erties of the background acitivty, varied systematically with the level of con-ditioning only for those cells that could be easily conditioned (as evidence in their changed responsiveness to the CS). Beta, in these cases, increased from the base level established in the unpaired habituation trials during the conditioning trials and then declined during the extinction trials. Beta did not correlate with the performance of any neurons that did not condition nor to those in an un-paired control group. Furthermore, no other measure such as the mean inter-stimulus interval, its variance, or for that matter, any of a set of other arbitrary ratios that O'Brien proposed, was closely associated in the same systematic man-ner as β with just those cells that displayed the ability to be conditioned. Thus β, even though it is a measure of background activity, in some way is indicative of neural plasticity.

Further support is, therefore, provided from this study for the suggestion that the properties of the very neurons in which the altered responsiveness was obser-ved were changing as a result of the training they experienced. Although it is not yet certain that the spontaneous or background activity that was measured in this case was a result of changes intrinsic to the responding neuron (background activity fluctuations could in principle, be produced by network effects too), there is a circumstantial argument, partially buttressed by Woody and Black-Cleworth's perviously discussed results, that these changes may be mediated by postsynaptic effects within the same neuron from which the spike action poten-tials were recorded.

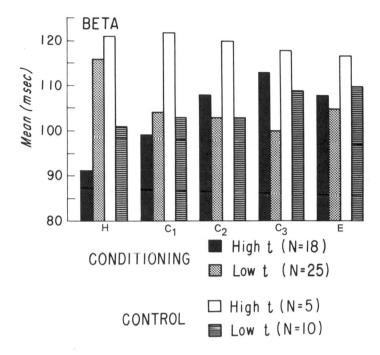

FIG. 8.23   Histogram showing the beta (β) values for the four kinds of neurons over the five-step course (H, C_1, C_2, C_3, E) of the O'Brien et al. experiment. Note that there is a progressive increase in β for the high conditioning (High t) group but not for the other neuron types. No other measure of the background activity displayed such a systematic change correlated with the training sequences for the High t group. (From O'Brien, Packham, & Brunnhoelzl, ©1973, with the permission of The American Physiological Society.)

We cannot say with assurance that this change in background activity is a direct indication of the storage of an engram, but clearly the behavior of the individual neuron is exhibiting a persistent change in its properties, possibly because of changes in the network of which it is a part, but also very possibly because of long-term changes in the state of the membrane of the individual neuron itself. Such evidence is logically, if not historically, the first clue to the solution of the mystery of just what the engram may be.

3.   Instrumental Conditioning of Single Units in Mammals

The classical conditioning experiments I have just described are examples of a paradigm that has been of interest to psychologists for most of the past century. In more recent years, however, operant or instrumental conditioning has come into prominent interest among psychologists. As I noted earlier, in operant conditioning paradigms, the critical response, some act instrumental in producing the subsequent reinforcement, is emitted on the basis of stimuli that are largely unknown and unknowable. The emitted response in the operant paradigm is reinforced or consolidated by the presentation of some positive or negative stimulus to the subject. Operant conditioning procedures thus allow the experimenter to reinforce behavior that is either "spontaneous" or much too complex to be elicited by simple and discrete stimuli.

Operant conditioning of individual neurons in the brain was probably first carried out by James and Margaret Olds (Olds & Olds, 1961). However, the more recent work of Eberhard Fetz of the University of Washington shall be the focus here. His work on monkeys (Fetz, 1974; Fetz & Baker, 1973) is especially interesting not only because of some of the techniques used but also because of the goals he and his co-workers set for themselves. Fetz strove to determine the relationship between responses of a single operantly conditioned neuron and the muscular responses learned concomitantly.

In Fetz' experiment, an electronic system was set up to trigger a food-pellet release when a particular frequency of spiking of a microelectrode-impaled neuron occurred. Whatever the original stimulus that elicited the burst of neural activity from the neuron, it was reliably demonstrated by Fetz and his colleagues that the spiking rate could be trained to either increase or decrease by appropriate reinforcements. Differential reinforcement of high rates of activity (DRH) with positive stimuli (food pellets) leads to increasingly high rates of activity, whereas differential reinforcement of zero rates of activity (DRO) leads to a conditioned reduction in the rate of spontaneously emitted bursting activity. So exquisitely sensitive is the procedure that two simultaneously impaled cells can be reinforced to perform in exactly opposite directions by reinforcing the animal with DRH and DRO respectively (Fetz & Baker, 1973). Thus the application of these powerful training procedures did produce the desired results—operant control of single neuronal activity.

Figure 8-24 shows the effect of alternating DRH (conditioning) and new reinforcement (extinction). Various instrumentally conditioned neurons, Fetz also noted, seemed to be selectively associated with particular muscular responses. Certain other neurons were apparently associated with the general response of major parts of the animal's body, whereas other neurons seemed to be associated with highly specific movements of only a single muscle. Not too surprisingly, other units seem to be associated with no visible response. By simultaneously recording electromyographic and neural responses in this operant conditioning paradigm, Fetz and his colleagues were able to show correlations between plastic behavior of the neurons of the motor cortex and the responses of particular muscle groups. The "motor field" of a neuron—a concept analogous to the receptive field of a sensory neuron—was thereby defined.

How powerful is the operant conditioning procedure? Perhaps the best answer to this question lies in Fetz' demonstration of its ability to deactivate individual neurons that had artificially been made epileptic by the application of

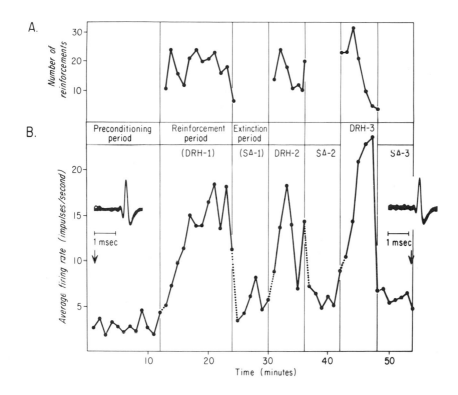

FIG. 8.24   Change in firing rate of a neuron as a function of being instrumentally conditioned for high firing rates. The "spontaneous" activity is quite controllable by the experimenter. Insets show multiple samples of the individual spike responses overlapped to confirm that these responses were from the same neuron. (From Fetz & Baker, ©1973, with the permission of The American Physiological Society.)

alumina creams to the surface of the monkey's cerebral cortex. These hyperactive cells could actually be *conditioned* to reduce their chemically induced high level of activity by reinforcing the periods of inactivity interspersed between seizures!

This extraordinary example of the power of operant conditioning techniques suggests the magnitude of its potential practical application. One must remember, however, that the theoretical value of this procedure, with regard to plastic mechanisms, is limited. Use of the technique does not require understanding of the underlying physiological process. The operant conditioning procedure reveals nothing about the nature of the cellular plastic changes involved in this or any other kind of learning. What Fetz' study does demonstrate is the ability of individual neurons to be operantly conditioned just like any other response. What it does not do is tell us anything about the nature of the plastic neural mechanism underlying this learning.

4.   A Neurophysiological Study of Unit Responses in the
     Frontal Lobes

In this section I move on to a more complicated form of learning—the delayed response, a task involving short-term memory, which is strongly influenced by activity in the frontal lobes of the brain as previously indicated in Chapter 5.

The association between the frontal lobes and the kind of short-term memory assayed by a delayed response task was first suggested by Jacobsen (1935) on the basis of ablation experiments. Animals with frontal lobe lesions seemed to lose the ability to remember the location of a food item that had been briefly exposed and then hidden for a period of time before a response was allowed.

The association between short-term memory and the frontal lobes was also supported by many other behavioral experiments. A particularly ingenious one (Fuster & Alexander, 1970), in which the frontal lobe was cryogenically cooled, demonstrated the reversibility of the process. With frozen frontal lobes, experimental animals exhibited the same decrement in performance as did specimens with a true surgical ablation. When the frontal lobes were allowed to thaw, the animals' delayed response scores returned to normal.

But what happens to individual frontal lobe neurons during the delayed response procedures? Fortunately, we have an elegant study of just this aspect of the problem to consider. Fuster (1973), following up on some work of Kubota and Niki (1971), set up an experimental situation with monkeys in which the delayed response paradigm was used to examine neuronal behavior. In addition to the usual behavioral apparatus and procedures, extracellular tungsten microelectrodes, attached to a skull-mounted pedestal (to allow the monkey free movement), were used to record the activity of individual neurons during the course of the delayed response experiment.

To help clarify the changes in the neuronal response, Fuster considered each trial to be composed of several sequential stages. The first stage was defined by the presentation of the cue. This involved raising an opaque screen that had initially blocked the view of the monkey from a scene that included a piece of apple in one of two wells. Figure 8-25 shows this apparatus. While the screen was open, two different objects were advanced to cover the two wells. The blocking screen was then lowered.

The second stage of the trial was defined as the delay period between the cue and the response. Nothing happened in this interval. The animal sat peering at the closed screen, presumably cogitating about the piece of apple with which he had been tantalized. The delay was variable and could be adjusted to suit the particular needs of a given experiment.

The third and final stage of the trial was defined as the response period. The viewing screen was opened and a barrier, which had prevented the monkey from taking the piece of apple during the cue and delay periods, was opened. The animal was allowed to keep the food only if he made the correct choice. Differences between the percentage of correct responses and chance (50%) indicated the degree to which the monkey remembered the location of the food.

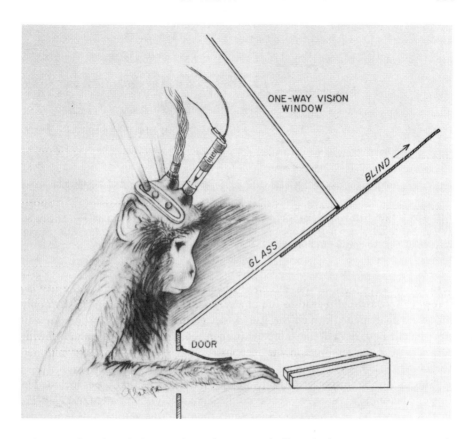

FIG. 8.25   Drawing of the experimental apparatus in Fuster's short-term memory experiment. (From Fuster, ©1973, with the permission of The American Physiological Society.)

Fuster's unique contribution to the literature of the delayed response was to record the activity of a sample of individual frontal lobe neurons of the monkey's brain. The main result of an extensive examination of many neurons was the discovery of seven different kinds of units present in the regions of the frontal lobe in which he probed. Incidentally, the region of the frontal lobe within which neurons were found that were correlated with delayed response behavior was considerably larger than that indicated by the ablation and cryogenic blocking techniques.

The seven types of cells were each characterized by a particular pattern of spiking activity during the three stages of each delayed response trial. Figure 8-26, for example, displays a sample firing record from what Fuster referred to as a D-type cell. Prior to the exposure of the stimulus in the cueing period, there was a relatively moderate level of background or "spontaneous" activity in this type of cell. During the cue, however, there actually was an apparent inhibition

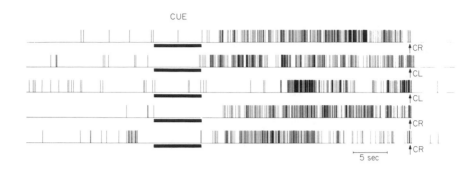

FIG. 8.26   Five trial records of a type D neuron showing the persistent neural activity between the stimulus cue and the opening of the door. (From Fuster, ©1973, with the permission of The American Physiological Society.)

resulting in a decrease in the amount of background activity. When the viewing screen closed, the cell began to fire at a very rapid rate that continued with only moderate abatement through the full extent of the delay period. When the barrier that had prevented the monkey from responding and the opaque viewing screen were both removed in the response period, the cell was again inhibited for a brief period.

This pattern of response was only one of the seven distinct types included in Fuster's taxonomy. All seven types are diagramatically represented in Fig. 8-27. In this figure, the horizontal axis represents time, and the vertical axis represents the momentary frequency of firing. In this diagram there are three types of cells, C, D, and I2, that have a particularly important and distinctive property. These three cell types display a response during the delay period that is noticeably different from the background activity either prior to the cue or following the response. Cell types C and D are both activated to a higher frequency of spiking during the delay, whereas cell type I2 is inhibited below its normal background activity. It seems likely that the polarity of the change is not important. Change in either direction would be an equally powerful information-carrying parameter that could serve to provide the memorial link between the cue and the opportunity to respond. The important result is the measurable change in the response of these cells in a way that indicates that they may be involved in some reverberatory trace that represents the information needed for the delayed response.

Fuster also examined the anatomical distribution of these types of cells in the frontal lobe. Figure 8-28 is a map of this region showing the locations of the individual units classified according to his seven category schema. In this diagram, there appears to be some tendency for cells of a similar type to be found near each other and for the C and D type cells (of particular interest as temporal bridges across the delay period) to be located in the fifth and sixth layers of the

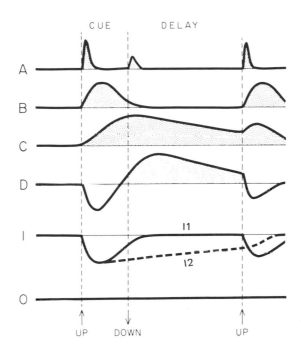

FIG. 8.27   The seven basic types of frontal cortex neuron response patterns observed by Fuster. The words "Up" and "Down" indicate movement, of the blind shown in Fig. 8.25. From Fuster, ©1973 with the permission of The American Physiological Society.)

frontal cortex. The main anatomical fact, as I mentioned previously, was that the C, D, and I2 cells seemed to be more widely distributed throughout the brain than had been suggested by the earlier ablation or cryogenic studies.

There are a number of possible artifacts in this sort of experiment, of course, for which careful controls must be maintained. The experimenter, in a study such as this, is obligated to determine, for example, if other regions, which had not been conventionally associated with such short-term memory processes, also contained any neurons with similar properties. If they did, the special association between the frontal lobes and the delayed response test suggested by Fuster's experiments would not be justified. It is also necessary, before accepting a special association between the C and D neurons, for example, and delayed responses, to show that the characteristic response pattern does not occur in a monkey who is not learning or has not learned anything.

These important control experiments were carried out by Fuster. First, he sampled an additional selection of neurons in the parietal cortex, a region that would not have been expected to be involved in the delayed response behavior, on the basis of earlier ablative studies. His results in this experiment reinforced

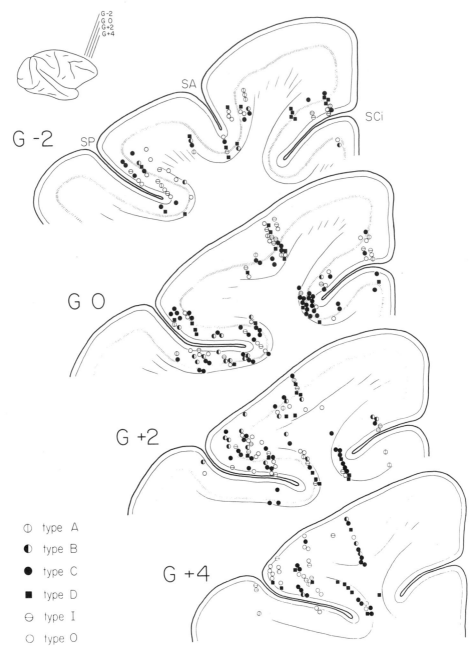

FIG. 8.28 Map of the frontal cortex of the monkey showing the location of the various types of the six different types of neurons. (From Fuster, ©1973, with the permission of The American Physiological Society.)

the general conclusion that the frontal lobe does seem to play a special role in this form of short-term memory. Neuronal responses in the parietal lobe seemed only to be associated with motor movement and did not display the same sustained pattern of activity during the delay period observed in the frontal lobes.

Second, Fuster studied the responses of individual frontal lobe neurons during mock trials in which untrained animals were used. A much smaller proportion of the cells studied in this case displayed the sort of sustained response change during the delay interval. Thus both controls supported the general conclusion of frontal involvement in delayed response.

Although these controls are only partial and not entirely conclusive (there are many other parts of the brain that might have been tested, and other explanations based on indirect feedback could have conceivably explained the lack of correlated results with naive monkeys), they are important as additional evidence in support of the argument that frontal lobe neurons do play some special role in short-term memory.

One of the most important conclusions to be drawn from Fuster's studies concerns the specific experimental conditions in which C- and D-type neurons, in particular, exhibited the characteristic increase in activity during the delay period. The special ability to continue responding during the delay occurred mainly in trained animals who had learned the "significance" of the stimulus. Thus the elevation of spike frequency in C and D neurons (or the inhibition of spike frequency in I2 neurons) was *presumably* contingent upon some symbolic aspect of the stimulus. The reinforcement had to be something that was of use to the monkey, such as food. These responses, therefore, were not purely sensory but also depended upon the monkey's "understanding" that this stimulus information would be useful if maintained.

The word *presumably* has been introduced in the preceding paragraph for a specific reason. In spite of the intrinsic elegance of Fuster's procedure and findings, it is by no means yet certain that these electrophysiological recordings are the true codes or transactional equivalents of the short-term memory process. We should be repeatedly reminded of many possible indirect pathways through which these response patterns might have been produced. In the event that the animal had learned to maintain a postural orientation to food during the delay, similar neuronal effects would likely have been produced. The essential message that Fuster's work bears is further support for the suggestion that the physiological equivalent of short-term memory, a few seconds or so in duration, is likely to be the reverberation of neural activity in neurons and neuron networks.

E. AN INTERIM SUMMARY

The several experimental approaches to single-cell correlates of learning that I have discussed in the previous sections do not all sing exactly the same tune, but there is a harmony of agreement between them. Some of the suggestions that emerge from these studies are those with which we are already familiar, and some are new. The work of Olds and his colleagues provides direct single neuron experimental support for Lashley's macroscopically based conclusion that the effects of learning occur at loci widely distributed throughout the nervous system. Although these studies do not show conclusively that learning itself, and by this I specifically mean the laying down of the trace Lashley would have called the engram, is so widely distributed, it is clear that the system of nuclei containing neurons that are involved, directly or indirectly in mediating learning, is widespread and highly interconnected.

Both Woody and O'Brien provide strongly suggestive electrophysiological evidence that the changes in responsiveness of single neurons are the result of processes that reside in the neuron itself. Woody's resistance measurements link membrane changes in the individual neurons to their altered responsiveness; O'Brien's data, assuming that the intrinsic background activity is also in large part a function of the state of the impaled neuron itself, makes the same link. Each of these studies thus provides indirect evidence that learning is mediated by a postsynaptic process (if the synaptic hypothesis to be discussed in the next chapter is acceptable in principle), rather than a presynaptic process.

Finally, Fuster's experiments on the frontal lobes and Thompson's (1976) on the hippocampus make it clear that short-term memory is most probably encoded by circulating patterns of neural activity altered by transient shifts in synaptic conductivity. This is in contrast to the very short-term sensory storage, which seems more likely to be related to persistent receptor biochemical effects, and very long-term storage which is probably better accounted for in terms of semipermanent changes in synaptic conductivity.

It would be most gratifying if we could now turn to some exemplar neurophysiological study of responses within the brain corresponding to long-term storage and specifically indicate what neural mechanisms might account for it. This, however, is not to be the case. One reason for this omission is an a priori incompatibility between the maximum account of time a neuron can be maintained at the tip of a microelectrode and the duration of long-term memory. At best, individual neurons have been continuously maintained for periods of only 2 days. Long-term memory is considered much more persistent. Thus, even if long-term memory were encoded by circulating responses in the nervous system, it would be very hard to detect the changes signaling their presence.

There is, however, a much more fundamental reason why long-term memory should not be sought at the tip of a microelectrode. The process of extremely persistent memorization is probably not mediated by the machinery of circulating or reverberating patterns of neuronal action potentials. As we see in the next chapter, almost all psychobiologists agree that long-term memory is more probably mediated by changes, probably occurring at the synapse, that involve membrane structure and a more permanent change in neuronal interconnectivity. Thus the microelectrode, a device for examining the dynamic state of a neuron, is intrinsically inappropriate for all except the most indirect studies of long-term memory. The more appropriate instruments to study the neural basis of long-term learning may ultimately turn out to be some tool of the anatomist, such as an electron micrograph, or of the biochemist, such as a measurement of protein concentration or synthesis. Correlates of long-term memory, in other words, are much more likely to be either actual physical changes at the level of magnification of the optical or electron microscope, or even more subtle molecular changes at a much more microscopic level than patterns of neuron activity.

Although I can speculate this far, the enigma of the engram remains as refractory to experimental approach as it was in Lashley's time. We still have no convincing proof of the exact nature of the memory trace. It is possible, if it is a synaptic process affecting network rearrangement, that it may be exceedingly difficult to detect the engram with any available technology. Distributed network arrangements do not lend themselves to examination with single microprobes or high-magnification microscopes. Discerning the global pattern change that most likely distinguishes long-term learning may be all but impossible with currently available technology.

In an important address (Thompson, 1976)[7] published just as the draft of this book was being finished, Richard Thompson of the University of California at Irvine asked, "How can the engram be identified?". His answer, as it only could be at present, was framed in terms of a "minimum list of criteria" that says more about what the engram is not than what it is. The engram, Thompson (1976) said, must exhibit:

a. "An eventual high correlation with learned changes in behavior"
b. A "lack of necessary correlation with stimuli"
c. An "absence of necessary correlation with motor response" [p. 223].

Clearly there is some doubt, given the looseness of these criteria, current technology, and the complexity of the problem, whether we will be able to recognize the engram if and when we finally see it.

Thus the engram remains as elusive in our time as it was previously. Furthermore, there is probably a family of engrams rather than a single one. The most general point that can be made at this stage in the development of psychobiology is that the engrams must be there—we do change our behavior as a result of experience—and they must be real biological processes or constellations of processes. This is a corollary of the essential premise of the science of psychobiology. Everything in the data base, and all reason and logic, point to the synapse as the most likely locus for the plastic neural changes that accompany long-term memory formation. The relevant processes, therefore, can only be going on at a subcellular level. These ultramicroscopic mechanisms determine the conductivity of the synapse and thus the nature of the interconnectivity between the involved neurons. It is to a discussion of such possible subcellular mechanisms of learning that I now turn.

---

[7]Thompson (1976) also provides an excellent review of a considerable body of material relevant to the discussion in this chapter to which the interested reader is referred.

9

Neural Correlates of Learning: Possible Mechanisms and Summary Models

A. POSSIBLE MECHANISMS OF NEURAL PLASTICITY

1. An Introductory Comment[1]

In the preceding chapter I considered a number of electrophysiological experiments that indicated that individual neurons within the nervous system are capable of responding to appropriate training by varying their characteristic activity patterns. The appropriate next step in the discussion of the biology of memory is the identification of possible and plausible molecular, membrane, and network organizational changes that could underlie the observed variation in neuronal responsivity.

The conceptual leap from membrane or biochemical mechanisms to neural functions is, however, a substantial one. It is equally as wide as that between neural net functions and behavior. At the outset of this discussion I must acknowledge that these conceptual gaps have not yet been bridged by anything even faintly resembling a convincing empirical data base or a comprehensive theoretical model. There is, as yet, no more adequate or generally accepted answer to the question of what biochemical and membrane mechanisms account for neuronal plasticity than there is to the question of how neuronal plasticity and the resulting changes in the network state account for learning.

---

[1]Just as the manuscript for this chapter was receiving its final touches and being prepared to be sent off to the copy editor, a new book was called to my attention by my colleague, Lester Rutledge of the University of Michigan, that is highly relevant to this chapter's content. Rosenzweig and Bennett (1976) have organized an exceedingly up-to-date and comprehensive discussion of the subject matter discussed here. I recommend this useful and comprehensive book to all who would like to delve deeper into the topic.

There is, however, one point on which most contemporary psychobiologists do agree; a fundamental premise, nearly universally accepted, is that the synapse in some way plays the critical and essential role in learning. This idea has had a long history. The original enunciation of this premise of the synaptic basis of learning is usually attributed to Tanzi (1893). More modern expressions of this same premise have been made by Hebb (1949), Gerard (1949), Eccles (1953), and Burns (1958). Eccles (1970; 1973a), in particular, has been the chief spokesman for the hypothesis of synaptic plasticity in recent years. How variations in synaptic conductivity, if the existing consensus is correct and not simply faddish foolishness, are transformed into adaptive and variable molar behavior, however, remains another expression of one of the most perplexing problems in modern psychobiology.

How could one go about crossing the enormous conceptual gulf between ultramicroscopic synaptic plasticity and molar behavior? The answer to this question is not evident. In spite of many attempts to apply anatomical and biochemical techniques to the analysis of changes occurring at synapses in what should be a straightforward way, the problem is almost always complicated by several confounding factors. For example, any study of the long-term effects of experience on neurons is almost certainly going to be heavily influenced by the concomitant effects of normal growth and development. Indeed, a number of authors have suggested that the process of learning (at the cellular level) and normal neuronal development may be mutually interdependent. Growth, for example, may progress only to the extent that experience triggers and modulates the developmental processes. On the other hand, some authors, most notably Greenough (1975) and Mark (1974), have virtually identified learning as but experientially controlled perturbations on the genetically determined growth process. Clearly, it is not yet possible to resolve this complex version of the nature-nurture controversy.

In this chapter my goals are somewhat more modest. I try to unravel a much simpler knot than the nature-nurture tangle by surveying the possible membrane, neuronal, and network changes that might serve as the substrate upon which molar learning could plausibly be based. The purpose of this chapter, therefore, is to consider the possible plastic mechanisms that might account for the observed neurophysiological changes discussed in Chapter 8 and also those alterations in the neural network that such synaptic changes may produce. A few hypotheses are discussed that suggest nonsynaptic bases for learning, but clearly, the keystone of modern psychobiological theories of learning are the variations in network junction conductivity that go under the umbrella rubric of synaptic plasticity.

The next section briefly introduces some of these nonsynaptic but neuronal hypotheses and then presents a brief review of current knowledge of synaptic functions possibly associated with neural network reorganization and thus with learning. I then consider some of the specific mechanisms that have been suggested to account for synaptic plasticity in particular. Later in this chapter I consider the theoretical systems of Holger Hydén and Karl Pribram. These two theories are among the most comprehensive discussions covering all levels of the problem. Each ties together much of the material discussed in Chapters 8 and 9. Because each has a different emphasis, the contrast serves to spotlight the basic similarities of all contemporary psychobiological theories of learning. Finally, I try to induce, from the details of the discussions of Chapters 8 and 9, the general principles of the relationship of neural plasticity and learning, best supported by the available data, with which most contemporary psychobiologists find little disagreement.

2. Nonsynaptic Neuronal Theories of Learning

a. *Special Neurons*

One class of neuronal theories of learning not directly involving the synapse is characterized by the suggestion that certain neurons in the central nervous system are particularly specialized by their anatomy and physiology for information storage. This hypothesis implies that the capacity to remember or exhibit plastic change is not a general property of all neurons but is restricted to only certain ones. One example of this special neuron approach to learning is Altman's (1967) renewal of a suggestion (originally made by Cajal many years ago) that the smallest neurons of the brain, the tiny "microneurons" that make up such a large portion of the nuclear mass, are plausible candidates to serve the special function of information storage. The arguments Altman cites in support of this hypothesis must necessarily be indirect, because microneurons are among the most difficult from which to record responses. Because they are not capable of long distance communication and generally are devoid of elongated axons, microneurons do not produce the easily detected and conspicuous spike action potentials. But microneurons, it is known from anatomical studies, are found in increasing numbers as one ascends the phylogenetic tree in rough agreement with increase in the ability of organisms to learn. Furthermore, these neurons develop slowly in embryological development just as does learning ability. All of these characteristics are used as indirect arguments by Altman to support the hypothesis that these microneurons play a key role in integration, in general, and in learning, in particular, and that role is not mediated by the kind of synaptic plasticity to be described later.

Another nonsynaptic, and indeed nonneuronal, hypothesis put forward by several neuroscientists attributes a possible role in learning to the neuroglia or glial cells of the brain. Glia are not neurons, but they are abundant in the central nervous system and have even been shown to be capable of producing a kind of action potential reflecting the activity in nearby neurons. Glia are sometimes invoked as a separate nonneuronal medium for the storage of information. They are proposed to play a special role in the macromolecular information storage theory of Hydén, discussed in greater detail later in this chapter. Even Pribram's "holographic" field theory, also discussed later in this chapter, is not inconsistent with the hypothesis of glial storage of the engram.

One possible way in which the glia might act as a mechanism for learning is by influencing synaptic conductivity, as suggested by Roitbak (1970) and diagrammed in Fig. 9-1. The essential aspect of his idea is that the glia are stimulated to grow by activity in adjacent neurons. After such growth, they tend to provide an insulating sheath, similar to myelin, that helps to maintain a high amplitude of the dendritic graded potentials by reduction of the shunt pathways

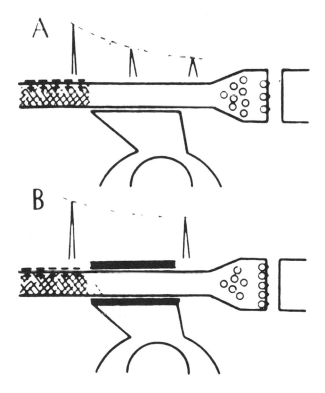

FIG. 9.1   Roitbak's hypothesis of how the insulating sheath of glial cells may act to maintain action potential amplitudes by reducing shunting pathways in nonregenerative regions of the axon. (From Roitbak, ©1970, with the permission of *Acta Neurobiologia Experimentalis.*)

that would otherwise act to dissipate electrotonic currents. According to Roit-bak's hypothesis, a given presynaptic potential is thus able to trigger the release of larger amounts of transmitter substance than it did prior to the glial growth. The larger amount of transmitter substance in turn produces a more effectively conducting synapse, and the overall neural network state is thereby altered.

b. Modulation of Spontaneous Activity

Another nonsynaptic possibility that might contribute in part to short-term information storage has been suggested by Frazier, Waziri, and Kandel (1965) and developed more fully by Kupfermann and Pinsker (1970). They suggest that the storage of information occurs when the endogenous rhythms of spontan-eously active neurons are modulated by repeated stimulation. This modulation is presumed to result from alterations of the same intraneuronal (membrane) mechanisms, whatever they were, that led this cell to act as a pacemaker; the membrane changes are presumed to be independent of any synaptic plasticity per se.

Kupfermann and Pinsker have suggested three plausible and conceptually distinct mechanisms that might account for the modulation of endogenous pace-maker activity. These are shown in the three plates of Fig. 9-2. Two alternative models (Fig. 9-2a and 9-2b) describe mechanisms corresponding to operant con-ditioning, and one models (Fig. 9-2c) a mechanism corresponding to classical conditioning.

In Fig. 9-2a, an increase in output response strength of a spontaneously ac-tive pacemaker is achieved by means of a feedback loop from that pacemaker neuron to a separate interneuron. The increase in activity with experience is nonspecific in this case, in that the feedback effects will be felt whether or not the cell upon which the feedback impinges is active at any particular moment. Temporal contiguity of the *input signal* and the trace of a delayed *feedback* signal are all that are required to produce an increase in the endogenous activity of the pacemaker cell.

On the other hand, Fig. 9-2b shows what is logically an equally effective means of increasing the activity in the pacemaker directly. Here the increase would be presumed to be most effective when the input signal occurred in synchrony with spontaneous spiking of two pacemakers.

Figure 9-2c depicts a mechanism that might account for classical condition-ing. A variable-frequency, spontaneously active pacemaker neuron produces responses that act to strengthen the response produced by a conditioned stim-ulus when the conditioned stimulus is paired with an unconditioned stimulus. The CS and the UCS both act on an interneuron as well as on the response neu-ron. Prior to the pairing, the CS is incapable of eliciting a response from the response neuron. Following pairing, however, the variable-frequency pacemaker neuron increases its output frequency, thus providing the priming necessary to allow the CS to activate the response cell.

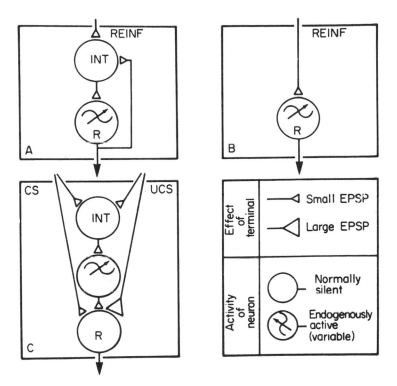

FIG. 9.2   Three models of conditioning based on changes in the activity levels of spontaneously active neurons. See text for details. (From Kupfermann & Pinsker, ©1970, with the permission of Academic Press.)

The important point in all three of these hypothetical models is that the effect is produced by an increase in the propensity of the endogenously or spontaneously active neuron to fire in a way that is, presumably, not a direct result of synaptic plasticity. Unfortunately, at the descriptive level at which Kupfermann and Pinsker have presented their model, it is not at all certain just what the membrane or biochemical changes are in the neuron that might account for this increase in pacemaker activity. Typically repetitive systems of this sort are driven by relaxation oscillation processes in which some condition builds up until it exceeds the threshold for the catastrophic discharge of that condition. The process then cyclically repeats itself. The current state of our knowledge about membrane mechanisms does not justify the assumption that the pacemaker or endogenously active neuron is driven by a relaxation oscillator of this sort, nor does it provide the basis for a guess as to the nature of the membrane mechanisms underlying the change in the frequency of firing.

c.   Nonsynaptic Ionic Effects

Although it is not possible to point specifically to any long-term effects at the level of ionic mechanisms that could account for the plastic changes in the resting and action potentials of the cell or plasma membrane, it is not implausible that such changes might account for nonsynaptic plastic changes in neurons. The Hodgkin-Huxley theory of membrane action (see Hodgkin, 1964, chap. 3; or Uttal, 1975b, chaps. 5 and 7, for more complete discussions of this theory of neuronal action potentials) involves a number of parameters that could produce persistent changes in membrane properties as a result of preceding experience. The sodium and potassium pumping actions, dependent as they are on metabolic and transport processes within the membrane, could be altered in their ability to transmit sodium out of or potassium into the neuron, as a result of prior experience. Thus the concentrations of these ions, the ones most intimately involved in the generation of membrane action potentials, might be persistently displaced from their normal equilibrium levels. For that matter, the proteinaceous channels in the plasma membrane, through which these ions pass, might also be altered in a behaviorally significant way by previous patterns of use and disuse.

Thus many different parameters of the Hodgkin-Huxley model appear able, in principle, to underlie neuronal plasticity completely independently of any synaptic effects. The results of Woody and Black-Cleworth (1973) described in Chapter 8, for example, suggest such a membrane effect in the form of a resistance change. A particularly sensitive locus on a neuron could be the point at which the graded local potentials are transformed into the spike action potential.

Is there any other evidence that such long-term membrane equilibrium changes actually occur? Surprisingly (from some conventional points of view), some reports of such effects have indeed been forthcoming recently. Brodwick and Junge (1972) have discovered a persistent alteration of potassium conductance as a result of multiple stimulations of neurons in *Aplysia*. Furthermore, Van Essen (1973) reports a similar long-duration effect on the sodium pumping process in the leech. However, additional work in this direction is required to more solidly determine whether these membrane effects represent a likely alternative to the contemporary consensus—the hypothesis of synaptic plasticity.

3.   The Synaptic Hypothesis

Some plausible alternatives to the synaptic hypothesis exist. Nevertheless, it takes no deep insight into the contemporary neurophysiological literature to realize that the majority of psychobiologists and neuroscientists today believe that the most salient learning effects must ultimately be attributed to the level of the synapse. Synaptic plasticity is generally assumed to be the most promising mechanism for producing changes in the status of the neural network and thus the most likely microscopic site of physiological correlates of learning. In the following section, I first consider in some detail the nature of the synapse, as it is perceived by modern neuroscience, and then attempt to classify the various ways in which synaptic plasticity relevant to learning may occur. Finally, I briefly discuss psychoactive drugs and hormones, chemicals that affect behavior probably because of their special affinity for synaptic mechanisms.

a.   The Synapse[2]

Before I can meaningfully consider how the neuronal microelements known as *synapses* might work to modify the activity of neurons and thus the state of neural networks, it is necessary to know something about their anatomy and physiology. The purpose of this section is to briefly review the basics of normal synaptic action as a basic prerequisite for the subsequent discussion of theories of synaptic plasticity.

The hypothesis that the nervous system is made up of individual, protoplasmically separate cells, demarcated by a continuous semipermeable plasma membrane and interacting only at particular junctions (synapses), is the fundamental premise of modern neuroanatomy. This hypothesis, known as *"the" neuron theory*, was not supported by direct proof, however, until the past 20 years or so, even though there was general agreement that the nervous system was not an interconnected reticulum for the last half-century.

Considering the infinitesimal dimensions of synapses, what are the convincing arguments that the intercellular contents of neurons on either side of a synapse are indeed separated by their respective plasma membranes? Eccles (1964) listed the following specific evidence for accepting the doctrine of cytoplasmic discontinuity between neurons:

1. Axonal degeneration produced by separating the axon from the cell body is often sharply demarcated at synaptic boundaries. Thus the metabolism of the axon beyond the synapse is separate and distinct from that preceding the synapse. That transneuronal degeneration that is observed may be associated with disuse rather than metabolic deficiencies.

2. Most chemical synapses insert a 1/2 to 1 millisecond delay in the transmission of a neural signal. This is equal to the delay produced by conduction over an inch or two of uninterrupted axon.

3. Special staining techniques, such as the Cajal silver stain, act selectively on a single neuron, and the stain is often sharply demarcated at the boundaries between neurons.

4. Electron micrographs show directly that the plasma membranes of two neurons are everywhere separate from each other in nearly all synapses (with the exception of a few kinds of electrical synapses).

---

[2]Some portions of this discussion of synapses have been adapted and updated from Uttal, 1975b.

Proceeding from the premise that synapses do not represent, in general, regions of cytoplasmic continuity[3] between neurons, we must next inquire into the mechanisms that account for the transmission of information across this cleft.

Synapses occur in a wide variety of forms between the many different kinds of neurons found in the multitude of animal species. Electron microscopes have revealed a rich world of synaptic forms. A few examples are shown in Fig. 9-3. In spite of this anatomical diversity, only two distinct kinds of synaptic action are known at present. The first is based upon direct electrical activation, similar to the way in which a nerve impulse is propagated along the axon itself. The second and apparently much more common (at least in vertebrates) mode of synaptic action is mediated by highly specialized transmitter chemicals released from the terminal or *presynaptic region* of the cell from which the information is coming. Information is transmitted by the diffusion of transmitter substance across the space between two neurons, producing an alteration in the membrane potential of the second or *postsynaptic cell*. I now consider each of these two forms of synaptic action in somewhat greater detail.

Electrical synapses.   Electrical synapses are believed to operate by direct electrotonic coupling of the electrochemical membrane potentials generated in the presynaptic neuron to the membrane of the postsynaptic neuron. For some time, the junction between the presynaptic neuron and the postsynaptic neuron in an electrical synapse was thought to be formed by an actual tight physical fusion of the two membranes. In recent years, however, higher-power electron microscopes have more often than not shown a very small gap of about 20 Å between the two membranes across an electrical synapse. Electrical synapses, therefore, are generally referred to as "gap junctions" (in those situations in which the membranes are separate) and less frequently as "tight junctions" (when the membranes are actually fused). This "gap" nomenclature, unfortunately, is somewhat misleading, because the presynaptic and postsynaptic membranes in a chemical synapse are separated by an even larger space, typically 200 Å. For clarity, therefore, the space between the membranes in a chemical synapse is now referred to as a synaptic *cleft* rather than as a *gap*.

Figure 9-4 shows a gap-type electrical synapse from the medulla of an electric catfish. The magnification, in this case, is enormous; this photograph is approximately 315,000 times larger than the original junction. Several important features of the gap junction are displayed in this figure, one of the most important being the blurred hint of a series of transverse connections between the postsynaptic and presynaptic membranes. It has been suggested that these tiny connections, only a few angstroms wide, may actually represent channels between the two neurons through which protoplasmic flow can occur, which is a curious

---

[3]We see later in this discussion that electron micrographs of some electrical synapses do show suspicious signs of possible cytoplasmic continuity between neurons.

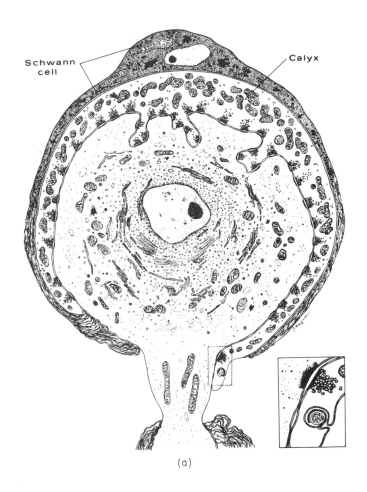

Schwann
cell

Calyx

(a)

FIG. 9.3 Examples of synapses drawn from McLennan's (1970) authoritative book on
Synaptic Transmission are reproduced here. (A) Synapse (shown in the inset) of a ciliary
ganglion cell from a chick (from de Lorenzo, ©1960, with the permission of The Rockefeller University Press); (B) A synaptic complex from the mammalian pulvinar. The main
dendrite (MD) branches to form secondary structures (CD) that have large numbers of syn-
aptic cells containing groups of synaptic vesicles. Some of the synapses are indicated as AA
(From Majorossy, Réthelyi, & Szentágothai, ©1965, with the permission of *J. fur Hirn
Forschung*); (C) synaptic contacts at the base of a Purkinje cell. Abbreviations indicated are:
P = the Purkinje cell body; Ba = basket cell axons; G = glia; and Ax = axon. (From Hámori
& Szentágothai, ©1965, with the permission of *Acta-Biologica*.)

621

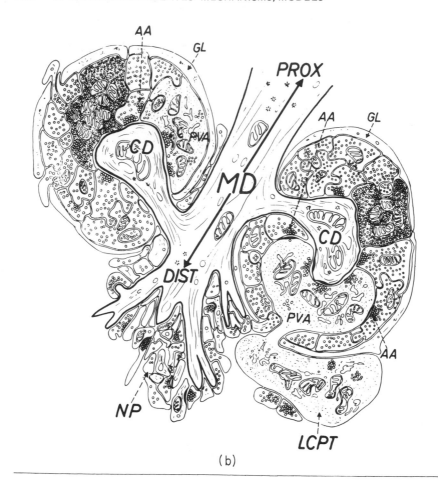

(b)

revival for this special case of the notion of a nervous reticulum, supposedly discarded long ago.

Until quite recently, the electrical synapse was thought to be only present in invertebrates and only extremely rarely, if ever, in vertebrates. It has now become clear, in particular through the work of M. V. L. Bennett and G. D. Pappas, that electrical synapses are very common in vertebrates up to and including mammals. (For reviews of this work, the reader is referred to Bennett, 1972; 1974.) The recent work by such workers as Baker and Llinas (1971), McDonald and Mitchell (1975), and Sotelo, Llinás, and Baker (1974) have provided further evidence that electrical synapses are quite common in a number of portions of the mammalian nervous system. Figure 9-5, for example, is a photomicrograph of a gap junction from the ventral cochlear nucleus of the rat at a magnification of 185,000.

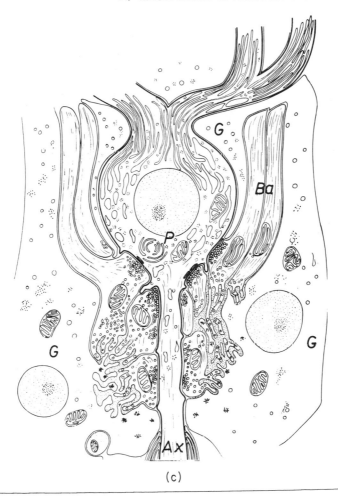

(c)

It is relatively common for electrical synapses to possess reciprocal electrotonic sensitivity between the involved dendrites. One can only guess at the exact physiological significance of this reciprocal interconnectivity, but it may play an important role in nervous system function as an amplifier of neural responses.

Some of the other special characteristics of the electrical synapse are described in a later section in which it is compared with the chemical synapse. The general action of the electrical synapse is very easy to summarize, however. The junction between two neurons at the point of an electrical synapse can simply be thought of as a resistor of relatively low value functioning in fundamentally the same way as any piece of plasma membrane might work to electrotonically conduct information. The means of transmission of information in the electrical synapse is thus the passive voltage driving of postsynaptic ions as a direct result of the presynaptic electrical potential.

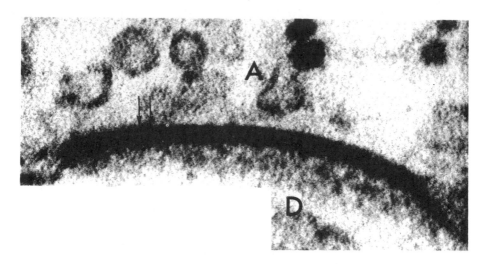

FIG. 9.4 A gap-type electrical synapse between an axon (A) and a dendrite (D) in the catfish's medulla. There is a faint suggestion at this enormous magnification (315,000X) of cross connections (arrows) that may possibly allow cytoplasmic continuity between the presynaptic and postsynaptic neuron. (From Pappas & Waxman, ©1972, with the permission of Raven Press.)

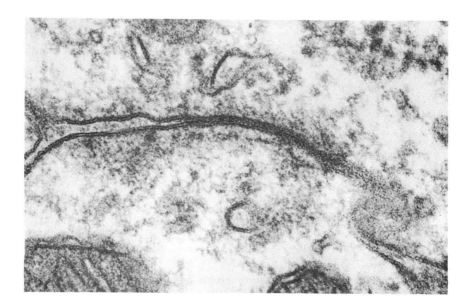

FIG. 9.5 A mammalian synaptic gap junction magnified approximately 185,000 times. (From Sotelo, Gentschev, & Zamora, © 1976, with the permission of Pergamon Press.)

Chemical synapses. The main factors of chemical synaptic action are illustrated in Fig. 9-6, which is adapted from a diagram originally drawn by Grundfest (1957). This figure emphasizes several important concepts. Note that even within the microscopic region of the chemical synapse—typically only a couple of hundred angstrom units in width—several different levels or modes of information coding can exist. Transmission in the presynaptic axon up to the region of the synapse takes place by means of frequency-coded spike action potentials. Presynaptic tissues then probably convert this pulse-coded information into a graded potential, which releases in a way not yet completely understood the transmitter chemical serving as a chemical code for the transmitted information. The transmitter chemical itself then diffuses, apparently in a purely passive manner (i.e., no active metabolic transport mechanism drives the transmitter molecules) across the synaptic cleft. The molecules of transmitter substance are subsequently captured by certain specialized receptor sites on the postsynaptic tissue, whose resting potential is altered to produce another graded postsynaptic potential.

The action of the transmitter substance on the postsynaptic potential and thus on the postsynaptic neuron may be either inhibitory or excitatory. If it is excitatory, it increases the amount of spike or graded action potential activity in the postsynaptic axon. If it is inhibitory, postsynaptic activity is reduced. Although inhibitory and excitatory transmitters are usually different chemicals, some transmitters (e.g., acetylcholine) can be either excitatory or inhibitory in different circumstances.

Now that I have characterized the general features of chemical synaptic action, let us consider the chemical transmission process in greater detail. The earliest evidence indicating the presence of some sort of chemical mediation of the synaptic transmission process was quite indirect. Investigators working in the first half of the twentieth century encountered a number of different chemicals that produced exceptionally strong neural effects. Loewi (1921), for example, demonstrated the very strong inhibitory effects of acetylcholine on heart rate. Cannon and his colleagues (Cannon & Bacq, 1931) found that epinephrine and some of its chemical relatives (specifically, norepinephrine) could accelerate or decelerate heart rate. In each case, the action was produced by a chemical normally emitted by stimulated portions of the parasympathetic and sympathetic nervous systems, respectively. The notion that parts of the nervous system both secrete and were receptors for chemicals thus became increasingly plausible.

It is now believed by neurophysiologists studying chemical synapses that the chemical transmitter substances are organized in a quantal fashion—an idea originally suggested by Del Castillo and Katz (1954). That is, many molecules of the chemical transmitter substance appear to be clustered into groups or packets of almost constant size that are released as units. One of the earliest and most compelling arguments for the packet concept was some work that dealt with very careful recordings of the microstructure of the postsynaptic potentials. Del

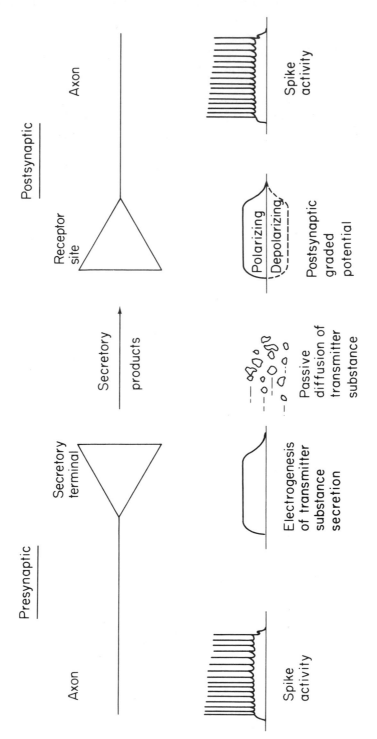

FIG. 9.6 Schematic sketch of the various stages of neuroelectric and chemical coding at a chemical synapse. (Adapted from Grundfest, 1957.)

Castillo and Katz (1954) observed in motor end plates, and Eccles, Eccles, Iggo, and Lundberg (1961) and Nishi and Koketsu (1960) observed in central neurons, that when a microelectrode was inserted into the postsynaptic tissue, spontaneous depolarizations occurred with rather irregular periodicity. These spontaneous depolarizations were very small, with an amplitude of only about .5 mV. Because of their small size, they have come to be called *miniature postsynaptic potentials.* It has been determined that the miniature postsynaptic potential results from the action of a relatively large and constant number of molecules (typically several thousand), because iontophoretic experiments in which only a few hundred ions are injected by a driving electrical field do not produce equivalent depolarizations.

Because the miniature potentials regularly occur spontaneously, are of relatively constant amplitude, and seem to result from the action of a substantial number of molecules, the idea that large numbers of molecules of the transmitter substance form constant size aggregates or packets has gained wide favor. Further direct support for this concept has come from electron micrographs of the sort shown in Fig. 9-7. The first observation of the vesicles, now believed to be the packets of transmitter substance, is usually attributed to De Robertis and Bennett (1954). Clusters of these structured vesicles can be seen in the presynaptic terminal in close proximity to the synaptic cleft. It is currently thought that the molecules separate either upon, or shortly after, the release and then travel independently to the postsynaptic receptor sites. Correspondence between the cleft size, the calculated diffusion time, and synaptic delays observed electrophysiologically, supports the notion that the molecules of the transmitter substance diffuse passively across the synaptic cleft.

Recently some important new information concerning the production and recycling of the synaptic vesicles that originally contain the molecules of transmitter substance has been developed by a number of laboratories (Douglas, Nagasawa, & Schultz, 1970; and Heuser & Reese, 1973). Heuser and Reese, in particular, have proposed a model of vesicle recycling that is extremely interesting. The general outline of their theory, based upon an experimental procedure that involved both electrical recordings of postsynaptic potentials and an ultrarapid fixation method for electron microscopic examination, is diagrammed in Fig. 9-8.

The cycle may be examined starting at the point (1) at which existing vesicles loaded with transmitter molecules migrate toward the plasma membrane of the neuron, presumably as a result of some stimulus applied to an earlier portion of the neuron. The vesicles merge with the plasma membrane releasing their contents into the synaptic cleft—a process that is called *exocytosis.* The remaining membranes of the vesicles gradually coalesce indistinguishably with the neuronal plasma membrane as shown at point (2). The increasing membrane area produced by this coalescence, however, is compensated for by a gradual reproduction of synaptic vesicles (pinocytosis) from a region of membrane near point (3), the boundary of the Schwann cell sheath of the cell. The vesicles so formed,

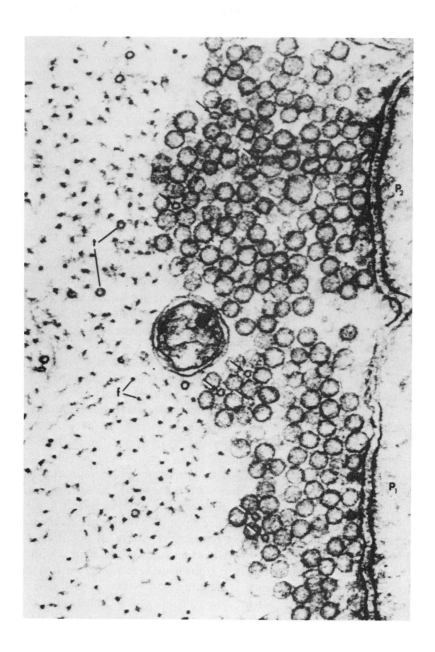

FIG. 9.7 Electronmicrograph of a synaptic region of a Muller cell from a lamprey. Note the synaptic vesicles clustered on the presynaptic side of the cell. P_1 and P_2 = two post-synaptic cells; t and f = microtubules and microfilaments, respectively. Arrows point to regular arrangement of vesicles around microtubules. Magnification is about 130,000X. (From Smith, Järlfors, & Beránek, ©1970, with the permission of The Rockefeller University Press.)

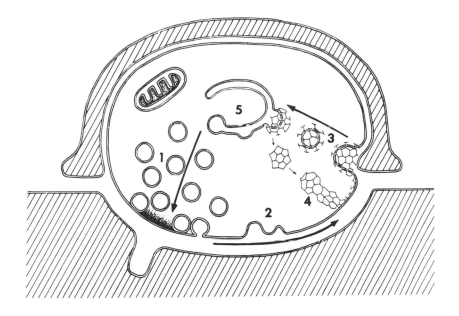

FIG. 9.8   Diagram depicting the metamorphasis of the synaptic vesicles. Numbered stages are described in the text. (From Heuser & Reese, ©1973, with the permission of The Rockefeller University Press.)

however, are coated with certain molecules that seem to prevent them from participating in the normal transmitter release process. It is likely, according to this research, that they do not, at this point, contain any of the transmitter substance.

Heuser and Reese propose that the newly formed and coated vesicles next migrate to the interior of the cell, where they form specialized structures known as *cisternae*. At this point (4), the molecules making up the vesicle coating material are disassociated from the newly regenerated vesicles and migrate back to the membrane where they are again used to coat the next generations of recycled vesicles. The cisternae, however, undergo a process akin to budding, at point (5), during which fully loaded (with transmitter substance) and active vesicles are produced that can fully participate in the synaptic transmission process, at point (1), which I have already described.

Like so many other theories of neuronal and membrane function, models of chemical synaptic function are in a rapid state of flux. In a very recent report, Marchbanks (1976) has suggested that the vesicles are, in fact, not receptacles for the transmitter substance actually used in synaptic conduction in some cases.

He feels that the acetylcholine that migrates across certain synaptic clefts does not appear to come from the vesicles. Rather, his observations suggest that it almost entirely comes from the pool of free acetylcholine in the presynaptic intracellular space. The acetylcholine in the vesicles, Marchbanks further hypothesizes, is actually only a buffer stored against possible depletion of the extravesicular (but intracellular) supply by heavy use. Furthermore, his work suggests that the stored acetylcholine is not actually contained within the vesicle but is more probably only attached to its surface much like the coating material is thought to be in Heuser and Reese's model.

A variety of biochemicals are now believed to act as synaptic transmitter substances in the nervous systems of various animals. For example, as I have already mentioned, acetylcholine has been shown to be an effective transmitter substance at several synapses. Although this substance was long thought to be solely involved in neuroeffector junctions and parasympathetic action in vertebrates, "cholinergic" synapses are now known to be more generally distributed throughout all animal phyla. Similarly, the catecholamine norepinephrine has classically been suggested as the main transmitter substance in the sympathetic portion of the autonomic nervous system, and epinephrine plays the same role in the parasympathetic portion. Other possible excitatory transmitter substances in mammalian brains include 5-hydroxytryptamine (serotonin), glutamic and aspartic acids, and dopamine, another catecholamine. Glutamates also seem to be excitatory transmitters in the squid.

Recent work indicates that some of the substances that had been thought to be exclusively excitatory may in fact be either excitatory or inhibitory, depending upon the nature of the receptor site. Acetylcholine, for example, is now known to serve either function in invertebrates like *Aplysia* (Wachtel & Kandel, 1967). It seems to be a general conclusion now that some transmitter substances may be both inhibitory and excitatory in different situations. The actual action of any transmitter seems to depend upon the nature of the receptor site and possibly even on the rate at which the substance is delivered (although variations in rate may simply serve to select different receptor sites). Nevertheless, even though a single substance may act to either inhibit or excite, a fundamental law of neurophysiology, Dale's principle, asserting that a single neuron is capable of producing only a single kind of transmitter substance, is still valid.

Substances that have classically been considered as solely inhibitory in mammalian brains include the amino acids glycine and GABA (gamma-aminobutyric acid). On the other hand, a substance like strychnine, although not strictly a natural transmitter substance, is known to inhibit the action of inhibitory transmitters and thus to produce a pseudoexcitatory effect. Strychnine's general effect is, therefore, to elicit neural activity, and in large doses this activation may be so strong as to result in severe convulsions. Strychnine appears to decrease the sensitivity of postsynaptic regions to the inhibitory substances that normally stabilize the neural net.

Another important synaptic chemical effect that should be kept distinct from the deactivation of inhibitory processes just described is the deactivation of the excitatory transmitter substances after they have migrated across the cleft by highly specific enzymes. For the system to maintain a high speed of response, it is obviously necessary that some active chemical means of deactivating excitatory transmitter substances must normally exist in the postsynaptic tissue. Otherwise the residual portion of the transmitter substance may exert a persistent influence and prolong the postsynaptic response. In cholinergic systems, for example, postsynaptic tissues seem to be rich in AChE (acetylcholine esterase), an enzyme that quickly breaks down acetylcholine. The synaptic effects of acetylcholine, therefore, last for only a few milliseconds before the residual transmitter molecules are destroyed. This is particularly important in speeding up the action of neurons and motor units, because perseveration of a response would reduce the speed at which changes could be made in the firing rate of the neuron.

It has also been suggested that some general anesthetic drugs work in a similar way by interfering with chemical synaptic transmission in the central nervous system. The postsynaptic sites, chemoreceptors that they are, are especially likely to bind a number of chemicals, but not all that are bound necessarily excite the neuron. Specifically, the suggestion has been made that blocking occurs when the anesthetic drug occupies many of the postsynaptic receptor sites without producing the effects required for nervous transmission. Because the sites are already occupied, any of the usual transmitter substance that might arrive would be ineffective. Other anesthetics, particularly local ones, must directly act to reduce axonal activity.

Although several major stages of the synaptic transmission process have been distinguished, not all are yet fully understood. It is not definitely known, for example, if spike action potentials produce an intermediate graded potential in presynaptic tissue or if the potentials detected there are merely degraded spikes. A question of equal importance concerns the action of the specific release mechanism. How does a graded potential release, or trigger the release, of transmitter molecules? In other words, what ionic mechanism suddenly stimulates extensive expulsion of transmitter chemicals when previously only infrequent spontaneous passages leading to miniature postsynaptic potentials occurred. About all that seems certain now is that calcium ions are intimately related somehow to the release of transmitter substances. The graded potentials produced in the presynaptic region by the spike action potentials seem to pull Ca^{++} ions into the cell. As these ions move into the neuron, the synaptic vesicles may tend to fuse more often with the membrane and thus more frequently release the molecules of the transmitter substance into the interneural cleft (if this is the correct model). These and related issues represent the frontier of current research in the field. A full and excellent discussion of synaptic biochemistry can be found in Albers, Siegel, Katzman, and Agranoff (1972) or in Dunn and Bondy (1974).

Bennett's (1974) collection of papers on synaptic transmission is an excellent source of general information about contemporary synaptic data and theory.

A comparison of electrical and chemical synapses.   It is important for the reader to understand that the distinction between an electrical and a chemical synapse does not mean that one is exclusively chemical or the other exclusively electrical. The voltages and currents that are the primary excitants in electrical synapses do result from the same sort of ionic flow processes that generate the electrical resting and action potentials. Although the chemical synapse seems to be relatively insensitive to electricity as a primary excitant (some neurophysiologists feel that it is completely inexcitable electrically), it does exhibit the same sort of electropotentials as any ion-membrane system. Because our technology for observing the magnitude and time course of these chemical events is almost exclusively an electrical one, chemical events can be only indirectly observed with the usual sort of electrophysiological electrodes and amplifiers.

The key difference between chemical and electrical synapses is the nature of the primary excitant that is best able to alter the resting potential of the postsynaptic region. In the epilog to his distinguished book, Eccles (1964) lists some more-specific distinguishing features of the chemical and electrical synapse, which have been paraphrased as follows:

1. A much smaller synaptic delay occurs across an electrical synapse than across a chemically mediated synapse.

2. The passive (electrotonic) spread of the generated postsynaptic potentials extends much further in an electrical than in a chemical synapse. An electrode placed in a presynaptic neuron will pick up much more of the activity in the postsynaptic neuron if the synapse is electrically mediated. In other words, electrical synapses are more closely electrically coupled than chemical ones.

3. The size of the synaptic cleft between two neurons is much larger in a chemically mediated synapse than in an electrical synapse, where the plasma membranes of the cells in some cases may actually be fused. This reduced spacing in an electrical synapse may partly explain the high level of electrical coupling described in (2).

4. Two neurons that electrically interact at a synapse are usually of roughly the same size. If the synaptic element of the first cell is very much smaller than that of the second cell, chemical transmission is almost obligatory, because direct electrical action between small presynaptic and large postsynaptic neurons would require some sort of an electrical energy amplification process. No such process is known to exist in electrical synapses.

In the past decade, considerable additional distinctions have been noted between these two forms of synapses. Bennett (1972) lists a number of others that can be paraphrased and added to the previous four criteria.

5. Individual chemical synapses are intrinsically unidirectional (rectifying) because of the asymmetrical physical arrangement of the source of the transmitter substance in the presynaptic neuron and the locations of the receptor sites in the postsynaptic neurons. Electrical synapses may possibly rectify, in some instances, but there appears to be conflicting evidence that this actually happens, and, in general, information flow seems to be possibly equally well in both directions.

6. Chemical inhibitory synapses are common, but direct inhibition is not observed in electrical synapses.

7. Electrical synapses are basically linear systems (following Ohm's Law), whereas chemical synapses are nonlinear (this is another way of saying that they amplify).

8. Temporal summation is common in chemical synapses but difficult to effect in electrical synapses because of the rapid decay of electrotonic spread.

b. *Possible Synaptic Plastic Mechanisms*

In this section I direct attention to the possible ways in which a synapse could conceivably change its properties such that its transmission conductivity would be altered as a result of previous activation. As we see later, there are many physiological possibilities that could account for such plasticity in the efficacy of a given synaptic junction.

It is important to reiterate that the changes I am about to describe must ultimately exert their influence on learning by means of the changes they produce in the state of the neuronal network. Thus any theories of learning based upon synaptic change are not, in any way, inconsistent with the more general concept of the network state. The important generalization to be kept in mind, regardless of the particular membrane mechanism invoked to account for the synaptic change, is that the overall effect of plasticity is to modulate the ease with which information can pass from a presynaptic to a postsynaptic cell and thus to reconfigure the monentary state of the overall neural network. The rest of the details are but the "technological" means by which this informational reconfiguration occurs.

John (1967), in his distinguished review of the mechanisms of memory, points out that there are really only three fundamentally different ways in which network reorganization can take place. Two of these are explicitly synaptic effects, and the third is a temporal process not directly involving synaptic plasticity. He refers to these three categories as the "Growth," "Shunt," and "Mode" hypotheses, respectively.

By the first of the two synaptic possibilities, the *growth hypothesis*, John means that the nervous system may create new pathways in the neural network as a result of the birth of new synaptic junctions. John's second possible synaptic means of altering network organization, which he refers to as the *shunt hypothesis*, asserts that there is actually very little growth in the interconnectivity pattern among the neurons in the network. Rather, he suggests that only a few of the multitude of preexisting and available synapses are selected from among the others by a process of differential facilitation.

John's third category, the *mode hypothesis*, is nonsynaptic but invokes transitory processes in which circulating patterns of neural impulses account for information storage and the details of synaptic transmissions at any place at any time. John (1967) defines a mode as a "temporal sequence of states in the network [p. 64]" with an increase in the probability of particular patterns of activity in the network. In brief, the idea is that circulating nerve action potentials are capable of modulating synaptic conductivity by providing, at the proper time, "gating signals" that permit an otherwise ineffective signal to pass through a junction.

It is important to note again, as this point in this discussion is passed, that much of John's thinking is based upon the concept of probabilities of groups of neural responses rather than upon specific deterministic mechanisms associated with individual neurons. His approach has a considerable a priori validity that can easily be lost sight of at the level of ultramicroscopic examination to which I direct the following discussion. It is vitally important to remember that each individual synapse is probably irrelevant to the molar behavior of the organism. Each synapse is but one of a myriad of similar structures contributing to the global response. In the realm of learning, as in the realm of perception, it is extremely difficult to understand how any individual synapse could be essential to any molar mental act. It seems far more likely that the relevance of these synapses is meaningful only in the statistical or probabilistic sense. It is the "central tendency" of the responses of a relatively large population of synapses that is important, not the individual synaptic response itself.

With this caveat in mind, I can now profitably turn to a consideration of the specific microscopic and individual synaptic mechanisms that might account for the reconfiguration of neural nets that, without a doubt, occurs during learning. I consider, in turn, one possible mechanism of plasticity in electrical synapses and then several of the possible mechanisms of plasticity in chemical synapses. Finally, observed changes involving the actual physical growth of old synapses, or even the birth of new synapses that might serve as explanations of variable synaptic conductivity, are discussed.

Plastic mechanisms in electrical synapses. The possible mechanisms underlying plastic functional change are numerous in chemical synapses. For many reasons, however, it has not been fashionable to consider the electrical synapse as a likely site of plasticity, particularly in discussions of the mammalian brain. Recently, however, Llinás (1974) has proposed a possible mechanism by which the action of an electrical synapse might be modified through the intervention of a nearby chemical synapse. Figure 9-9a shows Llinás' hypothesis of a possible arrangement of some of the neurons of the mammalian inferior olive. Note that two dendrites (IOD) are interconnected by electrical gap junctions (indicated by arrows) and that chemical synaptic terminals (ST) are also located nearby. Figure 9-9b shows how the electrical synapse could operate in the normal state. There is close electrical coupling between the two IODs, and one is able, therefore, to excite the other. This simple arrangement allows electrotonic currents to flow between the two IODs much in the way a closed switch operates. When the chemical synapse is activated and its transmitter substance is released, however, Llinás suggests that there may be a reduction in the effective membrane resistance of the presynaptic portion of the electrical junction that short circuits

INFERIOR OLIVE GLOMERULUS

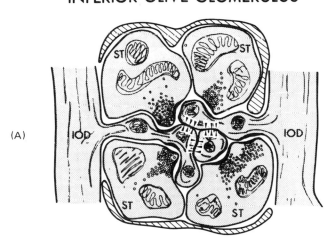

(A)

ELECTROTONIC COUPLING   ELECTROTONIC UNCOUPLING

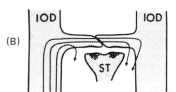

(B)

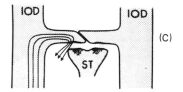

(C)

FIG. 9.9 A hypothetical model of a combined electrical and chemical system in the gomerulus of the inferior olive that might demonstrate plasticity in an electrical synapse. (From Llinás, ©1974, with the permission of The American Physiological Society.)

(or shunts) the ionic currents that had previously been effective in activating the postsynaptic electrical portion. The electrical synaptic circuit thus is rendered ineffective (corresponding to an opening of the switch, as shown in Fig. 9-9c), and the network of which this system is a part is thereby changed in state.

This single hypothesis of a chemically mediated electrical modulation is the only mechanism yet suggested that might allow an electrical synapse to exhibit the kind of plastic behavior required for the mediation of molar learning.

Nonstructural plastic mechanisms in chemical synapses. Quite unlike the situation with electrical synapses, the chemical synapse provides a plethora of candidate mechanisms that might account for the neural response variability observed to result from prior experience. In this section I consider some of the more plausible of these synaptic changes. The processes to be discussed occur on a molecular scale and, therefore, are observable only to the extent that they modify biochemical or physiological measures and not as growth or other anatomic changes. In the section to follow I consider changes that are better described in terms of the physical growth of old, or the birth of entirely new, synapses.

Presynaptic mechanisms. Some mechanisms of synaptic plasticity may be related to the presynaptic processes that control the release of transmitter substance. It is conceivable, for example, that the process by which an incoming spike action potential is converted to the transmitter releasing processes may be inhibited or enhanced by previous activation within the presynaptic neuron. It is also possible that a persistent hyperpolarization of the presynaptic membrane, by repeated activation, could result in a reduced ability to trigger transmitter release. There are, therefore, several points in the presynaptic portions of the synapse at which a plastic effect might be mediated.

Surprisingly, however, one of the most obvious presynaptic candidates to explain conditioned decrements in synaptic conductivity—depletion of the transmitter substance itself—turns out to be a relatively unlikely possibility. Transmitter substance is available in apparently large amounts relative to the quantity released by each synaptic activation either directly or in quickly available backup stores (see discussion of Marchbank's work on p. 629). Thus transmitter depletion at any conceivable realistic level of physiological activity seems to be unlikely. A transmitter substance depletion argument is also severely weakened by the fact that the general effects of repetitive stimulation are very often just the opposite of the prediction of a depletion hypothesis—a potentiation or increase rather than a decrease in synaptic conductivity. The converse of a depletion hypothesis—a mobilization of increased amounts of available transmitter substance—is, however, a possible basis of potentiated or enhanced synaptic plasticity.

In general, therefore, it now seems more likely that fluctuation in the probability of the release of transmitter molecules, rather than change in the amount of those molecules, is the best explanation of presynaptic plasticity. One suggestion is that the probability of transmitter release is closely related to the amount of ionic calcium present in the presynaptic terminal. For a summary of recent research on calcium ion effects, see Kupfermann (1975). For a discussion of the presynaptic blockade of transmitter release by botulinum toxin, see Kao. Drachman, and Price (1976).

Post-tetanic potentiation.   Another important mechanism of synaptic plasticity is known as *post-tetanic potentiation* (PTP). Although it is not certain whether PTP is a presynaptic or postsynaptic effect, it is of sufficient interest to be considered in detail at this point. Assume the following experimental preparation: A stimulating electrode is inserted into a presynaptic axon, and a recording electrode is placed somewhere in the postsynaptic neuron. The recording electrode may be recording either postsynaptic potentials in the region of the synaptic interface between the two cells, or spike activity in the axon. In either case, its purpose is to measure the change in activity of the postsynaptic cell as a function of presynaptic stimulation. Now assume that the presynaptic cell is actually stimulated with a train of electrical pulses. Such a pattern of stimulation is said to be *tetanic* because a similar stream of nerve impulses is thought to be responsible for the persistent contraction of a muscle, a phenomenon known as a *tetanus.*

The effect of a single tetanic stimulus burst on many types of synapses is the production of a prolonged hyper-responsiveness, or *potentiation*, of the preparation to a single test stimulus pulse. Post-tetanic (or *postactivation*) potentiation may be evidenced either by a greatly enlarged postsynaptic graded potential or by an increase in the number of postsynaptic spike action potentials produced by the single presynaptic test stimulus. Figure 9-10 shows a typical set of data illustrating the very long duration of potentiation obtainable. Although not all post-tetanic potentiations last as long or produce as large a change in relative response magnitude, this record is not grossly atypical and illustrates the very elongated periods of hyper-responsiveness obtained with this procedure.

Post-tetanic potentiation is of particular interest because it is one of the few single-cell plastic changes in vertebrates with durations comparable to those of behavioral phenomena. Eccles (1953) specifically has speculated that this type of increase in long-term cellular responsiveness may be one of the underlying mechanisms of human short-term memory. Because post-tetanic potentiation is transient and gradually does decrease, however, it could not possibly explain long-term memorial storage. Post-tetanic potentiation has been found frequently in vertebrate cerebral neurons, as well as in peripheral cells; thus it is apparently a ubiquitous phenomenon that may well have an important bearing on neural theories of short-term learning.

Bliss and Lomo (1970) have shown by a number of independent lines of research that post-tetanic potentiation occurs with great magnitude and with especially long persistence in the mammalian hippocampus, a structure already

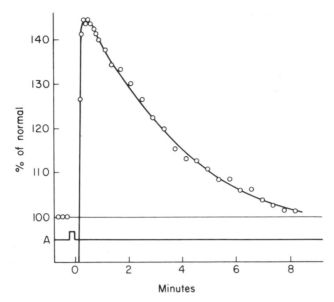

FIG. 9.10 Plot of the time course of post-tetanic potentiation as reflected in the amplitude of a postsynaptic graded potential. The pulse on line A indicates the occurrence of the
tetanic burst. (From Eccles, © 1953, after Liley & North, with the permission of Oxford
University Press/Clarendon.)

noted to be closely related to the control and regulation of learning, if not mediating the actual storage of information. Their demonstration showed that
hippocampal potentiation may last for several hours.

   Postsynaptic mechanisms.   In introducing this discussion of plastic effects
in chemical synapses, I noted that the changes occurring at the presynaptic
source of the transmitter substance were not the only plausible candidates to
explain the changes in synaptic conductivity; comparable changes at the receptor areas of the postsynaptic neuronal membrane might also be responsible. The
transduction process that converts the signal implicit in the diffusing transmitter chemical to a pattern of postsynaptic spike action potentials is also made
up of several steps. Any one of these steps might be altered to produce a change
in the efficiency of conduction.

   Some of the most plausible postsynaptic locations of plasticity are the receptor sites themselves, chemically tuned as they are to particular transmitter
substances. Deutsch (1973), for example, has specifically proposed that alterations in neuronal plasticity might be explained by a diminished or heightened
sensitivity to the specific transmitter substance on the part of receptor sites.
Furthermore, reductions in the postsynaptic neurosecretion of enzymes like
acetylcholinesterase, which are primarily responsible for the deactivation of the

transmitter substances, also might lead to abnormally prolonged efficiency of transmitter chemicals.

The nature of the receptor sites for synaptic transmitter substances is just beginning to be understood. The "sites," themselves, are probably protein molecules with the ability to selectively combine with the transmitter molecules in ways leading to changes in the postsynaptic plasma membrane properties. The induced membrane change may be in the form of a variation in the membrane permeability, resulting in transmembrane ion concentration shifts that are subsequently measured as postsynaptic potentials.

A very specific hypothesis of postsynaptic plasticity has been made by Mark (1974). He suggests that activity in a presynaptic neuron tends to build up high concentrations of calcium and sodium ions. The increase in intracellular sodium ions, in particular, produces an increase in the sodium pumping action that in turn produces an increase in the production of intracellular proteins whose structure is specific to that particular neuron. Mark assumes that the postsynaptic neuron then becomes sensitized to the "tailored" protein much as if it were an antibody. A postsynaptic neuron is thus tuned to fire more easily to a particular presynaptic neuron and to repress inputs from other presynaptic neurons. As a result of the selective sensitization of groups of neurons in this manner, the overall arrangement of the neural network assumes a new state, and the animal displays an altered form of molar behavior. This hypothetical process is diagrammed in Fig. 9-11.

Another possibility, of course, is an increase in the number of ultramicroscopic receptor sites rather than an increase in the efficiency of a constant number of sites. Such a possibility, however, is transacted at a molecular level that cannot be tested with the techniques currently available for measuring synaptic structure. The concept of an increase in the number of receptor sites bridges the gap from the mechanisms previously discussed (which are essentially changes in the molecular status of existing synapses) to consideration of another major possibility—the actual physical growth of new synaptic connections.

Growth of synapses—structural changes.   Although it is well established that regeneration of damaged tissue in the central nervous system does not usually occur, the reasons for this are not entirely clear. Central neurons do grow when incubated in vitro. Perhaps functional regeneration of central nervous tissue is poor simply because of the very dense packing of neurons in their normal state. There is, however, a considerable amount of evidence of the sprouting of what are called *dendritic spines*, which appear to contain synaptic connections, as a result of use and of their degeneration as a result of disuse. One of the first suggestions that physical growth of dendritic processes plays a role in learning was made by Ariens-Kappers (1917), who proposed a directed growth of dendrites from one neuron to another as a result of neural activity. The key idea was that

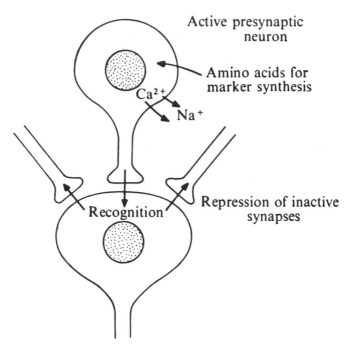

FIG. 9.11   Mark's theory of how synaptic use could lead to changes in conductivity. According to his model, activation of a presynaptic neuron is accompanied by an increase in the extrusion of Ca^{++} and Na^{+}. This changes the internal environment of the neuron so that it later has a tendency to take up a different kind of amino acid than usual. This leads to further changes in the specific proteins produced. The post synaptic neuron responds specifically to the protein, in a manner similar to an antibody-antigen reaction, thus changing the state of the neural network in a semipermanent way. (From Mark, ©1974, with the permission of The Oxford University Press.)

when these fibrils came into proximity with each other, membrane growth processes occurred that led to the creation of new synapses. Although the exact mechanism of such directed growth is not known (some workers have suggested that it is a function of the biochemicals secreted by the neurons themselves), the general process in which neural tissue grows toward or specializes around the regions from which it receives the highest level of stimulation is referred to as *neurobiotaxis*. Chemical biotaxis, in general, has been suggested as the means by which particular portions of the total genetic code (contained in all cells) are selected for expression by each cell during ontogeny.

Much later, Eccles (1953) contributed the next important step to the theory of synaptic growth. He proposed a more specific hypothesis—the swelling or ballooning of synapses with use—that has been extremely enduring in spite of the fact that it has only rarely been substantiated by direct observation.

Axons had long been suspected to swell as a function of usage (Hill, 1950), and Eccles suggested that a similar mechanism, although in a somewhat more delicate form, could account for the increased conductivity of synapses during learning. He further suggested that the swelling was a direct result of increased water uptake and that the increased synaptic size led to an increased synaptic conductivity simply because of a reduction in the membrane resistance and the changing distribution of presynaptic transmitter release sites.

Other workers (e.g., Ranck, 1964), noting that selective destruction of synapses can also be used to modify the state of the network in the same way that punching out holes in a paper card can enrich its information content, suggested that a process of selective synaptic degeneration might be a relevant structural change mediating learning at the molar level.

The notion that synapses may actually be either created or enlarged as a function of learning is one of the predominant themes of research in this field today. Cells of the mammalian brain, such as the great pyramidal neurons, have an extremely rich arborization consisting of spines projecting from all portions of the neuron—the cell body, the axon, or dendrites. Figure 9-12 is a drawing of a typical pyramidal cell (from layer 5 of the cerebral cortex of a rat) and indicates some of the nomenclature used in these investigations. A few of the spines on this neuron, which look like simple granules in low-power magnification, are enlarged in the inset to show both their detailed structure and the way in which the synaptic terminations are typically located at the most distal portion of the spines.

An important feature of these pyramidal neuron spines is their great variance in shape. Chang (1952) has proposed that the electrical resistance of a spine may vary as a function of its shape. Thus spines with long thin stalks, for simple physical reasons, would be expected to have a higher electrical resistance than short stumpy spines. The variation in synaptic resistance could, just as did synaptic swelling, directly affect the ability of a synapse to pass presynaptic graded currents and thus the general ability of the synaptic junction to convey information between the two neurons it interconnected. The hypothesis of a relationship between shape and conductivity is strongly supported by the work of Peters and Kaiserman-Abramof (1970), who have shown in a series of elegant microanatomical studies the extreme diversity of shape of dendritic spines found on pyramidal cells. Figure 9-13 shows the microanatomy of a sample of spines based on the observations of Peters and Kaiserman-Abramof and some estimates made by Rall (1974) of the membrane resistance these variously shaped spines should exhibit. Rall has carried this logic one step further by suggesting that systematic alterations in the geometry of the family of spines on a given neuron may be a function of the neuron's past experience. Thus changes in the microanatomy of synaptic spines must be added to our list of possible plastic synaptic mechanisms and thus of learning.

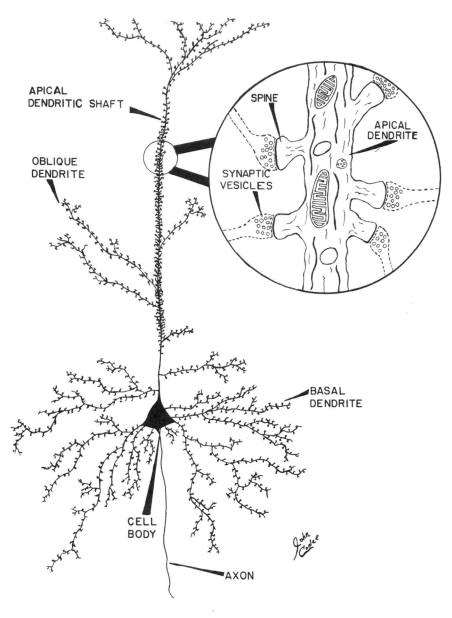

FIG. 9.12 Drawing of a cortical pyramidal neuron stained with a Golgi silver stain showing the major features of this type of cell and the details (inset) of the spiny synaptic interconnections. (From Greenough, ©1975, with the permission of *American Scientist,* Journal of Sigma Xi, The Scientific Research Society of North America.)

Shapes and lengths of dendritic spines	Dimensions	Estimates of spine stem resistance
1. Stubby	Average length 1.0 μ Range 0.5–1.5 μ	$R_{SS} \simeq 10^5$ to 10^6 ohm
2. Mushroom-shaped	Average length 1.5 μ Range 0.5–2.5 μ Average stem length 0.8 μ Average bulb dimensions 1.4 × 0.6 μ	$R_{SS} \simeq 10^6$ to 10^7 ohm
3. Thin	Average length 1.7 μ Range 0.5–4.0 μ Average stem length 1.1 μ Average bulb dimensions 0.6 μ Stem diam. 0.05 to 0.3 μ	$R_{SS} \simeq 10^7$ to 10^9 ohm

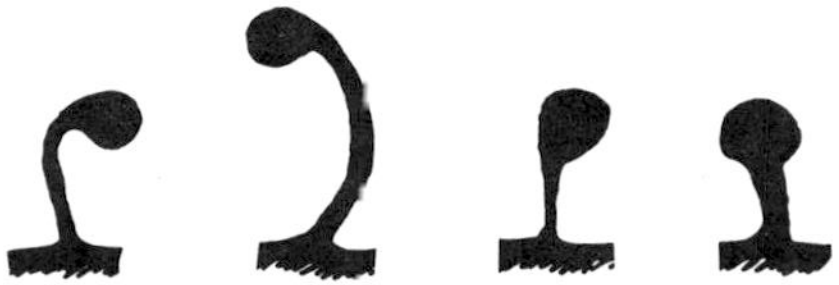

FIG. 9.13 Comparison of the shapes and stem resistances of pyramidal spines. This figure is an adaptation of one originally produced by Rall (1974) (who provided the estimates of spine stem resistance and who utilized the spine drawings and dimensions from Peters and Kaiserman-Abramof (1970). (Used with the permission of Rall and Peters & Kaiserman-Abramof and Brain Information Service/Brain Research Institute and The Wistar Press.)

Extensive changes have indeed been observed in the number and shapes of pyramidal neuron spines as a result of neuronal activity. In fact, the spine count seems to go up and down as a result of use and disuse (and as we see later, also possibly as a result of reinforcement) in a regular fashion on several different portions of the neuron. The technique used to make such measurements typically requires the manipulation of some aspect of the experimental animal's environment (either internal or external) and subsequent microscopic examination of postmortem specimens of brain tissue usually prepared with the Golgi silver stain. The Golgi stain, as I have noted, has the highly desirable property of staining most portions of a single neuron but only a relatively few of the all-too-numerous ones present in prepared tissue. Thus the anatomy of a single cell can be examined in detail in a field "cleared" of most of the surrounding neuronal tissue.

The technique for examining these structural effects of learning was developed to its current high levels by Valverde (1968). Valverde's now nearly classic study pointed out a considerable difference in the proliferation of dendritic spines in the occipital cortex, in particular when a mouse had one eye ennucleated at birth, compared to control areas of the brain. Figure 9-14, for example, shows two photographs of the apical dendrites from a pyramidal cell in the mouse's visual cortex. The experimental picture (Fig. 9-14b) is of a neuron from the side of the cortex contralateral to the ennucleated eye, and the control picture (Fig. 9-14a) is of a portion of a pyramidal neuron from the ipsilateral occipital cortex. Because the visual fibers are mostly crossed over in the mouse, this is a valuable built-in control. Obviously there is a substantial difference between the two photographs. Spines are much less frequent on the contralateral side of the brain to which the ennucleated eye would have projected and which, therefore, had received a much lower level of activation.

There are, of course, a large number of potential artifacts in this kind of research. It is possible that the effects are not visual but have something quite separate to do with mechanical or degenerative damage done by the ennucleation itself. One control in this case would be examination of the effects on other regions of the brain that are not primary visual projection areas. Valverde has carried out just this control and graphically displays the summarized spine counts for neurons in both the occipital and temporal lobes of the mouse's brain shown in Fig. 9-15. Obviously, the effect on spine growth of visual stimulation is restricted to the visual regions of the brain and are not general to nonvisual regions.

A simple interpretation of this deceptively complex experiment, however, still eludes us. The data are further confounded by the fact that ennucleation is a total and drastic reduction not only of the details and geometry of the visual stimulus but of all photic energy. Some more-recent studies have added to our understanding of the problem by showing that not only the total absence of light per se but also very much more subtle aspects of visual experience can produce similar spine count changes in particular regions of the visual cortex.

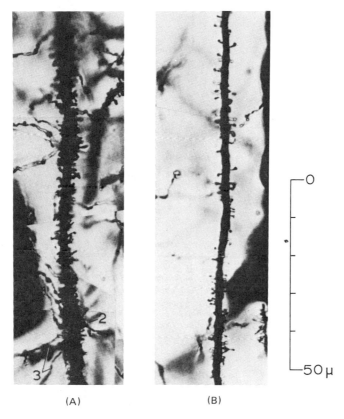

0

50 μ

(A)   (B)

FIG. 9.14   Photographs of two dendrites from the visual cortex of a 48-day-old mouse. The photo on the left shows the normal rich growth of dendritic spines and associated fibers (1, 2, and 3) on the side of the brain ipsilateral to an ennucleated eye. The photo on the right is from a pyramidal cell contralateral to the ennucleated eye. (From Valverde, ©1968, with the permission of Springer-Verlag, Inc.)

Globus, Rosenzweig, Bennett, and Diamond (1973), for example, have shown that both the spine count and the width of individual spines of pyramidal cells in the occipital cortex varies substantially as a result of whether rats lived in an "enriched" environment with many toys and much maze-running experience or in an "impoverished" environment with little stimulation. Interestingly, the spine counts and shape varied only on dendrites near the base cell body in this experiment. Spine counts and shapes on other portions of the dendritic tree of these cells changed only slightly if at all.

Greenough, Volkmar, and Juraska (1973) and Greenough and Volkmar (1973) have found essentially the same result in other portions of the brain. In their experiments, however, the most significant changes occurred in the infero-temporal cortex, and very few spine counts changed when comparisons were made in the frontal lobes. Because the temporal lobe is also tightly linked to

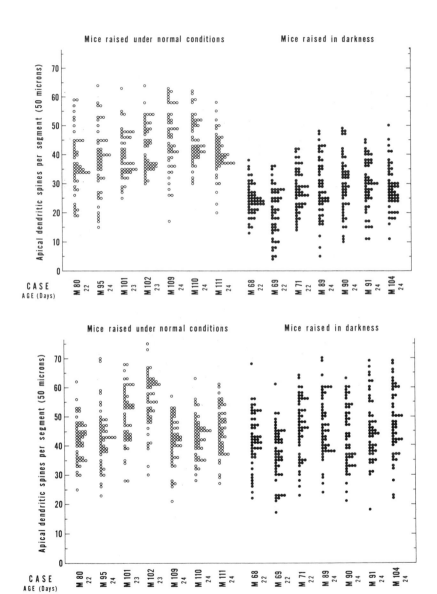

FIG. 9.15 Charts showing the number of spines on 50 micra segments of pyramidal cell dendrites as a function of location and rearing conditions. The upper figure compares the spine counts in the visual cortex for normal and dark-reared animals. There is obviously a difference as a result of the rearing conditions. The lower chart shows the counts for the temporal lobe. Little change is observed as a result of the rearing conditions in this region. Obviously the effect is specific to the visual projection regions. (From Valverde, ©1967, with the permission of Springer-Verlag, Inc.

visual inputs, and the effect is not universally found throughout the brain, further support is provided for the hypothesis that the microscopic anatomical changes in the shape of the synaptic spines are direct effects of very subtle aspects of the visual experience.

An interesting variation on this experimental theme has been carried out by Rutledge, Wright, and Duncan (1974), who used a more specifically designed learning paradigm on cats. These workers combined long-term (several weeks in duration) electrical brain stimulation with a classical conditioning paradigm in which the electrical brain stimulation served as the conditioned stimulus and a shock to the foot served as the unconditioned stimulus. The usual Golgi-type staining procedure was then used on postmortem brain samples to determine the effects of this conditioning procedure on neural and synaptic growth. These effects were compared to tissue samples taken from cats that had also received the brain stimulus and the foot shock but without pairing. Rutledge and his colleagues found a considerably greater increase in spine count when the CS and the UCS had been paired than when they had not been paired on the ipsilateral side of the brain. In addition, there seemed to be a considerably greater degree of sprouting in the brain regions contralateral to the side on which the electrical stimuli had been applied. Figure 9-16, for example, shows the difference between contralateral and ipsilateral brain tissue from a trained animal. The ipsilateral-contralateral difference seemed to be independent of whether the animal was trained, however. It occurred in all animals on the side opposite to the portion of the cortex to which the electrical stimulus had been applied even without pairing.

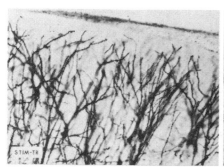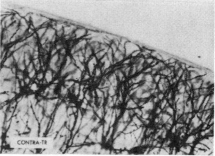

FIG. 9.16   Two photographs of dendritic growth in the cat's brain produced by electrical stimulation of the suprasylvan cortex. The picture on the left is from the side of the brain to which the electrical stimulation was applied; the picture on the right shows the much more extensive growth stimulated in the contralateral suprasylvan sulcus. The effect of stimulation therefore seems to be enhanced by some mediation by an intermediate synaptic connection. (From Rutledge, Wright, & Duncan, ©1974, with the permission of Academic Press.)

Why should the growth have been greater on the contralateral side even when the pairing had not been carried out? Rutledge and his colleagues suggest that this might be due to the fact that some sort of trans-synaptic activation is required to elicit neuron sprouting and growth. The fibers on the stimulated side of the brain were devoid of any trans-synaptic influence, for the most part; they were directly stimulated. The transcollosal connection to the other side of the cortex, however, is interrupted by synaptic junctions, and thus this criterion was met for the contralateral hemisphere.

Ipsilaterally the spine counts on the oblique and vertical portions of the dendritic tree were especially affected by the pairing aspect of the conditioning paradigm. Although the differences in spine counts were small, Rutledge believed that these results provided specific support for the hypothesis that synaptic spine growth was stimulated by the actual conditions of training that led to the acquisition of the skill and that they could not be attributed to simple stimulation effects. Thus he concluded that synaptic spine growth is a very likely correlate of learning per se.

The fact that trans-synaptic activation is also necessary for stimulation-elicited neural sprouting is also a significant and related result. It suggests that the kind of neural growth observed here is in some way closely associated with synaptic activation. The fact that the synapses are miniature neurosecretory organs may be also a part of this story. It is entirely possible that the contralateral sprouting as a result of electrical stimulation alone, and ipsilateral growth as a result of pairing, are both in some way "fertilized" by the chemicals secreted by the involved synapses.

In spite of the somewhat modest statistical differences obtained for spine counts in this study, it is a particularly important contribution. Rutledge and his colleagues provided one of the few studies in the literature that examines in detail the relative contribution of two experimental variables—simple use and CS-UCS pairing—and concludes that it is not neuronal use alone, in general, but the synaptic activation associated with learning, in particular, that accounts for synaptic neuronal growth.

An unusual opportunity to conclude this discussion of spine growth is provided by an exceedingly relevant study by Purpura (1974). Although all of the studies discussed so far have been carried out on infrahuman species of one sort or another, Purpura's study used a quite unusual experimental subject for this type of work—the human being. He compared the dendritic spine characteristics observed in retarded and normal youngsters. Figure 9-17 is a sample of his results from four different subjects. Plate A1 in this figure shows dendritic spines from a normal 6-month-old infant. This drawing has been marked with three of the standard spine shapes commonly found in microphotographs of this tissue and are classified as thin (TH), stubby (ST), or mushroom-shaped (MS). Plate B1 is a dendrite from a normal 7-year-old child who had been killed in an accident. The spines are thick and more or less similar to those shown in A1. The other two plates, A2 and B2, are from severely retarded human beings. A2 is from a living 10-month-old infant taken by biopsy, and B2 is a postmortem sample from a severely retarded 12-year-old child.

The difference between the spine shapes in the normal and retarded children is quite clear. The retarded children's dendritic spines have characteristically thin stalks and bulbous heads. The normal children have much shorter and stubbier spines. The spines are also obviously less abundant in the retarded children than they are in the normal children.

Purpura, of course, is not able to relate these microscopic anatomical differences to the specific behavioral dificiencies in other than a general way. However, these data, as well as those of others who have found similar results (e.g.,

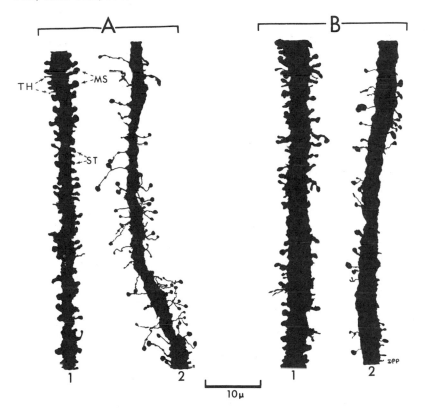

FIG. 9.17   Four cortical pyramidal cell neurons examined with the Golgi stain. (A1) is from a normal six-month-old infant; (A2) is from a retarded 10-month-old infant; (B1) is from a normal 7-year-old child; and (B2) is from a 12-year-old retarded child. Note that the normal two children show stubbier and denser spines (classified as TH = thin; ST = stubby; or MS = mushroom-shaped); the two retarded children show a much sparser sample of exceptionally long and thin spine stems. (From Purpura, ©1974, with the permission of The American Association for the Advancement of Science.)

Marin-Padilla, 1974), constitute a strong argument that the overall integrative ability of the brain's neural network can be modified by synaptic complexity in ways apparently closely associated with aspects of molar intellectual function. An obvious corollary of this hypothesis is that variations in the richness and complexity of this synaptic interconnectedness may be linked to variations in the ability to learn.

This then concludes our survey of some of the hypothetical or observed changes occurring at the synapse as a result of the organism's experience that could conceivably affect the organization of the neural network. This discussion of synaptic spines is also a transitional one; it especially emphatically recalls our attention to the probabilistic nature of the synaptic net. In the light of the microanatomy so far discussed, we may conclude that it is the average spine density and/or quality that matters rather than the presence or absence of any particular spine. A related inference is that the presence or absence of any single neuron in the net is equally insignificant. Rather, the organizational pattern of many neurons into an interacting net, as dictated by the synaptic interconnections, is the essence of brain's representation of mind, and changes in that pattern are the essential equivalents of learning.

The next question, therefore, concerns how this possible, plausible, and, in some cases, empirically observed synaptic plasticity produces the corresponding changes in the neural networks that are felt to be more directly linked to the molar aspects of the problem. Network organization and reorganization is, therefore, the topic of the next section of this chapter.

c. *Possible Network Changes Associated With Learning*

The following discussion deals with ideas that lie at the outermost boundary of speculation and credibility. The reason for this is simple. With the exception of a few instances in invertebrates (see, for example, the work of the *Aplysia* discussed in Chapter 8 and later in this section), there have been virtually no cases reported in the literature in which the individual actions of more than a few of the constituent neurons of an ensemble or network has been studied simultaneously. It is an oft-repeated axiom of this book that input-output relationships alone cannot possibly provide a unique solution to the problem of internal structure. Thus, almost without exception, each of the plausible network processes described are conceptual inventions based upon considerations of plausibility or of the activity of some model preparation far down the phylogenetic tree. Nevertheless, the exercise is useful because it reflects insights gleaned from laboratory experimentation and suggests what might be, even if it does not confirm what actually is.

It should also be appreciated that, from a certain point of view, almost all of the preceding discussion of the possible mechanisms of synaptic plasticity is irrelevant to the study of the representation of learning by neural networks. Although these mechanisms of synaptic plasticity are amenable to more direct investigation than the pattern's network organization, and they are exceedingly relevant to other conceptual levels, clearly they represent only the "technology" (i.e., the mechanisms) by which varying synaptic conductivity is effected. The mechanisms of altered synaptic conductivity themselves, however, are not the essence of learning. Rather, molar learning is much more likely encoded by changes in the state (i.e., the momentary pattern of organization) of the neural network than by the particular biochemical mechanisms that provide the means for the changes at each synapse. This is true in spite of the fact that study of network organization in vertebrates is beyond the scope of present research technology.

It is possible that several different network states can represent or encode the same molar processes. Given this logical possibility and the empirical fact that few studies have ever been carried out on neural ensembles in a way that could differentiate among the many equally plausible mechanisms of learning, little can be said with assurance concerning the particular network changes involved in vertebrate learning or any other cognitive process. What can be done is to take advantage of the speculations of such neuroscientists as Kupfermann and Pinsker (1970) concerning the kinds of neural network changes that might underlie one particular type of learning—classical conditioning.

In addition to the models shown in Fig. 9-2 that are based on variations in pacemaker response, Kupfermann and Pinsker have also invented hypothetical, simple neural networks that are reasonable models of the behavioral phenomena of classical conditioning based on synaptic plasticity. They emphasized, in the construction of these networks with varying synaptic conductivity, a very important feature of learning to which I have previously alluded only in passing; namely, that learning in general seems not to result simply from use. Rather, effective behavioral adaptation requires, in addition, some validation, success, or reinforcement of the response. Thus any proposed model of learning based on simple stimulus-response repetition or use alone is a less likely candidate than one requiring some kind of feedback of the utility of the response to the animal. A process like post-tetanic potentiation is not, therefore, of itself, likely to have all of the necessary features of a satisfactory model of learning. Kupfermann and Pinsker, therefore, add the important concept of specificity to their network model thus neurophysiologizing Neil Miller's definition of the behavioral aspects of learning presented on p. 517 in Chapter 8.

Drawing upon their laboratory studies of *Aplysia* and some of the theories of plausible synaptic plastic processes proposed in the previous section, Kupfermann and Pinsker suggest four neural networks that might equally well serve as models for classical conditioning. Figure 9-18 shows the four different models. The first (Model A) is based upon the notion that prior to conditioning a CS and

a UCS are both required to activate an interneuron (INT). After repetitive pairing of the CS and UCS, the CS acquires the ability to activate the interneuron.
The interneuron, therefore, is assumed to exhibit postsynaptic plastic behavior
at the point signified by the blackened synapse. The interneuron in Model A
serves the important function of making the action of the CS highly specific to
one particular conditioning situation.

In Model B, this interneuron is not present, but specificity can also be
achieved by a different strategem. All that is required is that the responding neuron (R) be activated during the paired presentation of the CS and the UCS. Thus
the two criteria—repetitiveness and reinforcement—for successful conditioning
are met. The repetitive activation of the plastic synapse occurs, at least some of
the time, in synchrony with the unconditioned response. The "successful use"
of R thus becomes a factor in the modulation of the EPSP at the plastic synapse
and in the increasing ability on the part of the CS to fire R.

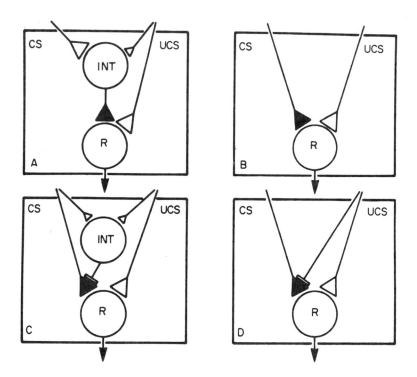

FIG. 9.18   Four different neural circuits, each of which is capable of modeling the type of
learning called *classical conditioning*. In each case, the essential plastic effect occurs at the
synapse indicated in black. See text for details. (From Kupfermann & Pinsker, ©1970, with
the permission of Academic Press.)

Both Models A and B produce response plasticity to the extent that they are capable of modulating the activity of the postsynaptic neuron (R). In each case the change in the synaptic efficacy is dependent upon the successful use of the R neuron. The synaptic changes produced, therefore, must be describable in terms of the postsynaptic receptor structure. In Models C and D, however, the critical (blackened) plastic synapse is altered presynaptically through the intervention of the UCS. In Model C, as in Model A, an interneuron is present that plays a modulating role on the critical synapse, whereas in Model D the plasticity is a direct result of the UCS acting on the neuron through which the CS is conducted.

The important point to be made by this discussion of these four alternative mechanisms is that they are all equally plausible network models. There is no present way to favor one model over any of the others as being more or less physiologically reasonable. Yet the situation modeled in this case is exceedingly simple. It involves only two or three "neurons." The number of equally plausible models, however, increases drastically with the number of neurons involved in the net. Networks that model realistic forms of vertebrate learning involve not three or four but thousands, millions, and even billions of neurons interacting through complex patterns of both inhibitory and excitatory connections. Is the situation, therefore, hopeless? Possibly not: One mitigating factor may lie in the fact that the units in Kupfermann and Pinsker's model can be thought of as representing ensembles of neurons collectively performing a single function rather than individual neurons.

This brief digression into network theory may be concluded by noting again the enormous gap between any physiological observations of synaptic plasticity on the one hand, and specific biochemical mechanisms at a more microscopic level and network effects at a more macroscopic level, on the other. The links between these levels, whereby molecular changes lead to synaptic plasticity, synaptic plasticity produces network changes, and network changes produce behavioral learning, are not yet understood.

d. *A Note on Psychochemistry*

The field of psychochemistry, which is concerned with behaviorally effective chemicals (drugs), is large enough to easily constitute another entire book. In this section, I only briefly mention some of the facts relevant to the effects of drugs on behavior. The reason for inserting these sections at this point, where they may seem to some readers to be irrelevant digressions, is that both drugs and hormones (the topic of the next section) are known to exert their influence at the level of the synapse. These chemicals modify behavior by thus modifying the connectivity of neural nets in much the same way that learning must do so. However, because the independent variables in a learning experiment are behavioral, we can never know what chemical processes are initially involved. However, when chemicals are used as independent variables, both macroscopic and microscopic analysis procedures can be used to describe the exact changes that occur at the membrane level. The analogy that may exist between these chemical effects and learning, therefore, is too close to be avoided. Models of synaptic effects produced by drugs and hormones are highly suggestive evidence of what may be going on in learning at the molecular and membrane levels.

Thompson (1975) classified psychocactive drugs into five categories: (a) sedatives and hypnotics, (b) stimulants, (c) anesthetics, analgesics, and paralytics, (d) psychotogenics (which induce psychotic symptoms), and (e) psychotherapeutics (which relieve psychotic symptoms). Table 9-1 lists various examples of these drugs and, as an aside, indicates which of them are addictive. The reader is referred to Thompson's book for a more detailed discussion of each of these categories.

This list, though only partial, is a fair indication of the wide variety of chemicals that can affect mental states. It is axiomatic within the general monistic and reductionistic philosophy of modern psychobiology that any drug affecting behavior does so because of its effects on some aspect of neural activity. And, indeed, much is known about the biochemical action of several of these psychoactive drugs. Local anesthetics, for example, are known to act directly on the plasma membrane of peripheral neurons to reduce ionic transport. They thereby can directly interfere with neural conduction. Some psychoactive substances are also known to act on particular regions of the central nervous system.

It seems likely, however, that most drugs that affect mental states act at the level of the most chemically sensitive parts of the central nervous system—the synapses themselves. Table 9-2, which has been abstracted from Dunn and Bondy (1974), lists a large number of drugs that are known to modify synaptic action by interfering with the release, diffusion, reception, or activation of transmitter substances. This table is organized in terms of the transmitter substances and indicates the drugs, the effect, and the presumed biochemical action of each where known.

The important point is that the state of the neural network can be altered by the action of specific chemicals on synapses. Certain regions of the brain are selectively affected by certain drugs, because they are particularly rich in one or another kind of synaptic transmitter substance. On the basis of which transmitter is predominantly used, certain subsystems of the brain can be defined. One well defined system, for example, includes those regions that mainly use serotonin as their transmitter substance and thus are sensitive to any drug that affects serotonin metabolism. These regions are concentrated in the raphe nuclei located near the interface between the lower midbrain and the upper pons (Snyder, 1976). Acetylcholine use probably also defines a separate system but it is widely distributed throughout the brain and has not yet been satisfactorily demarcated. On the other hand, a dopamine system, including the substantia nigra and basal ganglia, among other nuclei, is sharply defined by the predominant use of this transmitter substance in its constituent synapses. A norepinephrine system has also been defined. Figures 9-19, 9-20, and 9-22 show lateral and dorsal views of the norepinephrine and dopamine systems, respectively. Be-

TABLE 9.1

Classes of behaviorally effective drugs. (From Thompson, ©1967, after McIlwain, with the permission of Harper & Row, Publishers.)

Drug class	Group	Example	Evidence of addiction?
Sedatives and Hypnotics			
	General	Alcohol	yes
	Barbiturates	Phenobarbital	yes
	Bromides	Potassium bromide	no
	Chloral derivatives	Chloral hydrate	yes
Stimulants			
	Analeptics	Pentylenetetrazol	no
	Nicotinics	Nicotine	yes
	Psychotogenics	Lysergic acid diethylamide	
	Sympathomimetics	Amphetamine	yes
	Xanthines	Caffeine	yes
Anesthetics, analgesics, and paralytics	Analgesics	Opium derivatives	yes
	Local anesthetics	Cocaine	yes
		Procaine	no
	General anesthetics	Nitrous oxide	no
		Diethyl ether	no
		Chloroform	no
	Paralytics	*d*-tubocurarine	no
Psychotogenics			
	Cannabis sativa	Marijuana	no
	Ergot derivative	Lysergic acid diethlyamide	no
	Lophophora williamsii	Mescaline	no
	Psilocybe mexicana	Psilocybin	no
Psychotherapeutics			
	Anti-anxiety:		
	Propanediols	Meprobamate	yes
	Benzodiazephines	Chlordiazepoxide	yes
	Barbiturates	Phenobarbital	
	Antidepressant:		
	MAO inhibitors	Tranylcypromine	no
	Dibenzazepines	Imipramine	no
	Antipsychotic:		
	Rauwolfia alkaloids	Reserpine	no
	Phenothiazines	Chlorpromazine	no
	Stimulant	Amphetamine	

TABLE 9.2

Drugs that affect synaptic conductivity classified in terms of the neurotransmitter on which they exert their effects. (Adapted from Dunn & Bondy, 1974, with the permission of Spectrum Publishers.)

Drug	Effect	Mechanism
(a) Acetylcholine		
hemicholinium	lowers tissue ACh	blocks choline uptake
botulinus toxin	antagonist	blocks ACh release
d-tubocurarine (active principal of curare), gallamine (Flaxedil)	antagonists	reversibly block ACh receptors
naja naja toxin, α-bungarotoxin	antagonists	bind ACh receptor
atropine, scopolamine	antagonist	blocks muscarinic receptors
nicotine	nicotinic agonist	mimics ACh at nicotinic receptors
carbachol (carbamylcholine)	agonist	mimics ACh
(b) Catecholamines		
α-methyl-p-tyrosine (αMpT)	depletes catecholamines	inhibits tyrosine hydroxylase
reserpine	depletes catecholamines	inhibits vesicular storage (see also serotonin)
diethyldithiocarbarnate	depletes NE	inhibits DBH by chelating Cu^{2+}
amphetamine	noradrenergic agonist	probably multiple: stimulates release *and* mimics NE
phenoxybenzamine, ergot alkaloids, phentolamine	α-antagonist	blocks α-receptors
dichloroisoproterenol, propanolol	β-antagonist	blocks β-receptors
haloperidol, spiroperidol, phenothiazines (chlorpromazine, fluphenazine)		block dopamime receptors
lithium salts	depress NE	unknown
cocaine, amitryptyline, imipramine, desmethylimipramine (DMI)	deplete NE	inhibit NE reuptake
6-hydroxydopamine	destroys catecholamine-containing neurons	unknown; probably taken up into catacholaminergic cells by the selective reuptake systems

TABLE 9.2 *(continued)*

Drug	Effect	Mechanism
(c) Serotonin		
p-chlorophenylalanine (pCPA)	depletes 5HT	inhibits tryptophan hydroxylase (and tyrosine hydroxylase)
probenicid	elevates 5HT	blocks 5H1AA efflux
reserpine (see also catecholamines)	depletes 5HT	inhibits vesicular storage
amitryptyline	agonist	inhibits reuptake
methysergide, cinanserin, cyproheptadine	antagonist	block postsynaptic receptor
lysergic acid diethyl-amide (LSD)	complex effects	may both block and mimic 5HT ation (LSD also inhibits the degra-dation of substance P)
5, 6 dihydroxytrypt-amine	destroys 5HT containing neurones	unknown but probably analogous to 6-hydroxydopamine
(d) Gamma-aminobutyric acid		
hydroxylamine, amino-oxyacetic acid	increase GABA	inhibit GAD and GABA-T, but GAD less than GABA-T
tetanus toxin	cerebral excitant	inhibits GABA (and gly) release
bicuculline	cerebral excitant	blocks GABA receptors
picrotoxin	cerebral excitant	may block GABA receptors
(e) Glycine		
tetanus toxin	cerebral excitant	inhibits glycine (and GABA) release
strychnine	cerebral excitant (con-vulsant at higher doses)	blocks glycine receptor activity
(f) Glutamate		
glutamic acid diethyl ester	antagonist	blocks glutamate receptor
glutamic acid dimethyl ester	agonist	competitively blocks reuptake

NORADRENALINE

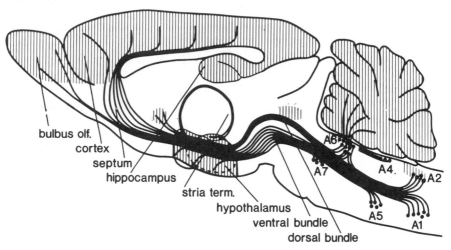

FIG. 9.19 A lateral diagram of the rat's brain showing the major ascending norepinephrine system. (From Ungerstedt, ©1971, with the permission of *Acta Physiologica Scandinavica*.)

DOPAMINE

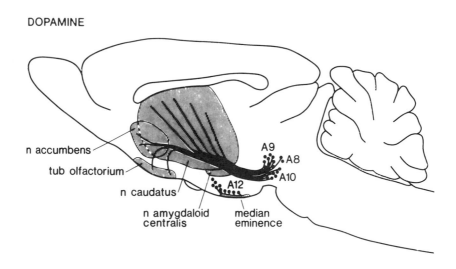

FIG. 9.20 A lateral diagram of the rat's brain showing the dopamine system. (From Ungerstedt, ©1971, with the permission of *Acta Physiological Scandinavica*.)

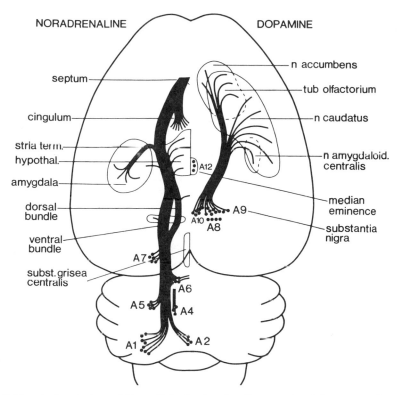

NORADRENALINE   DOPAMINE

FIG. 9.21 A dorsal view of the rat's brain showing the norepinephrine system (on the left-hand side) and the dopamine system (on the right-hand side). (From Ungerstedt, ©1971, with the permission of *Acta Physiologica Scandinavica*.)

cause of the localized sensitivities implied by the existence of these systems, it is certain that the application of certain of the psychologically active drugs selectively affect both specific nuclei and specific kinds of synapses. Drugs, therefore, can target particular regions of the brain in ways we did not previously have the power to accomplish.

The various systems are not independent, however, and must interact among themselves. Groves, Wilson, Young, and Rebec (1975) have pointed out the existence of a supersystem, as shown in Fig. 9-22. Within this complex are found interactions among the inhibitory dopamine, the excitatory acetylcholine, and the inhibitory GABA synaptic systems. This supersystem may be collectively involved in both behavioral and motor deterioration typical of Parkinson's disease.

To illustrate the current state of our knowledge concerning the details of the biochemical action of psychologically active drugs, let us consider two important papers dealing with synaptic opiate receptors (Snyder, 1975) and with the action of antipsychotic drugs (Iversen, 1975). These two papers were published

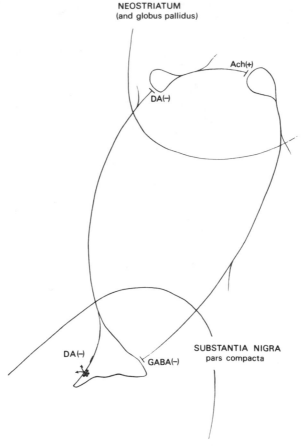

NEOSTRIATUM
(and globus pallidus)

Ach(+)

DA(-)

DA(-)   GABA(-)

SUBSTANTIA NIGRA
pars compacta

FIG. 9.22   A "supersystem" within the brain composed of subsystems that use dopamine, acetycholine, and GABA as the transmitter substances, respectively. This group of interlocking subsystems forms a "self-inhibiting" feedback loop that may be the basis of the action of some of the antipsychotic and psychotropic drugs. (From Groves, Wilson, Young, & Rebec, ©1975, with the permission of The American Association for the Advancement of Science.)

together after jointly sharing the distinguished F. O. Schmitt prize for neuroscience research in 1975.

Snyder's work deals with the action of poppy extracts, generically known as the opiates, on the nervous system. Specifically, he sought to determine where in the cell opiates work. It has been assumed that opium must be exerting its effects by being chemically bound to specific receptor sites on the neuron. But exactly where had not been known. Chemical analyses of the brain had shown the regions of the brain in which the highest level of opiate receptor binding occurs are the amygdala, the medial thalamus, and a number of the hypothalamic nuclei. Therefore, opiates seem to work selectively on the regions usually considered to be part of the limbic system.

Within these regions, Snyder was further able to determine the portions of the constituent neurons that seemed to possess the highest level of opiate binding activity. This was done by analyzing the binding capability of various fractions of neuron preparations that had been broken up and separated by a special centrifuging procedure. Snyder reported that little receptor activity (i.e., opiate binding) was found in any fraction of the centrifuged neuron other than in the region of the synapses. Indeed, very little receptor activity is found in the portion containing the synaptic vesicles; only the centrifuged fraction containing synaptic membranes are rich in the chemicals that must be the receptor materials. Although he could not say with certainty whether the receptors are in the presynaptic or postsynaptic regions, Snyder felt it was likely that opiates exert their influence (just as transmitter substances do) on receptor sites on the postsynaptic membranes.

Some progress has been made recently in identifying the molecular structure of the opiate receptor. Simon, Hiller, and Edelman (1975), using a chromatographic technique, have shown that the opiate receptor is most likely a macromolecule with a molecular weight of about 370,000. This may also be a fairly good general description of the heretofore mysterious postsynaptic receptor site.

Iversen (1975), in considering the action of the antipsychotic drugs, has gathered similar data. Drugs effective in treating schizophrenia, for example, are typically found to be most effective in changing neural activity in synapses using dopamine as their main transmitter substance. Iversen states that recent evidence suggests that antipsychotic drugs may possibly work presynaptically by increasing the rate at which dopamine is secreted. This suggests that some psychosis may, conversely, be the result of a deficiency in the release of this particular transmitter.

Perhaps the fairest thing to say with regard to the action of drugs on mental states, however, is that although a little is known about the manner in which they exert their effects at the synaptic membrane and biochemical levels, absolutely nothing is known of the neural network reorganizations they produce. Although chemicals have been successfully used in therapy, and although theories abound concerning the relationship of particular kinds of brain chemistry and specific behavioral disorders (most notably the relationship between the catecholamines, like dopamine, and schizophrenia, and between the manic-depressive syndrome and the biogenic amines), the details of the relationships are not yet known to the degree that would allow us to say "we understand" what happens when these drugs are administered. For all practical purposes, it must be admitted that both psychotherapeutics and psychotogenics are used without understanding and without a theoretical basis of their behavioral effects. They are usually discovered accidentally and applied according to hit-and-miss procedures.

Even the best research in the field of drug therapy for psychoses, therefore, is characterized by a "barefoot empiricism," and the most effective chemotherapies operate with little knowledge of the significant changes made in neural organization. Experiments reputed to have found specific chemical correlates of psychotic states [e.g., the reported low level of dopamine activity in schizophrenics, Wise & Stein (1973)] often turn out to be the results of unanticipated artifacts [e.g., the reduced levels of dopamine activity have been attributed to prolonged storage of the cadavers by Wyatt, Schwartz, Erdelyi, & Barchas, (1975)].

Some aspects of the chemistry of the synaptic effects produced by antipsychotic drugs, on the other hand, are relatively well-known. Figure 9-23 is a chart showing the relationship between the average clinical doses of a large variety of these substances and the concentrations that produce a 50% decrement in dopamine release by synapses. This figure is based on a study by Seeman and Lee (1975). Clearly, the clinical tradition, almost without realizing it, has resulted in dosage levels for a wide variety of drugs that seem to be highly correlated with a constant alteration of synaptic function. Nevertheless, there is no way to bridge the gap between this kind of knowledge of synaptic chemistry and knowledge of the network modifications that ultimately must correspond to the changes in behavior. When neurochemists examine the chemistry of the synapses, they are studying the technology of the neural elements. But this is a secondary aspect of the problem, and little progress has been made in understanding the essence of the main problem—the network state.

Sadly, this particular field of clinical psychobiology, so important in its personal and social implications, has contributed little to a fundamental understanding of the relationship between the brain and mind.

e. A Note on Hormones

Another powerful class of chemicals affecting behavior includes the substances known as *hormones.* Hormones are chemical substances secreted by the endocrine (ductless) glands of the body and thus are transported about the body in the blood. They are powerfully effective in regulating a wide variety of behaviors, as well as metabolic processes, and conversely are also produced in amounts and kinds that covary with mental states. For example, injection of the gonadal hormones (androgens or estrogens) can induce reproductive behavior specific to each of the sexes, and sexual activity seems to regulate the amount of hormones generated. Removal of the source of these gonadal hormones by castration can lead to serious deficiencies in the organism's sexual behavior, as well as in its growth and maturation. The effects of individual hormones are not simple; there are complicated interactions, for example, between the androgens and estrogens; androgenic effects in males seem to depend upon an adequate

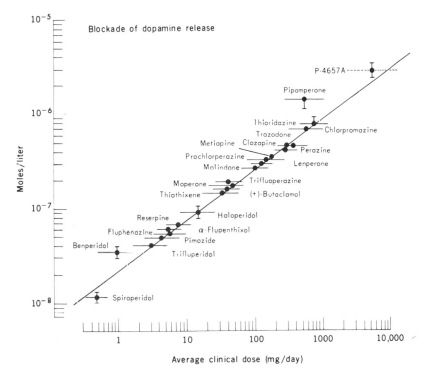

FIG. 9.23   A natural experiment in psychochemotherapeutics. This graph displays the relationship between the clinically effective dosages of various antischizophrenic drugs and their measured chemical ability to reduce the amount of dopamine released from the neostriatal region of the rat's brain. Amazingly, the chemical strength is linearly correlated with the clinically effective dose. (From Seeman & Lee, ©1975, with the permission of The American Association for the Advancement of Science.)

supply of estrogen [see Roy & Wade (1975) for a good, brief, and up-to-date summary of this problem].

Another hormonal influence on behavior is becoming clear. Pituitary hormones such as adrenocorticotrophic hormone (ACTH) and melanocyte-stimulating hormone (MSH) are thought to be intimately related to the acquisition of skills in instrumental conditioning experiments. This is particularly true in cases in which the reinforcement is the consummation of some basic drive. Although it cannot be asserted with certainty that the effect of these hormones is not an indirect one (perhaps they work by altering motivational levels or by varying the amount of protein available for synaptic growth) these hormonal effects may be quite direct and specifically mediated by their influence on transmission chemistry of specific types of synapses.

As in the case of the psychotherapeutic drugs themselves, there seem to be direct effects of some hormones on the brain, and it is most likely once again that these effects are mediated by interactions between the hormones and the synaptic transmitter substance. The brain is considered by many neuroscientists, therefore, to be a major hormonal receptor organ. For example, Fig. 9-24 shows the regions of the female rat brain in which estrogen concentrating neurons may be found.

On the other hand, the brain is also a neuroendocrine secretory organ. The hypothalamus, for example, secretes a hormone, vasopressin, that can affect the secretion rates of other endocrine glands or affect the blood pressure directly. An especially interesting related possibility is that behavioral states may be associated with the production of hormones in a way that would allow assays of those hormones to be used as diagnostic tools in psychotherapy [see Carroll, Curtis, & Mendelf (1976a; 1976b), for example].

Once again, the situation is opaque at the organizational and informational level at which mental processes must be represented. Although relationships have been shown between hormones and behavior and between hormones and synaptic effects, the exact relationship between the specific synaptic effects and behavior eludes us.

B.   GLOBAL THEORIES OF THE NEURAL BASIS OF LEARNING

In the introduction to this chapter I pointed out that there was little disagreement among the various theories of the neural basis of learning with regard to their basic premises. I asserted that the various theories differed mainly in terms of the attention given to one or another level or aspect of the problem and not in terms of any particular controversy among alternative explanations within any level. In this section, this point is expanded upon, and two modern theories of learning, one proposed by Hydén and the other by Pribram, that stand at the extremes in terms of their different emphasis on molecular biochemistry and field interactions, respectively, are discussed. The key point of this discussion that the reader should keep in mind is that upon close examination, there is more agreement among those theories than there is disagreement. Each accepts the central biochemical role of RNA metabolism; each hypothesizes a synaptic locus of the plastic neuronal effects; each believes that neurons must be concatenated into large networks to achieve their meaningful molar function; and each accepts the basic concept that the global activities of these networks can only be measured by examination of the compound action potentials that are the equivalent of the statistical sum of the actions of the individual units.

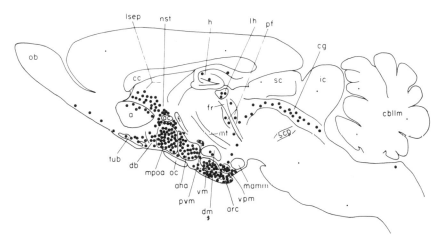

FIG. 9.24   This map of the brain shows the points at which estrogen binding sites have been located in the brain of the female rat. Abbreviations of the various nuclei indicated are: a = nucleus accumbens; ac = anterior commissure; aha = anterior hypothalamic area; arc = arcuate nucleus; cbllm = cerebellum; cc = corpus callosum; cg = central grey; db = diagonal band of Broca; dm = dorsomedial nucleus of the hypothalamus; f = fornix; fr = fasciculus retroflexus; h = hippocampus; ic = inferior colliculus; lh = lateral hanenula; lsep = lateral septum; mamm = mammillary bodies; mpoa = medial preoptic area; mt = mammillothalamic tract; nst = bed nucleus of the stria terminalis; ob = olfactory bulb; oc = optic chiasm; pf = nucleus parafascicularis; pvm = paraventricular nucleus (magnocellular); sc = superior colliculus; scp = superior cerebellar peduncle; tub = olfactory tubercle; vm = ventromedial nucleus; and vpm = ventral premammillary nucleus. (From Pfaff & Keiner, ©1973, with the permission of The Wistar Press.)

The two points of view to be discussed are not microtheories in the same way as those presented earlier in this chapter. Rather, although each has its own emphasis, the two examples now considered share the common characteristic that they both are more global attempts to describe the interactions among the several levels of the problem.

The most highly developed, clearly explained, and broadly conceived theory emphasizing the biochemical level is that proposed by Holger Hydén (1970). Most germane to the present discussion, however, is the fact that his theory transcends several levels from the most microscopic to the most macroscopic. Another example of a theory that crosses several conceptual levels is to be found in the work of Karl Pribram (e.g., Pribram, 1969; Pribram, Nuwer, & Baron, 1974). Pribram's model is based on a proposed analogy between learning and the optical hologram. This theory, which stresses the aggregate action of neurons, speculates about learning mechanisms that might use changing interference processes among waves of neural activity similar to interference patterns produced by optical systems as the basis of behavioral change.

Of the many possible neural models of learning and memory that could be presented, these two are the most useful, because the emphasis in each is among the most extreme in terms of the biological level emphasized. Hydén's emphasis is ultramicroscopic; Pribram's is just this side of the molar mental process itself. Discussing the details of these two alternative theoretical viewpoints reveals the contemporary consensus in sharpest contrast.

1. Hydén's Theory

As mentioned in Chapter 8, since the early 1960s there has been considerable interest and research effort directed toward elucidating what seems to be an important role of certain macromolecules in the memory process. The basic idea behind this work is that some of the large molecules, also known to be involved in genetic information storage and reproduction, and in particular RNA_t (transfer ribonucleic acid), may play important roles in mediating individuals as well as evolutionary memories. Although it is not certain, it seems likely that the idea was originally based only on the analogy between the two different meanings of the word *memory*—one defined in terms of the individual and one in terms of the species. Another more compelling influence, however, was the discovery that RNA_t and certain associated enzymes did play important biological roles in protein synthesis and, thus, ultimately in all growth processes. When early theories suggested that synaptic plasticity may also be framed in terms of growth, another logical link in an inferential chain implicating these macromolecules in memory was formed. The fact that the brain seems to be especially rich in the variety of types of RNA molecules compared to other organs of the body (Brown & Church, 1971) is also another suggestive argument that this particular biochemical is deeply involved in brain function, in general, and memory, in particular.

It is beyond the scope of this chapter to exhaustively consider the very large body of published reports in which biochemical changes have been shown to be associated with learning. The interested reader who wishes to look further at this problem should read two especially readable and thoughtful reviews by Agranoff (1974) and Horn, Rose, and Bateson (1973). Although both reviews strongly support the contributory role of the genetic macromolecules in learning, both also emphatically make the point that: "that macromolecular synthesis is involved in memory formation remains a hypothesis" (Agranoff, 1974, p. 618). This caveat is probably the key statement in this exceedingly complex field in which the biochemical and behavioral data have met and been compared.

One excellent example of the meaningful ways in which biochemical studies of learning can be carried out at the molar level is illustrated in the work of Bernard Agranoff and Roger Davis of the University of Michigan (Agranoff, 1967;

Davis & Agranoff, 1966; Agranoff, Davis, & Brink, 1965). They have shown that in the goldfish, formation of long-term memory seems to be selectively blocked by the injection of puromyacin. (Puromyacin is an antibiotic that is also known to act selectively to block the formation of new protein.) A fish that had successfully learned to avoid an electrical shock will act as if it were naive on subsequent retesting if this protein formation-blocking antibiotic is injected immediately following the original training. In all other regards, the fish appeared to be perfectly normal. There is no depression of the general metabolic functions (or activity) or any reduction of the fish's ability to initially learn the task. By selectively injecting puromyacin at different times following the training, a critical time period, presumably closely related to the time at which the consolidation of short-term into long-term memory occurs, can be identified. The consolidation was found to be complete in about 2 to 3 hours.

The point of these experiments is that they suggest that the consolidation process probably does involve the creation of new proteins in some manner and thus RNA_t. This conclusion, it must be repeated, does not mean that the memory itself is stored in the atomic configuration of a macromolecule, but rather that some aspect of a protein synthesis process (possibly including the growth of new synaptic membranes or enlargement of old ones) is involved in the consolidation of long-term memories.

On the other hand, macromolecules have been incorporated into learning theory in some ways that are now almost universally appreciated to be erroneous. Those psychobiologists who suggest that the macromolecules formed during learning are constructed with specific amino acid sequences in accord with the experience, and that these amino acid sequences represent a readable and specific code for experience, have a difficult row to hoe! I have already mentioned this work in Chapter 8. In general, any hypothesis that purports that memories can be chemically extracted and transferred with a high degree of specificity to other animals is not held in high regard by contemporary psychobiologists. Although the idea is seductively attractive and has attracted a large amount of popular attention, there is even less scientific proof for this extreme macromolecular coding version of the biochemical hypothesis than for the more general one that assumes merely that some sort of biochemical synthesis is in some undefined way involved in learning. For the reader who wishes to pursue this topic further, two useful sources that present more positive arguments for the controversial idea of memory transfer are Adam (1971) and Ungar (1970). Having briefly reviewed the relevant background, I can now discuss the kind of biochemical approach that is acceptable to contemporary psychobiology. I consider as my example of an acceptable model what is certainly the most specific and highly developed theory of biochemical involvement yet proposed. Holger Hydén (Hydén, 1970) has outlined a theory of memory that mainly emphasizes the RNA changes occurring within the brain as a result of learning.

The particular training paradigm he used to carry out his related empirical studies was an ingenious one. It took advantage of the anatomical organization of the rat brain to provide intrinsic controls. Rats, Hydén observed, like people, tend to be either dominantly right- or left-pawed. In rats particularly, the sensory-motor regions that control each paw are found almost entirely in the contralateral portion of the brain. Thus if an animal is trained to use the left paw on some task, Hydén suggested that any induced biochemical changes would be mainly found only in the right hemisphere. The left hemisphere, he felt, should be mainly unaffected with regard to its chemical constituents by the training trials. Although this premise of the study is open to criticism, as is the assumption that the effects of learning should be localized, it did turn out in this case that, upon analysis of brain tissue from the contralateral experimental and ipsilateral control areas, substantial differences in the RNA content were observed. Not only did the average amount of RNA increase from about 22 $\mu\mu$g to 31 $\mu\mu$g within each neuron from the contralateral side of the rat's brain, but there was also a substantial and significant change in the relative amounts of the RNA produced. The ratio of the four bases, adenine, guanine, cytosine, and uracil, which carry the code for the amino acids that are the building blocks in protein synthesis, changes drastically as a result of the training but only on the contralateral side of the brain. The changes in the ratios of the various bases are shown in Table 9-3 for the several conditions of Hydén's experiments. Clearly, Hydén's data indicates that learning is associated with changes in the biochemistry of related brain areas even if it is still impossible to say exactly what the role of the changes is in mediating synaptic plasticity.

Hydén's major contribution is the specific hypothesis he generated to explain the nature of these RNA changes and the possible link they may provide between the biochemical level and the individual neuroelectrical level. His theory also includes possible links with the ensemble network level and, in a more speculative manner, even between the ensemble and molar behavioral levels.

Before discussing the details of Hydén's theory, it is important to explicitly point out that this model, although involving structural specificity at the molecular level, is completely different in orientation than the molecular storage model embodied in the transfer experiments. The transfer theory specifically postulates that patterns of neural excitation produce macromolecular configurations that are themselves the repository of the engram. The learned behavior can be transferred between animals, it is asserted, because the necessary and sufficient information is encoded within the structure of the macromolecule by its specific structure.

Hydén's approach is quite different, and his disdain for the other kind of molecular theorizing is quite explicit. He says (Hydén, 1970): "At this point, I would like to stress that no data support the view that brain cells contain mech-

TABLE 9.3

Shifts in ratio of RNA bases produced as a result of learning. (From Hydén, ©1970, with the permission of Academic Press.)

	Controls Mean	Learning Mean	Change in percent	*P*
Adenine	18.4 ± .48	20.1 ± .11	+9.2	.02
Guanine	26.5 ± .64	28.7 ± .90	+8.3	.01
Cytosine	36.8 ± .97	31.5 ± .75	−14.4	.01
Uracil	18.3 ± .48	19.6 ± .56	+7.1	.05
$\frac{A + G}{C + U}$	0.81 ± .27	.95 ± .35	+17.3	.01
$\frac{G + C}{A + U}$	1.72 ± .054	1.51 ± 0.26	−12.2	.02

anistically taping 'memory molecules' that store information in a linear way. This is biological nonsense [p. 106]." Hydén's concept of the role of RNA, therefore, is quite different in essentials from that of the transfer theorists. He accepts the fact that biochemical changes are induced in RNA molecules but asserts that these changes represent the realization of preexisting and genetically determined structural patterns that are intrinsic and are not created as a specific result of the experience.

But how is this selective molecular production guided and controlled? The answer to this question is the essence of Hydén's theorietical contribution. He bases his answer upon quantitative estimates that only a small portion of the genetic information (the genotype) contained within a neuron is actually embodied in its molecular structure (the phenotype). Hydén suggests that portions of this extra encoded information, genetically available to produce proteins, are activated by the pattern of neural activity of the neuron. Thus specific new RNA sequences are not created by the learning experience as a result of training, but rather, existing RNA (i.e., within the genotype) is triggered to produce a specific phenotype protein. The specific nature of the produced proteins governing synaptic conductivity determines how and when the neuron will respond when subsequent input stimulus patterns are received. Ultimately, a richer than normal variety of RNA will be reflected in a richer than normal (and perhaps different) supply of protein molecules. These proteins determine the functional relationships between neurons and thus the interconnectivity characteristics of the neural network.

An important corollary of the premise that the genotype is only partially expressed in the phenotypic RNA synthesis, Hydén asserts, is that the particular phenotypes that are produced can be determined by the electrical and chemical environment of the gene. The particular environmental mechanism, which Hydén suggests to be capable of regulating which of the possible RNA codes will be actually expressed, is a change in the ionic equilibrium across the synaptic membrane produced by perturbations in the local electrical fields. These fields, in turn, are produced by the prevailing patterns of neural activity.

Thus, his chain of logic is: When a neuron is stimulated to respond with action potentials, these action potentials produce electrical fields that produce ionic equilibrium changes that select the specific phenotypic form of the RNA that will be produced from among all of the possible genotypic possibilities. The RNA, in turn, is able to direct the production of particular proteins, whose structure is directly associated with determining the subsequent patterns of neural activity by virtue of their involvement in synaptic conductivity and stimulus selectivity.

In particular, the produced proteins condition synapses to respond only when certain input conditions are met. Therefore, whether the neuron will respond in a retrial depends upon the key (the pattern of incoming neural activity) fitting the lock (the protein regulated synaptic sensitivities). An important advantage of this model is that each neuron is not limited to respond to a single pattern of activity. Rather, it is capable of participating in the action of a large number of neural nets to the extent that the appropriate proteins for each net have been manufactured within the cell and have conditioned the appropriate synapses.

Glia play an unusually important role in Hydén's theory. Glia have conventionally been thought to play merely a supportive (both mechanically and metabolically) role in the brain. Hydén, however, noting that glia are particularly efficient producers of RNA, suggested that there may actually be some transfer of appropriate RNA from glial cells to neurons after neural activity has stimulated the manufacture of the RNA in the glia.

Finally, Hydén suggested that three criteria must be met before a neuron will fire in a subsequent retrial situation that recalls information from the engram. First, the electrical pattern produced by the incoming activity must be appropriate to the original activity-produced specific proteins; second, the appropriate proteins must be present; and third, and most speculatively, there may actually be a requirement that some additional RNA be transferred from the glia to the neuron at the moment of retrieval. Figure 9-25 graphically depicts the various elements of Hydén's theory.

In summary, Hydén has proposed a model that emphasizes molecular changes to account for the plastic changes in individual neurons that produce selective functioning of a neural network. It is not a theory of molecular information storage per se (he does not propose that information is stored in molecules),

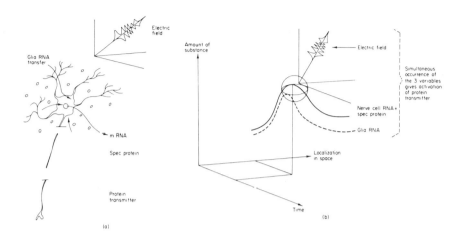

FIG. 9.25   Diagrammatic sketches of Hydén's molecularly oriented theory of learning. (A) shows the hypothetical process by which the neuron is modified and the specific proteins produced during the learning phase; (B) depicts the recall or retrieval process. The details of the model are described in the text. (From Hydén, ©1970, with the permission of Academic Press.)

but rather a model in which protein synthesis simply provides an alternative explanation of the basis of functional changes in synapses and neurons. Such an approach has a different emphasis but is not in conflict with any hypothetical mechanisms of synaptic plasticity discussed previously. It is entirely possible, and indeed quite likely, that the protein generation process Hydén invokes is the mechanism responsible for the synaptic conductivity changes. This is so because postsynaptic receptor sites are most probably proteins themselves as suggested by such studies as the work on opiate receptors discussed on p. 661.

Nor is Hydén's theory in conflict with the field theories of the kind I describe shortly. His molecular theory simply deals with mechanisms that might be thought of as the fine grain of the fields. It is a pleasant surprise to read Hydén's eclectic approach in contrast to some of the microtheories previously described. He continually refers to the role these molecular changes might have in defining the "Gestalt" of the nervous system and is clearly aware of the multiplicity of levels with which the problem of the neural basis of learning is concerned.

Hydén's theory is also consistent with a number of criteria that any successful neuronal theory of learning must satisfy. It does not depend on any particular locus in the brain in accord with Lashley's still generally accepted ideas of distributed memory, and it does not depend on circulating signals for the representation of long-term memory but invokes stable structural changes; but it does not deny other roles for patterns of circulating activity, and it is consistent with the many biochemical experiments showing RNA involvement in learning. Most important, however, is the fact that Hydén's perspective transcends many levels of the problem and provides at least the rudiments of a global approach to the neural basis of learning. In this regard, the general contribution of Hydén's theory may hold true even if it is incorrect in some biochemical, anatomical, or physiological details.

2.   A Field Model of Learning—Pribram's Theory

Another global theory of memory that transcends many levels of analysis is Karl Pribram's holographic hypothesis. The general approach embodied in this quantitative description of interacting neural fields is guided by many of the same criteria that characterize Hydén's thinking. Pribram was especially influenced by Lashley's original observation that memory seemed to be distributed rather widely throughout the nervous system as well as the more modern confirmations of the concept of distribution in the neurophysiological work of Galambos, Norton, & Frommer (1967) and Chow (1968).

The notion of interacting fields of neuronal activity had been around for a remarkably long period of time. Goldscheider (1906) was only one of many scientists, according to Pribram, who proposed interference-type theories as possible explanations of perceptual phenomena over 70 years ago, and we have already noted Lashley's adherence to this idea. Pribram and some of his co-workers (see, for example, Pribram, 1969; and Pribram, Nuwer, & Baron, 1974) have recently extended some of these notions of interference patterns from perception to memory. They accomplished this by merging new information concerning cellular plasticity with the mathematics developed to describe some novel optical systems that produce three-dimensional photographs called *holograms*.

Holography, originally conceived by Denis Gabor (1948; 1949) and first physically implemented by Emmet Leith and Juris Upatnieks (1962), is a lensless system of photography in which intereference among wave fronts of coherent light[4] is responsible for image storage and reconstruction. Figure 9-26 is a diagram of an optical system that can be used to make the images or holograms.

---

[4]Coherent light is produced by an electro-optical device known as a *laser*. The laser (an acronym for *l*ight *a*mplification by the *s*timulated *e*mission of *r*adiation) produces virtually monochromatic light in which all of the peaks of the electromagnetic waves are in phase. There is, therefore, an enormous amount of energy concentrated in what may appear to be a very small beam of light. But more important is that the light from a laser is highly directional (it may be directed from the earth to a target only a few feet wide on the moon), and any interference effects are regular and reinforced. This regularity of interference effects is in sharp contrast to the random and irregular interference of ordinary noncoherent light that, for example, may be produced by an incandescent source.

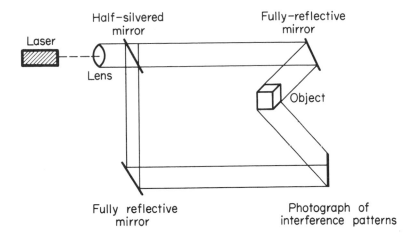

FIG. 9.26   The arrangement of a laser and some plane mirrors required to produce a photographic hologram.

A beam of coherent monochromatic light is shown directly on a photographic plate and at the same time on an object from which it is reflected to the plate. The reflected and direct light interact at the plane of the photographic plate to produce interference patterns that can image the object.

The photographic plate, if observed under normal light, will appear as a disorganized jumble of apparently irregular interference patterns. When another beam of coherent light (of the same frequency as that originally used) is passed through the plate, however, the light in that beam reconstructs the original image with great clarity.[5] The reconstruction system is shown in Fig. 9-27.

Two important features of holograms are particularly important, both in terms of the physics of the optical system and in terms of its use as a possible model of the neural basis of learning. First, the hologram is a totally distributed form of recording images. Any portion of the plate, no matter how small, contains all of the image. Although the image will be increasingly degraded (increasingly blurred) as a smaller portion of the photographic plate is used, all portions of the original object are represented everywhere on the plate.

Second, the hologram is intrinsically three-dimensional. Three-dimensional objects are recorded in a form that allows their stereoshapes to be reconstructed from the two-dimensional holographic plate. Thus a projected holographic image is seen in depth. As the viewer moves his head, he has different views of the scene over wide angles (as much as 160 degrees or so) before his viewpoint passes out of the line of the reconstructing light.

[5]It has recently been pointed out by Leith (1976) that, coherent light is not necessary to make a hologram but that it can be made with any light—even that from an ordinary incandescent bulb.

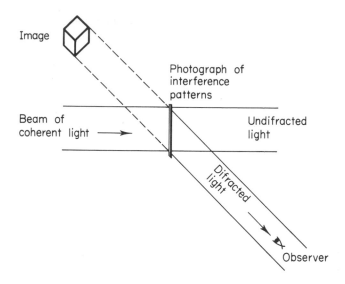

FIG. 9.27   The arrangement of the photographic hologram and a beam of coherent light that allows a three-dimensional image to be reconstructed.

Another important aspect of the hologram that Pribram and his colleagues stress in arguing for their model is the relevance of the Fourier transform mathematics that can be used to describe the interference of optical wavefronts. They note the other Fourier models of perception as being thus incorporated into their theory. As I noted in an earlier chapter, Fourier models are now suspect in terms of their actual neural implementation. This particular aspect of Pribram's theory, therefore, is probably open to the same criticisms.[6]

It is important to note that Pribram's approach should not be misconstrued to suggest that he believes there is actually an *optical* hologram in the head. Rather, Pribram is quite clear that the optical hologram is only an analog of the neural mechanism of the brain that he believes exhibits some of the same distributed transformational properties. It is the concept of interacting and distributed fields of neural activity rather than the particular physical mechanisms by which the fields are implemented that is the essence of his argument.

Pribram's holographic field theory, furthermore, does not deny an underlying neural microstructure. The entire discussion in the Pribram, Nuwer, and Baron

[6]The reader interested in an alternative model of memory, using autocorrelation functions as an alternative to Fourier transforms, should look at the work of Anderson (1968). The problem of the equivalence of the various models is discussed in greater detail in my earlier work (Uttal, 1975a), which describes an autocorrelation model of form detection. Another alternative model based on lateral interaction between center-surround antagonistic fields has been proposed by Grossberg (1973). All of these theories have common features and premises.

paper is based upon connectionistic and neural network ideas that are not at all deviant from the viewpoint that has been repeatedly expressed in this chapter. This is made highly explicit when they note (Pribram, Nuwer, & Baron, 1974): "In short, a neural hologram is the pattern of sensitivity values that corresponds to one element of an optical Fourier Hologram and it is a function of the junctional microstructure of the memory units [p. 440]."

The essence of Pribram's theory is that once a neural pattern has been established by alterations in the connectivity pattern, its retrieval is triggered by an input that produces a statistical pattern of nervous activity in the brain acting very like the reference wave in the optical hologram.

Pribram's theory, like John's approach, is intrinsically a statistical one. No one neuron is critical, and any portion of the neural net is capable of recording the engram even though, like the hologram, the resolution of the engram will be increasingly degraded, the smaller the storage region accessed. It is also possible for a particular part of the network to store the engram of several different memories simultaneously. This is an essential point of advantage for both Pribram's and Hydén's theories.

A hypothetical neural network that might carry out the operations required for retrieval of information from a holographic type of memory is shown in Fig. 9-28. Obviously this is a very general diagram, but its three levels of organization are quite representative and do emphasize the various stages of processing suggested by Pribram's theory.

Pribram has also proposed a specific mechanism to account for the plasticity of network interconnectivity. Like Hydén's, it also involves glia. Figure 9-29 (from Pribram, 1971) shows the details of this hypothetical glial memory mechanism. Pribram suggests that changes in the interconnectivity of a network, the neural equivalent of the engram, are mainly due to growth of dendrites. The dendrites, however, are blocked from making synaptic connections with other neurons by the ubiquitous glial cells. But glia can be stimulated by neural activity to divide, and the resulting cleavage space between the daughter cells provides a clear pathway for dendritic sprouting. Dendritic sprouting is enhanced, according to this hypothesis, as a result of extra RNA released by heavily activated neurons. Pribram's theory, thus, also incorporates specific glial and biochemical mechanisms. Indeed, on close comparison, Pribram's "field" theory can also be seen to incorporate most of the elements of Hydén's biochemical model. Although Pribram's emphasis is different from that of Hydén, there is little disagreement in general principle between the two theories, nor between either and any other contemporary neural theory of learning.

3. Neural Correlates of Memory and Learning—A Modern Perspective

The amount of growing interest directed at unraveling the neural basis of learning and the number of papers published on one or another aspect of the problem are striking. Indeed, Chapters 8 and 9 almost defied completion so rapidly did

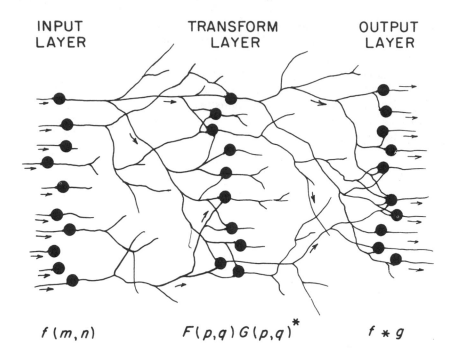

INPUT
LAYER

TRANSFORM
LAYER

OUTPUT
LAYER

$f(m,n)$ $F(p,q)G(p,q)^*$ $f * g$

FIG. 9.28   Pribram's neural analog of the optical hologram shown in Figure 9-27. The mathematical function reminds us that the process is akin to a Fourier transform (f*g) of the original stimulus pattern (f(m, n)). (From Pribram, Nuwer, & Baron, ©1974, with the permission of W. H. Freeman and Company.)

new relevant publications appear in the literature. The reader may wonder if all of this data could not help but evidence the existence of great and well-established knowledge. It is critically important, however, that a firm grasp be kept on the basic flaw in this belief. *The neural basis of learning is one of the most speculative bodies of knowledge in modern psychobiology.* Although there have been many biochemical and neural events recorded that correlate closely with the behavioral aspects of learning, the possibility that these correlated signals are only signs, in the sense defined in Chapter 6, is very high. Although no one questions the existence of electrophysiological and biochemical *correlates* of learning, it is essential to remain aware that most psychobiologists feel that it is still premature to assert that we have even begun to understand the actual *representational* relationship between learning and any of these neural or biochemical correlates.

Our understanding of the neural basis of learning, therefore, is based on reasonble conjecture, logical plausibility, and intuitive judgments that bridge the broad gaps between the various levels of inquiry and the great lacunnae in the

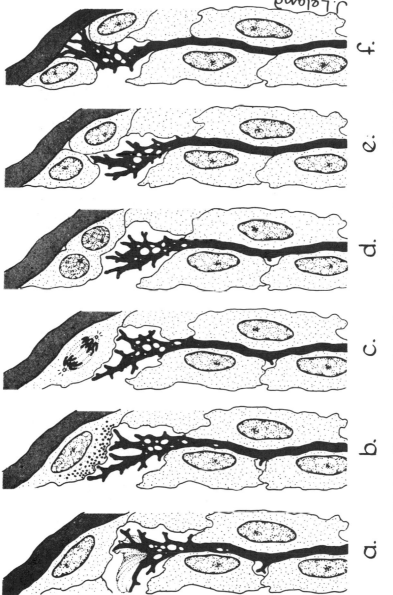

FIG. 9.29   The improvement of synaptic conductivity due to the division of glial cells following extensive use. This process, according to Pribram, may lie at the base of some kinds of synaptic plasticity. (From Pribram, ©1971, with the permission of Prentice-Hall, Inc.)

a.   b.   c.   d.   e.   f.

empirical data base. We are not really sure what the relationship is between macromolecular changes and membrane structure or what the effect is of membrane structure on the electrophysiological responses. The way in which neurophysiological responses are concatenated into network actions is also totally beyond our research technology. Perhaps most baffling of all is the "mysterious leap" from the ensemble action of literally billions of neurons to the behavioral observations or introspections of mental states.

Specific criticism can easily be made of most aspects of any of the speculative hypotheses. The basic concept that use and disuse of synapses leads to their growth or shrinkage runs counter to the equally fundamental fact that most kinds of learning at the molar level require some kind of contingent association with a reinforcer to produce learning. Simple use is usually ineffective at the molar level, and Rutledge's work suggests that it may be ineffective at the microscopic level as well. Activity alone, though demonstrably capable of altering synaptic conductivity, is, therefore, not even as a first approximation consistent with this basic characteristic of learning. Molecular theories that involve the production of specific proteins leave us with the still unresolved problem of how the composition of a protein might affect the firing propensities of a neuron. Hydén's hypothesis is one route to explaining this critically important read-out mechanism, but it too, admittedly, is not fully explanatory.

Undoubtedly, specific criticisms could be aimed at almost any aspect of any other contemporary theory of learning. It is notable that all but the most insensitive and dogmatic of the current theoreticians studying the neural basis of learning, in one place or another in their writing, insert a caveat that warns against uncritical acceptance of the implications and speculations of even their own models. This type of self-imposed criticism reflects a healthy and realistic acknowledgment of the many complex and unresolved problems incorporated in the study of the neural basis of learning.

Clearly, much current thinking about learning is going to be subject to drastic revision if not outright rejection in the years to come. Nevertheless, it is useful to look broadly at the material presented so far in an effort to extract the general principles of current consensual agreement, even if they are destined not to persist much longer. As we have seen in the earlier discussions of the viewpoints of Hydén and Pribram and many other contemporary psychobiologists, there is a common thread of agreement concerning the neural basis of learning. I now list the most significant general principles on which this agreement is based.

Principle No. 1: Learning is a multiple stage process.   Learning is not a single process but a coordinated cluster of processes varying in acquisition time and in duration of persistence. The most useful current classification of these learning processes is one based on hierarchal classification that includes after-images, iconic storage, and short-term, intermediate-term, and long-term memory. This behavior-based classification suggests the probable existence of different neural mechanisms underlying each kind of learning.

Principle No. 2: Learning is distributed in the brain.   Certain areas of the brain (e.g., the frontal lobes and the hippocampus) seem to be especially deeply involved in the control and regulation of learning. However, there seems to be little data at any analytic level that contradicts Lashley's early conclusion that the memory trace or engram resides in widely distributed regions of the brain. This fact suggests the unlikelihood of finding a location in which memory is stored and even more disappointingly, suggests that the search for the engram itself may be an impossible quest.

Principle No. 3: Learning is encoded by changes in the state of neural networks.   The distributed mechanism that represented memory is most probably encoded within a network of neurons of variable interconnectivity through which circulate transitory patterns of action potentials. The momentary activity state of the network is the physiological equivalent of mental activity, and changes in the pattern of interconnectivity that regulate that state are the equivalent of the dynamic process of learning at the molar levels.

Principle No. 4: A statistical rather than a single neuron mode of representation underlies learning.   Within this network, no one neuron is important. The code is represented by the central tendencies of an ensemble of neurons and their interactions. If not strictly a statistical process in its formal mathematical sense, the code is at least a function of coordinated activity of a host of neurons in the network.

Principle No. 5: The network states are functions of synaptic conductivity. Although there are a number of competing theories, the overwhelming consensus is that changes in the network state are mediated by plastic changes taking place at a multitude of synaptic junctions. Fluctuations in the conductivity of the synapses act to interconnect the neurons of the net in intricate, complicated, and dynamic patterns. Such synaptic versatility undoubtedly gives rise ultimately to the great variability observed in human behavior.

Principle No. 6: Synaptic conductivity changes may be short- or long-term. Fluctuating synaptic conductivity may be fairly transient and dependent upon the effects produced by the circulating neurophysiological responses as well as immediately preceding activity. The membrane effects that produce these short-term plastic synaptic changes are probably best described in terms of ionic equilibrium shifts and other transient changes in the ability of the membrane to conducted graded potentials or to respond to transmitter chemicals. Long-term changes in synaptic conductivity, on the other hand, include growth and birth of new synapses, degeneration of old synapses, and ultralong persistent changes in the properties of the membranes best described in terms of protein synthesis. The process of producing long-term synaptic changes from short-term ones is referred to as *consolidation.*

Principle No. 7: Long-term synaptic changes seem to involve RNA.   A host of biochemical studies has shown selective changes in the RNA_t content of cells that seem to be involved in learning. It is highly likely, therefore, that in some way as yet not well understood, RNA, DNA, and the proteins whose production these two genetic macromolecules control, are involved in long-term changes in synaptic conductivity.

Principle No. 8: Effective plastic change depends on relevant reinforcement. Simple use or disuse seems to be insufficient to guide the synaptic plastic changes described so far. Although, admittedly, it involves an immense logical leap, it seems that even at the most molecular level, reinforcement or some other kind of response validation is necessary to achieve plastic modifications.

In concluding this chapter, I come once again to the most vexing conceptual problem of all—the transitions between levels of analysis. How do molecular reactions affect membrane function, membrane function affect network organization, and so on? Although our technology successfully allows us to determine the characteristics of the processes occurring at the various biochemical, neurophysiological, network, and psychological levels, it is in each case uncertain exactly how the mechanisms at one level represent or encode the transactions at the next (higher) level. It is in the explanation of the upward transition between levels that speculation becomes most intense and the frailty of contemporary theory becomes most obvious. I can only conclude this chapter on the neural basis of learning by noting that in spite of the abundance of data, all too often discussions of the various aspects of the problem of the neural basis of learning end with the phrase: "At present, we do not yet know. . ."

10

Epilog — Emerging Principles of the Psychobiology of Mind

And so I have come to the conclusion of this survey of the theory and data base relevant to the mind-brain problem. I have considered a wide body of empirical material, many theories, and many of the fundamental concepts, premises, and difficulties that underlie this ultra-important human research activity. I have tried to indicate how the community of psychobiological scientists currently views the mind-brain problem as well as how it was viewed historically.

It should now be clear to each reader who has persisted to this point (as well as to those few wiser readers who actually started this book at its conclusion) that, in spite of all that has been said, there still is no fully satisfactory explanation of how neural activity is transformed into mental activity; there is, in fact, no universal theory of the "psychobiology of mind" that comes close to meeting the promise of this book's title. Rather, there is only a body of premises, empirical findings, and conceptual and paradigmatic perspectives, which feed backward and forward into each other, that collectively make up what may be properly called a *psychobiological science* of the relationship between neural structures on the one hand and psychological or mental processes on the other.

Nevertheless, I am convinced that a set of generally accepted principles does emerge from the synthesis that has been attempted here. Even if most of the details remain chaotic and a universal theory still eludes us, some global perspectives and reformulations of basic premises are beginning to solidify. It is the purpose of this concluding chapter to tease them out. At best this will be an incomplete exercise, because few of the questions that were asked in Chapter 1 can yet be answered. Nevertheless, however nebulous and faint, the glimmer of global wisdom perceptible within this mass of intricate detail and complex experimental design always has been and always will be the most important product of any scientific effort.

In this summary chapter, I present in list form what I believe to be the most important of these general principles without further justification, argument, or citation. Each principle has been more or less extensively discussed in the substantive chapters that preceded this. The list is a highly personal statement of my interpretation of the significance of the data and theories I have surveyed.

A preliminary statement of several especially important "metaprinciples" helps to provide an overview of the more specific principles presented later in this epilog. The first metaprinciple, though by no means the most important, is actually embodied within the overall organization of this book itself. It emphasizes the fact that most psychobiological research can be classified into a small number of broad problem categories. In this book I have stressed the triad of localization, representation, and dynamic change. As I see it, the essence of the psychobiological adventure in the past is almost entirely encompassed within these three broad categories. This suggested triad is a categorization of the empirical approaches that stresses three fundamental questions lying unspoken behind each particular psychobiological experiment: Where in the brain are particular processes mediated; how are molar mental processes represented by cellular action; and what plastic neural mechanisms underlie behavioral flexibility. Other research that may at first not fit well into this tripartite categorization usually turns out to be only a secondary aspect of these three main issues or to deal more with some technical matter of brain physiology or biochemistry than with the fundamental problem of the relation between brain and mind.

It should also be noted that each of the three fundamental questions embodies an implicit methodological paradigm or theoretical presumption that may not stand the tests of time. For example, we have seen how doubts have crept into the basic idea that psychological functions can be localized in any brainplace and also that microscopic single-cell responses are far from directly identifiable with molar mental processes for conceptual as well as empirical reasons. Possible indirect feedback effects cloud almost all neurophysiological studies of learning. Thus the triad of questions about which this book is organized is very likely to be a transient one, and other foci are quite likely to dominate research into the mind-brain problem in the future.

A second metaprinciple, repeatedly appearing in this book, provides a possible answer to the complex yet fundamental problem of determining at which of the many levels of research inquiry one should seek the neural essence of mental process. Although the molecular, membrane, cellular, and macroscopic nuclear levels all have been targets of psychobiological investigation, it seems to me that the compelling thrust of the entire body of current data is that the most important aspects of the nervous systems' contribution to mind are its information transduction, transmission, and processing properties. By emphasizing the flow of information, our answer to the question of level becomes independent of the particular biochemical or physiological process maintaining the structure or physiological action of neurons. In other words, this metaprinciple asserts that it is the pattern of activity and the organization of the paths of information flow, rather than the mechanics of the neural components, that really matter in the representation of mental process by nervous tissue.

In this light, the major conclusion of this book (as well as what I believe will be the major guiding theme of psychobiology in the century to come) is that the essential neural aspects of mental function are to be found in the organization of the networks into which either individual neurons or macroscopic brain nuclei are arranged. It is in the momentary states of activity within these networks that the true equivalents of mental processes are to be found. This metaprinciple emphasizes that the overall pattern of information coursing through the nervous system is indistinguishable in all denotative regards (in Feigl's terms) from the mental states of which we are individually aware and that are reflected in the molar behavior of the organism.

This principle of network-activity-state mental-process equivalence, therefore, is the key metaprinciple of modern psychobiology. Although stating it this way may not seem revolutionary, this network metaprinciple should be appreciated as a novel axiom running counter to the two premises that have dominated so much of recent research in psychobiology. The concepts that individual "centers" exist for particular functions in the central nervous system and that meaningful correlates of molar psychological states may be observed in the action of individual neurons are based on quite different premises than the essential idea of network state equivalents of psychological processes presented here.

The two main psychobiological research methodologies—comparisons of behavior with single-cell microelectrode recordings and the effect of ablative surgery on behavior—underlying these two older concepts have strongly contributed to this now obsolescent theoretical stress on single-cell representation and localized "centers." The findings of recent years make it clear, however, that both these techniques and the theoretical perspectives they have engendered have been incomplete.

Thus a further major conclusion of this synthesis is that it is now time to reshape our methodology as well as our theory. But this may be easier said than done. Neither the techniques for analyzing the simultaneous activity of many neurons as they interact in a network, nor the analytic mathematics required to model neuronal or nuclear networks, are yet adequately developed. The "many-body" problem remains as intractable in psychobiology as it is in physics.

A third metaprinciple permeating much of this book is the concept of symbolically coded representation of information patterns, i.e., there is no logical need for there to be a "picture in the head" for there to be a "picture in the mind." Isomorphism is not necessary; rather, encoded representations in any dimension may be used to represent messages originally presented in any other dimension.

These are the grandest metaprinciples and most global conclusions. They are the main foundations of the overall psychobiological perspective that I personally have achieved after studying the empirical data and the historical, technical, logical, and philosophical bases of psychobiology. Clearly, these broad generalities do not represent a revolutionary paradigmatic change from the perspective of most contemporary psychobiologists, but I hope they reflect the views of many of my colleagues.

Finally, there is another general perspective that should not be dignified with the approbation of "metaprinciple." Perhaps as a result of the critical stance that I took during my studies for this book, there is a rather negative "overtone" to much of the present discussion that deals with the issue of how far we have actually come toward the fulfillment of a psychobiological theory of mind. It appears to me, in general, that many psychobiologists have not been sufficiently rigorous in their attribution of psychological properties to neural mechanisms. Even the determination that a given neural mechanism or measurement is a sign of some psychological process is a far more difficult task than many of my colleagues seem willing to acknowledge. To establish psychoneural coding identity requires further tests of necessity and sufficiency that are not usually carried out. In general, all of us have been much too lenient and uncritical in accepting hypothetical links between observed electrophysiological or neuroanatomical data and psychological processes as either correlative or identity relationships. We have accepted concomitancy for identity, and analogy for homology, and have been willing to violate the elementary mathematical law that asserts that no internal mechanism can be uniquely specified solely from observations of input-output relationships. We have committed these errors with a degree of optimistic hopefulness that sometimes ignores the enormous logical, philosophical, and even empirical difficulties implicit in such cross-level identifications. In other words, electrical potentials from the brain are not necessarily equivalent to thoughts, as much as some of us want to believe, and may, as we have seen, be totally unrelated in a representational (coded) sense to even highly correlated psychological processes. Furthermore, it is surprising how frequently the simplest and most obvious psychological datum seems to shout that a particular neural model cannot be correct and yet how frequently we ignore these cries.

In looking over the book at this point, I must sadly say that I think psychobiologists "know" less now than they did 5 or 10 years ago concerning the mind-brain problem. Some previously widely held theories are no longer tenable and have not been replaced with equally well-accepted models. At least, I am sure that I am convinced of less now than I was 2 years ago when I started this work.

This viewpoint does not say, of course, that the mind and the brain are not uniquely and irrevocably intertwined. There is nothing dualistic about the fact that we have not yet definitively established links between the two sets of data or that the mind-brain problem remains the greatest challenge in the scientific adventure. My point is only that at present a considerable body of loose theorizing exists concerning mind-brain relationships that hopefully has been brought into clearer focus by the discussions in this book.

In the following list I state in a more positive way what I perceive to be the more particular and specific emerging principles of psychobiology. It is my hope that this analysis of the current state of psychobiology into a set of basic principles provides the reader with the necessary basis to synthesize his own global perspective.

1. Neural activity is the sole basis and only significant concomitant of mental activity. Although the specific links between mind and brain have not been established yet, this axiom must be basic to all of the principles that follow and is the keystone of all of modern psychobiology.

2. The brain, with its rich diversity of permanent and plastic interconnections, is the only plausible portion of the body in which patterned physiological activities identifiable with mind could reside.

3. The relation between brain activity and mental activity is direct. It is best summed up in terms of the principle of *psychoneural identity* or *equivalence*, which states that the linguistic terms of psychology and neurophysiology denote exactly the same mechanisms and processes. Briefly, mental processes and the relevant neural activities are related to the brain in exactly the same way; both are functions of this particular neural mechanism.

4. The particular mind-brain theory dominant at any time in history is a direct reflection of the contemporary technology and methodology available for the study of mental and neural processes. Vigorously championed models are always transient and are inevitably replaced by new views as the data base expands.

5. Psychobiology—the science of the relation between the brain and the mind—is beset by a number of fundamental and conceptual difficulties not found in either classical neurophysiology or psychology. The most fundamental difficulty lies in distinguishing between causal relationships and irrelevant but analogous concomitancy.

6. The mind-brain problem is actually a collection of many subproblems. Some are issues of great logical and conceptual complexity; others are merely issues of technical detail. The technical details sometimes tend to obscure the more fundamental conceptual issues.

7. Not all psychobiological questions are valid questions. Some are a priori unanswerable (e.g., how much energy is exerted by a thought?), and others lead to circular arguments (e.g., can the mind affect the brain?). Unfortunately, the decision as to which questions are good and which are logically defective is answered in different ways at different times.

8. Neurophysiological reductionism (i.e., the philosophy asserting that, in principle, psychological processes can be explained by neural ones) is a major

premise of modern psychobiology. Implicit within this philosophy is the idea that even though a full and comprehensive psychobiological theory does not yet exist, its ultimate formulation is certain. Also implicit in the strategic premise of reductionism is a philosophical viewpoint that assumes that the mind-brain relationship is fundamentally deterministic although in practice statistical methodologies must currently be used. This same philosophy also eschews theories of emergent properties as contrary to deterministic reductionism.

9. In principle, the behavior of the most complex brain can be predicted from full knowledge of the nature of the individual neurons only if one includes the details of interneuronal interactions. It is a premise of psychobiology that no new properties emerge solely as a result of concatenation. In practice, establishing the details of the interactions in a multi-object system quickly exceeds all possible computational ability even when the number of objects is relatively small.

10. The proper "level of inquiry," at which the most relevant aspects of neural action are found, is best phrased in the terms of the information flow within heavily interacting systems of neurons or brain nuclei that make up the microscopic and macroscopic networks respectively. The equivalent of the current mental state must ultimately be equivalent to the state of activity of some network at this instant. Although the nervous system is composed of neurons operating on the basis of sodium-potassium-chloride ion chemistry, these mechanical aspects of the neuron are of less importance than the interconnectivity, transmission, integration, and signal flow characteristics of the networks.

11. Measurements of mental processes can be as quantitative and as objective as the measurement of any physical parameters. In principle and in practice, the only difference between measurements in the physical and the mental worlds is the variance observed. Variance is largely explained in terms of multivariate influences; essentially the same degree of variance must be exhibited by psychological, neural, and physical functions when they are affected by the same number of factors with similar individual variabilities.

12. Encoded representations need not be isomorphic. Dimension changes are observed throughout the nervous system with spatial dimensions substituting for temporal dimensions, and quantitative dimensions being encoded by temporal dimensions, as two obvious examples. All conceivable reencodings seem plausible, and most have been observed. Symbolically (nonisomorphically) encoded representation seems to be a universal substitute for isomorphic replication within the nervous system. Mental images can exist without "pictures" in the head, just as transmitted television signals need not reproduce the two-dimensional geometry of the original scene until they arrive at their destination. This is the basic premise of coding or representation theory.

13. A wide variety of psychobiological theories of mind have been enunciated since antiquity, but modern psychobiology, most of its students agree, is

mechanistic, realistic, monistic, reductionistic, empiricistic, and methodologically behavioristic. Dualistic theories are still proposed by some psychobiologists, but dualism and psychobiology are internally and logically inconsistent. Psychobiological research must be based upon the monistic premise; otherwise, it is nonsensical.

14. Modern monistic psychobiology, in its most fundamental premises, is in profound logical and conceptual conflict with contemporary religious doctrine concerning human mortality.

15. The plan of the adult nervous system is superficially complicated but is easily understood if considered as the extended outgrowth of the basic tubular plan initiated during the earliest stages of embryological development.

16. Embryological development (ontogeny) is a partial recapitulation of the evolution of the species (phylogeny). Neuroembryology, therefore, is one of the main contemporary clues to the details of the brain's evolutionary development over the millenia.

17. Microembryology (the study of the development of individual neurons) is a potentially important source of information concerning the development of certain kinds of behavior and possibly even of learning or of the recovery of function following injury in adult animals.

18. The embryological and early postnatal development of the brain is influenced by many experiential, nutritional, environmental, and genetic factors.

19. It is uncertain whether the many gyri on the surface of the mammalian brain represent physiologically significant regions or are merely the result of quasirandom folding as the cortex enlarges during maturation.

20. Regions of the cerebral cortex may be classified on a number of different bases including cytoarchitectonic, evoked potential, and even biochemical criteria. The various classification systems do not always correspond.

21. Within the brain, major systems are defined by common anatomical interconnectivity, common synaptic transmitter substances, or common influences on certain kinds of behavior. Again, psychobiologists do not universally agree upon the anatomic limits or the behavioral role of the various "systems."

22. Although early microscopic studies prevented discernment of the basic orderly nature of neuronal arrangement in the nuclei of the brain, recent studies show a high degree of organization present at all levels of the nervous system from the peripheral receptor organs to the cerebral cortex. Individual cells define a volume of influence that may vary in shape from neuron to neuron, but most neuroanatomists accept order rather than randomness as the basic organizational property of brain tissue. In general, a lattice-like, three-dimensional network arrangement can be observed at all levels of the nervous system in microanatomical studies.

23. The lattice-like arrangement of neural tissue leads to the emergence of such organizational features as columns and layers. Interconnection between

these features and between their constituent neuronal elements can be elaborate and include feedforward, feedbackward, lateral, convergent, and divergent patterns. Inhibitory as well as excitatory connectives are universally observed throughout the nervous system.

24. Our knowledge of the operation of such heavily interconnected networks is still rudimentary, but rectifying synapses, refractory periods, and lateral inhibitory interactions are clearly all required to stabilize and organize the pattern of neural activity and to prevent repetitive firing of all constituent neurons.

25. A satisfactory definition of the mind and the separable mental processes is elusive. However, mind may be characterized as being individualistic, intrapersonal (observable only through interpersonally observed behavior), and indistinguishable in meaning from a host of other scientific and semipopular terms such as consciousness, soul, awareness, and so on.

26. The essential aspect of any definition of the mind is that it is process and not mechanism. Mind is one function of the brain and inseparable from that material mechanism. The task of psychobiology is to explain the relationship between the (neural) mechanism and the (mental) action. Without the mechanism, there could be no mental process. To restate a simplistic, but effective metaphor: Mind is to the nervous system as rotation is to the wheel.

27. It is not yet established whether the individual mental processes such as perception, learning, and motivation that are measured in specific experiments are, in principle, isolatable or only different aspects of a unitary mental process.

28. Historically, and to the present day, a host of fads, cults, and prescientific attempts to codify the relationship between mental processes and neural mechanisms has been suggested. Although these cults may satisfy various human needs, the fundamental relationship they propose between brain and mind is almost always theoretically incorrect. The assumption implicit in most of them, that the mind can affect the brain and other parts of the body, is logically unsupportable and of no theoretical value.

29. There is an indeterminancy principle operating in psychological research just as there is in physics. Psychological test probes themselves have been shown to affect the state of the nervous system in a way that can lead to misunderstandings of various effects in psychological research. This is not an example of the "mind affecting the body," however, but of stimuli altering the state of the neural mechanism.

30. The question of localization of mental processes in particular nuclei (or "centers") of the brain has a long and distinguished history. Psychobiologists, however, are now becoming aware that the effort to localize particular psychological functions in particular brain "centers" is probably misdirected. No single nucleus of the brain is solely responsible for any single mental process, and many nuclei are undoubtedly involved in even the most discrete psychological function. Most mental processes are not "localized" in the classic sense, therefore, but are mediated by clusters or networks of nuclei in strong cooperative and antagonistic interaction with each other.

31. Much of the empirical data presented in support of specific "centers" of localization has in recent years been shown to be spurious. Inadequate definition of the mental processes supposedly being manipulated, surgical mislocation of lesions, imprecise definitions of the limits of specific nuclei, mistaken identification of indirect inhibition as excitation, recovery of function, and noisy and variable data from human beings, all have contributed to an uncritical interpretation of the existing data base. A more fundamental difficulty, however, is that psychobiology possesses only the weakest technological means of studying the interactions in highly interconnected and redundant systems. This technical obstacle has impeded the emergence of the data base necessary for the formulation of a new nuclear network theory of macroscopic brain organization.

32. The brain is not a homogeneous mass. The anatomy, physiology, and psychobiology of the brain all attest to some degree of differentiation of function that has evolved for the many macroscopic nuclei. On the other hand, no nucleus acts as the unique locus of any mental function. Obviously, neither radical localization nor radical homgeneity theory is adequate. The emerging new perspective supports a theory in which networks of interacting nuclei must collectively operate to control any facet of behavior. Within the networks of nuclei, the psychological states are represented by networks of neurons.

33. A major trend over the years has been toward the discovery of multiple sensory representation systems above and beyond the classic "primary projection regions." For example, in some vertebrates, as many as a dozen different visual pathways have been discovered.

34. The major role of the many different brain regions in mammals now known to be responsive to visual inputs has been only partially analyzed. In general, the more central the region, the more complex are the processes that seem to be affected by its ablation. But again, the network interactions are profound, and paradoxical effects of multiple lesions often occur.

35. Although neither radical localization theory nor radical homogeneity theory is supported by contemporary research data, clearly there are regions of the brain that, when damaged, are more likely to produce behavior deficits of one kind than are other regions. Four trends may be observed in "localization" research:

a. Deficits in processes that depend heavily on sensory or motor communication (such as eating or drinking) have increasingly often been shown to result from transection of nearby conducting tracts rather than from ablation of the particular nucleus once invoked as the "center" of that process.

b. Many more nuclei than had been previously suspected can be shown to affect any given mental process.

c. Contradictory data is almost always available with regard to the behavioral effects of any brain lesion.

d. Many functions spontaneously recover after an initial period of deficit following brain damage.

36. The hemispheres of the brain are not identical in function. Nevertheless, it is unlikely that any psychological experiment using normal human subjects can speak directly to the issue of hemispheric specialization because of the normal rich cross-connections between the hemispheres. Transection of the corpus callosum and the other main commissures is required for good experimental design to test hypotheses of hemispheric specialization. Thus psychological experiments attempting to show hemispheric differentiation in normal subjects are probably fallacious.

37. It is often difficult to distinguish between representative localization (in which the mental process under study is actually mediated by mechanisms within a demarcated region) and partial localization of control or regulatory functions (which act to modify the time course or to sequence the mental process).

38. The various psychological processes intrinsically differ in their respective relevance to the question of localization. In principle, some processes (such as particular sensory modalities) may be localizable (at least within a system of nuclei), and others (such as motivation) may represent generalized weighting functions with no particular spatial meaning.

39. A major conceptual difficulty for localization research is created by the uncertainty of what it is that a psychobiologist is attempting to localize when he searches for a brain region in which to place some particular mental function. In other words, the spatial loci in the brain are far easier to specify than is the nature of the psychological process under investigation.

40. Polysensory and overlapping motor and sensory responsiveness seem to be increasingly observed in regions previously considered as dedicated to a single sensory modality.

41. Neural representation of psychological processes must ultimately be encoded by the activity state of complex networks of neurons. However, no neural models have yet been proposed that satisfactorily link the cellular network level of analysis with that of psychological processes, except in a few simple cases involving sensory communication.

42. The network state need not be "read" or decoded by any central receiving mechanism or homunculus. The existence of an appropriate though encoded state of network activity at some appropriate central locus is the necessary and sufficient equivalent of the mental process.

43. A neural code may be defined as a set of symbols (various kinds of neural action potentials) employed to represent images, messages, concepts, and meanings, and the set of rules governing the selection and use of these symbols.

44. There is no best code. Any system of symbols and rules can be used to represent any concept, no matter how complicated, although with varying degrees of efficiency.

45. Both single-cell activity and compound action potentials are possible signals of one or another aspect of mental activity. It is not possible to generalize from an observed correlation between a neural response and a psychological response, however, to the much stronger conclusion that the neural signal is the

psychoneural equivalent of or is identical to the mental process. True codes must be distinguished from signs by tests of necessity and sufficiency that go far beyond correlation no matter how high the observed correlation coefficient.

46. False identification of neural and psychological responses may be caused by confusion of signs and codes; dimensional alterations; ungeneralizable boundary effects; multiple, overlapping, and redundant coding; and variability within and between individuals and species. Perhaps most profound, however, is the misleading influence of distortions in our interpretation of the meaning of empirical data. The inability of all human beings, including psychobiologists, to adapt quickly to compelling new paradigms of thought and emerging new research data bases is profound.

47. There is a large body of psychophysical evidence reminding us that the input stimulus pattern is not the sole determinant of sensory and perceptual experiences. The brain does not act as a passive respondent to incoming messages but rather as an active "theoretician," "mapmaker," or "constructive hypothesis generator" that uses immediate stimulus input as only partial clues to the solution of the problem of modeling the outside world. The "solution" is a mental or cognitive state that is also functionally dependent upon logical and prejudicial meaningfulness and consistency with the previous experiences of the observer.

48. The sensory-coding aspect of the general psychobiological problem of representation is multidimensional. Often it has been mistakenly asserted that the relationship between neural signal frequency and perceptual magnitude is *the* coding problem. In fact, we also have to consider the full range of spatial, temporal, and qualitative dimensions of the perceptual response, as well as the large number of candidate neural codes. An $[m] \times [n]$ correlation matrix must be completed for each level of the ascending pathway, where $[m]$ is the set of common sensory dimensions, and $[n]$ is the set of candidate neural codes.

49. Because the psychophysical experiment deals with the organism as a black box and examines only the input and output, little can come from psychophysical experiments that can speak directly to the problem of internal neural representational or anatomical mechanisms. Two overtly similar perceptual processes may be represented by internal codes that are analogous in function but have totally different internal mechanisms and modes of operations. In only a few special cases does the molar behavior directly reflect the properties of internal single cells or cell classes. Inner anatomic arrangements cannot be uniquely determined by psychological experiments alone.

50. After one has passed beyond relatively peripheral models of contour enhancement, there is little to support any precise isomorphism of psychophysical data and neurophysiological findings at the single-cell level in the spatial, temporal, or qualitative sensory domains. Fine spatial, temporal, and qualitative discrimination seem to occur even though the cellular neural responses are widely diffuse in time and space. The codes may be entirely dissimilar from the percept in terms of the dimensions used internally.

51. Contrary to prior usage, the concept of coding or representation must be generalized to other aspects of the mind-body problem rather than limited to sensory communication. All psychological processes must be represented in some coded form somewhere in the nervous system. However, it should also be acknowledged that, because of the anchor provided by reference to the physical stimuli, most available data are obtained in the domain of sensory processes; only recently have data relevant to the problem of representation become available in other fields of cognition.

52. Many brain neurons have been shown to be more responsive to the particular spatio-temporal patterns of stimuli rather than to absolute energy magnitudes. These spatio-temporal feature sensitivities are determined by the organization of the network feeding into the neuron.

53. Although considerable controversy exists, it is exceedingly difficult to determine whether a discrete or a continuous organization of the cerebral cortex columns exists. Without the criteria of sharp boundaries and irregular order of orientation sensitivity, the two models of cortical organization fade into each other and cannot be distinguished.

54. The ability of feature-detecting neurons to be modified by experience during development of the organism has recently been called into question. It is now moot whether or not the organization of the receptive fields and other feature sensitivities are rigid or plastic over the life of the organism.

55. Many mathematical models of representation in sensory systems have been proposed. All of them deal with restricted stimulus sets and work only within the confines of a narrowly defined universe of discourse. Many such models are uncritically created because of convenient availability of mathematical apparatus and may display some superficial descriptive power because of the generality of the mathematics. However, almost all fail to incorporate fundamental psychophysical data to a satisfactory degree and thus seem to ignore both simple and complex aspects of human perceptual phenomena. In particular, both the basic premises of the Fourier model of visual form perception—narrowness of channels and independence of channels—have been challenged in recent years.

56. Neurophysiological data, when used to explain psychological phenomena, become neurophysiological theories.

57. Conversely, the attribution of molar behavioral descriptions to observed neural processes in model systems (e.g.,the retina or *Aplysia*) with which they may be analogous is also an act of theory building.

58. Some of the most serious difficulties for simplistic neural theories of mental processes arise from the following facts: Stimuli need only suggest forms to be perceived; there is often a considerable conflict between the time constants of the purported neural correlates and the associated psychological response; and spatial relationships differ between the neural models and the psychophysical processes. Furthermore, "subjective" responses may exist without identifiable isomorphic or even symbolically encoded neural correlates in the regions in

which they would be expected if other simple neural models are correct. This discrepancy suggests active high-level "interpretation" rather than peripheral, passive, and automatic responses to stimulus patterns.

59. Learning appears not to be a single process but a coordinated cluster of processes varying in acquisition time and in duration of persistence. Currently, the most useful classification of the set of learning processes is based upon a hierarchy including after-images, iconic storage, and short, intermediate, and long-term memory. This behavior-based classification suggests the probable existence of different neural mechanisms underlying each kind of learning but may also reflect, it should be acknowledged, the complex action of a dynamic and complex single process.

60. Certain areas of the brain (e.g., the frontal lobes and the hippocampus) seem to be especially deeply involved in the control and regulation of learning. There seems to be little data at any analytic level, however, contradicting Lashley's early conclusion that the memory trace or engram resides in widely distributed regions of the brain. This fact suggests the unlikelihood of finding a location in which memory is stored and, even more disappointingly, suggests that the search for the engram itself may be an impossible quest.

61. The distributed mechanism that represents memory is most probably encoded within a network of neurons of variable interconnectivity through which circulate transitory patterns of action potentials. The momentary activity state of the network is the physiological equivalent of mental activity. Changes in the pattern of interconnectivity and the resulting changes in network state are the equivalent to the dynamic process of learning at the molar levels.

62. Within this network, no one neuron is important. The code is represented by the central tendencies of an ensemble of neurons and their interactions. If not strictly a statistical process in its formal mathematical sense, the code for memory is, at least, a function of the aggregated activity of a host of neurons in the network.

63. Although there are a number of competing theories, the overwhelming consensus is that changes in the network state are mediated by plastic changes taking place at a multitude of synaptic junctions. Fluctuations in the conductivity of the synapses act to interconnect the neurons of the net in intricate, complicated, and dynamic patterns. Such synaptic versatility undoubtedly ultimately gives rise to the great variability observed in human behavior.

64. Fluctuating synaptic conductivity may be fairly transient and dependent upon the effects produced by the circulating neurophysiological responses as well as by the immediately preceding activity. Membrane effects producing these short-term, plastic, synaptic changes are probably best described in terms of ionic equilibrium shifts and other transient variations in the ability of the membrane to conduct graded potentials or to respond to transmitter chemicals. Long-term changes in synaptic conductivity, on the other hand, are probably best described in terms of the growth and birth of new synapses, degeneration of old

synapses, and ultralong persistent changes in the properties of the membranes produced by processes involving protein synthesis. The process of producing long-term synaptic changes from short-term ones is referred to as *consolidation*.

65. A host of biochemical studies has shown selective changes in the RNA_t content of cells that seem to be involved in learning. Although the exact mechanisms are not yet well understood, it is highly likely that RNA_t, RNA, DNA, and the proteins whose production these genetic macromolecules control, all are involved in long-term changes in synaptic conductivity.

66. Simple use or disuse seems to be insufficient to regulate the plastic synaptic changes described so far. Although, admittedly, it involves an immense logical leap, some evidence suggests that, even at the most molecular level, reinforcement or some other kind of response validation is necessary to achieve plastic modifications.

67. Many experimental studies of the neural basis of learning are equivocal because of a lack of control of possible feedback signals from effectors. In many of these cases, the "plastic" effects observed are likely to be mere reflections from proprioceptive receptors in effectors, and the actual plastic neural change takes place in other parts of the brain.

68. Finally, it should be reiterated that there is as yet no universal psychobiological theory of mind. The conceptual and logical problem of translating the data from one to another level (i.e., the molecular, membrane, cellular, microscopic network or macroscopic neuroanatomic, as well as the mental and behavioral) is enormously difficult. It is possible that our measurements of the functions of individual neurons, for example, may never be translatable into the language of percepts and feelings even if, in principle, psychoneural identity between these levels exists. The most fundamental problem of all, therefore, is still totally intractable; namely, how does a unified molar mental state arise out of the action of huge numbers of individual neurons?

Obviously, this book has not answered all the questions presented in Chapter 1. Many of them are unanswerable; many of them will not be a part of the mind-brain problem in the next few decades or centuries. As stated previously, I am now convinced that much less is known than I thought when I embarked on this enterprise. Many of the empirical foundation stones of physiological psychology accepted only a few years ago have turned out to be equivocal. Contradictory evidence has emerged to challenge some of the most tenaciously held premises. In a more profound sense, it appears that many of the techniques and approaches traditionally used to attack the various aspects of the mind-brain problem may be seriously flawed in fundamental concept.

Although I have not been able to provide a general solution to the mind-brain problem, I hope this book is useful to the degree that it has systematized the subproblems, the accomplishments, the implicit conceptual assumptions, and the various difficulties that have prevented and will prevent a complete solution for many years to come. The unsolved mind-brain problem thus remains the "world knot." Because of both its importance and its complexity, it still represents what many, including myself, consider to be the most exciting and important issue in contemporary science.

Bibliography

The bibliography for this book consists of two parts. The first part (A) is a set of suggested readings for each chapter or pair of chapters. Not all of the suggested readings are necessarily mentioned in the text. The second part (B) is a list of references for the publications actually cited in the text or in figure captions.

A. SUGGESTED READINGS

Chapters 1 and 2

Adam, G. *Biological aspects of perception, consciousness, and memory.* New York: Plenum, 1976.

Arbib, M. A. *The metaphorical brain: An introduction to cybernetics as artificial intelligence and brain theory.* New York: Wiley-Interscience, Wiley, 1972.

Armstrong, D. M. *A materialistic theory of the mind.* London: Routledge and Keegan Paul, 1968.

Boring, E. G. *Sensation and perception in the history of experimental psychology.* New York: Appleton-Century-Crofts, 1942.

Borst, C. (Ed.). *The mind brain identity theory.* London: Macmillan, 1970.

Campbell, K. *Body and mind.* Garden City, N.Y.: Doubleday Anchor, 1970.

Chappell, V. C. (Ed.). *The philosophy of mind.* Englewood Cliffs, N.J.: Prentice-Hall, 1962.

Corning, W. C., & Balaban, M. (Eds.). *The mind: Biological approaches to its functions.* New York: Wiley-Interscience, 1968.

Delafresnaye, J. F. (Ed.). *Brain and mechanisms and consciousness.* Springfield: C. C. Thomas, 1954.

Eccles, J. C. *The neurophysiological basis of mind: The principles of neurophysiology.* London and New York: Oxford University Press and Clarendon, 1953.

Eccles, J. C. (Ed.). *Brain and conscious experience.* New York: Springer-Verlag, 1966.

Eccles, J. C. *Facing reality*. Berlin: Springer-Verlag, 1970.

Eccles, J. C. *The understanding of the brain*. New York: McGraw-Hill, 1973.

Edwards, P. (Ed.). *The encyclopedia of philosophy* (Vols. 1-8). New York and London: Macmillan and Collier, 1967.

Encyclopaedia Britannica (Body and Mind; Knowledge, Theory of; Psychology). 1968 edition.

Fann, K. T. (Ed.). *Ludwig Wittgenstein: The man and his philosophy*. New York: Dell, 1967.

Feigl, H., Scriven, M., & Maxwell, G. (Eds.). *Minnesota studies in the philosophy of science. Vol. II: Concepts, theories and the mind-body problem*. Minneapolis: University of Minnesota Press, 1958.

Feigl, H., & Sellars, W. (Eds.). *Readings in philosophical analysis*. New York: Appleton-Century-Crofts, 1949.

Globus, G. G., Maxwell, G., & Savodnik, I. (Eds.). *Consciousness and the brain*. New York: Plenum, 1976.

Hook, S. (Ed.). *Dimensions of Mind: A Symposium*. New York: New York University, 1960.

James, W. *The principles of psychology*. New York: Henry Holt, 1890.

Kantor, J. R. *The scientific evolution of psychology* (Vol. I). Chicago: Principia Press, 1963.

Kantor, J. R. *The scientific evolution of psychology* (Vol II). Chicago: Principia Press, 1969.

Kantor, J. R. *The aim and progress of psychology and other sciences*. Chicago: Principia Press, 1971.

Kaufman, L. *Sight and mind: An introduction to visual perception*. New York: Oxford University Press, 1974.

Klein, D. B. *A history of scientific psychology: Its origins and philosophical backgrounds*. New York: Basic Books, 1970.

Koch, S. (Ed.). *Psychology: A study of a science. Study I. Conceptual and systematic* (Vol. 1). New York: McGraw-Hill, 1959.

Koch, S. (Ed.). *Psychology: A study of a science. Study II. Empirical substructure and relations with other sciences* (Vol. 4). New York: McGraw-Hill, 1962.

Koestler, A., & Smythies, J. R. (Eds.). *Beyond reductionism: New perspectives in the life sciences*. New York: Macmillan, 1969.

Mandelbaum, M. *Philosophy, science, and sense perception: Historical and critical studies*. Baltimore: Johns Hopkins Press, 1966.

Maslow, A. *A study in Wittgenstein's tractatus*. Berkeley: University of California Press, 1961.

McCulloch, W. S. *Embodiments of mind*. Cambridge: M.I.T. Press, 1965.

Minsky, M., & Papert, S. *Perceptrons: An introduction to computational geometry*. Cambridge: M.I.T. Press, 1969.

Ornstein, J. H. *The mind and the brain: A multi-aspect interpretation*. The Hague, Netherlands: Martinus Nijhoff, 1972.

Ornstein, R. E. *The psychology of consciousness*. San Francisco: Freeman, 1972.

Pepper, S. C. *World hypotheses: A study in evidence*. Berkeley: University of California Press, 1970.

Pitcher, G. (Ed.). *Wittgenstein, the philosophical investigations*. New York: Doubleday & Co., 1966.

Polten, E. P. *Critique of the psycho-physical identity theory*. The Hague, Netherlands: Mouton & Co., 1973.

Pribram, K. H. *Languages of the brain*. Englewood Cliffs, N.J.: Prentice-Hall, 1971.

Robinson, D. N. *The enlightened machine: An analytical introduction to neuropsychology*. Encino, Calif.: Dickenson Publishing Co., 1973.

Robinson, D. N. *An intellectual history of psychology*. New York: Macmillan, 1976.

Rosenblatt, F. *Principles of neurodynamics: Perceptrons and the theory of brain mechanisms*. Washington, D.C.: Spartan Books, 1962.

Rosenblueth, A. *Mind and brain: A philosophy of science.* Cambridge: M.I.T. Press, 1970

Ryle, G. *The concept of mind.* New York: Barnes & Noble, 1949.

Sahakian, W. S. (Ed.). *History of psychology: A source book in systematic psychology.* Itasca, Ill.: F. E. Peacock Publishers, 1968.

Sayre, K. M., & Crosson, F. J. (Eds.). *The modeling of mind: computers and intelligence.* Notre Dame: University of Notre Dame Press, 1963.

Scher, J. M. (Ed.). *Theories of the mind.* New York: Free Press of Glencoe, 1962.

Schrodinger, E. *Mind and matter.* Cambridge: Cambridge University Press, 1958.

Sherrington, C. *Man on his nature.* Cambridge: Cambridge University Press, 1963.

Smythies, J. R. (Ed.). *Brain and mind: Modern concepts of the nature of mind.* London: Routledge & Kegan Paul, 1965.

Vesey, G. N. A. (Ed.). *Body and mind: Readings in philosophy.* London: George Allen & Unwin Ltd., 1964.

Wiener, N. *Cybernetics, or control and communication in the animal and the machine.* New York: Wiley, 1951.

Wittgenstein, L. *Tractatus logico-philosophicus* (D. F. Pears & B. F. McGuinness, trans.). London, 1961. (Reprinted from 1922).

Wittgenstein, L. *Philosophical investigations* (G. E. M. Anscombe, trans.). New York: Macmillan, 1953.

Wittgenstein, L. *The blue and brown books.* New York: Harper & Row, 1958.

Chapter 3

Allan, F. D. *Essentials of human embryology* (2nd ed.). New York: Oxford University Press, 1969.

Beritoff, J. S. *Neural mechanisms of higher vertebrate behavior.* London and Boston: Little, Brown, 1965.

Blinkov, S. M., & Glezer, I. I. *The human brain in figures and tables: A quantitative handbook.* New York: Basic Books and Plenum Press, 1968.

Burns, B. D. *The mammalian cerebral cortex.* London: Edward Arnold, 1958.

Carpenter, M. B. *Human neuroanatomy* (7th ed.). Baltimore: Williams and Wilkins, 1976.

Clarke, E., & O'Malley, C. D. *The human brain and spinal cord: A historical study.* Berkeley: University of California Press, 1968.

Crosby, E. C., Humphrey, T., & Lauer, E. W. *Correlative anatomy of the nervous system.* New York: Macmillan, 1962.

Desmedt, J. E. (Ed.). *New developments in electromyography and clinical neurophysiology. Vol. 3: Human reflexes, pathophysiology of motor systems, methodology of human reflexes.* Basel, Switzerland: S. Karger, 1973.

Eccles, J. C., Ito, M., & Szentágothai, J. *The cerebellum as a neuronal machine.* Berlin: Springer-Verlag, 1967.

Fichtelius, K-E., & Sjölander, S. *Smarter than man? Intelligence in whales, dolphins, and humans.* New York: Pantheon Books (Random House), 1972.

Goss, C. M. (Ed.). *Gray's anatomy of the human body* (29th ed.). Philadelphia: Lea & Febiger, 1973.

Hamilton, W. J., & Mossman, H. W. *Human embryology: Prenatal development of form and function* (4th ed.). Cambridge: W. Heffer & Sons, 1972.

Isaacson, R. L. *The limbic system.* New York: Plenum Press, 1974.

Jung, R. (Ed.). *Handbook of sensory physiology. Vol. VII/3: Central processing of visual information, Part B: Visual centers in the brain.* Berlin: Springer-Verlag, 1973.

Kuhlenbeck, H. *The central nervous system of vertebrates. Vol. 1: Propaedeutics to comparative neurology.* New York: Academic Press, 1967.

Kuhlenbeck, H. *The central nervous system of vertebrates. Vol. 3, Part I: Structural elements: Biology of nervous tissue.* New York: Academic Press, 1970.

Mark, R. *Memory and nerve cell connections.* Oxford: Clarendon Press, 1974.

Matzke, H. A., & Foltz, F. M. *Synopsis of neuroanatomy.* New York: Oxford University Press, 1967.

McCormick, J. B. *Atlas and demonstration technique of the central nervous system.* Springfield, Ill.: C. C. Thomas, 1961.

Patten, B. M. *Foundations of embryology* (2nd ed.). New York: McGraw-Hill, 1964.

Pease, D. C. (Ed.). *Cellular aspects of neural growth and differentiation.* Berkeley: University of California Press, 1971.

Petsche, H., & Brazier, M. A. B. (Eds.). *Synchronization of EEG activity in epilepsies.* New York: Springer-Verlag, 1972.

Ranson, S. W. *The anatomy of the nervous system* (10th ed.) (Revised by S. L. Clark). Philadelphia: Saunders, 1959.

Rosenblith, W. A. (Ed.). *Sensory communication.* Cambridge and New York: M.I.T. Press and Wiley, 1961.

Schadé, J. P. *The peripheral nervous system.* Amsterdam: Elsevier Publishing Co., 1966.

Schmitt, F. O. (Ed.). *The neurosciences: Second study program.* New York: The Rockefeller University Press, 1970.

Schmitt, F. O., & Worden, F. G. (Eds.). *The neurosciences: Third study program.* Cambridge: The M.I.T. Press, 1974.

Shepherd, G. M. *The synaptic organization of the brain: An introduction.* New York: Oxford University Press, 1974.

Sholl, D. A. *The organization of the cerebral cortex.* London and New York: Methuen & Co. and John Wiley, 1956.

Spalteholz, W., & Spanner, R. *Atlas of human anatomy* (16th ed.). Amsterdam and Philadelphia: Scheltema & Holkema NV and F. A. Davis Co., 1967.

Stein, D. G., & Rosen, J. J. *Basic structure and function in the central nervous system.* New York: Macmillan, 1974.

Szentágothai, J., & Arbib, M.A. *Conceptual models of neural organization.* Cambridge, Mass.: M. I. T. Press, 1975.

Truex, R. C., & Carpenter, M. B. *Human neuroanatomy* (16th ed.). Baltimore: Williams and Wilkins, 1969.

von Bonin, G. *Essay on the cerebral cortex.* Springfield, Ill.: C. C. Thomas, 1950.

Chapter 4

Beloff, J. *The existence of mind.* London: MacGibbon & Kee, 1962.

Broadbent, D. E. *Decision and stress.* London: Academic Press, 1971.

Chappell, V. C. (Ed.). *The philosophy of mind.* Englewood Cliffs, N.J.: Prentice-Hall, 1962.

Corning, W. C., & Balaban, M. (Eds.). *The mind: Biological approaches to its functions.* New York: Wiley-Interscience, 1968.

Corso, J. F. *The experimental psychology of sensory behavior.* New York: Holt, Rinehart & Winston, 1967.

Deutsch, F. (Ed.). *On the mysterious leap from the mind to the body.* New York: International Universities Press, 1959.

Eccles, J. C. *Facing reality.* Berlin: Springer-Verlag, 1970.

Helson, H., & Bevan, W. (Eds.). *Contemporary approaches to psychology.* Princeton, N.J.: Van Nostrand, 1967.

Hook, S. (Ed.). *Dimensions of mind: A symposium.* New York: New York University, 1960.

Kantor, J. R. *The aim and progress of psychology and other sciences.* Chicago: Principia Press, 1971.

Kaufman, L. *Sight and mind: An introduction to visual perception.* New York: Oxford University Press, 1974.

Kling, J. W., & Riggs, L. A. (Eds.). *Woodworth & Schlosberg's experimental psychology* (3rd ed.). New York: Holt, Rinehart & Winston, 1971.

Kneale, W. *On having a mind.* Cambridge: Cambridge University Press, 1962.

Koch, S. (Ed.). *Psychology: A study of a science. Study I. Conceptual and systematic. Volume 1. Sensory, perceptual, and physiological formulations.* New York: McGraw-Hill, 1959.

Koch, S. (Ed.). *Psychology: A study of a science. Study II. Empirical substructure and relations with other sciences. Volume 4. Biologically oriented fields: Their place in psychology and in biological science.* New York: McGraw-Hill, 1962.

Marks, L. E. *Sensory processes: The new psychophysics.* New York: Academic Press, 1974.

Marx, M. H., & Hillix, W. A. *Systems and theories in psychology* (2nd ed.). New York: McGraw-Hill, 1973.

Maslow, A. *A study of Wittgenstein's Tractatus.* Berkeley: University of California Press, 1961.

Ornstein, J. H. *The mind and the brain: A multi-aspect interpretation.* The Hague, Netherlands: Martinus Nijhoff, 1972.

Ornstein, R. E. *The psychology of consciousness.* San Francisco: Freeman, 1972.

Polten, E. P. *Critique of the psycho-physical identity theory.* The Hague, Netherlands: Mouton, 1973.

Rosenblueth, A. *Mind and brain: A philosophy of science.* Cambridge: M.I.T. Press, 1970.

Ryle, G. *The concept of mind.* New York: Barnes & Noble, 1949.

Sahakian, W. S. (Ed.). *History of psychology: A source book in systematic psychology.* Itasca, Ill.: Peacock, 1968.

Scher, J. M. (Ed.). *Theories of the mind.* New York: Free Press of Glencoe, 1962.

Schrödinger, E. *Mind and matter.* Cambridge: Cambridge University Press, 1958.

Smythies, J. R. (Ed.). *Brain and mind: Modern concepts of the nature of mind.* London: Routledge & Kegan Paul, 1965.

Stevens, S. S. (Ed.). *Handbook of experimental psychology.* New York: Wiley, 1951.

Vesey, G. N. A. (Ed.). *Body and mind: Readings in philosophy.* London: Allen & Unwin, 1964.

Chapter 5

Altman, J. *Organic foundations of animal behavior.* New York: Holt, Rinehart & Winston, 1966.

Arbib, M. A. *The metaphorical brain: An introduction to cybernetics as artificial intelligence and brain theory.* New York: Wiley-Interscience, Wiley, 1972.

Baru, A. V., & Karaseva, T. A. *The brain and hearing: Hearing disturbances associated with local brain lesions.* New York: Consultants Bureau, 1972.

Beatty, J. *Introduction to Physiological psychology: Information processing in the nervous system.* Monterey, Calif.: Brooks/Cole, 1975.

Beckenbach, E. F., & Tompkins, C. B. (Eds.). *Concepts of communication: Interpersonal, intrapersonal and mathematical.* New York: Wiley, 1971.

Beritoff, J. S. *Neural mechanisms of higher vertebrate behavior.* Boston: Little, Brown, 1965.

Brazier, M. A. B. (Ed.). *The central nervous system and behavior: Transactions of the first conference, February 23, 24, 25, and 26, 1958.* Madison, N.J.: Madison Printing Co., 1959. (a)

Brazier, M. A. B. (Ed.). *The central nervous system and behavior: Transactions of the second conference, February 22, 23, 24, and 25, 1959.* Madison, N.J.: Madison Printing Co., 1959. (b)

Carterette, E. C. (Ed.). *Brain function. Vol.III: Speech, language and communication.* Berkeley, Calif.: University of California Press, 1966.

Crosby, E. C., Humphrey, T., & Lauer, E. W. *Correlative anatomy of the nervous system.* New York: Macmillan, 1962.

Delafresnaye, J. F. (Ed.). *Brain mechanisms and consciousness.* Springfield, Ill.: C. C. Thomas, 1954.

Eccles, J. C. (Ed.). *Brain and conscious experience.* New York: Springer-Verlag, 1966.

Eccles, J. C. *The understanding of the brain.* New York: McGraw-Hill, 1973.

Edwards, P. (Ed.). *The encyclopedia of philosophy.* New York: Macmillan, 1967.

Eidelberg, E., & Stein, D. G. Functional recovery after lesions of the nervous system. *Neurosciences Research Program Bulletin,* 1974, *12*(2), 189-303.

Field, J. (Ed.). *Handbook of physiology. Section 1: Neurophysiology* (Vol. I). Washington, D.C.: American Physiological Society, 1959.

Fulton, J. F., & Wilson, L. G. *Selected readings in the history of physiology* (2nd ed.). Springfield: C. C. Thomas, 1966.

Gazzaniga, M. S. *The bisected brain.* New York: Appleton-Century-Crofts, 1970.

Gazzaniga, M. S., & Blakemore, C. (Eds.). *Handbook of psychobiology.* New York: Academic Press, 1975.

Gellhorn, E. (Ed.). *Biological foundations of emotion: Research and commentary.* Glenview, Ill.: Scott, Foresman & Co., 1968.

Glass, D. C. (Ed.). *Neurophysiology and emotion.* New York: Rockefeller University Press and Russell Sage Foundation, 1967.

Harlow, H. F., & Woolsey, C. N. (Eds.). *Biological and biochemical bases of behavior.* Madison: University of Wisconsin Press, 1958.

Haymaker, W., Anderson, E., & Nauta, W. J. H. (Eds.). *The hypothalamus.* Springfield, Ill.: C. C. Thomas, 1969.

Ingle, D. J., & Sprague, J. M. Sensorimotor function of the midbrain tectum. *Neurosciences Research Program Bulletin,* 1975, *13* (2), 167-228.

Isaacson, R. L. *The limbic system.* New York: Plenum Press, 1974.

Jasper, H. H., Proctor, L. D., Knighton, R. S., Noshay, W. C., & Costello, R. T. (Eds.). *Reticular formation of the brain.* Boston: Little, Brown, 1958.

Jerison, H. J. *Evolution of the brain and intelligence.* New York: Academic Press, 1973.

Jung, R. (Ed.). *Handbook of sensory physiology. Vol. VII/3: Central processing of visual information, Part A.* New York: Springer-Verlag, 1973. (a)

Jung, R. (Ed.). *Handbook of sensory physiology. Vol. VII/3: Central processing of visual information, Part B.* New York: Springer-Verlag, 1973. (b)

Kantor, J. R. *The aim and progress of psychology and other sciences.* Chicago: Principia Press, 1971.

Koch, S. (Ed.). *Psychology: A study of a science. Study II. Empirical substructure and relations with other sciences. Vol. 4. Biologically oriented fields: Their place in psychology and in biological science.* New York: McGraw-Hill, 1962.
Program Bulletin. 1974, *12* (4), 511-656.

Luria, A. R. *Higher cortical functions in man.* New York: Consultants Bureau and Basic Books, 1966. (a)

Luria, A. R. *Human brain and psychological processes.* New York: Harper & Row, 1966.(b)

Luria, A. R. *The working brain: An introduction to neuropsychology.* New York: Basic Books, 1973.

McCleary, R. A., & Moore, R. Y. *Subcortical mechanisms of behavior: The psychological functions of primitive parts of the brain.* New York: Basic Books, 1965.

Myers, R. D. (Ed.). *Methods in psychobiology. Vol. 1. Laboratory techniques in neuro-psychology and neurobiology.* London and New York: Academic Press, 1971.

Newton, G., & Riesen, A. H. (Eds.). *Advances in psychobiology* (Vol. 2). New York: Wiley-Interscience, Wiley, 1974.

Oatley, K. *Brain mechanisms and mind.* New York: Dutton, 1972.

Penfield, W. *The Sherrington lectures V: The excitable cortex in conscious man.* Liverpool, England: Liverpool University Press, 1958.

Penfield, W., & Roberts, L. *Speech and brain-mechanisms.* Princeton, N.J.: Princeton University Press, 1959.

Polyak, S. *The vertebrate visual system.* Chicago: University of Chicago Press, 1957.

Pribram, K. H. *Languages of the brain: Experimental paradoxes and principles in neuro-psychology.* Englewood Cliffs, N.J.: Prentice-Hall, 1971.

Pribram, K. H., & Luria, A. R. (Eds.). *Psychophysiology of the frontal lobes.* New York: Academic Press, 1973.

Quarton, G. C., Melnechuk, T., & Schmitt, F. O. (Eds.). *The neurosciences: A study program.* New York: Rockefeller University Press, 1967.

Riklan, M., & Levita, E. *Subcortical correlates of human behavior: A psychological study of thalamic and basal ganglia surgery.* Baltimore: Williams & Wilkins, 1969.

Ruch, T. C., & Patton, H. D. (Eds.). *Physiology and biophysics* (19th ed.). Philadelphia: Saunders, 1965.

Russell, R. W. (Ed.). *Frontiers in physiological psychology.* New York: Academic Press, 1966.

Schmitt, F. O., & Worden, F. G. (Eds.). *The neurosciences: Third study program.* Cambridge: M.I.T. Press, 1974.

Stein, D. G., & Rosen, J. J. *Basic structure and function in the central nervous system.* New York: Macmillan, 1974. (a)

Stein, D. G., & Rosen, J. J. *Motivation and emotion.* New York: Macmillan, 1974. (b)

Stellar, E., & Sprague, J. M. (Eds.). *Progress in physiological psychology* (Vol. 1). New York: Academic Press, 1966.

Stellar, E., & Sprague, J. M. (Eds.). *Progress in physiological psychology* (Vol. 2). New York: Academic Press, 1968.

Teitelbaum, P. *Physiological psychology: Fundamental principles.* Englewood Cliffs, N.J.: Prentice-Hall, 1967.

Thompson, R. F. *Introduction to physiological psychology.* New York: Harper & Row, 1975.

Valenstein, E. S. *Brain control.* New York: Wiley-Interscience, Wiley, 1973. (a)

Valenstein, E. S. (Ed.). *Brain stimulation and motivation: Research and commentary.* Glenview, Ill.: Scott, Foresman & Co., 1973. (b)

Warren, J. M., & Akert, K. *The frontal granular cortex and behavior: A symposium.* New York: McGraw-Hill, 1964.

Whalen, R. E., Thompson, R. F., Verzeano, M., & Weinberger, N. M. (Eds.). *The neural control of behavior.* New York: Academic Press, 1970.

Whipple, H. E. Sensory evoked response in man. *Annals of the New York Academy of Sciences,* 1964, *112* (1), 1-546.

Wolstenholme, G. E. W., & O'Connor, C. M. (Eds.). *Ciba Foundation symposium on the neurological basis of behaviour.* London: Churchill, 1958.

Chapters 6 and 7

Brazier, M. *A history of the electrical activity of the brain.* London: Pitman Medical Publishing Co., 1961.

Cassirer, E. *The philosophy of symbolic forms. Vol. I: Language.* New Haven: Yale University Press, 1965.

Cobb, W., & Morocutti, C. (Eds.). *The evoked potentials* (Proceedings of an International Meeting, Siena, Italy, June 30-July 2, 1966). Amsterdam: Elsevier Publishing Co., 1967.

Donchin, E., & Lindsley, D. B. (Eds.). *Average evoked potentials: Methods, results, and evaluations.* (National Aeronautics and Space Administration.) Washington, D.C.: U.S. Government Printing Office, 1969.

Fodor, J. A. *The language of thought.* New York: Thomas Y. Crowell Company, 1975.

Gazzaniga, M. S., & Blakemore, C. (Eds.). *Handbook of psychobiology.* New York: Academic Press, 1975.

Grüsser, O. -J., Klinke, R. (Eds.). *Pattern recognition in biological and technical systems.* (Proceedings of the 4th Congress of the Deutsche Gesellschaft für Kybernetik, Berlin, April 6-9, 1970.) Berlin: Springer-Verlag, 1971.

Ingle, D. J., & Shein, H. M. (Eds.). *Model systems in biological psychiatry.* Cambridge: M.I.T. Press, 1975.

Karczmar, A. G., & Eccles, J. C. (Eds.). *Brain and human behavior.* Berlin: Springer-Verlag, 1972.

Katchalsky, A., Rowland, V., & Blumenthal, R. Dynamic patterns of brain cell assemblies. *Neurosciences Research Program Bulletin.* 1974, *12*(1), 1-87.

Kaufman, L. *Sight and mind: An introduction to visual perception.* New York: Oxford University Press, 1974.

Leibovic, K. N. (Ed.). *Information processing in the nervous system* (Proceedings of a Symposium at the State University of New York at Buffalo, October 21-24, 1968). New York: Springer-Verlag, 1969.

MacKay, D. M. Evoked brain potentials as indicators of sensory information processing. *Neurosciences Research Program Bulletin,* 1969, 7 (3), 181-276.

Morris, C. *Signs, language and behavior.* New York: Braziller, 1955.

Perkel, D. H., & Bullock, T. H. Neural coding: A report based on an NRP work session. *Neurosciences Research Program Bulletin,* 1968, *6*(3), 221-348.

Reichardt, W. (Ed.). *Proceedings of the International School of Physics "Enrico Fermi". Course 43: Processing of optical data by organisms and by machines.* New York: Academic Press, 1969.

Schmitt, F. O., & Worden, F. G. (Eds.). *The neurosciences: Third study program.* Cambridge: M.I.T. Press, 1974.

Somjen, G. *Sensory coding in the mammalian nervous system.* New York: Appleton-Century-Crofts, 1972.

Uttal, W. R. *The psychobiology of sensory coding.* New York: Harper & Row, 1973.

Uttal, W. R. *Cellular neurophysiology and integration: An interpretive introduction.* Hillsdale, N.J.: Lawrence Erlbaum Associates, 1975.

Whalen, R. E., Thompson, R. F., Verzeano, M., & Weinberger, N. M. (Eds.). *The neural control of behavior.* New York: Academic Press, 1970.

Chapters 8 and 9

Ádám, G. (Ed.). *Biology of memory* (Proceedings of the Symposium held at the Biological Research Institute in Tihany, Hungary, September 1-4, 1969). New York: Plenum Press, 1971.

Adams, J. A. *Learning and memory: An introduction.* Homewood, Illinois: Dorsey Press, 1976.

Anderson, J., & Bower, G. *Human associative learning.* New York: Winston-Wiley, 1973.

Bennett, M. V. L. (Ed.). *Synaptic transmission and neuronal interaction.* New York: Raven Press, 1974.

Boakes, R. A., & Halliday, M. S. (Eds.). *Inhibition and learning.* London: Academic Press, 1972.

Chase, M. H. (Ed.). *Operant control of brain activity. Perspectives in the brain sciences* (Vol. 2). Los Angeles: Brain Information Service/Brain Research Institute, University of California, 1974.

Deutsch, D., & Deutsch, J. A. (Eds.). *Short-term memory.* New York: Academic Press, 1975.

Deutsch, J. A. (Ed.). *The physiological basis of memory.* New York: Academic Press, 1973.

Dunn, A. J., & Bondy, S. C. *Functional chemistry of the brain.* Flushing, New York: Spectrum Publications, 1974.

Eccles, J. C. *The physiology of synapses.* New York: Academic Press, 1964.

Eccles, J. C. *Facing reality.* New York: Springer-Verlag, 1970.

Eccles, J. C. *The understanding of the brain.* New York: McGraw-Hill, 1973.

Estes, W. K. (Ed.). *Handbook of learning and cognitive processes.* Hillsdale, N.J.: Lawrence Erlbaum Associates, 1975.

Gazzaniga, M. S., & Blakemore, C. (Eds.). *Handbook of psychobiology.* New York: Academic Press, 1975.

Isaacson, R. L. *The limbic system.* New York: Plenum Press, 1974.

John, E. R. *Mechanisms of memory.* New York: Academic Press, 1967.

Kimble, D. P. (Ed.). *The anatomy of memory* (Vol. 1) (Proceedings of the First Conference on Learning, Remembering, and Forgetting held in Princeton, New Jersey, from September 29 to October 2, 1963). Palo Alto: Sciences and Behavior Books, Inc., 1965.

Kintsch, W. *Learning, memory and conceptual processes.* New York: Wiley, 1970.

Lindsay, P. H., & Norman, D. A. *Human information processing: An introduction to psychology.* New York: Academic Press, 1972.

Mark, R. *Memory and nerve cell connections.* London: Oxford University Press, 1974.

Murdock, B. B., Jr. *Human memory: Theory and data.* Hillsdale, N.J.: Lawrence Erlbaum Associates, 1974.

Norman, D. A. *Memory and attention.* New York: Wiley, 1969.

Pappas, G. D., & Purpura, D. P. (Eds.). *Structure and function of synapses.* New York: Raven Press, 1972.

Penfield, W., & Roberts, L. *Speech and brain-mechanisms.* Princeton: Princeton University Press, 1959.

Pribram, K. H. *Languages of the brain.* Englewood Cliffs, N.J.: Prentice-Hall, 1971.

Pribram, K. H., & Broadbent, D. E. (Eds.). *Biology of memory.* New York: Academic Press, 1970.

Quarton, G. D., Melnechuk, T., & Schmitt, F. O. (Eds.). *The neurosciences: A study program.* New York: Rockefeller University Press, 1967.

Schmitt, F. O. (Ed.). *The neurosciences: Second study program.* New York: Rockefeller University Press, 1970.

Schmitt, F. O., & Worden F. G. (Eds.). *The neurosciences: Third study program.* Cambridge: M. I. T. Press, 1974.

Shepherd, G. M. *The synaptic organization of the brain: An introduction.* New York: Oxford University Press, 1974.

Stein, D. G., & Rosen, J. J. *Learning and memory.* New York: Macmillan, 1974.

Stellar, E., & Sprague, J. M. (Eds.). *Progress in physiological psychology* (Vol. 1). New York: Academic Press, 1966.

Stellar, E., & Sprague, J. M. (Eds.). *Progress in physiological psychology* (Vol. 2). New York: Academic Press, 1968.

Thompson, R. F. *Introduction to physiological psychology.* New York: Harper & Row, 1975.

Ungar, G. (Ed.). *Molecular Mechanisms in memory and learning.* New York: Plenum Press, 1970.

Uttal, W. R. *Cellular neurophysiology and integration: An interpretive introduction.* Hillsdale, N.J.: Lawrence Erlbaum Associates, 1975.

Woody, C. D., Brown, K. A., Crow, T.J., Jr., & Knispel, J. D. (Eds.). *Cellular mechanisms subserving changes in neuronal activity* (Research Report #3). Los Angeles: Brain Information Service/Brain Research Institute, University of California, 1974.

Young, J. Z. *The memory system of the brain.* Berkeley and Los Angeles: University of California Press, 1966.

B. REFERENCES

Ádám, G. (Ed.). *Biology of memory.* (Proceedings of the Symposium held at the Biological Research Institute in Tihany, Hungary, September 1-4, 1969.) New York: Plenum Press, 1971.

Adams, J. A. *Learning and memory: An introduction.* Homewood, Ill.: Dorsey, 1976.

Adey, W. R. Neurophysiological correlates of information transaction and storage in brain tissue. In E. Stellar & J. M. Sprague (Eds.), *Progress in physiological psychology* (Vol. 1). New York: Academic Press, 1966.

Adey, W. R., & Walter, D. O. Application of phase detection and averaging techniques in computer analysis of EEG records in the cat. *Experimental Neurology,* 1963, *7,* 186-209.

Agranoff, B. W. Agents that block memory. In G. C. Quarton, T. Melnechuck, & F. O. Schmitt (Eds.), *The neurosciences: A study program.* New York: Rockefeller University Press, 1967.

Agranoff, B. W. Biochemistry of learning processes: Biochemical concomitants of the storage of behavioral information. In L. Jaenicke (Ed.), *Biochemistry of sensory functions.* Gesellschaft der Biologische Chemie. Berlin: Springer-Verlag, 1974.

Agranoff, B. W., Davis, R. E., & Brink, J. J. Memory fixation in the goldfish. *Proceedings of the National Academy of Science-U.S.,* 1965, *54,* 788-793.

Agranoff, B. W., Springer, A. D., & Quarton, G. C. Biochemistry of memory and learning. In P. J. Vinken & G. W. Bruyn (Eds.), *Handbook of clinical neurology* (Vol. 27). Amsterdam: North Holland, 1976.

Aidley, D. J. *The physiology of excitable cells.* New York: Cambridge University Press, 1971.

Akimoto, H., & Creutzfeldt, O. D. Reaktionen von Neuronen des optischen Cortex nach elektrischer Reizung unspezifisher Thalamuskerne. *Archiv für Psychiatrie und Nervenkrankheiten,* 1957/1958, *196,* 494-519.

Albers, W., Siegel, G., Katzman, R., & Agranoff, B. W. (Eds.). *Basic neurochemistry.* Boston: Little, Brown, 1972.

Allman, J. M., & Kaas, J. H. A representation of the visual field in the caudal third of the middle temporal gyrus of the owl monkey *(Aotus trivirgatus). Brain Research,* 1971, *31,* 85-105.

Allman, J. M., Kaas, J. H., Lane, R. H., & Miezin, F. M. A crescent-shaped cortical visual area surrounding the middle temporal area (MT) in the owl monkey *(Aotus trivirgatus). Anatomical Record,* 1973, *175,* 263-264.

Alpern, M., Rushton, W. A. H., & Torii, S. The size of rod signals. *Journal of Physiology,* 1970, *206,* 193-208.

Altman, J. Postnatal growth and differentiation of the mammalian brain, with implications for a morphological theory of memory. In G. C. Quarton, T. Melnechuk, & F. O. Schmitt (Eds.), *The neurosciences: A study program.* New York: Rockefeller University Press, 1967.

Amassian, V. E. Studies on organization of a somesthetic association area including a single unit analysis. *Journal of Neurophysiology,* 1954, *17,* 39-58.

Amassian, V. E., Waller, H. J., & Macy, J., Jr. Neural mechanism of the primary somatosensory evoked potential. *Annals of the New York Academy of Sciences,* 1964, *112,* 5-32.

Amatniek, E. Measurement of bioelectric potentials with microelectrodes and neutralized input capacity amplifiers. *I.R.E. Transaction Medical Electronics,* 1958, *PGME10,* 3-14.

Anand, B. K., & Brobeck, J. R. Hypothalamic control of food intake in rats and cats. *Yale Journal of Biology and Medicine,* 1951, *24,* 123-140.

Anderson, J. A. A memory storage model utilizing spatial correlation functions. *Kybernetik,* 1968, *5,* 113-119.

Anderson, J. A. A simple neural network generating an interactive memory. *Mathematical Biosciences,* 1972, *14,* 197-220.

Anderson, J., & Bower, G. *Human associative memory.* New York: Halstead Press, 1973.

Andersson, B., & McCann, S. M. A further study of polydipsia evoked by hypothalamic stimulation in the goat. *Acta Physiologica Scandinavica,* 1955, *33,* 333-346.

Andersson, S., & Gernandt, B. E. Cortical projection of vestibular nerve in cat. *Acta Otolaryngologica,* 1954, supplement, *116,* 10-18.

Anstis, S. M. What does visual perception tell us about visual coding? In M. S. Gazzaniga & C. Blakemore (Eds.), *Handbook of psychobiology.* New York: Academic Press, 1975.

Aquinas, St. Thomas. *Summa Theologica.* In W. S. Sahakian (Ed.), *History of psychology: A source book in systematic psychology.* Itasca, Ill.: Peacock, 1968.

Arbib, M. A. *The metaphorical brain: An introduction to cybernetics as artificial intelligence and brain theory.* New York: Wiley-Interscience, 1972.

Arden, G. B. Complex receptive fields and responses to moving objects in cells of the rabbit's lateral geniculate body. *Journal of Physiology,* 1963, *166,* 468-488.

Ariens-Kappers, C. V. Further contributions on neurobiotaxis IX. *Journal of Comparative Neurology,* 1917, *27,* 261-298.

Armstrong, D. M. *Bodily sensations.* London and New York: Routledge & Kegan Paul and Humanities Press, 1962.

Ashby, W. R. *Design for a brain* (2nd ed.). New York: Wiley, 1960.

Atkinson, R. C., & Shiffrin, R. M. Human memory: A proposed system and its control process. In K. W. Spence & J. T. Spence (Eds.), *The psychology of learning and motivation.* New York: Academic Press, 1968.

Atkinson, R. C., & Shiffrin, R. M. The control of short-term memory. *Scientific American,* 1971, *225,* 82-91.

Averbach, E., & Coriell, A. Short term memory in vision. *Bell System Technical Journal,* 1961, *40,* 309-328.

Baddeley, A. D., & Dale, H. C. A. The effects of semantic similarity on retroactive interference in long- and short-term memory. *Journal of Verbal Learning and Verbal Behavior,* 1966, *5,* 417-420.

Baker, R., & Llinás, R. Electrotonic coupling between neurones in the rat mesencephalic nucleus. *Journal of Physiology,* 1971, *212,* 45-63.

Ball, G. G., Micco, D. J., Jr., & Berntson, G. G. Cerebellar stimulation in the rat: Complex stimulation-bound oral behaviors and self-stimulation. *Physiology and Behavior,* 1974, *13,* 123-127.

Bard, P. On emotional expression after decortication with some remarks on theoretical views. *Psychological Review,* 1934, *41,* pp. 309-329; 424-449.

Bard, P., & Mountcastle, V. B. Some forebrain mechanisms involved in expression of rage with special reference to suppression of angry behavior. *Research Publications. Association for Research on Nervous and Mental Disease,* 1947, *27,* 363-404.

Barlow, H. B. Optic nerve impulses and Weber's law. *Cold Spring Harbor Symposia on Quantitative Biology,* 1965, *30,* 539-546.

Barlow, H. B., Blakemore, C., & Pettigrew, J. D. The neural mechanism of binocular depth discrimination. *Journal of Physiology,* 1967, *193,* 327-342.

Barlow, H. B., & Hill, R. M. Selective sensitivity to direction of movement in ganglion cells of the rabbit retina. *Science,* 1963, *139,* 412-414.

Barlow, H. B., Hill, R. M., & Levick, W. R. Retinal ganglion cells responding selectively to direction and speed of image in the rabbit. *Journal of Physiology,* 1964, *173,* 337-407.

Barlow, H. B., & Levick, W. R. The mechanism of directionally selective units in rabbit's retina. *Journal of Physiology,* 1965, *178,* 477-504.

Barlow, H. B., Narasimhan, R., & Rosenfeld, A. Visual pattern recognition in machines and animals. *Science,* 1972, *177,* 567-575.

Barondes, J. H., & Cohen, H. D. Puromycin effect on successive phases of memory storage. *Science,* 1966, *151,* 594-595.

Basmajian, J. V. Electromyography: Single motor unit train. In R. F. Thompson & M. M. Patterson (Eds.), *Bioelectric recording techniques* (Vol. IC). New York: Academic Press, 1974.

Baumgarten, R., von, & Jung, R. Microelectrode studies on the visual cortex. *Revue Neurologique,* 1952, *87,* 151-155.

Baumgartner, G., & Jung, R. Convergence of specific and unspecific afferent impulses on neurones of the visual cortex. *Electroencephalography and Clinical Neurophysiology,* 1956, *8,* 163-164.

Beck, E. C. Electrophysiology and behavior. *Annual Review of Psychology,* 1975, *26,* 233-262.

Begleiter, H., & Porjesz, B. Evoked brain potentials as indicators of decision-making. *Science,* 1975, *187,* 754-755. (a)

Begleiter, H., & Porjesz, B. Letter. *Science,* 1975, *190,* 1006. (b)

Békésy, G., von. Funneling in the nervous system and its role in loudness and sensation intensity in the skin. *Journal of the Acoustical Society of America,* 1958, *30,* 399-412.

Békésy, G., von. Interaction of paired sensory stimuli and conduction in peripheral nerves. *Journal of Applied Physiology,* 1963, *18,* 1276-1284.

Bell, C. *Idea of a new anatomy of the brain submitted for the observation of his friends.* London: Strahan & Preston, 1811.

Beloff, J. *The existence of mind.* London: MacGibbon & Kee, 1962.

Benjamin, R. M., & Welker, W. I. Somatic receiving areas of cerebral cortex of squirrel monkey *(Saimiri sciureus). Journal of Neurophysiology,* 1957, *20,* 286-299.

Bennett, M. V. L. A comparison of electrically and chemically mediated transmission. In G. D. Pappas & D. P. Purpura (Eds.), *Structure and function of synapses.* New York: Raven Press, 1972.

Bennett, M. V. L. (Ed.). *Synaptic transmission and neuronal interaction.* New York: Raven Press, 1974.

Berlucchi, G., & Buchtel, H. A. Some trends in the neurological study of learning. In M. S. Gazzaniga & C. Blakemore (Eds.), *Handbook of psychobiology.* New York: Academic Press, 1975.

Bernard, M. C. *Lessons on the physiology and pathology of the nervous system.* London: Baillière Tindall Ltd., 1858.

Bernstein, J. Untersuchungen zur Thermodynamik der bioelektrischen Strome. Erster Theil. *Pflüger's Archives of the European Journal of Physiology,* 1902, *92,* 521.

Bernston, G. G. Blockade and release of hypothalamically and naturally elicited aggressive behaviors in cats following midbrain lesions. *Journal of Comparative and Physiological Psychology,* 1972, *81,* 541-554.

Bernston, G. G. Attack, grooming, and threat elicited by stimulation of the pontine tegmentum in cats. *Physiology and Behavior,* 1973, *11,* 81-87.

Bernston, G. G., & Beatie, M. S. Functional differentiation within hypothalamic behavioral systems in the cat. *Physiological Psychology,* 1975, *3,* 183-188.

Bernston, G. G., Potolicchio, S. J., Jr., & Miller, N. E. Evidence for higher functions of the cerebellum: Eating and grooming elicited by cerebellar stimulation in cats. *Proceedings of the National Academy of Science-U.S.*, 1973, *70*, 2497-2499.

Bever, T. G., & Chiarello, R. J. Cerebral dominance in musicians and nonmusicians. *Science*, 1974, *185*, 537-539.

Bindra, D. The problem of subjective experience: Puzzlement on reading R. W. Sperry's "A modified concept of consciousness." *Psychological Review*, 1970, *77*, 581-584.

Blake, R., & Hirsch, H. V. B. Deficits in binocular depth perception in cats after alternating monocular deprivation. *Science*, 1975, *190*, 1114-1116.

Blakemore, C., & Campbell, F. W. On the existence of neurones in the human visual system selectively sensitive to the orientation and size of retinal images. *Journal of Physiology*, 1969, *203*, 237-260.

Blakemore, C., & Cooper, G. F. Development of the brain depends on the visual environment. *Nature*, 1970, 228, 477-478.

Blakemore, C., & Cooper, G. F. Modification of the visual cortex by experience. *Brain Research*, 1971, 31, 366.

Blakemore, C., & Mitchell, D. E. Environmental modification of the visual cortex and the neural basis of learning and memory. *Nature* (London), 1973, *241*, 467-468.

Blakemore, C., Nachmias, J., & Sutton, P. The perceived spatial frequency shift: Evidence for frequency selective neurons in the human brain. *Journal of Physiology*, 1970, *210*, 727-750.

Bliss, T. V. P., & Lömo, T. Plasticity in a monosynaptic cortical pathway. *Journal of Physiology*, 1970, *207*, 61P.

Bodian, D. The generalized vertebrate neuron. *Science*, 1962, *137*, 323-326.

Boring, E. G. *A history of experimental psychology* (2nd ed.). New York: Appleton-Century-Crofts, 1950.

Bower, G. H. Cognitive psychology: An introduction. In W. K. Estes (Ed.), *Handbook of learning and cognitive processes*. Hillsdale, N.J.: Lawrence Erlbaum Associates, 1975.

Boycott, B. B., & Kolb, H. The connexions between bipolar cells and photoreceptors in the retina of the domestic cat. *Journal of Comparative Neurology*, 1973, *148*, 91-114.

Bradbury, S. *The evolution of the microscope*. Oxford: Pergamon Press, 1967.

Braun, J. J. Neocortex and feeding behavior in the rat. *Journal of Comparative and Physiological Psychology*, 1975, *89*, 507-522.

Brazier, M. A. B. The historical development of neurophysiology. In J. Field, H. W. Magoun, V. E. Hall (Eds.), *Handbook of physiology. Section 1: Neurophysiology* (Vol. I). Washington, D. C.: American Physiological Society, 1959.

Brazier, M. A. B. *A hsitory of the electrical activity of the brain*. London: Pitman Medical Publishing Company, 1961.

Breen, T. E. The effect of occipital and pretectal lesions on retention of easy and difficult brightness discriminations in the rat. Unpublished doctoral dissertation, Louisiana State University, 1965.

Breitmeyer, B., & Ganz, L. Implications of sustained and transient channels for theories of visual pattern masking saccadic suppression, and information processing. *Psychological Review*, 1976, *83*, 1-36.

Bremer, F. Cerveau "isolé" et physiologie du sommeil. *Comptes Rendus. Société de Biologie*, 1935, *118*, 1235-1241.

Bremer, F. L'activité cérébrale au cours du sommeil et de la narcose. Contribution a l'étude du mécanisme du sommeil. *Bulletin de L'Académie Royale de Medecine de Belgique*, 1937, *2*, 6ᵉ série, 68-86.

Bridgman, P. W. *The logic of modern physics*. New York: Macmillan, 1927.

Broadbent, D. E. *Perception and communication*. New York: Pergamon, 1958.

Broadbent, D. E. *Decision and stress*. London: Academic Press, 1971.

Broca, P. Remarques sur la siège de la faculte du language articule, suives d'une observation d'aphemie (perte de la parole). *Bulletins de la Société Anatomique de Paris*, Tome VI, 1861, *36*, 330-357.

Broadmann, K. Beiträge zurhistologischen Lokalisation der Grosshirnrinde. VI. Mitteilung: Die Cortexgliederung des Menschen. *Journal für Psychologie und Neurologie, Leipzig*, 1908, *10*, 231-246.

Brodmann, K. *Vergleichende Lokalisationslehre der Grosshinrnrinde*. Leipzig, Germany: Barth, 1908.

Brodwick, M. S., & Junge, D. Post-stimulus hyperpolarization and slow potassium conductance increase in *Aplysia* giant neurone. *Journal of Physiology*, 1972, *223*, 549-570.

Brooks, B., & Jung, R. Neuronal physiology of the visual cortex. In R. Jung (Ed.), *Visual centers in the brain*. Berlin: Springer-Verlag, 1973.

Brown, I. R., & Church, R. B. RNA transcription from nonrepetitive DNA in the mouse. *Biochemical and Biophysical Research Communications*, 1971, *42*, 850-856.

Bruner, J., & Kennedy, D. Habituation: Occurrence at a neuromuscular junction. *Science*, 1970, *169*, 92-94.

Buerger, A. A., & Fennessy, A. Long term alteration of leg position due to shock avoidance by spinal rats. *Experimental Neurology*, 1971, *30*, 195-211.

Bullock, T. H. On the anatomy of the giant neurons of the visceral ganglion of *Aplysia*. In E. Florey (Ed.), *Nervous inhibition*. New York: Pergamon, 1961.

Burns, B. D. Electrophysiologic basis of normal and psychotic function. In Garrattini & Ghetti (Eds.), *Psychotropic drugs*. Amsterdam: Elsevier, 1957.

Burns, B. D. *The mammalian cerebral cortex*. London: Edward Arnold Ltd., 1958.

Butcher, L. L., & Fox, S. S. Motor effects of copper in the caudate nucleus: Reversible lesions with ion exchange resin beads. *Science*, 1968, *160*, 1237 1239.

Butter, C. M. Habituation of responses to novel stimuli in monkey's with selective frontal lesions. *Science*, 1964, *144*, 313-314.

Byrne, J., Castellucci, V., & Kandel, E. R. Receptive fields and response properties of mechanoreceptor neurons innervating siphon skin and mantle shelf in *Aplysia. Journal of Neurophysiology*, 1974, *37*, 1041-1064.

Byrne, W. L., Samuel, D., Bennett, E. L., Rosenzweig, M. R., Wasserman, E., Wagner, A. R., Gardner, F., Galambos, R., Berger, B. D., Margules, D. L., Fenichel, R. L., Stein, L., Corson, J. A., Enesco, H. E., Chorover, S. L., Holt, C. E., III, Schiller, P. H., Chiappetta, L., Jarvik, M. E., Leaf, R. C., Dutcher, J. D., Horovitz, Z. P., & Carlson, P. L. Memory transfer, *Science*, 1966, *153*, 658-659.

Cajal, S. Ramon y. *Histologie du Système Nerveaux de l'Homme et des Vertébrés* (Vol. II). Paris: Maloine, 1911.

Campbell, F. W., Cooper, G. F., & Enroth-Cugell, C. The spatial selectivity of the visual cells of the cat. *Journal of Physiology*, 1969, *203*, 223-235.

Campbell, F. W., Cooper, G. F., Robson, J. G., & Sachs, M. B. The spatial selectivity of the visual cells of the cat and the squirrel monkey. *Journal of Physiology*, 1969, *204*, 120-121.

Campbell, F. W., & Maffei, L. Electrophysiological evidence for the existence of orientation and size detectors in the human visual system. *Journal of Physiology*, 1970, *207*, 635-652.

Campbell, F. W., Nachmias, J., & Jukes, J. Spatial-frequency discrimination in human vision. *Journal of the Optical Society of America*, 1970, *60*, 555-559.

Campbell, F. W., & Robson, J. G. Application of Fourier analysis to the visibility of gratings. *Journal of Physiology*, 1968, *197*, 551-566.

Campbell, S. K., Parker, T. D., & Welker, W. I. Somatotopic organization of the external cuneate nucleus in albino rats. *Brain Research*, 1974, *77*, 1-23.

Cannon, W. B. The James-Lange theory of emotions: A critical examination and an alternative theory. *American Journal of Psychology*, 1927, *39*, 106-124.

Cannon, W. B., & Bacq, Z. M. Studies on the conditions of activity in endocrine organs. XXVI. A hormone produced by sympathetic action on smooth muscle. *American Journal of Physiology,* 1931, *96,* 392-412.

Carpenter, M. B. *Human neuroanatomy* (7th ed.). Baltimore: Williams & Wilkins, 1976.

Carroll, B. J., Curtis, G. G., & Mendelf, J. Neuro-endocrine regulation in depression. I. Limbic system-adrene-cortical dysfunctions. *Archives of General Psychiatry,* 1976, *33,* 1051-1058. (a)

Carroll, B. J., Curtis, G. G., & Mendelf, J. Neuro-endocrine regulation in depression. II. Discrimination of depressed from non-depressed patients. *Archives of General Psychiatry,* 1976, *33,* 1051-1058. (b)

Cassirer, E. *[The philosophy of symbolic forms* (Vol. 1). *Language]* (R. Manheim, trans.). New Haven: Yale University Press, 1953.

Castelluci, V., Pinsker, H., Kupfermann, I., & Kandel, E. R. Neuronal mechanisms of habituation and dishabituation of the gill-withdrawn reflex in *Aplysia. Science,* 1970, *167,* 1745-1748.

Caton, R. The electric current of the brain. *British Medical Journal,* 1875, *2,* 278-296.

Chang, H. T. Cortical neurons with particular reference to the apical dendrites. *Cold Spring Harbor Symposium on Quantitative Biology,* 1952, *17,* 189-202.

Chomsky, N. *Syntactic structures.* The Hague: Mouton, 1957.

Chomsky, N. *Aspects of the theory of syntax.* Cambridge, Mass.: M.I.T. Press, 1965.

Chow, K. L. Visual discrimination after ablation of optic tract and visual cortex in cats. *Brain Research,* 1968, *9,* 363-366.

Chusid, J. G. *Correlative neuroanatomy and functional neurology* (16th ed.). Los Altos, Calif.: Lange Medical Publications, 1974.

Clark, T. K., Caggiula, A. R., McConnell, R. A., & Antelman, S. M. Sexual inhibition is reduced by rostral midbrain lesions in the male rat. *Science,* 1975, *190,* 169-171.

Clemente, C. D., & Chase, M. H. Neurological substrates of aggressive behavior. *Annual Review of Physiology,* 1973, *35,* 329-356.

Cobb, S. (In S. Cobb, H. M. Fox, P. H. Gates, S. Gifford, P. H. Knapp, A. O. Ludwig, W. F. Murphy, C. Mushatt, E. V. Semrand, J. L. Weinberger, F. Deutsch) Is the term "mysterious leap" warranted? In F. Deutsch (Ed.), *On the mysterious leap from the mind to the body.* New York: International Universities Press, 1959.

Cobb, W., & Morocutti, C. (Eds.). *The evoked potentials.* (Proceedings of an International Meeting, Siena, Italy, June 30-July 2, 1966.) Amsterdam: Elsevier, 1967.

Conrad, K. New problems of aphasia. *Brain,* 1954, *77,* 491-509.

Coombs, C. H., Dawes, R. M., & Tversky, A. *Mathematical psychology: An elementary introduction.* Englewood Cliffs, N.J.: Prentice-Hall, 1970.

Coombs, C. H., & Huang, L. Tests of a portfolio theory of risk preference. *Journal of Experimental Psychology,* 1970, *85,* 23-29.

Coombs, C. H., & Meyer, D. E. Risk-preference in coin toss games. *Journal of Mathematical Psychology,* 1969, *6,* 514-527.

Corning, W. C., & Balaban, M. *The mind: Biological approaches to its functions.* New York: Wiley, 1968.

Corso, J. F. *The experimental psychology of sensory behavior.* New York: Holt, Rinehart & Winston, 1967.

Courchesne, E., Hillyard, S. A., & Galambos, R. Stimulus novelty, task relevance and the visual evoked potential in man. *Electroencephalography and Clinical Neurophysiology,* 1975, *39,* 131-143.

Cowan, W. M., Gottlieb, D. I., Hendrickson, A. E., Price, J. L., & Woolsey, T. A. The autoradiographic demonstration of axonal connections in the central nervous system. *Brain Research,* 1972, *37,* 21-51.

Creutzfeldt, O. D., & Akimoto, M. Konvergenz und gegenseitige Beeinflussung aus der Retina und den unspezifischen Thalamuskernen an einzelnen Neuronen des optischen Cortex. *Archiv für Psychiatrie und Nervenkrankheiten*, 1957/1958, *196*, 520-538.

Creutzfeldt, O., & Baumgartner, G. Reactions of neurones in the occipital cortex to electrical stimuli applied to the intralaminar thalamus. *Electroencephalography and Clinical Neurophysiology*, 1955, *7*, 664-665.

Creutzfeldt, O. D., & Heggelund, P. Neural plasticity in visual cortex of adult cats after exposure to visual patterns. *Science*, 1975, *188*, 1025-1027.

Crosby, E. C., Humphrey, T., & Lauer, E. W. *Correlative anatomy of the nervous system.* New York: Macmillan, 1962.

Cucnod, M. Commissural pathways in interhemispheric transfer of visual information in the pigeon. In F. O. Schmitt & F. G. Worden (Eds.), *The neurosciences: Third study program.* Cambridge, Mass.: M.I.T. Press, 1974.

Curtis, H. J., & Cole, K. S. Membrane resting and action potentials from the squid giant axon. *Journal of Cellular and Comparative Physiology*, 1942, *19*, 135-144.

Dagan, D., Vernon, L. H., & Hoyle, G. Neuromimes: Self-exciting alternate firing pattern models. *Science*, 1975, *188*, 1035-1036.

Dalby, D. A., Meyer, D. R., & Meyer, P. M. Effects of occipital neocortical lesions upon visual discriminations in the cat. *Physiology and Behavior*, 1970, *5*, 727-734.

Davis, R. E., & Agranoff, B. W. Stages of memory function in goldfish: Evidence for an environmental trigger. *Proceedings of the National Academy of Science-U.S.*, 1966, *55*, 555-559.

Dawson, G. D. Cerebral responses to electrical stimulation of peripheral nerve in man. *Journal of Neurology, Neurosurgery and Psychiatry*, 1947, *10*, 137-140.

Dawson, G. D. Cerebral responses to nerve stimulation in man. *British Medical Bulletin*, 1950, *6*, 329.

Dawson, G. D. A summation technique for the detection of small evoked potentials. *Electroencephalography and Clinical Neurophysiology*, 1954, *1*, 65-84.

Dawson, G. D., & Scott, J. W. The recording of nerve action potentials through skin in man. *Journal of Neurology, Neurosurgery, and Psychiatry*, 1949, *12*, 259-273.

Dean, P. Effects of inferotemporal lesions on the behavior of monkeys. *Psychological Bulletin*, 1976, *83*, 41-71.

Del Castillo, J., & Katz, B. Quantal components of the end-plate potential. *Journal of Physiology*, 1954, *124*, 560-573.

De Lorenzo, A. J. The fine structure of synapses in the ciliary ganglion on the chick. *Journal of Biophysics, Biochemistry, and Cytology*, 1960, *7*, 31-36.

Denning, H. *Lehrbuch der Inneren Medizin.* Band II, 7 Aufl., Stuttgart, Germany: Georg Thieme Verlag, 1966.

De Robertis, E., & Bennett, H. S. Submicroscopic vesicular component in the synapse. *Federation Proceedings*, 1954, *13*, 35. (Abstract)

Desiraju, T. Transformations of discharges of neurons of parietal association cortex during sleep and wakefulness in monkey. *Journal of Neurophysiology*, 1972, *35*, 326-332.

Deutsch, J. A. A theory of shape recognition. *British Journal of Psychology*, 1955, *46*, 30-37.

Deutsch, J. A. (Ed.). *The physiological basis of memory.* New York: Academic Press, 1973.

Deutsch, J. A., & Deutsch, D. *Physiological psychology.* Homewood, Ill.: Dorsey Press, 1966.

DeValois, R. L., Abramov, I., & Jacobs, G. H. Analysis of response patterns of LGN cells. *Journal of the Optical Society of America*, 1966, *56*, 966-977.

DeValois, R. L., & Pease, P. L. Contours and contrast: Responses of monkey lateral geniculate nucleus cells to luminance and color figures. *Science*, 1971, *171*, 694-696.

Disterhoft, J. F., & Olds, J. Differential development of conditioned unit changes in thalamus and cortex of rat. *Journal of Neurophysiology*, 1972, *35*, 665-679.

Dodwell, P. C. *Visual pattern recognition*. New York: Holt, Rinehart & Winston, 1970.

Donaldson, P. E. K. *Electronic apparatus for biological research*. New York: Academic Press, 1958.

Donchin, E. Letter. *Science*, 1975, *190*, 1004-1005.

Donchin, E., & Lindsley, D. B. (Eds.). *Average evoked potentials: Methods, results, and evaluations*. (National Aeronautics and Space Administration.) Washington, D.C.: U.S. Government Printing Office, 1969.

Donders, F. C. Die Schnelligkeit psychischer Processe. *Archiv für Anatomie, Physiologie und Wissenschaftliche Medicin, Leipzig*, 1868, 657-681.

Douglas, R. J. Pavlovian conditioning and the brain. In R. A. Boakes & M. S. Halliday (Eds.), *Inhibition and learning*. London: Academic Press, 1972.

Douglas, R. J., & Pribram, K. H. Learning and limbic lesions. *Neuropsychologia*, 1966, *4*, 197-220.

Douglas, W. W., Nagasawa, J., & Schultz, R. A. Electron microscopic studies on the mechanism of secretion of posterior putuitary hormones and significance of microvesicles ('Synaptic vesicles'): Evidence of secretion by exocytosis and formation of microvesicles as a byproduct of this process. *Society for Endocrinology. Memoirs*. 1970, *19*, 353.

Dow, B. M., & Dubner, R. Visual receptive fields and responses to movement in an association area of cat cerebral cortex. *Journal of Neurophysiology*, 1969, *32*, 773-784.

Dow, B. M., & Dubner, R. Single-unit responses to moving visual stimuli in middle suprasylvian gyrus of the cat. *Journal of Neurophysiology*, 1971, *34*, 47-55.

Dowling, J. E., & Boycott, B. B. Organization of the primate retina: Electron microscopy. *Proceedings of the Royal Society*, Series B, 1966, *166*, 80-111.

Dräger, U. C., & Hubel, D. H. Responses to visual stimulation and relationship between visual, auditory, and somatosensory inputs in mouse superior colliculus. *Journal of Neurophysiology*, 1975, *38*, 690-713.

Dubin, M. W. The inner plexiform layer of the vertebrate retina: A quantitative and comparative electron microscopic analysis. *Journal of Comparative Neurology*, 1970, *140*, 479-505.

Dubner, R., & Rutledge, L. T. Recording and analysis of converging input upon neurons in cat association cortex. *Journal of Neurophysiology*, 1964, *27*, 620-634.

Du Bois-Reymond, E. *Untersuchungen über thierische elektricität*. (Vols. I-II). Berlin: Reimer, 1948-1949.

Ducasse, C. In defense of dualism. In S. Hook (Ed.), *Dimensions of mind: A symposium*. New York: New York University, 1960.

Duddell, W. D. B. Oscillographs. *The electrician*. September 10, 1897.

Dunn, A. J., & Bondy, S. C. *Functional chemistry of the brain*. Flushing, N.Y.: Spectrum, 1974.

Durant, W. *The age of faith*. New York: Simon & Schuster, 1950.

Earley, K. A very special brain. *The Sciences* (New York Academy of Science), December 1974, 25-27.

Ebbesson, S. O. E. On the organization of central visual pathways in vertebrates. *Brain, Behavior and Evolution*, 1970, *3*, 178-194.

Eccles, J. C. *The neurophysiological basis of mind: The principles of neurophysiology*. Oxford: Clarendon Press, 1953.

Eccles, J. C. *The physiology of nerve cells*. Baltimore: Johns Hopkins Press, 1957.

Eccles, J. C. *The physiology of synapses*. Berlin: Springer-Verlag, 1964.

Eccles, J. C. (Ed.). *Brain and conscious experience*. New York: Springer-Verlag, 1966.

Eccles, J. C. *Facing reality*. Berlin: Springer-Verlag, 1970.

Eccles, J. C. *The understanding of the brain*. New York: McGraw-Hill, 1973. (a)

Eccles, J. C. Preface to *Critique of the psycho-physical identity theory*, by E. P. Polten. The Hague: Mouton, 1973. (b)

Eccles, J. C., Eccles, R. M., Iggo, A., & Lundberg, A. Electron-physiological investigations of Renshaw cells. *Journal of Physiology*, 1961, *159*, 461-478.

Eccles, J. C., Ito, M., & Szentágothai, J. *The cerebellum as a neuronal machine*. Berlin: Springer-Verlag, 1967.

Edwards, P. (Ed.). *The encyclopedia of philosophy* (Vols. 1-8). New York and London: Macmillan and Collier Macmillan, 1967.

Eichenbaum, H., Butter, C. M., & Agranoff, B. W. Radioautographic localization of inhibition of protein synthesis in specific regions of monkey brain. *Brain Research*, 1973, *61*, 438-441.

Encyclopaedia Britannica, 1968 edition.

Enroth-Cugell, C., & Robson, J. G. The contrast sensitivity of retinal ganglion cells of the cat. *Journal of Physiology*, 1966, *187*, 517-552.

Epstein, A. N., & Teitelbaum, P. Role of adipsia in lateral hypothalamic stimulation. *Science*, 1960, *132*, 1491.

Epstein, R., & Tauc, L. Heterosynaptic facilitation and post-tetanic potentiation in *Aplysia* nervous system. *Journal of Physiology*, 1970, *209*, 1-23.

Erlanger, J., & Gasser, H. S. Action currents of individual fibers. In J. F. Fulton & L. G. Wilson (Eds.), *Selected readings in the history of physiology*. Springfield, Ill.: C. C. Thomas, 1924.

Erlanger, J., & Gasser, H. S. *Electrical signs of nervous activity*. Philadelphia: University of Pennsylvania Press, 1937.

Ervin, F. R., & Anders, T. R. Normal and pathological memory: Data and a conceptual scheme. In F. O. Schmitt (Ed.), *The neurosciences: Second study program*. New York: Rockefeller University Press, 1970.

Estes, W. K. (Ed.). *Handbook of learning and cognitive processes*. Hillsdale, N.J.: Lawrence Erlbaum Associates, 1975.

Eysenck, H. J., Arnold, W., & Meili, R. (Eds.). *Encyclopaedia of psychology*. New York: Herder & Herder, 1972.

Fechner, G. T. *Element der Psychphysik*. Leipzig, Germany: Breitkopf & Härterl, 1860.

Feder, R., & Ranck, J. B., Jr. Studies on single neurons in dorsal hippocampal formation and septum in unrestrained rats. Part II. Hippocampal slow waves and theta cell firing during bar pressing and other behaviors. *Experimental Neurology*, 1973, *41*, 532-555.

Fehmi, L. G., Adkins, J. W., & Lindsley, D. B. Electrophysiological correlates of visual perceptual masking in monkeys. *Experimental Brain Research*, 1969, *7*, 299-316.

Fehrer, E., & Raab, D. Reaction time to stimuli masked by metacontrast. *Journal of Experimental Psychology*, 1962, *63*, 143-147.

Feigl, H. The mental and the physical. In H. Feigl et al. (Eds.), *The Minnesota studies in the philosophy of science* (Vol. II). *Concepts, theories and the mind-body problem*. Minneapolis: University of Minnesota Press, 1958.

Feigl, H. Mind-body *not* a pseudoproblem. In S. Hook (Ed.), *Dimensions of mind: A symposium*. New York: New York University, 1960.

Fentress, J. C. Specific and nonspecific factors in the causation of behavior. In P. P. G. Bateson & P. H. Klopfer (Eds.), *Perspectives in ethology*. New York: Plenum Press, 1973.

Fetz, E. E. Operant control of single unit activity and correlated motor responses. In M. H. Chase (Ed.), *Operant control of brain activity*. *Perspectives in the Brain Sciences* (Vol. 2). Los Angeles: Brain Information Service/Brain Research Institute, University of California, 1974.

Fetz, E. E., & Baker, M. A. Operantly conditioned patterns of precentral unit activity and correlated responses in adjacent cells and contralateral muscles. *Journal of Neurophysiology*, 1973, *36*, 179-204.

Finger, S., Walbran, B., & Stein, D. G. Brain damage and behavioral recovery: Serial lesion phenomena. *Brain Research,* 1973, *63,* 1-18.

Fink, R. P., & Heimer, L. Two methods for selective silver impregnation of degenerating axons and their synaptic endings in the central nervous system. *Brain Research,* 1967, *4,* 369-374.

Flexner, L. B., Flexner, J. B., Roberts, R. B., & de la Haba, G. Loss of recent memory in mice as related to regional inhibition of cerebral protein synthesis. *Proceedings of the National Academy of Science-U.S.,* 1964, *52,* 1165-1169.

Fonberg, E. Improvement produced by lateral amygdala lesions on the instrumental alimentary performance impaired by dorso medial amygdala lesions in dogs. *Physiology and Behavior,* 1975, *14,* 711-717.

Forbes, A., & Thatcher, C. Amplication of action currents with the electron tube in recording with the string galvanometer. *American Journal of Physiology,* 1920, *52,* 409-471.

Fox, S. S., & Norman, R. J. Functional congruence: An index of neural homogeneity and a new measure of brain activity. *Science,* 1968, *159,* 1257-1259.

Fox, S. S., & O'Brien, J. H. Duplication of evoked potential waveform by curve of probability of firing of a single cell. *Science,* 1965, *147,* 888-890.

Fraisse, P. Visual perceptive simultaneity and masking of letters successively presented. *Perception and Psychophysics,* 1966, *1,* 285-287.

Frazier, W. T., Kandel, E. R., Kupfermann, I., Waziri, R., & Coggeshall, R. E. Morphological and functional properties of identified neurons in the abdominal ganglion of *Aplysia californica. Journal of Neurophysiology,* 1967, *30,* 1288-1351.

Frazier, W. T., Waziri, R., & Kandel, E. Alterations in the frequency of spontaneous activity in *Aplysia* neurons with contingent and noncontingent nerve stimulation. *Federation Proceedings,* 1965, *24,* 522.

French, G. M. Locomotor effects of regional ablation of frontal cortex in rhesus monkeys. *Journal of Comparative and Physiological Psychology,* 1959, *52,* 18-24.

Freund, H. J. Neuronal mechanisms in the lateral geniculate body. In R. Jung (Ed.), *Handbook of sensory physiology.* New York: Springer-Verlag, 1973.

Fritsch, G., & Hitzig, E. Ueber die elektrische Erregbarkeit des Grosshirns. *Archiv für Anatomie, Physiologie und Wissenschaftliche Medicin,* 1970, *37,* 300-332.

Fulton, J. F., & Wilson, L. G. *Selected readings in the history of physiology* (2nd ed.). Springfield, Ill.: C. C. Thomas, 1966.

Fuortes, M. G. F., & Simon, E. J. Interactions leading to horizontal cell responses in the turtle retina. *Jounal of Physiology,* 1974, *240,* 177-198.

Fuster, J. M. Unit activity in prefrontal cortex during delayed-response performance: Neuronal correlates of transient memory. *Journal of Neurophysiology,* 1973, *36,* 61-78.

Fuster, J. M., & Alexander, G. E. Delayed response deficit by cryogenic depression of frontal cortex. *Brain Research,* 1970, *20,* 85-90.

Fuster, J. M., Creutzfeldt, O. D., & Straschill, M. Intracellular recording of neuronal activity in the visual system. *Zeitschrift fuer Vergleichende Physiologie,* 1965, *49,* 605-622.

Gabor, D. A new microscopic principle. *Nature,* 1948, *161,* 777.

Gabor, D. Microscopy by reconstructed wave fronts. *Proceedings of the Royal Society of London,* 1949, *A197,* 454-487.

Galambos, R., Norton, T. T., & Frommer, C. P. Optic tract lesions sparing pattern vision in cats. *Experimental Neurology,* 1967, *18,* 8-25.

Galbraith, G. C., & Gliddon, J. B. Letter. *Science,* 1975, *190,* 292-294.

Galeano, C. Electrophysiological studies of learning in simplified nervous system preparations. In G. H. Bourne (Ed.), *The structure and function of nervous tissue* (Vol. V). New York: Academic Press, 1972.

Gall, F. J., & Spurzheim, J. C. Recherches sur le système nerveux en général, et sur celui du cerveau en particulier. *Académie de Sciences. Paris. Memoirs.* 1808.

Galvani, L. *[Commentary on the effect of electricity of muscular motion]* (R. M. Green, trans.). New Haven: Licht, 1953. (Originally published, 1791)

Ganz, L., Fitch, M., & Satterburg, J. A. The selective effect of visual deprivation on receptive field shape determined neurophysiologically. *Experimental Neurology,* 1968, *22,* 614-637.

Gardner, R. A., & Gardner, B. T. Teaching sign language to a chimpanzee. *Science,* 1969, *165,* 664-672.

Gasser, H. S. Recruitment of nerve fibers. *American Journal of Physiology,* 1938, *121,* 193-202.

Gazzaniga, M. S. *The bisected brain.* New York: Appleton-Century-Crofts, 1970.

Gazzaniga, M. S. Brain mechanisms and behavior. In M. S. Gazzaniga & C. Blakemore (Eds.), *Handbook of Psychobiology.* New York: Academic Press, 1975.

Gazzaniga, M. S., Szer, I., & Crane, A. Modifying drinking behavior in the adipsic rat. *Experimental Neurology,* 1974, *42,* 484-489.

Geffen, L. B., Livett, B. G., & Rush, R. A. Immunohistochemical localization of protein components of catecholamine storage vesicles. *Journal of Physiology,* 1969, *204,* 593-605.

Gelber, B. Investigations of the behavior of parmecium aurealia: I. Modification of behavior after training with reinforcement. *Journal of Comparative and Physiological Psychology,* 1952, *45,* 58-65.

Geldard, F. A. *The human senses* (2nd ed.). New York: Wiley, 1972.

Gerard, R. W. Physiology and psychiatry. *American Journal of Psychiatry,* 1949, *106,* 161-173.

Gescheider, G. A. *Psychophysics: Method and theory.* Hillsdale, N.J.: Lawrence Erlbaum Associates, 1976.

Geschwind, N. The organization of language and the brain. *Science,* 1970, *17,* 940-944.

Gilinsky, A. Orientation-specific effects of patterns of adapting light on visual acuity. *Journal of the Optical Society of America,* 1968, *58,* 13-18.

Ginsburg, A. P. Psychological correlates of a model of the human visual system. *IEEE Proceedings,* 1971, NAECON, 283-390.

Ginsburg, A. P. Critique of Sachar. *Science,* in press.

Ginsburg, A. P., Carl, J. W., Kabrisky, M., Hall, C. F., & Gill, R. A. Psychological aspects of a model for the classification of visual images. In J. Rose (Ed.), *Advances in Cybernetics and systems* (Vol. III). London: Gordon & Breach, 1976.

Globus, G. G. Unexpected symmetries in the "world knot." *Science,* 1973, *180,* 1129-1136.

Globus, A., Rosenzweig, M. R., Bennett, E. L., & Diamond, M. C. Effects of differential experience on dendritic spine counts in rat cerebral cortex. *Journal of Comparative and Physiological Psychology,* 1973, *82,* 175-181.

Gold, P. E., Macri, J., & McGaugh, J. L. Retrograde amnesia produced by subseizure amygdala stimulation. *Behavioral Biology,* 1973, *9,* 671-680.

Golda, V., Nováková, V., & Sterc, J. Effects of dorsal, mediobasal and laterobasal septal lesions in the rat: Reflexive fighting and pain thresholds. *Experimental Neurology,* 1975, *48,* 189-200.

Goldenson, R. M. (Ed.). *The encyclopaedia of human behavior: Psychology, psychiatry and mental health.* Garden City, N.Y.: Doubleday, 1970.

Goldscheider, A. Über die materiellen Veränderungen bei der Assoziationsbildung. *Neurologisches Centralblatt,* 1906, *25,* 146.

Goldstein, M. Enzymes involved in the catalysis of catecholamine biosynthesis. In N. Marks & R. Rodnight (Eds.), *Research methods in neurochemistry* (Vol. 1). New York: Plenum Press, 1972.

Goss, C. M. (Ed.). *Gray's Anatomy of the human body* (29th ed.). Philadelphia: Lea & Febiger, 1973.

Gourlay, K. D., Uttal, W. R., & Powers, M. K. VRS—A programming system for visual electrophysiological research. *Behavioral Research Methods and Instrumentation*, 1974, *6*, 281-287.

Graham, J., & Gerard, R. W. Membrane potentials and excitation of impaled single muscle fibers. *Journal of Cellular and Comparative Physiology*, 1946, *28*, 99-117.

Graham, N., & Rogowitz, B. E. Spatial pooling properties deduced from the detectability of FM and quasi AM gratings: A reanalysis. *Vision Research*, 1976, *16*, 1021-1026.

Graybiel, A. M. Studies on the anatomical organization of posterior association cortex. In F. O. Schmitt & F. G. Worden (Eds.), *The neurosciences: Third study program.* Cambridge, Mass.: M.I.T. Press, 1974.

Green, D. M., & Swets, J. A. *Signal detection theory and psychophysics.* New York: Wiley, 1966.

Greenough, W. T. Experiential modification of the developing brain. *American Scientist*, 1975, *63*, 37-46.

Greenough, W. T., & Volkmar, F. R. Pattern of dendritic branching in occipital cortex of rats reared in complex environments. *Experimental Neurology*, 1973, *40*, 491-504.

Greenough, W. T., Volkmar, F. R., & Juraska, J. M. Effects of rearing complexity on dendritic branching in frontolateral and temporal cortex of the rat. *Experimental Neurology*, 1973, *41*, 371-378.

Grobstein, P., & Chow, K. L. Receptive field development and individual expereince. *Science*, 1975, *190*, 352-358.

Gross, C. G. Visual functions of inferotemporal cortex. In R. Jung (Ed.), *Handbook of sensory physiology* (Vol. 7, Pt. 3B). Berlin: Springer-Verlag, 1973.

Gross, C. G., Bender, D. B., & Rocha-Miranda, C. E. Visual receptive fields of neurons in inferotemporal cortex of the monkey. *Science*, 1969, *166*, 1303-1306.

Gross, C. G., Bender, D. B., & Rocha-Miranda, C. E. Inferotemporal cortex: A single unit analysis. In F. O. Schmitt & F. G. Worden (Eds.), *The neurosciences: Third study program.* Cambridge, Mass.: M. I. T. Press, 1974.

Gross, C. G., & Carey, F. M. Transfer of learned responses by RNA injection: Failure of attempts to replicate, *Science*, 1965, *150*, 1749.

Gross, C. G., Rocha-Miranda, C. E., and Bender, D. B. Visual properties of neurons in inferotemporal cortex of the macaque. *Journal of Neurophysiology*, 1972, *35*, 96-111.

Gross, C. G., Schiller, P. H., Wells, C., & Gerstein, G. L. Single unit activity in temporal association cortex of the monkey. *Journal of Neurophysiology*, 1967, *30*, 833-843.

Grossberg, S. Contour enhancement, short term memory, and constancies in reverberating neural networks. *Studies in Applied Mathematics*, 1973, *52*, 213-257.

Grossman, S. P. Role of the hypothalamus in the regulation of food and water intake. *Psychological Review*, 1975, *82*, 200-224.

Groves, P. M., DeMarco, R., & Thompson, R. F. Habituation and sensitization of spinal interneuron activity in acute spinal cat. *Brain Research*, 1969, *14*, 521-525.

Groves, P. M., Glanzman, D. L., Patterson, M. M., & Thompson, R. F. Excitability of cutaneous afferent terminals during habituation and sensitization in acute spinal cat. *Brain Research*, 1970, *18*, 388-392.

Groves, P. M., Wilson, C. J., Young, S. J., & Rebec, G. V. Self-inhibition by dopaminergic neurons. *Science*, 1975, *190*, 522-529.

Grundfest, H. Electrical inexcitability of synapses and some consequences in the central nervous system. *Physiological Reviews*, 1957, *37*, 337-361.

Grüsser, O. -J., & Grüsser-Cornehls, U. Mikroelektrodenuntersuchungen zur Konvergenz vestibulärer und retinaler Afferenzen an einzelran Neuronen des optischen Cortex der Katze. *Pflüger's Archiv für die gesamte Physiologie des Menschen und der Tiere*, 1960, *270*, 227-238.

Grüsser, O. -J., Grüsser-Cornehls, U., & Saur, G. Reaktionen einzelner Neurone im optischen Cortex der Katze nach elektrischer Polarisation de Labyrinths. *Pflüger's Archiv für die gestamte Physiologie des Menschen und der Tiere*, 1959, *269*, 593-612.

Guthrie, E. R. *The psychology of learning* (Rev. ed.). New York: Harper & Row, 1952.

Guyer, M., Fox, J., & Hamburger, H. Format effects in the Prisoner's Dilemma game. *Journal of Conflict Resolution*, 1973, *17*, 719-744.

Halas, E. S., Beardsley, J. V., & Sandlie, M. E. Conditioned neuronal responses at various levels in conditioning paradigms. *Electroencephalography and Clinical Neurophysiology*, 1970, *28*, 468-477.

Hamilton, W. J., & Mossman, H. W. *Human embryology: Prenatal development of form and function* (4th ed.). Cambridge, England: W. Heffei & Sons, 1972.

Hámori, J., & Szentágothai, J. The Purkinji cell baskets: Ultrastructure of an inhibitory synapse. *Acta-Biologica* (Academiae Scientiarum Hungaricae), 1965, *15*, 465-479.

Harlow, H. J. The formation of learning sets. *Psychological Review*, 1949, *56*, 51-65.

Harmon, L. D. Studies with artificial neurons. I: Properties and functions of an artificial neuron. *Kybernetik*, 1961, *1*, 89-101.

Hartline, H. K., & Ratliff, F. Inhibitory interaction of receptor units in the eye of *Limulus*. *Journal of General Physiology*, 1957, *40*, 357-376.

Hartline, H. K., Wagner, H. G., & Ratliff, F. Inhibition in the eye of *Limulus*. *Journal of General Physiology*, 1956, *39*, 651-673.

Harvey, J. A., & Hunt, H. F. Effect of septal lesions on thirst in the rat as indicated by water consumption and operant responding for water reward. *Journal of Comparative and Phsyiological Psychology*, 1965, *5*, 49-56.

Haymaker, W., Anderson, E., & Nauta, W. J. H. (Eds.). *The hypothalamus*. Springfield, Ill.: C. C. Thomas, 1969.

Hayward, J. N., Ott, L. H., Stuart, D. G., & Cheshire, F. C. Peliter biothermodes. *American Journal of Medical Electronics*, 1965, *4*, 11-19.

Hebb, D. O. *The organization of behavior*. New York: Wiley, 1949.

Hebb, D. O. *A textbook of psychology*. Philadelphia: Saunders, 1958.

Hecht, S., Schlaer, A., & Pirenne, M. H. Energy, quanta, and vision. *Journal of General Physiology*, 1942, *25*, 819-840.

Heimer, L. Selective silver-impregnation of degenerating axoplasm. In W. J. H. Nauta & S. O. E. Ebbeson (Eds.), *Contemporary Research methods in neuroanatomy*. New York: Springer-Verlag, 1970.

Heimer, L. The olfactory connections of the diencephalon in the rat. *Brain, Behavior and Evolution*, 1972, *6*, 484-523.

Henning, G. B., Hertz, B. G., & Broadbent, D. E. Some experiments bearing on the hypothesis that the visual system analyses spatial patterns in independent bands of spatial frequency. *Vision Research*, 1975, *15*, 887-897.

Hensel, H., & Boman, K. K. Afferent impulses in cutaneous sensory nerves in human subjects. *Journal of Neurophysiology*, 1960, *23*, 564-577.

Hetherington, A. N., & Ranson, S. W. The spontaneous activity and food intake of rats with hypothalamic lesions. *American Journal of Physiology*, 1942, *136*, 609-617.

Heuser, J. E., & Reese, T. S. Evidence for recycling of synaptic vesicle membrane during transmitter release at the frog neuromuscular junction. *The Journal of Cell Biology*, 1973, *57*, 315-344.

Hilgard, E. R. *Theories of learning*. New York: Appleton-Century-Crofts, 1948.

Hill, D. K. The volume change resulting from stimulation of a giant nerve fibre. *Journal of Physiology*, 1950, *111*, 304-327.

Hinde, R. A. *Animal behavior*. New York: McGraw-Hill, 1970.

Hirsch, H. V. B., & Spinelli, D. N. Visual experience modifies distributor of horizontally and vertically oriented receptive fields in cats. *Science*, 1970, *168*, 869-871.

Hirsch, H. V., & Spinelli, D. N. Modification of the distribution of receptive field orientation in cats by selective visual exposure during development. *Experimental Brain Research*, 1971, *12*, 509-527.

Hirsh, I. J., & Sherrick, C. E. Perceived order in different sense modalities. *Journal of Experimental Psychology*, 1961, *62*, 423-432.

Höber, R. Eine Methode, die elektrische Leitfähigkeit im Innern von Zellen zu messen. *Archiv für die gesamte Physiologie*, 1910, *133*, 237-259.

Höber, R. Ein zweites Verfahren, die Leitfähigkeit im Innern von Zellen zu messen. *Archiv für die gesamte Physiologie*, 1912, *148*, 189-221.

Hodgkin, A. L. The ionic basis of nervous conduction. *Science*, 1964, *145*, 1148-1154.

Hodgkin, A. L. *The conduction of the nervous impulse.* Springfield, Illinois: C. C. Thomas, 1967.

Hodgkin, A. L., & Huxley, A. F. Action potentials recorded from inside a nerve fibre. *Nature*, 1939, *144*, 710.

Hodgkin, A. L., & Huxley, A. F. A quantitative description of membrane current and its application to conduction with excitation in nerve. *Journal of Physiology*, 1952, *117*, 500-544.

Hodos, W., & Campbell, C. B. G. *Scala naturae:* Why there is no theory in comparative psychology. *Psychological Reveiw*, 1969, *76*, 337-350.

Hogben, J. H., & Di Lollo, V. Practice-induced decrement of suppression in metacontrast and apparent motion. Paper presented at Psychonomic Society, November 11-13, 1976.

Hook, S. (Ed.). *Dimensions of mind: A symposium.* New York: New York University, 1960.

Horn, G. Changes in neuronal activity and their relationship to behavior. In G. Horn & R. A. Hinde (Eds.), *Short-term changes in neural activity and behaviour.* London: Cambridge University Press, 1970.

Horn, G., Rose, S. P. R., & Bateson, P. P. G. Experience and plasticity in the central nervous system. *Science*, 1973, *181*, 506-514.

Horridge, G. A. Learning of leg position by the ventral nerve cord in headless insects. *Proceedings of the Royal Society. Series B.*, 1962, *157*, 33-52.

Horridge, G. A. The interpretation of behavior in terms of interneurons. In M. A. B. Brazier (Ed.), *The interneuron.* Berkeley: University of California Press, 1969.

Hoyle, G., & Burrows, M. Neural mechanisms underlying behavior in locust *Schistocerca gregaria.* I. Physiology of identified motor neurons in the metathoracic ganglion. *Journal of Neurobiology*, 1973, *4*, 3-41. (a)

Hoyle, G., & Burrows, M. Nueral mechanisms underlying behavior in locust *Schistocerca gregaria.* II. Integrative activity in metathoracic neurons. *Journal of Neurobiology*, 1973, *4*, 43-67. (b)

Hubel, D. H. Tungsten microelectrode for recording from single units. *Science*, 1957, *125*, 549-550.

Hubel, D. H. Cortical unit responses to visual stimuli in nonanesthetized cats. *American Journal of Ophthalmology*, 1958, *46*, 110-121.

Hubel, D. H. Single unit activity in striate cortex of unrestrained cats. *Journal of Physiology*, 1959, *147*, 226-238.

Hubel, D. H., & Wiesel, T. N. Receptive fields of single neurons in the cat's striate cortex. *Journal of Physiology*, 1959, *148*, 574-591.

Hubel, D. H., & Wiesel, T. N. Receptive fields, binocular interaction and functional architecture in the cat's visual cortex. *Journal of Physiology*, 1962, *160*, 106-154.

Hubel, D. H., & Wiesel, T. N. Shape and arrangement of columns in cat's striate cortex. *Journal of Physiology*, 1963, *165*, 559-568.

Hubel, D. H., & Wiesel, T. N. Receptive fields and functional architecture in two nonstriate visual areas (18 and 19) of the cat. *Journal of Neurophysiology*, 1965, *28*, 229-289.

Hubel, D. H., & Wiesel, T. N. Receptive fields and functional architecture of monkey striate cortex. *Journal of Physiology,* 1968, *195,* 215-243.

Hubel, D. H., & Wiesel, T. N. Visual area of the lateral suprasylvian gyrus (Clare-Bishop area) of the cat. *Journal of Physiology,* 1969, *202,* 251-260.

Hubel, D. H., & Wiesel, T. N. Stereoscopic vision in macaque monkey. *Nature* (London), 1970, *225,* 41-42.

Hubel, D. H., & Wiesel, T. N. Laminar and columnar distribution of geniculo-cortical fibers in the macaque monkey. *Journal of Comparative Neurology,* 1972, *146,* 421-450.

Hubel, D. H., & Wiesel, T. N. Sequence regularity and geometry of orientation columns in the monkey striate cortex. *Journal of Comparative Neurology,* 1974, *158,* 267-294.

Hughes, R. R. *An introduction to clinical electroencephalography.* Bristol, England: Wright & Sons, 1961.

Hull, C. L. *Principles of behavior.* New York: Appleton-Centruy-Crofts, 1943.

Hyden, H. Biochemical changes in glial cells and nerve cells at varying activity. In *Biochemistry of the central nervous system.* Fourth International Congress of Biochemistry, Vienna. New York-London: Pergamon, 1959.

Hydén, H. Biochemical changes accompanying learning. In G. C. Quarton, T. Melnechuk, & F. O. Schmitt (Eds.), *The neurosciences: A study program.* New York: Rockefeller University Press, 1967.

Hydén, H. The question of a molecular basis for the memory trace. In K. H. Pribram & D. E. Broadbent (Eds.), *Biology of memory.* New York: Academic Press, 1970.

Hyvärinen, J., & Poranen, A. Function of the parietal associative area 7 as revealed from cellular discharges in alert monkeys. *Brain,* 1974, *97,* 673-692.

Ingle, D. J., & Shein, H. M. (Eds.). *Model systems in biological psychiatry.* Cambridge, Mass.: M.I.T. Press, 1975.

Irwin, D. A., & Rebert, C. S. Slow potential changes in cat brain during classical appetitive conditioning of jaw movements using two levels of reward. *Electroencephalography and Clinical Neurophysiology,* 1970, *28,* 119-126.

Isaacson, R. L. *The limbic system.* New York: Plenum Press, 1974.

Isaacson, R. L., Douglas, R. J., & Moore, R. Y. The effect of radical hippocampal ablation on acquisition of avoidance response. *Journal of Comparative and Physilogical Psychology,* 1961, *54,* 625-628.

Ito, M., & Olds, J. Unit activity during self-stimulation behavior. *Journal of Neurophysiology,* 1971, *34,* 263-273.

Iversen, L. L. Dopamine receptors in the brain. *Science,* 1975, *188,* 1084-1089.

Iversen, S. D. Brain lesions and memory in animals. In J. A. Deutsch (Ed.). *The physiological basis of memory.* New York: Academic Press, 1973.

Jackson, J. H. *Selected writings of John Hughlings Jackson* (Vol. 2). (J. Taylor, Ed.) London: Hodder & Stoughton, 1931.

Jacobsen, C. F. Functions of the frontal association area in primates. *Archives of Neurology and Psychiatry,* 1935, *33,* 558-569.

Jacobsen, C. F. The functions of the frontal association areas in monkeys. *Comparative Psychological Monograph,* 1936, *13,* 1-60.

Jacobson, M. Development of neuronal specificity in retinal ganglion cells of *Xenopus. Developmental Biology,* 1968, *17,* 202-218. (a)

Jacobson, M. Cessation of DNA synthesis in retinal ganglion cells correlated with the time of specification of their central connections. *Developmental Biology,* 1968, *17,* 219-232. (b)

James, W. *The principles of psychology.* New York: Henry Holt, 1890.

Jasper, H. H., & Doane, B. Neurophysiological mechanisms in learning. In E. Stellar & J. M. Sprague (Eds.), *Progress in physiological psychology* (Vol. 2). New York: Academic Press, 1968.

Jasper, H. H., Ricci, G., & Doane, B. Microelectrode analysis of cortical cell discharge during avoidance conditioning in the monkey. In H. H. Jasper & G. D. Smirnov (Eds.), *The Moscow Colloquium on electroencephalography of higher nervous activity. Electroencephalography and Clinical Neurophysiology,* 1960, *13,* supplement, 137-155.

Jeans, J. H. *An introduction to the kinetic theory of gases.* New York: Macmillan, 1940.

Jenness, D. Auditory evoked-response differentiation with discrimination learning in humans. *Journal of Comparative and Physiological Psychology,* 1972, *80,* 75-90.

Jerison, H. J. *Evolution of the brain and intelligence.* New York-London: Academic Press, 1973.

Jerison, H. J. Paleoneurology and the evolution of mind. *Scientific American,* 1976, *234,* 90-101.

John, E. R. Switchboard versus statistical theories of learning and memory. *Science,* 1972, *177,* 850-864.

Johnston, V. S., & Chesney, G. L. Electrophysiological correlates of meaning. *Science,* 1974, *186,* 944-946.

Johnston, V. S., & Chesney, G. L. Letter. *Science,* 1975, *190,* 294.

Jones, P. D., & Holding, D. H. Extremely long-term persistence of the McCullough effect. *Journal of Experimental Psychology: Human Perception and Performance,* 1975, *1,* 323-327.

Jouvet, M. The states of sleep. *Scientific American,* 1967, *216,* 62-72.

Jung, R. Coordination of specific and nonspecific afferent impulses at single neurons of the visual cortex. In H. H. Jasper, et al. (Eds.), *Reticular formation of the brain.* Boston: Little, Brown, 1958.

Jung, R. (Ed.). *The handbook of sensory physiology.* New York: Springer-Verlag, 1973.

Jung, R., Baumgarten, R. von, & Baumgartner, G. Mikroableitungen von einzelnen Nueronen im optischen Cortex der Katze: Die lichtaktivierten B-neurone. *Archiv für Psychiatrie und Nervenkrankheiten,* 1952, *189,* 521-538.

Jung, R., & Baumgartner, G. Hemmungsmechanismen und bremsende Stabilisierung an einzelnen Neuronen des optischen Cortex: Ein Bietrag zur Koordination corticaler Erregungsvorgänge. *Pflüger's Archiv für die gestamte Physiologie des Menschen und der Tiere,* 1955, *261,* 434-456.

Jung, R., Kornhuber, H. H., & da Fonseca, J. S. Multisensory convergence on cortical neurons: Neuronal effects of visual, acoustic and vestibular stimuli in the superior convolutions of the cat's cortex. *Progress in Brain Research,* 1963, *1,* 207-240.

Kaada, B. R. Brain mechanisms related to aggression behavior. In C. D. Clemente & D. B. Lendsley (Eds.), *Agression and defense, brain function* (Vol. 15). Berkeley: University of California Press, 1967.

Kandel, E. R. An invertebrate system for the cellular analysis of simple behaviors and their modifications. In F. O. Schmitt & F. G. Worden (Eds.), *The neurosciences: Third study program.* Cambridge, Mass.: M.I.T. Press, 1974.

Kandel, E. R., & Spencer, W. A. Cellular neurophysiological approaches in the study of learning. *Physiological Review,* 1968, 48, 65-134.

Kandel, E. R. & Tauc, L. Mechanism of prolonged heterosynaptic facilitation. *Nature,* 1964, *202,* 145-147.

Kandel, E. R., & Tauc, L. Heterosynaptic facilitation in neurons of the abdominal ganglion of *Aplysia depilans. Journal of Physiology,* 1965, *181,* 1-27. (a)

Kandel, E. R., & Tauc, L. Mechanism of heterosynaptic facilitation in the giant cell of the abdominal ganglion of *Aplysia depilans. Journal of Physiology,* 1965, *181,* 28-47. (b)

Kaniza, G. Subjective contours. *Scientific American,* 1976, *234,* 48-52.

Kantor, J. R. The evolution of mind. *Psychological Review,* 1935, *42,* 455-465.

Kantor, J. R. *The aim and progress of psychology and other sciences.* Chicago: Principia Press, 1971.

Kao, I., Drachman, D. B., & Price, D. L. Botulinum toxin: Mechanisms of presynaptic blockade. *Science,* 1976, *193,* 1256-1258.

Karten, H. J. The organization of the avian telencephalon and some speculations on the phylogeny of the amniote telecephalon. *Annals of the New York Academy of Science,* 1969, *167,* 164-179.

Katchalsky, A., Rowland, V., & Blumenthal, R. Dynamic patterns of brain cell assemblies. *Neurosciences Research Program Bulletin,* 1974, *12,* (1), 1-87.

Katz, B. *Nerve, muscle and synapse.* New York: McGraw-Hill, 1966.

Katz, J. J. & Halstead, W. C. Protein organization and mental function. *Comparative Psychology Monographs,* 1950, *20,* 1.

Kaufman, L. *Sight and mind: An introduction to visual perception.* New York: Oxford University Press, 1974,

Keesey, R. E., & Powley, T. L. Hypothalamic regulation of body weight. *American Scientist,* 1975, *63,* 558-565.

Kellogg, W. N. Is 'spinal conditioning,' conditioning? Reply to 'a comment.' *Journal of Experimental Psychology,* 1947, *37,* 263-265.

Kelly, J. P., & Van Essen, D. C. Cell structure and function in the visual cortex of the cat. *Journal of Physiology,* 1974, *238,* 515-547.

Kennedy, C., Des Rosiers, M. H., Jehle, J. W., Reivich, M., Sharpe, F., & Sokoloff, L. Mapping of functional neural pathways by autoradiographic survey of local metabolic rate with [^{14}C] deoxyglucose. *Science,* 1975, *187,* 850-853.

Kerwin, J., & Reitman, W. *Video game #3: A Go protocol with comments.* (Information Processing Working Paper #20 (IP-20)). Unpublished manuscript, Mental Health Research Institute, University of Michigan, Ann Arbor, September 1973.

Kesner, R. A neural system analysis of memory storage and retrieval. *Psychological Bulletin,* 1973, *80,* 177-203.

Kesner, R. P., & Doty, R. W. Amnesia produced in cats by local seizure activity initiated from the amygdala. *Experimental Neurology,* 1968, *21,* 58-68.

Kety, S. S. A biologist examines the mind and behavior. *Science,* 1960, *132,* 1867-1869.

Kety, S. S. The biogenic amines in the central nervous system: Their possible roles in arousal, emotion, and learning. In F. O. Schmitt (Ed.), *The neurosciences: Second study program.* New York: Rockefeller University Press, 1970.

Kievit, J., & Kuypers, G. J. M.   Basal forebrain and hypothalamic connections to frontal and parietal cortex in the rhesus monkey. *Science,* 1975, *187,* 660-662.

Kim, C., Choi, H., Kim, J. K., Kim, M. S., Huh, M. K., & Moon, Y. B. Sleep pattern of hippocampectomized cat. *Brain Research,* 1971, *29,* 223-236.

Kimble, D. P. Hippocampus and internal inhibition. *Psychological Bulletin,* 1968, *70,* 285-295.

King-Smith, P. E., & Kulikowski, J. J. The detection of gratings by independent activation of line detectors. *Journal of Physiology* (London), 1975, *247,* 237-271.

Kintsch, W. *Learning, memory and conceptual processes.* New York: Wiley, 1970.

Kintsch, W. *The representation of meaning in memory.* New York: Halstead Press, 1974.

Kleist, K. *Gehirnpathologie.* Leipzig, Germany: Barth, 1934.

Klüver, H. Visual functions after removal of the occipital lobes. *Journal of Psychology,* 1941, *11,* 23-45.

Klüver, H., & Bucy, P. C. "Psychic blindness" and other symptoms following bilateral temporal lobectomy in rhesus monkeys. *American Journal of Physiology,* 1937, *119,* 352-353.

Klüver, H., & Bucy, P. C. An analysis of certain effects of bilateral temporal lobectomy in the rhesus monkey, with special reference to "psychic blindness." *Journal of Psychology,* 1938, *5,* 33-54.

Koch, S. Behaviourism. In *Encyclopaedia britannica* (Vol. 3). 1968.

Kolers, P. A. The role of shape and geometry in picture recognition. In B. S. Lipkin & A. Rosenfeld (Eds.), *Picture processing and psychopictorics.* New York: Academic Press, 1970.

Kornhuber, H. H., & da Fonseca, J. S. Convergence of vestibular, visual and auditory afferents at single neurons of the cat's cortex. *Fifth International Congress of EEG and Clinical Neurophysiology,* Rome, 1961. Excerpta Medica, International Congress Series, 1961.

Kozak, W., Rodieck, R. W., & Bishop, P. O. Responses of single units in lateral geniculate nucleus of cat to moving visual patterns. *Journal of Neurophysiology,* 1965, *28,* 19-47.

Krantz, D. H., Luce, R. D., Suppes, P., & Tversky, A. *Foundations of Measurement* (Vol. I). *Additive and Polynomial Representations.* New York-London: Academic Press, 1971.

Krasne, F. B. Excitation and habituation of the crayfish escape reflex: The depolarizing response in lateral giant fibers of the isolated abdomen. *Journal of Experimental Biology,* 1969, *50,* 29-46.

Krasne, F. B. Learning in crustacea. In W. C. Corning, J. A. Dyal, & A. O. D. Willows (Eds.), *Invertebrate learning: Arthropods and gastropod mollusks.* New York-London: Plenum Press, 1973.

Krasne, F. B. Aspects of plasticity in the crayfish central nervous system. In C. D. Woody, K. A. Brown, T. J. Crow, Jr., & J. D. Knispel (Eds.), *Cellular mechanisms subserving changes in neuronal activity.* Research Report #3. Los Angeles: Brain Information Service/Brain Research Institute, University of California, 1974.

Kristensson, K., Olsson, Y., & Sjöstrand, J. Axonal uptake and retrograde transport of exogenous proteins in the hypoglossal nerve. *Brain Research,* 1971, *32,* 399-406.

Kristan, W. B., Jr. Plasticity of firing patterns in neurons of *Aplysia* pleural ganglion. *Journal of Neurophysiology,* 1971, *34,* 321-336.

Kubota, K., & Niki, H. Prefrontal cortical unit activity and delayed alternation performance in monkeys. *Journal of Neurophysiology,* 1971, *34,* 337-347.

Kuffler, S. W. Discharge patterns and functional organization of mammalian retina. *Journal of Neurophysiology,* 1953, *16,* 37-68.

Kuffler, S. W., & Nicholls, J. G. The physiology of neuroglial cells. *Reviews of Physiology, Biochemistry and Experimental Pharmacology,* 1966, *57,* 1-90.

Kuhlenbeck, H. *The central nervous system of vertebrates* (Vol. 1). *Propaedeutics to comparative neurology.* New York: Academic Press, 1967.

Kuhn, T. S. *The structure of scientific revolutions* (2nd ed.). Chicago: University of Chicago Press, 1970.

Kulikowski, J. J., & King-Smith, P. E. Spatial arrangement of line, edge and grating detectors revealed by subthreshold summation. *Vision Research,* 1973, *13,* 1455-1478.

Kupfermann, I. Neurophysiology of learning. *Annual Review of Psychology,* 1975, *26,* 367-391.

Kupfermann, I., Carew, T. J., & Kandel, E. R. Local, reflex and central commands controlling gill and siphon movements in *Aplysia. Journal of Neurophysiology,* 1974, *37,* 966-1019.

Kupfermann, I., Castellucci, V., Pinsker, H., & Kandel, E. Neuronal correlates of habituation and dishabituation of the gill-withdrawn reflex in *Aplysia. Science,* 1970, *167,* 1743-1745.

Kupfermann, I., & Kandel, E. R. Neuronal controls of a behavioral response mediated by the abdominal ganglion of *Aplysia. Science,* 1969, *164,* 847-850.

Kupfermann, I., & Pinsker, H. Cellular models of learning and cellular mechanisms of plasticity in *Aplysia.* In K. H. Pribram & D. E. Broadbent (Eds.), *Biology of memory.* New York: Academic Press, 1970.

Kuypers, G. J. M., Szwarcbart, M. K., Mishkin, M., & Rosvold, H. E. Occipitotemporal cortico-cortical connections in the rhesus monkey. *Experimental Neurology,* 1965, *11,* 245-262.

Langer, S. K. *Feeling and form: A theory of art.* New York: Scribner, 1953.

Langer, S. K. *Mind: An essay on human feelings.* Baltimore: Johns Hopkins Press, 1967.

Lasek, R. J. Axonal transport and the use of intracellular markers in neuroanatomical investigations. *Federation Proceedings,* 1975, *34,* 1603-1611.

Lasek, R., Joseph, B. J., & Whitlock, D. G. Evaluation of an autoradiographic neuroanatomical tracing method. *Brain Research,* 1968, *8,* 319-336.

Lashley, K. S. The problem of cerebral organization in vision. *Biological Symposium,* 1942, *7,* 301-322.

Lashley, K. S. In search of the engram. In D. G. Stein & J. J. Rosen (Eds.), *Learning and memory.* New York: Macmillan, 1974. (Reprinted from *Society of Experimental Biology Symposium No. 4: Physiological Mechanisms in Animal Behaviour* (Cambridge University Press), 1950, 454-482.)

Lashley, K. S., Chow, K. L., & Semmes, J. An examination of the electrical field theory of cerebral integration. *Psychological Review,* 1951, *58,* 123-136.

LaVail, J. H. The retrograde transport method. *Federation Proceedings,* 1975, *34,* 1618-1624.

LaVail, J. H., & LaVail, M. M. Retrograde axonal transport in the central nervous system. *Science,* 1972, *176,* 1415-1417.

Leao, A. A. P. Further observations on the spreading depression of activity in the cerebral cortex. *Journal of Neurophysiology,* 1947, *10,* 409-414.

Leck, I. Causation of neural tube defects: Clues from epidemiology. *British Medical Bulletin,* 1974, *30,* 158-163.

Leeper, R. A study of a neglected portion of the field of learning—the development of sensory organization. *Journal of Genetic Psychology,* 1935, *46,* 41-75.

Leeuwenhoek, A. van An extract of a letter from Mr. A. Van Leeuwenhoek to the Royal Society containing his observations on the seeds of cotton, palm, or date-stones, cloves, nutmegs, gooseberries, currents, tulips, caffia, lime-tree: On the skin of the hand, and pores, of sweat, the crystalline humour, optic nerves, gall, and scales of fish: And the figures of several salt particles, etc. *Royal Society of London, Philosophical Transactions,* 1693, *17,* 949-960.

Leiman, A. L., & Christian, C. N. Electrophysiological analyses of learning and memory. In J. A. Deutsch (Ed.), *The physiological basis of memory.* New York: Academic Press, 1973.

Leith, E. N. White light hologram. *Scientific American,* 1976, *235,* 80-95.

Leith, E. N., & Upatnieks, J. Reconstructed wavefronts and communication theory. *Journal of the Optical Society of America,* 1962, *52,* 1123-1130.

Lendaris, G. G., & Stanley, G. L. Diffraction-pattern sampling for automatic pattern recognition. *IEEE Proceedings,* 1970, *58,* 198-216.

Lennenberg, E. H. Language and brain: Developmental aspects. *Neurosciences Research Program Bulletin,* 1974, *12,* 511-656.

Lennox-Buchthal, M. A. Single units in monkey, *cercocebus torquatus atys,* cortex with narrow spectral responsiveness. *Vision Research,* 1962, *2,* 1-15.

Lettvin, J. Y., Maturana, H. R., McCulloch, W. S., & Pitts, W. H. What the frog's eye tells the frog's brain. *Institute of Radio Engineers Proceedings,* 1959, *47,* 1940-1951.

Leventhal, A. G., & Hirsch, H. V. B. Cortical effect of early selective exposure to diagonal lines. *Science,* 1975, *190,* 902-904.

LeVere, T. E. Neural stability, sparing, and behavioral recovery following brain damage. *Psychological Review,* 1975, *82,* 344-358.

Levinthal, C., Macagno, E., & Tountas, C. Computer-aided reconstruction from serial sections. *Federation Proceedings,* 1974, *33,* 2336-2340.

Li, C.-L., Oritz-Golvin, A., Chou, S. N., & Howard, S. Y. Cortical intracellular potentials in response to stimulation of lateral geniculate body. *Journal of Neurophysiology,* 1960, *23,* 592-601.

Libet, B., Alberts, W. W., Wright, E. W., Jr., & Feinstein, B. Responses of human somato-sensory cortex to stimuli below threshold for conscious sensation. *Science,* 1967, *158,* 1597-1600.

Ling, G., & Gerard, R. W. The normal membrane potential of frog sartorius fibers. *Journal of Cellular and Comparative Physiology,* 1949, *34,* 383-385.

Lipetz, L. E. The relation of physiological and psychological aspects of sensory intensity. In W. R. Loewenstein (Ed.), *Principles of receptor physiology.* New York: Springer-Verlag, 1971.

Llinás, R. Motor aspects of cerebellar control. (18th Bowditch Lecture.) *The Physiologist,* 1974, *17,* 19-46.

Llinás, R. The cortex of the cerebellum. *Scientific American,* 1975, *232,* 56-71.

Loewi, O. Über humorale Übertragbarkeit der Herznervenwirkung. I. Mitteilung. *Pflüger's Archives of the European Journal of Physiology,* 1921, *189,* 239-242.

Lömo, T., & Mollica, A. Attività di singole unità della corteccia ottica primaria durante stimolazioni luminose acustiche, olfattive e dolorifiche, nel coniglio senze narcosi. *Bolletino della Societa Italiana di Biologia Sperimentale,* 1959, *35,* 1879-1882.

Lömo, T., & Mollica, A. Activity of single units in the primary optic cortex in the unanesthetized rabbit during visual, acoustic, olfactory and painful stimulation. *Archives Italiennes de Biologie,* 1962, *100,* 86-120.

Lorente de Nó, R. The cerebral cortex: Architecture, intracortical connections and motor projections. In J. F. Fulton (Ed.), *Physiology of the nervous system.* London-New York-Toronto: Oxford University Press, 1938.

Lorenz, K. Z. Analogy as a source of knowledge. *Science,* 1974, *185,* 229-234.

Lovell, K. L., & Eisenstein, E. M. Dark avoidance learning and memory disruption by carbon dioxide in cockroaches. *Physiology and Behavior,* 1973, *10,* 835-840.

Lubar, J. F., & Wolf, J. W. Increased basal water and food ingestion in cingulectomized rats. *Psychonomic Science,* 1964, *1,* 289-290.

Luce, R. D., & Mo, S. S. M. Magnitude estimation of heaviness by individual subjects: A test of a probabilistic response theory. *British Journal of Mathematical and Statistical Psychology,* 1965, *18,* (Part 2), 159-174.

Luria, A. R. *Higher cortical functions in man.* New York: Consultants Bureau and Basic Books, 1966. (a)

Luria, A. R. *Human brain and psychological processes.* New York: Harper & Row, 1966. (b)

Luria, A. R. *Traumatic aphasia: Its syndromes, psychology, and treatment.* The Hague: Mouton, 1970.

Luria, A. R. Aphasia reconsidered. *Cortex,* 1972, *8,* 34-40.

Luria, A. R. *The working brain: An introduction to neuropsychology.* New York: Basic Books, 1973.

Lynch, G., Gall, C., Mensah, P., & Cotman, C. W. Horseradish peroxidase histochemistry: A new method for tracing efferent projections in the central nervous system. *Brain Research,* 1974, *65,* 373-380.

Lynn, R. *Attention, arousal and the orientation reaction.* New York: Pergamon, 1966.

MacKay, D. M. Interactive processes in visual perception. In W. A. Rosenblith (Ed.), *Sensory communication.* Cambridge, Mass. and New York: M.I.T. Press and Wiley, 1961.

MacKay, D. M. Evoked brain potentials as indicators of sensory information processing. *Neurosciences Research Program Bulletin,* 1969, *7*(3), 181-276.

MacLean, P. D. Psychosomatic disease and "visceral brain"; recent developments bearing on Papez' theory of emotion. *Psychosematic Medicine,* 1949, *11,* 338-353.

Maffei, L., Fiorentini, A., & Bisti, S. Neural correlate of perceptual adaptation to gratings. *Science,* 1973, *182,* 1036-1038.

Magendie, F. Experiences sur les fonctions des racines des nerfs rachidiens. *Journal de Physiologyie Experimentale et Pathologique,* 1822, *2,* 276-279.

Magoun, H. W. The ascending reticular system and wakefulness. In J. F. Delafresnaye (Ed), *Brain mechanism and consciousness.* Oxford: Blackwell, 1954.

Magoun, H. W. Early development of ideas relating the mind with the brain. In G. E. W. Wolstenholme & C. M. O'Connor (Eds.), *Neurological basis of behavior*. London: J. and A. Churchill Ltd., 1958.

Magoun, H. W. *The waking brain* (2nd ed.). Springfield, Ill.: C. C. Thomas, 1963.

Majorossy, K., Réthelyi, M., & Szentágothai, J. The large glomerular synapse of the pulvinar. *Journal für Hirn Forschung*, 1965, *7*, 415-432.

Marchbanks, R. M. The role of synaptic vesicles in transmission. *Experimental Brain Research*, 1976, *24*, 16.

Marg, E., Adams, J. E., & Rutkin, B. Receptive fields of cells in the human visual cortex. *Experientia* (Basel, Switzerland), 1968, *24*, 313-316.

Marin-Padilla, M. Structural organization of the cerebral cortex (motor area) in human chromosomal aberrations. A Golgi Study. I. D_1 (13-15) Trisomy, Patau Syndrome. *Brain Research*, 1974, *66*, 375-391.

Mark, R. *Memory and nerve cell connections*. London: Oxford University Press, 1974.

Marks, L. E. *Sensory processes: The new psychophysics*. New York: Academic Press, 1974.

Marshall, J. F., Richardson, J. S., & Teitelbaum, P. Nigrostriatal bundle damage and the lateral hypothalamic syndrome. *Journal of Comparative and Physiological Psychology*, 1974, *87*, 808-830.

Marx, M. H., & Hillix, W. A. *Systems and theories in psychology* (2nd ed.). New York: McGraw-Hill, 1973.

Masland, R. L. Manifestations of structural defects of the nervous system. In E. F. Beckenbach & C. B. Tompkins (Eds.), *Concepts of communication: Interpersonal, intrapersonal, and mathematical*. New York. Wiley, 1971.

Maslow, A. *A study of Wittgenstein's Tractatus*. Berkeley: University of California Press, 1961.

Maturana, H. R., & Frenk, S. Directional movement and horizontal edge detectors in the pigeon retina. *Science*, 1963, *142*, 977-979.

Maynard, D. M. Simpler networks. *Annals of the New York Academy of Sciences*, 1972, *193*, 59-72.

McConnell, J. V. Memory transfer through cannibalism in planarians. *Journal of Neuropsychiatry*, supplement 1, 1962, *3*, S42-S48.

McCulloch, W. S. Why the mind is in the head. In L. A. Jeffress (Ed.), *Cerebral mechanisms in behavior (The Hixon Symposium)*. New York: Wiley, 1951.

McCulloch, W. S., & Pitts, W. A logical calculus of the idea imminent in nervous activity. *Bulletin of Mathematical Biophysics*, 1943, *5*, 115.

McCullough, C. Color adaptation of edge-detectors in the human visual system. *Science*, 1965, *149*, 1115-1116.

McDonald, D. M., & Mitchell, R. A. The innervation of glomus cells, ganglion cells and blood vessels in the rat carotid body: A quantitative ultrastructural analysis. *Journal of Neurocytology*, 1975, *4*, 117-230.

McGaugh, J. L. A multi-trace view of memory storage processes. In D. Bovet, F. Bovet-Nitti, & A. Oliverio (Eds.), *Attuali orientamenti della ricerce sull'aprendimento e la memoria*. Rome: Academia Nazionale dei Lincei, 1968.

McGaugh, J. L. Facilitation of memory storage processes. In S. Gogoch (Ed.), *The future of the brain sciences*. New York: Plenum Press, 1969.

McLennan, H. *Synaptic transmission* (2nd ed.). Philadelphia: Saunders, 1970.

McNew, B. R., & Thompson, R. Effect of posterior thalamic lesions on retention of a brightness discrimination motivated by thirst. *Journal of Comparative and Physiological Psychology*, 1966, *62*, 125-128.

McNew, J. J. Role of the red nucleus in visually guided behavior in the rat. *Journal of Comparative and Physiological Psychology*, 1968, *65*, 282-289.

Melton, A. W. Short and long term postperceptual memory: Dichotomy or continuum. In K. Pribram & D. Broadbent (Eds.), *Biology of memory*. New York: Academic Press, 1970.

Melzack, R., & Wall, P. D. Pain mechanisms: A new theory. *Science,* 1965, *150,* 971-979.

Meyer, D. R. Some features of the dorsolateral frontal and inferotemporal syndromes in monkeys. *Acta Neurobiologiae Experimentalis,* 1972, *32,* 235-260.

Meyer, P. M., Dalby, D. A., Glendenning, K. K., Lauber, S. M., & Meyer, D. R., Behavior of cats with lesions of the septal forebrain or anterior sigmoid neocortex. *Journal of Comparative and Physiological Psychology,* 1973, *85,* 491-501.

Michael, C. R. Receptive fields of directionally selective units in the optic nerve of the ground squirrel. *Science,* 1967, *152,* 1092-1095.

Michael, C. R. Receptive fields of single optic nerve fibers in a mammal with an all-cone retina. II. Directionally selective units. *Journal of Neurophysiology,* 1968, *31,* 257-267.

Michaels, R. R., Huber, M. J., & McCann, D. S. Evaluation of transcendental meditation as a method of reducing stress. *Science,* 1976, *192,* 1242-1244.

Miller, N. E. Certain facts of learning relevant to the search for its physical basis. In G. C. Quarton, T. Melnechuk, & F. O. Schmitt (Eds.), *The neurosciences: A study program.* New York: Rockefeller University Press, 1967.

Miller, N. E., & Dworkin, B. R. Visceral learning: Recent difficulties with curarized rats and significant problems for human research. In P. A. Obrist, A. H. Black, J. Brener, & L. V. DiCara (Eds.), *Cardiovascular psychophysiology.* Chicago: Aldine, 1974.

Milner, B. Amnesia following operation on the temporal lobes. In C. W. M. Whitty & O. L. Zangwill (Eds.), *Amnesia.* London: Butterworths, 1966.

Milner, B., & Penfield, W. The effect of hippocampal lesions on recent memory. *Transactions of the American Neurological Association,* 1955, 42-48.

Minsky, M. Steps toward artificial intelligence. In E. A. Feigenbaum & J. Feldman (Eds.), *Computers and thought.* New York: McGraw-Hill, 1963.

Minsky, M., & Papert, S. *Perceptrons: An introduction to computational geometry.* Cambridge, Mass.: M.I.T. Press, 1969.

Mishkin, M. Visual discrimination performance following partial ablations of the temporal lobe. II. Ventral surface versus hippocampus. *Journal of Comparative and Physiological Psychology,* 1954, *47,* 187-193.

Mishkin, M. Visual mechanisms beyond the striate cortex. In R. Russell (Ed.), *Frontiers of physiological psychology.* New York: Academic Press, 1966.

Mishkin, M. Cortical visual areas and their interaction. In A. G. Karczmar & J. C. Eccles (Eds.), *The brain and human behavior.* Berlin: Springer-Verlag, 1972.

Morrell, F. Microelectrode and steady potential studies suggesting a dendritic locus of closure. In H. H. Jasper & G. D. Smirnov (Eds.), *The Moscow Colloquium on electroencephalography of higher nervous activity. Electroencephalography and Clinical Neurophysiology,* 1960, *13,* supplement, 65-79.

Morris, C. *Signs, language and behavior.* New York: Braziller, 1955.

Moruzzi, G., & Magoun, H. W. Brain stem reticular formation and activation of the EEG. *Electroencephalography and Clinical Neurophysiology,* 1949, *1,* 455-473.

Motokawa, K., Taira, N., & Okuda, J. Spectral responses of single units in the primate visual cortex. *Tohoku Journal of Experimental Medicine,* 1962, *78,* 320-337.

Mountcastle, V. B. Modality and topographic properties of single neurons of cat's somatic sensory cortex. *Journal of Neurophysiology,* 1957, *20,* 508-534.

Mountcastle, V. B. (Ed.). *Medical physiology* (12th ed.). St. Louis: Mosby, 1968.

Mountcastle, V. B., Lynch, J. C., Georgopoulos, A., Sakata, H., & Acuna, C. Posterior parietal association cortex of the monkey: Command functions for operations within extrapersonal space. *Journal of Neurophysiology,* 1975, *38,* 871-908.

Mountcastle, V. B., Poggio, G. F., & Werner, G. The relation of thalamic cell response to peripheral stimuli varied over an intensive continuum. *Journal of Neurophysiology,* 1963, *26,* 807-843.

Müller, J. *Hanbuch der Physiologie des Menschen* (Vol. II). Coblentz, Germany: Hölscher, 1840.

Murata, K., Cramer, H., & Bach-Y-Rita, A. Neuronal convergence of noxious, acoustic, and visual stimuli in the visual cortex of the cat. *Journal of Neurophysiology*, 1965, *28*, 1223-1240.

Murata, K., & Kameda, K. The activity of single cortical neurones of unrestrained cats during sleep and wakefulness. *Archives Italiennes de Biologie*, 1963, *101*, 306-331.

Murdock, B. B., Jr. *Human memory: Theory and data*. Hillsdale, N.J.: Lawrence Erlbaum Associates, 1974.

Murphy, W. F. (In S. Cobb, H. M. Fox, P. H. Gates, S. Gifford, P. H. Knapp, A. O. Ludwig, W. F. Murphy, C. Mushatt, E. V. Semrad, J. L. Weinberger, F. Deutsch) Is the term "mysterious leap" warranted? In F. Deutsch (Ed.), *On the mysterious leap from the mind to the body*. New York: International Universities Press, 1959.

Myers, R. D. (Ed.). *Methods in psychobiology* (Vol. 1). *Laboratory techniques in neuropsychology and neurobiology*. London-New York: Academic Press, 1971.

Myers, R. D. (Ed.). *Methods in psychobiology* (Vol. 2). *Specialized techniques in neuropsychology and neurobiology*. London-New York: Academic Press, 1972.

Myers, R. D. Visual deficits after lesions of brain stem tegmentum in cats. *Archives of Neurology*, 1964, *11*, 73-90.

Myers, R. E., & Sperry, R. W. Interocular transfer of a visual form discrimination habit in cats after section of the optic chiasm and corpus callosum. *Anatomical Record*, 1953, *175*, 351-352.

Nauta, W. J. H. A summary of the limbic system. Mimeographed informal communication.

Nauta, W. J. H., & Gygax. P. A. Silver impregnation of degenerating axon terminals of the central nervous system: (1) technic; (2) chemical notes. *Stain Technology*, 1954, *26*, 5-11.

Nauta, W. J. H., & Karten, H. J. A general profile of the vertebrate brain, with sidelights on the ancestry of cerebral cortex. In F. O. Schmitt (Ed.), *The neurosciences: Second study program*. New York: Rockefeller University Press, 1970.

Neale, J. H., Neale, E. A., & Agranoff, B. W. Radioautography of the optic tectum of the goldfish after intraocular injection of [^{3}H] proline. *Science*, 1972, *176*, 407-410.

Neild, T. O., & Thomas, R. C. New design for a chloride-sensitive micro-electrode. *Journal of Physiology*, 1973, *231*, 7-8P.

Neill, D. B., & Linn, C. L. Deficits in consummatory responses to regulatory challenges following basal ganglia lesions in rats. *Physiology and Behavior*, 1975, *14*, 617-624.

Neisser, U. *Cognitive psychology*. New York: Appleton-Century-Crofts, 1967.

Nicholls, J. G., & Purves, D. Monosynaptic chemical and electrical connections between sensory and motor cells in the central nervous system of the leech. *Journal of Physiology*, 1970, *209*, 642-667.

Nishi, S., & Koketsu, K. Electrical properties and activities of single sympathetic neurons in frogs. *Journal of Cellular and Comparative Physiology*, 1960, *55*, 15-30.

Noda, H., Creutzfeldt, O. D., & Freeman, R. B., Jr. Binocular interaction in the visual cortex of the awake cat. *Experimental Brain Research*, 1971, *12*, 406-427.

Noda, H., Freeman, R. B., Jr., Gies, B., & Creutzfeldt, O. D. Neuronal responses in the visual cortex of awake cats to stationary and moving targets. *Experimental Brain Research*, 1971, *12*, 389-405.

O'Brien, J. H., & Fox, S. S. Single-cell activity in cat motor cortex. I. Modifications during classical conditioning procedures. *Journal of Neurophysiology*, 1969, *32*, 267-284. (a)

O'Brien, J. H., & Fox, S. S. Single-cell activity in cat motor cortex. II. Functional characteristics of the cell related to conditioning changes. *Journal of Neurophysiology*, 1969, *32*, 285-296 (b)

O'Brien, J. H., & Packham, S. C. Habituation of cell activity in cat postcruciate cortex. *Journal of Comparative and Physiological Psychology*, 1974, *87*, 781-786.

O'Brien, J. H., Packham, S. C., & Brunnhoelzl, W. W. Features of spike train related to learning. *Journal of Neurophysiology*, 1973, *36*, 1051-1061.

Ochs, S. *Elements of neurophysiology*. New York: Wiley, 1965.

Olds, J. Hypothalamic substrates of reward. *Physiological Review*, 1962, *42*, 554-604.

Olds, J., Disterhoft, J. F., Segal, M., Kornblith, C. L., & Hirsh, R. Learning centers of rat brain mapped by measuring latencies of conditioned unit responses. *Journal of Neurophysiology*, 1972, *35*, 202-219.

Olds, J., & Milner, P. Positive reinforcement produced by electrical stimulation of septal area and other regions of the rat brain. *Journal of Comparative and Physiological Psychology*. 1954, *47*, 419-427.

Olds, J., & Olds, M. E. Interference and learning in paleocortical systems. In J. F. Delafresnaye (Ed.), *Brain mechanisms and learning*. Oxford: Blackwell, 1961.

Olszewski, J. The cytoarchitecture of the human reticular formation. In J. F. Delafresnaye (Ed.), *Brain mechanisms and consciousness*. Springfield, Ill.: C. C. Thomas, 1954.

Orkand, R. K., Nicholls, J. G., & Kuffler, S. W. Effect of nerve impulses on the membrane potential of glial cells in the central nervous system of amphibia. *Journal of Neurophysiology*, 1966, *29*, 788-806.

Ornstein, J. H. *The mind and the brain: A multi-aspect interpretation*. The Hague: Martinus Nijhoff, 1972.

Pagano, R. R., Rose, R. M., Stivers, R. M., & Warrenburg, S. Sleep during transcendental meditation. *Science*, 1976, *191*, 308-310.

Papez, J. W. A proposed mechanism of emotion. *Archives of Neurology and Psychiatry*, 1937, *38*, 725-744.

Pappas, G. D., & Waxman, S. G. Synaptic fine structure—morphological correlates of chemical and electrotonic transmission. In G. D. Pappas & D. P. Purpura (Eds.), *Structure and function of synapses*. New York: Raven Press, 1972.

Parker, T. D., Strachan, D. D., & Welker, W. I. Tungsten ball microelectrode for extracellular single-unit recording. *Electroencephalography and Neurophysiology*, 1973, *35*, 647-651.

Pasik, T., & Pasik, P. The visual world of monkeys deprived of striate cortex: Effective stimulus parameters and the importance of the accessory optic system. *Vision Research*, 1971, supplement #3, 419-435.

Patrissi, G., & Stein, D. G. Temporal factors in recovery of function after brain damage. *Experimental Neurology*, 1975, *47*, 470-480.

Patterson, K., & Bradshaw, J. L. Differential hemispheric mediation of nonverbal visual stimuli. *Journal of Experimental Psychology: Human Perception and Performance*, 1975, *1*, 246-252.

Patterson, M. M., Cegavske, C. G., & Thompson, R. F. Effects of a classical conditioning paradigm on hind-limb flexor nerve response in immobilized spinal cats. *Journal of Comparative and Physiological Psychology*, 1973, *84*, 88-97.

Patton, H. D. Special properties of nerve trunks and tracts. In T. C. Ruch & H. D. Patton (Eds.), *Physiology and biophysics* (19th ed.). Philadelphia: Saunders, 1965.

Pellegrino, L. J., & Cushman, A. J. *A stereotaxic atlas of the rat brain*. New York: Appleton-Century-Crofts, 1967.

Penfield, W., and Jasper, H. H. *Epilepsy and the functional anatomy of the human brain*. Boston: Little, Brown, 1954.

Penfield, W., & Rasmussen, T. *The cerebral cortex of man*. New York: Macmillan, 1950.

Penfield, W., & Roberts, L. *Speech and brain-mechanisms*. Princeton, N.J.: Princeton University Press, 1959.

Pepper, S. C. A neural-identity theory of mind. In S. Hood (Ed.), *Dimensions of mind: A symposium.* New York: New York University, 1960.

Peretz, B. Habituation and dishabituation in the absence of a central nervous system. *Science,* 1970, *169,* 379-381.

Perkel, D. H., & Bullock, T. H. Neural coding: A report based on an NRP work session. *Neurosciences Research Program Bulletin,* 1968, *6* (3), 221-348.

Perkel, D. H., & Mulloney, B. Letter. *Sciences,* 1974, *188,* 1036.

Peters, A., & Kaiserman-Abramof, I. R. The small pyramidal neuron of the rat cerebral cortex. The perikaryon, dendrites and spines. *American Journal of Anatomy,* 1970, *127,* 321-356.

Peterson, L. R., & Peterson, M. J. Short-term retention of individual verbal items. *Journal of Experimental Psychology,* 1959, *58,* 193-198.

Peterson, W. W., Birdsall, T. G., & Fox, W. C. Theory of signal detectability. *IEEE Transaction on Information Theory* (formerly IRE Professional Group on Information Theory), 1954, *4,* 171-212.

Pettigrew, J. D., & Daniels, J. D. Gamma-aminobutyric acid antagonism in visual cortex: Different effects on simple, complex, and hypercomplex neurons. *Science,* 1973, *182,* 81-83.

Pettigrew, J. D., & Freeman, R. D. Visual experience without lines: Effect on developing cortical neurons. *Science,* 1973, *182,* 599 601.

Pettigrew, J. D., Nikara, T., & Bishop, P. O. Responses to moving slits by single units in cat striate cortex. *Experimental Brain Research,* 1968, *6,* 373-390.

Pfaff, D. W., and Keiner, M. Atlas of estradiol-concentrating cells in the central nervous system of the female rat. *Journal of Comparative Neurology,* 1973, *151,* 121.

Pfaffmann, C. The sense of taste. In J. Field (Ed.), *Handbook of physiology. Section I: Neurophysiology* (Vol. I). Washington, D. C.: American Physiological Society, 1959.

Picton, T., & Hillyard, S. A. Human auditory evoked potentials. II: Effects of attention. *Electroencephalography and Clinical Neurophysiology,* 1974, *36,* 191-199.

Pinsker, H., Kupfermann, I., Castellucci, V., & Kandel, E. Habituation and dishabituation of the gill-withdrawal reflex in *Aplysia. Science,* 1970, *167,* 1740-1742.

Pitman, R. M., Tweedle, C. D., & Cohen, M. J. Branching of central neurons intracellular cobalt injection for light and electron microscopy. *Science,* 1972, *176,* 412-414.

Pitts, W., & McCulloch, W. S. How we know universals; the perception of auditory and visual forms. *Bulletin of Mathematical Biophysics,* 1947, *9,* 127.

Poggio, G. F., & Viernstein, L. J. Time series analysis of impulse sequences of thalamic somatic sensory neurons. *Journal of Neurophysiology,* 1964, *27,* 517-545.

Pollen, D. A., Lee, J. R., & Taylor, J. H. How does the striate cortex begin the reconstruction of the visual world? *Science,* 1971, *173,* 74-77.

Polten, E. P. *Critique of the psycho-physical identity theory.* The Hague: Mouton, 1973.

Polyak, S. *The vertebrate visual system.* Chicago: University of Chicago Press, 1957.

Pomeranz, B., & Chung, S. H. Dendritic-tree anatomy codes form-vision physiology in tadpole retina. *Science,* 1970, *170,* 983 984.

Porter, K. R., & Bonneville, M. A. *Fine structure of cells and tissues* (4th ed.). Philadelphia: Lea & Febiger, 1968.

Posner, M. I. Psychobiology of attention. In M. S. Gazzaniga & C. Blakemore (Eds.), *Handbook of psychobiology.* New York: Academic Press, 1975.

Powell, E. W., & Hines, G. The limbic system: An interface. *Behavioral Biology,* 1974, *12,* 149-164.

Premack, D. Language in a chimpanzee. *Science,* 1971, *172,* 808-822.

Pribram, K. H. A review of theory in physiological psychology. *Annual Review of Psychology,* 1960, *11,* 1-40.

Pribram, K. H. The neurophysiology of remembering. *Scientific American,* 1969, *220,* 73-86.

Pribram, K. H. *Languages of the brain.* Englewood Cliffs, N.J.: Prentice-Hall, 1971.

Pribram, K. H. (Ed.). *Psychophysiology of the frontal lobes.* New York: Academic Press, 1973.

Pribram, K. H., & McGuinness, D. Arousal, activation, and effort in the control of attention. *Psychological Review,* 1975, *82,* 116-149.

Pribram, K. H., Nuwer, M., & Baron, R. J. The holographic hypothesis of memory structure in brain function and perception. In D. H. Krantz (Ed.), *Contemporary developments in mathematical psychology* (Vol. II). San Francisco: Freeman, 1974.

Proctor, F., Riklan, M., Cooper, I. S., & Teuber, H. L. Judgement of visual and postural vertical by Parkinsonian patients. *Neurology,* 1964, *14,* 287-293.

Prokasy, W. F., & Raskin, D. C. (Eds.). *Electrodermal activity and psychological research.* New York: Academic Press, 1974.

Purpura, D. P. Nature of electrocortical potentials and synaptic organizations in cerebral and cerebellar cortex. *International Review of Neurobiology,* 1959, *1,* 47-163.

Purpura, D. P. Dendritic spine 'dysgenesis' and mental retardation. *Science,* 1974, *186,* 1126-1128.

Radinsky, L. B. Outlines of canid and felid brain evolution. *Annals of the New York Academy of Science,* 1969, *167,* 277-288.

Rall, W. Dendritic spines, synaptic potency and neuronal plasticity. In C. D. Woody, K. A. Brown, T. J. Crow, Jr., & J. D. Knispel (Eds.), *Cellular mechanisms subserving changes in neuronal activity.* Los Angeles: Brain Information Service/Brain Research Institute, University of California, 1974.

Ranck, J. B., Jr. Synaptic 'learning' due to electroosmosis: A theory. *Science,* 1964, *144,* 187-189.

Ranck, J. B., Jr. Studies on single neurons in dorsal hippocampal formation and septum in unrestrained rats. Part I. Behavioral correlates and firing repertoires. *Experimental Neurology,* 1973, *41,* 461-531.

Random house unabridged dictionary (1966 ed.). Westminster, Md.: Random House.

Ranson, S. W. *The anatomy of the nervous system: Its development and function* (10th ed.) (revised by S. L. Clark). Philadelphia: Saunders, 1959.

Ranson, S. W., & Clark, S. L. *The anatomy of the nervous system.* Philadelphia: Saunders, 1959.

Rapoport, A. Information processing in the nervous system. *International Congress of Physiological Sciences: Lecture and Symposium,* 1962, *3,* 16-23.

Rapoport, A., & Chammah, A. M. *Prisoner's Dilemma: A study in conflict and cooperation.* Ann Arbor: University of Michigan Press, 1965.

Rapoport, A., & Guyer, M. A taxonomy of 2 X 2 games. *General Systems,* 1966, *11,* 203-214.

Ratcliff, R., & Murdock, B. B., Jr. Retrieval processes in recognition memory. *Psychological Review,* 1976, *83,* 190-215.

Ratliff, F. *Mach bands: Quantitative studies on neural networks in the retina.* San Francisco: Holden-Day, 1965.

Ratner, S. C. Conditioning of decerebrate worms, *Lumbricus terrestris. Journal of Comparative Physiology and Psychology,* 1962, *55,* 174-177.

Raviola, E., & Gilula, N. B. Intramembrane organization of specialized contacts in the outer plexiform layer of the retina. *Journal of Cell Biology,* 1975, *65,* 192-222.

Regan, D. *Evoked potentials in psychology, sensory physiology and clinical medicine.* London: Chapman & Hall, 1972.

Rexed, B. A cytoarchitectonic atlas of the spinal cord in the cat. *Journal of Comparative Neurology,* 1954, *100,* 297-379.

Ribot, T. A. *Les maladies de la mémoire.* Paris: Baillière, 1881.

Riccio, D. C., Hodges, L. A., & Randall, P. K. Retrograde amnesia produced by hypothermia in rats. *Journal of Comparative and Physiological Psychology,* 1968, *66,* 618-622.

Rice, R. W., & Campbell, J. F. Effects of neocortical ablations on eating elicited by hypothalamic stimulation. *Experimental Neurology,* 1973, *39,* 359-371.

Richardson, A. *Mental imagery.* New York: Springer, 1969.

Richman, D. P., Stewart, R. M., Hutchinson, J. W., & Caviness, V. S., Jr. Mechanical model of brain convolutional development. *Science,* 1975, *189,* 18-21.

Riklan, M., & Levita, E. *Subcortical correlates of human behavior: A psychological study of thalamic and basal ganglia surgery.* Baltimore: Williams & Wilkins, 1969.

Rocha-Miranda, C. E., Bender, D. B., Gross, C. G., & Mishkin, M. Visual activation of neurons in inferotemporal cortex depends on striate cortex and forebrain commissures. *Journal of Neurophysiology,* 1975, *38,* 475-491.

Rodieck, R. *The vertebrate retina: Principles of structure and function.* San Francisco: Freeman, 1973.

Rodieck, R. W., Kiang, N. Y. S., & Gerstein, G. L. Some quantitative methods for the study of spontaneous activity of single neurons. *Biophysical Journal,* 1962, *2,* 351-368.

Rodieck, R. W., & Stone, J. Response of cat retinal ganglion cells to moving visual patterns. *Journal of Neurophysiology,* 1965, *28,* 819-832.

Roitbak, A. I. A new hypothesis concerning the mechanisms of formation of the conditioned reflex. *Acta Neurobiologiae Experimentalis,* 1970, *30,* 81-94.

Romer, A. S. *The vertebrate body.* Philadelphia: Saunders, 1949.

Rosenblatt, F. *Principles of neurodynamics: Perceptrons and the theory of brain mechanisms.* Washington, D. C.: Spartan Books, 1962.

Rosenblith, W. A. (Ed.). *Sensory communication.* Cambridge, Mass. and New York: M.I.T. Press and Wiley, 1961.

Rosenblueth, A. *Mind and brain: A philosophy of science.* Cambridge, Mass.: M.I.T. Press, 1970.

Rosenzweig, M. R., & Bennett, E. L. (Eds.). *Neural mechanisms of learning and memory.* Cambridge, Mass: M.I.T. Press, 1976.

Rosner, B. S. Neural factors limiting cutaneous spatiotemporal discriminations. In W. A. Rosenblith (Ed.), *Sensory communication.* Cambridge and New York: M.I.T. Press and Wiley, 1961.

Roth, W. T., Kopell, B. S., Tinklenberg, J. R., Darley, C. F., Sikora, R., & Vesecky, T. B. The contingent negative variation during a memory retrieval task. *Electroencephalography and Clinical Neurophysiology,* 1975, *38,* 171-174.

Rowland, V., & Goldstone, M. Appetitively conditioned and drive-related bioelectric baseline shift in cat cortex. *Electroencephalography and Clinical Neurophysiology,* 1963, *15,* 474-485.

Roy, E. J., & Wade, G. N. Role of estrogens in androgen-induced spontaneous activity in male rats. *Journal of Comparative and Physiological Psychology,* 1975, *89,* 573-579.

Rudell, A. P., & Fox, S. S. Operant controlled neural event: Functional bioelectric coding in primary components of cortical evoked potential in cat brain. *Journal of Neurophysiology,* 1972, *35,* 892-902.

Russell, R. W., & Espir, M. L. E. *Traumatic aphasia.* London: Oxford University Press, 1961.

Russell, C., & Russell, W. M. S. Raw materials for a definition of mind. In J. M. Scher (Ed.), *Theories of the mind.* New York: Free Press of Glencoe, 1962.

Rutledge, L. T., Wright, C., & Duncan, J. Morphological changes in pyramidal cells of mammalian neocortex associated with increased use. *Experimental Neurology,* 1974, *44,* 209-228.

Ryle, G. *The concept of mind.* New York: Barnes & Noble, 1949.

Sachs, M. B., Nachmias, J., & Robson, J. G. Spatial-frequency channels in human vision. *Journal of the Optical Society of America,* 1971, *61,* 1176-1186.

Saito, H., Yamamoto, M., Iwai, E., & Nakahama, H. Behavioral and electrophysiological correlates during flash-frequency discrimination learning in monkeys. *Electroencephalography and Clinical Neurophysiology,* 1973, *34,* 449-460.

Sakata, H., Takaoka, Y., Kawarasaki, A., & Shibutani, H. Somatosensory properties of neurons in the superior parietal cortex (area 5) of the rhesus monkey. *Brain Research,* 1973, *64,* 85-102.

Sakitt, B. Locus of short-term visual storage. *Science,* 1975, *190,* 1318-1319.

Sakitt, B. Iconic memory. *Psychological Review,* 1976, *83,* 257-276.

Schachar, R. A. The "pincushion grid" illusion. *Sceince,* 1976, *192,* 389-390.

Schaefer, H. Psychosomatic problems of vegetative regulatory functions. In J. C. Eccles (Ed.), *Brain and conscious experience.* New York: Springer-Verlag, 1966.

Schaller, G. B. *The mountain gorilla: Ecology and behavior.* Chicago: University of Chicago Press, 1963.

Schaller, G. B. *The deer and the tiger: A study of wildlife in India.* Chicago: University of Chicago Press, 1967.

Schaller, G. B. *The Serengeti lion: A study of predator-prey relations.* Chicago: University of Chicago Press, 1972.

Schaltenbrand, G. *Allgemeine neurologie.* Stuttgart, Germany: George Thieme Verlag, 1969.

Scheibel, M. E., & Scheibel, A. B. Structural substrates for integrative patterns in the brain stem reticular core. In H. H. Jasper, L. D. Proctor, R. S. Knighton, W. S. Noshay, & R. T. Costello (Eds.), *Reticular formation of the brain.* Boston: Little, Brown, 1958.

Scheibel, M. E., & Scheibel, A. B. Some structuro-functional substrates of development in young cats. *Electroencephalography and Clinical Neurophysiology,* 1963, supplement 24, 235-246.

Scheibel, M. E., & Scheibel, A. B. Terminal axonal patterns in cat spinal cord. I. The lateral corteospinal tract. *Brain Research,* 1966, *2,* 303-350.

Scheibel, M. E., & Scheibel, A. B. Terminal axonal patterns in cat spinal cord. II. The dorsal horn. *Brain Research,* 1968, *9,* 32-58.

Scheibel, M. E., & Scheibel, A. B. Terminal axonal patterns in cat spinal cord. III. Primary afferent collaterals. *Brain Research,* 1969, *13,* 417-443.

Scher, J. M. (Ed.). *Theories of the mind.* New York: Free Press of Glencoe, 1962.

Schiller, P. H. Single unit analysis of backward visual masking and metacontrast in the cat lateral geniculate necleus. *Vision Research,* 1968, *8,* 855-866.

Schiller, P. H. Behavioral and electrophysiological studies of visual masking. In K. N. Leibovic (Ed.), *Information processing in the nervous system.* New York: Springer-Verlag, 1969.

Schiller, P. H., & Koerner, F. Discharge characteristics of single units in superior colliculus of the alert rhesus monkey. *Journal of Neurophysiology,* 1971, *34,* 920-936.

Schmidt, R. F. (Ed.). *Fundamentals of neurophysiology.* New York: Springer-Verlag, 1975.

Schmitt, O. H., & Dubbert, D. R. Tissue stimulators utilizing radio frequency coupling. *Review of Scientific Instruments,* 1949, *20,* 170-173.

Schneider, G. E. Two visual systems. *Science,* 1969, *163,* 895-902.

Schuman, H. Two sources of antiwar sentiment in America. *American Journal of Sociology,* 1972, *78,* 513-536.

Seeman, P., & Lee, T. Antipsychotic drugs: Direct correlation between clinical potency and presynaptic action on dopamine neurons. *Science,* 1975, *188,* 1217-1219.

Segal, M. Flow of conditioned responses in limbic telencephalic system of the rat. *Journal of Neurophysiology,* 1973, *36,* 840-854.

Segal, M., & Olds, J. Behavior of units in hippocampal circuit of the rat during learning. *Journal of Neurophysiology,* 1972, *35,* 680-690.

Segal, M., & Olds, J. Activity of units in the hippocampal circuit of the rat during differential classical conditioning. *Journal of Comparative and Physiological Psychology,* 1973, *82,* 195-204.

Segundo, J. P., & Bell, C. C. Habituation of single nerve cells in the vertebrate nervous system. In G. Horn & R. A. Hinde (Eds.), *Short-term changes in neural activity and behaviour.* London: Cambridge University Press, 1970.

Segundo, J. P., & Perkel, D. H. The nerve cells as an analyzer of spike trains. In M. A. B. Brazier (Ed.), *The interneuron.* Berkeley: University of California Press, 1969.

Sellinger, O. Z., & Petiet, P. D. Horseradish peroxidase uptake *in vivo* by neuronal and glial lysosomes. *Experimental Neurology,* 1973, *38,* 370-385.

Selverston, A. I., & Mulloney, B. Synaptic and structural analysis of a small neural system. In F. O. Schmitt & F. G. Worden (Eds.), *The neurosciences: Third study program.* Cambridge, Mass.: M.I.T. Press, 1974.

Semon, R. *The mneme.* London: Allen & Unwin, 1904.

Shaw, C., Yinon, U., & Auerbach, E. Diminution of evoked neuronal activity in the visual cortex of pattern deprived rats. *Experimental Neurology,* 1974, *45,* 42-49.

Sherman, S. M. Monocularly deprived cats: Improvement of the deprived eye's vision by visual decortication. *Science,* 1974, *186,* 267-269.

Shiffrin, R. M., & Atkinson, R. C. Storage and retrieval processes in long-term memory. *Psychological Review,* 1969, *76,* 179-193.

Sholl, D. A. *The organization of the cerebral cortex.* London and New York: Methuen and Wiley, 1956.

Shurrager, P. S., & Culler, E. Conditioning in the spinal dog. *Journal of Experimental Psychology,* 1940, *26,* 133-159.

Sideroff, S., Bueno, O., Hirsch, A., Weyand, T., & McGaugh, J. L. Retrograde amnesia initiated by low-level stimulation of hippocampal cytoarchitectonic areas. *Experimental Neurology,* 1974, *43,* 285-297.

Sillito, A. M. The contribution of inhibitory mechanisms to the receptive field properties of neurons in the striate cortex of the cat. *Journal of Physiology,* 1975, *250,* 305-329.

Silver, I. A. Other electrodes. In P. E. K. Donaldson (Ed.), *Electronic apparatus for biological research.* New York: Academic Press, 1958.

Simmons, F. B., Epley, J. M., Lummis, R. C., Guttman, N., Frishkopf, L. S., Harmon, L. D., & Zwicker, E. Auditory nerve: Electrical stimulation in man. *Science,* 1965, *148,* 104-106.

Simon, E. J., Hiller, J. M., & Edelman, I. Solubilization of a sterospecific opiate-macromolecular complex from rat brain. *Science,* 1975, *190,* 389-390.

Sjöstrand, F. S. A search for the circuitry of directional selectivity and neural adaptation through three-dimensional analysis of the outer plexiform layer of the rabbit retina. *Journal of Ultrastructure Research,* 1974, *49,* 60-156.

Sjöstrand, F. S. The outer plexiform layer of the rabbit retina, an important data processing center. *Vision Research,* 1976, *16,* 1-14.

Skinner, B. F. *The behavior of organisms.* New York: Appleton, 1938.

Skinner, B. F. Operant behavior. In W. K. Honig (Ed.), *Operant behavior: Areas of research and application.* New York: Appleton, 1966.

Skinner, B. F. *Beyond freedom and dignity.* New York: Knopf, 1971.

Skrebitsky, V. G. Nonspecific influences on neuronal firing in the central visual pathway. *Experimental Brain Research,* 1969, *9,* 269-283.

Smith, D. S., Järlfors, U., & Beránek, R. The organization synaptic axoplasm in the lamprey (*Petromyzon marinus*) central nervous system. *Journal of Cell Biology,* 1970, *46,* 199-219.

Smythies, J. R. (Ed.). *Brain and mind: Modern concepts of the nature of mind.* London: Routledge & Kegan Paul, 1965.

Snyder, S. H. The opiate receptor. *Neurosciences Research Program Bulletin,* 1975, *13,* supplement, 1-27.

Snyder, S. H. Catecholamines, serotonin, and histamine. In G. J. Siegel, R. W. Albers, R. Katzman, and B. W. Agranoff (Eds.), *Basic neurochemistry.* Boston: Little, Brown, 1976.

Sokolov, E. N., Polyansky, V. B., & Bagdonas, A. Dynamics of the single unit reactions in the visual cortex of the unanesthetized rabbit. *Vision Research,* 1970, *10,* 11-28.

Somjen, G. *Sensory coding in the mammalian nervous system.* New York: Appleton-Century-Crofts, 1972.

Sommerhoff, G. *Logic of the living brain.* London: Wiley, 1974.

Sotelo, C., Gentschev, R., & Zamora, A. J. Gap junctions in ventral cochlear nucleus of the rat. A possible new example of electrotonic junctions in the mammalian C.N.S. *Neuroscience,* 1976, *1,* 5-7.

Sotelo, C., Llinás, R., & Baker, R. Structural study of inferior olivary nucleus of the cat: Morphological correlates of electrotonic coupling. *Journal of Neurophysiology,* 1974, *37,* 541-559.

Spalteholz, W., & Spanner, R. *Atlas of human anatomy* (16th ed.). Philadelphia: Davis, 1967.

Spehlmann, R. Acetylcholine and prostigmine electrophoresis at visual cortex neurons. *Journal of Neurophysiology,* 1963, *26,* 127-139.

Spehlmann, R., & Kapp, H. Die Wirkung lokaler Mikroelektrophorese von Acetylcholin auf einzelne Neurone des visuellen Cortex. *Pflüger's Archiv für die gestamte Physiologie des Menschen und der Tiere,* 1961, *274,* 37-38.

Sperling, G. The information available in brief visual presentation. *Psychological Monographs,* 1960, *74,* (11) Whole No. 498.

Sperling, G. Successive approximations to a model for short term memory. *Acta Psychologica,* 1967, *28,* 285.

Sperry, R. W. Mechanisms of neural maturation. In S. S. Stevens (Ed.), *Handbook of experimental psychology,* New York: Wiley, 1951.

Sperry, R. W. Brain bisection and mechanisms of consciousness. In J. C. Eccles (Ed.), *Brain and conscious experience.* New York: Springer-Verlag, 1966.

Sperry, R. W. Split-brain approach to learning problems. In G. C. Quarton, T. Melnechuck, and F. O. Schmitt (Eds.), *The neurosciences: A study program.* New York: Rockefeller University Press, 1967.

Sperry, R. W. A modified concept of consciousness. *Psychological Review,* 1969, *76,* 532-536.

Sperry, R. W. An objective approach to subjective experience: Further explanation of a hypothesis. *Psychological Review,* 1970, *77,* 585-590. (a)

Sperry, R. W. Perception in the absence of the neocortical commissures. *Perception and Its Disorders,* Research Publication, *48,* The Association for Research In Nervous and Mental Disease, 1970. (b)

Sperry, R. W., Miner, R., & Myers, R. E. Visual pattern perception following subpial slicing and tantalum wire implantations in the visual cortex. *Journal of Comparative and Physiological Psychology,* 1955, *48,* 50-58.

Spinelli, D. N. Receptive field organization of ganglion cells in the cat's retina. *Experimental Neurology,* 1967, *19,* 291-315.

Spinelli, D. N., Bridgeman, B., & Owens, S. Technical note: A simple single-unit microelectrode recording system. *Medical and Biological Engineering,* 1970, *8,* 599-602.

Spinelli, D. N., Hirsch, H. V. B., Phelps, R. W., & Metzler, J. Visual experience as a determinant of the response characteristics of cortical receptive fields in cats. *Experimental Brain Research,* 1972, *15,* 289-304.

Spinelli, D. N., & Pribram, K. H. Neural correlates of stimulus response and reinforcement. *Brain Research,* 1970, *17,* 377-385.

Sprague, J. M., Levitt, M., Robson, K., Liu, C. N., Stellar, E., & Chambers, W. W. A neuro-anatomical and behavioral analysis of the syndromes resulting from midbrain lemniscal and reticular lesions in the cat. *Archives Italiennes de Biologie,* 1963, *101,* 225-295.

Squires, K. C., Squires, N. K., & Hillyard, S. A. Decision-related cortical potentials during an auditory signal detection task with cued observation intervals. *Journal of Experimental Psychology: Human Perception and Performance,* 1975, *1,* 268-279.

Stebbins, W. C., Clark, W. W., Pearson, R. D., & Weiland, N. G. Noise- and drug-induced hearing loss in monkeys. In J. E. Hawkins, M. Lawrence, & W. P. Work (Eds.), *Advances in oto-rhino-laryngology* (Vol. 20). Basel, Switzerland: S. Karger, 1973.

Stedman's medical dictionary (22nd ed.). Baltimore: Williams & Wilkins Company, 1972.

Stellar, E. The physiology of motivation. *Psychological Review,* 1954, *61,* 5-22.

Sternberg, S. High-speed scanning in human memory. *Science,* 1966, *153,* 652-654.

Sternberg, S. Memory-scanning: Mental processes revealed by reaction-time experiments. *American Scientist,* 1969, *57,* 421-457.

Stevens, C. F. *Neurophysiology: A primer.* New York: Wiley, 1966.

Stevens, S. S. (Ed.). *Handbook of experimental psychology.* New York: Wiley, 1951.

Stevens, S. S. Neural events and the psychophysical law. *Science,* 1970, *170,* 1043-1050.

Stevens, S. S. Sensory power functions and neural events. In W. R. Loewenstein (Ed.), *Principles of receptor physiology.* New York: Springer-Verlag, 1971.

Stone, J., & Hoffman, K. P. Very slow-conducting ganglion cells in the cat's retina. A major new functional type? *Brain Research,* 1972, *43,* 610-616.

Stowell, H. Letter. *Science,* 1975, *190,* 1005-1006.

Stretton, A. O. W., & Kravitz, E. A. Neuronal geometry: Determination with a technique of intracellular dye injection. *Science,* 1968, *162,* 132-134.

Stromeyer, C. F., III, & Julesz, B. Spatial-frequency masking in vision: Critical bands and spread of masking. *Journal of the Optical Society of America,* 1972, *62,* 1221-1232.

Stromeyer, C. F., III, & Klein, S. Evidence against narrow-band spatial frequency channels in human vision: The detectability of frequency modulated gratings. *Vision Research,* 1975, *15,* 899-910.

Strong, O. S., & Elwyn, A. *Human neuroanatomy.* Baltimore: Williams & Wilkins, 1959.

Stroud, J. The fine structure of psychological time. In H. Quastler (Ed.), *Information theory in psychology.* Glencoe, Ill.: Free Press, 1955.

Stryker, M. P., & Sherk, H. Modification of cortical orientation selectivity in the cat by restricted visual experience: A reexamination. *Science,* 1975, *190,* 904-906.

Sutherland, N. S. Visual discrimination in animals. *British Medical Bulletin,* 1964, *20,* 54-59.

Sutton, S., Braren, M., Zubin, J., & John, E. R. Evoked-potential correlates of stimulus uncertainty. *Science,* 1965, *150,* 1187-1188.

Swammerdam, J. Experiment to demonstrate contraction of frog muscle. In J. F. Fulton & L. G. Wilson (Eds.), *Selected readings in the history of physiology.* Springfield, Ill.: C. C. Thomas, 1966.

Szentágothai, J. Glomerular synapses, complex synaptic arrangements, and their operational significance. In F. O. Schmitt (Ed.), *The neurosciences. Second study program.* New York: Rockefeller University Press, 1970.

Szentágothai, J. Memory functions and the structural organization of the brain. In G. Ádám (Ed.), *Biology of memory.* (Proceedings of the Symposium held at the Biological Research Institute in Tihany, Hungary, September 1-4, 1969) New York: Plenum Press, 1971.

Szentágothai, J. The basic neuronal circuit on the neocortex. In H. Petsche & M. A. Brazier (Eds.), *Synchronization of EEG activity in epilepsies.* (A Symposium organized by the Austrian Academy of Sciences, Vienna, Austria, September 12-13, 1971) New York: Springer-Verlag, 1972.

Szentágothai, J. Neural and synaptic architecture of the lateral geniculate nucleus. In R. Jung (Ed.), *Visual centers in the brain*. Berlin: Springer-Verlag, 1973. (a)

Szentágothai, J. Synaptology of the visual cortex. In R. Jung (Ed.), *Visual centers in the brain*. Berlin: Springer-Verlag, 1973. (b)

Szentágothai, J. The "module-concept" in cerebral cortex architecture. In press.

Szentágothai, J., & Arbib, M. A. *Conceptual models of neural organization*. Cambridge, Mass.: M.I.T. Press, 1975.

Szentágothai, J., & Réthelyi, M. Cyto- and neuropil architecture of the spinal cord. In J. E. Desmedt (Ed.), *New developments in electromyography and clinical neurophysiology* (Vol. 3). Basel, Switzerland: S. Karger, 1973.

Tanner, W. P., Jr., & Swets, J. A. A decision-making theory of visual detection. *Psychological Review*, 1954, *61*, 401-409.

Tanzi, E. I fatti e le induzioni nell'odierna istologia del sistema nervosa. *Rivista Sperimentale di Freniatria*, 1893, *19*, 419-472.

Tauc, L., & Epstein, R. Heterosynaptic facilitation as a distinct mechanism in *Aplysia*. *Nature*, 1967, *214*, 724-725.

Teitelbaum, P., & Epstein, A. N. The lateral hypothalamic syndrome: Recovery of feeding and drinking after lateral hypothalamic lesions. *Psychological Review*, 1962, *69*, 74-90.

Teyler, T. J., Baum, W. M., & Patterson, M. M. (Eds.). Behavioral and biological issues in the learning paradigm. *Physiological Psychology*, 1975, *3* (1), 65-72.

Thomas, R. C. Measurement of current produced by the sodium pump in a snail neurone. *Journal of Physiology*, 1968, *195*, 23-24P.

Thomas, R. C. New design for sodium-sensitive glass micro-electrode. *Journal of Physiology*, 1970, *210* (2), 82-83P.

Thompson, R. F. *Foundations of physiological psychology*. New York: Harper & Row, 1967.

Thompson, R. F. Localization of the "visual memory system" in the white rat. *Journal of Comparative and Physiological Psychology Monograph*, 1969, *69*, (4, Pt.2).

Thompson, R. F. *Introduction to Physiological psychology*. New York: Harper & Row, 1975.

Thompson, R. F. The search for the engram. *American Psychologist*, 1976, 31, 209-227.

Thompson, R. F., Johnson, R. H., & Hoopes, J. J. Organization of auditory, somatic sensory, and visual projection to association fields of cerebral cortex in the cat. *Journal of Neurophysiology*, 1963, *26*, 343-364.

Thompson, R. F., Lesse, H., & Rich. I. Dissociation of visual and auditory habits following pretectal lesions in rats and cats. *Journal of Comparative Neurology*, 1963, *121*, 161-172.

Thompson, R. F., Lukaszewska, I., Schweigerdt, A., & McNew, J. J. Retention of visual and kinesthetic discriminations in rats following pretecto-diencephalic and ventral mesencephalic damage. *Journal of Comparative and Physiological Psychology*, 1967, *63*, 458-468.

Thompson, R. F., Mayers, K. S., Robertson, R. T., & Patterson, C. J. Number coding in association cortex of the cat. *Science*, 1970, *168*, 271-273.

Thompson, R. F., & Myers, R. E. Brainstem mechanisms underlying visually guided responses in the Rhesus monkey. *Journal of Comparative and Physiological Psychology*, 1971, *74*, 479-512.

Thompson, R. F., & Patterson, M. M. *Bioelectric recording techniques. Part A. Cellular processes and brain potentials*. New York: Academic Press, 1973.

Thompson, R. F., & Patterson, M. M. *Bioelectric recording techniques. Part B. Electroencephalography and human brain potentials*. New York: Academic Press, 1974. (a)

Thompson, R. F., & Patterson, M. M. *Bioelectric recording techniques. Part C. Receptor and effector processes*. New York: Academic Press, 1974. (b)

Thompson, R. F., & Rich, I. A discrete diencephalic pretectal area critical for the retention of visual habits in the rat. *Experimental Neurology*, 1961, *4*, 436-443.

Thompson, R. F., & Spencer, W. A. Habituation: A model phenomenon for the study of neuronal substrates of behavior. *Psychological Review*, 1966, *73*, 16-43.

Thorne, M. Visual discrimination performance in rats following nucleus posterior thalamic and di-mesencephalic juncture damage. *Journal of Comparative and Physiological Psychology*, 1970, *71*, 136-146.

Tolman, E. C. *Purposive behavior in animals and men.* New York: Appleton-Century-Crofts, 1932.

Tolman, E. C., & Honzik, C. H. Insight in rats. *University of California Publications in Psychology*, 1930, *4*, 215-232.

Towe, A. L. Notes on the hypothesis of columnar organization in somatosensory cerebral cortex. *Brain, Behavior, and Evolution*, 1975, *11*, 16-47.

Trevarthen, C. B. Two mechanisms of vision in primates. *Psychologische Forschung*, 1968, *31*, 299-337.

Truex, R. C., & Carpenter, M. B. *Human neuroanatomy* (6th ed.). Baltimore: Williams & Wilkins, 1969.

Ungar, G. Chemical transfer of learning: Its stimulus specificity. *Federation Proceedings*, 1966, *25*, 207.

Ungar, G. (Ed.), *Molecular mechanisms in memory and learning.* New York: Plenum Press, 1970.

Ungar, G., & Oceguera-Navarro, C. Transfer of habituation by material extracted from brain. *Nature*, 1965, *207*, 301-302.

Ungerstedt, U. Sterotaxic mapping of the monoamine pathway in the rat brain. *Acta Physiologica Scandinavica*, 1971, *82*, supplement 367, 1-48.

Uttal, W. R. A comparison of neural and psychophysical responses in the somesthetic system. *Journal of Comparative and Physiological Psychology*, 1959, *52*, 485-490.

Uttal, W. R. Evoked brain potentials: Signs or codes? *Perspectives in Biology and Medicine*, 1967, *10*, 627-639.

Uttal, W. R. Masking of alphabetic character recognition by dynamic visual noise (DVN). *Perception and Psychophysics*, 1969, *6*, 121-128.

Uttal, W. R. On the physiological basis of masking with dotted visual noise. *Perception and Psychophysics*, 1970, *7*, 321-327.

Uttal, W. R. A masking approach to the problem of form perception. *Perception and Psychophysics*, 1971, *9*, 296-298.

Uttal, W. R. (Ed.). *Sensory coding: Selected readings.* Boston: Little, Brown, 1972.

Uttal, W. R. *The psychobiology of sensory coding.* New York: Harper & Row, 1973.

Uttal, W. R. *An autocorrelation theory of form detection.* Hillsdale, N. J.: Lawrence Erlbaum Associates, 1975. (a)

Uttal, W. R. *Cellular neurophysiology and integration: An interpretive introduction.* Hillsdale, N.J.: Lawrence Erlbaum Associates, 1975. (b)

Uttal, W. R., & Cook, L. Systematics of the evoked somatosensory cortical potential: A psychophysical-electrophysiological comparison. In R. Katzman (Ed.), *Sensory evoked response in man.* New York: New York Academy of Sciences, 1964.

Uttal, W. R., & Hieronymus, R. Spatio-temporal effects in visual gap detection. *Perception and Psychophysics*, 1970, *8*, 321-325.

Uttal, W. R., & Kasprzak, H. The caudal photoreceptor of the crayfish: A quantitative study of responses to intensity, temporal and wavelength variables. *AFIPS Conference Proceedings*, 1962, *21*, 159-169.

Uttal, W. R., & Krissoff, M. The response of the somesthetic system to patterned trains of electrical stimuli: An approach to the problem of sensory coding. In D. R. Kenshalo (Ed.), *The skin senses.* Springfield, Ill.: C. C. Thomas, 1968.

Valenstein, E. S. Stability and plasticity of motivation systems. In F. O. Schmitt (Ed.), *The neurosciences: Second study program.* New York: Rockefeller University Press, 1970.

Valenstein, E. S. (Ed.). *Brain stimulation and motivation: Research and commentary.* Glenview, Ill.: Scott, Foresman & Company, 1973.

Valverde, F. Apical dendritic spines of the visual cortex and light deprivation in the mouse. *Experimental Brain Research,* 1967, *3,* 337-352.

Valverde, F. Structural changes in the area striata of the mouse after enucleation. *Experimental Brain Research,* 1968, *5,* 274-292.

Van Essen, D. C. The contribution of membrane hyperpolarization to adaptation and conduction block in sensory neurones of the leech. *Journal of Physiology,* 1973, *230,* 509-534.

Van Lawick-Goodall, J. *The behavior of free-living chimpanzees in the Gombe Stream Reserve.* London: Baillière, Tindell & Cassell, 1968.

Van Lawick-Goodall, J. *In the shadow of man.* Boston: Houghton Mifflin, 1971.

Verzeano, M. The synchronization of brain waves. *Acta Neurologica Latinoamerica,* 1963, *9,* 297-307.

Vinogradova, O. U., & Lindsley, D. F. Extinction of reactions to sensory stimuli in single neurons of visual cortex in unanesthetized rabbits. *Federation Proceedings,* 1964, *23,* 241-246.

Vom Saal, F. S., Hamilton, L. W., & Gandelman, R. J. Faster acquisition of an olfactory discrimination following septal lesions in male albino rats. *Physiology and Behavior,* 1975, *14,* 697-703.

Wachtel, H., & Kandel, E. R. A direct synaptic connection mediating both excitation and inhibition. *Sceince,* 1967, *158,* 1206-1208.

Wall, P. D., & Cronly-Dillon, J. R. Pain, itch, and vibration. *AMA Archives of Neurology,* 1960, *2,* 365-375.

Walter, W. G. The contingent negative variation: An electrical sign of significant association in the human brain. *Science,* 1964, *146,* 434.

Warner, R. R., & Coleman, J. R. Electron probe analysis of calcium transport by small intestine. *Journal of Cell Biology.* 1975, *64,* 54-74.

Warren, R. M. Perceptual restoration of missing speech sounds. *Science,* 1970, *167,* 392-393.

Wartzok, D., & Marks, W. B. Directionally selective units recorded in optic tectum of the goldfish. *Journal of Neurophysiology,* 1973, *36,* 588-604.

Wasserman, G. S., & Kong, K.-L. Illusory correlation of brightness enhancement and transients in the nervous system. *Science,* 1974, *184,* 911-913.

Watson, J. B. Psychology as the behaviorist views it. *Psychological Review,* 1913, *20,* 158-177.

Weber, E. H. *De pulsu, resorpitione, auditu et tactu: Annotationes anatomicae et physiologicae.* Leipzig, Germany: Koehlor, 1834.

Weiskrantz, L. Behavioral analysis of the monkey's visual nervous system. *Proceedings of the Royal Society of London,* Series B, 1972, *182,* 427-455.

Weiskrantz, L. The interaction between occipital and temporal cortex in vision: An overview. In F. O. Schmitt & F. G. Worden (Eds.), *The neurosciences: Third study program.* Cambridge, Mass.: M.I.T. Press, 1974.

Weisstein, N. What the frog's eye tells the human brain: Single cell analyzers in the human visual system. *Psychological Bulletin,* 1969, *72,* 157-176.

Weisstein, N. Neural symbolic activity: A psychophysical measure. *Science,* 1970, *168,* 1489-1491.

Weisstein, N., & Bisaha, J. Gratings mask bars and bars mask gratings: Visual frequency response to aperiodic stimuli. *Science,* 1972, *176,* 1047-1049.

Weisstein, N., Matthews, M., & Berbaum, K. Illusory contours can mask real contours. Paper presented at Psychonomic Society, Boston, November, 1974.

Weisstein, N., Ozog, G., & Szoc, R. A comparison and elaboration of two models of metacontrast. *Psychological Review,* 1975, *82,* 325-343.

Welker, W. I. A method for preparing brain casts. *The Anatomical Record,* 1967, *158,* 239-244.

Welker, W. I. Ontogeny of play and exploratory behaviors: A definition of problems and a search for new conceptual solutions. In H. Moltz (Ed.), *The ontogeny of vertebrate behavior.* New York: Academic Press, 1971.

Welker, W. I. Principles of organization of the ventrobasal complex in mammals. *Brain, Behavior and Evolution,* 1973, *7,* 253-336.

Welker, W. I. Brain evolution in mammals: A review of concepts, problems, and methods. In R. B. Masteron, M. E. Bitterman, B. Campbell, & N. Hotton (Eds.) *Evolution of brain and behavior in vertebrates.* Potomac, Md.: Lawrence Erlbaum Associates, 1976.

Welker, W. I., & Campos, G. B. Physiological significance of sulci in somatic sensory cerebral cortex in mammals of the family *Procyonidae. Journal of Comparative Neurology,* 1963, *120,* 19-36.

Welker, W. I., & Seidenstein, S. Somatic sensory representation in the cerebral cortex of the raccoon *(Procynon lotor). Journal of Comparative Neurology,* 1959, *111,* 469-502.

Werner, G. Personal communication, 1974.

Wernicke, C. *Der aphasische symtomenkomplex.* Brieslau, Germany: Cohn & Weigert, 1874.

Wever, E. G. *Theory of hearing.* New York: Wiley, 1949.

Wiener, N. *Cybernetics.* New York: Wiley, 1948.

Wiesel, T. N., & Hubel, D. H. Single-cell responses in striate cortex of kittens deprived of vision in one eye. *Journal of Neurophysiology,* 1963, *26,* 1003-1017.

Wiesel, T. N., & Hubel, D. H. Comparison of the effects of unilateral and bilateral eye closure on cortical unit responses in kittens. *Journal of Neurophysiology,* 1965, *28,* 1029-1040. (a)

Wiesel, T. N., & Hubel, D. H. Extent of recovery from the effects of visual deprivation in kittens. *Journal of Neurophysiology,* 1965, *28,* 1060-1072. (b)

Wiesel, T. N., & Hubel, D. H. Ordered arrangement of orientation columns in monkeys lacking visual experience. *Journal of Comparative Neurology,* 1974, *158,* 307-318.

Willmer, E. N. *Cytology and evolution.* New York: Academic Press, 1970.

Wise, C. D., & Stein, L. Dopamine β-hydroxylase deficits in the brains of schizophrenic patients. *Science,* 1973, *181,* 344-346.

Wittgenstein, L. [*Tractatus logico-philosophicus*] (D. F. Pears & B. F. McGuinness, trans.). London, 1961. (Reprinted from 1922)

Wittgenstein, L. [*Philosophical investigations*] (G. E. M. Anscombe, trans.). New York: Macmillan, 1953.

Wittgenstein, L. *The blue and brown books.* New York: Harper & Row, 1958.

Wolstenholme, G. E. W., & O'Connor, C. M. (Eds.). *Ciba Foundation Symposium on the neurological basis of behavior.* London: J. & A. Churchill, 1958.

Woody, C. D. Conditioned eye blink: Gross potential activity at coronal-precruciate cortex of the cat. *Journal of Neurophysiology,* 1970, *33,* 838-850.

Woody, C. D., & Black-Cleworth, P. Differences in excitability of cortical neurons as a function of motor projection in conditioned cats. *Journal of Neurophysiology,* 1973, *36,* 1104-1116.

Woody, C. D., Brown, K. A., Crow, T. J., Jr., & Knispel, J. D. (Eds.) *Cellular mechanisms subserving changes in neuronal activity.* Research Report #3. Los Angeles: Brain Information Service/Brain Research Institute, University of Californai, 1974.

Woody, C. D., & Engel, J., Jr. Changes in unit activity and thresholds to electrical microstimulation at coronal-precruciate cortex of cat with classical conditioning of different facial movements. *Journal of Neurophysiology,* 1972, *35,* 230-241.

Woody, C. D., Vassilevsky, N. N., & Engel, J., Jr. Conditioned eye blink: Unit activity at coronal-precruciate cortex of the cat. *Journal of Neurophysiology,* 1970, *33,* 851-864.

Woolsey, C. N. Pattern of localization in sensory and motor areas of the cerebral cortex. In *The biology of mental health and disease: The Twenty-seventh Annual Conference of the Milbank Memorial Fund.* New York: Hoeber, 1952.

Woolsey, C. N. Organization of cortical auditory system. In W. A. Rosenblith (Ed.), *Sensory communication.* Cambridge, Mass. and New York: M.I.T. Press and Wiley, 1961.

Wundt, W. Vorlesungen über die Menschen und Thierseele. In W. S. Sahakian (Ed.), *History of psychology: A source book in systematic psychology.* Itasca, Ill.: Peacock, 1968.

Wurtz, R. Visual cortex neurons: Response to stimuli during rapid eye movements. *Science,* 1968, *162,* 1148.

Wurtz, R. H. Visual receptive fields of striate cortex neurons in awake monkeys. *Journal of Neurophysiology,* 1969, *32,* 727-742. (a)

Wurtz, R. H. Response of striate cortex neurons to stimuli during rapid eye movements in the monkey. *Journal of Neurophysiology,* 1969, *32,* 975-986. (b)

Wurtz, R. H. Comparison of effects of eye movements and stimulus movements on striate cortex neurons of the monkey. *Journal of Neurophysiology,* 1969, *32,* 987-994. (c)

Wurtz, R. H., & Goldberg, M. E. Activity of superior colliculus in behaving monkey. IV. Effects of lesions on eye movements. *Journal of Neurophysiology,* 1972, *35,* 587-596.

Wyatt, H. J., & Daw, N. W. Directionally sensitive ganglion cells in the rabbit retina: Specificity for stimulus direction, size and speed. *Journal of Neurophysiology,* 1975, *38,* 613-626.

Wyatt, R. J., Schwartz, M. A., Erdelyi, E., & Barchas, J. D. Dopamine β-hydroxylase activity in brains of chronic schizophrenic patients. *Science,* 1975, *187,* 368-370.

Wyers, E. J., & Deadwyler, S. A. Duration and nature of retrograde amnesia produced by stimulation of caudate nucleus. *Physiology and Behavior,* 1971, *6,* 97-103.

Wyers, E. J., Peeke, H. V. S., Williston, J. S., & Herz, M. J. Retroactive impairment of passive avoidance learning by stimulation of the caudate nucleus. *Experimental Neurology,* 1968, *22,* 350-366.

Young, J. A. The giant nerve fibres and epistellar body of cephalopods. *Quarterly Journal of Microscopical Science,* 1936, *78,* 367.

Young, J. Z. Learning and discrimination in the octopus. *Biological Review,* 1961, *36,* 32-96.

Young, R. W. Visual cells. *Scientific American,* 1970, *223,* 80-91.

Zaidel, E. Linguistic competence and related functions in the right hemisphere of man following cerebral commissurotomy and himispherectomy. Ph. D. thesis, California Institute of Technology, Pasadena, 1973.

Zaidel, E. Language, dichotic listening, and the disconnected hemispheres. Paper presented at the Conference on Human Brain Function, University of California, Los Angeles, September 27, 1974.

Zaidel, E. A technique for presenting lateralized visual input with prolonged exposure. *Vision Research,* 1975, *15,* 283-289.

Zanchetti, A. Subcortical mechanisms in arousal and emotional behavior. In G. C. Quarton, T. Melnechuk, & F. O. Schmitt, (Eds.), *The neurosciences: A study program.* New York: Rockefeller Universtiy Press, 1967.

Zeigler, H. P. Feeding behavior in the pigeon: A neurobehavioral analysis. In I. Goodman & M. Schein (Eds.), *Birds: Brain and behavior.* New York: Academic Press, 1974.

Zeigler, H. P. Feeding Behavior of the pigeon. In J. Rosenblatt, R. A. Hinde, E. Shaw, and C. Beer (Eds.), *Advances in the study of Behavior,* Vol. 6. New York: Academic Press, 1976.

Zeigler, H. P., & Karten, H. J. Brain mechanisms and feeding behavior in the pigeon *(Columbia livia):* I. Quinto-frontal structures. *Journal of Comparative Neurology,* 1973, *152,* 59-82.

Zeki, S. M. Cortical projections from two prestriate areas in the monkey. *Brain Research,* 1971, *34,* 19-35.

Zilber-Gachelin, N. F., & Chartier, M. P. Modification of the motor reflex responses due to repetition of the peripheral stimulus in the cockroach. *Journal of Experimental Biology,* 1973, *59,* 359-403.

Zinnes, E. Scaling. *Annual Review of Psychology,* 1969, *20,* 447-478.

Zornetzer, S. F., & McGaugh, J. L. Effects of frontal brain electroshock stimulation on EEG activity and memory in rats: Relationship to ECS-produced retrograde amnesia. *Journal of Neurobiology,* 1970, *1,* 379-394.

Author Index

Subject Index